W9-CLW-606

CLINTON'S SECRET WARS

ALSO BY RICHARD SALE

Traitors: The Worst Acts of Treason in American History from
Benedict Arnold to Robert Hanssen

The Blackstone Rangers

CLINTON'S SECRET WARS

★ ★

THE

EVOLUTION

OF A

COMMANDER IN CHIEF

RICHARD SALE

THOMAS DUNNE BOOKS
ST. MARTIN'S PRESS ✿ NEW YORK

THOMAS DUNNE BOOKS.
An imprint of St. Martin's Press.

CLINTON'S SECRET WARS. Copyright © 2009 by Richard Sale. All rights reserved.
Printed in the United States of America. For information, address St. Martin's Press,
175 Fifth Avenue, New York, N.Y. 10010.

ISBN-13: 978-0-312-37366-5 (alk. paper)

TO MY LOVELY WIFE,

CAROL,

WHO FOR TWENTY-TWO YEARS

HAS BEEN MY COMPANION

AND PARTNER

IN A LIFE OF LOVE,

GROWTH, PASSION,

AND ENRICHING JOY.

CONTENTS

PREFACE

This book is an attempt to right a wrong. The popular image of Bill Clinton as a foreign policy leader is one of a man who was tardy, vacillating, irresolute, always timidly reluctant to use force and heading an administration lacking in singleness of focus or ruthlessness of drive. I believe this picture to be grossly unfair and submit that President Clinton's performance deserves a far more balanced examination than it so far has received. This book deals with some of the covert actions and secret programs that the Clinton administration undertook during his two terms, for Clinton worked largely undercover in a serious crisis. His designs often depended on secrecy for their success, and as a result, one of the most highly publicized presidents was one of its most covert, and one who participated in his own cover-up of these activities. But no one should be misled. It is clear that President Clinton learned to act with focused intensity and implacability of purpose when a serious crisis came.

I understand that there are many Americans who on instinct and principle distrust covert actions. To these people, these activities violate the law (they do, or they would not be covert); they are meddlesome and sneaky; and such skeptics feel that American democratic ideals, the growth of personal liberty, dislike of power, consideration for the weak or infirm, are best spread by example, not by plots. But I believe covert acts are absolutely necessary in a case like the Balkans, given the spineless inertia exhibited by the Europeans in the face of clear and proven atrocity.

Of all the presidents, Clinton in foreign affairs reminds me most of

Presidents Franklin Roosevelt and Dwight Eisenhower, the latter, who as a former military commander, had a deep visceral repugnance when it came to using the military, yet none at all when it came to using covert operations to accomplish certain vital U.S. ends. Thought to be pliant and weak, Clinton exhibited an initial uncertainty and clearly made some early major stumbles, but he quickly learned to put his own stamp on foreign policy, "making it his policy, not the mere product of bureaucratic momentum," in the words of advisor Dick Morris. In Clinton, what first appeared to be wincing dissimulation, indecision, and procrastination were, in fact, symptoms of a mind able to wait amid a hurricane of pressure or ridicule in order to weigh a vast and complicated array of difficult choices whose consequences he could not foresee but that could possibly cause serious, even fatal, damage to his presidency and prestige.

Clinton slowly grew into a man who had the inner hardness to make very tough decisions. A reluctance to use force is not a refusal to use it. Clinton used force in Haiti and Somalia, and if disaster occurred in the latter place, Clinton's military let him down, not the other way around, according to former CENTCOM commander Gen. Anthony Zinni. As this book will show, Clinton was often extremely pugnacious. Only days after the February 5, 1994, Serb bombing of the Markala marketplace in Sarajevo, the president set afoot preliminary plans for a covert operation that would remove from power the Serb bully Slobodan Milosevic, and within a year of taking office, Clinton had put U.S. Special Forces in Bosnia, poised to extract Canadian peacekeepers from Srebrenica in a daring night operation that involved helicopters and air defense suppression aircraft. In the end, the operation stood down, but Clinton had been determined to go through with it, in spite of its perilous risks and a public hostile to involvement.

Historically, the election of Bill Clinton could not have come at a worse time. Few realize that like Harry Truman, Clinton gained office when the powers of the presidency had been sharply cut back. With the Cold War gone, congressional and political voices once again arose to warn that America would do better to give its attention to problems at home than to lose its way by casting its attention abroad and going in search of "distant monsters" to destroy, as John Quincy Adams had said. Clinton himself had begun as one of those voices in his campaign, criticizing his predecessor for being too occupied in attending to matters abroad at the expense of those at home. But the necessities of circumstance quickly forced Clinton to change.

"No other modern president inherited a stronger, safer international position than Bill Clinton," said commentator William Hyland, yet just the opposite was the case. People had underestimated the degree of political unanimity imposed by the Cold War. With that conflict ended, instead of a smaller, safer era, the world of the 1990s was larger and more volatile, breaking up into multiple movements of nationalism that were often aggressive, suspicious, and unsure. Instead of stability, a new savage life emerged that would be characterized by the democratization of warfare where conflicts between nations had been replaced by small wars of extermination between ethnic groups.

Few appear to have recognized the change. Clinton is too often described as being fearful of the bold stroke when it came to courageously intervening in crises like Somalia or Bosnia. But who was not? The U.S. military shrank from any involvement in Bosnia the way a deer might shy away from dogs. Was the United Nations more resolute? Was NATO? The Europeans impudently declared that the slaughters of Yugoslavia were their problem and then allowed a spirit of paralyzed bafflement to settle over everything they did. What resulted was little more than futile dithering. Was Clinton more reluctant to bring himself to the point of action than his own American public in the Bosnian debacle? I don't believe so. At the time of some of the worst Balkan massacres, 70 percent of the U.S. public was against intervening. As Arthur Schlesinger noted, the most widespread thought was, Why should a son or a daughter die in some remote place where the victory had no meaning for the welfare of the United States? The American public couldn't distinguish between peacekeeping and combat.

Was Congress any better? During the Kosovo savagery, the Republican-led U.S. Congress hardly acquitted itself with any distinction: the Senate voted to approve air strikes to stop the mass murder, true, but the House didn't get around to it until a month later. On April 29, 1999, the House voted not to allow ground forces into Kosovo unless Clinton first obtained explicit approval, and then in a tie vote, failed to signal its approval for the ongoing air campaign.

Clinton was a politician. That is not simply an obvious remark. Without a party, a statesman is nothing. If the leader of a political faction goes beyond the wishes of his associates and allies, and emancipates himself from their control, he may be sidelined, ignored, or suppressed. If Abraham Lincoln appeared morally cowardly at times when it came to the question of slavery, seeming to do so little and the little he did was done feebly and too late, it was chiefly because he had to wait for the vast majority to catch up with his views. Clinton, like Lincoln, could not afford to get too far ahead of his public on such a potentially explosive issue as Bosnia. A politician doesn't simply live in a political environment, he lives *by means* of it. His responses to the challenges in that environment must be appropriate and effective or he perishes. However fitfully or slowly, Clinton always moved ahead on a path he had chosen, and, unlike his successor, George W. Bush, he never attempted to suspend or muffle dissent. In the end, like the quick and brilliant learner he was, Clinton dealt with the tyranny in Iraq and the murderousness in the Balkans with exceptional moral strength, tactical dexterity, and strategic skill, often making daring decisions in secret. In cases where it really counted, he displayed an inner steel, a strength, that has been little noticed and less praised.

When Clinton was elected, no country in the West had yet understood the special kind of evil that Osama bin Laden's al Qaeda represented. (When the first World Trade Center bombing occurred in 1993, Clinton initially thought the culprits to be Serbs, just as he later did in the 1995 Oklahoma City bombing.) In brief, no one at that time had ever seen a terrorist movement that lacked a national base in any country but consisted of a network of loosely connected, almost autonomous cells, dedicated to the spread of Islam—using the mass murder of innocents of any religion who did not endorse bin Laden's religious-political agenda as its means of expansion. Iran's Ayatollah Khomeini had proved a key initial figure here. In 1979 in a world where Muslims were tending toward secular, pro-Western models, he reversed the direction of history. One of the reasons President Jimmy Carter had been so ineffective in Iran is that the world had never seen a movement of liberation that looked not to the future with its secular moderation, but to religion and the past, embracing a more primitive, stringent form of Islam instead of a more progressive, less restrictive, and more modern species of it.

For years, U.S. Middle East policy bordered on the fear of Iranian expansion to the point of myopic obsession. The fact that Clinton had the adventurous courage to free himself of this fear and allowed Iranian arms to be shipped to the Bosnian Muslims, his use of Croatian proxies to alter the balance of power on the ground combined with his ruthlessly effective tactics to deny al Qaeda a foothold in the Balkans, are to me presidential accomplishments of the first distinction.

As for the 1993 Somalia crisis, it was a nightmare that Clinton did not create. The chief failure, according to former CENTCOM commander Gen. Anthony Zinni, lay with the snarled mess that was the chain of command. According to Zinni, the Pentagon had five separate systems of command and control, the Delta people had their own, the Rangers had their own, none of them working in coordination with the others. As I show, when the CIA obtained intelligence that could have avoided the Black

Hawk Down incident, the Defense Department officials didn't act on it and the result was disaster.

Clinton had to learn to overcome his early dislike of the CIA. According to Tyler Drumheller, a former senior CIA official who worked in clandestine operations, Clinton came in with a deep suspicion of the agency, but nonetheless seemed focused on how to revamp it for the post–Cold War era, a focus we shared with Europe. And Drumheller himself soon learned to appreciate the new president. "Clinton was actually very good to work with. He could be tough as hell. When it came to the war with Serbia, he was concerned only to get the job done. Civilian casualties didn't bother him at all." Clinton National Security Advisor Tony Lake said of the president: "He grew into being able to make the tough decisions."

The covert operation that toppled Milosevic and sent him as a prisoner to The Hague is still being taught today at the CIA as an example of the effectiveness of a relatively bloodless coup that uses both open and covert means. I first wanted to do this book because of that operation. It represented to me one of those splendid and exhilarating moments of history when men and woman of unflinching resolution and noble purpose overcame their fear and reclaimed their dignity and humanity, risking everything by stubbornly refusing any longer to be mere tools of another person's will. In fact, this book is intended to credit and honor the president, his advisors, and the men and women in the field or in overseas posts who made such a moment of supreme self-assertion possible for the Serb people. This book is intended as a tribute to them as well.

A NOTE ON SOURCES

This book is based on hundreds of hours of interviews with over fifty former top Clinton administration officials. Since the book deals mainly with information that is still highly classified, most were conducted on a "background" basis—meaning that people agreed to talk only on the condition that they would not be identified by name. Indeed, in several cases, a source would agree to have "a conversation that never took place."

Since several sources have recently become members of President Barack Obama's administration, at least three who had agreed to be quoted have withdrawn their names.

In addition to former White House officials, I interviewed members of Congress and their staff, former senior Defense Intelligence Agency officials, Treasury Department officials, and former National Security Agency officials. They did not want their names to be used.

Some have remained on the record. Richard Holbrooke, the architect of the Dayton Accords and a key negotiator with Serb leader Slobodan Milosevic in 1999, not only helped with facts and insights, but read parts of the draft.

Former U.S. ambassador to Croatia Peter Galbraith offered invaluable help. We had multiple, detailed interviews and e-mail exchanges, and he was generous in offering to read parts of the draft. Special thanks go to his wife, Tune Bringa, a U.N. worker in Bosnia, who was one of the first to discover the horror of the 1995 massacre at Srebrenica. Her reading of that section was invaluable.

With special thanks to Gen. Wesley Clark for reading parts of the draft.

On the Israel and Iraq sections, special appreciation goes to former State Department officials Ned Walker and David Mack.

I also wish to acknowledge the help of former Foreign Service officer Louis Sell, who shared his knowledge and was patient with my many questions.

I did not interview former President Clinton because I wanted no taint of authorization and knew that many topics in this book would be ones on which he simply could not comment.

As UPI's intelligence correspondent from 2001 to 2005, I developed many priceless mentors and guides, many of whom continue with their help to this day. My deepest thanks go to:

Andrew Bacevich, Bob Baer, Roger Barnett, Milt Bearden, Stan Bedlington, J. Rand Beers, Rachel Bronson, Whitley Bruner, Kurt Campbell, Vince Cannistraro, Sandy Charles, Andrew Cockburn, Angelo Codevilla, Steve Cohen, Tony Cordesman, Ivo Daalder, Jack Devine, Tyler Drumheller, Fritz Ermarth, Ric Francona, Graham Fuller, Toby Gati, Rohan Gunaratna, Gen. Joe Hoar, ret., Charles Jefferson, Larry Johnson, Kenneth Katz, Martha Kessler, Mike Kraft, Richard Kerr, Pat Lang, David Long, Gal Luft, David Manners, Warren Marik, Phoebe Marr, Roy Neel, Robert Oakley, Mike O'Hanlon, Ken Pollack, B. Raman, Paul Redmond, Peter Rodman, Marc Sageman, Gary Sick, John Shattuck, Dimitri Simes, Nancy Soderberg, Phil Stoddard, Greg Thielmann, Lt. Gen. Bernard Trainor, ret., Courtney West, Wayne White, Burt Wides, Judith Yaphe, Warren Zimmermann, Gen. Anthony Zinni, ret.

I have benefited greatly from the guidance and advice of my editors at St. Martin's, Tom Dunne and Rob Kirkpatrick. Rob especially was a steady and unremitting hand that kept the craft on course amidst the odd storm occasionally streaming past. Both Tom and Rob expertly took a vast amount of material and turned it into a finished book. Together with their assiduous copy editor, Fred Chase, they have my affectionate thanks. I also want to thank my assiduous agent, Joe Vallely, for his counsel and encouragement. Special appreciation goes to my wife, Carol, whose hawk's eye did such expert copyediting. She worked like a slave in a mine without complaint.

Arthur Schlesinger once said that in grading presidential leadership, the reputation of a U.S. commander in chief was at its lowest point ten to fifteen years after his death. The ratings of Theodore Roosevelt and Woodrow Wilson were at rock bottom for at least a decade after their deaths. FDR's and John Kennedy's were embarrassingly bad as well. Happily Bill

Clinton with all his gifts and flaws is very much still with us, but it should humble us to think that in the present, we write from "the hollow of the wave," as Schlesinger put it with his usual grace and deftness. Every generation judges presidents through the prism of its own experience with all its bias, faddish prejudices, and personal idiosyncrasies. Judging from history, it would seem that the early assessments of Clinton are likely to be wildly off the mark, mine included. My purpose here has been to bring about a basic reexamination. If that occurs, that is enough.

PART ONE

THE

TRANSFORMATIONAL

PRESIDENT

THE DILEMMAS OF LEADERSHIP

Summer daylight was fading outside the long, tall windows of the Lincoln Bedroom. Present were senior policymakers, gathered in the residence rather than the West Wing, because the residence has a side door through which cabinet members could enter without being spotted by the press. The mood in the room was gloomy and subdued.[1] The White House serving staff was usually clad in their formal whites at such occasions, but this evening they had on somber, close-fitting black jackets. Their faces were grave. They moved silently among the senior officials, stopping now and then to bend a bit at the waist to politely extend silver trays full of tiny canapés, shrimp, and saucers of cocktail sauce. Few of the tense, unsmiling guests took anything to eat. Cocktails with gin, whiskey, or vodka were available but those who had a drink stuck to Diet Coke or club soda with cubes of ice. The air was tense. This meeting was not social, but top secret, and its agenda was a grim one.

President Bill Clinton was about to perform his first major act as the country's commander in chief: he was about to launch air strikes against Iraqi dictator Saddam Hussein in Baghdad. It would be the first use of military force in Clinton's presidency.

It had begun with special assistant to the president Richard Clarke, a man of boundless energy who had a high forehead, thinning red hair, and hard, intense eyes. Every day those eyes fell on hundreds of intelligence reports, embassy messages, and translations from foreign media, forwarded to him from the White House Situation Room. It was on a Sunday in June that he spotted an item that froze his blood: an Arab-language newspaper in London was reporting that Kuwaiti police had foiled an assassination attempt by Iraq on the former U.S. president.[2]

Two months before, in April, former President George H. W. Bush had returned in a triumphant visit to Kuwait, the country where less than two years before, U.S.-led forces had routed formidable masses of Iraqi troops, sending them fleeing north in headlong panic. Bush had arrived in Kuwait City to receive an award from the Kuwaiti royal family and his reception had been hearty, tumultuous, and grateful. As far as anyone knew, the trip had gone off without incident.

Clarke was perplexed. He had been given no intelligence of the assassination attempt from the Central Intelligence Agency, the Federal Bureau of Investigation, or even the Department of State. Clarke immediately picked up a secure phone and called the U.S. ambassador to Kuwait, Ryan Crocker. Clarke asked Crocker if he had seen the item. Crocker said he hadn't and then chattered effusively about the exhilarating time Bush had had in Kuwait. And then suddenly a great light broke over Crocker. Surely, he asked, surely Clarke wasn't suggesting that he ask the Kuwaitis about the report of the plot? Clarke knew that under new rules a National Security Council staffer wasn't allowed to ask a U.S. ambassador to do *anything*, and after chatting a bit more, they ended the conversation.

But Crocker would hear a message even when it hadn't been said. On Monday, a sealed envelope lay on Clarke's desk. It was so sensitive that it could not be sent electronically from the Situation Room. Crocker had come through. There was no doubt—the Kuwaitis had foiled a scheme by Iraq to kill the former president. Clarke quickly called National Security Advisor Tony Lake, a brilliant, mild, bespectacled man who looked like a college professor. "Saddam tried to kill Bush," Clarke said.

Crocker had startled the Kuwaitis by saying that the United States already knew of the plot. He startled them even more when he demanded that the United States be given access to the prisoners. There were sixteen in all, but only two were Iraqis. Saddam's plan was chillingly savage. The Iraqis had been recruited in Basra and given a Toyota Land Cruiser, then driven into Kuwait thanks to a whiskey-smuggling ring. The Land Cruiser had been fitted to a bomb, and then the vehicle was to be driven to a place near the university in Kuwait City.[3] The bomb would be exploded when Bush's motorcade went past. It had enough explosive power to level four city blocks. It probably would have worked, except for bad luck. The jittery driver of the Land Cruiser had gotten mixed up in a traffic accident, and Kuwaiti police discovered the bomb and began to make arrests.

Soon, teams from the FBI, the CIA, and the Secret Service were on their way to Kuwait. Clinton quickly demanded two parallel investigations, one by law enforcement, the other by U.S. intelligence. The U.S. team members were far from displaying the slightest trace of enthusiasm. Everyone knew Saddam capable of any kind of human meanness, a creature capable of killing the man who had humiliated him before all of the world, yet, in a surprising display of inertia, the team members felt they were wasting time on a wild-goose chase. Iraq's secret police operated with the greatest stealth and cunning. How likely was it, the U.S. investigators scoffed, that a Toyota Land Cruiser could be impudently driven all the way in over the Kuwait-Iraq border, packed full of explosives, and allowed parking in an area close enough to the route of President Bush's motorcade? Such a plan was clearly preposterous. It was true the Kuwaiti officials had confessions from the suspects, but who would put any faith in those, especially since they were likely the result of torture or coercion?

But as the U.S. operatives, known as spooks, began interviewing suspects, their attitude drastically altered. They were both amazed and disconcerted by the degree of technical detail the suspects divulged about the makings of the bomb. Finally, after hours of careful interviews, the U.S. forensic experts were led in to see the bomb itself. They went over it with great care, like doctors examining a patient, until they had no more doubts. The bomb's construction bore the same distinctive signature of other Iraqi murder bombs they'd seen. As Secretary of State Warren Christopher said, "It was the forensic equivalent of a DNA match."[4]

On June 23, National Security Advisor Lake, whose appearance belied his energy and depth of insight, had his usual Wednesday lunch with Secretary of Defense Les Aspin, a loquacious, disorganized former congressman, along with Secretary of State Christopher, laconic by temperament. Lake called Clarke. Clarke and one person from the State Department and Department of Defense were to develop a plan, a checklist for targets of retaliation.

The pressing question was what course of action should the United States take now that it had solid proof of a direct link to Iraq? A focused, frowning Clinton had to decide. Should the United States wait for the verdict of the Kuwaiti courts? Beyond any other consideration, a message of unmistakeable menace had to be sent to Saddam. Would the death of the suspects by hanging be enough to send a deterring message to Saddam? Air strikes would. But should the United States do it unilaterally or obtain prior approval from the U.N. Security Council?

Secretary of State Christopher came to play a prominent part in the outcome. The decision was made to strike unilaterally. As Christopher put the case, "A plot to kill a former president was an attack on our nation." Working from a target list developed by the Joint Chiefs of Staff and the CIA, Christopher argued that, out of concern for legal grounds, the strike should be limited to hitting one facility, the headquarters of the Mukhabarat, the Iraqi secret police, in the Al Mansur district of Baghdad—a building that sat amid other tempting targets like the headquarters of the Baath Party to the south, the Mukhabarat Directorate, M-19, for covert procurement to the north, the Special Republican Guard headquarters, or the headquarters of the Air Defense Command and the like. Soon Aspin, Lake, and the imposing chairman of the Joint Chiefs, Gen. Colin Powell, appeared to brief Clinton. As they talked, Clinton stayed busy jotting notes on a small pad, peppering the DOD officials with questions: "Are we sure the evidence is compelling? Is this a truly proportionate response? How can we minimize harm to innocent civilians?" Clinton had even pressed Powell on what would be the best time to strike. Christopher had already said the strike should be made on a Saturday night, to keep casualties to a minimum.

Finally on that fateful late afternoon in the residence, Clinton, tardy as always, ambled into the Lincoln Bedroom and opened the meeting. All the heavyweights were there: Christopher; Vice President Al Gore, solid, imposing and hawkish; along with Lake and Powell. As head of the Joint Chiefs, it would be Powell who would lead the secret meeting. Powell at that time stood at the summit of his public reputation, a figure of extraordinary renown. Whether it was in the Congress, in the White House, or in the media, he was seen as being perhaps *the* major player in Washington, his political skills, his canny knowledge, his effectiveness rivaling, if they did not overshadow, even the president's. It was widely said that it had been principally his generalship that lay behind America's stunning victory in the Gulf War, but in spite of that Powell was not a belligerent man. He never looked for a fight. When it came to the use of military force, he embodied a cautious sagacity that bordered on the timid. "The reluctant warrior," as one reporter had put it, and Powell had been deeply pleased. He had served in Vietnam and experienced its full bitterness. What pugnacious voices in the Pentagon or Congress saw as a quick victory, a sure thing, almost a pushover, Powell saw as something liable to be more difficult, bloody, heartbreaking, and trying to the spirit than anyone at first thought. Any military action was therefore not to be undertaken lightly. Generals moved to glory over long rows of graves. Instead, Powell believed that in foreign affairs a country should move forward like Frederick the Great, only after a detailed, careful, painstaking assessment of possible risks and rewards.

"I detected a common thread running through the careers of officers who ran aground even though they were clearly able," he said. "They fought what they found foolish or irrelevant, and consequently did not survive to do what they considered vital." He never forgot to "pay the king his shilling." He accommodated. He acquiesced. He advanced.[5]

His greatest fame rested on his Powell Doctrine. If a war became necessary, "You had to do it right," he said. "You've got to be decisive. You've got to go in massively. You've got to be wise and fight in a way that keeps casualties to a minimum." This seems perfectly sound, but it is also a way of hedging your bets. The doctrine provides an escape hatch, as a commentator once observed. "When the day of reckoning comes, you can always say, 'We didn't go in massively enough. We lost because we didn't go in to win.'" Powell had made grave errors in conducting the war against Iraq but they were only known and lamented inside the corridors of the Pentagon. Few outside knew of them.

Now standing before the Clinton heavyweights, Powell was about to "conduct a graduate level tutorial for a national security freshman," as he put it later.[6] No one in the room had ever served in the military. The campaign had exposed Clinton as a draft dodger, someone who had gamed the system, employing the grossest deceit to manipulate it, and thereby escape doing military service, as had many senior American public figures like Dick Cheney, the Wyoming congressman who had been secretary of defense during Desert Storm. So initially the pairing of Powell and Clinton could have proved awkward. Not only had Clinton dodged the draft, but he had strongly opposed the Vietnam War. The thought that he had become not simply a president but commander in chief had been slow to sink in with Clinton. In the beginning the new president hadn't yet known how to give a military salute. When the time came, he would furtively touch only his fingertips to his bowed head, making nearby observers cringe. The matter was discussed by senior White House staff, and finally Tony Lake had been dragooned to talk to the president about it. Lake hadn't served in the military, but he had served in Vietnam as a Foreign Service officer, and senior staff had decided that Clinton's salute "came under the heading of national security." After their private talk, a new crispness entered Clinton's salute and remained there.

Now it was Powell's time. The Pentagon had already mulled over possible targets, finally settling on Baghdad. As Powell began, he was all courtesy and all command as he walked the new president through the proposed strike against Baghdad. The weapons would be cruise missiles. He went on to explain what the attack might achieve, what could go wrong, possible

Iraqi reactions, and the decisions the president would have to make at each stage. Clinton had imposed only a few limitations. He wanted the weapons to hit Baghdad at midnight, so as not to fall on the Muslim holy day of Friday. He wanted to kill as few people as possible. On the stroke of 4:22 P.M., EDT, on June 26, 1993, 12:22 A.M., June 27, in Baghdad, cruise missiles were fired at Saddam's intelligence headquarters from a U.S. destroyer and cruiser in the Red Sea. As they soared away, smoke furrowing and spreading wide from their tails, Clinton was in the Oval Office at the old-fashioned desk made from the timbers of the British warship HMS *Resolute*, a gift from Queen Victoria, with the phone to his ear. Clinton had already consulted his counterparts in neighboring Arab countries like Egypt, Saudi Arabia, and Kuwait, and they had been supportive. Clinton then called George Bush. "We've completed our investigation," he said. "It was clearly directed against you. I've ordered a cruise missile attack." Clinton closed the call by assuring Bush he'd done everything to minimize the loss of life.

"You'll be judged by whether you hit the target," Warren Christopher had said with typical bluntness. He was a laconic man from North Dakota who didn't mince words, and he was right.

Throughout the incident, the deeply scrutinizing eyes of Colin Powell had remained fastened on Clinton, wondering if the new president had the cold inner hardness required for such a strike, closely watching the president's behavior, his ability to concentrate and choose, assessing his control of his emotions.

Clinton had, at times, appeared to wobble. When he had first been given the target, his only comment was, "Well, this may teach him a lesson, but if it doesn't we'll have to do more."

As the operation went forward, and as Clinton made phone calls notifying congressional leaders, Clarke came in to say that the missiles had been launched. He was floored when Clinton asked, "Well, when will we get the pictures from the missiles?" Clarke replied the missiles had no cameras, but they would know from satellites the next morning about the degree of the damage.

"Why don't the missiles have cameras in them?" Clinton asked, a bit irked.

Clarke explained that if Washington were able to communicate with the weapons, they could be interfered with or diverted.

Clinton was appalled. "We can't communicate with the missiles? What if I wanted to turn them back?"[7]

Clarke grew flustered, stammering, "Because you can't . . . there's no mechanism to."

But Clinton was about to go on television and tell the American people he had ordered Saddam's intelligence headquarters blown up. He needed some proof it had been. Clarke notified Lake, who called the number two man at the CIA, Admiral William Studeman. Studeman said they had to wait.

In the meantime, Clinton had called CNN on his own. The network had no one in Baghdad, but its cameraman in the Jordan bureau "had a cousin in Baghdad who lived close to the Iraqi intelligence headquarters." As stupefaction and horror spread through the room, Clinton said CNN had reached the man, and Clinton quoted him as saying, "The whole place blew up." So Clinton was sure enough of his results to go ahead with his TV speech.

CNN confirmed that twenty-three cruise missiles had crashed and exploded into the secret police headquarters, which was deserted at night. Unfortunately, one of the missiles went astray, killing Leilah Attar, Iraq's leading female artist.

Throughout, Powell remained impressed. Clinton, he felt, had "remained cool and resolute," he said afterward.[8]

Few at the Pentagon were impressed. To DOD officials the strike confirmed their worst misgivings and contemptuous suspicions. Military strikes "are not supposed to be a gesture," one said to me. "A military power consists of the power to injure on a large scale." Strikes were to kill and maim, destroy and lay waste. The purpose was to get quickly to your enemy so you could hit him and cause him excruciating, crippling pain. Clinton had responded, sure, but what had he actually accomplished? Killed a night watchman at Saddam's intelligence headquarters? To prove what? That Saddam could be targeted? After severely damaging most of Baghdad with a thousand-hour string of air assaults in 1991, surely Saddam knew he could be hit. "It was like watching a girl throw a softball," one disgusted former senior Pentagon official said to me of the operation. And the fact was that Clinton's election had filled his military critics in the Pentagon with genuine alarm. Clinton's retaliation on Iraq was not an auspicious beginning for men who belonged to a "can do" culture whose chief purpose was to blow up buildings and kill people. To them when you struck at an enemy you aimed to hit him with pulverizing force.

But the Pentagon carping overlooked a paramount fact: Saddam Hussein never again attempted a terrorist assault on any American anywhere.

2

PRESIDENT OF ALL THE PEOPLE

Few men entered the office of the president of the United States with such huge potential for accomplishment as William Jefferson Clinton. He was the first Democrat to be elected in twelve years, and his victory over incumbent President George H. W. Bush came as a startling upset to many, even to some of Clinton's most fervent supporters. Clinton's emergence as president-elect seemed to materialize out of nowhere, but the truth was the bulk of his adult life had been spent in politics. There are always a few rare people who can early sense their fate. Clinton was one of these. Somehow early in life, Clinton acquired a romantic image of himself and what he could become, and even in his teens, he had already begun to think of himself as a person with a special and exceptional destiny. It is not unusual for young men to have such dreams, but it is extraordinary when the dreamer does not allow them to expire. In 1968, when only twenty-two years old, Clinton told friends that he one day wanted to be president, and he was not self-deceived. In the end he would capture the presidency, not once but twice, and stand alone on that pinnacle of predominance that he had so early in life chosen to climb.

Clinton was the total political animal, armed with a vast arsenal of talents and abilities. Politics for Clinton was the ultimate expression of his most persistent, innate personal characteristics. Everything he did was politically driven and had as its motive the goal of advancing his political career. To him, politics and policy were closely interlinked because politics was the *only* means by which idealism and philosophy could be turned into measures that would help ordinary people more easily bear their life's burdens. If Clinton could be said to have a political creed, it was his unwavering belief that politics was the prime instrument of human betterment.

In the incumbent President George H. W. Bush, Clinton had faced an opponent who appeared entrenched and invulnerable. After all, Bush had won the Persian Gulf War that year, the largest conflict since World War II, and he had presided with masterly sureness over incredibly difficult matters such as the reunification of Germany, the fall of the Soviet Union, and the reorientation to the West of what had been the Eastern Bloc countries, now called merely Central Europe. In brief, George Bush was a man who not only knew what he was doing but he could make others believe that he knew. Against a popular and towering figure like Bush, few were going to make a big wager on an unimportant young nobody from Arkansas.

Skeptics, however, had underestimated the newcomer's talents.

Perhaps Clinton's most important gift was his temperament. As Walter Bagehot said of Lord Palmerston, Clinton had in him "all that a common man has" but something more. Clinton seemed touched by a larger spirit, and like FDR, Clinton's ability to read personalities surpassed the uncanny. An advisor, Leon Panetta, quickly grasped this. Clinton, he said, "can walk into any group, anywhere, anytime. And for whatever it is, it's those magic antennae that go out that can sense what an audience is about, who they are, are they conservative or liberal, or this or that—he can pick it up and he can speak to them, and have them in his pocket."[1]

He could make the merely ceremonial seem intensely personal. FDR's speechwriter Samuel Rosenberg once wrote of Roosevelt, "He could make a casual visitor believe that he had been waiting all day for this hour to arrive. Only a person who really loved human beings could give that impression."[2] Like FDR, Clinton knew by instinct that the people wanted down-to-earth leaders who could touch their hearts, and his ability to hit the best approach was unsurpassed in its emotional rightness and perceptive sincerity. During the first campaign, he was shaking hands on a rope line when he came abreast of a couple with a disabled child. As expected, he first gave special focus to the child, but then Clinton turned and gazed directly at his brother. "Your parents have their hands full, you know that," he told the boy. "But don't ever forget, they love you just as much."

His oral skills were superb and decisive. The culminating showplace for this gift was put on display when the Democratic Leadership Council appeared with a handful of Democratic hopefuls including Jay Rockefeller, Al Gore, and Richard Gephardt. Clinton had no prepared text, but he began to talk about the problems of the "forgotten" middle class of America and asked, "Why in the world haven't the Democrats been able to take advantage of these conditions?

"I'll tell you why, because so many of the people who need to vote for us, the very burdened middle class we're talking about, have not trusted us in national elections to defend our national interests abroad, or to take their tax money and spend it with discipline."

Then Clinton said, "Our burden is to give people a new choice, rooted in the old values, a new choice that is simple, that offers *opportunity*, demands responsibility, gives citizens more say, provides them with responsive government—all because we recognize that we are a *community*.

"We are all in this together, and we will go up or down together."[3] It was something FDR might have said.

All in all, the campaign of 1992 was a curious one. Clinton hated to antagonize, and his utterances were designed to gain the support of a wide variety of people. What resulted was a lot of talk of job growth, protection on the job, welfare reform, economic stimulus, and health care programs, but many wondered how definite a program he was actually offering. To his critics, it was simply an assortment of proposals, some well conceived, but others vague to the point of uselessness. Clinton seemed better at assailing the policies of his predecessor than proclaiming fresh and definite ones of his own.

But there is campaigning and there is governing. To gain the White House is one thing; to assemble an effective governing group is another. Bill Clinton entered office with the highest negative ratings of any president in modern times, and no other president would tarnish his victory by committing so many grievous stumbles during the first months in office as Bill Clinton. The concern of Clinton's victorious campaign manager, Mickey Kantor, the fifty-three-year-old lawyer who had worked to elect Clinton since 1987, was to ensure the new group acted and made major decisions within the first hundred days, the traditional after-election truce where Clinton would hopefully be free of the curse of organized, concerted opposition to his designs. The most immediate and pressing issue in the wake of triumph was who would be in charge of the transition. To Kantor, speed was the only thing that mattered. The transition period was to be exploited with the utmost energy, and Kantor urged this with all the force of his soul.

Clinton's campaigns were always whirlwind, cyclonic affairs, and he had visited more cities than any previous president in his race for the White House. The problem was that he had expended more strength than he had and entered his presidency without a voice or a spark of energy. When the pestering Kantor kept urging decisive steps be taken, Clinton's wife, Hillary, bridled into open, ugly revolt. Henry Cisneros, a Hispanic, and soon to be the new secretary of housing and urban development, was at a meeting when, as Kantor exhorted Bill Clinton to take prompt actions, the first lady suddenly got a hard, inflexible face. "Don't do that!" she snarled. "You're not going to push him! Look at how exhausted he is! We are not going to be pushed! *So back off!*"

The lethal tone of the imperial "We" froze the blood of those who were there.

It is a commonplace that no initial presidential appointment is as important as that of the White House chief of staff. The White House was the engine of the country's political power and to govern effectively a president had to have a clear staff structure and competent subordinates. Kantor was forced out, and Clinton then turned to Warren Christopher to handle the job. Christopher was twenty-one years older than the president. He was a lawyer by profession, a highly disciplined workhorse, an outwardly modest almost maddeningly meticulous man, but hardly a furious driver. In fact, he lacked energy of life, and when he could, shrank from confrontation. Leon Panetta, a new member of Clinton's economic team, described Christopher as "a facilitator, he's someone who will try and work with you and sense what you're thinking, try and get it done, but he's not someone who will say, 'Look, you son of a bitch, do that!'" Christopher, his talents always those of a deputy, was not likely to stir alarm in his president, who then proceeded to pick for the job the most manageable man instead of the most capable one.

So even as the administration was supposed to be poised to act with energy on its first programs, the White House was forced to work under the handicap of having no competent chief of staff. After a lot of deft, last-minute footwork, Clinton finally moved Christopher from chief of staff to secretary of state, perhaps the most important cabinet job in his administration, and for the chief of staff, the president called in an old kindergarten friend from Arkansas, Thomas "Mac" McLarty, called "Mac the Nice." McLarty never mastered the complexities of his job and was finally replaced by the forceful, well-organized Leon Panetta. Perhaps the most unfortunate part of the whole episode is that the poor appointments left many veteran and expert Democrats sitting idly on the sidelines—people like skilled diplomats Richard Holbrooke and Tom Donilon.

To many, Clinton's very style of leadership exhibited a maddening, scatterbrained informality that seemed to feed the internal chaos reigning in the White House. The young president did not like using executive authority to impose decisions but preferred to take time to forge a loose consensus first. Clinton's nature had an accommodating, reconciling streak, due, in my opinion, to having grown up in a household where, thanks to a violent and alcoholic stepfather, the menace of physical abuse was always there at the edge of domestic life. Clinton's childhood had been its own horrible, little hell of private pain, and it had made him almost compulsive in his efforts to avoid conflict. The administration's top expert on Russia, Strobe Talbott, noted that Clinton, when negotiating with a foreign official, began every discussion by saying, "I agree with that, I agree with that," to the dignitary's assertion, whether he did in fact agree or not.

Whatever the causes, the initial behavior of his cabinet was unfocused, disorganized, contradictory, and embarrassingly amateurish. Attending the initial meeting of Clinton's foreign policy experts, Gen. Colin Powell, soon to depart as chairman of the Joint Chiefs, was dismayed by the relaxed, unhurried, informal, frat house style of the new leadership. At one of his first White House meetings, Powell was sitting in the room with the Principals when he noticed that neither Vice President Gore nor the president had arrived. Powell, like Clinton's inner staff, was just starting to learn that the president had trouble sticking with schedules and was almost always late. Tardiness, of course, was only a minor annoyance. What worried Powell more was the lack of focused purpose or any sense of intellectual efficiency among assembled staff. As they sat there waiting for Clinton, National Security Advisor Tony Lake occupied the chairman's seat, but he didn't move to take the lead. Secretary of Defense Les Aspin was also there, but he too didn't propose anything, and the elderly Christopher was, by habit, used to waiting to hear what the policy was to be instead of attempting to play any part in its formulation.

When Vice President Gore had finally shown up, the participants had to get up and shuffle around the table to make a place for him, and by the time Clinton came in, they had made sure a place had been saved for him. Yet even after Clinton at last sat down, Powell found the atmosphere disconcerting. He was accustomed to secretaries of state like George Shultz and James Baker, who, at such meetings, were all courtesy, all business—and all command. In Powell's words, they strode in "like chieftains" and quickly got down to solid matters of fact. By contrast, this meeting was like a discussion at a think tank, meandering, inconclusive. Such gatherings were like "graduate student bull sessions," Powell would say later. The informality was so ingrained that there was no established sense of hierarchy—staffers were able to sound off and waste time, and Powell was shocked when a subordinate of Lake's argued with his chief in front of everyone.

Yet Powell was not blind to Clinton's talents. The general enjoyed the incandescent brilliance and refreshing candor, and the breadth of knowledge that Clinton brought to these meetings because the president was able to "put history, politics and policy into perspective." But Clinton didn't demand any intensity of concentration and instead allowed the talk to disjointedly wander where it would and usually the group would come up with what sounded like a good plan, turn it over a bit, adjourn, and then, upon thinking it over once more, realized it wasn't such a great plan after all and they would start from scratch at the next meeting.

The White House was adrift.

3

THE SPREADING OF DARKNESS

In 1990, only a handful of people in Europe or America saw the big storm coming in the Balkans. The ominous signs had been there, the darkening thunderclouds on the horizon, the little malignant flickers of lightning fluttering in them, the little gusts of Serbian nationalism beginning to stiffen to a gale, but from 1980 to 1990, they remained merely signs. As the decade of the 1980s ended, the mood of Europe was hopeful, and everywhere there was a new resolution of purpose and everything seemed easy and possible. Much of this mood was due to the incredible disappearance of the Soviet Union from the stage of history. The demise of the "evil empire" was unprecedented. No one had ever seen anything like it. The USSR was not conquered, it was not destroyed, and it was not overthrown. It simply swayed and abruptly collapsed with a rickety crash. A superpower, a large industrial state with a nuclear arsenal, had simply ceased to exist and its ruin injected Europe, or at least its western half, with a huge sense of relief.

To Clinton, the demise of the Soviet Union and the freeing of the former Eastern Bloc states offered a dazzling and unrepeatable opportunity. It was a chance for the United States to take the lead in building "a free, peaceful, undivided Europe," driven by the "inexorable logic of globalization," as Clinton put it. All over the continent and in Washington there was talk of the full and free circulation of goods, services, capital, and people. The trappings of national sovereignty were giving way to fresh cooperation among transnational agencies.

To be sure there were obstacles to overcome. The former Eastern Bloc countries were burdened with obsolescent, malfunctioning plants and management methods combined with vast environmental desecration. For them, to become members of the new Europe[1] was their only real option, yet it would take time for their sick economies to recuperate, modernize, obtain foreign aid, and secure new markets. Membership in the European Community glowed brightly like gold on the horizon.

In the Balkans, considered one of the more backward and impoverished regions on the continent, even Yugoslavia had appeared promising. Journalist David Halberstam once called Yugoslavia "stapled together," but the phrase is more striking than accurate. The country was the post–World War I offspring of President Woodrow Wilson's commitment to self-determination for small countries, and America, along with France, was one of its godfathers.[2] It was also a multiethnic state made up of six republics that subsumed five nations, three religions, and two alphabets. For example, two of the republics, Slovenia and Croatia, were Catholic and had formerly been part of the Austro-Hungarian Empire. Both used the Latin alphabet. Serbia, Montenegro, Macedonia, and Bosnia had been ruled for centuries by the Ottoman Empire. They were Orthodox in religion and used the Cyrillic alphabet. The republic of Bosnia was Muslim and Islamic.

As Warren Zimmermann, the last U.S. ambassador to Belgrade, observed, Yugoslavia at its best "stood for civility and tolerance among peoples with different ethnic backgrounds and different historical experiences."[3]

To naive policymakers in the former Bush administration, it seemed clear that Belgrade would make the peaceful transition from a subsidized socialist economy to market-driven capitalism while being careful to preserve those features of socialism still popular with the public—low prices, cheap rents, guaranteed jobs, and the like. That was not in doubt. The chief question was who in that country would head and direct this liberalizing reform, and the Bush administration thought it had already found its man. His name was Slobodan Milosevic, a dumpy little man with a big, high forehead and ears like the handles on teacups. He was a Serb whose career had been in international banking, he had been to America, and he was thought by some senior Bush officials to be an economic liberal.

To National Security Advisor Tony Lake, the Bush administration's misconception of Milosevic was understandable. Lake had read the intelligence reports; he had talked with Zimmermann and other State Department officials. The Serb made a stunning first impression. His English was clear, forceful, and competent. He dressed well. His cherubic cheeks gave him the innocence of a baby. He drank scotch on the rocks and smoked Italian cigarettes. His manner was affable, and then there was his mind, clear, lucid, well briefed, quick and insightful, abounding in skillful pretense. Best of all, instead of reciting the usual clumsily cut polygons of communist dogma, Milosevic seemed remarkably open to free markets and privatization.

Milosevic proved anything but. Not only did he despise private property, he was a communist and Serb imperialist, believing that the Serbs were underdogs who had wrongfully been denied their rightful destiny to be the real rulers of Yugoslavia. Milosevic had proved a master at whipping up the more ignorant segments of the Serb populace, manipulating them through their resentments, able to mobilize them to aggressive conquest by means of the ruthless suppression of Yugoslavia's minorities, killing them to displace them and steal their land.

Shadows were growing up everywhere, and some new and sinister menace was clearly on the march.

It was perhaps ironic that Bosnia had been the issue where Clinton had been most sharply critical of his predecessor. The United States had recognized Bosnian independence on April 7, 1992, and Serb attacks to sabotage its secession from Serbia began shortly thereafter. In his campaign, Clinton had long been in the habit of saying more than he meant, and in a speech to black teenagers of an East St. Louis high school, he'd pledged, "We may have to use military force. I would begin with air power against the Serbs to restore the basic conditions of humanity."[4] Longing to appear high-minded, Clinton said he viewed Bosnia as a "moral problem" that had to be faced, a statement viewed with indifferent skepticism in Europe whose foreign policy was based on calculations of interest, not morality. They had heard it all before. From Thomas Jefferson through Wilson and Roosevelt, America has always believed that the spread of democratic values reflected its very essence.[5] President Jimmy Carter had said, "We cannot look away when a government tortures its own people or jails them for their beliefs or denies minorities fair treatment or the right to emigrate or the right to worship." During his inaugural speech, Clinton had echoed that idealism, saying, "Our hopes, our hearts and hands are with those on every continent who are developing democracy and freedom." In the campaign, Clinton had harshly taken Bush to task for not having challenged the blockade of Sarajevo and for giving "short shrift" to the yearnings for independence on the part of those in Bosnia and Croatia.

When it came to foreign affairs, Clinton was quick to sense political danger, as he did when it came to the Balkans. Clinton was now commander in chief, he was president, and he had the power to move the country in a definite direction. Yet he seemed not to know yet what that direction should be. During his presidency, John Kennedy had preferred acting to waiting. By contrast, Clinton preferred passive waiting to acting. The foreign policy challenges were certainly there, and Clinton had inherited some dangerous ones. Yet the domestic political terrain through which Clinton moved was not promising even for a president with foreign policy ambitions. The country was full of a confusing alignment of political forces: a reluctant military, a hostile Congress, an unstable public that was basically isolationist. Part of the blame for the public's indifference to Bosnia rested with the new president. During the campaign, Clinton had said the presidency at that moment "rested on foreign policy" but that foreign policy was not something the majority of the American people "really cared about." In fact, some polls said between 60 and 70 percent of Americans were against any foreign involvement.[6]

As usual, Clinton had an unerring sense of the public mood. By the early 1990s, there had been a distinct narrowing of the American public focus away from the serious and improving to those objects, topics, and activities whose intent was to amuse, entertain, and distract. American concern for collective security and for the readiness of U.S. armed forces, the responsibilities of possessing great power, was moving from the center of interest to the periphery. We as a people were tired of foreign conflicts, of complex alliances, of the frightening shadows of distant fears. It was time to refocus, to give our fixation with foreign affairs a rest. If there were things going very wrong in America, and clearly there were, let the politicians handle these things for a change. Americans wanted action, but on the economy. That was what Clinton had been elected to do so let him do it. What was wrong if America took a new interest in itself?

Lt. Gen. John Shalikashvili, about to become Colin Powell's successor as chairman of the Joint Chiefs of Staff, observed, "What took place at that moment was what I would call a holiday from leadership." He added that the Europeans were not up to dealing with the crisis, and America for some reason had taken time off. As former Middle East Institute president Phil Stoddard said, "It was all Life, Liberty, and the Pursuit of Apathy."

There was no way for leadership to rouse a happy, smug, peaceful, self-centered populace to indignant rage over distant and remote doings such as those in the Balkans. To ask Americans to leave home to go and die for the sake of foreigners being persecuted by Serbs was to ask the impossible or, worse, the ridiculous. Clinton advisors like Dick Morris at one moment believed that Clinton's foreign policy team kept him insulated from new ideas on the topic, yet Morris himself was constantly telling the president, "You're too young now to run your own foreign policy, so let Lake and

Christopher do it." And Morris would add: "You don't want to be Lyndon Johnson. . . . It's the Democrats' disease to take the same compassion that motivates their domestic policies and let it lure them into heroic but ill-considered foreign wars."[7]

It would be an incident on a cold, rainy day in Washington in April 1993 that would belatedly jolt Clinton into realizing that if he wasn't making a priority of the plight of Bosnia, others were. On April 22, Clinton had attended the official opening of the United States Holocaust Memorial Museum, a short walk from the National Mall. As he moved through the exhibits, it struck Clinton that the Nazi crimes against the Jews and the Serbian crimes against Croats and Bosnians shared repulsive, sinister similarities—forced deportations, concentration camps, mass rapes, the widespread massacre of enemies including women and children. In Washington that day, the shelling of Sarajevo and the Muslim city of Srebrenica and the multiplying horrors were weighing on many minds. For two hours Clinton wandered through the Holocaust exhibits, staring at the four thousand used shoes, at the boxcars that had hauled victims to the extermination camps.

At the dedication ceremony, Clinton was preceded by Elie Wiesel, a survivor of Auschwitz who had written a minor classic in his memoir, *Night.* Wiesel, standing erect in the thin drizzle and gray air, gripping the podium, had asked the audience how the murderers could have done what they had and gone on living? Then he turned to impale Clinton with a stare. "Mr. President, let me tell you something," he began. "I [was] in the former Yugoslavia last fall. I cannot sleep since what I have seen. As a Jew I am saying that we must do something to stop the bloodshed in that country. People fight with each other and children die. Why? Again, something must be done."[8]

Clinton had jolted as if he'd been jabbed by a stick. The crowd applauded with real verve, while the subdued, shaken president, still off balance, had managed only a few faint claps. He had not realized until that moment what a poor figure he had been when it came to foreign policy. When asked afterward if he saw in Wiesel's remarks a personal challenge, Clinton said, "I think it was a challenge to the United States and to me and to the West to take further initiatives in Bosnia," and he said he accepted it as such.[9]

But what actions would he take was the question.

A STARLESS DARK

Any attempt to forge a new approach to Bosnia would be done by the Clinton Principals Committee, made up of Secretary of Defense Les Aspin, Secretary of State Warren Christopher, Chairman of the Joint Chiefs Gen. Colin Powell, National Security Advisor Tony Lake, Lake's deputy, Samuel "Sandy" Berger, and either Vice President Al Gore or his deputy on the National Security Council, Leon Fuerth, CIA director James Woolsey, and Madeleine Albright, the U.S. ambassador to the United Nations, in a newly created cabinet position. They gathered in the Situation Room, a small, drab, windowless room in the basement of the West Wing. Being underground it offered protection against any eavesdropping or penetration by hostile lasers that could pick up conversations from vibrations on the windowpanes, and was equipped for audiovisual presentations or secure teleconferences with overseas installations.

A dozen or so chairs would be squeezed around a central, oblong table reserved for the ranking Principals in attendance. Lake usually sat at the end of the table with Aspin on his immediate right and Christopher on his left. If Clinton attended, he usually sat at the other end of the table, facing Lake. Everyone prepared for the gathering very carefully. Christopher relates how he always held a "prebrief" in his office to discuss what he intended to say. He would gather his information from the State Department offices, including geographical bureaus like Europe or functional bureaus like Politico-Military Affairs. The Principals meeting itself could go on for a few minutes or many hours, especially among Democratic liberals.

Lake was one of the few in the new group to retain a clear head and an equally clear conviction that Clinton's presidency would in the end not stand or fall because of success or failure in reducing the national deficit, but on how effectively Clinton responded to the growing butchery of Muslims in Bosnia. Lake had already seen Jimmy Carter turned out of office because he was unable to extract U.S. hostages from Iran, and the stakes were the same here. Bosnia was turning into a nightmare of inhumanity, ugly fires of crisis were burning out of control, and America had to assert mastery over this faraway war before it asserted its own monstrous and ungovernable rules.

Lake knew that no president ever gets a clean slate, and the Bush administration had handed off to Clinton a horribly botched and ineffectual policy for the Balkans. By 1991, against the wishes of President Bush, Yugoslavia had split into six pieces. Catholic Slovenia, the most economically advanced, had been the first to leave and the first of four wars broke out. When the Serb army moved in to retake Slovenia, Belgrade's troops floundered into an embarrassing defeat after only ten days. Within a few weeks, spoiling to restore its lost esteem, the Serb army then attacked Croatia. Throughout the summer of 1991, like a row of toppled trees, major Croatian towns fell to the irresistible tide of Serb forces until they had lost a third of their country to the Serbs.

Bosnia would be next.

It was a landlocked, basically Muslim country to the south and west. Recognized as independent by the European Community on April 6, 1992, Bosnia was endorsed by the United States the next day, chiefly because Saudi Arabia and other Muslim nations had been instrumental in persuading Bush to support Bosnian independence. There was little choice. Bush owed the Saudis, who had allowed the United States to use its soil as a base to expel Saddam Hussein from Kuwait, plus the oil kingdom had also liberally used its funds to bribe Muslim allies such as Egypt and even Syria to support the venture, in Syria's case paying $6 billion, according to former CIA officials.

No sooner had Bosnia become a free republic than the pent-up, loathing fury of the Serbs burst out with the intent of destroying it. Bosnia was home to the bulk of the Serb arms industry, and Milosevic had planned to infiltrate the republic, corrupt it, and by sheer brutality and massacre keep it within the Yugoslav Federation or FRY, the latter now a rump state consisting of Serbia and Montenegro. While in public guaranteeing Bosnia's right to independence, in January of 1992, Milosevic had secretly ordered all Serb army officers born in Bosnia to return and organize. That spring, even as the Serb army publicly announced it was withdrawing, the bulk of its members had remained in Bosnia, waiting. That same month, the Yugoslav National Army (JNA) launched a huge assault to seize eastern Bosnia, attacking the city of Zvornik, shelling the town from inside Serbia. U.S. and NATO intelligence reports reported that Milosevic had smuggled eighty thousand JNA troops into the country before the attack. The whole operation was conducted with extraordinary and ruthless skill.

In the village of Biscani, Muslim captives, herded into camps, were first told they would be shot at dawn the next day. They were then forced to sing Serb nationalist songs to their jeering, scoffing captors, and the Serbs would exultantly brag that they had raped their captives' wives before killing them. The Muslim men were forced to perform sexual acts on each other, even to murder each other for the pleasure of their guards. Then at gunpoint they had to dig mass graves and collect and bury the bodies of their friends and neighbors. These same horrors occurred in places like Banja Luka. By July 1992, there were 1.1 million refugees clogging the roads.

Events continued to hurtle toward catastrophe. Soon, Serb paramilitaries had placed the Bosnian capital of Sarajevo under siege. The city's population, cut off from food and water, would be the target of incessant, systematic, and murderous shelling. By the end of June, the Bosnian government claimed that 7,200 people were dead and that another 30,000 were unaccounted for. To knowledgeable onlookers in the Clinton campaign like Lake, Albright, and soon to be Vice President Gore, the Serb design was clear. According to U.S. intelligence reports, the Serbs were planning to partition the country and they were going to divide Sarajevo as the East and West had once divided Berlin, including building a wall through its heart, except the Serbs were going to grab the plum industrial and commercial parts of the city and its choice residential districts. Even as Milosevic consolidated his gains by pious and fraudulent denials that he had any control over the Bosnia Serbs, he was secretly masterminding the operation. The tempo of attacks stepped up.

Although not yet in government, members of the Clinton camp felt unshakably convinced that something had to be done, a defiant stand had to be made. Yet to their intense disgust, the Bush administration deliberately held its response to a very low key. Until now, the Western democracies had avoided the pain of making choices and they planned to continue in the same, diffident, safe course. Any attempt at a staunch, activist policy by the administration would come up against the indifference of the general public, who could not be relied on to give their general or wholehearted backing. As a result, the reaction of the Bush State Department had been to try and keep the issue off the public radar. When reports surfaced of one hundred

Serb concentration camps, no one in the administration followed up. George Kenney, a State Department official who resigned over the matter, alleged that State Department policy was concealing genocide and that the plan was "let's pretend this isn't happening."[1]

"The basic Bush position was that it was too late for the West to mount an effective resistance, especially in an election year," a former Bush advisor said.

The world had observed this species of flaccid moral fiber before, but not since the 1930s, when the British had responded to Hitler's arming Germany with the astoundingly dense stratagem of announcing that London would unilaterally disarm. At that time, the line taken by British prime minister Ramsay MacDonald had been that the security in Europe was to be sought "not by military but by moral means." But MacDonald's world of the 1930s now happily belonged to the ages, and this was 1992. Yet incredibly, almost the very same timid song, anxious to gain favor by not offending a rampant evil force, was being played once again.

One of the most pathetic of the appeasing voices had been that of British prime minister John Major, who had told Parliament that military intervention in the Balkans was out of the question. He put his faith in pressure and diplomacy, he said, as if diplomacy needed no military underpinning. President Bush, in an effort to do *something*, had issued a rallying cry meant to stop ethnic cleansing when he urged the United Nations to pass a resolution authorizing the use of military force, *not* to curb Serb aggression, but to ensure the delivery of humanitarian aid to Serbian victims. Sensing an opponent who was unwilling to fight, the Serbs in reply closed the airport of the Bosnian capital city of Sarajevo, ending deliveries of aid.

Major's reaction was characteristic: "All the advice tells me that we cannot use force. . . . It is the nature of the Yugoslav tragedy that solutions cannot be imposed from without."[2]

To his credit, President Bush *had* inflicted some punishment on Belgrade. The United States had withdrawn its last ambassador and worked with the Europeans to suspend the rump states of Yugoslavia, Serbia and Montenegro, from international organizations, but the collective will of the West to take decisive action to halt the slaughter fell apart like soggy blotting paper. After the bitter experience of Vietnam, the Pentagon was through with nation building and opposed any open-ended commitment to Bosnia. Even plans to use force to guarantee delivery of humanitarian aid were opposed by Secretary of Defense Dick Cheney and General Powell, who said such missions could take place *only* under U.N. auspices, the conditions of which everyone knew would be crippling and inadequate. To underline their pessimistic gloom, they also incessantly made the point that Bosnia was more like Vietnam than Iraq.

Within the Bush White House, several ideas were floated at Friday morning meetings—imposing a unilateral naval blockade of ports to enforce sanctions, especially the port of Bar in Montenegro, cutting off the oil pipeline that ran into Serbia from Romania, launching unilateral air strikes against Serb artillery in the hills around Sarajevo. These suggestions went nowhere, smothered in their crib. The Pentagon even opposed trying to put together a Gulf War–type coalition that would have included visits by Secretary of State James Baker to the key European capitals.

The Bush group finally agreed that any use of force would only occur under U.N. auspices and with explicit prior congressional support (which the group knew it was certain not to get). In addition, there would be no U.S. troops deployed on the ground; that decision severely hobbled the incoming president since no Republican-controlled Congress was likely to reverse it.

After the Serbs seized the Sarajevo airport, the United Nations finally issued a forty-eight-hour ultimatum for them to open the airport or face air attacks, and the Europeans had followed with their own strong deadline. The U.N. flag soon flew over Sarajevo while the heavy Serb guns still ringed the city from the surrounding hills, biding their time. After senior Bush officials like Secretary of State Lawrence Eagleburger and National Security Advisor Brent Scowcroft left office, they suddenly came out with strong positions on Bosnia that had by no means been made manifest during their White House tenure. Eagleburger grandly declared, "From beginning to end, to right now, I am telling you I don't know any way for it to stop except with the massive use of military force."[3] Scowcroft also said almost the same thing.

Yet contradicting this hollow bravado, toward the end of Bush's term his senior officials practically fell over themselves rushing for the sidelines of the crisis. Baker had declared, "This [is] not an American problem and it should be left to the Europeans," even though the Europeans were against using force and were clearly callow and inexperienced. Baker further weakened the U.S. case for action by saying privately, "We have no dog in this fight."[4]

President Bush would then act to slip another crippling hitch around his successor's future policies by announcing that Bosnia was *not* vital to American interests. Eagleburger then pitched in to blame the victims, saying in 1992: "Until the Bosnians, Serbs and Croats decide to stop killing each other, there is nothing the world can do about it."[5] In other words, never mind Serb aggression; all sides were equally guilty.

In his memoirs, Baker is proud of U.S. reluctance to use force. He said Bush's determination that American forces would not fight a fourth war in Europe in the twentieth century was "absolutely the right decision."

But thanks to Bush's policy on Bosnia, Clinton's ability to handle the crisis had been crippled. The nightmare on Europe's doorsteps continued to build.

5

THE PRESENT STATE OF EVIL IN THE WORLD

By early February of 1993, just days after the inauguration of Bill Clinton, the United States joined with other major democracies and the United Nations in efforts to mount programs of humanitarian aid to the stricken population of Bosnia. At a long Principals meeting on February 5, Clinton had haphazardly said, "for humanitarian reasons, if no other," the United States had to take the lead on Bosnia. Several European countries had put peacekeepers on the ground, forces quite incapable of keeping the peace, but deployed all the same. The United States had not sent any, but Clinton still put on a bold front. "If the United States doesn't act in situations like this, nothing will happen," he said. The president added that a failure to do so would be "to give up American leadership," but this was simply posturing.

On February 10, the tone of the United States continued to take on a new truculence. Christopher declared that "over the past two years the states of the former Yugoslavia have descended into a dark period of terror and bloodshed," mainly due, he said, to the Bush inaction. He added, "Our conscience revolts at the idea of passively accepting such brutality."[1]

One might have expected some definite, hard-driving actions by America after such tough talk, but for some time neither Clinton nor Christopher ever came to the point of transforming platitudes into policy. Decisions were made, chief of which was to initiate airdrops of food into the Muslim-held areas of Bosnia, shrunken now to only a third of the country. America would also ask for enforcement of a no-fly zone over certain areas and urged a tightening of the U.N.-imposed economic sanctions on Serbia. America would repeat its warnings to Serbia not to stir up trouble in the Muslim province of Kosovo.

When it came to the no-fly zone and most of the new program, the allies were opposed, as was the U.S. military. To no one's surprise, General Powell was one of the first on the American side to demur over the question of airdrops. He was doubtful about whether airdrops done at night from ten thousand feet were the safest way to get food to the Muslims. One story surfaced that a large load of food attached to a wooden sled had wrecked a farmer's back shed, turning his plot into a lumpy garden of containers of dried "Chicken Stew," powdered "Cherry Drink," "Iodized Salt," and "Dried Peach Dessert." Powell soon returned to the meetings to say that the Pentagon had studied the matter and instead of dropping large loads of food attached by parachute to wooden sleds, the planes would simply drop thousands of Meals Ready to Eat, small foil packages that wouldn't hurt anyone if they accidentally should land on some civilian's head.

In any case, the Serbs would soon prove the key obstacle to the program. Relief convoys were being constantly stopped by Serbs who searched the drivers and trucks, and did everything possible to obstruct and delay any movement of food. Convoys were sometimes held up for days, then allowed to take a modest amount of food, far below the delivery quotas, and only to forestall any attempts by the West to resort to force to ensure the arrival of relief. The hostility of the Serbs was methodical and unrelenting. They positioned themselves near the areas targeted for food drops and not only did they intercept the supplies, they often shot at aircraft or fired on the people, who at times fought like animals over the contents. The program was further undercut by the U.S. military, who fretted constantly over the administration's not having set a definite end date for the program. Rankled at the carping, Clinton and Gore stubbornly declared the airdrops would continue.

Yet clearly the Clinton group had quietly dropped the pledges of tough action that they'd given during the campaign. The Serbs had run amok, and the region was entering a darkening tunnel in which its inhabitants would face carnage and horror not seen since the ugliest days of World War II, and yet Europe had decided to treat Milosevic's criminal land grab as a humanitarian crisis, as if it were a natural disaster like an earthquake or a flood that one could only clean up after. Of course, sending food to Milosevic's victims was action of a kind, but it hardly deterred Milosevic in his plans of brutal conquest nor did it act to keep innocent people from being forced from their homes or killed.

Former British prime minister Margaret Thatcher told a newspaper,

"You can't keep feeding these people and then letting them be killed," she said, but no one was listening.

The U.N.'s next action was equally weak and ineffective. Britain and France were opposed to any forceful measures that might smack of military adventure. The United Nations had managed to deploy a small number of peacekeepers called the United Nations Protection Force (UNPROFOR) on the ground to stop the fighting, help distribute aid, and protect the inhabitants in Bosnia, but the presence of the peacekeepers was equivalent to erecting a small number of tissue-paper tents in the path of a hurricane. There was a total of twenty thousand in the U.N. force but they were widely dispersed, lightly equipped, and tied to static positions, only at times able to help move relief convoys through while the fighting raged around them. The cold truth was that the U.N. forces had neither the vision, the will, or the weapons to accomplish much of any worth, and instead of putting a brake on the spreading slaughter, they were instant pawns of the Serbs, becoming readily available hostages whose seizure could be used to block any attempt by the West to launch air strikes to punish Belgrade for any number of cease-fires it had violated. For the Serb forces, the U.N. peacekeepers amounted to a gift to Milosevic.

Perhaps what is most stunning is how the Clinton administration moved from its own determined, moral center on the issue of Bosnia to fall weakly into step with Europe and the United Nations. In the beginning Clinton had depicted this as an inhuman war caused by Serb aggressors that had to be stopped at all costs. Now suddenly it had become a humanitarian matter, which meant basically that the new president had accepted the United Nations, the European, and the former administration's vision of the conflict, a view that was basically pro-Serb. If the United Nations possessed anything, it was a belief in its blameless rectitude and the pure disinterest of its motives. It embraced the principle of neutrality as sacrosanct. But it was neutral in name only because neutrality simply provided a charter for inaction and a legalization of Serb gains. In the summer of 1992, as Bosnia was suffering dismemberment from widespread Serb attacks, a trio of U.N. officials, former Secretary of State Cyrus Vance, former British foreign secretary David Owen, and U.N. secretary-general Boutros Boutros-Ghali, demanded that the international community cease its calls for military intervention, saying that such threats would jeopardize a forthcoming peace agreement in 1993.

Unfortunately, under the terms of that agreement, much of what Serbia had stolen at gunpoint would remain in Serb hands. An agreement would end the war, but it would hardly guarantee the right of refugees to return to their expropriated homes or act to right other wrongs. As journalist David Rieff put it, "The U.N. wanted to get aid through to facilitate a peace. . . . The terms of the peace were, from the standpoint of UNPROFOR, almost irrelevant. All that the United Nations required was that 'the parties' agree to it."

Rieff then added with great insight, "If the purpose of a mission is to stop a war, and one side [Serbia] having won, appears ready to settle, while the other side [Bosnia], feeling its cause to be just but having turned out to be the loser, is determined to fight on, then those running this [U.N.] mission are likely to find that most of the time their interests coincide with those of the victors. They and the victors want peace. The vanquished, possessed of the notion that they have right on their side, refuse to accept their defeat. Given these convergences, it is only a small step to the victors and the international organization understanding that, when all is said and done, they share the same goal. That goal was forcing a Muslim surrender and obtaining a settlement on Serb terms."[2]

Only one human being acutely understood the full import of the weakness of the United Nations and the Clinton administration. Bosnian president Alija Izetbegovic was seventy years old and had endured eight years in Tito's jails. (Josip Broz, known as Tito, was Yugoslavia's first post-war leader.) American diplomat Richard Holbrooke had praised the Bosnian and described his allegiance to his Bosnian state "a remarkable tribute to his courage and determination." Not that Izetbegovic was an easy man to work with. Holbrooke had also noticed that the Muslim's eyes had "a cold and distant look" from so much suffering, yet realized it was his inexorable grip on his living faith of a Bosnian homeland for Muslims that had sustained him through his ordeals. He was not a lover of democracy, only a Muslim patriot. As Henry Kissinger noted, "Leaders of independence struggles tended to be heroes, and heroes do not generally make comfortable companions."[3] The same was true here.

In April of 1992, Izetbegovic had declared Bosnia independent of the rump state of Yugoslavia because he saw it as a unified state. Immediately, Belgrade told him to withdraw Bosnia's independence, Izetbegovic had refused, and the assaults had begun. Desperate alarm rose in Izetbegovic as the slaughter spread and he became aware of the dimension and character of the crisis closing in on his country.

"It was unbelievable almost," he said. "The civilians being killed, the pictures [showing] the dead bodies of women in the street. I thought it was a photo-montage. I could not believe my eyes. I couldn't believe it was possible."

Izetbegovic ordered a general mobilization of his own forces but they were poorly trained and pitifully underarmed. Sarajevo was a city dominated by high hills, and the Serbs placed their heavy guns on them, raining down on the inhabitants a systematic and murderous fire. Soon the city had run out of food and water. People were living in cellars like animals. Hospitals became indistinguishable from grubby morgues. So many people died that the inhabitants began to bury fresh corpses in their gardens. The Serbs even cut the gas lines, prompting the mordant joke, "What's the difference between Sarajevo and Auschwitz? At Auschwitz they had gas." The Serb method of conquest for capturing a place was exceptionally simple—first reduce it to rubble.

Another potential point of Muslim disaster was the city of Srebrenica, a light industrial city and once an old Roman silver mining site, about a two-hour drive from Sarajevo. Shaped like a finger, nestled far down between high bluffs, the Serb grip of the place was crushing out its life. The inhabitants were suffering horrors, every degree of debility and deprivation. Babies were dying of hunger, dogs were feeding off corpses, people were sleeping in the streets. The city's original inhabitants were beginning to die of starvation, reduced to eating acorns and leaves, or grinding down the hard cores of corn cobs to make cakes from the coarse powder. Televised images were going out daily to TVs all over the West, and a wave of warlike repulsion swept over the Europeans and Americans. Thanks to the influence of Gore, Lake, and Albright, pressure was being applied on the United Nations and the Europeans to enforce a no-fly zone against the Serbs to end Serb harassment of relief convoys. The British sniffily replied to this option by refusing to deploy their aircraft. This angered Christopher, who said if the Serbs continued to interfere with relief, the United States would press to lift the arms embargo against the Muslims and help arm Muslim troops. Christopher claimed this would "level the playing field" even if it escalated the fighting. In reply, Lord Owen haughtily scoffed that it would only "level the killing field," and the fruitless allied bickering went on.[4]

For Lake, the most pressing question was how to interest his commander in chief in the urgent issues of foreign policy. Lake was in his fifties, an energetic, brilliant, strategic thinker who had served as director of State Department Planning under President Carter. In the fall of 1991, Clinton arrived in Boston to give a speech on the economy, and Lake had met with the young, dark-haired George Stephanopoulos, a key Clinton advisor, and Hillary Clinton. Lake and Stephanopoulos would be quick to form a friendship, sensing in the other a similarity of temperament, outlook, and taste. Within a few weeks, Lake and Clinton finally sat down for a chat. The talk centered chiefly on domestic concerns. Lake's neighbors in western Massachusetts were suffering severe economic hardship, and Clinton was quite taken by Lake's stories and anecdotes of their plight. For his part, Lake thought Clinton exceptionally bright. He was clearly a man who could take in at a glance, and retain in his mind, a whole printed page. Lake joined Clinton as a speechwriter.

What he liked most was that Clinton tried to come to his conclusions thanks to an authentic process of thinking things out. Lake had written speeches before, but with Clinton, Lake experienced a new depth of critical scrutiny. The candidate simply didn't accept what was put before him. He would go carefully over the words and as he read, he would say, "Yes, I agree with that," or "Yes, I believe that," instead of accepting it because the audience might agree with it. Hopes in the European and American press had soared at the advent of Clinton's election, expecting a new hard line in the Balkans, but to everyone, including Lake, the reality was like a douche of ice water. Downcast and discouraged, he quickly discovered that, in his words, foreign policy had become "a wholly owned subsidiary" of Clinton's domestic agenda, and as the weeks wore away, no clear-cut policy emerged even as the Balkan tragedy rapidly deepened in intensity and scope.[5]

Lake had been the author of Clinton's hard-nosed words on the Balkans and while Lake had employed them as a tool to discredit Bush, the words had also been a statement of intent for Lake. Lake was many things, but he was not a man of insincerities. He believed that life had a moral element, and that a statesman, like any other human being, was confronted by an act that was either more moral and upright or less moral and upright, and that it was incumbent on the responsible official to do the first and refrain from the second.

Yet as the days passed, Lake more and more found Clinton's lack of passion for foreign affairs both puzzling and disheartening. Foreign policy had never been a Clinton strength, and Lake had certainly seen Clinton's casual tendency to neglect foreign affairs issues early on. At the Democratic convention, when Clinton had given his acceptance speech, a senior official on the Council on Foreign Relations, Leslie Gelb, noted that Clinton had devoted 141 words out of 4,300 to foreign policy, hardly a good sign. (President Kennedy, on the other hand, had given short shrift to domestic issues in his inaugural, but nobody had noticed or criticized.)

In addition, Clinton displayed little eagerness for meetings with foreign leaders and had been dilatory in answering their congratulatory calls when he became president. It didn't bode well.

Nor was Lake alone in his misgivings. Clinton's prospective secretary of state, Warren Christopher, had also discovered early that the focus of Clinton was entirely on developing and implementing his domestic agenda, chiefly economic reform. Before Clinton's election, Christopher had met Clinton late one night in Los Angeles, his purpose was to greet the nominee and walk him to his hotel so the man could nap. Christopher soon discovered the incredible loquacity of the brilliant candidate who clearly preferred talking to sleeping. For several hours, Clinton peppered an incredulous Christopher with questions about the presidents that Christopher had served. He wanted to know what he thought had gotten them elected—was it policy or personality? He was especially intrigued by Lyndon Johnson and clearly admired his civil rights and anti-poverty legacy. Vietnam was not brought up.

If Christopher and Lake had their doubts, so did Clinton's CIA director, James Woolsey, an intelligent, quiet-spoken professorial man who was a Republican appointed as a sop, but whose views soon caused him to be shunned by the White House staff the way sheep might shun a wolf. Before he left the CIA in 1995, the relations between the White House and the CIA had entirely deteriorated. Woolsey's hardened view was that Clinton and his national security team were "entirely uninterested in foreign affairs." According to him, the foreign policy group had no drive to frame a comprehensive strategy and, in addition, was neglecting doing any stringent, thorough analysis of any of the "big" issues. Certainly, the new president had forged a good relationship with Russia, he was being gentle with China, but with issues like Bosnia, or Haiti, or Somalia, Woolsey, like Lake, felt that the chief aim of the White House was to manage these crises with the aim of limiting any damage or possible disruption to domestic programs, especially deficit reduction.

Woolsey maintained that Clinton's only real foreign interest was in foreign trade, as evidenced by his passage of NAFTA, the North American Free Trade Agreement.[6]

Even when Clinton talked of foreign policy, he lost his fire, his manner becoming awkwardly diffident and stilted, losing those qualities of empathy, energy, and delight that he always brought to the discussion of his domestic programs.

The one country that Clinton did appear to be interested in was Russia, but it was always "episodic and desultory," a former White House official said. The only other country he knew much about was Japan because, as governor of Arkansas, Japan had provided a market for the state's rice crop.

When it came to Bosnia, what sent a shudder down Lake's back was not simply the war but the way it was being fought. Within thirty days of being attacked by the Serbs, 12 percent of Bosnia's population of 500,000 people had been ruthlessly uprooted. Serbs had destroyed Catholic churches and thousands of mosques and razed 67,000 Muslim homes. One American, soon to play a major administration role in trying to curb the spreading Balkan catastrophe, had seen the Muslim expulsions himself and thus was an invaluable witness to the sinister crisis closing on Bosnia. His name was Richard Holbrooke. Dark-haired, extremely intense, and intellectually brilliant, Holbrooke was born in 1941, the son of an immigrant Jewish family. He had lived in Scarsdale, a chic bedroom community forty minutes outside New York City. What Holbrooke had was a towering ambition and a superb arsenal of talents. He hungered to be one of those who act, decide, and achieve, and from a young age had possessed that inner confidence that is the father to all intellectual originality and moral fearlessness. Pretensions and titles meant nothing to him. As a young Foreign Service officer stationed in the Mekong Delta he hadn't hesitated to contradict Gen. William Westmoreland, the overall commander of U.S. forces in Vietnam. Westmoreland had thought him a presumptuous upstart.

"How old are you?" challenged the general.

"Twenty-four," replied Holbrooke.

"What makes you think you know so much?"

Holbrooke shot right back. "I don't know," he said, "but I've been here two years and spent all my time in the field."

In 1995, Gen. Wesley Clark, who had begun to work on Bosnia the summer of that year, was surprised that even at that late date, Pentagon leaders were relying on intelligence reports, diplomatic cables, and the world's press for its information about the unspeakable evils occurring in Bosnia. Yet Holbrooke had gotten his initial firsthand look in the summer of 1992, just as the Clinton campaign was gearing up. Gen. George Patton had said, "One look is worth a thousand reports," and Holbrooke had first gone to Croatia and Bosnia as part of a fact-finding mission for the International Rescue Committee, on whose board he served. Accompanied by a former U.S. ambassador to Turkey and Thailand, and a former assistant secretary of state under Richard Nixon, the party arrived in Zagreb, the Croatian capital. There Holbrooke got his first bad scare when a group drove to a checkpoint at a bridge to find an angry-looking man clad in a slovenly uniform, wearing Reeboks and smoking, who suddenly began waving an automatic rifle in their direction. The militia man was drunk and nothing had happened, but it had been extremely unnerving. Holbrooke had never seen so many men carrying weapons, not even in Cambodia or Vietnam.

The party returned to Zagreb, but restless and liking to keep on the move, Holbrooke had headed for the town of Banja Luka on the edge of the Serb-controlled areas of western Croatia. When he arrived he found a town devastated by war, a field of ruined, blackened, roofless shells of houses, and badly damaged, littered streets. Holbrooke's room in the Hotel Basna was small and stiflingly hot. On August 14, he was awakened by a loud noise and the sound of gunfire. He dressed, went out, hastened down a street and saw a clump of journalists with cameras. As he moved forward, he came upon a scene of sickening surprise. Before him, under gunpoint, was a long line of grim, bedraggled, shabby people carrying suitcases. The line straggled for blocks. Holbrooke saw they were sobbing, distraught, and completely disheartened, all waiting to enter this one stone building. The building was a Serb headquarters, the Office of Population Resettlement and Property Exchange. The footsore, distressed people would disappear inside for a few minutes, then come out grim-faced to get on a waiting bus.

Holbrooke was witnessing ethnic cleansing, a curiously neutral phrase that had originated from the U.S. embassy in Belgrade. When it was used by State Department spokesperson Margaret Tutwiler at a midday briefing, it instantly caught fire. The truth, however, is always concrete, and Holbrooke saw the reality behind the abstract phrase. He had that special gift to be able to understand a historical process as it was happening. The waiting line of people were Muslims, many of whose families had lived in this place for centuries, and to save their lives and escape the horror and brutality, they were being coerced into signing away their property and homes. If they signed over ownership, either to their neighbors or the authorities, the Serbs pledged they would get a safe passage to Croatia. At least that was what they had been told. The houses and property extorted from the owners would then be given to Serbs who were there specifically to displace and supplant the Muslims. Under the Milosevic system, this was not seen as theft, extortion, or exploitation, but simply a way of building Greater Serbia. So thousands of Muslims gave up their homes, cars, businesses, money, and luxury goods, fearing for their lives at the hands of the authorities or roving, vicious paramilitary gangs. The final indignity was that the newly exiled people were charged a fee for being driven from their town after having been robbed. Thousands simply walked out, making for safety, tramping through the mountains for days on end. Some were too weak and died on the way.

Holbrooke was profoundly shaken. After boarding a bus himself, his vehicle passed destroyed houses lining the route, and the farther they went, the worse the destruction. Here and there loomed an unmarked house, wrecked and empty, and Holbrooke could see that the destruction was not from combat but from a "systematic and methodical program in which Serbs had fingered their Muslim neighbors."[7]

That was bad enough, for Lake and others a fresh horror began to crystallize as they realized that whole classes of Bosnian Muslims were starting to disappear. Professionals like doctors, lawyers, teachers, police officials, and political leaders who made up the elite of the towns began to vanish. Muslims were being deported en masse, loaded onto cattle cars and sent away, never to be seen or heard of again. For prisoners, packed tightly together like sheep in a pen, the conditions inside the cars were deadly. There was no fresh air, no water, and no food. There were no toilets, just holes cut in the floors, and sickening piles of excrement rose in the cars. Stench stifled the air. Many died.

American reporters soon broke the ugly news that the Serbs had constructed over one hundred concentration camps in Bosnia. They had names like Trnopolje or Manjaca, but the worst was an open mine pit in the north called Omarska. Conditions there were ghastly. Inmates lived out in the open. There was no food or water, and, starving, the inmates had eaten the grass down to the bare ground. In mud up to their knees, having no shelter or warmth, they began to die, little figures with sticklike arms, and huge, bulbous heads with oddly lighted eyes atop their awkward, shrunken bodies.

Bosnia's Muslims had become Europe's new Jews.

6

AN ECHOING CAVE OF WINDS

In spite of the worsening Bosnian crisis, the discussions of the Clinton Principals Committee on foreign policy resembled an echoing cave of winds. All was drift and improvisation. Clinton was like a man groping for a wall switch in the dark. The Constitution gave the president very wide latitude for initiating policies when it came to foreign affairs, but Clinton ignored them, having basically embraced a policy of wary, profound, self-protecting caution. Not knowing what else to do, his foreign policy team dragged out all the old, discarded Bush options: blockades, sending an aircraft carrier into the Adriatic Sea, launching air strikes. Hours upon hours were spent in examining, analyzing, discussing, but no step was ever taken.

To Lake, this was intolerable. It might be dangerous to be strong or dangerous to be weak, but it was far more dangerous to be weak. In a fever of savagery, Milosevic had launched a rampage of murder, rape and pillage, beheadings, forced transport of entire populations against the Muslims in an effort to create his new Serbian state, his assaults arousing increasing Muslim hatred, and the Serbs employing additional brutality in response. The pro-Serb Europeans were worse than useless, and it was up to America, Lake felt, to prevent the worst from happening in the Balkans and that came down to threatening the use of force. Only diplomacy backed by force could make any diplomacy credible, and America could not afford to waste any more time. What Lake feared most was that each successful Serb encroachment would be accepted by the United Nations as inevitable, and the foreign powers would be less and less inclined to call a halt to Serb aggression and lose their will to resist. Lake believed that there was a real opportunity for Clinton to take a robust stand, but that opportunity had to be *seized*, and in Clinton, Lake found no drive or passion for action. Clinton disliked inconvenient facts, and Lake, a deferent man, didn't insist on the president's accepting them. So Lake floundered, unable to make the weight of his views felt where they counted.

Part of the paralysis was due to Clinton's advisors being so fearfully, tragically divided between hawks and doves, the gun-shy and the decided. Perhaps the most towering and unchallengeable of the Pentagon doves was Colin Powell. During the previous administration, Powell had been extraordinarily effective in strangling any discussions involving the U.S. military in Bosnia. In Principals meetings, like rivets spat from a gun, he would pepper Bush and Scowcroft with questions: If the United States took part in multilateral air strikes, what were the targets to be? Serbian artillery in the hills? What if they were hit and damaged and the Serbs didn't back down? Would further air attacks drive the Serbs to the conference table? If they didn't, what then? What if Serbs put targets close to civilian installations, then what?

When Ambassador Zimmermann had once suggested that such bombing would carry a potent message of warning to the Serb leadership to cease its aggression, Powell brushed off the remark. When Scowcroft argued that for the sake of credibility, America might have to do what was necessary to prevail, even to the point of using ground troops, Powell was incredulous. Out came the mantra: you could not deploy U.S. troops without first having a clear goal, applying overwhelming force, and having a definite exit strategy before you began. The resolve to act sank out of sight beneath Powell's objections. As Zimmermann noted, "The Vietnam Syndrome and the Powell Doctrine proved powerful dampers on action by the Bush administration, particularly in an election year."[1]

Once again finding himself a leading voice within the new White House, Powell would endlessly make the point that America could not be expected to be the world's policeman and that the necessary support by the American people could never be galvanized or sustained for the degree of force required in Bosnia. In his view Bosnia was a potential military nightmare. Sending American forces over there was like launching loose straws into a huge maelstrom where the wisps would end up spinning aimlessly in tightening spirals until they were finally sucked down into a terrible abyss. Bosnia was not like Iraq, he said, it was like Vietnam.

This view was widespread. Even Christopher, whose views blew hot and cold when it came to Bosnia, was disconcerted when, in a February briefing given him privately by a three-star general, he was told that if the United States went into Bosnia, it would require a field force of 400,000 troops. Hearing this, the color had drained from Christopher's face, and there vanished in him any craving for rapid action.

During one meeting, as Powell droned on, one of the hawks in the room sat and listened with cold and skeptical disdain. Madeleine Albright, Clinton's ambassador to the United Nations, was not the type to be captured by anyone's preconceptions. Possessed of singular pugnacity and an inflexible will, she had from the beginning of the Balkans crisis manifested the fewest doubts about the necessity for using force. She had urged its use so often and on so many occasions that she had gotten on Powell's nerves. Once she would begin to outline her reasons, Powell would lose his temper and warn, "Madeleine, you're at it again."

At the time of the Clinton campaign, Albright had clearly become a part of the Democrats' influential inner circle. She had worked for former Senator Ed Muskie, for Zbigniew Brzezinski at Carter's NSC, and more and more people found her personally impressive. Clinton had come back to her Georgetown house one night after a fund-raising to hear her ideas on foreign policy and was impressed by her. He had promised to choose a cabinet that "looked like America," and when aides presented him with a list of people being considered for top positions, his eye had fallen on Albright's name, and he marked "good" beside it in the margin. She was appointed to head the transition team at the National Security Council, getting a West Wing basement office.

Albright had from the beginning bombarded Clinton with confidential memoranda that in the most vehement and uncompromising language had urged the use of force against the Serbs. From working at the United Nations, she saw that the events in Bosnia were of grave concern to the Europeans, and both her inferences were indisputable: violence in Bosnia was a threat to Europe and would eventually threaten American interests as well. To the impatient Albright, Powell, with all his pussyfooting caution, was a man who harped drearily on a single string. She grew weary of seeing Powell using a red laser pointer on maps of Bosnia to argue how difficult the Balkan terrain would prove or when asked what it would take to free the Sarajevo airport, listen as the general mechanically recited how any military action would take tens of thousands of troops, cost billions of dollars, and probably end in numerous casualties or an open-ended commitment like Vietnam. "Time and again he led us up the hill of possibilities and dropped us off on the other side with the practical equivalent of 'No can do,'" she said. Finally, sick of Powell's enormous, ineradicable, habitual caution, Albright

burst out in a wrath of exasperated patience: "What are you saving this superb military for, Colin, if we can't use it?" Powell was so incensed he later
said, "I thought I would have an aneurysm."[2]

But if she had enraged Powell, she also irked Lake, his personal dislike of
Albright acting to align his sympathies with a man whose positions he essentially opposed. Albright bored Lake. To him, her mind ran along a single
track. Lake liked Powell better as a person, and the general had taken Lake
aside to talk to him about the dangers of airpower, putting a human face on
the predicament. "You're putting a young kid in a fighter-bomber that is going about 500 miles an hour and asking him to take out something [an artillery piece] which looks to him like a tiny little tube." In 1994, at the
suggestion of the Air Force chief of staff, Lake had taken a ride in an F-15
and they had put him through a short training course, seating him in the
cockpit and telling him how to pull the cord to eject if the flight came to
that. The Air Force technicians had added that Lake shouldn't worry. "Either way, sir, you're going to end up in the hospital." Lake was a sensitive
man with a ready fund of sympathy, and could feel for the young lives a
course of military action would place at risk.

President Clinton up until that point had cleverly skirted the truly dangerous reefs of the crisis while proclaiming himself a master captain. The
administration's messages were always mixed. If Clinton came out for airdrops of food, his officials were quick to signal that the president was not
obsessed with foreign policy and there would be no deep U.S. involvement
in Bosnia—after all, one of Clinton's most effective arguments in his campaign against Bush was that the president paid far too much attention to
foreign countries far away and far too little to his own.

To no one's surprise, now that the time had come for Clinton to act with
decisive force and commanding vigor, neither he nor his team had the focused will or any definite, workable ideas to propose that would halt the war.
No objectives were laid out, no options argued, no decisions made. Pressure
was exerted on Clinton by associates who felt that any redirection of focus
from the domestic economic agenda to a foreign crisis amounted almost to
disloyalty to his voters. So for Clinton, a policy of no risks, no commitments,
a policy "of avoiding alien entanglements" was more sensible than one of aggressive intervention and collective security. Clearly Clinton would not address the topic of Bosnia until it had entered the domestic bloodstream and
until then, instead of leading creatively and resolutely, Clinton retreated, seeing his real mission not to guide public opinion, slowly shifting its attitudes,
but instead to stay in step with it, suiting his policies to existing conditions.

The tuition for this piece of procrastination was high—the deaths of hundreds of thousands of innocent human beings.

Meanwhile, as the situation in Srebrenica continued to deteriorate, a desperate hour of decision was approaching. On March 25, Clinton summoned the Principals and told them it was time for fresh, strong ideas. "The old policy was running out," as he would say later. It was, and faster than he realized.

7

DANSE MACABRE

A year had gone by since Sarajevo had been first besieged and throughout that time the city endured the ordeal of constant attack, and it was by now too late for the White House to pretend that nothing was happening or ignore Yugoslavian president Slobodan Milosevic, the renegade predator who was behind it. When they had entered office, Warren Christopher's State Department specialists, Tony Lake's National Security Council staff, and the rest had studied the old Bush dossiers on the main actors in the Bosnian tragedy ranging from the Croatian president, Franjo Tudjman, to the president of the Federal Republic of Yugoslavia, Slobodan Milosevic. Milosevic was the chief author of the massacres, the rapes, the wholesale displacement of populations, the vast despoilment of Muslim property. Tudjman certainly possessed as brutal and avaricious character as Milosevic, but his forces had been mauled by the Serbs, stalemating the Croats' long-held ambition of carving up Bosnia into an appendage of Croatia. Within the White House, everyone studying the issue was acquainted with the characters of these men. They saw with tolerable clarity that Milosevic would simply keep going until he was stopped, yet they appeared to lack any coherent idea of how to effectively do this. What was still missing was a strategic rationale.

Meanwhile, there had been what some might call "progress."

The Europeans were pushing for acceptance by all sides of the Vance-Owen peace plan, which would have partitioned the country into Serb, Croat, and Muslim territories. Under terms of the plan, the Serbs would have the major share of the war's spoils. With 34 percent of the population, the Serbs would get 50 percent of the country (they already controlled 70 percent thanks to force of arms). With 44 percent of the population, the Muslims would be jam-packed into isolated, landlocked pockets with access to the outside world dependent on Croatian or Serbian goodwill. Sarajevo would be divided into ten districts.

The Vance-Owen plan would have brought peace, but it would also have ratified Serb aggression. As Senator Joe Biden remarked at the time, the British were displaying the same flabbiness of fiber that they had in the 1930s. The main sentiment of the Europeans was that it was too late to try and save the Bosnians, and there was unspoken skepticism as to whether the life of a European would be worth losing to do it. The irony was that for the first time since the end of World War II, America had turned a major security issue over to the Europeans instead of strenuously asserting its own leadership.

To their credit, Clinton, Christopher, and others had not liked the Vance-Owen plan, which they felt was proof that crime truly paid if done on a large enough scale. Hold up a liquor store and you were a petty criminal, but overrun thousands of square miles, murder the inhabitants, and steal their land, and you were suddenly seen as a serious force that had to be included in peace negotiations. Senior officials at the State Department were especially hostile to the different ethnic "cantons" of the plan and labeled the result of the plan as a "partition" of an independent state. White House resistance rose. The Principals Committee began to explore some means of equalizing the forces in play, such as arming the Bosnian Muslims and using American combat planes to bomb the Serbs. The NATO alliance was now engaged in its first test of combat since its inception, but decisive force was not a phrase in its vocabulary, and, further, its ability to act was hobbled by crippling authority at the United Nations. The United Nations had its finger on the trigger of military action, not NATO.

The major push for increasing U.S. military pressure was coming from the usual hawkish quarters. Secretary of Defense Les Aspin was opposed. He preferred a cease-fire in place, and among the doves there was the feeling that the doctrine of force was incompatible with continued diplomacy— the fighting started when the talking ceased and the talking was still going on. As usual, Powell was employing his deftly lethal questioning to disembowel any designs on the part of anyone to try and entice military involvement. "Tell me what the objective is?" he'd say. "Tell me what it will take; tell me what the consequences are? If we bomb the Serb targets in Bosnia and that doesn't bring them to the conference table, then what?"[1]

It is a common myth that intelligence helps shape policy, but the opposite is true. Policy, or the lack of it, usually shapes and fashions intelligence.

Powell soon came to meetings armed with a Defense Intelligence Agency estimate that dealt with targets, climate, coverage, and geographical conditions in Bosnia and Serbia. According to the DIA there were a number of targets that could be struck in Serbia itself, including bridges, military facilities, command and control centers, and fuel dumps. Hitting them would dent the reputation of Milosevic's invincibility, but what if he didn't negotiate? Iraq's Saddam Hussein had, after all, survived extensive allied bombing in the Gulf War.

The intelligence assessment pointed out that the artillery of the Bosnian Serbs was hidden high up in the severe, forbidding mountainous country, and which, except for summer, was often concealed under deep cloud cover, masked from aerial reconnaissance. What if the Bosnian Serbs moved their artillery and had heavy weapons next to homes, schoolhouses, and hospitals? What then? The assessment ended by saying that the only really effective strategy was to deploy three divisions of ground troops in conjunction with the bombing, and, even if this succeeded and a peace was reached, an agreement would only validate Bosnian territory seized by Serbs at the point of a gun.

Lifting the arms embargo had been another recent, if tentative, Clinton exploration. Izetbegovic had suggested this course years ago, because he knew, as well as Clinton's staff, that the U.N. arms embargo had benefited the aggressor and weakened Belgrade's victims since the Serbs had a military and the Muslims, who although they had men, had very few modern arms or equipment, except for a trickle coming in from Muslim countries. For months, with a singular tenacity of purpose and extraordinary strength of reserve, Lake, Albright, and Gore had been working to end the embargo on the Bosnian Muslims while threatening air strikes on the Bosnian Serbs if they continued their aggression. If the Serbs launched an all-out effort to crush the Muslims before they could stand their own ground, NATO would hit them with air strikes that would include American combat planes. The European allies knew that obtaining more arms for the Muslims meant an intensification of fighting on the ground, endangering their forces, and they were strongly opposed.

Unfortunately, the menace advancing on Srebrenica was an especially sinister one. The Serb general about to take Srebrenica was a primal, unbridled force by the name of Ratko Mladic. In his early attacks on the city, Mladic had in cold blood targeted hospitals, parks, water treatment plants, and refugee centers, using terror with great and ruthless skill. On April 12, his mortars and artillery had killed fifty-six people in an hour. One shell had landed in a schoolyard where children were playing soccer. A U.N. official saw the aftermath: fourteen dead bodies, body parts and flesh clinging to the fence, the ground literally soaked in blood as if the grass had been sprayed with red paint. A little girl of six was left lying decapitated.[2]

The White House was checking with the operations center at the U.S.-European Command at Stuttgart, a flood of intelligence was pouring in from State and the NSC staff, and the president's aides pulled together a coherent picture of the situation on the ground. President Clinton was briefed closely on the Serb advances, receiving daily briefings from Lake, the CIA, and State. The U.N. Security Council issued an ultimatum that the Serbs were to stop shelling and move their weapons away. Mladic didn't pay the least attention. He took Muslim village after village, and finally paused at the edge of the city.

Srebrenica was by now in desperate straits. Home to thirty thousand people before the Serb onslaught, it was now bursting with eighty thousand, many of them refugees. New arrivals, near starvation, poured like a river into the place, driven from their small towns, having lived on herbs, grass, half-boiled pumpkins. As one observer said, people began to pack the town as tightly as matches in a box. Lake's ambition rested on the hope that the brutalities that were arousing the indignation of much of the civilized world might act to alter the Europeans' views. In his private talks with the president, Al Gore saw that Clinton was deeply concerned about the injustices done to the Muslims, his face reddening in anger as he listened to the recital of Serb crimes.

Yet never were the inconsistencies in Clinton's character shown more clearly than in what followed. The president had publicly promised in April to make a hard decision on Bosnia, but none came. Throughout the early part of the month, there were more meetings of the Principals, flurries of activity, and more promises of action. Clinton finally promised a major decision by the last week of the month, but then, before acting, he began to sound, not like Albright or Gore, but like Powell. Suddenly Clinton's key advisors were enduring a fusillade of cautious presidential objections phrased as questions: What is the limiting principle of this option as opposed to that? What is our real objective? Within this option what lies within our control and what doesn't? Yes, the United States *could* act unilaterally but it would make agreement with allies and gaining domestic support more difficult.

Lake, for one, thought all of this mere radishes. NATO, strongly urged by the United States, could stop Milosevic if it was determined to do so at all hazards. But Clinton would not commit. "Clinton is not sequential," a former advisor said. "When you put a list in front of some people—of what is important and not important—they go down the list. Clinton goes around

the problem. He circles and circles it."³ Finally, on April 17–18, with Srebrenica clearly moving toward calamity, Lake used the crisis to try and spur
Clinton into a decision that pledged the United States would lift the arms
embargo and would use air strikes to keep the Serbs from crushing the
Muslims before they could effectively utilize their weapons. America would
also push for a cease-fire and the protection of Muslim enclaves. Lake was
immensely pleased with the plan and even Christopher, normally hesitant,
agreed. He and Lake spent hour upon hour perfecting a statement for the
president to give publicly. Inside the White House, Lake was admired for
having been the driving force behind the new policy. The president would
listen to Lake. As an advisor said confidently, "The President will come out
where Tony is."

On April 19, Mladic took the city.

The surrender of Srebrenica hit the West like an earthquake. At a stroke,
it reduced the Vance-Owen plan to an absurdity and the whole machinery
of appeasement crumbled into nothingness. Under terms of the treaty, Srebrenica was a Muslim area. With the surrender was it to be a Muslim area
under the military control of the Serbs?

The initial U.N. response was one of trying to disguise its failure, mainly
to save face but to neuter U.S. pressure for military intervention. In a panic,
it tried to disguise the city's surrender by saying that the Bosnian Muslims
had "reached a disarmament agreement" with the Serbs, a staggering lie.
Then secretly, Owen and Vance began to set in motion double-faced schemes
to rescue their work from destruction. The U.N. Security Council had
slapped a comprehensive set of sanctions against Belgrade that would have
frozen its assets abroad and barred transshipments through Serbia and
Montenegro. Milosevic could not afford these sanctions and continue with
his war. The Serbs didn't like the plan because under its terms it would have
to give back huge swaths of land seized by conquest, and this would reduce
more than a third of what the Serbs controlled and deny them the unbro-
ken, single landmass of Greater Serbia so much desired by Milosevic. Vance
and Owen secretly promised that the Serbs would not police those territories, only the United Nations.

Milosevic agreed to the plan, saying later that he could obstruct any
implementation and end by getting his Serb state. He felt certain that once
he agreed there would be no steady pressure for its actual implementation.
The Bosnian Muslims hated the plan because it so splintered the Muslim territories as to render the centralized Bosnian government null and void, but
when they heard the Serbs had signed, they agreed to as well, certain the
Bosnian Serbs would be holdouts.

All this was done hurriedly, secretly, quietly; but for the rest of the world, the fog had finally rolled away and the certainty of Serb aggression had emerged along with the need for a firm and rapid response. Surely only a simpleton could be bluffed into puzzled inaction at this point. Instead, the spectacle broke upon the world of the allies floundering about in confused and inept dismay. British prime minister Major called for "tough, swift measures," but wasn't able to quite name what they would be. The airlift of supplies for starving people was called off. In fact, thanks to Serb interference, the U.N. relief effort was on the brink of disaster. The Serbs were still shelling the city, and they continued to shell the Sarajevo airport.

Once again, Lake saw the surrender as a chance to prod Clinton into more decisive action, and at first Clinton seemed to stand foursquare. He initially announced he was "considering air strikes," but the quick Serb-U.N. cease-fire gave him the way out he was looking for, and he paused, announcing the situation "had eased." Clinton said he would wait and see. To his hawks, Clinton, like the Europeans, appeared to be mainly interested in developing alibis for inaction. By contrast, Albright called for America to launch unilateral air strikes, her stance supported by a dozen memoranda from State that urged arming the Bosnian forces, a position also backed by Lake and leaders of both the Republicans and Democrats in the Congress.

President Clinton, spurred by his pollsters and advisors, tried to put on a bold face. "America should lead," he declared, although, not unilaterally. He then sounded a ringing moral note, "Ethnic cleansing is the kind of inhumanity the Holocaust took to the nth degree. You have to stand up against it."[4]

One is reminded of Winston Churchill's words in the 1930s after a speech by British prime minister Anthony Eden denouncing some new aggression of Hitler's: "They are brave words," said Churchill, "but actions would have spoken louder."

The horizon in Srebrenica continued to darken and in another spasm of bravado, Clinton once again announced that he was ready to take "stronger action" within days. Amazingly enough he did. Powell flew to Brussels to perfect plans for allied air strikes. NATO and the Pentagon assembled an armada of over a hundred planes that took off from bases in Italy and Germany, heading for the Adriatic as a scare tactic. There were other plans under discussion to use American airpower to protect Muslim enclaves under attack.

It appeared that all the Serb cards that had been laid out on the table were at last going to be called. But many in the United Nations were wringing their hands, waiting for what Milosevic would do. As NATO hung fire, the situation was made for Milosevic's superb skills in waging psychological warfare. He could detect among the allies the rifts, the reservations, the differences, especially their deeply entrenched disinclination to act, and, in a surprising move, the Serb suddenly declared that he would intervene to halt the Bosnian Serbs. He would cut off all supplies to his proxies except food, and, pressured by the British, he intervened to prevent General Mladic from officially taking Srebrenica in a public way that might have upped the pressure for American intervention.

Clinton was still talking tough, but then, inexplicably, he stalled. His resolve left him, and he grasped for deliverance at the new plan. The Bosnian Serbs, who had rejected the plan, were summoned to a summit in Athens by Vance and Owen where they discovered they'd been bushwhacked—Milosevic and Izetbegovic had already agreed to the plan. They were the only holdouts. The three Bosnian Serb delegates realized they would not be allowed to leave and go home until they had signed the agreement. They signed, but, unfortunately, they did not have the necessary parliamentary authority to make their agreement stick.[5]

Once the agreement of the Bosnian Serbs was announced, the West began to pull back. The summit had been a cynical delaying ploy on the part of Milosevic, but Lord Owen brayed fatuously, "The bombers have had their day, this is the start of what I suspect will be an irreversible process towards peace." Clinton responded coldly, "We will judge intentions by actions," but he said he would give the Serbs another chance. Trying to put on a bold front, the United Nations declared Srebrenica a "safe area" even though Serb shells still fell like stones on the city's helpless citizens. The war continued as it always had, with the Serbs on the attack. When Clinton then said, "America is ready and will do its part," the president was sounding as if he were preparing to fight when, in fact, he had no intention of doing so.

As days went by a torture of apprehension was eating away at President Clinton. Lake and Gore were pushing hard to go in, arm the Muslims, and get out. Clinton himself commented that the policy was "a very clear, specifically defined strategy" with "very clear tactical objectives." But Milosevic executed another skilled feint when he asked for time for the Bosnian Serbs to have a referendum on approving the Vance-Owen plan and Clinton weakly gave ground once again. Privately, Russian and European pressure had been brought to bear on him. Tough action on Milosevic would cause Russian leader Boris Yeltsin no end of trouble with hard-liners in his parliament, and Yeltsin's friendship with Clinton was important.

The United States rejected the Vance-Owen plan ostensibly because it would reward Milosevic's criminal aggression, but enforcing the agreement would have required 45,000 U.S. troops on the ground, violating the one sacrosanct premise of U.S. Bosnian policy since the Bush days—no use of ground troops. More days passed, and the Clinton idea of unilateral U.S. air strikes was retracted, even though Serbia was bringing helicopters into the area near Sarajevo which flouted all previous allied ideas such as setting up an exclusion zone, a border blockade, and establishing safe areas that were really safe. Within the administration, nothing was studied with a view to acting, but rather the opposite. Clinton put an empty scowl on weakness when he outlined certain conditions such as forfeiting any unilateral U.S. action if Europe agreed to set up a war crimes tribunal, guarantee the territorial integrity of the province of Kosovo, and strengthen boundaries around Sarajevo.

More days passed, and in the end, the Clinton idea of unilaterally using U.S. planes was retracted. Owen, Vance, and even some of the doves on Clinton's own staff, convinced him to agree that he would abandon acting independently if a war crimes commission was established, guarantees were made to Kosovo's Albanians, and boundaries would be withdrawn to strengthen Sarajevo. A vast sigh of relief went up from Europe, and when news of the U.S. conditions was leaked, Clinton received a grateful phone call from John Major for the president's sudden change of heart. The wounded citizens in Sarajevo were left cowering in their cellars.

Resolve was quick to melt to mere rhetoric. On April 20 at a photo op, Clinton said, "The United States should always seek an opportunity to stand up against—or speak out against—inhumanity," as if the difference between the two was not momentous.

The stage was now set for the final empty, pathetic gesture. Already knowing Europe's intense dislike of "lift and strike," Clinton sent Christopher to consult with the Europeans on the discredited policy. (Prime Minister Major told Christopher that the British government would fall if he accepted it.) Christopher, never a forceful man, had behind him no presidential muscle, no weight of the president's authority to ram through a consensus of some kind. To the Europeans, America, having refused to commit any troops on the ground, had forfeited its leverage and credibility. They would receive Christopher politely, but with a courtesy lacking in warmth. Then, in Christopher's absence, Clinton seemed to lose sight of the Bosnian military realities altogether and would subside into a kind of hypnotic daze. He had gotten ahold of Robert Kaplan's book *Balkan Ghosts*, which presented the area as "a hopeless case, a cauldron of mysterious squabbles and ancient animosities, murderous hatreds fueled by memories of persecution and massacre."[6] It was a tar baby, a swath of quicksand that no intelligent president would dare to put a foot in. And suddenly Clinton was echoing the

Europeans. Many in the European leadership, instead of seeing Milosevic for the pitiless, greedy manipulator he was, quietly held to the mistaken semiconscious view that the mounting violence in the Balkans was due to some flaw in the Slavic temperament, which was depraved by nature, addicted to endless quarreling and the hoarding of grudges.

After a talk with the president, rumpled Les Aspin called Christopher to alert him that Clinton "is going south on the policy. His heart isn't in it." So selling lift and strike no longer had presidential backing. Dogged and always disciplined, Christopher completed his trip, but he returned like a kicked dog. Clinton later tried to airbrush the farce. "There was a lot more agreement than you think," he said.[7]

The fiasco provided rhetorical benefits for everyone. The Clinton administration could accuse the Europeans of gullibility when it came to the Serbs, and the Europeans could point out that the Americans, with no troops on the ground, were back in the habit of parading their self-righteousness while reneging on their responsibilities.

Christopher returned in a foul mood and quickly blew up in a froth of injured frustration. He said he found nothing in the alliance but "indifference, timidity, self-delusion and hypocrisy."[8] Yet oddly enough an obscene mood of relief permeated the White House. Failure let the leaders off the hook. On May 18, Clinton reversed his earlier stance. Executing one of those remarkable somersaults for which he was already famous, he announced America was no longer to lead on Bosnia. He talked of "ancient hatreds" and said it was up to Europe to deal with the Serbs. He said the United States was prepared to commit troops once all the parties had agreed on a peace plan (in other words when the war was over). He then left the Serbs an out by saying that there had been "atrocities on both sides," which was true, but hardly the issue.

Clinton tried to convince his hearers that the United States was not abandoning the Muslims, and that America still believed in lifting the arms embargo against the Bosnian government and in limited "compensatory air action" to allow the Muslims "a level playing field" in their fight with the Serbs. The words fell flat. "The strategy was, this thing is . . . Let's not make it a quagmire," said a White House official. "That's what the lift and strike, and limited air strikes, was about."

On May 22, a Joint Action Plan was put forward by France, Russia, the United States, the United Kingdom, and Spain, but it proposed no action whatsoever. The United States sent some troops to Macedonia, where U.N. forces were already deployed, but it was done simply for the sake of appearances.

Meanwhile, Izetbegovic was in a sputtering rage, saying publicly that Clinton had abandoned Bosnia to a carve-up. The Bosnian president saw the whole Srebrenica episode for what it was—that Europe and America had been completely outwitted and outmaneuvered by the crafty Milosevic and that what mattered to the West more than halting slaughter and war was preserving the unity of the alliance.

Clinton then proceeded to weaken his position on Bosnia even further. He was no longer concerned with saving the territorial integrity of the Bosnian state, but announced instead that he was looking for an agreement that would give "reasonable land for Muslims." He added, "My preference is for a multiethnic state in Bosnia. But if the parties themselves, including the Bosnian government—genuinely and honestly agree to a different solution, then the United States would have to look at it very seriously."

This was Clinton at his worst and weakest, a leader who, at a moment of genuine testing, would wince, relent, and refrain from action. Ever since Clinton's tough campaign talks, Bosnia had incessantly posed the unavoidable and fundamental question of what sort of principles were to prevail in the world and to what extent the United States would act to establish their supremacy. It was now clear to all that his "policy" in Bosnia had been mere rhetoric that disguised a planned and consistent retreat from a principled stand. The leader of the free world had drastically undercut the Bosnian Muslims at a time when the Serbs were planning to wipe them off the map of Europe.

8

THE PRINCE OF TENNESSEE

The relation between Bill Clinton and Al Gore was an amazing and unprecedented partnership from the very first. During the campaign, Warren Christopher had been put in charge of finding a running mate for the presidential candidate, and it was a search so secret it could have involved the development of some new species of atomic weapon. In the Jones Day law firm in downtown Washington, working in unmarked rooms, was a team of five lawyers who carefully assessed an original list of forty candidates, who had been subdivided into lists of eight. The "C" list included the names of people who had been named just so they could be told later that they had been considered to avoid hurting their feelings. The "B" list included the unlikely but not impossible, but it was the "A" list, ten pages single-spaced, that really counted. The vetting of all the candidates had been overseen by Harry McPherson, a former LBJ aide.[1]

It had been a lengthy and tedious process. Information on candidates had been derived from computer sources and a scattering of interviews, sent to Christopher, and by Memorial Day forwarded to Clinton. There had already been some who had rejected Clinton's overtures. A thirty-minute interview with Senator Jay Rockefeller from West Virginia had stretched into two hours, but as sincere and sensitive as Rockefeller proved, in the end he was not really interested. Colin Powell and Western governor Bill Richardson had been polite and prompt in their refusals.

Work went on, and Christopher finally struck real ore with a name taken from a priority list of fifteen candidates. When the ten-page memo was passed on to Clinton, it immediately struck his interest. The prospect's name was Al Gore, whom Clinton had met in Tallahassee, Florida, back in the 1960s. The pros were telling Christopher that Gore would supplement Clinton in his weak areas like foreign policy, arms control, and the environment. Gore was a Vietnam vet with strong, centrist positions on defense issues. Gore had run for president in 1988 with Richard Holbrooke as his foreign policy advisor, and Gore's background held no surprises. Nor did Gore's Senate record raise any red flags. In fact, Gore's outlook on the purposes of government, its basic mission to better the lives of ordinary citizens; the importance of improving world trade as a means of increasing U.S. security and reducing the causes of war; and his intimate connections to the current leadership in Russia, all told heavily in his favor.[2]

The pros were excellent and the cons—the deficits—were surmountable. Yes, Gore's presence on the ticket offered no regional balance, and he was said to have a "wooden" public personality. (He did, but only in public; in private he was funny, lively, and quick.) The really serious question was would he prove a deferent and loyal subordinate? He could be quite assertive and like most men of character and intelligence, he knew his own value. He'd been called "a political opportunist" but that was like calling him an "office seeker"—it was merely saying the same thing twice. Gore was also hard on staff, not driving them any harder than he drove himself, but, as a relentless micromanager, he was demanding to work with, and many of his staff had quit after the 1988 campaign. In bullying staff or having a temper, Gore was not different from Clinton himself or Lyndon Johnson or scores of others who held authority in Washington. If in their campaigns, they were champions of the rights of the "little man" or the "forgotten man," that compassion did not extend to the office. There, any worker was the target of querulous tantrums, insults, humiliations, and slights almost as if presidents, vice presidents, NSC chiefs, and the like took a special delight in savaging those who were vulnerable and could not fight back.

McPherson was a thorough man and called sources all over the world to try and dig up dirt on Gore. The responses were all mild. No one used the occasion to settle a debt or run him down. Gore, he found, was ambitious, intelligent, and well informed. When McPherson and his gumshoes went to talk to Gore at an apartment his family maintained in the Methodist Building across from the Supreme Court, Gore had answered the door. The room was furnished in the manner of the old-fashioned South, flounces, heavy curtains, tables covered with petticoat layers. It was there that Gore had written his widely admired book, *Earth in the Balance: Ecology and the Human Spirit*. Soon the visitors were served tuna fish sandwiches, and they were quick to get a taste of their prospect's temper. When policy was brought up, Gore said with some sharpness that Clinton's proposal for a middle-class tax cut would never happen. He said he had tried something similar before, and it had never gotten airborne. McPherson asked Gore about his friends, and Gore hung fire. He had been a loner in the Senate, as men of original thought and feeling often are, but the hesitation worried McPherson. He went away musing to himself, "So he has no friends."

Leon Fuerth, a key Gore aid, was like a second brain for Al Gore, a second soul. A man with a poker face and a crop of salt-and-pepper hair, faintly resembling Republican advisor Bill Bennett, Fuerth has been at Gore's side during all the major issues of his political career.

He was free of any ideological bent beyond advancing what he believed were the strengths of American interests, but it was Fuerth who often pushed Gore to take tough stands and made him understand that foreign policy was at the bottom based on the threat of force. Gore consulted him on everything. Lake told *The Washington Post* he admired the way Fuerth "could chew on an issue like a bulldog," a tenacity he held in common with his mentor.[3]

Gore was taken to meet Clinton the night of June 30, placed inside a sealed red SUV, driven to the Senate building, then transferred vehicles to proceed to the Washington Hilton, up the service elevator to a suite reserved under aide Mark Gearan's wife's maiden name, Herlihy. As David Maraniss, Gore's biographer, wrote, "He and Clinton met like college pals who had not seen each other since the 1960s and who picked up where they'd left off."[4] They had gone into a bedroom to talk and closed the door, but according to accounts, rather than compete, they sensed an immediate emotional congruity and began to talk as if they were trying to frame a strategy to take on the rest of the world. Usually such interviews lasted an hour, but this one took fire from its own energy and drive. On and on it went as Gearan and two other aides, Gary Ginsburg and Bruce Lindsey, watched TV, eaten up by impatience. Finally one went to the door and knocked, thinking what the hell is going on in there?

The door opened to reveal their jackets off and shirttails hanging out. "No, no," Clinton called. "We're doing fine. Don't worry about us," and the door shut again.

But back in the SUV, as Gore was being taken home, he wasn't giving anything away. "Wow, that went well," one of them said. But Gore was not to be seduced. Silence met the remark. One of the aides felt that Gore was exhausted, having spent all his resources in the performance of his life. But another felt that he was being canny. His reaction would be reported and to seem pleased would be a weakness, to talk would be indiscreet and that would almost amount to betrayal. He simply rode in silence.

Clinton knew he had found a prize, a man of disciplined substance, hardness of will, and someone he could trust to do a thing the way he had wanted it done, the kind of trust he had in Hillary. Of course there was a last-minute round of calls searching for unpleasant surprises, but there were none. When Clinton called Marty Peretz, now at CNN and a former student with Gore at Harvard, Peretz said offhandedly, "Gore will not knife you in the back."

More digging and detective work ensued, but Gore's family life was solid. He was not, as advisor David Gergen had said of Clinton, "a hard dog to keep on the porch." When McPherson met Gore again at the Methodist Building apartment on a hot summer day, the sounds of traffic coming through the open window, he tried to ask Gore if he had *any* disconcerting secrets that might emerge, but fumbled the question, only to look up and find Gore had fixed him with a look. "There won't be any problems," Gore said, ending that.

Then Clinton decided. According to Christopher, Gore got the news of his offer in Rio de Janeiro where he was attending a U.N. conference on the environment. Gore wanted the job but realized he was in a foreign country and asked permission to make the final answer after he returned home. Christopher met Clinton in Little Rock on June 25.

Meanwhile, Gore took his family, and inner circle, down to his Carthage, Tennessee, home on the Fourth of July. Two of his old aides, Peter Knight and Roy Neel, were there among others. It was the night of July 5 that Clinton called Peretz. On July 8, the call from Clinton came. At 11:30 that night, Gore took the call in his bedroom, then Tipper, his wife, got on the line. When it was finished, jubilation reigned in the house. No one slept that night. In the morning Mark Gearan waited at the airport to accompany Gore to Little Rock.

The news of Gore's appointment electrified the country. These two young, good-looking vital men with handsome families matched the country's aspirations and its taste. They took the convention by storm, and afterward Christopher said he had never met so many people who stopped and thanked him for his part in putting the two men together. It soon proved that if Walter Mondale had been the breakthrough in being the first vice president to join the president at every Oval Office meeting, Gore was the breakthrough in genuine influence and absolute control of some White House issues. For one thing, foreign policy with Gore was an abiding and serious interest that he pursued with uncompromising zeal. Christopher had watched how, under Carter, Mondale had wielded unprecedented power even though the president and vice president had often differed on issues. Christopher felt the vice president should "be given meaningful policy assignments that would draw on his special talents," and Clinton agreed.

Gore would prove the most outstanding beneficiary of the post–World War II trend that the VP should have an active substantial role in foreign policy. Partly this was due to the ordeal and travails of Harry Truman. Throughout World War II, Roosevelt essentially had been his own secretary of state and had confined Truman's official duties to wreath-laying ceremonies at the funerals of foreign dignitaries. When FDR died in April of 1945, Truman, who had only met the president eight times in Truman's whole career, found he knew nothing of what Roosevelt had set afoot in the world. The gloomy days after Roosevelt's death were an endless ordeal of having to master complex and multidimensional issues. As a result of his tormenting hours of insufficiency, Truman vowed no vice president would be as ill-informed in foreign affairs as he had been, and he began the critical practice of allowing the vice president to sit with the president's cabinet, with the president keeping the VP fully briefed on crucial matters.[5]

Unlike Truman, Gore was no novice. After eight years in the Congress, Gore had obtained a shrewd knowledge of the world's workings. His mind was copious and supple and in spite of his stiffness he operated often with the grace of strength. His mind brought a keen discernment to any matter, and he was instantly aware of the vital elements of a situation. One feeling in his character dominated all others—a desire to excel, not just in this area or that, but everywhere, in everything.

There was something else. A profound aversion for injustice was central to his makeup. While a high school football player, Gore was known for seeking out and fighting a player from another team who had "played dirty" against him or against a teammate. He was not one to back off, but possessed that dangerous pugnacity born of indignation.

Gore attacked intellectual matters with the same relentless perseverance. Gore thought out the details of his conceptions with the minutest care. When Gore took an interest in nuclear weapons in the 1980s, he set aside eight hours every week for thirteen months to master the subject, and he emerged from the study with his own strategic plan. "He is a quick study, but when he has to, he really puts in the time to understand the issues," said Larry Haas, who worked on Gore's Reinventing Government initiative. "He is committed to being very, very knowledgeable on policy," Haas said.

Gore's managing style differed drastically from that of his boss. Where

Clinton's efforts to concentrate resembled an attempt to shovel fleas across a barnyard, Gore was sober and highly disciplined with a capacity for intense focus, a ruthless ability to stay fixed on an issue. Clinton had been spoiled by having been waited on hand and foot for eight years as governor of Arkansas. Plus Clinton's goals were all centered on the domestic. Foreign policy had no real hold over his mind and meeting opposition or complexity or an obstacle in pursuing it, he veered off into areas where he could enjoy assured success.

Gore came at things with a much greater sense of self-confident accomplishment, and he tried to get Clinton to pace himself, to control his schedule, and set aside more time to examine every facet of his private thoughts, a practice Gore never failed to perform in his own case. Gore "will set aside large chunks of time and will sit down and think these things through," as his chief of staff, Jack Quinn, said. "He never shoots from the hip, he is thoughtful, he is prepared, he's careful." Plus, Gore had a capacity for rapid decision and an expressed impatience with Clinton's fluttered dithering. "To him, Gore, governing is a series of decisions, many of them uncomfortable; you have to make them and move on." As a result, Gore was soon known as the steadiest and strongest advisor the president had. And while he deeply respected Clinton, he was not above getting annoyed with his senior partner. Once, when Clinton was rambling inconclusively about his deficit bill, asking mournfully "What can I do?" Gore snapped tersely, "You can get with the program."

When the chaos in the White House had gotten almost totally out of hand, Gore donated his own chief of staff, Roy Neel, to help bolster Clinton's man, Mac McLarty. When Mac the Nice proved inadequate to the requirements, Gore personally persuaded Clinton to replace McLarty with Leon Panetta.

But there was something about Gore that enforced respect and Clinton felt it.

Gore was one person that Clinton would listen to, aides reported. "When a lot of people talk, you'll see the president looking around the room," said Mike McCurry, the White House spokesman. "When Gore talks, the president is absolutely riveted.

"You can search but you won't find a major policy decision in this administration that President Clinton has made without discussing it with the vice president," he added.

On another occasion McCurry said, "Gore is very good at forcing issues, at bringing issues to closure." And a former Albright advisor said, "Everything Gore did was to further a line of activity. He never took his eye off his goal, and he never rested till he obtained it."

When it came to Bosnia, Gore saw that events on every side were moving toward catastrophe, and yet it was clear that most of the new cabinet sat on the verge of a precipice and didn't realize it because they never looked down. To Gore, the question was what price America was prepared to pay to honor its principles in the world, and Gore felt America must pay whatever it might cost, however high the price. Yet as open and honest as Gore was, he was always "a trifled covert" in the way he worked, according to former close associates. As Andrew Jackson once said of Martin Van Buren, "He rows towards his goal with muffled oars." In the midst of people he trusted, he would generously open his own mind. But when he left that circle, he kept his ultimate designs between himself and old friends like his assistant Leon Fuerth. Gore was a deep and accurate reader of the talent in the room. Foreign policy was in the hands of doves, men like Christopher, who were attempting to guess where the president was going and trying to get there first, or like Lake, who wanted strong action, but whose will was divided and ambivalent about the use of force and its ultimate implications— "gun-shy," as Holbrooke bluntly said.

As the Bosnian crisis grew more doubtful and more dark, Gore moved with great and patient care. You could not prevail or win the applause of a group until you had first won its approval. Most of his policies were at odds with those in the most powerful positions. There was no gain to be had in open opposition. There was gain to be had only in developing a coalition of those who differed, those, who like him, were in favor of a more active intervention in Bosnian affairs—those who wanted to reach out and strike a blow rather than wait passively to have the Serbs inflict another horror on the world.

Gore had dealt with complicated situations before and he quietly went to work. He knew that if you would change policy you must first change personnel, and he would now patiently set up his own parallel government of hawks to counter that of the doves.

THE COURTIER

Many who were close to Clinton felt he often confused being busy with being alive. After the bad news of Bosnia, and with the collapse of the Vance-Owen plan, Serb expansion continuing, and a fresh war flaring up between Croats and Muslims, Clinton went on the road. He seemed to regain his self-confidence and energy by seeing the enormous enlivening effect his words and presence had on people. His warm geniality, his quick adroitness and pointedness of repartee, his power to inspire, brought his heart back to life and restored his sense of being "president of all the people."

All the same, the recent defeats had hurt, and many of his speeches lacked fire. He talked to defense workers, town meetings, gang members, and civic groups, and returned to gear up to fight for his reconciliation bill, a key compromise measure dealing with changes in taxes and spending to reconcile them with his goal of budget reduction. His political standing was shaky, and if he lost this fight, it would be a major defeat. If he began to be seen unable to retaliate, he would be treated as weak and someone not to be feared, and it would likely seal the fate of his ambitious domestic agenda. So when he returned, Clinton was all energy in the White House. He was everywhere, exhorting, calling, persuading, encouraging, and the bill did get out of the House Ways and Means Committee, which some felt was a major victory.

Clinton himself knew that his main fault was that he spread his focus too broadly over too many matters to fasten public attention to what politically mattered most. Yet thanks to his efforts, the House passed the bill on May 27.

Even that success was offset by *The Wall Street Journal* observation that his public standing remained very low.

He passed through two more blunders, a disastrous failed appointment for another attorney general, Lani Guinier, a friend of Hillary, who had written articles that challenged a few of the basic gospels of the Constitution and who had to be nudged aside, and then came the Ruth Bader Ginsburg matter. Looking for someone to nominate to the Supreme Court, Clinton advisor Bernie Nussbaum spotted a judge on the federal appeals court in Washington, Ruth Bader Ginsburg. A former Harvard Law School professor and chief judge of the U.S. Court of Appeals in Boston, Steve Breyer, had been Clinton's first choice, but it was discovered Breyer had not paid Social Security taxes on a domestic worker, and Bader Ginsburg was to be the fall-back if circumstances required. Ginsburg had loitered at the bottom of Clinton's long list of possible appointees, but now the scrutiny of her suddenly sharpened.

Gore had been very pro-Breyer, but the winds had changed direction, and he backed off. Ginsburg's story captivated Clinton. From a woman unable to get a job at a law firm after graduating from Columbia Law School, Ginsburg had gone on to argue cases before the Supreme Court that had strengthened women's rights. Gore was unimpressed and made remarks to the effect that Ginsburg was "charismatically challenged."[1]

It got worse. It was found her record was drab and that her votes had often been conservative rather than liberal. But in a meeting Ginsburg read a statement about her life that brought Clinton to tears and she got the job in March, Clinton's first appointment to the Supreme Court. Many women's groups had wanted a more liberal nominee but Clinton's choice made clear that when he made a decision, it was not inveterate firmness or a meticulous assessment that counted most but whatever wayward emotion had engulfed his heart at the time. Yet more disconcerting developments in the form of poisonous cabals were taking place in the White House under his nose.

Warren Christopher would call Al Gore "the most influential vice president in history," but on his return from Europe, one of Christopher's first moves was to quietly undercut Gore's good standing as the president's advisor.[2] As secretary of state, Christopher was not a man fertile in strategy; his brain harbored no sweeping, encompassing foreign policy schemes sound in their conception and proposing momentous results in their successful execution. When entering office, talking to the Senate Foreign Relations Committee of Clinton's plans to address "the great challenges in the era of change," Haiti, Somalia, and Bosnia did not make Christopher's list. His top goals were opening Japan's markets, passage of the North America Free

Trade Agreement, successful talks on tariffs, and promoting the integration of East Asian and Pacific economies with the U.S. economy. The "highest priority" was promoting successful reform in Russia. There was not a word mentioned about failed states or ethnic conflict.

A former head of State Department policy planning, Samuel Lewis, said of Christopher, "Frankly, I found that Christopher was not interested in either policy or planning." At the time there was a steady stream of horrifying cables pouring into the State Department detailing war crimes carried out against civilians and depicting the desperate predicament of the Muslims. There had also been a string of resignations by senior State Department officials, the most prominent being former Ambassador Zimmermann, who said he had quit because he'd felt a growing unease as he saw America sacrificing important principles in the "unseemly struggle to stay uninvolved." There was much resentment over the way Christopher deliberately tried to define the conflict "as an issue where U.S. leadership was not imperative to resolve it."

Under criticism, Christopher closed tightly like a clam. The department resignations only caused him to retire into the ranks of his closest advisors. Sealed off in the fortress of his seventh floor office, he surrounded himself with his personal staff and undersecretaries of state, who were all political appointees. Lewis noted that when a topic gets touchy it is the instinct of the White House NSC or State Department to tighten the circle of people who are trusted and have access. Christopher asked Assistant Secretary of State Steven Oxman to exclude the former Yugoslavia desk from all policy discussions. It worked for a while, but soon Christopher's minions required their expertise. There was a more constrained atmosphere, less free, a little more fearful. Christopher didn't like the free flow of talk, he didn't like those who were tough, sharp-examining, and he didn't reach out much but manifested a neurotic desire for secrecy. You controlled the decision making by controlling the secrecy, making the circle of decision makers as small as you could, confining matters to those who were most loyal and most committed to you and the president or at least your idea of the president.

Christopher then changed his method by asking for policy options, targeting small groups of senior diplomats who had put together alternatives through discussion before presenting him with an act he could veto or adopt. This meant there was little opportunity for alternative views to make their way to his office.

He was always happy to parcel out the heavy questions for debate to others: Russia to Deputy Secretary of State Strobe Talbott, Asia to Assistant Secretary of State Winston Lord, and the Middle East to special envoy Dennis Ross.

Clinton's desire for weak subordinates was coming back to haunt him in Christopher's case. As a former White House official said, Christopher had been picked not because he was a man of outstanding ability but because he was a weak, cautious man who could be managed. Clinton wanted no rivals nearby, no forceful character likely to wander off the reservation and strike out on trails of his own. The flame of life burned low in Christopher, and when once asked why he'd chosen him, Clinton had said because Christopher "gave off no heat."

Christopher's relation with the president was that of father-son, mentor-student, similar to what Clinton felt for Secretary of Treasury Lloyd Bentsen. But at the bottom, he was simply an operative, the classic clean-up man who came to the hotel room and wiped it down for fingerprints after a mishap—an efficient, anonymous, discreet creature careful to erase evidence from the earlier messes that had been made. Christopher was the man of the small step. He was the classic functionary, a footling, a "heel-clicker," as one of his former colleagues put it. He was the classic courtier, the man who pretends "not to notice wrongs done him, who smiles at his enemies, controls his temper, disguises his passions, and speaks and acts [in most cases] against his real opinions." His chief aim as secretary was to ensure his access to the president and thus safeguard the power of his own influence. As in most cases, the good of Clinton often became confused with the good of Christopher, and, after his European failure, if Christopher was determined to do one thing, it was to get rid of Bosnia as an issue, to drive it off the front pages, to keep it out of the American mind.

Christopher was convinced that any attempt to move out ahead of Europe on Bosnia was an error that would irreparably damage the Clinton presidency and that presidency he saw as having been specifically delivered to his safekeeping. Following his return from Europe, in May 1992, Christopher met with Clinton advisors like George Stephanopoulos and pollster Stanley Greenberg. Christopher put the blame for the debacle on the Bosnian Muslims and said the Serbs weren't looking for peaceful solutions to their problems. The Balkans was a bottomless morass. It was a lose-lose issue. Christopher then scheduled two private talks with the president, both designed to emasculate the upsurging influence of Gore. In Christopher's view, Gore gave long, overly detailed answers to brief questions, was a little too sure of himself, a little too insistent in his views, and the extremity of his opinions was "going to get us into war." A short time after, as Gore was about to leave town, Christopher scheduled another short meeting with the president. Since Gore usually was present at such meetings, an alert source gave a heads-up to Gore chief of staff Roy Neel. Gore tried to reschedule his trip and return to the White House but couldn't, and at that second meeting, Christopher again cautioned Clinton about Gore's overzealousness when it came to using force.

Christopher had in fact been the hidden hand pulling the levers that set in motion a series of last-minute feints during the surrender of Srebrenica designed to disguise the vacuum of Clinton's policy. After the failure of Christopher's trip, the pretense for having avoided such failure began. The word "commitment" suddenly began to appear in the press, although no one knew exactly what it meant. Next, the United States sent troops to Macedonia in a completely meaningless exercise, while behind the scenes Christopher had tried to counter the U.N. action in labeling the six Muslim enclaves as "safe areas," since he saw this as siding with the Muslims.

Shortly thereafter, Christopher had met with his political operative and press man, Tom Donilon, a brilliant young staff chief, in an expensive Washington restaurant and produced a yellow-lined pad with items, which if carried out, would quietly bury U.S. concerns over Bosnia. Out of that meeting came the Joint Action Plan, another meaningless label since it was a plan only in name and required no American resources. It merely sanctioned Serb aggression and offered a lame substitute for lift and strike. Many in the press saw through this mumbo jumbo, but Christopher was unfazed. He had an invulnerable sense of his own rectitude in the line of conduct he was pursuing.

Gore was not Christopher's only target. Les Aspin had also gotten on his nerves. Aspin, who was supposed to be managing the largest, most conservative, bitterly contentious entity in the world, the Pentagon, had set up policy shops instantly nettling Christopher, who felt these encroached on the State Department's domain. Was Aspin managing DOD or was he running his own think tank? The military was wary of Aspin. He exuded no cold edge, no capacity for ruthlessness. He didn't dress the part, but was always rumpled, he was too affable, he didn't intimidate or carry himself the way a commander should. The charge that stung most deeply was that he ran the Pentagon like a congressional committee. But his leadership style closely reflected his president's. People sat around and discussed something, and there was a lack of that fiery determined drive that was intent on producing action.

The defect lay with Christopher as much as with Aspin. As secretary of state, Christopher should have been creating an atmosphere of collegiality, an expansive ambience where people felt they were equally involved in a common purpose, that their views were valued as being important. Instead, Christopher was out busily putting up fences that marked his territory as separate from everyone else's. His European failure intensified his sense of narrow territoriality, advisors said.

Perhaps the most serious crisis was the souring of relations between Christopher and Tony Lake. Lake was feeling more and more a discarded figure, powerless and inconsolable. Christopher, the man with no grasp of the large, had instead rooted his esteem in his mastery of the small. Samuel Johnson once said all stupid people think they're cunning. Christopher wasn't stupid, but he was a schemer and he was unwise. From the very first when it came to National Security Advisor Lake, Christopher had a great consciousness of turf and had worked to circumscribe Lake's role. For one thing, Christopher would be the administration spokesman for policy and Christopher asked that Lake stay off television. If there were pronouncements to be made, then Christopher would make them. In addition, Lake was to keep clear of diplomacy. It was the secretary's job to formulate diplomacy, based of course on options developed by the National Security Council. And policy was the secretary's job, not Lake's. This pared down the scope of Lake's job quite a bit. Usually the NSC brought policy options to the president and State forged its own as well. Now the NSC was to be an appendage of State, and this stung Lake, but he allowed his resentment to simmer. If Christopher wanted him in a corner, he would be happy to stay there. Policy would suffer and Christopher would come to see he was wrong, but Lake was content to wait.

Christopher's strictures were based on his knowledge of the past. He knew from the Carter days that the State Department and the NSC were terrific rivals and the Carter presidency had seen vicious backstairs infighting with Secretary of State Cyrus Vance having been shut out of some major issues. Since its formation in 1947, the NSC had been expanding its scope and power at the expense of the State Department and, to a lesser extent, DOD and other foreign policy agencies. The NSC was intended to be a planning agency to introduce broad policy initiatives, but over the years that mission had changed to protecting presidential interests and promoting the White House perspective in foreign policy affairs. Christopher was aware that a new administration usually loaded the NSC with its own loyalists, and that they tended to be adroit, skilled operators rather than career diplomats, and their influence had aggressively expanded. Christopher sought to keep them in check.

Foreign governments were aware of the growth of power and influence of the NSC staff and when they wanted the American government's ear, they turned to the NSC. Henry Kissinger and Zbigniew Brzezinski both had been involved with negotiations with foreign governments. There was

no way to un-ring the bell, and the struggle between ambitious NSC operatives and State professionals to seize power over policy was constant, bitter,
and intense, a source of endless friction. Both groups played by their own
rules, guarded their own information, and used every bureaucratic device to
gain precedence over the other. Of course, each thought itself objective but
every agency had its own agenda and style. As Lake noted, a cable begun
with leisurely phrasing laced with "on the one hand" or "on the other hand"
was likely to be State. If its headline hit you head-on, full of facts and data
but its interpretation and analysis were not entirely clear or particularly well
thought out, it was from Defense. According to Lake, the CIA produced the
best analysis. But in any case, for the president to obtain a fair and well-
founded view, he needed the output of all three. However much State deserved deference as the chief foreign policy agency, this wasn't possible, any
more than Defense could be allowed to shape military issues on its own.

The situation had grown more complex with the new communications
networks that flowed into the White House Situation Room to monitor the
cable traffic of the foreign affairs agencies with greater efficiency, and using
back channels provided by the CIA to communicate with American embassies and foreign governments, bypassing State. Christopher was determined
to see the NSC operational role held to a minimum because he thought
State deserved deference from the NSC. He knew that State had its own
agenda and point of view and thought it deserved first consideration. Out
of this would come tragedy.

The Bosnian nightmare was spreading faster than the efforts to contain it.
Christopher was convinced that Bosnia posed the danger of taking the
United States and Clinton's presidency where they didn't want to go, but he
missed the fact that the tide of circumstances was beginning to flow with
irresistible force toward a different direction and outcome. There was still a
sense among policymakers that when hawks asked for action, they were
asking the impossible. Meeting after meeting ended with gloomy agreement that nothing or little could be done. Yet the real difficulty lay with
Clinton too busy trying to do too many things so that he had no clear sight
of the developing geopolitical realities.

Clinton had been occupied all summer trying to develop additional congressional support for his budget bill with mixed results. The latest version
was embroiled in various disputes, reflecting the shallowness of his Democratic support in Congress. However, in July as Clinton was preparing to
leave for a G-7 summit in Japan, he had been profoundly disconcerted by
televised pictures of Sarajevo under siege.

Clinton, a flammable man, could be jarred into action by images. When the president was talking to his old friend from his Rhodes Scholar days, Strobe Talbott, Clinton complained of the spectacle of Bosnia spiraling into anarchy, and he was sharply critical of the incoherence of the advice he was getting from his foreign policy team, remarking: "Some people are saying don't just stand there, do something, but others are saying don't do something, just stand there." Clinton by then was intensely aware of the potential damage in doing nothing, but still had no clear ideas governing the kinds of things that should be done.

Talbott was not Clinton's only confidant. The president had also spoken to Christopher, who, still smarting from his European fiasco, once again simply hung fire and thought that safety lay in doing nothing. He was convinced that the Europeans had mastered all the arts of sticking fast in the mud. It would be a disaster if the United States embarked on a program only to look behind and find that no one in Europe was following.

On a Sunday in July, as Clinton was leaving to fly to South Korea, he was stopped by Lake, who, taken up with writing the trade agreement to be discussed in Japan, alerted Clinton that a special raid involving helicopters was about to be launched against Somali warlord Mohammad Farah Aideed. Unfortunately, this was news Clinton did not seem to take in. Until then, instead of displaying that implacable purpose that allows for real accomplishment, Clinton had been on the look out for dodges, omissions, possible loopholes for avoiding real action. Now he suddenly spoke in a direct, stern and forceful tone meant to convey to Lake that he wanted options developed to relieve the people of Sarajevo. Christopher had put Bosnia in the "too hard to do" box but in a dazzling change of mind, the secretary was caught with one foot in the air as Clinton said he was considering the use of American ground troops to relieve Sarajevo.

The wholesale shelling by the Serbs had demolished much of the city, from the homes and apartments of its people to the official buildings of its government. Sections of the city had been destroyed, and buildings had been gutted. Much of Novo Sarajevo had been obliterated and so had much of the apartment city of Dobrinja near the airport. To travel through the confrontation lines in Dobrinja and near the airport in Butmir was to journey through a no-man's-land marked by checkpoints and bunkers, along sniper screens of overturned trailers and wooden blockades, and through outlying villages eviscerated by the shelling. The Clinton hawks wanted bold action that their experience told them was required. Political appointees were telling Clinton that the United States couldn't be sure of success, and intervention would jeopardize projects on other fronts such as U.S.-Russia relations.

But on this subject Clinton exhibited a certain, undeviating fixity of intention. In Hawaii, where Aspin and Lake had accompanied the president before his flight to Japan, Clinton said to Lake that he should be vigorously pursuing the Sarajevo initiative.

Lake later called and asked Aspin how the options were coming, and at a Principals meeting on July 13, Powell's deputy, Adm. David Jeremiah, stifled any actionable plan by claiming huge numbers of troops would be required, about seventy thousand, and which the airport at Sarajevo simply couldn't handle. This was somewhat disingenuous. In 1992, the DIA had done a "road reconnaissance" survey in the former Yugoslavia, designed to make an estimate of the "trafficality" of surface roads to see if they could endure the weight of U.S. armored units and especially to ensure that the country's bridges could sustain the weight of the main U.S. battle tank, the Abrams. Former DIA Col. Pat Lang added, "All bridges had to be classified." The survey was done by Col. Robert Herrick, the American military attaché in Zagreb, Croatia, and a member of the U.S. Army Corps of Engineers. The American military attachés in Belgrade and Sarajevo were also involved. Jeremiah noted there were other ground operations involving smaller numbers of troops but said he disliked the options.

But the president had indicated he favored unilateral actions, and suddenly that option was emerging as a serious one. Christopher, with his finger in the wind, testing caution, did an amazing about-face, suddenly declaring that decisive air strikes, with the United States acting alone if necessary, might induce the Serbs to negotiate a truce. It was a stunner, Christopher had reversed himself entirely. With his knack of ingratiation, Christopher's responses were based on selfish calculation. "When Christopher smells the president going a certain way, that's where he goes," said an observer. The discussion continued, and as usual the hawks and doves spoke from their respective camps. Albright was for the use of troops as long as their use was first explained to the American people. Aspin was against it, calling the option "a nonstarter." Lake said the issue should be thoroughly explored. In response to Christopher, others objected that U.S. intervention might harden Muslim attitudes and prompt them to hold out for a better deal. Once again, Aspin also thought this a nonstarter for obvious reasons, brandishing the word "quagmire," whose use always petrified any discussion into frozen stillness.

In truth, action was required. A CIA study showed that most of the city's inhabitants were on the verge of starvation. Without aid many would die that winter. Ideas sprang up everywhere, but no decision was reached. After the meeting, as the momentum built for unilateral U.S. action, Christopher began to use Donilon to leak to the Washington papers the falsehood that he had been in favor of tough, unilateral action all along, not acknowledging that the impulse had come from the president.

There were more meetings featuring the military's usual attempts to cut back the number of troops, lowered now to 25,000, but Leon Panetta wondered where the funds were to pay for the deployment and began a frantic scouring of the budget. Aspin in Italy asked NATO if a small group of six thousand troops would work, but the answer was a sharp no. Aspin did not have his heart in the plan. The whole idea would "overload" an already overcrowded agenda, and it would take up too much of the president's time. Aspin also felt sending troops would only legitimize Serbian aggression.

Lake tried to cobble together a plan that he believed would remove almost everyone's misgivings, aimed at Congress, the public, DOD, and the other government groups. A key element was that NATO, not the United Nations, would exercise command and control, and, secondly, that the deployment would have a clear deadline. Aspin was pessimistic. The deployment would result in more people being killed, it would ratify ethnic cleansing, there would be more refugees, he said. He did agree that NATO should take the lead, as this was what the organization had been created for in the first place.

A new obstacle appeared when the U.N. secretary-general, Boutros Boutros-Ghali, announced that only he and the United Nations, not NATO, had the authority to order military intervention. As this news spread, everyone's heart sank into their shoes. U.N. control greatly pleased the British and French, who from the first had disguised their reluctance to be involved by insisting that the United Nations had to wield final approval for action, the last thing that organization was likely to do.

Yet the plan wasn't jettisoned, at least not just yet. Clinton had made a public commitment. He had tensed for action. But once again, his behavior was equivocal. His whole foreign policy was vague and platitudinous, and he never went to the American people to try and explain why the plan was required and deserved their approval. Clinton made no effort to educate the American public as to what was at stake. There was no attempt to communicate the genuine realities on the ground. Clinton, like Roosevelt in his first term, was more of a "pussyfooting politician" than a general leader. Why did Clinton allow himself to be immobilized by public indifference? His mind was elsewhere. Roosevelt once said, "There are those who come from England, France and Germany who point to the fact that every crisis of the past three years has been muddled through with the hope that each succeeding crisis will be met peacefully in one way or another in the next few years." He said he hoped the view was right but that it went "against one's common sense."[3]

Such wishful thinking still tended to dominate Clinton's thought. As Elizabeth Drew said, "his policy was all over the place . . . he was passive, and changeable—like a cork bobbing about on the waves." His sympathy pulled him toward rescue, but his deep anxieties about his domestic agenda, his determination not to move until he was guaranteed some certainty of advantage, again held him back. Lacking guidelines from the administration, the hawks in the international community stood by helplessly.

The plan crumbled to muck like an eroding sand castle. The Serbs soon loosened their hold, letting enough supplies come into the city so that the world could see that Sarajevo wasn't being "strangled," and in mid-August announced peace talks, provided, of course, that the United States or NATO didn't bomb. Once again, American policy had talked tough only to fizzle out in delay and fuzziness of purpose. Lake, the strongest advocate for action, hadn't possessed the most prominent voice nor commanded the deciding power. Clinton had again advocated action, then pulled back. It was as if Clinton's emotional reactions to events drove him to action, but as the emotions faded or were directed elsewhere, his ideas for policy died in their tracks. Once again the giant had paused, irresolute, muscle-bound, anxious to avoid a fall.

Unfortunately, paralysis wasn't possible. A far more dangerous crisis loomed just over the horizon in Bosnia.

10

SHAPING A SECRET STRATEGY

Where in Bosnia could the West make a stand against Milosevic? That was the cardinal problem facing Clinton. What measures could be undertaken to break the military stalemate and move the parties toward peace? The United Nations was powerless, the United States had no troops there, the U.N. chain of command virtually prohibited any air strikes against the Serbs, who, sensing the West's weakness, insolently continued to do whatever they chose. Paralysis and perplexity reigned, and many were the meetings in which the participants were moody, divided, and unhappy. As the months dragged by, U.S. policymakers had consistently lacked the ability to fix and discern the center of gravity of the Balkan conflict. Said former ambassador to Croatia Peter Galbraith, "They weren't asking, 'What is really the most important place on our radar?' They were avoiding the question."

In Washington, the Deputies Committee[1] made up of subordinates of the Principals Committee, had for months been awash in military and intelligence studies of the Serb forces. They had studied plans, and analyses and options, and not much had happened at first, but then out of the welter of competing ideas would come a winner that would end by altering the military balance in Bosnia, and the answer to the question at last came clear: "Croatia."

The risk in undertaking such a policy would be immense. If the U.S. public would not support foreign involvement, then such involvement must be hidden and held in the strictest secrecy. The purpose of U.S. policy was to bring the Serbs to the conference table, and they would go there only if forced to go, and the best American brains bent their best efforts devising a strategy of two parts: the first would be to arm the Bosnian Muslims; and the second element would be to secretly arm, aid, and train the Croatian military to a NATO standard and then turn it loose on the Bosnian Serbs. Where Yugoslavian president Slobodan Milosevic had always been indifferent to his military and lacked any skills of command, Croatian president Franjo Tudjman was a furiously driving and able officer, and his troops were first-rate.

Apparently, the idea for this dual program first emerged in August of 1993 at a Deputies meeting; then it was presented at a Principals meeting that fall. But there was a problem—at the time American policymakers were discussing a joint force of Croats and Muslims, the two were locked in a completely pointless fratricidal war, full of the greatest bitterness and savagery. As Galbraith said, "It was insane." Here, the marauding Serbs controlled 70 percent of Bosnia, ruling it with the utmost brutality, and instead of finding common cause, the Croats and Muslims were slaughtering each other over territorial scraps, leaving the Serb oppressors unmolested.

Peppery little Leon Fuerth and the NSC's European expert Sandy Vershbow are said to have come up with the original idea of how to counter the continuing Serb onslaughts. Fuerth was already playing a key part in maintaining harsh pressure against Belgrade. After the collapse of Srebrenica, the U.N. Security Council had passed sanctions against the rump state of Yugoslavia. The provisions froze Belgrade's assets abroad and transshipments through Serbia and Montenegro, in what was the most comprehensive set of mandatory sanctions in U.N. history. The cost of Milosevic's war was already sending his economy back to the dark ages, and Belgrade's tottering financial structure was honeycombed with fraud, the funding for the war coming mainly from a variety of Ponzi schemes, fake bank offerings, and other shady ploys perpetrated against the Serb people. An entire criminal gang, masking itself as Belgrade's government, had battened itself on the political system and was drinking its blood dry.

Leon Fuerth was not a member of the Council on Foreign Relations, yet he was at the center of policymaking on a wide range of international issues, virtually the day-to-day manager of U.S.-Russia relations, in addition to his other duties. It was Fuerth's job to administer the sanctions, and they would prove a "primary pillar" in tightening the economic pressure on Belgrade. Memoranda written by Fuerth at the request of Gore became the list of the essential conditions agreed to with the allies and Russia that had to be met before there would be any easing of sanctions. Former colleagues say that Fuerth was a wonder to watch. He always thought before he spoke; he had unusual depth of mind; and he could carry a crushing workload.

While others fidgeted and wavered, Fuerth and Vershbow had cast their eye on the leader of Croatia as possibly the man who could do the job. "What we were looking for was strong leadership," and that meant Tudjman, according to a former senior administration official. The difficulty was that Tudjman was hardly a savory figure. He had a square, severe, jowly face, framed by severe wire-rimmed spectacles, and his followers deified him. "God in heaven and Tudjman in the homeland" was a popular slogan.

Many U.S. policymakers thought Tudjman and Milosevic were a lot alike. One former U.S. official said, "Tudjman was a Stalin, Milosevic a Hitler." Both were authoritarian centralizers with no affection for anything democratic. Ambassador Zimmermann said that with Tudjman and Milosevic, you had the two chief former Yugoslavian republics being led by men "who are the very embodiments of the ethnic resentments of their people."

Croatia bore the stain of having been a Hitler-backed ally during World War II, responsible for some of the worst atrocities committed against the Serbs, a fact that Tudjman soft-pedaled, asserting lamely that the Utashi militia had simply been an expression of Croatia's desire for a homeland. Its big advantage in the eyes of U.S. policymakers was that it wasn't Slav, it wasn't Muslim, it was Catholic.

Yet Tudjman was also an obscene racist who had once made the repulsive statement, "Thank God my wife is not a Jew or a Serb." He and Milosevic had a genius for irritating each other's vanities. After his election in the early 1990s as president, the new Croatian flag resembled in ways the old, loathed fascist one, but Tudjman's public was callow, unaware of his moral crudities, declaring stoutly, "Tudjman is our Milosevic." When the Croats finally hammered out a new constitution in 1990, the document abruptly declared that Serbs were not true Croatians and asserted that the Serbs living in Croatia were no longer a nation but a national minority, the same sort of divisive racism that Milosevic had employed with such devastating effect. The constitution declared that the Cyrillic alphabet beloved of the Serbs was no longer the national script in Croatia. All of this left the Serbs affronted, alienated, and angry.

But the stakes for America were too high for this to matter. "In times of violence choose the least ugly faction," said the poet Robinson Jeffers, and although Tudjman was not a name to be harmoniously associated with the idea of civic decency or a just and humane democracy, there was little choice. Galbraith believed that unless the Croat-Muslim war was stopped soon, it might never be stopped. "Bosnia was a moral problem," Galbraith said with passion. "My God, you had women in high heels who were being shot down or blown apart by shells just trying to get to work. You had horrible slaughter. Someone had to do something."

For Galbraith, everything of importance that he had to do, everything of real meaning to himself and to the nation, would be done in Croatia, or Bosnia would become another Middle East, "full of instability, constant terrorism, chaos," as he would later say. To others, he had compared the area as resembling "Lebanon being next to Cyprus." Galbraith saw clearly that the darkest forces of the soul fed the conflict. Racial and religious contempt, added to unremitting animosity and suspicion, had soon soured into a deadly brew that came to drip venom into a very unstable situation. On the part of both warring parties, ineradicable hatred had entered the most personal recesses of wish and will.

The war had to be stopped at all costs. If the Croatian forces got the proper armaments and were taught the proper tactics, given unofficial U.S. guidance, leadership, and intelligence, Tudjman's forces had the ability to hit the Serbs a blow of pulverizing impact that would alter the balance of power.

The footwork that secured Galbraith's appointment as U.S. ambassador to Croatia was nothing short of miraculous. What Gore and his staff were looking for was the proper human instrument to negotiate with Tudjman, and they found it in this hard-driving young staffer on the Senate Foreign Relations Committee named Peter Galbraith. Had the intense, passionate young man taken his views to anyone but Fuerth and Vershbow initially, Galbraith may well have been the wrong man in the wrong place with the wrong idea and been ignored, yet when he made the case to Fuerth, Fuerth realized that he was suddenly hearing a passionate recitation of his own ideas.

To Fuerth, Galbraith's ideas were music. One of Fuerth's few Foreign Service postings, made in the 1970s, had been to Zagreb, the capital of Croatia, so he had some familiarity with it. The more meetings that Fuerth and Vershbow had with Galbraith and the more he talked, the more the hawks saw that he had a clear perception of the actual facts combined with a shrewd, farsighted judgment of their implications. He had a quick grasp of the possibilities within a situation. Gore was keeping Clinton apprised, traipsing in and out of the president's office several times a day to discuss details, and Gore's articulate, definite enthusiasm fired up the president with a sense of hopeful possibility.

As it worked out, the appointment of Galbraith, a daring step, was done just in the nick of time. It would be only by a hairbreadth that Galbraith wangled his chance to make the difference he craved. Throughout the fall of 1993, the senior State Department leadership had been a hotbed of cold feet when it came to Bosnia. The topic was still in Christopher's "too hard to do" box, and Christopher, who harbored a vast distaste for Tudjman, had set in motion plans to downgrade U.S.-Croatia relations and withdraw the U.S. ambassador. Gore got wind of it and the race was on. According to Galbraith, the Croatia desk officer, Steve Walker, "practically bundled Galbraith out the door" before the Christopher changes took effect. By the time Christopher reacted, he was too late. Galbraith had a Senate hearing on January 9, 1994, was nominated on the 19th, had a six-day waiting rule suspended, and on January 26 was presenting his credentials in Zagreb to Tudjman. Galbraith would later laugh and say his was "probably one of the fastest appointments in history—I basically staffed my own nomination."

Galbraith was the son of the famous economist John Kenneth Galbraith, and like many excitable, intellectual men, was something of an eccentric. He cared little for appearances, often showing up at conferences with his hair uncombed and standing up all over the place like chicken feathers, the knot of his tie loosened, his dress shirt hastily tucked into his belt on one side. He was habitually late. He reminds one of General Ulysses Grant, who always went about in his mud-spattered private's uniform. But Galbraith harbored a genuine interest in refugees and humanitarian problems, and manifested a personal fearlessness about going to some of the more violent, harsh, and squalid spots on the face of the earth to obtain his information firsthand.

In 1991 when Saddam had begun the slaughter of Iraq's Kurds, Galbraith had been the staff director of the Senate Foreign Relations Committee, and his interest had instantly flared high and hot at the slaughter. When secretary of state George Shultz had put in place the rule about "no contacts with the Iraqi opposition," Galbraith had been quick to see a significant useful source of intelligence in the Kurds. Eventually an improvised system was set up by which the Kurds would telegraph their intelligence to Iran, where it went from there to Damascus, and from there by phone to the Kurds' office in Detroit. Then it would be faxed to Galbraith's office on the Hill. "This was not stupid stuff," he said. "One [report] was about an allied pilot who had been shot down. But [it] was picked up by a lieutenant from naval intelligence who couldn't have been less interested."[2] Galbraith had returned to Washington to play a decisive part in gaining White House support for easing the humanitarian crisis that had resulted from Saddam's attack.

By the time of Galbraith's appointment as ambassador to Croatia, any European toughness of intent, any stores of urgent, propellant energy had run dry, and Europe's resolve about Bosnia was rapidly draining away, like a spent wave, sliding in retreat down the steep slope of a beach. Galbraith had long felt Christopher and others were simply refusing to see and absorb the horror of what was happening in Bosnia. He also saw that this was not all due to timid spinelessness or fear of U.S. involvement. A new process had begun that was not going to stop. His new opportunity was not only a great opportunity, it was in the hands of a tirelessly energetic young man.

11

MARK OF DESOLATION

The White House system of management, the lack of intense, studied attention to the concrete, minute details of foreign policy, was about to plunge Clinton into one of the greatest failures and embarrassments of his presidential career. If he had been weak in foreign policy, if he had embraced a policy of drift and timid caution, it was partly because of a deep-seated fear of incurring any loss of American lives. "The fear of suffering any American casualties anywhere in the world was extremely profound," said a former presidential aide. Yet Clinton was about to lose eighteen American lives.

The crisis was partly of his own making. Clinton was clearly a man congenitally incapable of *not* talking, and during his presidential campaign, he had pledged to avoid future Vietnams by requiring other countries to share the dirty work in places such as Bosnia where an international authority would be responsible for directing operations. To irk Bush, Clinton had promised to send American troops into Somalia on a humanitarian mission to relieve hunger among 700,000 to 1.5 million people who were essentially living without the basic services of a functioning government. A vicious civil war was raging among tribal chiefs, and no mechanism existed for distributing food to the needy and desperate who were on the verge of starvation. Bush had hesitated for a time, but badly stung by Clinton's attacks about his paralysis in the Balkans, the lame-duck president had finally sent American troops to Somalia to quell the damaging criticisms, especially after NBC News broadcast images of the gaunt faces of frail, withering small children, and the vehement outburst of sympathy forced him to take the plunge.

Somalia had come into being after World War II, with British Somaliland in the north, the U.N. Trust Territory, and the old Italian Somaliland
to the south. It was a key location on the Horn of Africa. The United States
had used the naval base at Berbera in the north and we had sent some aid,
but the shipments were canceled in 1988 after human rights violations. Relations soured further. The U.S. embassy was closed and in 1990, Americans
were evacuated.

After the brutal dictator General Mohamed Siad Barre had been overthrown, two antagonistic factions had sprung up; one headed by business-
man and rival president Ali Mahdi Muhammad, and the other, the son of a
camel driver and a charismatic natural killer by the name of Mohammad
Farah Aideed, head of the Habr Gidr clan. The fighting for power began in
1991 and it was a real war of atrocity. The chaos and depredations were
made worse by drought, and the United Nations sent in a small group of
Pakistani peacekeepers to try and distribute food aid, which was usually
looted by members of armed clans. The situation grew worse, and the United
States airdropped 45,000 tons of food, but the clans blocked the Pakistanis
from entering the capital of Mogadishu to guard the food. The United Nations wanted to use force, and on December 9, 1992, the Security Council
voted to go in. On that same day, a small number of U.S. Marines began to
land.

The event, Operation Restore Hope, was extraordinary. The government of Somalia had not asked for the aid or the troops, the U.S. mission
had no congressional authorization, nor was it sent in response to any community invitation. Bush had said the mission would be brief, and the United
States would be out by inauguration day. But military deployments are never
prompt. In effect, the intervention had been in response to public outrage in
the United States and hadn't been well thought out. What was causing the
starvation was domestic internal chaos, and the Bush measure didn't attempt to deal with that. The gift of food was designed to treat the symptoms of civil disorder caused by a group of clans with no sense of civic or
general welfare and who clung to no end beyond wielding power. The aid
was designed to treat the symptoms not the disease.

At its peak there were 28,000 U.S. troops in Somalia, but they were to
be out quickly, to be replaced by U.N. troops, or at least that was the story.
Yet in January, redheaded, fiery Richard Clarke, appointed by Clinton to be
the first national coordinator for security, infrastructure protection and
counterterrorism, had a curious meeting with Tony Lake in the Presidential
Transition Office, located on a private floor in a building on Vermont Avenue.
There was a bustle of activity, a sea of résumés, and at a desk the bespectacled

figure of Lake, whom Clarke had never met. Lake was overwhelmed but polite. He thanked Clarke for coming, then said he gathered they didn't have much to worry about regarding Somalia because U.S. forces would be "largely out by inauguration day."

A surprised Clarke said that, "No, actually, the U.S. deployment into Somalia would not be complete till the end of January." Clarke then showed Lake the plan for scheduled deployments.

"The U.N. is dragging its feet, Mr. Lake."

Lake's eyes sharpened. "We were told that the U.N. would take over." Clarke noted that Lake's shocked reaction was like that of a man who'd just been told he had cancer.[1]

By March, the Congress still hadn't challenged the legality of the operation, and officials were talking as if the affair was about to wind up. Again, the senior levels of the Clinton administration appeared to be barely aware of the operation. The administrative powers were vague and fluctuating, often without clear responsibility or effective coordination.

Meanwhile the civil war blazed on, and soon U.N. Envoy Robert Oakley, the U.S. ambassador to Somalia from 1982 to 1984, was sent by the United Nations to try to forge some sort of cease-fire between the tribes. Oakley, a straight, direct, rough-hewn man, knew the players and read not only their characters but grasped the factors at play in the situation. As a young Foreign Service officer he had served with Holbrooke and Lake in Saigon, and since had held a number of positions in hot spots like Zaire and Pakistan. Oakley knew that in such places the faculty of intrigue is often a key source of influence. To know with whom to be silent, to know with whom to speak and just how much to say, to be able to drop casual observations, to have a keen sense of what others meant even though they did not say it; to know what someone was planning in secret even though they attest to the opposite—such were his skills. Using all his tact, insight, and persuasion, Oakley had fifteen warlords sign up to create an interim government, and to everyone's amazement, there had resulted a fragile, edgy kind of peace that was able to hold.

But Oakley had not counted on another factor, the grandiose ambitions of U.N. secretary-general Boutros Boutros-Ghali. Boutros-Ghali was an Egyptian Copt, a member of one of the world's oldest Christian sects but in a Muslim country. He was waspish, petulant, gossipy, an ambitious man who could lose sight of larger issues in his anxiety to enlarge his authority and aggrandize himself. He had an exaggerated estimate of his intellect matched only by his outsized sense of self-importance. As a Copt in Egypt, he had never been allowed to rise to the top of the tree and he seethed with a sense of a destiny denied. Now he saw in Somalia a chance to enact a grand dream of "reconstruction, reconciliation, and rehabilitation" of Somalia at the hands of the United Nations and under his direction.

His own experience should have led him to a more cautious examination of his premises. When he visited Mogadishu in January of 1993 on a one-day visit, he was forced to take refuge with the U.S. Marines when hundreds of Somalis pelted U.N. headquarters with rocks and garbage, and desecrated the U.N. flag. Swelling crowds gathered before the building to chant, "Down, down with Boutros-Ghali," throwing stones, cans, and grapefruit rinds.

The mob had been sent by Aideed, who suspected Boutros-Ghali of supporting the rival Darod clan of Ali Mahdi Muhammad.

As the White House began to turn over control of Operation Restore Hope to U.N. forces, it was Boutros-Ghali who urged the United States to stay longer and broaden the U.N. mandate to disarm the population. Colin Powell had approved this and many of his colleagues felt it was a way of not having to send any American troops to relieve Sarajevo. But one of his colleagues, General Joe Hoar, thought the idea of disarming Mogadishu, the capital of the country, to be "idiotic." Hoar said, "We hadn't been able to disarm Los Angeles or New York and we were going to disarm Somalia?"[2] But pressure was coming from Boutros-Ghali, who said he believed that Somalia would be the place to set afoot a new, more vigorous and high-profile United Nations program of national reconstruction. He also warned direly that if the United States did not support this venture, it would be "a disaster for all our multilateral efforts." As Oakley knew, the clan warfare and famine had so far killed 350,000 Somalis, and while not lacking in sympathy, the seasoned diplomat thought Somalia the last place to successfully build a democratic nation.

Oakley was a realist. Any foreign or outside power suffered disaster when it tried to apply its influence to inappropriate institutions or circumstances. Democracy was not a plant suitable for any and all places; Oakley did not believe that the promotion of democracy should constitute a major, even an overriding, objective of American policy on a global scale. He did not believe that such efforts would have much effect against the strength of habit and custom or the absence of any participatory popular institutions. He was suspicious of the notion that inside every tribesman there lurked a liberal democrat trying to get out if only given the chance. To Oakley, once the tribesman gained power, he was far more likely to treat his tormentors as his tormentors had treated him, an objective having little to do with spreading democracy. So he cast a cold eye.

The CIA held the same view. Given its colonial past, Somalia was not going to welcome a foreign presence, which would have to operate in hostile conditions whose meaning the United States barely grasped.

The Oakley team, backed by Frank Wisner, the undersecretary of defense, and Marine Lt. Gen. Robert Johnston, began to enact a very careful, tactful program. Oakley viewed the Somali warlords as human beings. "Treat a warlord like a statesman, and he'll behave like a statesman. Treat him like a warlord, and he'll act like a warlord." The structure of the country was tribal, social, political, and economic, not military. It was fine to talk of modernizing the society and broadening the base of government, but this was simply seeing the place through our own attitudes. If Somalia was a frighteningly foreign culture, Oakley still believed that even a man like Aideed could be reasoned with and had a sense of responsibility if it were appealed to in the right way.

To Oakley, Aideed was a legitimate leader. Yes, he used terror, he shot his own men and blamed the killings on the United Nations, and he used starvation to strengthen his base. But he embodied certain valid national forces of his people. Of course, Aideed knew that to give in to foreign pressure would have destroyed his prestige and rendered him a foreign pawn.

Under Oakley and Johnston, detailed procedures were set up. What the U.N.-U.S. mission sought to do was rid the streets of Mogadishu of "technicals"—open-backed pickup trucks mounted with .30 caliber machine guns—which were responsible for most of the violence. Thanks to careful, painstaking talks, the Somalis agreed that the technicals were to be placed in compounds, and the compounds were to be inspected by U.N. troops. "Above all, there weren't to be any surprises," said Marine Gen. Joe Hoar, head of the Central Command with responsibility for Somalia. The U.N. people took pains to talk to Aideed every single day by telephone and keep him apprised of any U.N. moves. If a U.N. convoy was going to inspect a compound, Aideed was given a five-day notice. The Somalis appreciated the courtesy and there were no incidents.

The whole situation worsened with the advent of Adm. Jonathan Howe. Boutros-Ghali had asked for an American to be in charge and Lake had persuaded Howe, a Scowcroft deputy, to take this job. Doctrinaire, inflexible, with an absolute confidence in the rightness of his judgments, Howe harbored a ferocious dislike of Aideed, seeing him as devious, unstable, brutal, corrupt, and wildly unpredictable. The state of the city had shocked the admiral, the looting, the rampant unemployment, the disfigured damage to the structures. Howe thought Aideed the seat of all wickedness—a dangerously intolerant and immoderate judgment for a foreigner operating on strange soil to make. Where Oakley merely saw Aideed as the inevitable product of the anarchic chaos, he knew that if you killed Aideed, you were very likely to end up with someone just like him or even worse.

In May, matters in Mogadishu were relatively quiet. Oakley with his mastery of personalities, his endless tact and patience, his skill in outwaiting obstacles, delays, and frustrations, along with Marine Lt. Gen. Robert Johnston, the senior U.S. representative, had won agreement from Aideed to end the clan warfare. The U.S.-sponsored agreement, worked out in Addis Ababa, Ethiopia, included a disarmament conference to be sponsored by Aideed in Mogadishu. But Howe began to try to marginalize Aideed, and, as time passed, tensions worsened between Aideed and the U.N. personnel. In addition, a nettled animosity had developed between Oakley and Howe that threatened to undermine the frail peace.[3] The two men couldn't stand each other, colleagues said, and, bit by bit, the procedures so carefully implemented and put in place "began to fall through the cracks," as Hoar said. The daily telephone calls, so important to keeping open the channels of communication, began to be ignored.

Aideed was aware of Howe's hatred and saw in him allies of his old adversary, Gen. Siad Barre, and Boutros-Ghali, who had always been a close ally of his old enemy. Howe's personal determination to rid Somalia of Aideed gained support from the State Department with the arrival of the new U.S. envoy, Robert Gosende, who had the support of Christopher and Peter Tarnoff, undersecretary of state for political affairs, who also viewed Aideed as the sink of all foulness and the chief obstacle to progress.

It was soon clear that America saw Aideed as a target to be hunted down. The careful procedures deteriorated further. As a mutual search for a modus operandi evaporated, mistrust and suspicion began to surface, and a little chain of ugly clashes and incidents erupted between the Somalis and U.N. forces. Power in Somalia was paid for in blood, and when Aideed's clan had overthrown General Barre, Aideed had lost men, and he felt his rule was his by just claim.

The building rancor burst out on June 5 with the slaughter of twenty-four Pakistani peacekeepers. It was greeted everywhere as an act of mindless violence, yet Gen. Anthony Zinni makes clear this was not a mere piece of Somali perversity. "The war erupted when peacekeepers took down the Aideed radio station. We allowed Aideed to keep his station as long as he let us have ours. When he preached hate, we did too. But every now and then, we would say to him, Lower your rhetoric and we'll lower ours, and both sides would tone it down."[4]

On June 5, the Pakistanis decided to conduct an inspection, but because of the decay in the system of phone calls to Aideed, no advance warning of the convoy was given. "That day they sent a U.N. officer to say they were going to do an inspection but the Somalis said, 'Give us some time to notify people,' but there was not time," Zinni said. When the Pakistanis destroyed the station, it was a place in the heart of Aideed's followers, and after the attack, Somalis came running from all directions. They confronted the Pakistanis, killed two dozen of them, and then the mob began destroying food stations and other U.N. installations. Aideed claimed the Pakistanis had launched a premeditated attack.[5]

On June 6, Madeleine Albright at the United Nations in New York agreed that whoever had killed the Pakistanis had to be captured and punished. Albright pushed this option without first bothering to consult with Lake or the NSC, according to Hoar.[6] Clinton knew little of this. There never was a single Principals meeting on Somalia until after eighteen U.S. Rangers had been killed in October. The Deputies Committee had done most of the staff studies and analysis, and passed it up to the Principals, where informal decisions were made without a thorough analysis of possible consequences. The Clinton administration had simply adopted a poorly thought out mission from the Bush administration.

Lake hadn't considered the June 6 decision a big deal. There was some talk of trying to mute the "us versus them" aspect of the struggle to keep it from becoming a melodrama, but Howe's blood was up. With a twist of the kaleidoscope, the U.N. mission had assumed an entirely different pattern. What had begun as an impulse to aid a country's population and try to rebuild it now changed into a manhunt. For Admiral Howe, punishment was simply a kind of fair repayment for what had happened to the Pakistanis. Howe posted a reward of $25,000 for the capture of Aideed, whose followers posted the sum of $1 million for the capture of "Animal Howe." Berger later said when Howe put up the reward, "we felt it didn't make a lot of sense," but he added that Howe was calling the shots and wasn't to be second-guessed.

Howe sent in a request to Washington for the dispatch of a Delta Force group to kidnap Aideed as part of a plan of punishment. Once Aideed was in custody, the Delta Force would whisk the Somali to a third-country ship anchored off the coast of Kenya. A tribunal of African judges, assembled by the CIA, would then try Aideed for murder. This request was thought dubious and was denied.

It didn't deter Howe, who now set out to capture Aideed with the forces already in country. To keep down collateral damage, Howe first sent out helicopters announcing the times of the raids, a tactic mocked wildly by the

Somalis. Then on July 12, Howe sent in a force against an Aideed head-quarters, the Abdi House, using helicopters and TOW missiles. A total of seventy-three Somalis were killed, and when reporters rushed to cover the event, four were murdered by mobs.

Clarke said Aideed could have been captured at that time, but that the U.S. military "let him go."

On that same date, July 12, Aideed and several of his aides left Mogadishu for Khartoum, Sudan, where they attended a People's Arab and Islamic Conference chaired by Hassan Abdallah al-Turabi, the Sudanese leader, who sponsored terrorism against the United States and backed the spread of Islam throughout the Horn of Africa. Turabi had ties to Abdul-Rahman Ahmad Ali Tour, who had proclaimed the Islamic code or Sharia as the law of Somalia and had henceforth received financial and military aid from Iran and Sudan. "Certainly General Aideed was receiving some technical and logistical aid from Sudan as part of a fledgling military alliance in 1992," this source said.

The decision to fight U.S. forces in Somalia was a direct result of Sudan's strategy, according to a U.S. government analyst. Robert Oakley, who had served as U.S. ambassador to Somalia, disagrees, but he concedes that Sudan was very nervous about U.S. intervention. "The Sudanese thought that they were next, that after we were finished in Somalia we would strike at Sudan."[7] Hezbollah, the fundamentalist Islamic militia, for example, published documents at the time alerting factions that Sudan was the next U.S. target. "It was a totally mistaken idea," Oakley said.

In any case, the effect of the Abdi House assault was to unite the country behind Aideed. Even moderates who had opposed him dropped their opposition. Howe began to use backchannel communications to persuade Washington to okay the dispatch of Delta, with such obsessional insistence his colleagues called him "Jonathan Ahab." But there was no serious discussion among senior White House officials of the viability of using Delta. In August, when Christopher was on vacation in Santa Barbara, Peter Tarnoff was in touch with him by phone. But it was summer, and the attention of the Principals was elsewhere.

After four American soldiers were killed in August, Howe was given his Delta Force. General Hoar had been against it: "Any raid to capture Aideed had only a 25 percent chance of success. Only if it had had an 80 percent chance of success would I have approved it. It was as dumb as shit." Throughout July and August, the White House gave no green light.

On two occasions Hoar voiced his misgivings about any attempted raid to Lake and Berger, and another time, he warned Aspin and his deputy,

William Perry, that the raid was dubious. Aideed was on his home turf; he was a former police chief in the city and knew every alleyway, every rat hole, every escape route. Yet in spite of this deep-seated reluctance, no one had thought to brief Clinton.

Meanwhile, Aideed was moving about in the open, but there was so much loose talk of an impending U.S. raid he quietly went to ground and disappeared. The CIA had dispatched teams who were well connected. The Delta team arrived on August 23. Knowing that Aideed had become elusive and that searches for a single man had not worked well in Panama or Nicaragua or other places in the past, the Delta team was going to put Aideed out of business by capturing his aides and destroying his military infrastructure.

The first attempt to snatch Aideed had proved an outright farce. On August 30, Rangers slid down ropes from helicopters to assault an empty building and capture a man who resembled Aideed but, in fact, was a member of the U.N. mission. Aspin wailed, "We look like the gang who couldn't shoot straight," and Powell felt the mishap an unforgivable amateur error. The Pentagon spokesperson, Kathleen deLaski, simply lied. "This is not an effort to go after one man," she said.

The White House was toughening its rhetoric, firm in its belief that if the United States was staunch enough, Aideed would weaken, a view that drastically undersold the resilience, the hatred of foreigners, and morale on the other side. On August 27, Aspin gave a speech that said America would remain in Somalia until it was disarmed, a statement that stiffened backs in the Congress, especially that of Senator Robert Byrd, who threatened to cut back the mission.

Powell began to feel that force should be applied and the hunt for Aideed proceed, according to Hoar. "He didn't like it; he thought it was necessary," he said. Powell called Lake and said they should go ahead.

Suddenly the currents of decision began to run in a different direction. The bulk of Clinton advisors felt that a political solution was by far the most desirable, not a military one, which appeared to have little chance of success. "Engagement is not endorsement," said Hoar. To isolate Aideed and see him as a fugitive was to make it impossible to have any influence over him. A political solution made Aideed an indispensable commodity and gave a promise of success. Pushing the political angle, Clinton at one point asked if there were a way to simply cordon off the southern part of Mogadishu where Aideed was hiding instead of raiding it, but was told it was militarily "infeasible."

As the administration began to change policy, no new instructions were issued to the Delta Force in the field. Clinton, in fact, was acting in the misguided belief that the raids had ended. What resulted was the usual confusion, a two-track policy that was attempting to put together a diplomatic package while still continuing to try and hunt down Aideed. Several times Clinton seemed bewildered by the military effort, asking angrily, "Why the hell are we chasing after him?"

Clinton clearly preferred diplomacy, siding with Hoar and others who felt Howe's policy of combined arrogance and ignorance would issue in folly and disaster.

"None of these men had the remotest notion of how to handle this," Hoar said.[8]

On September 12, Clinton had a long, thoughtful conversation with former President Jimmy Carter, who had met Aideed while visiting Somalia and had received letters from the warlord in which Aideed had protested his innocence. Carter told Clinton that the key to success in Somalia was a political settlement and the hard line of Howe began to lose hearers in the White House. At the same time there was rising reluctance to approve the fighting in the Congress, and Democrats had their hands full trying to contend with it.

Aideed, in the meantime, was running free and was making America look inept, muscle-bound, clumsy, and foolish.

Once again an ugly incident brought the episode to a new and dangerous crisis point. On September 5, Aideed's augmented forces ambushed a Nigerian U.N. contingent, killing seven soldiers. It took a massive intervention by U.S.-U.N. forces to relieve the hard-pressed Nigerians, according to U.S. government officials. The U.S. military was eager to strike a blow back, and on the 9th, when American and Pakistani soldiers were trying to clear a roadblock, Somali mobs rioted and Army Cobra gunships fired missiles into the crowd, killing more than a hundred Somalis. On the 13th, fierce fighting took place between U.S. and Aideed forces in which a Cobra gunship attacked a hospital being used as a Somali headquarters and storage facility. Aideed charged that the United States had killed civilians, and on September 15, Aideed launched mortar attacks against the U.N. compound, and when women and children stoned U.N. patrols, the U.N. patrols opened fire, U.S. officials said. Uneasiness was intense.

On the ground, the CIA had teams that were working hard to keep an eye on Aideed lieutenants. One key CIA team leader, code-named Condor, was an African-American by the name of Ernie Shanklin, a brilliant and intrepid covert operator. When the United States could not capture Aideed, it decided to kidnap two of his top leaders, what one former U.S. military source called "tier-one personalities"—of top importance—Omar Salad, Aideed's main political advisor, and his ostensible minister of interior, Abdi "Qeybdid" Hassan Salad Awale. They were described as "hard-liners, men with blood on their hands," Shanklin said later.[9]

Fluent in Arabic, Shanklin and his team did an excellent job of keeping track of the two lieutenants, at great risk to themselves. Shanklin was aware that on October 3 there was to be an all-out effort to kidnap the two Aideed men. Task Force Ranger was an assault force made up of Delta's C Squadron, a top Army commando unit, and Rangers from Company B, 3rd Battalion of the Army's 75th Infantry, backed up by three surveillance helicopters, a spy plane, four MH-6 Little Bird helicopters and eight Black Hawk troop-carrying helicopters. The force was supported on the ground by eight Humvees carrying Rangers, Delta operators, and four members of the Navy's SEAL Team Six, the Sea, Air, Land group of the Navy's Special Forces. Together this force totaled 160 men.

Clearly, Aideed had some advance knowledge of the plan. According to Oakley, the fight on October 3 was "a spontaneous response" fueled by the previous U.S. killing of Somalis. "It was primarily a Somali operation. They had the motives and the tactical knowledge," he said. But Shanklin disagrees with this. He and his team had observed the continuing growth of Aideed's forces and concluded it was "by design, not something anyone missed." He added that the CIA was reporting that 150 to 200 fighters a day were arriving in Mogadishu. "To most people that would indicate a massing of troops," he said. The U.S. military disagreed. Shanklin said the Army command saw the attacks as individual incidents, not the probing of a larger and well-organized force.

The main assault was scheduled for October 3, but on the 2nd, Shanklin received electrifying news. The two Aideed henchmen, Salad and Awale, had been spotted in a tea house not four hundred yards from the main U.S. command base where the Delta Force was housed. Shanklin hastened to the tea house and confirmed the sighting with his own eyes. It was now a question of striking at top speed. Shanklin and his men notified the command of Gen. William Garrison. They had the top priority targets under surveillance. All that was required was a ten-man "snatch team" to come and kidnap them, and render the necessity for the next day's larger operation null and void. With growing urgency, Shanklin kept reporting in, repeating his requests over and over. There was no word. The pressure of time lay on the matter and Shanklin tried again. All it would take was ten guys, he said.

Again there was no answer. Then finally came the dismal reply. "We're going to wait until tomorrow," Shanklin was told. He couldn't believe his ears.

Years later he would say, "It was perfect for a snatch job. We could have had them both and it would have only taken ten men."

Garrison's reaction was to wait until the next day and send a big, high-profile force in to seize the men in broad daylight, this source said. The force easily seized the two Aideed aides when they walked into a trap. However, in the fight, two high-tech MH-660 Black Hawk[10] helicopters were shot down, two more crash-landed; eighteen Rangers were killed and seventy-seven wounded by the angry mob. Bodies were desecrated. There was an angry convulsion in Congress, Clinton's credentials as commander in chief were jeered at, and his humiliation was profound.

Zinni blamed the command system on the ground. "You had five different chains of command each acting independently, the Delta guys off doing their own thing in isolation, and so were all the others. No one did anything in a coordinated fashion."[11]

But Clinton, standing amid a firestorm of congressional criticism, told some legislators who wanted to cut and run, "We started this mission for the right reason, and we're going to finish it in the right way."[12] If Clinton stared straight into the face of the debacle, others tried to avert their eyes, and Clinton began to realize he had soft spots amid his foreign policy group. One was Christopher. When Clinton had met with congressional leaders, Christopher hadn't said much, and in meetings the day before the secretary had been mute. On Thursday, Christopher didn't come to the usual pre-meeting at the White House, and he departed quickly after another meeting with congressional leaders. It was clear he felt the topic was dangerously contaminated, and was staying away from it. The secretary of state was a marked man, although that would only emerge over time. Gore had been the opposite. "Gore never tried to evade a shred of responsibility," said a former aide.

Clinton's anguish was profound. How could a rational and responsible government have become involved in such an ill-starred adventure? But he confronted the failure with unflinching steadiness and a sense of his own responsibility for it. "What plagued me most was that when I approved the use of force to apprehend Aideed, I did not envision anything like a day-time assault in a crowded, hostile neighborhood. I assumed we would try and get him when he was on the move. I thought I was approving a police action by U.S. troops." He'd had no idea he'd been authorizing "a military assault in hostile territory."

The operation had not been approved by General Hoar. The damage to the administration in the Congress was hardly to be underestimated.

Clinton accepted his blame in the matter with sturdy equanimity. When the father of a dead Delta Medal of Honor Winner, Randy Shugart, met with Clinton at the White House, he told Clinton he wasn't fit to be commander in chief. Clinton later said, "He could say anything he wanted as far as I was concerned."[13]

Clinton's next steps were calm, composed, and determined. He had followed the Pentagon's advice, and the Pentagon had been wrong, just as Howe had been wrong earlier. The first of the bitter lessons learned was not to rely on experts. Clinton had to make sure he had the unfettered and confidential advice of his most astute advisors. After this, he would broaden the range of his advice, consulting experts and generalists in whom he trusted. He made the resolution that presidential interest *had* to be present in decisions of this kind of magnitude. He was still baffled at how men as competent and knowledgeable as Powell and Aspin had let this matter get away from them.

What was required was political reconciliation in the Congress, having the strength to accept disaster, and begin efforts to recoup the situation.

During one meeting, as the president sat red-faced in the Cabinet Room, listening to Christopher, it was clear that, like Kennedy, he would hear them out, but any actions he took would be his own. Clinton sat doodling and finally, after everyone had talked themselves out, he looked up. "Okay, here is what we're going to do," he said. "We are not running away with our tail between our legs. We're staying. We are also not going to flatten Mogadishu because the world knows we could do that.

"We are going to send in more troops, with tanks and aircraft and anything they need. We are going to show force. If anybody fucks with us, we'll respond. And we're going to get the U.N. to finally show up and take over."

In the days that followed, America secretly placed snipers on the roofs and walls of the U.N. compounds. Any Somalis in the area were shot on sight. It was an ugly and unreported little war. Six months later, America handed over the operation to U.N. peacekeeping forces. But something in Clinton had hardened, and he emerged from the crisis a different man.

12

THE WANT OF SUCCESS

Aspin was not to survive the Somalia fiasco. He had never been a proper fit for defense secretary with his absentminded professor demeanor, his rumpled suits, and his tendency to think out loud. To the uniformed Pentagon, a real commander could, if needed, be fierce, peremptory, and glacial. Aspin never came close to projecting that kind of decisiveness. He was too amiable, too informal and shambling in manner to inspire much more than contemptuous ridicule among the senior military. Gore had already spoken to Clinton about the shortcomings and defects of Aspin's performance, but it fell to Tony Lake to give Aspin the bad news during a mid-December White House meeting.

When Aspin entered Lake's office, the national security advisor announced he had some bad news.

"What, you're not leaving?" said Aspin, concerned.

"No, Les," said Lake. "You are."

The scramble to find a successor began. Senator Warren Rudman was approached but turned the job down. Bobby Ray Inman, a former senior intelligence official, was briefly considered as a candidate, but too many complications surfaced there and he withdrew. Gore was said to have suggested Aspin's number two man, William Perry. Gen. Wesley Clark had been impressed by the magnificence of Perry's office, whose window looked out over the Potomac toward Washington. There were plush carpets, multiple sitting areas, a large desk set in the center, portraits on the walls, several phones, and a computer. As Clark said, "The room spoke of authority from every angle."

Perry was the perfect appointment, the number two man who turned out to be the perfect number one. In late 1992, a discussion had taken place between Lake and Berger about what characteristics made up the ideal public official, and they agreed on four basic categories: there was the individual who was talented but high-maintenance, someone like Holbrooke; talented but low-maintenance; not very talented but low-maintenance; and not very talented but high-maintenance. The rarest and most invaluable specimen, they agreed, was highly talented and low-maintenance, and that description fit Perry more than anyone else. A person like Perry could subordinate his ego to serve a common purpose, be driven by the loftiest motives of inner loyalty, and complete projects, not because of the glory of execution, but because the innate worth of the program was worth the best and most selfless efforts. So Perry was appointed, and at a stroke, much of the military's misgivings about Clinton vanished.

Perry was a prize. He had a keen mind, a serious demeanor, tenacious in his grasp of the chief points of an issue. He was not folksy or a populist as so many in the White House were. He was focused, articulate, precise and with an original depth of mind. He had a Ph.D. in mathematics from Penn State and he had been an aggressive promoter of stealth and other advanced technologies working with defense industries in California. His intimate knowledge of weapons systems immediately boosted his stock among the uniformed military. He spoke carefully in crafted, precise sentences that were models of urbane lucidity. He had an ability to instantly discern what the crux of an issue was.

On Bosnia, he was far more of a hawk than Aspin had been, much more inclined to strike at the Serbs with airpower. Perhaps of most importance, he felt a certain sympathy for small countries, not seeing them as failed versions of America. They understood what they had made themselves and they believed their societies expressed their authentic character, and Perry felt that one got along with them best by trying to understand how they saw the world, and what they wanted to do in it and with it. It might be very different from what you might do, but it was valid for them. To Perry, variety and difference were not merely a fact of the world but a splendid fact of it. He was sensitive in other ways to people's feelings as well. Once Clinton was twenty minutes late to a summit meeting with French president Jacques Chirac and German prime minister Helmut Kohl. They were fuming, on the edge of rage, and Perry had engaged and calmed them until at last Clinton came in.

Perry was one problem solved, but Clinton still wasn't happy with his foreign policy staff. In December of 1994, just after political consultant Dick Morris went to work for him, Clinton asked him whether he thought he should change secretaries of state. "How about Sam Nunn?" he suggested.

Morris told Clinton that Nunn would lose the Democratic Senate seat in Georgia. Clinton said Nunn was going to retire in 1996 anyway.

"He'd be a very good choice," said Morris, "but would he be loyal to you? Would he freelance?"

The question about Nunn was hardly a ringing endorsement of Christopher. Word of Clinton's dissatisfaction made its way like a bad smell to the nose of Christopher, who offered to step aside, only forcing Clinton, who had no replacement, to tell Christopher he wanted him to stay on.

Clinton's relations with Lake were becoming strained. Lake was fifty-three, had a mild manner and quiet voice that concealed a fiercely competitive nature. His character housed a vast streak of intolerant impatience. "Talk faster," he'd snarl at a staff meeting. He also had a lightning wit. When they talked of Saudi terrorist mastermind Osama bin Laden, Lake had once interrupted to say, "Aahh, the fiftieth child syndrome."

A former colleague said Lake ran his office "like a baseball club" and that back in his days when he was policy planning chief at State he had a bat and ball up on his office wall. Lake believed in collegiality, and he looked to Christopher to provide it. Yet the secretary was growing increasingly full of narrow intrigue and yielding to the cravings of territoriality at the expense of the harmonious functioning of the whole.

Lake did what he could, but there was still no policy. He had an office staff of thirty and within that a close inner circle of about seven to whom he gave all the work of importance. Lake was good at delegating, with a talent for perceiving the crux of an issue, but he was a poor administrator. "Lake never made full use of his troops," said a former State Department official who knew him well. He "wasn't a bitter, nasty, kick 'em up, knock 'em down person like Paul Wolfowitz or Peter Rodman," said a senior Bush Defense Department official, "who took very eager, sincere gifted men and bullied them into cowed compliance."

Lake's problems with Clinton stemmed from some air of constraint that lay between them. Among men of similar disposition, there will arise a general feeling of pleasure, an emotional congruence, and the two will be drawn together by a feeling of mutual sympathy. To people like Gore, Lake lacked inner iron when it came to Bosnia. He was hard-line one minute, given to appeasement the next. For Gore, the atrocities merely hardened his will. Lake seemed befuddled, believing that perhaps nothing could really be effectively done. He was a Wilsonian, believing that America was mighty but good, that American power was basically unselfish and its mission in the world was redemptive.

Lake hadn't known Clinton before the campaign, and they could banter and trade light jokes, but there was no depth of friendship there, no letting go, no opening of one heart to another. This crimped Clinton's style, which was at home in the most informal, wide-ranging ability to discuss whatever was on his mind. To Clinton there was something unsympathetic about Lake; he was a man with a small personality in some ways, a good man, an idealist, but a man missing something called heart. Clinton could sense that Lake was not in full sympathy with him, he always tiptoed around him, never exploding at him, the way he did others, as if he sensed something prissy and easily hurt in Lake and wanted not to bruise it. Once on a trip, Clinton overstepped and did explode at Lake over some minor irritation. Clinton had a volcanic temper and an imperfect means of controlling it, and his squalls disappeared as quickly as they came, but Lake was profoundly offended, seeking out presidential aide Bruce Lindsey and saying, "If he ever does that again, I'll quit."

The inner White House group, people like George Stephanopoulos, Dick Morris, David Gergen, were all political animals to the core and utterly baffled Lake. Their energies went to swapping information, gathering intelligence, trying to shape the news, trying to romance reporters. As Stephanopoulos said, "In the end a political campaign boils down to talk, talk, and more talk. What are they saying? What are we saying? What are they saying about what we're saying in response to their question? And so on and so on." To Lake what was important was that a man had truths of his own—clear, firm positions on matters he regarded as important to how he viewed himself and the world and his role in it. To Lake, politics was derivative and secondary in the agenda of human activities. It drained people of life and intimacy and was supremely trivial because it focused on the role of human beings as mere citizens. Plus, political methods were dubious since they tried to move the masses by every means except appealing to their intelligence. Lake felt superior to politics, felt that to go on TV to mouth vague platitudes was demeaning. He also resented the little indignities such as having, as a senior person, to appear at meetings of junior staff to ensure that foreign policy events had been included on the president's calendar. Nor did he ever forget that foreign policy was, in this group, at least, always viewed as an inconvenience, secondary to the domestic agenda.

As an operator, Lake was considered sly, crafty, and proprietary about his information and not above filtering it carefully to the president when it showed himself to advantage. He was ruinously touchy, and extremely mistrustful of his colleagues, believing that chances of betrayal increased with the entrance of a second person into the room. He was afraid of leaks, afraid of being accused of making them, and as his term wore on he was an increasingly perplexed, unhappy, almost discarded man.

If Lake's star had begun to set, Gore's power was gaining. He began his day by joining the president, Lake, Deputy National Security Advisor Sandy Berger, and occasionally the White House chief of staff to meet with someone from the CIA who gave a briefing on the world's events that had happened overnight. Gore's functions were steadily expanding, and he had been able to reach selectively into important areas of foreign policy that had previously been reserved for the secretary of state.

As the Serb campaign of steady brutality and intimidation continued, it was clear to Gore that Bosnia was the key issue, and that the target was none other than the Serb leader Slobodan Milosevic. What Gore saw was that for Milosevic war was indispensable for the Serb to realize his ambitions. It was one thing to, like Lake, say that policy should be based on a higher morality, but if your opponent had no morals, what then? No world order had ever been based on a higher morality. To Gore it was a question of blackmail. The world seemed eager to be blackmailed as long as it could continue to slumber in soft and blissful peace. Such a feeling was repellent to him. To him there were dividends in daring, and the Deputies Committee, subordinate to the Principals Committee, began to try to fashion the means to deal with Serbia.

Behind the scenes, Gore was telling Clinton that the president had to pay more attention to foreign policy, act decisively, and accept the consequences.

This was more easily said than done. Clinton was wary of being out in front of the American people. He had a sound knowledge of history. He wanted to retain alternative tactical lines of action, including a line of retreat. Clinton had a keen sense that no policy on Bosnia would work without public support, and he tried to use polling data to discover approaches to the public that might work to garner their support.

The polls of Dick Morris were not encouraging. About 40 percent of the U.S. public was isolationist and wanted no foreign policy at all. In one poll Morris asked if the United States should intervene to protect our interests abroad and act as a global police officer and only 14 percent agreed to this. He then asked if America should act as a peacemaker, using U.S. influence to resolve disputes. A total of 37 percent agreed that this role was proper for America. But another 37 percent rejected any role for America.

Another difficulty emerged when it was found that Americans really didn't understand the difference between peacekeeping and combat.

If the U.S. public couldn't muster the understanding, then it would be bypassed, and Clinton would embrace duplicity and secrecy to advance his aims. More and more, Gore began to be seen as one of the Clinton group's ruling spirits, an earnest, convincing voice that was all business, whose views had force because they were sound. To the hawks, Gore's closely reasoned arguments, based on historical precedents and clearly, pointedly stated, were like a gust of fresh air. When Gore spoke, he put heart into people.

Suddenly, the foreign policy situation was enlarging.

Gore saw Milosevic's aggression as a test of spine and principle and made others feel the same. His influence within Clinton's inner circle began to spread and make itself felt. Little by little, energetic activists who had been in the periphery of Bosnian policy were, under Gore, being brought back into the center of the action. The installation of Gore had begun a process under which the vice president was able to quietly assemble his own administration team operating quietly but effectively within Bill Clinton's established but ineffectual group. All the men entering government had known each other a long time. Strobe Talbott, who would become Clinton's Russia hand, had known Richard Holbrooke for over twenty years, ever since Talbott had been a *Time* magazine correspondent and Holbrooke had been the editor of *Foreign Policy* magazine. In the late 1980s, when Holbrooke had been waiting for nomination to a Democratic position and Talbott had been correspondent, they had taken a trip to the Soviet Union, including the Balkan states, and Talbott was struck by Holbrooke's inexhaustible curiosity about matters, the depth of his knowledge, and the passion of his interest. Holbrooke was keenly aware of what was taking place in Europe and was passionate in his view about what the U.S. role could be in shaping events. While his own position was uncertain, Holbrooke had gone head down into helping Talbott see what the scope of his future activities might be. In the past the responsibility for the Soviet Union had come under the authority of a regional assistant secretary of state responsible for Europe. The Soviet Union was a giant country of eleven time zones and this organization made little sense. With the collapse of the USSR, what had once been a monolith had fractured into fifteen new countries. It was not a pretty sight, but the Soviet empire had transformed into a mosaic of messy pluralism. What Talbott was being offered was a position of eye-opening grandeur, ambassador at large and special advisor to the secretary of state on the new independent states of the former Soviet

Union, reporting directly to Secretary of State Christopher; he would take the position in November of 1993.

Holbrooke himself was about to emerge from exile. He had learned Roman dramatist Seneca's bitter lesson that a friend in power was a friend lost. Lake and Holbrooke shared a past, and the election of 1992 had reunited them. Both had arrived in Vietnam at about the same time in 1963, and in both men, although close friends, there had always been at work a quiet rivalry. There was, to be sure, mutual affection and admiration, but it was not unmixed with wariness, hostility, and suspicion. They were like runners in the same race, always aware of where the other was in the pack and whether he was gaining ground. Both possessed outstanding energy, character, and intellect, but of the two, Lake had been the more fortunate, born to a more genteel class with better social and political connections, and, as a result, Lake had always appeared more finished in the ways of life, more able to glide adroitly to the front rank, always the man able to obtain the more envied place. By contrast, Holbrooke was raw, brilliant, a man of incredible force, but unpolished, always compelled to forge his own connections by means of his own wit and resources, always appearing a bit tactless, crass, and thrusting in his ambition.

Holbrooke had attended Brown, where he had been editor of the newspaper. He then tried to get a job with *The New York Times* but failed. The Foreign Service exam is based on a year's worth of *New York Times* reporting, a fact still not widely known. Holbrooke studied the *Times*, took the exam, and passed. When he entered the Foreign Service School, he discovered that Tony Lake was his classmate. They found that they liked each other, and after classes, would go out to drink. On weekends they played softball and the first hint of Lake's determination never to come in second surfaced when he showed up to play wearing spikes.

In Vietnam, both men had held good jobs, acting as aides to Ambassadors Henry Cabot Lodge and Maxwell Taylor. When Holbrooke got married in Saigon, Lake signed the wedding certificate and Holbrooke stood as godfather for one of Lake's children. But the urge of the one to outshine the other, to prove tougher or smarter, or more clever or better informed, remained in play. Lake opposed the Vietnam War and eventually ended up working for Henry Kissinger. After Kissinger lied to Lake about the war in Cambodia, Lake resigned. He was a man of genuine decency and had the manhood to suffer for his convictions.

Both men ended up in the Democratic Party in the late 1970s in the

Carter administration. Lake had gotten the plum position of head of State policy planning while Holbrooke had been assistant secretary of state for East Asia. With the election of Clinton, the longtime friendship of both men began to fray.

Most men who offer good advice think of it as a generous gift to be made use of by better and more enlightened men, and they neglect the fact that excellent advice is sometimes found to be off-putting simply because it is excellent, and that it tends to upstage and reprove the better men in their own understandings. Holbrooke, the former foreign policy advisor to Gore in his 1988 campaign, had been a firsthand witness of ethnic cleansing, and in September of 1992, he wrote for *Newsweek* of the "inadequate reaction so far, by the United States and to an even greater degree the European community," which he said could undermine "the dreams of a common European House." He urged the United States to act with boldness and strength to counter the Serbs.

Holbrooke was perhaps alone at the time in seeing the coming crisis as posing "staggering political, strategic, and humanitarian" problems to the West. On January 13, 1993, one week before Clinton was to assume office, Holbrooke wrote a memo to Warren Christopher and Lake that said clearly, "Bosnia will be the key test of American policy in Europe." Holbrooke, like most truly insightful men, thought he was giving a helpful heads-up, but he was writing to the wrong men on the wrong topic at the wrong time. For people to whom even good advice comes as a surprise, the best advice is unpleasant and displeasing, and Lake was very much displeased.

Instead of being rewarded for his insight, Holbrooke was reduced to a species of street beggar, hungry and in need, and trying to be noticed. His name was already in circulation within the new administration. He had been briefly considered for secretary of state but was discounted for the faults of personality—a vulgar eagerness to be in the limelight, accused of having a character too overbearing, entirely too forceful, that tended to dominate any gathering he was in, a man suffering from a compulsion of always having to be right—an allegation that ignored the fact that he usually was.

Holbrooke *was* obnoxious, a man who saw the complete dimensions of things with such clarity and quickness that those who disagreed were seen by him as being willfully perverse rather than stupid. He had a prodigious memory, able like the British historian Thomas Macaulay to glance at a page of print and commit most of it to memory. He had the talent of seeing in a situation where the key to manipulating it lay, and his insight into people was superb. He had a tendency to inflict his problems on his superiors, but he was fearless and could not be intimidated. Wiles and craft made Milosevic cunning, devious, and revengeful, but he met his match in Holbrooke.

In the meantime, Holbrooke was dead in the water. Anxious to serve and contribute, he was reduced to stewing in baffled frustration. He thought that if he were edged out of the position of deputy undersecretary or deputy secretary, he might become ambassador to Japan, an area of interest, but hardly major given the brewing crisis in the Balkans. Any hopes he had melted into thin air when former Vice President and presidential candidate Walter Mondale, whose wife had a voracious interest in Japanese art, was given the position. Holbrooke was downcast. "I have never seen him so dejected and out of heart," said an associate. Holbrooke was forced to look on as the top State Department job went to the elderly Christopher because like Abraham Lincoln's win in 1860, he had made the fewest enemies. And like Theodore Roosevelt or Woodrow Wilson or FDR, Clinton was going to act as his own secretary of state. Clinton wanted in his secretary a mere tactician, a functionary with control over his ego who wouldn't get in the way and in Christopher he had that man.

Holbrooke fumed. By blood and instinct, he always craved to be where the action was, and he felt he could bring something valuable to the new group. Suddenly, Holbrooke made a decision. He called Sandy Berger and told him he was ready to support Clinton in any way he could. With Christmas approaching, Holbrooke got a call from Lake informing his old friend he, Lake, was now Clinton's National Security advisor. Given their rivalry, one would have thought the news would have stung Holbrooke like a slash from a whip, but it didn't. Holbrooke gave his congratulations, and offered his assistance. The two men talked of the old days in Saigon and Lake promised his friend he would keep in touch.

After sending in his January 13 memo on the Balkans, Holbrooke found Lake did not bother to tender a reply, so Holbrooke waited, and after much impatient nail-biting, fretting, and fuming, Holbrooke finally yielded to weakness and called and asked his friend if he had received it, and Lake, using the halfhearted response to annihilate, told him it was useful, but that it contained items that "would undercut us at the United Nations." A few weeks later, the extent of Lake's ill will was made clear when Lake appointed Reginald Bartholomew, a former ambassador to the United Nations and Lebanon, as special negotiator for Bosnia.

Yet certain people kept an eye on him. Holbrooke was a talent, a man who had rarely failed in anything he had attempted in life. Thanks to a kind word from Berger, Holbrooke received a phone call offering him the position of U.S. ambassador to Germany. His spirits soared, and he accepted on the spot.

By the fall of 1994, he would make another stunning move—Holbrooke would be appointed assistant secretary of state for European and Canadian affairs.

13

HAMMER ON THE ANVIL

English philosopher Thomas Hobbes had said it took a "strong power of imagination to be able to feel pity," but Peter Galbraith had to a great degree that admirable and generous power of responding to the unfortunate. He was a humane man, with a real courtesy of heart, quick to consider, not his own welfare, but what was due to others by just claim. He showed kindness, and felt mutual sympathy for any people of any country who were the victims of government mistreatment or police abuse. He had a passionate, intolerant hatred of injustice, a trait he shared with Madeleine Albright, and when he saw the ghastly atrocities of the Balkans, he realized with great sorrow that the only rule there was the ancient one of survival at any cost. Yet even if they had been maneuvered into a place where they couldn't say no or exercise full supervision, senior administration officials still resented Galbraith for being unpredictable and a glory hound who liked to see his name in the press.

A chief difficulty facing Galbraith lay with the disorganization the Clinton people had inherited from the previous Bush administration. One outstanding disaster was State's Office of East European Affairs. It had, for years, handled a mere six countries, Poland, Romania, Hungary, Bulgaria, Czechoslovakia, and East Germany, the former Eastern Bloc. Now, without warning, it was handling fifteen countries, all of the above, plus the republics of what had formerly been the Soviet Union and Yugoslavia. During the Cold War, the State office had for decades been a sleepy backwater, with haphazard staffing. "You didn't say in the old days, who is the best person to go to Romania, you said, 'How can we get rid of Joe?' and you sent Joe," said Galbraith. Now, without warning, the office had been thrust to the forefront.[1]

This hardly made Christopher happy. With the appointment of Peter Galbraith as ambassador to Croatia, the cautious Christopher was faced with the same problem he had to confront with Holbrooke. Here Christopher had a man over whom he didn't exercise full authority, a go-getter he couldn't quite control, an activist with an abundance of energy and fierce drive with a tendency to ignore his orders, a man like General Grant, whose career was full of attempts to take action on his own initiative, always running up against the limits of his office. So when Galbraith got the job, he found his promotion met, incredibly, with silence from Christopher and the upper levels of State. As a result, Galbraith was sent out with no instructions from the State Department, whose senior officials "didn't really have much enthusiasm for any U.S. involvement," as Galbraith would say later. Since Galbraith had no orders to follow, he cunningly devised his own agenda. He would do everything he could to end the war, work vigorously to facilitate humanitarian assistance, and take whatever action was necessary to end the atrocities. He knew no one was going to tell him not to do those things, he said, because the orders to cease and desist would have to come by cable, and "cables like that tend to leak," he said, and would embarrass the administration.

In any case, the State Department's snubbing of him had left him freedom of action and Galbraith set right to work. Croatian president Franjo Tudjman had proved to be prickly in the past because he had felt Bosnia was an artificial creation of the former Yugoslavian state and had no legitimacy. To Galbraith this was nonsense, and he began working to counter Tudjman's attempts to undermine Bosnia's territorial security and to persuade him to grant the Muslims the status of "constituent nation"—an idea to which until now Tudjman had been opposed, even though he was making the same demand for Bosnia's Croatians.

Galbraith saw from the first that the points of leverage on Tudjman were lying out in the open. Croatia would not be Croatia unless it found itself in the front rank. Tudjman would bring glory to his country and himself. That Croatia thought itself different from the rest of the Balkans could be seen everywhere. Zagreb, except for its Gypsies, was racially homogeneous. Its outlying parts looked like those of any other European city, and were remarkable for their quaint, picturesque nineteenth-century architecture, and Zagreb's bustling center boasted impressive construction sites and modern office buildings. Billboards advertised major brands: Mercedes cars, Benetton sweaters, and so forth. Zagreb clearly saw itself as a European, not a Balkan, city. Its cars displayed the letters "HR," the abbreviation for Croatia, surrounded by the twelve gold stars of the European Union. In its in-flight magazine, Croatian Airlines declared, "Today with its million inhabitants, Zagreb is in many ways a Mittel European city." Croatia, in other words, was Middle European, the countries to the south were Mediterranean. The declarations were more wish than fact, but unfulfilled desires leave doors open for entry and manipulation.

Galbraith's program had full White House backing from the first and from the first he took a tough line designed to end Croatia's designs to expand its territory at the expense of its neighbors. The new ambassador and others bluntly told Tudjman that Croatia might go ahead and grab its chunk of Bosnia from the Muslims, but a third of Tudjman's country was in the hands of the Serbs, and if he tried to move on Bosnia, he could forget about any help from Washington in regaining Croatia's land. It was as simple as that. Documents were then presented to Tudjman by Galbraith that made it clear that if Tudjman continued his land grabs, he would be regarded as a pariah. In addition, Washington would ensure that Croatia's economy be punished by strict and severe sanctions. "I saw the documents—the language was very tough," said one former senior administration official. Clearly the White House had approved the language.

Tudjman didn't budge, but it didn't matter. Galbraith was a man in a hurry. He acknowledges that "people at State felt I was doing a lot more than they wanted to see done," but Galbraith ignored this. He secretly sent a cutout to visit several Croatian concentration camps in Bosnia where starving Muslim prisoners were being kept in appalling conditions. Evidence and documentation in hand, Galbraith then warned Tudjman and the Croatian leadership that he thought anyone in charge of these camps could very easily be seen as war criminals. Then Galbraith went public. The Croatians were shocked to suddenly find that world opinion was seeing them as being no better than their Serb aggressors. The bulk of the Croatian public felt the camps to be inhuman and morally intolerable. The special U.S. envoy, Charles Redman, asked Tudjman how he wanted history to view him, and this proved to be a key point of the man's makeup. Said Galbraith, "Tudjman had a pride in his country and a belief in his chief role came to him as second nature. De Gaulle always saw France and himself as one and the same thing. There was a lot of de Gaulle in Tudjman." Since Croatia could not be Croatia without greatness, Tudjman would be the instrument of making sure the country's rights were respected in the eyes of the world. His ambition made him change his policy.

There followed all sorts of obstructions, all sorts of intricate maneuvering, including the use of U.S. covert funds, and, then, very quietly, hardline Croatians who were opposed to any truce with the Bosnians were mysteriously asked to take long vacations from their jobs. They did so. Then the United States began to tread quietly up the back stairs to certain offices in the United Nations, and lo and behold, in February, the United Nations abruptly told Croatia it had a deadline of two weeks to pull its troops out of Bosnia or suffer the consequences. It was a harsh, inflexible ultimatum. As concern spread through Croatia's leadership, like a storm spreading through tossing trees, the Clinton people brought basic bribery to bear. Croatia wanted to join the European Union, and it wanted to be a part of NATO as well. When Tudjman consulted Galbraith and others, their reply was blunt: form a federation with the Muslims. Once this was done, the United States would help speed Croatia's political, economic, and military integration with the West. Galbraith was poised to make a speech saying that Croatia would be part of the West or if stubborn, it could end up sharing Serbia's renegade, despised, and isolated status. Croatia could not expect Western support when its armies remained in Bosnia Herzegovina. It was as simple as that.

With the steady, ominous tightening of pressure, shifts in policy began. The Croatian Foreign Ministry sent for Galbraith. Suddenly there was a new entity, the Muslim-Croat Federation, and Tudjman, who had tried to set up a Croatian state-let at the expense of the Muslims, was suddenly speaking in praise of a common cause with the Muslims playing an equal part. The new federation would prove to be an effective base for the first Clinton covert operations in that theater of war. It was March of 1994, only a year after Elie Wiesel had embarrassed Clinton at the Holocaust Museum opening.

The benefits for Tudjman were immediate. "We rewarded him for his good behavior by giving him access to the highest levels of the U.S. government," a former White House official said. Suddenly Tudjman was savoring unhurried contacts with the chairman of the Joint Chiefs of Staff, while Tudjman's secretary of defense, Gojiko Susak, became "an equal partner" with Secretary of Defense William Perry, who "treated him with respect," according to a former administration official.

The Muslims were already getting a trickle of arms. Iranian deliveries of them had begun in 1992, and Iranian Revolutionary Guards were deployed late that same year to begin a training program for the Bosnian army. By 1993, there were about five hundred Iranians, a number that would be drastically reduced after the Dayton Accords of 1995. Bosnian president Alija Izetbegovic had visited Iran in 1991 to try to solicit assistance and Iran was the first country to recognize Bosnia's independence. Also heavily involved was Turkey. The U.S. worry was that, without aid, Bosnia would "go down the tubes," in Galbraith's words, and the new Washington agreement had a provision that was hidden from the prying eyes of the nosy world. Clinton had approved it personally, working as he best liked to work, in secret. The U.N. arms embargo was in effect, but thanks to the new federation, the Clinton hawks had activated a hidden provision that allowed Iran and other Muslim countries, mainly Turkey, Pakistan, and Malaysia, to expand their arms shipments to the Bosnian Muslims. Saudi Arabia would supply the funds, and soon flights of Iranian aircraft began to land at Krk, and the CIA KH-11 satellites began to spot big Iranian planes at Turkish bases. (The source of the weapons was mainly the former Warsaw Pact.) Turkey was, in fact, the most important supplier of arms to Bosnia. In one of the varied operations, modified U.S. Air Force C-130s would fly from bases in the U.K. and Germany to pick up the arms in Turkish Cyprus. The cargo would then be flown over the Adriatic to Croatia and from there to Bosnia. Turkey had been in on the deal as early as 1993, then Ankara had arranged with Iran to open a smuggling route to bring arms to fellow Muslims. After the Washington agreement, Hungary, Uganda, Brunei, and Malaysia would also send consignments and cargoes.[2]

But the whole episode of gaining Tudjman's approval for arming Bosnian Muslims was indicative of an instance where Tudjman—the canny, quick-witted devious man who liked to play games—had finally run into people who played a better, slicker, more adroit one than he did. It had happened like this: In the spring of 1994, when the desperately unarmed Muslims went to Tudjman and asked him for arms (Croatia was siphoning off arms intended for Bosnia), the Croat leader had been on his stilts and contemptuously refused. Galbraith had argued the matter with him, but he had refused to budge. Finally, Tudjman outsmarted himself. To end the tiresome, probing pleadings from Galbraith, Tudjman had asked the matter to be referred to Washington, confident that the old Bush policy of withholding arms from the Muslims was still in place. (The Bush administration had "shit plaid" in the words of a U.S. official after an earlier shipment of Iranian arms had been stopped at the Zagreb airport. Since then America had strictly enforced the embargo.)

Fortunately, times had changed. During the spring of 1993, the Saudis were attempting to collect a past due payment for their support of Bush senior during the Persian Gulf War, and to Riyadh that meant only one

thing—aiding Arab schemes to supply arms on the sly to the Bosnian Muslims. In June in Washington, Clinton met with Prince Turki al-Faisal, the
urbane, polished chief of Saudi intelligence, to discuss the matter. Turki's
articulate urging that America take the lead in supplying Bosnian arms met
with no enthusiasm from Clinton, who told Turki that doing so would place
additional dangerous, fraying strains on NATO unity. But no sooner had
Turki departed than Clinton set in motion plans to get arms to Bosnia's
Muslims, putting so much personal authority behind the idea that it suddenly became a serious, overriding priority. The scheme was at first derailed mainly by Lake because of his fear that it would be leaked to the U.S.
press, creating new, widening divides of hostile differences within NATO.
It is of interest here that one of the most inexhaustible, aggressive advocates
of the plan was none other than Richard Holbrooke, soon to be appointed
assistant secretary of state.

Never shy about putting his oar in anything disputatious, Holbrooke
had earlier suggested using third-party countries to smuggle in the arms.
Lake, who had proved so halfhearted on covert operations when it came to
Iraq, apparently had lost his moral touchiness when it came to this operation, and State Department lawyers were, in fact, taken by the attractive-
ness of using Pakistan, Turkey, and Iran to supply the Bosnian weapons.

Galbraith, like the restless Holbrooke, was convinced that sending arms
to the Bosnians was essential to ending the war there. Galbraith had already
tried to give the matter a push on April 16, 1994, when he had talked to a
Muslim leader from Zagreb, Iman Sefko Omerbasic, who unfortunately
later told the Iranians of the conversation, a message intercepted by U.S.
intelligence. Galbraith was all unresting energy in his exertions. He was also
trying to prod the prodigious, dead mass of the State Department into stirring to some sort of life. Galbraith made his case with his usual coherence
and vigor, and laid out a subtle rationale. Washington did not have to say it
approved the shipments of arms; it only had to say it had no objections to
such shipments by other unnamed countries. Galbraith made clear that the
United States would continue to strictly enforce the arms embargo on itself, but it would cease to enforce it when it came to other countries.

Having made his case, Galbraith waited, a thing he was not good at.
Then he waited and waited some more. He was on the verge of snatching
out his hair when he finally had his answer: "You have no instructions," said
Washington. When he read the answer, Galbraith felt furiously vexed,
puzzled, and disappointed. More weak inaction, one more sample of State's
temporizing and "chickenshit timidity." But when he called the NSC,

Jenonne Walker, the staffer there, told him that he and envoy Charles Redman had carried the day. "Your instructions are to say that you have no instructions," she said, adding that when Tony Lake had passed the message
on to her during a flight returning from Nixon's funeral, "He said it with a
smile and a raised eyebrow." The great light broke over Galbraith at last. He
rushed to Tudjman. "Mr. President, I have no instructions," he joyfully told
the Croat. He added, "Please pay attention to what I am not saying." And
Redman's message also said that the United States was not in a position to
object to arms going to Bosnia. In the aftermath, Galbraith played his public part perfectly, telling a *New York Times* reporter that he would be "shocked,
I repeat, shocked," to learn that arms were flowing into Bosnia.

In fact, the State Department legal experts had been studying the matter
for some time and at last found comfort. They had been able to conclude
that using foreign countries to supply Bosnian arms was not a "covert action," and, therefore, Clinton could not be called to account by Congress.
Covert diplomacy was perfectly legal if done under State Department or
NSC auspices and supervision, said the State Department lawyers. Clinton's Russia hand, the debonair Strobe Talbott, deputy secretary of state,
and Lake on the NSC had proved to be the men able to work the secret
levers of power on this issue. It was the two of them, aided by State Department lawyer Jim O'Brien, who formulated the "no instructions" gambit for
Galbraith that would give America plausible deniability when the dogs of
bias and accusation began to bark. Clinton was told of the plan on April 27
while on Air Force One. For Lake, it was a deft stroke, presenting the gun-shy
Christopher with the hard truth that he'd been ruthlessly bypassed and stuck
with a done deal that he was powerless to alter. Simply because there was no
Presidential Finding and no official covert action and because the NSC was
basically running the operation, Galbraith had to cut the CIA station chief in
Zagreb, Marc Kelton, out of the loop, nor was the agency notified in Washington, a fact that nettled the agency and later caused difficulties.

In any case, the weapons began to reach Bosnia. Only a trickle at first,
but quickly strengthening to a stream that turned to a swollen flood. Former senior DIA official Col. Pat Lang told me that the Bosnian sales were
"guaranteed by the DSAA," the Defense Security Assistance Agency, at the
Pentagon, but a former senior administration official denied this, saying
the weapons were paid for out of the Pentagon's secret budget for Special
Operations. In any case, simply allowing other countries to militarily arm
while not seeming to be able to discern it was being done, was working as

well as the Clinton hawks had hoped it would. As diplomat Louis Sell records, "Over the next 18 months, the arms supplies to the Bosnians, together with the growing military cooperation, gradually shifted the military balance in Bosnia against the Bosnian Serbs," and shattered the image of Serb invincibility.

14

FACING ADVERSITY

For Clinton, 1994 would be a year when his resolution, steadiness, and tenacity of purpose would be tested to the utmost. The president would describe it as "one of the hardest of my life."[1] It began in January with the personal heartbreak of losing his beloved mother, and ended in political disaster when his party lost control of both houses of Congress. Yet it was also the year he seemed to finally gain access to some new depth of inner strength. While his Bosnia policy still remained one of caution, his tactic to hold the line and delay decisions, he would be forced by circumstances to act decisively and fearlessly in situations of extreme intricacy and peril.

As we have seen, many of Clinton's problems were the result of careless statements made in exhilarating circumstances where any threat of consequences wasn't apparent at the time. Although lacking any dominating interest in foreign policy, Clinton was an internationalist and a liberal to whom foreign markets and the expansion of trade were the critical determinants of policy, their end being the spread of democracy and the betterment of human welfare around the world. In Clinton's view, it was by means of American ideals that the United States forged its link to the common people of the planet, and he tended to align himself with John Adams, who believed that America improved more rapidly by making efforts at home rather than by intervening abroad.

The promotion of human rights was a top concern of Clinton just as it had been for Carter. As Arthur Schlesinger said, since human rights "must find their sanctions and laws in human institutions, and given the limitations

of the role of national states, the long-term hope lies in international organizations."[2] America was not isolated, and however exalted its principles, its
actions in foreign policy gained legitimacy by acting within alliances, and
Clinton had chosen the United Nations as the instrument for carrying out
U.S. leadership. As usual, he had overstated his case rather thoughtlessly
during the 1992 campaign. For one, he had endorsed a standing U.N. army.
(Given his draft-dodging record and the "gays in the military" farce, this
only acted to further estrange his own military.) Then in 1993, he provoked
a frightful cacophony when a draft policy directive that agreed to place
U.S. forces under U.N. command was leaked to Congress. Just before the
Black Hawks had been shot down, in late September, he had given a speech
before the United Nations General Assembly in which he urged more professional competence in U.N. peacekeeping efforts, and he also suggested
stricter restraints on peacekeeping missions. The United Nations had to be
astute and selective in what it did. "The United Nations cannot become engaged in every one of the world's conflicts; if the American people are to say
yes to U.N. peacekeeping, the United Nations must know when to say no."

But for all of his commitment to the idea of collective security, which so
often had allowed Clinton to take a back seat and duck trouble at home, he
was beginning to find the United Nations and NATO a dog collar when it
came to Bosnia. NATO "unity" was a hilarious oxymoron. The organization
had nineteen members, and just as one human estimates the worth of his
work in relation to another, every member put its own interest first and saw
the conflict through the prism of its own history and institutions, and its
own internal concerns. For some Europeans, history acted to distort any
clear, lucid sight of the present. Many British and French had a soft spot for
the Serbs since Serbia had been an ally in two world wars. Plus, there was a
great mistrust of Bosnia's closeness to Iran, with an abhorrence to seeing
anything like a fundamentalist Islamic state established in Europe. The British and others had seen the evil of Ayatollah Khomeini's work in Iran, his
return to barbarity, stoning of adulterers, the eradication of the rights of
women, and they felt that Izetbegovic was an agent spreading the same
horrible virus. And just as the Greeks were volunteering soldiers to the
Serbs and just as Israel was selling Belgrade artillery shells and mortars, so
the British and French had a bias that robbed the actions of any severe or
criticizing spirit when it came to Belgrade. As a result, when it came to confronting Milosevic, NATO and the United Nations had both dwindled into
something timid and inept, practically cowering in a corner.

Building a consensus and forging a common purpose within such a cum-
brous system was proving to be a nightmare. The structural defects of the

two-body system were a disaster, one of the most handicapping being the U.N.-NATO chain of command. The whispered truth was there was no "unity of command" within NATO. "Every military success depends on having a clearly defined line of command," retired four-star Gen. Joe Hoar said recently. This meant that at every level, every officer was compelled to report to only one superior, so there would be "no danger of competing or conflicting orders in a fast-breaking combat situation," in the words of Secretary of Defense William Perry. Confusion or compromise on this concept could result in disaster, as it had in Somalia. It was Perry who told Talbott while on a flight to Moscow, "Air power was needed immediately while the fighting was still taking place."[3] But this was impossible under the existing NATO setup.

As it stood, the NATO chain of command went from airborne surveillance through an airborne command and control C-130 aircraft to the Combined Air Operations Center at Vicenza, Italy, where the Combined Air Force Component commander was the approving officer for any air strike. There was another, second chain of command that went from U.N. Protection Force (UNPROFOR) forward air controllers on the ground through the Bosnian Operations Center located in Kiseljak, Bosnia, and then to the capital of Zagreb. The UNPROFOR commander would ask the U.N. headquarters in New York for permission to deploy live weapons. To get anything like a prompt or efficient response to any request for airpower had been out of the question from the first.

It would take a horrible tragedy to cause the competing tensions between the Europeans and the Americans to explode with redoubled vehemence.

February 5, 1994, was a bright, sunny day when the earth seems to awaken, the air is warm and scented, and people gratefully gulp down drafts of spring. Sarajevo's Markala open market was packed with animated, happy people. At 12:37 P.M., masses of them shuffled among the stalls, talking eagerly. Without warning, a mortar shell, one of 500,000 tank, mortar, or artillery shells to fall on the capital in a twenty-two-month period, came hurtling down in silence. It struck an overhead shop canopy made of plastic just before it hit and exploded to send thousands of fragments of red-hot metal into the shoppers. The active, cheerful place turned into a slaughterhouse. In a matter of seconds, sixty-nine people had been turned from human beings into ghastly objects. Another two hundred were wounded.

At the news, a horrified revulsion swept through the West. The slaughter broke the heart of Bosnian president Izetbegovic. At a news conference, calling February 5 "a black and terrible day," he said, "We Bosnians feel con-demned to death. Every government that supports the arms embargo against this country is an accomplice to acts of atrocity such as this."[4] The outrage spread. In every Western capital erupted harsh demands for NATO to prevent a recurrence of such an atrocity by sending combat aircraft to patrol the skies of Sarajevo.

Clinton was incensed by the attack, launching a remarkable flood of expletives as he watched the television in the White House. At a Principals meeting he ordered Albright to argue at the United Nations that NATO must intervene and that authority for such action already existed in U.N. Security Council resolutions. Such views suddenly found new supporters, including the shaky titmouse, Douglas Hurd, the British foreign secretary, usually the first to throw up his hands in horror at the idea of air strikes, who peeped shrilly that he too wanted action. Even the French were pushing for a more active role for NATO.

For a brief moment it appeared that the West had ceased to shrink from the irrevocable and was poised to risk the desperate and punitive. All parties were demanding harsh action. Unfortunately, the appearance was misleading. Clinton would descend into a mood of black wrath when he discovered that British U.N. officials were working feverishly to un-dercut any fresh military response by the West, instead quick to side with the Bosnian Serbs, whose habit was to deal with their own atrocities by blaming them on someone else. The Bosnian Serb leader, a poet and bushy-haired psychiatrist named Radovan Karadzic, blamed the Muslims for the shelling and ordered his forces to block all humanitarian convoys into Sarajevo until the U.N. peacekeepers declared the Serbs to be inno-cent.

The Bosnian Serbs would garner unsuspected suuport in blaming the Muslims from an entirely surprising quarter, the new U.N. commander in Bosnia, Gen. Michael Rose. Rose was a three-star general with a forceful and colorful personality but narrow, unsound, and petty ideas. The son of an In-dian army officer, Rose was seen as a "brush fire wars" man. He had joined the Coldstream Guards, then the elite British Special Air Service, similar to America's Delta group. As a commanding officer, he had dealt with the 1980 Iranian embassy siege in London, and then served in the 1982 Falklands War, and in Northern Ireland, ending as commander for Bosnia.

In Bosnia, he was famous for being a Serb appeaser. "British policy de-signs in the Balkans were so conservative, they aroused mistrust," according to one former State Department official. The United Nations had given its peacekeeping forces the power to protect themselves using NATO air strikes, under the terms of Resolution 836, which called for the use of force in response to armed incursions or bombardment. This measure was hardly ever ordered because Rose incessantly depicted the Bosnian Muslims as provocateurs, staging incidents to attract the world's sympathy. Rose often accused the Muslims of making the "safe area" concept unworkable because they left their forces within the enclaves when in fact they were allowed to do this under the U.N. resolution. Rose also often hinted that the world would be better off if the Muslims were disarmed.

New York Times correspondent Roger Cohen grew heartily sick of Rose and the United Nations and NATO, both of which, he said, had a tendency to portray the war "in terms that justified its paralysis." As an example, he quoted Rose as saying that the plight of Sarajevo inhabitants enduring daily shelling was "not very conducive to security," or that the siege of Sarajevo was not really a siege but a "militarily advantageous encirclement"[5] for the Serbs along with other equally wretched examples of meaningless euphemism. Rose was especially detested because he constantly accused the Croats or Bosnians of breaking cease-fires and "other misdemeanors." In the view of Washington, Rose simply had the "wrong agenda" and was "fucking up the script," in the words of a former senior Albright advisor.

Rose had in his office a photo that showed a Red Cross vehicle destroyed by a bomb. The caption read, "Nice one, NATO," but while the photo was a fake, to Cohen, Rose appeared to fatuously embrace the message that intervention in this war was a waste. Commenting on NATO, Rose once remarked that the U.N. "is too blunt an instrument to use in diplomacy. In these small wars it is simply too big to be effective."[6] He also gave a terse if somewhat defeatist summary of British policy. "If someone wants to fight a war here on moral or political grounds, fine, great, but count us out. Hitting one tank is peacekeeping. Command and control, infrastructure, logistics, that is war."

But UNPROFOR wasn't keeping the peace. The initiatives of peace or war still remained with arbitrary Serb whims. The only tune Rose knew by heart was one that depicted the sinister intent of the Bosnian Muslims to stage incidents that would act to widen the war. Washington went so far as to accuse Rose of actions that almost bordered on "collaboration" with the Serbs, such as not pressuring his forward air controllers to report promptly on Serb violations in the eastern Gorazde Safe Area. Plus there was a general feeling that he didn't report "when the Serbs were up to something," according to a former U.S. official. When Rose blamed the marketplace attack on the Muslims, it deeply rankled Clinton, who rejected the claim immediately, ordering Albright to work through the United Nations to try and fix the blame, and he ordered the U.S. military to help evacuate the wounded from the city. It was clear to Clinton that the new international climate of pitiless resolve must not be wasted, and he and others saw in Rose's efforts a crafty U.N. attempt to head off the West's desire for military action against the Serbs by baldly presenting supposition as if it were fact. Twenty-two innocent civilians had been butchered in the Market Place attack, and capitals around the world were calling for air strikes or for air patrols that would prevent another slaughter. Even the French were demanding intervention, borne along by overwhelming pressure like a chip in a flood. Yet the U.N. was so opposed to action, that it used its cat's paw, General Rose, to work in a crafty attempt to undermine any anti-Serb action by the West.

The British diplomat David Owen thought a NATO strike would anger the Russians and split the alliance, and soon General Rose flew to Brussels. At Brussels, the British lied that there was no need to bomb the Bosnian Serbs because General Rose was on the verge of reaching a demilitarization agreement with them. NATO Secretary-General, Manfred Woerner of Germany, after a quick look, informed the Clinton White House, that in fact no such agreement existed. General Rose did finally produce a four-point plan that included an immediate cease-fire and withdrawal of Serb heavy weapons from around Sarajevo, but it imposed no penalties for violations and its chief effect was to infuriate President Clinton. "He was absolutely furious," said a former aide. "Clinton was going around saying, 'No one realizes what shits the British are.'" Woerner summarized the document as saying that it asked the Serbs "to please behave yourselves."

The West had also underestimated the shameless insolence of the Bosnian Serbs. Karadzic, suddenly all chest-beating bravado, announced his men would shoot down as many NATO planes as possible and take U.N. peacekeepers hostages, and, as if falling into step, General Rose kept claiming, quite falsely, that the Serbs were turning over heavy weapons, pointing to the Lukaavica barracks where a few ancient, rusted old relics had been put on display in a shameless piece of public relations. In fact, the Bosnian Serbs were ignoring Rose, who began to have his staff turn out daily progress reports on Serb disarmament when in fact no progress was occurring. The Bosnian Serbs continued as cocky and unrepentant as before. On February 12, they had inserted a new condition for their cooperation in giving up their weapons. They would only turn them in if the Bosnian Muslims first withdrew their front-line forces, a demand that even Rose had not dared make. It was a stinging slap in NATO's face, but Rose was undeterred. He met with the Serbs and the two parties continued to haggle over the Serb areas to be disarmed. The Serbs finally agreed to sites around Sarajevo, but when one of Izetbegovic's advisors saw the locations on a map, he angrily thumped the table, and the Bosnian president, seeing the map, was beside himself with rage. If the West agreed, it would still leave Serb weapons on the same strategic heights where they had been shelling the city for the last twenty-two months. In other words, Rose had been entirely outwitted; the Bosnian Serbs ended by turning their backs on his proposal.

Even within NATO, bitter internal divisions once again surfaced over the meaning of the word "control." What did it mean that Serb weapons were under NATO's control? On February 9, when NATO made its statement, the meaning had seemed clear. Now people were asking was it NATO or the United Nations who was to take the lead. Control did not mean mere monitoring, NATO said. It meant that Serb weapons would be placed under NATO's lock and key. But the tireless Rose worked to weaken this as well, claiming that the United Nations should have the final say. Everyone knew the pro-Serb weakness of NATO and when Clinton heard of this, witnesses said he grew red with anger. It was further proof that Rose was attempting to water down the ultimatum.

It would be the Russians that came to the rescue. The relationship between the inner circles of Russian and U.S. leaders was exceptionally close, and it would be last-minute Russian diplomacy that resulted in the Serbs pulling back their weapons. Russian leader Boris Yeltsin, close to Clinton, pledged to send Russian peacekeepers into the newly disarmed areas, and within hours, Russian convoys were on the move. Rose was not consulted about the Russian deployment.

The world was about to discover it was dealing with a different Bill Clinton, more fierce, more purposeful, more relentless. For months the nation of America had seemed more impressive than the people who ran it. Clinton's usual action in foreign policy was to take no action. His real mission as president was to modify and alter public opinion in a direction closer to American interests as he saw them. But he followed public opinion instead of leading it, or, when he did lead, it was with his eye always on a line of retreat. But at last Clinton was beginning to possess a greater sense of his own leadership. His presidency had been built around the power of his personality, and he was beginning to wield that power.

Clinton had aggressive instincts. During the same spring, North Korea and America had come dangerously close to a collision over Pyongyang's attempts to develop a nuclear weapon. At that time, Clinton's aggressiveness had blazed like a torch. A Defense Department official later said the United States had "skirted dangerously close" to a military clash, and later it emerged that Clinton had exhibited such driving combativeness and tenacity that South Korean president Kim Young Sam had made dozens of calls trying to back Clinton off his hard stance regarding the use of force. Now the Bosnian Serbs were about to deal with that same man.

As the crisis intensified, Clinton was taking bold, forceful steps. He was all furious drive, and his advisors caught glimpses of some fresh, inner steel. In place of scattered, sporadic efforts, there now could be seen a unified, wholehearted drive. Within a week of the marketplace massacre, Clinton personally launched his first covert action of the war, authorizing the use of U.S. Special Forces on the ground in Bosnia. When Srebrenica had "surrendered" to Serb Gen. Ratko Mladic, the Serb had allowed 140 Canadian soldiers into the city to help collect weapons and render aid. As they were about to leave, Muslim residents, fearing slaughter if the Canadians left, had closed the roads. Without hesitation, Clinton met on February 12 with Canadian prime minister Jean Chrétien, and they hammered out an agreement based on a secret Pentagon–National Security Agency memorandum prepared for the Canadian Chief of Defence staff. The plan was called Operation Royal Castor/Blue Jay.[7]

Scheduled for February 24, the operation was a daring one. If the Canadians came under attack by Serb forces, the United States would employ electronic warfare aircraft to jam Serb radars and communications, supported by U.S. combat aircraft "using whatever degree of force was required."[8] Not only would the Canadians be rescued but the administration would remove a Dutch unit of peacekeepers as well.

At a meeting in Naples on February 22 between the commanders of Canadian Joint Task Force Two and U.S. officials the die was cast. A total of 156 people including the 140 Canadian soldiers, six U.N. humanitarian workers, six members of the Dutch group, and four Doctors Without Borders personnel would be withdrawn by Sea Stallion helicopters. That same day U.S. Special Forces arrived in Zagreb, Croatia, from Italy. A fleet of fearsome C-130 gunships and F/A-18 fighter aircraft were to provide close air support for the mission, attacking Serb ground targets. The operation would occur at night, only a few hours from takeoff to landing to and from Brindisi, Italy. The White House received data in real time on its screens in the Situation Room. Everything moved ahead. On February 24, U.S. Special Forces were flown into Srebrenica from Italy. But there was no need. The Serbs had accepted the NATO ultimatum on the 21st. The siege of Sarajevo was ended.

It was the first time that NATO had threatened force, but the threat had been successful.

15

TO BE USED AND PUSHED ASIDE

It was only a few days after the February 5 Sarajevo bombing that Clinton gave approval for the CIA to begin planning a covert operation that would topple Serbian leader Slobodan Milosevic from power. Once signed, the congressional committees would be notified of the "finding" that authorized the agency to use any and all means to deliver Milosevic into international custody for trial as a war criminal. After it was signed, it would be classified as "sensitive compartmented information, Top Secret/Codeword," but it wasn't signed yet.

The beginning draft of the finding was an executive matter "subject to White House control," said a former CIA official. Albright, Fuerth, and especially Gore saw that no great day of change would come to the Balkans until Milosevic was shoved out. If at home you changed policy by changing personnel, the same rule applied to international affairs. The influence of the Gore group was on the rise, and Galbraith and Holbrooke, as well as Albright and Gore, knew how to drive toward a goal with unremitting ruthlessness, and they would do so with great steadiness over the next four years. Commenting on the finding, another former CIA official said, "It was immediately after the first [Sarajevo] marketplace bombing, I mean, only a couple of days," that the planning began. The task went to the CIA's Directorate of Operations, the DO, whose operatives, working with White House lawyers, began developing a blueprint. The U.S. presence would remain a hidden hand and be part of the subterfuge. Milosevic's ouster would have to appear to come from his people, even if they had little practice in the give-and-take of democracy and little understanding of free elections. Milosevic was the cause of violence, of war, the man responsible for the declining standard of living in his own country. He had lost a war with the Slovenes. Could the United States aid his enemies without being discovered? Could the United States arm the Bosnian Muslims, or engage the Croatians? Whatever the case, there was now in play a movement to remove Milosevic.

A chief requirement of the plan was to infiltrate Milosevic's inner circle. The targets were to be key officials of his military and security services. His finances would be targets as well. The plan would follow a blueprint laid out by CIA director William Casey back in the 1980s that would use U.S. corporations to help in smuggling funds for the operation or providing corporate cover for secret operatives or using front companies. In some cases, corporate executives who traveled in the region would be used since they made excellent sources and could provide a picture of the political temper. These executives would then be debriefed by the National Collections Division of the CIA, a group that has offices in some thirty U.S. cities. Also to be employed were nongovernmental organizations or NGOs.

"The [covert operations] planners were a small group at the beginning. Some were seen as not being aggressive enough, so they were replaced," said another CIA operative. But the pace picked up. "The White House was in earnest," the former official said.

Milosevic was not an insignificant enemy. As the self-styled "protector of all the Serbs," he would best the West for years and prove a wily, cunning opponent. The agency, the NSC, and the White House were awash in biographical profiles prepared on him by the CIA's Bureau of Leadership Analysis, a targeting office. One official there known for outstanding work was Gerald Post. Sources ranged from State Department records, memoranda, and summaries of conversations to more abstract analysis.

With Milosevic, the gutter had come to power in Serbia. As a man and character, he was disturbingly cold, his nature free of soft, benevolent, yielding, or sympathetic feelings toward people (with the exception of his family). He came from a school of diplomacy whose instruments were savagery, deceit, intrigue, and financial corruption. He came from a school of thought where the restraints of decency and moral responsibility in your opponents acted to leave them open to your attacks, and attack them he did with extraordinary and ruthless skill. He would realize his designs through a program of despoilment, pillage, rape, murder, all done coldly and methodically. The insidious viciousness of his conduct embodied the maxim "War and pity do not mix." His wars would surpass all wars in atrocity except

Hitler's and Stalin's, his slaughter of innocent people was the worst the
world had seen since those two monstrous dictators had strutted on history's center stage. In the end, Milosevic loved only power, lived for the pos-
session of it, craved to expand it, exulted in the coercions and brutalities of
its exercise. Power for him was the supreme authority, and in the 1980s, he
set out to build up his portion of it with great speed and effectiveness—
through under-the-table deals that double-crossed old benefactors and colleagues, through purges, through smear and slander, through stirring up
and making use of the old, sour, gnarled hatreds between the Serbian factions. He began with small betrayals, with small purges of members of his
party who weren't subject to his influence. Then, at some point, the Serb
leader saw a great design opening out before his imagination: a state called
Greater Serbia. He would be its creator and ruler, it would be under his control, and he would enjoy to the full the delicious sensations of command.

His methods of rousing the masses must be noted for their effectiveness.
The career of Milosevic was a triumph of calculated purpose, and he would
become the greatest manipulator of mass emotion since Adolf Hitler. "The
public is an idiot," Lord Salisbury once said. Milosevic understood, just as
Hitler had, that whoever controls the streets comes to control the country,
and in his rise to power Milosevic secretly began to use the masses very
cleverly, staging phony demonstrations that heightened their resentful feelings of persecution and discontent. The Serbs were never the aggressors in
Milosevic's version. In despoiling the country, Milosevic was simply trying
to right a wrong. He would provoke the flammable resentment of the Serbs
in Kosovo, transform it into an instrument for expanding his own power,
radicalize the Serbs living in Croatia and Bosnia, and make them his accomplices in seizing great masses of what had been Yugoslavia.

At the time of the marketplace bombing of 1994, Milosevic always
claimed that the Bosnian Serbs were independent of him and that Belgrade
denied them supplies. However, as he would later admit, Belgrade was using
portable bridges over the Drina River to get weapons to the Bosnian Serbs
and there were unauthorized flights between Serbia and Bosnia. As Milosevic
would later boast, his supposed boycott "was a never a real blockade" but "a
clever political maneuver to reduce the severity of the sanctions."[1]

The major goal of U.S. policy was to secure a cease-fire and peace agreement for the region. Clinton and his advisors regarded the Bosnian Serbs as
incorrigible, lacking in human decency and completely unreliable. If the
West were to secure an agreement, it would probably have to negotiate with
Milosevic. But he would be used, flattered, then, a cease-fire reached, he
would be pushed aside.

The idea that Clinton would use the CIA to get rid of Milosevic meant he first had to rebuild his frayed ties to the organization. The souring of relations between the agency and White House had been a surprise because the relationship had begun on such a promising footing. Robert Gates was a former CIA national intelligence officer on the Soviet Union, a former NSC staffer under Nixon, Gerald Ford, and Carter. In 1991, he had become a very capable and hard-driving CIA director. No sooner had Clinton been elected than Gates flew to the Governor's Mansion in Little Rock. The agency had set up a temporary headquarters, complete with secure communications and armed guards, at a Comfort Inn close to the city's airport. Gates was planning to leave the CIA shortly but had agreed to remain at his post to brief the president-elect on security issues. Already Clinton had recognized two such concerns, terrorism and drug trafficking, but it was clear he had a lot to learn.

When the door opened for Gates, it revealed a rumpled, frazzled Clinton, keeping himself awake by drinking oceans of coffee, but mentally receptive and alert. In talking, one thing Gates noted and liked immediately was the absence in Clinton of any ingrained suspicion or moral superciliousness regarding the craft of intelligence, an attitude unlike that of President Carter or former presidential candidate Michael Dukakis. The two men got along famously, and during the transition months, after Gates left, he dispatched his deputy director for intelligence to the Comfort Inn from which there began to issue a river of sensitive intelligence reports, all devoured voraciously by the new leader-elect of America. Soon, Clinton was receiving the President's Daily Brief, and he asked the agency to do a series of specialized intelligence studies, which they put promptly in his hands.

But when Gates left the agency, so did the rapport between the CIA and the incoming president. With Gates gone, the agency needed a new director, but the Clinton transition team was disorderly, and on the matter of director they procrastinated. There was the usual dithering about political balance. Clinton had a number of liberals in his cabinet and might it be prudent to put in someone who was slightly right-wing? The answer was yes. After reviewing candidates, Clinton called a fifty-one-year-old lawyer named James Woolsey, a former Army captain, a tall, dome-headed man with a genial manner and soft gray eyes. The voice retained a slight twang from his boyhood in northeastern Oklahoma, and in the beginning Clinton and Woolsey were delighted to find they shared similarities. Woolsey was from rural, small-town country yet had worked with such distinction that he, like Clinton, had been awarded a Rhodes Scholarship, plus he was a graduate of

Yale Law School, like Clinton, and, like Clinton, had had been a vociferous opponent of the Vietnam War in spite of his military service. Before becoming CIA director, he had become close to the far-right-wing and Likudnic supporter of Israel, Senator Henry "Scoop" Jackson, whose staffer Richard Perle had been caught by an FBI tap giving classified information to the Israeli embassy.

As *Washington Post* reporter Steve Coll points out, the CIA director has three invaluable functions in relation to the White House that are his and his alone. First, he meets face-to-face each day with the president and has an unparalleled opportunity to forge a personal friendship through which to exert his influence. Since the president is the only one who can authorize a covert action, such a foothold can prove to be of unique worth. Second, the director must take on the care and feeding of the two congressional intelligence oversight committees. Third, he has to be a leader of his intelligence professionals at the agency. Woolsey, some said, would later prove a disaster in doing all three.

It began well enough. When Woolsey arrived at the mansion, he and Clinton sat and talked about football at the University of Oklahoma and the University of Arkansas, where Clinton had briefly been a Razorback when he joined its ROTC program to prevent being drafted to serve in Vietnam. They had talked about good fishing holes in the Ozarks, and ranged over many things, saying only a few words about the function and future of the CIA. Clinton did take care to make a point. He did not feel, he said, that the CIA director should advise the president on policy. Woolsey agreed, saying that the director "ought to call the intelligence straight." The visit ended, and Woolsey left, pleased, but also noticing that he hadn't been offered any job.[2]

That came the next day. A staffer called Woolsey's hotel and asked him to be at the Governor's Mansion by noon. There would be a press conference at 12:30 said the staffer. "Wait," said Woolsey. The press conference was fine, but, "Does the president want me to be the director of the CIA?" he asked. The staffer didn't know, so Woolsey called up Warren Christopher, who was running the transition. Christopher told him to come to the press conference—everything would get straightened out there. "But am I being offered the job?" asked Woolsey. Christopher told him to hang on, made another call, then came back on line. Yes, Woolsey was being offered the job. Just come to the press conference, and they would straighten it out there, said Christopher.

They almost did. Woolsey arrived at the Governor's Mansion to find the Clintons, Secretary of Defense Les Aspin, National Security Advisor Tony Lake, the Gores, and National Security Council staffer Sandy Berger already gathered there. Also present were some political aides including Dee Dee Myers. They immediately tried to prepare Woolsey to field questions they anticipated would be asked by the press when the new national security team was introduced to the public. What worried everyone was the fear that the team would appear merely a bunch of retreads from the Carter administration, but to Woolsey, that was exactly what they were. Thinking of a point that might tell on the reporters, Woolsey told the group that he had served in President George H. W. Bush's administration, leading an arms reduction team dealing with conventional forces in Europe. Myers was taken aback. "Admiral, I didn't know you served in the Bush administration," and Woolsey, embarrassed, blushingly made the correction that he had actually risen to a captain in the army. "Oh, we'll have to change the press release," Myers said.

From there, the relation went downhill.

In Washington, access to the presidency is power. Woolsey and the rest of the agency soon found they were situated on the periphery. Unlike Bush, Clinton did not invite senior clandestine officers to weekends at Camp David or to White House Christmas parties. Thomas Twetten, who would help head Clinton's 1996 effort to overthrow Saddam Hussein, perceived Clinton as "personally afraid of any connection with the CIA" due to what Twetten believed were long-standing suspicions of it but also "to avoid immersing himself in foreign policy problems." The fact that the agency had grown more right-wing and Republican during the years Ronald Reagan was president was a factor, because, as a result of their politics, they tended to see Clinton as a soft, liberal Democrat with a weakness of will. Some, of course, were veterans of the Vietnam War and would not forgive Clinton's opposition to it.

To his critics, Woolsey's biggest failure was his own inability to capture the interest or loyalty of the men he was to lead. Toward the real spies in the Directorate of Operations, former colleagues said the new director manifested a vast mistrust from the first, and for their part, they noticed in him an aloofness that offended, mixed with arrogance when it came to the rightness of his own ideas and observations. Woolsey was considered by some to be an egotist liable to stretch the facts to support a dubious point. For his part, former agency critics of Woolsey said he viewed his subordinates as a kind of trap meant to waylay him. He heard a lot about the agency's cabals, divisions, cliques and avoided insiders as if straining to keep clear of some kind of worldly contamination. They in turn were affronted and turned a cold shoulder.

His critics claimed that Woolsey disliked covert operations and human spying. According to them, when it came to intelligence, his overmastering professional interest centered on the technical collection of intelligence, the capabilities of which he believed had dangerously declined. Woolsey disputes this. He believes human intelligence and technical intelligence work together. "There's no doubt that your assets on the ground spot for the satellites, and the satellites help the guys on the ground. There is no antagonism there. At least, I didn't feel any."

The problem was that as he entered his tenure as director he faced a major crisis in the Congress. The chairman of the Senate Intelligence Committee, Dennis DeConcini, a Democrat from Arizona, had inaugurated "alarming and unprecedented" CIA budget cuts, not only in satellite collection systems but also in supercomputers, a key weapon of the spy war. At a time when the country faced terror, DeConcini was planning such deep cuts in agency personnel that, Woolsey said, "I could not have hired new people without a reduction in force."

Even more disturbing, said Woolsey, was the large reduction of the number of interpreters and translators of Persian (Farsi) and Arabic, languages spoken in areas vital to U.S. strategic interests. "The world was entering a dangerous age," he said. "The dragon of the Cold War was dead but we now had a world full of poisonous snakes. The cuts were simply awful."

Woolsey spent most of his days arguing with DeConcini to restore agency budget funds. Finally, DeConcini said to Woolsey, "If the president gives me a call, I'll reconsider." In spite of his efforts, Woolsey said he "simply could not make it happen." To White House advisors, Woolsey seemed to delight in acting with arrogant contentiousness toward key figures in Congress on whose good opinion the agency depended for vital support. He was his own worst enemy. That he had no choice but to defend his agency was ignored.

Political differences also proved damaging. The White House was anxious to replace Haitian military junta leader Raoul Cédras with Jean-Bertrand Aristide. One of Woolsey's best Haiti analysts, Brian Latell, pointed out before Congress that Aristide's human rights violations were almost as gross as those of Cédras. Woolsey stood by his analyst. He was scorned for not being a team player and was soon being called "a grating character . . . arrogant, tin-eared and brittle." Worse, he had acted to estrange the president of the United States, the agency's most important and indispensable client. Part of this was due to Clinton's own intellectual efficiency. He disliked briefings that took too much time, especially when he could speed-read anything the CIA sent him, and he would read the daily brief, annotate it, and send it back. As Woolsey describes his relationship with the president: "I did not have a bad relation with Clinton. I didn't have one at all." He was fired in January 1995.

Clinton never really liked the CIA. During the Carter administration, prompted by Vice President Walter Mondale, who had extreme prejudices against covert operations, Carter brought in Adm. Stansfield Turner to do a housecleaning of the Directorate of Operations. As a result a lot of agents were fired, and a great deal of covert capability was destroyed. Apparently, the agency was going to rely more on technical means and less on human assets. The result was a disaster, as seen in Iran where the United States had no sources of any worth. In the beginning, Clinton reflected this old attitude. "He thought we could get by with fewer spies," a former aide said.

The president clearly understood that if Milosevic were to be deposed and disgraced, the United States had to build an airtight case against him. Holbrooke had said from the beginning that some Serbs had to be convicted of war crimes and Milosevic's involvement in the Balkan atrocities had to be made clear before all the world. Albright here displayed tenacity in setting in motion an effort that by September of 1994 involved dispatching a CIA team of spooks to Bosnia to interview refugees. The CIA agents were accompanied by a team of FBI sketch artists who produced portraits of torturers, rapists, and murderers. There are two versions of this CIA-FBI relationship. One is that it was a genuine instance of heartfelt cooperation and the other is that the FBI offered the sketch artists to keep the CIA out of its computer data. (The latter is probably closer to the truth.)

Within three months, using refugee reports, satellite reconnaissance and imagery, and press articles, the administration had solid evidence about the Serb displacement of tens of thousands of people, mostly Muslims, from their lands. CIA explosives experts determined that tens of thousands of mosques had been deliberately dynamited and not destroyed by battlefield fighting as the Serbs had claimed. In addition, it was established that over 3,600 villages had been razed and 90 percent of the atrocities in the region had been caused by Serb forces. Evidence also indicated that the Serb leader had personally planned and approved of such vicious acts.

Clinton closely followed the data. After being handed a sheaf of reports by Lake, Clinton read them, put them down and spat, "This is disgusting."

By December, only three months later, the agency and the Clinton administration had assembled a pretty complete picture of ethnic cleansing and Serb crimes. At times, Clinton would allow the U.N. Commission of Experts on War Crimes to inspect the evidence, but it was forbidden to keep it or copy it or make it public. Finally in May of 1995, some dissatisfied administration official leaked the data to *The New York Times*, infuriating Department of Defense officials who were still stubbornly opposed to any U.S. military involvement and felt the articles might inflame a fresh public impetus to take action.

There were other good reasons for the secrecy. Threats to peacekeepers were the topmost concern. Clinton's own policy group was profoundly split, as sharing such information with foreign human rights investigators might compromise U.S. intelligence sources and methods. Plus, photos could not identify who had ordered the slaughters, which was now a major aim.

Additional capabilities were strengthened. When he had been president, George H. W. Bush had instituted U-2 flights over key Serb areas. President Clinton had no intention of letting these measures lapse and was no sooner in office than he stepped up the number of U-2 flights overflying the former Yugoslavia.[3] Clinton even streamlined the process. The pictures were to be transmitted to a ground facility in Italy for processing, saving hours over the previous procedure that involved flying the film to the U.K. The National Security Agency's interception of Serb communications was also increased. The Serb forces had only crude electronic countermeasures (ECM) to shield their communications, and U.S. intelligence was busy reading them all. Clinton was using this information to keep track of the military balance in the region, a top priority, along with the amount of military aid being given the Bosnian Serbs by Belgrade.

Clinton also began to beef up intelligence collection begun by his predecessor. In 1992, when the head of the Defense Intelligence Agency had approached the group's head of human intelligence, Col. Pat Lang, a decorated Vietnam veteran and a teacher of Arabic at West Point, had given him a detailed brief of a new program that would use the human sources of former Eastern Bloc countries.[4] Lang was dispatched to make approaches to the intelligence services in Hungary, Czechoslovakia, and Poland, countries friendly to reform and all of which sought to eventually enter NATO. The United States was anxious to strengthen ties to these services first and foremost to keep them from backsliding into the Russian orbit. But of key importance was the fact that these former Soviet services enjoyed excellent liaison with other services in the area, meaning intelligence officers in Serbia, Croatia, and Kosovo, among others. There were pockets of Poles, Czechs, Slovenes, and Hungarians salted throughout Bosnia and the rest of the former Yugoslavia. If America worked with skill, it could use these services to wire Serbia's leadership for penetration, surveillance, and targeting.

One of the DIA's first stops was Hungary, and in Budapest, Lang found the scene there eerie because the headquarters of Hungarian intelligence, in the city of Pest, was in the same building that had housed that function during the Hapsburg monarchy. "There was an astounding continuity," Lang said. Sitting down with Hungarian officials, the pitch went like this: The heads of these services were asked if they still worked for the Soviets. "The answer was heaven's no!" said Lang.

They were then asked how and if they could help. Of course, they could help. What the United States offered was money and equipment, including sophisticated Inmarsat transmitter/receivers, and when the time came, the United States would ask for the former Warsaw Pact agents to meet U.S. intelligence collection requirements. They agreed. "They were extremely good," said Lang.

The reaction of the DIA's new recruits was far from uniform. The Hungarians were eager and full of verve, and the Clinton covert operation that toppled Milosevic in 2000 would come to be based in the U.S. embassy in Budapest. In fact, when it was opened, the new Serb leader, Vojislav Kostunica, called it "interference in Serbia's internal affairs," with good reason. In any case, the Poles were "former KGB and they were a bit sullen, not overjoyed to be working with the DIA," said Lang, "but they were cooperative— they produced." The Czech service was perhaps the most interesting. The new head of Czech intelligence was a former army captain who'd been imprisoned by the communists, and then, after his release, had worked as a stagehand at a theater where future Czech president Václav Havel was having his plays performed. "The former stagehand proved to be first-rate," said Lang. In the meantime, what was sought was information on Serb troop dispositions, air defense systems, Serb paramilitaries and their chain of command, force dispositions, the Yugoslav National Army's (JNA) order of battle, and the like. Identifying threats to U.N. peacekeepers was also a top priority.

Shortly after Lang left, the DIA's first case officer, Emily Francona, arrived in Budapest and began interviewing refugees, gathering details of war crimes.

The hawks were gaining traction.

16

THE RETURN OF HELL

The congressional elections of November 8, 1994, completely floored Bill Clinton. "The heart went out of him; he was dazed, almost stunned," said a former official. Early omens of the disaster could be seen wherever one looked, but Clinton hadn't seen them. His longtime consultant Stanley Greenberg, the highly energetic man with the Groucho Marx mustache and bushy hair, had delivered a memo intended for the president and first lady that warned Clinton they faced a political disaster in November "unless we move urgently to change the mood of the country." The memo went on to say that the results of a recent focus group made clear that when the consultants had asked for descriptions of Clinton, the replies most often received had said the new president was "in over his head," followed by "indecisive" and "immature."[1]

Not even Clinton's staff had been able to envisage the magnitude of the disaster. In the first place, Democratic turnout was very low, an important statement in itself. In the House, fifty-two Democrats lost, all of them moderates. In the Senate, eight seats were gone, and in the states, eleven governorships. The House Republicans now outnumbered the Democrats 230–204, and in the Senate 53–47.

Clearly Clinton wasn't coming across as a leader of all the people. Historically the classic test of a new president is his ability to lead Congress. This meant a display of firm focus and energy from the first moment of power, using careful handling of patronage, good timing, an almost constant and adroit pressure skillfully applied, and that test Clinton had clearly failed.

To some he was pushing ahead the most ambitious domestic legislative agenda since Lyndon Johnson: the North America Free Trade Agreement, national service, direct student loans, the Brady gun control bill, a large expansion of Head Start. By December of 1993, the economy was on the move; unemployment was down to 6.4 percent, the lowest since 1991. Purchases of new homes were climbing.

Clinton, however, was always under a cloud, always dogged at every step by some allegation of improper conduct or some dubious financial transaction. There was the scandal over whether he had manipulated the system to avoid the Vietnam draft. (He had.) Then Gennifer Flowers, a onetime lounge singer and Arkansas state government employee, accused Clinton of a twelve-year extramarital affair. Then the Paula Jones lawsuit had emerged. Jones, another Arkansas state employee, had been allegedly approached by a state trooper who asked on behalf of Clinton if she would perform oral sex on the governor. (Other stories of Clinton using his state police to arrange assignations with women would emerge.) In the fall of 1993, in what would turn out to be another major scandal, questions had arisen over the involvement of both Hillary and Bill in a 1978 planned resort development in the Ozarks called Whitewater. In many ways, he didn't seem quite up to the job. The way he ran the White House hardly inspired confidence. There was still a lack of experienced staff people; there were too many meetings, a lack of coherent structure, staffers who wandered into the Oval Office without warning, no system for making decisions. As a longtime friend said, "There's no system" (when it came to decisions). Clinton "had a decision-making method that is a postponement process." Nor was there any finality once a decision was made—it was rehashed and revisited again and again.

Perhaps the blackest mark against him was his lackluster performance in foreign policy. Again and again, there were shameless retractions of campaign promises. When asked during his campaign about relations with Iraq, Clinton had been glib, saying that as a president he would consider normal relations with Saddam Hussein if the dictator improved his behavior. "I'm a Baptist," said Clinton. "I believe in deathbed conversions." When this hit a sour note with the press, provoking some nasty criticism, Clinton claimed that the reports had been a distortion. They hadn't been. He had twice talked publicly of normalizing relations with Saddam.

Then there had been Haiti, a humanitarian disaster waiting to happen. A military junta was standing on the neck of the place's impoverished people, there were horrible atrocities, and many there wanted to flee to America. Clinton, opposing Bush's policy of nonadmittance, said Haitian refugees would be welcome in the United States until, shortly after his election, U.S. satellite photos revealed hundreds, even thousands of Haitians swarming like disturbed ants in their country's woods, cutting down trees to make boats. The idea of Miami disappearing under a tidal wave of immigrants prompted Clinton to hastily recant. The refugees were no longer welcome. Then there had been the disaster in Somalia, estranging him even further from a military that had taken deep offense over Clinton's early plan to use executive authority to ensure gays could serve in the military, As *The Washington Post*'s Bob Woodward put it, "Clinton was coming to a central understanding: he was not in control of his nation's destiny, the first duty of all presidents."[2]

Clinton did not recover quickly from his election failure. All his efforts to distinguish himself that had led him to this high place, his voracious determination to make a mark that would endure and exalt his name, had apparently been for nothing. The bounce had left his step. Few had seen him so quiet and down. He would alternate between fits of infantile torpor where he would stare into space to a nervous irritability that would respond instantly and viciously to any real or imagined slight. As usual Clinton blamed his consultants, his staff, the fates, but not himself. When an advisor urged he pull himself together and get on with his presidency, Clinton lost control of himself, screaming that the main problem was that the public didn't know the degree or importance of his accomplishments. In one four-hour session with advisors, he went ballistic when one of them suggested he hadn't taken enough strong stands. "Don't ever say that to me again!" Clinton shouted. The problem was not his not having taken stands, it was that he didn't "have any help around here."

Unfortunately, events were on the move.

By May 1995, fresh disaster was beginning to build up in the Balkans. The fury of an elemental malign force had begun again to sweep through the region. Within the allied alliance, all was still drift and appeasement. Even the United States had declared that NATO unity was more important than Bosnia, and Tony Lake had said in a draft memo that "since the stick of military pressure is no longer viable, it should be abandoned."

The month of May saw Sarajevo experience its bloodiest fighting in fifteen months. Messages of alarm began to arrive at the White House Situation Room. Day by day, hour by hour, affairs grew worse. NATO and the United Nations exhibited their usual withdrawal into paralyzed indecision, looking on while the Bosnian Serbs, who had a year before been forced by the United Nations to withdraw their tanks and cannons and mortars from the mountains and ridges surrounding the city, suddenly came and took them back. Without warning, the Serb forces, dressed in camouflage uniforms, moved into the weapons collection sites and picked up artillery pieces, armored vehicles, mortars, utterly ignoring the French U.N. blue helmets charged with controlling those arms. The Serbs then simply drove away with them. The same process was repeated the next day by other parties of raiding Serbs.

This galling piece of impudence was the work of Milosevic's very capable general, Ratko Mladic. But the new commander of U.N. troops in Bosnia, British Lt. Gen. Rupert Smith, was no weakling like Rose. Smith was a combative man, and nothing aroused in him a furious urge to fight more than Mladic's cocksure, brutal arrogance. Young, intense, dark-haired, Smith knew that men like Mladic could only be stopped by brute force, and Smith finally got approval for a mild bombing raid that took out two Serb ammunition bunkers. On May 24, Bosnian Serb General Mladic used his new arsenal to unleash a merciless barrage, smashing the city with over three thousand shells in violation of a ban the year before of heavy weapons in the area. Smith demanded air attacks, but he was given only a bit of what he wanted and not in the way he wanted it. When Smith mounted another U.N. pinprick raid by NATO aircraft on May 25, the Serbs replied by indiscriminately shelling all six safe areas in retaliation. In Sarajevo, a Serb shell had careened into a crowded café packed with students, killing seventy-one people, most of whom were under twenty-five, and wounding 250.

When Smith hit back with whatever he could get, taking out six bunkers in the ammunition depot at Pale, the Serbs, with the most brazen lawless insolence, replied by taking 350 peacekeepers hostage. Instead of feeling outrage and increasing support of Smith, the U.N. hierarchy began to work quickly to undermine him. At a meeting on May 29, the U.N. secretary-general's special envoy Yasushi Akashi said Smith's decision for strikes had proved "the ineffectiveness of air strikes as a way to confront the Serbs." U.N. commander French Gen. Bernard Janvier issued new guidelines. U.N. headquarters in New York was no longer able to approve large-scale air strikes for U.N. officials in the former Yugoslavia like Smith. From now on it would be only U.N. secretary-general Boutros-Ghali who would have the authority to personally turn the key for any air strikes. Smith had no authority to order them anymore.[3]

The Serb war against the Bosnian Muslims had reached a new turning point. General Mladic knew he did not have enough resources to fight a long and indefinite war, and he knew he needed to conquer the Croats and Bosnian Muslims in the spring of 1995. At the top of his list of targets were the six Muslim enclaves.

By July, Mladic's forces had thrown a noose around the city of Srebrenica, and it was clear some sort of terrible climax was approaching. The Serb general was moving with a frightening, savage determination, and at any moment the city's isolation might be complete.

Srebrenica could not have been in worse shape. It was bursting to the brim with refugees from Serb assaults on the surrounding small towns. A gagging, sickening stench rose from the overcrowded apartments where people were living twelve to a room. At night people slept on the bathroom or kitchen floors. Buildings were infested with rats, fleas, and lice. Any trace of personal dignity or privacy had vanished. Grandparents, parents, aunts, uncles, and little children slept, fornicated, ate, defecated publicly in one room. A single toilet had hordes of users. The city's sewage system could not handle the load and overflowed, filling the air outside with an insufferable stink. Rotting piles of garbage lay in a vile litter in the streets where they'd been dumped a year before. With the Serbs blocking resupply convoys, there was no fuel for vehicles that could take away the trash. The people were starving. After mid-June almost half the population was without any food. Soup kitchens had been opened to feed the most infirm and feeble, but there were not enough ingredients to keep them operational.[4]

The deputy mayor of Srebrenica, Hamdija Fejzic, asked the Dutch peacekeeping commander, Lt. Col. Thomas Karresmans, to send a letter to UNPROFOR superiors in Tuzla and Sarajevo, and in a June 17 letter, Karresmans wrote, "The people were dying a slow death before the eyes of Europe," adding that he expected people would begin to die of starvation within ten days. At the same time he made an emotional appeal to the world, saying that Srebrenica "had already been the largest concentration camp in the world for three years" from which "the exhausted and hungry eyes of its citizens" were looking to "the powerful of the earth for help." The Serbs, he wrote, were willfully interfering with the delivery of humanitarian aid. In the last five and a half months, only a half kilo of baby food and two kilos of powdered milk per child had been distributed. The humanitarian convoys had only been able to complete 65 percent of their runs and been able to deliver only 30 percent of scheduled quantities. In addition, the lack of goods had sapped the morale of the underarmed Bosnian Muslim forces almost as much as it had the general population.

The time for rescue had come, and some set their teeth and sat down to wait with expectation. Nothing came. The machinery of the United Nations and NATO was ponderous and difficult to set in motion. Patience was required and so was time. Unfortunately, time had run out. For Mladic it was now or never.

The city fell on July 11, with one Dutch outpost after another taken by the Serbs. Yet clearly something was amiss. The International Committee of the Red Cross had coordinated the deportation of refugees from the city by convoy on July 12 and 13. As these had arrived, the ICRC had noticed that 90 percent of the arrivals were women, children, and elderly men. This was disconcerting and puzzling, since this meant roughly between ten thousand to twenty thousand people, mainly young males, were missing.

Alarm began to spread, but supposition had not yet solidified into verifiable fact and no technical evidence would emerge until August 4. There was a stiffening gale of disquieting reports of mass atrocity, but no evidence. Milosevic, a man without tenderness, without honor, without scruples or remorse, was already retailing preposterous lies—yes, he said, men were missing from Srebrenica, but it was because they had yielded to frantic, unreasoning panic and fled into the woods when the Serbs entered the town. Perhaps they had already emerged and rejoined their families and the families were refusing to admit it, to embarrass the Serbs. For the time being, Milosevic's incredible affront was swallowed in silence.

Initial corroboration of mass executions came from someone who had barely escaped being killed himself. At Tuzla in Croatia, there were teams of U.N. workers interviewing Srebrenica refugees. Among them was a young Norwegian woman, Tune Bringa, who was taking down reports of rape, stories of transport buses being stopped and young women being taken off and violated. Bringa was a member of U.N. special envoy Akashi's policy analysis staff, working with people like Doug Perry and Peggy Hicks from UN-PROFOR's human rights section. The tarmac at the Tuzla airport was teeming with thousands of newly arrived refugees, the U.N. staffers using loudspeakers to encourage people to come forward.

Suddenly a man in his early forties with a bloody head appeared, shouting frantically, "I need to speak to the United Nations! I need to speak to the United Nations!" An excited crowd formed around him asking, "Have you seen my brother?" Or, "Have you seen my husband?" The man shouldered them aside and yelled again, "I need to speak to the United Nations!" Bringa took the man aside, and saw that a bullet had grazed his head. Speaking fluent Bosnian, she took down his story.

He had been in the stadium at Potocari when he heard Mladic taunting the Muslim men, "Where is your Alija now?" referring to the Bosnian president. He had then been taken to a school where he spent a horrific night watching Serb soldiers as they kept pulling men off trucks. He described hearing gunfire followed by screams. He was then taken by a truck to a field near Konjevic Polje where he was forced off and watched in horror as a line of men ahead of him were machine-gunned in front of an open pit. He was next in line, and as the Serbs opened fire, he fell on top of the dead bodies in the pit. Rushing to complete their work, the soldiers ordered another line of captives forward. They were shot and their corpses covered the body of the survivor. He lay still until dark, rigid with terror at the thought that Serb bulldozers might rumble in and bury him alive in the corpse-filled pit. When the Serbs finally left, he cried out, "Is anyone still alive?" Someone was. A seventeen-year-old boy answered, and together they fled through the woods to Tuzla.

The man with the bullet graze on his temple showed Bringa the burn marks where his wrists had been tied with rope.

Bringa immediately understood the significance of the man's account. It explained what had happened to Srebrenica's missing men and boys. Bringa also knew the United Nations and knew that her boss, Akashi, was not a man of daring, energy, or action. She was afraid the man's account would sink out of sight in the murk of the U.N. bureaucracy. Akashi would demand extensive corroboration before he would forward a report of massacre that might prompt a resolute, fierce military response. That evening Bringa flew back to Zagreb to see a man she had been dating, the U.S. ambassador to Croatia, Peter Galbraith. Galbraith had been recalled to Washington July 5 for talks but had since returned.

In a distraught voice, she described what she had heard and asked what Galbraith could do. "This doesn't belong in some drawer somewhere!" she said. "This is critical! This can't simply end up in a drawer somewhere!" She was convinced the United Nations would try and suppress reports of the massacre.

Galbraith didn't say anything, but after they talked he immediately went to his office and dictated a "NODIS" or "No Distribution" cable entitled: "Possible Mass Execution of Srebrenica Is Reason to Save Zepa," another enclave under Mladic attack. He recounted Bringa's story, urging "reconsideration of air strikes" to help protect Zepa. Galbraith's cable ended somberly, "There may be no survivors of the men rounded up in Srebrenica." Assistant Secretary of State Richard Holbrooke personally put Galbraith's cable in the secretary's hands, saying, "Chris, this is the human side of what's happening!" By mid-July, Galbraith was convinced the missing Muslim men were dead.

Christopher responded to Galbraith's cable by sending John Shattuck, the assistant secretary of state for democracy, human rights, and labor, to Croatia. Shattuck's reports were disturbing. The diplomat not only interviewed Bringa's witness, he also talked with the seventeen-year-old who had escaped with the older survivor. Shattuck gathered more solid, detailed information and finally came up with an estimate of ten thousand people from Srebrenica missing and possibly killed. Shattuck gave his estimate to Christopher on August 4.

The assembled accounts were horrifying. At a place called Nova Kasaba, northwest of the city, Muslim men ranging from teenagers to those in their sixties and seventies had had their hands bound behind their backs, were lined up, and then shot. Serbs moved among them putting bullets into anybody they thought might harbor life. One of the Serb executioners had handed his rifle to the horrified driver of a bus. "You kill one," he ordered. Everyone was to be implicated.

For hours and hours, as more and more buses arrived, Muslim men were slaughtered like deer.

For Madeleine Albright, the U.S. ambassador to the United Nations, the nightmare of Srebrenica began early the morning of July 11. Stuart Seldowitz, political officer on the U.N. mission staff, walked into the office of U.N. undersecretary Shashi Tharoor. In Albright's words, Tharoor was "the ultimate diplomat, articulate, analytical, suave." She knew Seldowitz well and had never before heard his voice betray emotion, but it did today. He related to her that he had seen Tharoor's face that morning filled with shock and grief. When asked why, Tharoor had said, "I think we're facing a humanitarian disaster of historic proportions. There are reports of mass killings in Srebrenica." Seldowitz had hastened across the street to phone Albright, who called Washington. As she was talking, a young assistant was saying on another phone, "No, no, I understand." When Albright hung up, the aide gave her his phone. On the other end was the young, handsome Bosnian ambassador to the United Nations, Mohammed Sacirbey. He was crying.

A somber Principals meeting began in Washington. The mood was gloom, fixed, and unyielding, permeated by subtle, implacable hostility for the Bosnian Serbs. Gore had a hard, stony face. "We cannot acquiesce in genocide," he said. Albright said simply, "We need to tell our allies, this is it."

The fact is that no Western intelligence service predicted the fall of Srebrenica. The United States had entirely missed the imminent takeover because collecting intelligence on the eastern enclaves had been assigned a very low priority. The common assumption was that some U.S.-Serb or NATO-Serb clash was inevitable, and the crucial allied target would be the destruction of Milosevic's sophisticated Russian-built air defense systems. The United States bent every exertion to collecting additional data on these, even though the systems were not unfamiliar. In fact, in terms of U.S. policy, the enclaves had slipped in importance. But at the time of the city's fall, data on Serb air defense systems enjoyed an unchallenged priority.

The importance of this choice was made clear on June 2, 1995, when a NATO U-2 Senior Span signals intelligence aircraft intercepted radar emissions from a Serb SA-5 Gainful surface-to-air missile in northwestern Bosnia that indicated it was tracking a NATO plane. Because of equipment problems, that data was not relayed to the National Security Agency headquarters at Fort Meade, Maryland. The pilot, Scott O'Grady, was shot down and disappeared into Serbia. No one knew if he was dead or alive.

Clinton's basic capacity for warmth and compassionate sympathy was made clear on July 7, when, after a late strategy session, he was alone with consultant Dick Morris in the president's dressing room just off the president's bedroom in the White House residence. Clinton was playing solitaire and he and Morris were talking about a balanced budget speech, when the president took a call. Clinton listened, and then said with force, "You got him? You got him?" His face beamed with joy and he stomped his feet in glee. After he hung up, he pulled his fist passionately toward himself and yelled in exultation, "Yes!" like a fan at a prizefight. Clinton then slumped in a chair and vast relief spread over his face. O'Grady had been rescued.

It had been submarines in the Adriatic as well as signals intelligence aircraft that had first picked up signals sent by O'Grady in Serbia that he was alive and kicking but on the run. As he dodged Serb search parties combing the countryside for him, Clinton sent U.S. Special Forces to go in and successfully extract him.

As disquieting reports of mass atrocities in Srebrenica continued to surface, U.S. intelligence collection began to pick up its pace. The United States not only had to adjust its plans but change the way it thought about them. America was flying U-2R reconnaissance aircraft operated by the CIA's National Reconnaissance Office or the Defense Airborne Reconnaissance Office (DARO), run by the Defense Intelligence Agency. The U-2R was a formidable aircraft that could shoot eleven kilometers of high-resolution film per flight, almost twenty-eight miles. The aircraft flew over Bosnia twice a week, each flight charted on the basis of intelligence requirements approved in Washington. Some of the film on Serb air defenses was analyzed within eighteen hours, but analysts were lacking and warehouses of film lay unanalyzed.

Now with allegations of slaughter being made publicly, solid substantiation was needed, but CIA analysts confronted hundreds of miles of film—literally hundreds of thousands of images of various sites, at various times, with no clue as to where among that vast, cluttered mass glinted the gold of incriminating evidence that would withstand any scrutiny. As a Dutch analyst said, "Where exactly would the analyst have looked? They did not know if the executions had been carried out on a road to the north or south of Srebrenica. They did not know which enlargements to make of which sectors on a sweep of forty kilometers by ten kilometers. It is, moreover, extremely difficult to identify a small group of people about to be executed."[5] It would be a human intelligence source, not technical, that made the breakthrough. Working for the DIA, this person, unknown to Bringa or Galbraith, had drawings of sites, lists of times, exact dates, names of Serb perpetrators. He gave detailed briefings of his work to the CIA's Balkan Task Force, whose analysts had begun their careful scrutiny of the U-2 film. The analysts soon found what they were looking for. A U-2 photo, taken July 13, showed the Nova Kasaba soccer field in Srebrenica. The CIA analysts marked the photo with red arrows that pointed toward two dark clumps where approximately six hundred prisoners stood in a huddle together. A second photo, taken July 27, showed three areas where the grass had been upturned, and light-colored dirt beneath could be seen. Tracks from heavy vehicles also appeared sharp and clear. On August 2, Clinton was told of the photo, probably by CIA director John Deutch who had replaced Woolsey after he resigned. It was shown to him by one of the Principals on August 4. It came from a U-2 flight from the Royal Air Force base at Alconbury in Britain, operated by the Defense Intelligence Agency.[6]

The Serbs kept up their straight-faced lies, but they were beginning to fizzle out and fall flat. The allies had already convened negotiations to discuss Srebrenica in Belgrade on July 15. Attending were U.N. special envoy Akashi, EU envoy Carl Bildt, U.N. negotiator Thorwald Stoltenberg of Germany, Gen. Rupert Smith, Milosevic, and General Mladic. Before one meeting convened, the U.S. embassy in Belgrade gave the U.S. negotiators a high-resolution U-2 photo, which a staff member left out on the central table at the talks. After viewing it, Mladic was visibly shaken and discomfited. (This photo was not one of those used later by Albright at the United Nations.)

When Albright went after the accomplishment of a goal, it was always with a certain savage, frightening determination, and she exhibited this now. Those photos had to be declassified and made public at all costs, and her fixity of position had CIA director Deutch distraught. By its very nature, the agency is paranoid about releasing material that could compromise sources and methods, and Deutch dug in to resist with every means in his power. Albright was unfazed, and State Department lawyers were tenacious in their support. Clinton supported Albright from behind the scenes, wanting to see the material made public. Toby Gati, then chief of the Bureau of Intelligence and Research at the State Department said, "The intelligence community was not very happy with her. She pushed [the matter] very far."[7]

The climax occurred the morning of August 10. The U.N. Security Council met in closed session, and, when it was Albright's turn to speak, she powerfully described two incidents, one involving a forty-one-year-old man who had been brought to a field at Nova Kasaba where lines of Muslim men were machine-gunned, and the other involving a seventeen-year-old boy. Albright spoke with great strength, clarity, and passion. She had already shown the Dutch military attaché to the permanent representation in New York, Maj. E. A. W. Koestal, a gruesome photo of the arm of a corpse protruding from the soil. This photo was not released to protect sources and methods, but Albright released the rest.[8]

The normally buzzing, noisy room fell silent as the photos were passed around. It was all there. Later that afternoon, the Security Council assembled in formal session to demand that the Pale Serbs give immediate access to Sarajevo. There were the usual displays of cross-purposes and contradictions, but further fuzziness and delay were no longer possible. After all the dark and murk, it was finally becoming light enough to see and the sight was sickening. In America, repulsion and outrage were welling up everywhere. Among the Bosnian Muslims, a terrible cry of vindictive indignation rose from every throat.

17

THE RIVALS

To his critics, Clinton's policy on Bosnia still appeared to be beset by obstacles, frustrations, dissensions, and failures on all sides. Even to some of his advisors, Clinton's caution was clearly crippling him. To many insiders he was acting as if he no longer dared to undertake any enterprise the success of which he could not calculate beforehand with a maximum of certainty. Whereas in the case of a domestic matter like welfare reform, Clinton would work until he knew the thing "inside and outside, upside and downside," in foreign policy he was displaying no confidence, no sureness of mastery. The president appeared to have a baffling lack of capacity to drive a plan through to its conclusion.

Even as dark shadows had grown around the Muslim enclaves, to all appearances nothing had changed. The cornerstone of U.S. policy continued to be not deploying any U.S. troops to Bosnia. Along with this was the ambition to preserve allied unity, prevent a widening of the war, and push forward diplomatic efforts that everyone knew were going nowhere. The conduct of the crisis stumbled from one day to the next, preserving an unstable equilibrium.

Clinton clearly realized the defects of this ad-hoc approach. On June 14, 1995, as he was about to meet with the new French president, Jacques Chirac, Clinton was blunt about his Bosnia policy defects: "We have no clear mission. No one is in control of events." Gore had joined in, declaring that the Europeans were "self-delusional" in repudiating strong NATO action to support the U.N. forces. NATO looked weak and the United States even weaker. "The need to protect and preserve the alliance is driving our policy. It is driving us into a brick wall with Congress," the vice president said. Clinton cut in: "We need to get the policy straight." What he wanted was a new, coherent strategy. He wanted to hear something new, he said.[1]

Since late May, ferment had been at work. The underlying premises were these: how could the Bosnian Serbs be brought to the negotiating table, and how could the allies be persuaded to accept the massive use of airpower to help that happen?

Albright, who had become the lead hawk, had very definite ideas. The United States must have a peace agreement by the end of the year. To do that, force had to be used to forward Serb movement toward diplomacy. This meant removing from the United Nations any authority over air strikes. She had another conviction. The United Nations must be made to realize that its forces were a dead cat around the neck of any effective plan of action, a part of the problem, rather than a part of the solution. U.N. peacekeepers did not keep the peace, but often ended up passive accomplices to the most hideous war crimes. Worse, their presence prevented the lifting of the arms embargo and prevented NATO from engaging in prolonged and devastating air strikes against the predatory Serbs. Perhaps instead of trying to keep them there, the United States should quietly pressure them to get out.

In the past, everyone had made statements to the effect that U.N. withdrawal of its forces would be disastrous, mainly because Bosnia would then become an American responsibility. But ducking responsibility was weakening America's credibility all over the world. The U.S. reluctance to act was placing American leadership at risk.

Let UNPROFOR withdraw, and then press the Serb leader Slobodan Milosevic to recognize Bosnia in return for limited sanctions relief. Albright put all this in a memo and gave it to the president. When Clinton read the memo, he enthusiastically agreed. When Lake saw it, he also agreed with its basic thrust. Lake had raised similar concerns in an earlier meeting with Clinton, and he soon was meeting with Albright at her house for Chinese food as they dissected ideas for refining the new approach. They both agreed that America had to seize the leadership of the crisis as it had in early 1994 when it brokered the formation of the Croat-Muslim Federation. They also needed to put together a bunch of carrots and sticks to ensure a peace agreement was reached by the end of the year.

Everyone began producing papers. Albright's was an extended version of her memo called "Elements of a New Strategy." Lake put forward his "Endgame" strategy. And suddenly the State and Defense departments, and the NSC, were busy doing policy reviews.[2] As was usual with Secretary of

State Christopher, he was wary and cautious. The promise of success tendered by Albright and Lake was by no means worth the possibility of failure. He resisted the idea of the withdrawal of U.N. forces, since their extraction would involve U.S. forces and put the Clinton presidency in political peril. His key proposal urged that efforts be made to have Milosevic recognize Bosnia as part of a new diplomatic initiative. Dealing with the Bosnian Serbs like Mladic would be like dealing with madmen. If Milosevic delivered, sanctions would be lifted, not merely suspended.

The Defense Department basically took the position to go on with things as they were.

Then came Lake's turn. He argued that the administration needed a peace agreement by the end of the year that would preserve Bosnia as a single state. He suggested a number of things including pressuring UNPROFOR to withdraw and having NATO issue a new ultimatum to the Serbs to remove their heavy weapons around Sarajevo. If Belgrade didn't end its support for the Bosnian Serbs, there would be air strikes at targets inside Serbia as well as Bosnia, and sanctions could be tightened. The arms embargo should be lifted multilaterally, but if the Europeans hung fire, then unilaterally. Toward the end of the meeting, Clinton came in, as Lake had arranged. The current policy "is doing enormous damage to our standing in the world," Clinton said. "The only time we've ever made progress is when we've geared up NATO to pose a threat to the Serbs." The administration needed to get out of the rut it was in, he said, then left.[3]

It was clear in the case of Lake and Albright that their recommendations meant a hardening of U.S. policy, and it was also clear that many senior Clinton advisors were casting aside any lingering remnants of esteem they had once entertained for the United Nations and many of the Europeans. The allies were vacillating, timid, and had a horror of risk. Plus they were treacherous. They manipulated the whole United Nations dual key system of approval for air strikes to their own advantage and the result was always paralysis and inaction. Nor had Clinton forgotten Rose's double cross of 1994 or the rude treatment of Christopher by the British a year earlier. Clinton had moved to neutralize Rose and the British basic favoritism toward Belgrade. On July 4, 1994, when Rose was traveling, the Americans opened their embassy next door to the British residency in Sarajevo. Since U.S. ambassador Victor Jackovich and his staff operated mainly from Vienna, it was only a part-time embassy, yet it was still a busy one.

In his memoirs, Rose alleges that the United States was monitoring his conversations throughout 1994 and 1995, and that the information was sent directly to the U.S. military command in Naples, Italy; a statement happily confirmed by former U.S. intelligence officials. In Rose's traffic with U.N. headquarters in New York, the NSA always had its ear flatly pressed to his door. Of course, Rose was also monitored by the Serbs, Muslims, and Bosnian Serbs, but Rose rightly claimed that the Americans spied on him because they thought him too pro-Serb.

Even the links of the senior UNPROFOR became a major target for the NSA. America provided secure links between Sarajevo and General Rose's office and later to that of his successor, Gen. Rupert Smith, a hard-liner where Rose had been a soft one. The links were encrypted. The talk normally went via a secure link, known as the tactical satellite radio (TacSat), which consisted of two components, a receiver and a transmitter. Smith was to discover to his dismay one day that the TacSat was rigged. Smith had just called London and Washington and had lengthy conversations on sensitive matters. He used the TacSat. Then, expected at a meeting at the neighboring U.S. embassy, Smith hastened over with an aide and was astounded to hear his own voice emanating from an embassy room, repeating his conversation of a half hour before. An embassy staffer was making a report on it, and not long after, a Smith staffer alerted his boss to the extra transmitter NSA had rigged in his TacSat. The infuriated Smith threw the thing in the trash and got a TacSat from the British Special Air Service, the British equivalent of Delta Force or SEAL Team Six.[4]

But Smith and Rose hadn't been singled out—the entire UNPROFOR headquarters in Sarape was a special NSA target, and to counter this the building often swarmed with British sweep teams searching for bugs. Some were found but were thought to belong to the Bosnians or Serbs. Within the compound, the UNPROFOR headquarters had three interconnected containers that housed the top secret communications equipment and only the Americans could enter those containers—"they were the only nationality," said an aide to Rose and Smith.[5] It vacuumed up not only all the UNPROFOR transmissions but even those of the mujahedeen fighters in Bosnia although no U.S. admission was ever made of this.

When the Serbs captured Srebrenica in July 1995 and rumors of massacre began to surface, the new president of France, Jacques Chirac, and Clinton had spoken on the phone. Chirac was in a fine fury. "We must do something!" he said excitedly. "Yes, we must act," said Clinton. Chirac declared that he wanted to use French paratroopers to retake the town, a reckless, romantic, highly emotional plan, which, while showy, would have left the Pentagon cold. Clinton's answer was deflating: Would it really make that great a difference? he asked.

Only a few days later, on July 14, Chirac called again, storming and ranting, talking of World War II and of the West's not resisting Hitler's takeover of the Sudetenland in Czechoslovakia, implying that France might have to pull out of the U.N. peacekeepers. "We can't imagine that the U.N. force will remain only to observe and to be, in a way, accomplices in the situation," Chirac snapped. "If that is the case it is better to withdraw."

The words stung Clinton like a slash from a whip. Chirac, the leader of a secondary world power, was talking to the leader of the mightiest in the history of the world, implying he was weak.

Chirac had upstaged Clinton once before. On June 14, President Chirac paid his first visit to Washington, meeting with congressional leaders, and later had gone to the White House for a small, private dinner. It was a warm, magical June night, and after Chirac and his wife had said their goodbyes, the president and first lady danced alone to the easy music of the Marine Band.

The next day both men attended the G-7 conference in Halifax, and the heads of state had been content to talk of Europe without really going into details on Bosnia. Not Chirac. Chirac was, above all, a hard man. He was a campaign-hardened veteran of the Algerian War and exuded an air of limitless endurance and ferocious tenacity. The war in Algiers had been one where the government had had the force to confront and the will to use the force, and it had done so, sometimes not to its credit. But perhaps as a result, Chirac didn't think in grays but in blacks and whites, knowing absolutely that in a fight one side would endure a clear-cut defeat, the other a hard-earned victory on which to build its pride.

The war in Algeria had resembled the war in Yugoslavia in its vicious atrocity and the fact that so many noncombatants were targets. To Clinton, what was refreshing about Chirac was that he was absolutely devoid of the pro-Serb bias of his predecessor, François Mitterrand, and he was not afraid to say so. The Greeks, because of the shared religion of the Orthodox Church, had sympathized with the Serbs from the first. In a conversation, when Greek prime minister Andreas Papandreou began to defend the Serb actions, Chirac had abruptly cut him off. "Don't speak to me of any religious war," he said. "These people are without faith, without any sense of law. They are terrorists." Chirac was aware that the accumulating stress from the dissensions, the warring factions, the incessant impotent squabbling within the European Union, were tearing it apart, and he strongly balked at this. Unity of Europe was a thing on which he placed a supreme value. Hostility between systems or cultures or nationalities was not irreconcilable. He had seen after World War II how Germany and France were able to put away past pain and work together for ends that would benefit them both. Chirac was not about to allow fratricidal violence in the Balkans to damage that ideal of European unity. Too much blood had been spilled. He has a Gascoigne's pride—he never forgot an insult or a service.

That day in Halifax, he chose to upstage Clinton.[6] "He was concerned not just about the future of Europe or NATO or Balkan atrocities but the glory that was France," as Clinton biographer John Harris noted. Many of Chirac's hearers were full of contemptuous disdain, seeing in this outburst another evidence of France's addiction to colorful but empty dramatics. Even though Chirac, the old paratrooper, may have had a streak of self-promoting vainglory, it was mixed with a genuine pugnacity, and the elemental force of his eruption startled the attendees. Chirac was a head-down fighter, and he wanted tougher rules of engagement in Bosnia, he wanted to take on the Serbs, he wanted *action*. The passion, intensity, and conviction of his performance, his old seasoned warrior's vigor, his resolve, his unbridled intensity, acted to elbow Bill Clinton, the chief leader of the free world, from his spot at the world's center stage. Clinton's eclipse was made more bitter when, returning to France after his second American visit, Chirac announced that the position of leader of the free world was "vacant."

It was another slap in the face (Clinton would react to Chirac's words in a tantrum on the putting green in which the president gave vent to a distilled, bitter fury, the exquisite rage of pure impotence, for forty-five minutes). Chirac's insult came at a time when Clinton was beginning to exhibit the fixed determination of an indomitable will. He had been working in secret with Lake on the "Endgame" strategy, and when Lake had told him the new strategy meant putting his presidency on the line, Clinton met that moment of major testing with a manner that was unflinching. He wanted the strategy and would endure the risk.

In the case of Chirac's sneer, what tortured Clinton was the clear knowledge that he had *not* been inactive. The new Lake strategy was only one element; the U.S. arming and training of the Croats was another. Clinton, like FDR, was very much at home with subterfuge, and the truth was that he *had* acted; but the action had not been taken in public but *in secret*. He could not make public covert programs without destroying them. He knew that the key to success of his activities in Croatia depended on patience, on their being perfected out of sight of public criticism. To his critics, Clinton's policy blunders on Bosnia had risen to a tall, stark pile. The U.S. covert actions, which no one in America knew of and which his spook teams had contrived and executed with hazard, skill, and difficulty, had as yet produced no visible results. As these covert programs were gathering in mass, extensiveness, and strength, they were like a precious fruit that had to be kept in the dark to fully ripen. They could not be rushed. Plus Clinton said nothing until the world saw that they had brought success, and even then America's hand in them had to stay hidden. Nor could he know in advance how successfully they would work or if they would work fully and in time.

The U.S.-Croat intelligence operations were known to a tiny circle, but a Croatian military offensive combined with new diplomatic initiatives might turn the tide.

And in fact they would. "What we did in Croatia made Clinton's first term," said Galbraith.

And Galbraith would prove to be right, but until then Clinton was a man who had to spar for time.

"COVENANTS WITHOUT SWORDS
BE BUT WORDS"

—*Thomas Hobbes*

A chain of events was about to unfold with lightning rapidity that would scatter the Bosnian Serbs like a covey of birds and change the whole dynamic of the ground war in Bosnia. David Gergen, one of Clinton's advisors, said the president had two sides to his nature. "He went from a goo-goo to a man wanting to win at any cost." Now the president was all pugnacity. The world had only caught glimpses of that inner steel now and then, but a new inner toughness was becoming central in Clinton. America had a new policy and it was being driven by the president.

On July 21, 1995, European and American officials met in London at a meeting called by British prime minister John Major. America was represented by Secretary of State Warren Christopher, Secretary of Defense William Perry, and Chairman of the Joint Chiefs Gen. John Shalikashvili. Clinton, who had formidable powers of persuasion, had called Chirac on July 18 and while Chirac said he still preferred some kind of ground operation, he would not stand in the way of the U.S. proposal for a decisive air campaign.

That was a major victory. Once the meeting began, the British wanted things to continue as they had. They wanted the United Nations to continue to control air strikes, which meant no air strikes would occur. As late as July 27, having already been voted down, both the French and British had still wanted to retain the cumbersome dual key system of approval for air strikes. Unfortunately for them, Clinton had thrown his full weight into gaining success, and he had numerous phone conversations with the Europeans to try and bring them on board. The prestige of his office told on his opponents. Perry and Shalikashvili were immovable, and on July 25, during a thirteen-hour debate at the North Atlantic Council, America finally saw its basic demands met. By August 1, the bickering was over and Clinton had an agreement that said any Serb attack on Gorazde, one of the few remaining enclaves, would be met by sustained air strikes targeting Serb installations or forces all over Bosnia. Nor would NATO have to wait to respond to a Serb attack but could strike if it only detected Serb preparations for one. Authority for calling in air strikes would rest with General Smith, the UNPROFOR commander, *not* the U.N. civilian leadership. The attacks would continue even if peacekeepers had been taken hostage.

Squabbles immediately erupted on how to implement this decision. Boutros-Ghali obstinately refused to relinquish his authority over air strikes until two phone calls from Christopher made clear he had no choice. Even as he gave in, the vain, self-regarding Egyptian dictated a cable that made it sound as if the decision had been his own idea: "I have decided to delegate the necessary authority," he began, but the matter was no longer in Boutros-Ghali's hands. The French insisted that final authority for air strikes go to Gen. Bernard Janvier, the U.N. commander and the man who had basically dithered impotently and had not moved to stop the Serbs from taking Srebrenica. Even London tried to insert a limiting condition, asking that the threat of strikes apply only to Gorazde and nowhere else, but this failed.[1]

The United States stood firm, and the agreement would put in place the structure that would make possible the bombing of the Serbs after they blew up the Sarajevo marketplace on August 25.

The 2001 war in Afghanistan would be widely hailed as a campaign where, for the first time, the Pentagon had brilliantly used a force of foreign proxies to secure military success. In fact, the Afghan war was but a faint echo of Clinton's secret strategic cooperation with Croatia, where Tudjman's forces would defeat the Bosnian Serbs and drive them to the negotiating table.

By the summer of 1995, Croatia's U.S.-directed upgrading and modernizing of Zagreb's military forces had been extremely extensive, including a complete reorganization of the Croatian Defense Ministry. Slowly, the military balance was shifting against Serbia, thanks to internal economic mismanagement and a spiritually discouraged and impoverished population led by Milosevic, who was very far from being a master of war. By contrast, Tudjman's newly trained and outfitted forces, while not on a level with the Serb regular army, certainly outclassed the forces of the Bosnian Serbs. And from poorly armed, ragtag bands of guerrilla fighters, the Bosnian Muslim forces were now able to conduct coordinated, large-scale operations, thanks to a new structure of command and control.[2]

In March, Tudjman, eager to the initiative, had wanted to launch an attack, but was talked out of it by Gore.[3] But planning was already under way, the target to be western Slavonia, part of the Serb Republika Srpska, a renegade state-let set up in Croatia by the insidious machinations of Milosevic and Mladic in 1991. With forests and wooded hills, the area was strategically important. Bordered by the Drava and Sava rivers, it was a clear route to the Hungarian border, and, if captured, it would sever the link between Zagreb and Osijek, ruining forever Milosevic's Greater Serbia plan.

Called Operation Flash, the Croatian plan had actually been the brainchild of U.S. Gen. John Galvin, former Supreme Area Commander for Europe (SACEUR). For Flash, the United States had provided Croatia not only encryption equipment for its divisions, but the CIA was flying Predator drones from the island of Krk. The Clinton administration had also provided Tudjman's forces with NSA intercepts of Serbian communications.

One evening in April, the U.S. military attaché in Zagreb, Col. Robert Herrick, who had earlier done the road and port surveys for the DIA, was summoned to the Croatia Ministry of Police and told that Operation Flash would "begin in a few hours' time," according to a participant. Accompanied by his assistant, Sgt. Ivan Sarac, an American-Croatian, at exactly midnight, the two Americans were told that Croat operation staff was moving from the Police to the Defense Ministry, and that Herrick and Sarac were to move there as well. At dawn the battle began, and from then on Herrick constantly received updates on the operation, immediately forwarding them to Lake, who briefed President Clinton in the White House. In a two-day blitz, the ferocity of the Croat attack swept the board clean of Bosnian Serb chips. Backed by twenty tanks, three thousand Croat troops drove the Serb Krajina forces out of western Slavonia, cutting the crucial link to Hungary.[4]

Clinton had cast a keen eye on the battle. He was "quick-triggered and dynamic," a former aide said, listening with intensity to the battle's progress, eagerly absorbing updates each morning, exhibiting the same informed, professional interest in detail, coupled with "a certain fertility of comment and question." The mood in the White House was a jubilant one. The Pentagon coordinated the action via Herrick, while the CIA activities were coordinated by the Zagreb station chief, Marc Kelton, who himself was working closely with Miroslav Tudjman, head of SIS, the Croatian intelligence service. Then had come Srebrenica. Clinton knew that the Serbs would not come to peace talks unless forced to by defeats on the battlefield. This meant a major Croatian operation must be made. Called Ouja or Operation

Storm, it raised some major objections within the defense and intelligence communities. The Pentagon, always heavy, sluggish, and irresolute, was opposed, while the CIA predicted complete disaster for the Croats. To these two bodies, the plan was impetuous to the point of being reckless. If the attack failed, it was argued, that would be bad enough, but if it succeeded it could bring in the Serb national army, which would mangle the Croats and widen the war.[5]

Tudjman was certain he would win. He was a hard, grim, remorseless, driving spirit, and he had a sharp eye for weakness. For some time he had told Washington that the Krajina Serbs were overextended and could be had. Too much Serb military equipment had been sucked up for the assaults on the eastern enclaves, and, as far as he was concerned, the door to opportunity stood wide open. Galbraith thought so too. The time was perfect he felt for the Croats to be turned loose. The Serbs were busy assaulting Bihar, an enclave, and if the assault succeeded, the world would be witness to the massacre of forty thousand Muslims. If the Croats took Krajina, yes, it would be unpleasant, there would be some atrocities, but the Serbs would be driven off their lands, lands infamously obtained by subversion and savage conquest. Like Galbraith, Holbrooke took this position, arguing for an attack.

Retired U.S. Gen. Carl Vuono had, weeks before, held a top-level secret meeting at Brioni Island off the Croatian coast with Croatian Gen. Varimar Cervenko, chief architect of the coming campaign. For months the United States had been secretly aiding the Croats in intelligence collection, using airborne and other platforms including networks of agents to gather information on the movement of Serb troops, penetrating their communications systems, their codes, and also helping the Croats to designate shelling points for any future attack. The NSA Bosnian group was also targeting traffic between the towns of Pale, Hans Pijesak, and general military communications in Belgrade.

In the meantime, squabbling went on in Washington. Advocates for the assault explained, urged, justified, while the opposition rebutted, expressed gloom and misgiving, and shook its head. Finally the chatter died down. The president had made up his mind, and the doubt and second-guessing that plagues any commander's vision suddenly dissolved and everything came clear. Clinton was convinced a determined push could be made. The more he thought of the attack, the more he thought it an excellent card to play. Like Tudjman, he too thought it would force the Serbs to give up lands they had held unlawfully for years.

But the United States needed plausible deniability, and Ambassador

Galbraith had flown in for talks with Tudjman on July 31. The U.S. military attaché, Colonel Herrick, played a key part in helping to coordinate and oversee preparations. "I personally know that Herrick was at times in northern Croatia observing rehearsals of the coming attack," said Galbraith. In August of 2001, Markivca Rubic, the former Croatian army head of counterintelligence, said, "The Pentagon and the CIA were completely supervising Ouja or Storm." He claimed that he'd gotten a message from Herrick saying the United States didn't oppose the operation if Croatia performed it "quickly and cleanly," hopefully completing it within five days. According to a source who attended the Galbraith-Tudjman talks, the United States did not give a green light to the operation. "It was phrased more like, 'We appreciate your efforts to rescue Bihac.'" Said Galbraith, "The main thing is we didn't say to Tudjman, 'Don't do it.'"[6]

In any case, the need for action received a vital shove from an unexpected quarter. Senator Bob Dole, already eyeing a run against Clinton in 1996, had for months been pushing for a lifting of the arms embargo against Bosnia, and he had assembled a veto-proof majority. When the measure passed, Clinton saw he was about to lose control over a fundamental issue of foreign policy. The administration had to go back on the offensive.

The final okay for the operation prior to Storm went from Clinton to Lake and to Defense Secretary Perry to senior Croat officials in Zagreb, including Rubic, Miroslav Tudjman of SIS, and Miro Medimurac, another top SIS intelligence official, who, for a long time, had held extensive consultations with American military and intelligence agencies.[7]

The last steps were taken in feverish haste, and then a nerve-testing silence fell over everything. On August 4, without warning, over 200,000 Croats backed by heavy tanks and heavily armored personnel carriers launched a lightning dawn assault along seven fronts of the Krajina area. The attack was a perfect NATO model. It was highly coordinated, swift, and hit with pulverizing impact. Croat MiG 21s destroyed Serb air defense systems, military communications nodes, command and control installations— savaging anything that stayed in the open to try and fight. Storm kept powering ahead in a fit of fury, rampaging through Serb towns that were scourged. From inside Croatian Gen. Ante Gotovina's military base, U.S. officials were provided with real-time data that was transmitted to the White House Situation Room. The Pentagon was also forwarding to Gotovina data being gathered by the CIA on possible Serb movements.

During the three-day campaign, CIA Predator drones were able to show Serb forces massing for a surprise counterattack, enabling the Croats to surprise it and turn it back. U.S. officials also said that on the opening day of battle, two U.S. electronic warfare aircraft jammed key Krajina Serb positions. Jim Mitchell, a NATO spokesman in Aviano, Italy, acknowledged that two Navy pilots flying Grumann EA-6B Prowler electronic warfare planes were over the battlefield at the request of the U.N. military commander. Serb reports that NATO or U.S. planes bombed an air defense radar were "completely false," according to former U.S. officials. In addition, the U.S. missile sites deployed near Udbina airport assisted the Croats in protecting their forces against any attacks by Serb aircraft that had occurred earlier in the war.

Within hours, a huge tide of forty thousand Bosnian Serbs were flooding east in full spate. In a mere four days, Krajina, a great crescent of land gobbled up by the Serbs in 1991, was swept clean by the Croats, who seized village after village, murdering or expelling their inhabitants and burning their houses to the ground. In the meantime, Bosnian Muslims attacked the Serbs as well. Tens of thousands of refugees were clogging the roads in maddened chaos, clinging to tractors, riding in cars or horse-drawn carts, moving in a panicked flood over the border from Bosnia. Soon the red and white checkerboard Croatian flag was flying over the Krajina capital of Knin. Bodies of Serbs lay in the streets, dozens of houses were afire amid billows of smoke, cars were burning, the streets were strewn with cast-off clothing and blankets. A State Department cable noted that in Knin, food had been set out on the tables of houses, laundry hung from the clotheslines, all the signs of life were there. What was missing were the people.[8]

For Clinton, the gloves had come off. Some essential fury had slipped its leash at last.

The Croatian attack struck with enormous impact, and the morale of the Bosnian Serbs crumpled like a paper cup hit by a sledge hammer. They were stupefied by its immensity, its endless, savage violence, its sustained, severe, disorienting shocks. As Milosevic's delusion of invulnerability eroded before his eyes, the Serb leader began a strange withdrawal inward. Surprise breeds shock, shock breeds disorganization and loss of morale, these breed unnecessary errors and the result is disaster. If the Bosnian Serbs had gotten heavily bombed, so did Milosevic. Never renowned for his physical courage, he began heavily drinking brandy. When he arrived at a meeting with Carl Bildt, Lord Owen's successor as EU envoy to Yugoslavia, and British diplomat David Austin, Milosevic couldn't even speak coherently.[9] Austin said of the bombing, "Milosevic believed it would never happen."

As Milan Milutinovic, Milosevic's foreign minister, conducted the Bildt-Austin meeting, Milosevic just sat there, on the verge of coma, awakening now and then to mumble, "You've got to stop the bombing. It's intolerable," before drifting off again.

As Bildt said, Milosevic was "obsessed—distracted by the thought that the bombing was going to destroy everything, and he was in no condition to discuss anything else." Milosevic had come to believe in the myth that he had created, and now NATO bombs were destroying it, along with his carefully amassed power, and he was numbing his pain of defeat with more fruit brandy. There was reason for dismay. NATO by then had destroyed the Bosnian Serbs' military and communications infrastructure in only two weeks. On September 12, the Serbs got a greater shock when missile attacks destroyed the bridges across the Drina River, the route over which had come the weapons from Belgrade in the past. On September 13, Milosevic asked for an immediate cease-fire followed by an international peace conference, but Holbrooke refused in order for the Croats and Bosnians to gain more ground.

In truth, the Bosnian Serbs had suffered a terrible defeat. Their cities were in ruins, their homes pillaged. Everything left behind was blackened, burned, sodden, or otherwise ruined. A total of 200,000 Serb refugees were pushing into Serbia from Croatia after the collapse of Krajina, and they were not at all welcome. Yet on they came. Even Mladic, the brutal, swaggering, fearless Mladic, had gone to pieces as well, sending a long, pathetic rambling fax to the United Nations about how poor little Serbia was being ill-used once again, and attempting to depict the bombings as worse than Hitler's bombing raids on Belgrade in 1941. The American officials who read the fax thought him seriously unhinged.

And in the meantime, the Croat Muslim forces were sweeping ahead in an irresistible tide, approaching within striking distance of Banja Luka, a city that Milosevic had eyed as an alternative power base. Senior American policymakers saw the situation with a blinding clarity. If Banja Luka fell to the Croats, Milosevic might possibly be ousted from power at home, and the United States would have no central point of Serbian authority with which to deal. In Sarajevo, President Izetbegovic and his generals wanted to push the Serbs until they broke in two. Holbrooke turned stony and stubborn. He was frank with Izetbegovic—he warned the Bosnian leader that he was "shooting craps" with Bosnia's destiny, and it couldn't be allowed. Izetegovic acknowledged that without Washington support his military forces would suffer. Under American help, they had developed a genuine military infrastructure and their combat tactics were becoming more effective. Izetbegovic agreed to stop, but only if the siege of Sarajevo was lifted, and its water, gas, and electricity were turned on. It was done. After a seige of 1,200 days and twelve thousand dead, Sarajevo was free.

To American policymakers, a central tenet was that Milosevic had to be kept in power to end the Bosnian war. This conviction blinded them to the future, and no one seemed to foresee how many people would be killed or uprooted when the Serb leader later turned on his Muslims in Kosovo. The attitude was "one thing at a time," said former U.S. diplomat Louis Sell.

So American pressure had not allowed Banja Luka to fall. There were CIA estimates that if Banja Luka fell, the defeat might draw the Yugoslav National Army into the war, and Holbrooke had warned Tudjman off. Milosevic was now anxious to get talking. When the Serb suggested that Holbrooke meet with Mladic and Karadzic, Holbrooke agreed, but only on the strict condition that they "cut through the shit" and have a real discussion. There were to be no "historical lectures, no bullshit." When the meeting occurred, Mladic blundered immediately. He began whining again about poor, brave, misused little Serbia, and Holbrooke got up and left, saying to Milosevic, "Mr. President, you told us we were here to be serious. If we're not serious, we have to go."

What impressed Milosevic most about this was that Holbrooke seemed to have his own charter of authority that allowed him scope of action and independence of decision. Milosevic believed that, in ways, Holbrooke was as ruthless and authoritarian as he was.

Holbrooke was never one to waste time. In the offensive, he sensed a way to gain advantages for upcoming talks. In his memoir, *To End a War,* he speaks of talking with Tudjman, telling him his attack was of great value for speeding up the prospect of negotiations, and then directing Tudjman to take certain key Serb towns such as Most, Prijedor, and Bosanki, all important towns that had become worldwide symbols of ethnic cleansing. The CIA and other U.S. intelligence services had greatly feared that the regular Serb army might reenter the war, and when a member of Holbrooke's team urged Tudjman to halt his offensive, one of Holbrooke's most polished and toughest team members slid his boss a note across the table, "Dick, we 'hired' these guys to be our junkyard dogs because we were desperate. We need to try and 'control' them. But this is no time to get squeamish about things. This is the first time the Serb wave has been reversed. That is essential for us to get stability, so we can get out."[10] Holbrooke agreed. He told Croatian defense minister Susak, "Nothing we said today should be construed to mean that we want you to stop the rest of the offensive, other than Banja Luka. Speed is important. We can't say so publicly, but please take Sanski, Most, Prijedor and Bosanski Novi. And do it quickly before the Serbs regroup."[11]

This was all part of Holbrooke's belief that positions held by friendly forces would prove to be the most powerful determinant when it came to discussing territorial divisions with your enemy at the conference table.

The new unleashed aggressiveness of Clinton would get a further unexpected gift that would end the war in Bosnia. On August 25, 1995, the Serbs fired a shell into the Markala open air marketplace on Marshal Tito Boulevard. The shells were 120 millimeter, and they hit the place where sixty-nine people had died in 1994; this time they dismembered thirty-seven Sarajevans. According to writer Barbara Demick, five people in the immediate neighborhood were killed. "Mremia Ziga, 42, was feeling ill and left work to see the doctor. Heading down Marshal Tito at midday, she walked directly into the trajectory of an incoming 120-mm mortar shell" and was instantly killed. Adnan Ibrahimagic, twenty-seven, was supposed to have left town the previous Friday to meet his mother in Austria but hadn't gone. That noon he was heading for a takeout lunch when the shell landed. His death photo showed his "skinny, teen-age body, dead, slumped over a railing outside the [lunch] shop. His friend, 16, Dario Glouhi, had both his legs amputated in an attempt by surgeons to save his life. He died anyway."

Clinton heard of the massacre with dark fury and quickly signed the "lethal finding" for the CIA to take the lead in toppling Milosevic, while notifying the appropriate congressional committees.

Holbrooke grasped instantly what the consequences of this Serb callous recklessness were. "The brutal stupidity of the Bosnian Serbs had given us an unexpected last chance to do what should have been done three years earlier. I told Strobe Talbott [the acting secretary of state] to start NATO air strikes against the Bosnian Serbs—not minor retaliatory 'pinpricks' but a serious, and if possible, sustained air campaign."[12] He was in luck—United Nations or British or other officials who had opposed the use of force were on vacation or unavailable. U.N. secretary-general Boutros Boutros-Ghali, who had opposed all air strikes, happened to be on a flight when the bombing began and was unreachable. His stand-in, Kofi Annan, found himself in charge and asked U.N. officials to temporarily relinquish their authority to veto air strikes in Bosnia. They did. Holbrooke would later say that Annan's action landed him Boutros-Ghali's job.

So the NATO air strikes began. The huge assault was called Operation Deliberate Force and it not only moved the peace talks forward, it did much to redraw the map that would be under discussion. For two weeks beginning at the end of August, NATO pilots flew 3,500 sorties, taking out Serb antiaircraft batteries, radar sites, ammunition depots, command bunkers, and key bridges. As the Croatians continued their attacks, the NATO missions almost acted as a kind of inadvertent air cover that would end up changing the balance of power in Bosnia. By the end of September, the Serbs had lost enough territory to bring their holdings from 70 percent of Croatia to less than half.

Now the hawks like Galbraith, Albright, General Wesley Clark and others heard encouragement instead of caution. Clinton was on vacation in Wyoming when the strikes began, and when he heard, he closed his eyes, whispering with passion, "Whhhoooopppeee." It was full of relief and vindictive satisfaction. Waiting for the strikes to begin had been a time of frightful nervous tension. It was a solemn moment as well: U.S. diplomats had died in Bosnia, and 200,000 innocent people had perished there. For months Clinton's foreign policy team had not appeared to be of much advantage to the world, and throughout that time, the president had schemed, labored, and doggedly persisted in trying to bring this moment about, the burden weighing on him with an oppression of almost unbearable responsibility. So now it was done, and a fierce, exulting joy reigned along with the relief. When Lake called to brief him, Clinton said in a metallic voice, "Hit them hard." Said a former staffer, "Clinton was like a guy who had won a close game. He had finally arrived at a place it had cost him such suffering to reach." *The Washington Post* on August 30, 1995, ran the headline: "A Joyous Cry of 'At Last.'"

Holbrooke with his indomitable drive had always considered bombing as part of a negotiating strategy. But for all the administration inside talk of reining in the offensive and wanting Galbraith to deliver a message ordering the Croats to halt advances, Holbrooke and his team never received that instruction officially, and Galbraith urged Tudjman to press ahead. Finally, the assaults ground to a halt, and the diplomatic sparring that would end the war in Dayton had begun.

19

"THE STRIFE OF WILLS, THE WARS OF PRECEDENCE"

—Lucretius

They came in on October 31, 1995. A cold wind and rain were whipping the airfield at Dayton, Ohio. Bosnian president Alija Izetbegovic's mood on arrival was apprehensive, nervous, and sour. When asked, he would say only that he was seeking "peace with justice" in a glum way that showed he was very doubtful of getting it. The Croatian president, Franjo Tudjman, the military victor, proved to be a grandiose boor, full of vacuous swagger. He was in fact despotic and unscrupulous, his character little better than that of Yugoslav president Slobodan Milosevic, who was heading the Bosnian Serbs. Tudjman would die in 1999, but had he lived, he would have been put on trial for war crimes for having set up a network of concentration camps and for the murder and expulsion of Serbs in Operation Storm. The Bosnian Izetbegovic, swarthy and diminutive, a militant Islamic, couldn't stand to set eyes on Tudjman, even though they would be negotiating partners.

Of the three groups arriving, the Serbs were perhaps the most divided. By August 30, the day before the preparatory U.S. team arrived in Belgrade, Milosevic had already gained complete authority to negotiate on behalf of the Bosnian Serbs—a strange choice really, since neither Serbia nor Montenegro, the remaining Yugoslav republics, was at war in Bosnia. In late August, Milosevic had summoned Karadzic and Mladic to Belgrade to bludgeon new concessions from the glum, defeated, abject men. Milosevic insisted on having full power to delegate and conclude a peace, and said that if he didn't get it Serbia would impose a total, ruinous blockade on Republika Srpska. "It's crucial to stop the war immediately," he announced.

He even used the prestige of the Serbian Orthodox patriarch to extort authority from Karadzic. That Milosevic emerged victorious is not surprising, given his tone and methods. During the previous May when Mladic had taken four hundred U.N. peacekeepers hostage, and NATO responded with air strikes, Milosevic announced that the taking of hostages had "humiliated all Serbs," and said he was dispatching the head of his secret police, Jovica Stanisic, to Bosnia to get the hostages released, telling Ivor Roberts, the British chargé d'affaires in Belgrade, that Stanisic would tell Karadzic to release the hostages and "that I will have him killed if he doesn't. . . . He knows I can do it."[1] One Bosnian Serb leader had called the threat of a blockade a dagger in the back, but agreed to cede authority nonetheless.

The site of the talks had been chosen with care. One lesson learned in putting together the Croat-Muslim Federation had been that the parties had to be kept together, even if in separate rooms, until they were able to agree. Charles Redman, the special envoy who had worked with Galbraith, had for days gone doggedly between one room to another, bearing draft after new draft until the Croats and Muslims had signed. So the site was key. The delegates must inhabit a location that had limited access to the media. No one would make significant progress if every time the talks ran aground, some delegation could rush crying its woes to the television networks. That must not happen. Holbrooke was determined to keep a tight grasp over the proceedings.

A Holbrooke aide, Tom Donilon, was assigned to find the right place for the talks called "Site X." Patrick Kennedy, the assistant secretary of state for administrative affairs, did the grunt work, sending his aide, Ken Messner, to hear out Holbrooke's requirements. Holbrooke was obsessive. "Every detail mattered," Messner said. Nine delegations were coming, the five Contact Group countries, the EU representative Carl Bildt, the world's press, the idly curious.

Sharp eyes ran down lists of possible places: Camp David was quickly rejected as too close to Washington, too much identified with the 1978 Middle East peace talks, to be a serious candidate. Many other places were looked at, weighed, probed, then rejected. Finally, Kennedy suggested that a military base would be best, and the Air Force offered Wright-Patterson in Dayton, Ohio. Dayton was famous as the birthplace of the Wright brothers. But for Holbrooke, Dayton was not just a place, it was a living embodiment of what the Balkans could become. Dayton, Ohio, was in the American heartland, but the state's people were drawn from every part of Central and Southeastern Europe. In fact, there were more Serbs and Hungarians living in nearby Cleveland than any other American city, and in Dayton, the different ethnic groups lived in peace, their competition restricted "to softball games, church rivalries, and the occasional barroom fight," as Holbrooke put it.[2] Perhaps it would dawn on some of the Balkan visitors that what had been done in Dayton could perhaps be done in Bosnia.

In the meantime, Rosemary Pauli, a Kennedy aide, drove around the sprawling base, which contained 23,000 military personnel. They found it had five visiting officers quarters grouped around a central parking lot. With some work, it would be perfect.

As teams spread out across Europe to gain support, Holbrooke knew that the coming talks must make decisions on as many issues as possible, including the details required to implement the agreement. As the time for the talks crept closer, NATO was still attacking Serb forces in Bosnia, but the fighting on the ground was beginning to wind down. On October 11, for the first time in years, a cease-fire fell into place, and in Sarajevo, lights began to flicker on in the city, ending a siege in which twelve thousand had died. Clinton wanted a final decision on Wright-Patterson, and Holbrooke, taking a weekend on Long Island, tried to call him by cell phone. The White House switchboard forbids such calls, so Holbrooke went into a service station phone booth. When Clinton answered, he said, "Is this the envoy to *The Washington Post?*" referring to a recent praising article. "How did you get such an article?" Clinton continued. "I can't get them to say anything nice about me."[3]

But the decision had been made. Dayton was to be the place.

The essentials of what would be the Dayton Accords had already been put in place by September 9 after a hectic flurry of U.S. diplomacy coaxed Milosevic and Izetbegovic into agreeing on basic principles, later ratified at a meeting of the foreign ministers in Geneva. The strategy had been put together by Lake, with the help of Sandy Vershbow and Bosnia expert Nelson Drew. Albright and Lake had always suffered from a certain mutual, competitive distrust, but that had thankfully been laid aside, and her ideas had proved valuable to the final arrangements. Under terms of the new principles, Bosnia would be divided into two "entities," one belonging to the Croat-Muslim Federation, comprising 51 percent of the land, while the Bosnian Serb Republic would get the remaining 49 percent and retain its name of Republika Srpska. In other words, the Bosnian Muslims would have to swallow the disagreeable necessity of having a Serb entity within Bosnia that would retain a special relationship with Belgrade. This was why Izetbegovic was plunged into gloom. His stubbornly held dream of a "unitary" Bosnian Muslim state was dead on arrival.

There were other issues, the chief ones being the fate of Sarajevo and the enclave of Gorazde. Under attack by Serbs, Gorazde had held out, and since the Bosnian Muslims had paid for it by a sea of blood, they were intent on keeping it, demanding it be linked by secure corridor to the capital of Sarajevo. The Bosnian Serbs refused, so clearly the climb to any agreement on such touchy matters would prove to be a steep road. And of all people, Milosevic would help the Americans reach the top.

The Americans certainly knew the stakes. Obtaining a peace agreement on Bosnia could mean Clinton's reelection, and Clinton by now had a clear insight into the character of the Serb leadership. Holbrooke had defined the war in Bosnia as a "human rights war," and Clinton shared that assessment. The record of Milosevic was one of injury, oppression, and exploitation. In pursuit of his dream of a Greater Serbia, he had started four wars that had perhaps killed 250,000 Croats and Bosnian Muslims. It was the cruelty of the Serb behavior that most disturbed Clinton and his advisors. Milosevic not only conquered anyone who opposed him, but afterward he hated and despised those he had defeated, eager to deprive them not only of every right and protection but of every mercy as well. It was therefore ironic that Milosevic's authority was essential to the success of America in the talks, yet cold, dispassionate analysis left no other choice. "What we were looking for was someone who could speak with a single voice for all the Serbs," said a former senior advisor. Radovan Karadzic, an indicted war criminal and president of the Republika Srpska, was out of the question, as was Mladic. "We could never agree on anything with them," the former official said. Both Mladic and Karadzic would have been subject to arrest if they set a foot on U.S. soil.

Of course, Milosevic was a war criminal too, but this was suppressed. For years, U.S. intelligence intercepts had been collected on Serb government links between Belgrade and Pale, the Bosnian Serb capital and home of Karadzic. These intercepts showed that Milosevic had from the first given major, substantial support to the Bosnian Serbs in their ethnic cleansing. He had known ahead of time of their goals, means, methods, and results. If it had chosen, the Clinton administration could have had Milosevic indicted for war crimes on the basis of what the intercepts contained. (They were later used in the Serb's 2001 indictment at The Hague.) During a White House meeting between U.N. negotiator Carl Bildt and Vice President Gore before the talks, Gore had read portions of the intercepts to Bildt, who later said he could not recall the meeting. (Gore could not be reached for comment.) But former U.S. intelligence officials confirmed the story, and Larry Johnson, a former CIA official, commented that the way the intercepts were suppressed "is hardly a good use of intelligence."[4] Yet there was no choice. To keep the peace process alive, the Clinton administration would use Milosevic, squeeze him like a rind, then toss him away.

Clinton, mixed with confidence in his ability to prevail in the confrontation, was about to play a ruthless game. Clinton would do to Milosevic as he had been done by. At Dayton, the United States was going to pursue peace by means of perfidy. Milosevic, the deceiver, was going to be deceived. It was not the time for policymakers to pride themselves on some false moral delicacy. Any means would be employed to reach agreement and prevent Bosnia from descending again into chaos and savagery.

Clinton had long before settled on Holbrooke as ideal for the job of presiding over the talks. In a farewell toast to Holbrooke at a Washington dinner five years later, Clinton said, "After all, everyone in the Balkans is crazy and everyone has a giant ego. Who else could you send?"

As the talks approached, the American had more and more become a single-track embodiment of will, a man impatient, fiery, and indefatigable. Holbrooke's unrelenting tenacity of ambition by now had become as vast as Oliver Cromwell's and was just as merciless. He had always done laborious and thankless jobs conscientiously, he had never defaulted on an opportunity offered, and every exertion of his adult life had brought him to this culminating pinnacle.

He knew the obstacles. The prevailing mood among the arriving parties would be one of prejudiced mistrust and rancid, unremitting animosity. After all, they had all been at war with each other and had been or still remained enemies. Within recent years, Serbs had attacked and fought Croats, Croats had attacked and fought Muslims and vice versa, then both the latter had joined together to fight against the Bosnian Serbs. All the negotiating groups had been involved in and tainted by bloody and savage contests in which all pretense, every noble illusion of words, forms, and institutions had been stripped away to reveal human nature at its most vile and shameless. Not only would there would be the falsity, the lordliness, and overweening conceit of Milosevic to put up with, but each group would arrive with its own obsessions with ethnic or national prestige, its own narrow mania for preserving or acquiring territory, its own preoccupation with coming out on top at the talks at all costs. To the Bosnian president, the Serbs were mere animals. For their part, the Bosnian Serbs detested everyone, especially the Croats, but reserving for Muslims a profound and embittered abhorrence, which the Muslims returned in kind. All the participants would squabble, stall, balk, obstruct, bicker, and they would turn the talks into a shambles unless some force swept down on them to hammer, punish, bully, and coerce them without cease. To Holbrooke, it was essential to have the delegates in one place, keep them under control, and force them to remain in daily contact with each other until they came up with results, even if agreement was only a simple yielding to mere exasperated weariness. If Holbrooke was certain of anything, it was that he would somehow measure up to the greatness of the event. He would be the hammer, never letting up. It was perfect for him; he didn't tire, he was invulnerable to strain, he had an incredible power of focus. He could outlast anyone.

Throughout the Dayton negotiations, Milosevic put on a prize performance. Now safely ensconced at Wright-Patterson, he regained his bravado. He was upbeat and confident, full of a sense of possibility, seeming to bask delightedly in the prominence bestowed on him by the event. Milosevic acted as if he had confidence to burn. Yes, he believed that the talks would succeed, trumpeting pompously, "We attach the greatest importance to [the] peace initiative of the United States."[5] When the first day ended and the other exhausted delegates went to bed, Milosevic felt frisky and so Holbrooke and Warren Christopher took him to Packy's Sports Bar, an officers restaurant on the base furnished with huge pictures of Bob Hope, each table having its own small speaker, while four giant TV screens were turned to CNN and ESPN and other all-sports channels. As Christopher watched Milosevic turn on the charm, he later observed that had Slobo been born in a different place and given a different education, he would have been "a successful politician in a democratic system."

But if Milosevic thought his charm, his swagger, his ability to intimidate were going to carry the day, if he thought he was going to drive a hard bargain and go away a winner, he was wrong. At home his grip on the tiller of power was beginning to slip, and he was psychologically damaged and off balance from the defeat in Krajina. The huge new waves of Bosnian Serb refugees arriving in Serbia in an endless, nightmarish, slow-moving river of vehicles: tractors, cars, horse-drawn carts, with soldiers, the elderly, families with young children, all mingled together, glum and dispirited, was acting to depress his popular standing even further. At the sight of the refugees, humiliated outrage had swept Serbia. Not only that, but his public knew that under his leadership, Yugoslavia had gone from a country on the brink of the First World to a place in the Third. Plus Milosevic had lost much of his hold not only of his professional middle class, but even among his military, police, and security establishments. In Belgrade he had been struck and appalled by the graffiti to be seen scrawled on the city's walls:

"Pair off in twos: dead, hungry, dead, hungry." At a soccer match, fifty thousand fans had chanted, "Slobo, you have betrayed Krajina," and Radoje Kontic, the Yugolsav deputy prime minister, began drinking heavily after his children told him they "pissed on his premiership."

That the Americans were not going to baby the Serb leader was quickly made clear. Back in Belgrade, they had rudely put him in his place. No longer were the Serb's assertions to be respectfully taken at face value. Milosevic had always maintained that the Bosnian Serb Republika Srpska was independent of Belgrade and militarily self-sufficient. But what was clear was that for months Serbia supplied tanks, artillery, heavy weapons, technical recommendations, soldiers, integrated air defense systems, supply flights, and financial assistance to the Bosnian Serbs. Also, Milosevic was laundering funds for this operation via the Austrian Central Bank, banks in Cyprus, and a number of banks in Moscow. U.S. intelligence officials complained that if a financial embargo had been in place, Milosevic could not even have afforded to pay the salaries of Bosnian Serb VJS officers.

All this was well known to U.S. intelligence and it was time to let Milosevic know that the United States knew. So while in Belgrade, Holbrooke asked the CIA to prepare a "sanitized" file that laid out the ties between a butcher and terrorist named Arkan and the Yugoslav army. Holbrooke raised the subject on October 17 and again at a lunch two days later. Milosevic acted with his typical brass. When confronted with Shattuck's information, he blithely denied it. "No, no, no," said Milosevic. "Your information is wrong." Milosevic calmly went on eating. He had refused to touch the document, as if it were a poisonous snake coiled on the table. When the meal ended, a Serb official went up to Jim Pardew, a director of the Balkan Task Force at the Pentagon, and told him he had left his paper on the table. "No, I didn't forget it," Pardew said. "It belongs to President Milosevic."

The Dayton talks began on November 1. Holbrooke and others were dismayed to find that because the participants of the European Union held so many contradicting and divergent views it could not negotiate as a single entity, even while its fellow members undermined and hamstrung the group's leader, Carl Bildt. That was one problem. Another was the Bosnian Serbs, who had suddenly turned truculent, demanding that Sarajevo be divided like Cold War Berlin, and that the city's airport be moved so that Serb settlers could occupy the land instead. The Americans listened to this with mounting incredulity, and then, after declaring that such views were totally unrealistic, had simply walked out. From then on, no one talked to the Bosnian Serbs. "Pay no attention to those guys," Milosevic said to Holbrooke. "I'll make sure they accept the final agreement."[6]

The degree to which Milosevic treated his former proxies, the Bosnian Serbs, with scathing, contemptuous disdain startled and puzzled the Americans. But Milosevic had always considered people disposable, as mere objects and raw material, but even given that, the British and Americans had been shocked at the corrosive rudeness they saw on display. At one point, Holbrooke asked him if his friends, the Bosnian Serbs, would agree to a point, and Milosevic interrupted, "They are not my friends. They are not my colleagues. They are shit."

Milosevic aggressively ignored the Bosnian Serbs and spent all his time with the president of Montenegro, Momir Bulatovic. When, in desperation, one Bosnian Serb leader began bombarding Holbrooke with angry letters demanding to know what was happening, Holbrooke showed Milosevic the letters, and the Serb took each one, crumpled it up without reading it, and threw it in the trash.

It was the British diplomat David Austin, who had been in earlier negotiating sessions in Belgrade, some lasting ten hours or more, who was stunned by the extent of Milosevic's power. "Serbia was run by one man," Austin said. "Milosevic gave the impression he had nothing to do but talk to us. He had an intellectual arrogance that nobody else in the country could do it. He knew the subject intimately. He took decisions, made concessions, and he never had to consult with anybody. He just did it. This was a very odd way to operate." Austin also observed, "He liked a good argument and discussion and seemed to be enjoying it. He was good at it, although quite often he would marshal facts which were not facts at all."[7]

Having lifted the siege of Sarajevo, Milosevic continued to spend highly jovial nights drinking scotch at Packy's, and in spite of downing a great many drinks, the Serb still remained able to render his own rather touching and acceptable rendition of "Tenderly" and other Tin Pan Alley tunes and flirt with his favorite waitress, Vicky. Izetbegovic only sat unsmiling, listening sullenly while the Serb sang.

But when it came to business, Milosevic was no fumbler. Like Stalin, he possessed a range of formidable mental talents: the ability to see through veneers, his rapid assimilation of the facts, his informed, shrewd persistent attention to detail. He liked to argue from the facts, and if the facts were incomplete or not in his favor, he fabricated and marshaled what appeared to be facts and fought with those. He seldom used a prepared text and never turned to an aide to refresh his memory. He was extraordinarily talented in spotting the weakness in a statement or argument. That plus the unbridled ferocity of his will, his ability to trample and brutalize the sensitivities of another in the pursuit of his goal, also gave him a significant advantage. Yet when he wanted something, Milosevic could be pleasant and accommodating. He would speak in an authoritative baritone, and his personality had a genuine aura of authority that arrested the attention. Like Holbrooke, his capacity for retention of information verged on the astounding, reacting quickly, relevantly, able to fish up the obscure, overlooked, demolishing fact with ease. He had a mind on which nothing was lost.

Gen. Wesley Clark said of him, "I've spent hundreds of hours dealing with Milosevic. He's a very shrewd, forceful, tough, wily negotiator. He's not afraid to make bold decisions. . . . He plays by his own rules, and he has his own standards of rationality."[8]

Like Dwight Eisenhower, Milosevic knew how to act his anger, knew when to stage a tantrum, when to jump up, tear up papers, or stalk out of a room,[9] and he was always looking for weaknesses in people that would off-set his own. Milosevic was still Milosevic, testing people when he could, liking to intimidate them when the occasion arose. Holbrooke learned to go on the attack at the first signs of this. The more outspoken Milosevic became, the harsher Holbrooke was and the less fastidious were his methods. He would use the haughtily ironical, the sarcastic, the sly, the base, the quixotic, brutal clarity, combined with unexpected shifts of approaches and unexpected lines of argument, to best his opponent, and Milosevic was aware he was encountering an opponent of a new and formidable caliber.

Yet Milosevic still retained in his hand some key cards, and he would play them with great skill. Holbrooke's weakness was his urgent need for success. Milosevic's weakness was his necessity to get sanctions lifted. Who would weaken first? The issues kept coming: Sarajevo, disputes over bits of territory, new elections, a new Muslim-Croat Federation agreement, this odd bit of the map versus that. No side ever accepted the offer that came from the other without first trying to change it. In one instance, the Bosnian Muslims resorted to flagrant deceit, agreeing to a change on the map that gave away not their territory but Croatian land to the Serbs. As the days wore away, frustration and anxiety began to build in Holbrooke. A negotiation could lose its focus and momentum, the urge to obtain agreement could run out of gas. He tried everything he knew, every ruse, every trick, every ploy, yet he could never bring the great moment nearer, could never make it happen. The talks were fast reaching the point where they had to go forward or go under.

It was Milosevic who broke the deadlock. He began to act like a Mafia godfather, eager in his generosity to dispense gifts to the deserving. At one point the Bosnian Serbs were squabbling about Sarajevo, they wanted each of the three parties to have a sector like Cold War Berlin (a thing that Clinton had urged Holbrooke to avoid), when to everyone's stunned surprise and without Milosevic having consulted the Bosnian Serb leader, Karadzic, Milosevic suddenly gave the whole city and its suburbs to the Bosnian Muslims, forcing the evacuation of 100,000 more Serbs from its suburbs. He said to Holbrooke, "Izetbegovic has earned Sarajevo by not abandoning it. He's one tough guy. It's his."[10]

These words were the most astonishing and unexpected of the conference and stunned Holbrooke and another negotiator, State Department official Chris Hill. But the Serb's bait hid a clever hook. Milosevic was angling to retain the vital center of the city. His gift did not quite unify Sarajevo but the reverse, a prime Serb war aim. When his ploy was pointed out to him, Milosevic exploded at Hill in a rage: "I'm giving you Sarajevo, and you talk such bullshit!"[11]

But he later gave in, removing this obstacle while announcing to his former victims, "You deserve Sarajevo because you fought for it and those cowards killed you from the hills," an amazing way to speak of his own proxies who had acted at his direction.

At one point, Milosevic stumbled into trouble. By mistake, he had given concessions that totaled 55 percent for the federation instead of the agreed on 51 percent. When this was pointed out by the U.S. Defense Mapping Agency, Milosevic flew into a rage. "You tricked me," he said to Holbrooke and Christopher. "How can I trust you?" he said angrily. "This is my bottom line with the Republika Srpska. We agreed to this before Dayton."[12]

Days dragged on. The problem of Gorazde was solved when the enclave was linked by secure corridor to Sarajevo. Agreements were reached on other areas. Yet as more time passed, the Bosnian Muslims grew obstinate, in that state of mind where the will crowds out the ability to make sound judgments. Izetbegovic was sullen, unreasonable, sulky. He exasperated Christopher so much that the usually unflappable lawyer lost his temper. It was only a few days later that Holbrooke's moment of supreme crisis approached. He was determined to carry the talks to successful completion, but the unrealistic, bickering Bosnian Muslims were not about to budge, and immense pressure would have to be exerted on them or the talks were doomed. A mood of desperate resolution settled on Holbrooke. He took U.S. diplomat Chris Hill aside, saying, "This next meeting may be the most important of [your career]. We can get this agreement or we can lose it. Forget Washington. It's entirely in our hands. We just go into the meeting with an absolute determination to succeed."

By then it was clear that Milosevic and Tudjman were going to sign an agreement whether Izetbegovic did or not. Even the Bosnian seemed aware of this. So when the senior Americans entered the room to meet with the three main Bosnians, it was time to let the dice fly high. The Americans had made proposals, amendments, retractions, counterproposals, come up with new suggestions, introduced fresh compromises, yet met with no response. Time had about run out, and America required an immediate answer about an agreement. This was as good a deal as Izetbegovic was going to get and Holbrooke was sick of this state of paralyzed bafflement. Izetbegovic had to make up his mind. A long, agonizing pause began. No one spoke. It was to be now or never. Decide. Finally, Izetbegovic said, "It is not a just peace." He paused. Everyone held their breath. Time passed. Then he at last said wearily, "But my people need peace."

President Clinton made the announcement from the Rose Garden. "After nearly four years, 250,000 killed, two million refugees, and atrocities that have appalled people all over the world, the people of Bosnia finally have a chance to turn from the horror of war to the promise of peace."

Still, Milosevic at Dayton didn't do badly at all. If he was defeated, he wasn't forced from the field. Throughout the whole Dayton gathering, Milosevic had his mind set on a single object—the lifting of sanctions. Six days into the talks, he suddenly asked for 23,000 tons of heating oil and for the resumption of national gas supplies. It was a political necessity—if he were to sell out the Bosnian Serbs, the benefits for his own immediate public had to be solid and spectacular. It was a testament to his political skill that he convinced people who hated him like Izetbegovic and Bosnia's prime minister, Haris Silajdzic, to be his allies. So the heat went on in Belgrade, just as it had in Sarajevo.

At the close of the talks, Clinton had mechanically praised Milosevic's "contribution to peace" and, commending him as a guarantor of the agreement, had used his influence to ensure the U.N. sanctions were lifted. By November 2 they had been, and the EU companies rushed in hordes to Belgrade to do business.

The Serb leader's handling of Bosnia was a notable display of his devious cunning. By giving away Sarajevo, he was not being generous but taking pains to ensure that Bosnia would never live again as a multiethnic country. One U.S. source said the Bosnia settlement was done to make sure Dayton wouldn't work because to function you had to have an integrated capital of Serbs and Bosnians, and Milosevic had placed them apart forever. Serbs would not live in a Sarajevo dominated by Muslims. Plus the Bosnian Serb Republic, an entity created by infamous means, would retain its own armies, its police forces, its own courts and political structures. It would even keep its Serb name of the Republika Srpska, an enduring sore in the side of the Bosnian Muslims.

For veteran diplomat Louis Sell, it was amazing to watch the "two-tiered game" that Milosevic played. He had appointed Mladic as a general, had authorized the massacre of perhaps 100,000 Bosnian Muslims; he had supplied the special police units, put bridges over the Drina to bring in heavy weapons, and in general been behind so much of the carnage; it was incredible that he was still viewed as the one force that could be depended on to bring peace to the region. U.S. diplomat Sell had likened it to hiring the arsonist who had set numerous fires to be the person to come and put them out.

There was still some sputtering going on. Croatia was interested in eastern Slavonia, and there was some pulling back and forth over minor points on the map, but the people most swindled by the agreement had been the Bosnian Muslims. Yet what could be done? If they got much less than they felt they deserved, the United States would make it up by modernizing their army and by providing aid for the reconstruction of their country. But to Izetbegovic, economic aid meant nothing real or rewarding. Gone forever was his dream of a unified Muslim state.

Milosevic remained as full of sly cunning as ever.

Not until the talks had almost closed did Milosevic show the Bosnian Serbs the maps that gave away Sarajevo. They angrily refused to sign. No matter. Milosevic told the Americans not to worry. And the Bosnian Serbs got on the airplane looking bedraggled, crushed, and defeated, but once back in Belgrade, Milosevic summoned Karadzic to a meeting at a villa and obtained his initials on the agreement by threatening to arrest him and the rest of the Pale leadership if they didn't go along.

So Holbrooke had won. The war had ended. Or, as he would later ask, had he really brought peace or merely the absence of war? In any case, the settlement demanded that twenty thousand American peacekeepers be deployed. Any mention of U.S. ground troops set the Pentagon, and most of the administration, to sucking their knuckles in anxiety. But Clinton had hardened. He was about to enter a reelection campaign, and the polls showed 70 percent of Americans against such deployment. But Clinton was through being advised. He was through with his fear of being unpopular with his public. There were worse things, and, in what was a tremendous decision of personal courage, he agreed to deployment.

No one remembered Valéry's wise saying that the "only treaties that ought to count are those which would affect settlement between ulterior motives," and in the jubilant triumph of the hour, no one saw in far-off Kosovo a silent gathering together of the fates.[13]

PART TWO

FORWARD TO BAGHDAD

20

"HUMAN, ALL TOO HUMAN"

—Friedrich Nietzsche

Like President Bill Clinton's crises in Haiti or Somalia, the American duel with Saddam Hussein was something the young president had inherited from the Bush administration. Unfortunately, like Bosnia, the Bush administration had framed no coherent plan for dealing with Iraq once the Persian Gulf War ended, so the allied/U.S. victory over Saddam fizzled out in a huge, incoherent muddle, plagued with factors that hadn't been understood, measures that hadn't been taken, calculations that had been mistakenly made, along with serious issues no one had quite foreseen.

First of all, the ground war had ended prematurely in February 1991, mainly for reasons of public relations. The stated goal of the campaign was the immediate and unconditional withdrawal of Iraqi forces from Kuwait, but U.S. commanders had been told that the destruction of the Iraqi forces, especially the eight divisions of Saddam's elite Republican Guard, had been the real goal of their ground campaign.

The war ended before its key military objectives had been reached. The point of throwing a punch in war is that you put behind it everything you have. A chief goal had been to destroy the Republican Guard, but the pulverizing, roundhouse punch from the enveloping allied army in the west landed on empty air, a fact that some U.S. officials are still defensive about to this day. "We never planned to destroy the Guard," a former White House official said, asking not to be named. A former senior U.S. intelligence official agreed. "The policy was to get rid of Saddam, not his army. The center of gravity for Iraq was the Republican Guard. It had to remain in being—to be left with sufficient forces to be able to prevent chaos and ensure the orderly functioning of the state. Otherwise, we would have seen the looting, the burning of ministries, the complete breakdown of law and order that we saw in 2003."

But many, including retired Marine Corps Lt. Gen. Bernard Trainor, think this lame and idiotic. "In my view a golden opportunity was missed. The Iraqis were over a barrel and vulnerable. The United States could have presented the Iraqi generals an offer they couldn't refuse—depose Saddam and we will recognize the interim government of Iraq, or we will continue and annihilate your army." Thus Saddam would be gone, but Iraq would "still be a bulwark against Iran and perhaps open to reform."[1]

The expectation of the White House was that the defeat of Iraq would topple Saddam. Defeat always disintegrates, slashing like a knife through old bonds, ties, and loyalties, and in February of 1991, with his defeated, panicked forces hungry, thirsty, and exhausted, Saddam may have thought his wartime travails had ended (after all, he had survived), but his rule was actually hovering on the verge of collapse. As the soundly whipped Iraqi troops streamed home, they were in a dangerous mood, filled with bitter rage at Saddam for having led them into a fight and then allowed them to be "chased like rats" out of Kuwait, in the words of one Iraqi officer. Soon, it became clear a great convulsion was under way in the country. Shia cities in the south toppled like dominoes. The floodgates of revolt had opened; the rampaging currents were carrying everything before them. Soon, Saddam had lost control of fourteen of Iraq's eighteen provinces. With his eyes riveted on the spreading disorders in the south, Saddam underwent a fresh shock: the Kurds had risen to the north. But thanks to incompetent surrender negotiations conducted by the allied commander, Gen. Norman Schwarzkopf, who had been asked by an Iraqi official for permission to use their helicopters for transport since combat had damaged its roads, Saddam Hussein was allowed to fly his helicopters and the United Nations and America stood by helplessly while he used them to slaughter his rebellious military, his Shia, and his Kurds, causing a vast humanitarian crisis.

Within the Bush administration, there had already been high-level discussions about how to deal with Saddam. Said a former senior CIA official, "At the end of the Gulf War, we wanted no sweeping away of Saddam's regime, but a toppling of Saddam. This may have meant killing Saddam, his two sons, and a couple of other family members, but we wanted a six-month transitional government, and then we would hold free elections. We would put in clean people."[2]

The Bush administration specifically favored Gen. Sultan Hashimi to head the transitional government. In 1991, Hashimi, who was from an old Mosul family in eastern Iraq, had surrendered to Schwarzkopf, and the CIA and other administration officials thought him the perfect figure to head the transitional government. "The question was, what kind of government would make sense?" the former senior CIA official said. The Iraqi Shia religious parties were opposed to any transitional government because the new government would have been Sunni and secular, a fact whose meaning the CIA hadn't yet grasped. "We were outwitted. We had no idea then of the Shia agenda to try and come to power," said the former CIA official. So the transition plans went nowhere.

Having botched the chance to destroy Saddam and mishandled his surrender, the Bush administration then put in place a policy to contain Saddam using U.N.-backed economic sanctions, no-fly zones, and U.N. weapons inspections of Iraqi facilities. In August 1990, when Saddam was mobilizing his forces against Kuwait, the U.N. Security Council passed its first sanctions resolution against Iraq. (That resolution would remain in effect until 2003.) In April 1991 after Desert Storm, this was followed by Resolution 687, which was linked to Iraq's suspected WMD, weapons of mass destruction, programs. The tool to unearth the truth about the extent of Saddam's weapons was to be the United Nations Special Commission (UNSCOM) working closely with the International Atomic Energy Agency or IAEA, the Vienna-based nuclear watchdog organization assigned to oversee Iraq's disarmament.

With Resolution 687, the United Nations showed it was in earnest. Thus in the resolution Saddam was forever enjoined against developing such weapons or even "nuclear weapons usable material." It was a jumble of a document. One part said that once Iraq had complied with all of the WMD requirements, sanctions would be lifted; in another part, exports to Iraq were to be conditioned on "the policies and practices of the Iraqi government," language lamentably vague. But the bottom line was harsh: if Iraq wished to import or export any types of goods excepting medical supplies and humanitarian aid, it would have to fully disarm its chemical, biological, and nuclear WMD including missile delivery systems. Resolution 687 contained other stringent injunctions regarding the repayment of Iraq's foreign debts and compensation for damage inflicted on Kuwait. The resolution had concluded: "the Iraqi people may soon face another imminent catastrophe, which could include epidemic and famine, if massive life-supporting needs aren't rapidly met."[3] Along with the resolution, the United States offered to establish a program that would exchange Iraqi oil for food and humanitarian goods to meet basic necessities. Iraq was given only fifteen days to give intelligence on the location, amounts, and types of its WMD arsenal. The United Nations was given 120 days to determine if Saddam had fully complied.

Iraq had no intention of complying. With his usual self-confidence, Saddam thought he could outwit the United Nations. "The Special Commission is a temporary measure. We will fool them and we will bribe them and the matter will be over in a few months," he said.[4] In the meantime, he would terrorize potential domestic rivals and begin to stonewall the U.N. WMD inspectors.

Inspections soon began with a game of hide and seek that would last for over a decade.

Bush was increasingly unhappy with the stubborn deceit and unyielding defiance of Saddam, and his far-right Republicans were impatient with the strategy of punishment by means of long-term attrition. They soon raised a clamor in the Congress, demanding that the White House stop fooling around and oust Saddam. President Bush succumbed to the pressure, and in October of 1991, he signed a document marked "Top Secret" authorizing the CIA to mount a covert operation to "create the conditions for the removal of Saddam Hussein from power," using any and all means "up to and including lethal force."

21

DUAL CONTAINMENT

In early 1993, having captured the White House, Bill Clinton and his administration set policies toward the two major Middle East troublemakers, Iraq and Iran, aimed at containing them both. When it came to Iraq, President Clinton said the United States would use its military force and political alliances to ensure that Iraq could "no longer threaten its neighbors . . . or suppress its people with impunity."[1] He added that his administration would continue to support a U.S.-military presence in Kurdistan, which had become semi-autonomous under ambiguous international control but which could be used as a base of operations against Baghdad.

Strict sanctions would continue to be clamped on Iraq until it agreed to disarm and was found to be in full compliance with all U.N. resolutions dealing with disclosure of its WMD programs. About two hundred U.S. combat aircraft were deployed to patrol the Iraq no-fly zones, flying from bases in Turkey, Saudi Arabia, and other Gulf states, and an additional fifteen thousand U.S. military were posted to the region. The policy appeared to work well during the first year, and National Security Advisor Tony Lake had confidence in it, noting that U.S. success was due in large measure "because we have an understanding with our regional friends about the common threats and how to deal with them."

As for Iran, America would use the threat of force and economic pressure to curb the ayatollahs until they agreed to stop attempting to acquire WMD, ceased abusing human rights, and stopped supporting international terrorism. Iran had also been on a $10 billion weapons buying spree, snapping up

MiG-29 Russian fighters, two hundred T-72 Russian tanks, and three Russian Kilo-class submarines, sales the administration hoped to end.

Unfortunately, while Clinton's policies looked good on paper, they were halfhearted at best, done with a minimum of resources, and no steady, implacable energy of will, according to former senior administration officials. As we have seen, advancing Clinton's domestic agenda was the top priority. Everything else was to be left on the back burner. At some point, circumstances would force Clinton to stand up to bad actors like Saddam Hussein and pound him for his aggression, but so far the new president had not made any major false moves, and every step Clinton had taken had been weighed with his political future in mind. What gripped him with all its force was his ambition to stay in office for as long as possible. The worship of power and political success were mainstays of his life. As far as public opinion went, Clinton wouldn't fall behind, and he wouldn't get more than a step ahead. Most of the time he would simply go along.

This ignored completely the fact that tensions with Iran were on the climb. When Clinton came into office, Iran already had in place a more aggressive foreign policy targeted at the United States. U.S. intelligence had amassed evidence that Tehran was increasing its covert action and terrorist activities. For months in the early 1990s, Iran had undertaken surveillance of U.S. installations and assets to develop pre-attack profiles for bombings, suicide attacks, and even targeted killings. The Iranian teams also studied the security procedures at U.S. installations, followed American personnel to and from work, and had learned where they lived. Iran acted with impunity because it did not hold America in any fear. It had not been lost on Tehran that the Reagan administration had not retaliated against Iran for its role in the horrendous 1980s bombings in Lebanon even though Iran had clearly crossed an unmistakable line.

As a result, Tehran assumed that Clinton, like Bush and Reagan, would also shrink from taking decisive action no matter what it did.

The early days of the new administration seemed further proof to the Iranians that America would remain indecisive and passive. Early Clinton efforts to contain Iran didn't accomplish much. American attempts to shut down Russian or Chinese military and nuclear technology sales to Tehran went nowhere. Gore, in particular, had a lot of screaming fights with his friend Russian prime minister Viktor Chernomyrdin in which he won pledges by the Russian to cut back on sales to Iran, only to see such sales continue as they had. The Bush administration had earlier scaled back sanctions on Iran, and the United States soon became the largest single buyer of Iranian oil that was bought through the overseas subsidiaries of U.S. oil companies, and the pursuit of additional commerce had acted to put the brake on any genuine tightening of U.S. pressure on Iran. By 1995, even as Iran's aggressive foreign policy shifted to high gear, the United States was Iran's third largest trading partner, the largest purchaser of its oil, and the sixth largest buyer of its exports. Iran and America weren't friends, but when it came to trade, it seemed they didn't mind being accomplices.

All the warring, incoherent elements in the American attitude toward Iran were exposed to the world's gaze when Conoco, an American oil company, was awarded a $1 billion contract by Tehran. In Congress, outrage quickly rose heavenward. Conoco said that it had had over twenty meetings with the State Department, which had given them assurances that the deal would be approved, yet on March 14, Clinton denounced the deal and the next day signed an executive order that prohibited *all* oil development deals with Iran, hoping to smother the issue for good. Iranian soft-liners had thought the deal might thaw relations with Washington, but Iranian hard-liners saw it as a further display of Washington weakness, a further manifestation of American hypocrisy. On May 6, Clinton signed another executive order banning financial and commercial transactions with Iran, including trade.

The new hostile Republican Congress headed by House Speaker Newt Gingrich, trying to cut a fancy figure to impress Israel's right wing, asked Clinton why his administration hadn't mounted a covert action to topple Iran's mullahs from power. The speaker then added $18 million to the CIA's budget for that purpose, but it was empty posturing. With the collapse of the CIA-run operation in Frankfurt, the United States had no human assets left in Iran.

Clinton's other bitter enemy in the Middle East, Saddam Hussein, was not going to wait before testing his adversary and obtaining his own appraisal. The Iraqi leader decided to probe the inner iron of the new president only seventeen days after his inauguration by suddenly targeting U.S. aircraft with his air defense radars in northern Iraq, ending his self-declared cease-fire in the U.S. no-fly zones.[2] Suddenly, inside U.S. aircraft cockpits, warning signals flashed alerting the pilots that they were being targeted. The U.S. planes, F-16s and F-4s, replied by firing deadly volleys of cluster bombs and antiradiation missiles, severely damaging the missile sites. This displeased the French, who had business ties with Saddam, and the French foreign minister Roland Dumas, complained the strike "went beyond U.N. Security Council resolutions." While British prime minister John Major and the House of Commons supported the action, both parties had earlier balked at a more ambitious plan that would have hammered a dozen more Iraqi sites. Russia for its part "regretted" the strike and called for coordinated decisions before any more air assaults, chiefly because Russian leader Boris Yeltsin had hard-liners who were accusing him of taking his cues in foreign policy from America. In other words, Russian leadership was working to woo its domestic constituency rather than back America when it came to Iraq.

Clinton was brief and brusque about the strike, "It is the *American* policy," and Warren Christopher said, "The United States intends to protect our pilots." Alas, the clash was just the first lightning flicker of the coming storm.

When it came to the Arab-Israeli dispute, the feeling among some of Clinton's advisors was that Clinton should take care to step very wide of the issue. The dispute was a bottomless morass, and chances for any substantial breakthrough were extremely bleak at best. During the previous administration, the government of Yitzhak Shamir clearly planned to keep most if not all of the territory captured by the Israelis during the Six Day War of 1967. Egypt and Israel were at peace, but no other Arab countries appeared involved in any search for common ground. In addition, any new plan was likely to harden opposition around it. Any new initiative would merely waste time and words. Lake, for example, who had only a superficial knowledge of the Middle East, saw no need for presidential activism in that region, which he felt should be left to the secretary of state, Warren Christopher, who also wanted to keep the new administration from becoming snarled and immobilized by any Middle East peace process.

Clinton had other ideas. One night in Washington at a dinner at the Israeli embassy early in 1995, a senior Israeli diplomat strongly took issue with *New York Times* columnist William Safire, a strong supporter of Israel, over a piece the latter had recently written. The Israeli let loose and mauled Safire, derisively declaring that the American had been duped and manipulated by press agents for the opposition coalition in Israel, and Safire, his own heat up, responded with a biting, passionate vigor that bordered on rudeness. Warren Christopher, who overheard the exchange, turned pale, when the gravelly-voiced Israeli suddenly reached and laid his hand on Christopher's arm, through a cloud of cigarette smoke, saying: "Relax. We [two] can do this because we go way back." The Israeli was Prime Minister Yitzhak Rabin.[3] This cordiality was new, making clear once and for all that America was dealing with quite a different Rabin than it had in the past. The Israeli prime minister had held an earlier term in that office when Jimmy Carter had been president, and the two had not taken to each other at all. Stiff and cold, Rabin had radiated mistrust and wariness. Carter, who had warm feelings for Israel as "the land of the Bible," had tried to charm the Israeli, asking Rabin, after a state dinner, if he would like to look in at

Carter's daughter, Amy, who was asleep in a White House bedroom. "No, thank you," said a curt Rabin.[4] When Secretary of State Cyrus Vance talked with Rabin, he fared little better. The Israelis saw Carter as being "too quick to criticize Israel, and too inclined to be responsive to the Arabs," in the words of Dennis Ross, Clinton's chief Arab-Israeli negotiator.[5]

However, years had passed, Bill Clinton was president, and Rabin had become a transformed man.

President Clinton had first spoken to Rabin in March of 1993 during the second week of the transition. For Clinton, the Arab-Israeli dispute remained a stale deadlock similar to the wars between Catholics and Protestants in the sixteenth and seventeenth centuries. In both cases, the parties had claims that appeared to be absolute, each had thought their values universal, and each thought their claims mutually exculsive and therefore incapable of compromise. At the time of the religious wars, both sides had been driven by various types of necessity, but it had seemed inconceivable to most people that two forms of the Christian religion could coexist within a given country. It was the discovery of tolerance, the ability of both sides to slowly begin to put themselves in the other's place, that altered the whole platform on which the struggle was being waged; this was basically through the realization that members of the hostile party were also human beings and fundamentally were like each other. Yet people are not mere slaves of condition, and personalities make a difference. The person that makes such a discovery clearly has a mind that is superior to circumstance and possesses the fearless originality of thought, the moderation, decency, and generosity of emotion to reach new conclusions and try new approaches. Yitzhak Rabin was such a man, and he would begin a new epoch in the Middle East. Rabin had been present at the creation of Israel and was very much responsible for its survival. Thanks to the structure of his mind and the largeness of his spirit, he would add a new and hopeful dynamic to the seemingly unending Arab-Israeli dispute.

His mind had a capacity to deliberate on great, weighty matters plus Rabin had a lavish, responsive, and generous nature that savored the pleasure brought by the small things in life. For example, in Jerusalem, he lived in a house that had a roof garden, and having once studied engineering, he took great pleasure in showing Christopher an automatic watering system he'd designed.

Unlike most military men who see things in black and white, the world appeared to Rabin in shades of gray. He was a man of artful compromises, with the strength to adjust to realities no matter how painful they were. As profound an analyst as he was, he never saw the facts through the prism of politics. Politics distorted the facts, simplified and deformed them to the point of falsity, and Rabin trusted his ability to perceive the facts without distortion, and he had the inner calm of a man with absolute confidence in his ability to discern what the real truth was.

He trusted few people completely, but when he gave his trust it was without craftiness or reservation. Rabin appeared to many a hard man, but at the appearance of his wife or the mention of her name, his face would soften and his manner became gentle; and he expressed great and selfless kindness to his friends.

A new epoch in Israeli-Arab relations began in Augustr of 1993, when Rabin called Warren Christopher with the news that Israel and the PLO, the Palestine Liberation Organization, had signed a peace agreement negotiated in Oslo, Norway. This was the same PLO that previous Israeli prime ministers refused to see as equals and as a result had rejected any dealings with them. Never before now had the Israelis sat down for talks with the PLO.[6] Yet the new Oslo agreement shone with the brilliance of real progress: there was the extension of formal mutual recognition between the two bodies and the signing of the Declaration of Principles on interim self-government arrangements for the West Bank and Gaza. The agreement also dealt with matters that included increased security for Israel and compensation, economic aid, and refugee relocation for the Palestinians.

Although Warren Christopher knew of the agreement by August 26, White House aides didn't learn of the agreement until September 8, only a few days before it was to be signed in Washington, and as with all political events, the first concern was with appearances, having Rabin and Yasser Arafat, longtime PLO leader, shake hands without Arafat kissing Rabin, and convincing Arafat not to show up as a peacemaker wearing his famous pistol. Warren Christopher had played a key part in keeping both sides from being hung up on conditions, thrashing helplessly about in legal tangles, and avoiding roads that led nowhere.

When Clinton had read the agreement, even though a final treaty remained light-years away, he saw that the principles agreed to at Oslo were eminently level-headed and just. On September 10, when Clinton met with Rabin on the White House lawn, he simply listened as Rabin displayed an amazing breadth of insight and sympathy. Rabin told Clinton he realized that Israel had always been obsessive in viewing the seized Arab land as essential to its security. The prevailing wisdom had always declared that such land would act as a buffer and was therefore indispensable. But Rabin, who had a first-rate military mind, had outgrown that view. He told Clinton that the territories captured in the 1967 war were no longer necessary to Israeli security but rather had become a source of insecurity. Both Clinton and Rabin knew that the West Bank had become "Lebanonized," full of contending factions, and was therefore unstable. Before the Palestinian uprising in the West Bank, the Intifada, Palestinians had been careful for the most part to first attack *only* Israeli settlers settled illegally on Palestinian land, then Israeli military targets, leaving for last innocent civilians inside Israel. Unfortunately, as the occupation continued, violence was spreading and becoming more indiscriminate and vicious.

Rabin understood the axiom of former senior Indian CIA official B. Raman, an expert in terrorism, that said, "Behind all terror lies a grievance." Rabin had seen in the 1989 Intifada outbreak the anger of a people who felt they were being denied their rights, and he saw that angry, insulted Palestinians did not make Israeli civilians safer. Rabin had also realized during the Gulf War, when Saddam had fired Scud missiles at Israeli cities, that a land buffer did not mean safety either. Finally, Rabin was concerned with Palestinian civil rights. If Tel Aviv kept the West Bank indefinitely, the Israeli government would have to decide if Palestinians living there could vote in Israeli elections, as did those who lived within the 1967 borders. If the Palestinians had the right to vote, given the "Arab womb," the higher birth rate of Muslims, how long would it be before Israel was no longer a Jewish state?

The next item on Rabin's list was to make some sort of a deal to return the Golan Heights, gained during the 1967 war, to Syria where it belonged.

Clinton sensed the ennobling inner quality of Rabin, the Israeli military man who had spent most of his life fighting Arabs, yet who, by power of character, had risen to think beyond his background, his ideological biases, prejudices, and partisanship—all in the determination to realize a solid, healing peace between the two peoples. It was the dream Rabin dreamed, and Clinton said to himself, "I was determined to help him achieve his dream of peace," and under Rabin progress between Israel and the PLO continued.[7]

The day of the signing was a Monday. It was a bright, sweltering day, and a horde of press had appeared in the Palm Room where a young aide, trying to bring order from chaos, rushed about saying, "Israeli press over here, PLO folks over there." Suddenly former President George Bush, looking tall, tan, and fit, appeared. Someone called out, "Make room for the president, make room for the president," and Bush, as he shouldered his way along, kept repeating modestly, "Ex . . . Ex . . . Ex."[8]

The South Lawn soon filled with a mob that included former secretaries of state—including William Rogers, Henry Kissinger, Alexander Haig, James Baker, and Lawrence Eagleburger—former Presidents Bush and Carter, and congressman, foreign diplomats, Arabs in kaffiyehs, Arab-American leaders and Jewish-American leaders. Shimon Peres, who loved crowds, was there, but Rabin was visibly tense, aware that since Peres, his longtime rival, was leader of the Israeli delegation, he thus outranked him. Yasser Arafat, wearing an olive green uniform (without his pistol), seemed a bit bewildered at having moved from the periphery of politics to front and center of the world's stage.

The document was signed on the same table where the Egyptian-Israeli peace had been signed at Camp David in 1979, and Clinton would be the first to speak. The president had awakened at 3 A.M. and read the entire Book of Joshua, worked on his speech, and walked through every step of the ceremony. As he rose to address the crowd, he was poised and at ease, prompting Christopher to say later, Clinton "seems to thrive on the pressure that builds before a major public appearance," and how he often added to that pressure by incessantly making changes in what he was to say, some made en route to the event, driving his aides to the edge of madness.[9] Clinton's remarks were full of heart and feeling, emphasizing the history of the region and the contributions of those who had preceded him as president. Christopher said the note he set was perfect.[10]

Yet Rabin, who followed him, struggling to control his emotions, said in his deep, gravelly voice, "This signing . . . today . . . it's not so easy, neither for myself as a soldier in Israel's war, or for the people of Israel . . ." He paused and gained a grip on himself, then said: "Let me say to you, the Palestinians, we are destined to live together on the same soil in the same land . . . we who have fought against you, the Palestinians, we say to you in a loud and clear voice, enough of the blood and tears. Enough!"

With a new set of facts on the ground, with the possibility of progress no longer a possibility but a genuine fact, fresh opportunities opened everywhere. Yasser Arafat, a terrorist, persona non grata in the United States until the 1990s, had just appeared as an honored, invited White House guest! The world was just adjusting to the Palestinians, the Israelis, and the United States all working together as mutually dependent partners, when another stunning event occurred. By the fall of 1993, Rabin and King Hussein of Jordan had developed a warm friendship for each other. For years Jordan had held secret meetings with the Israelis on security issues and the men had gotten to know each other. The king, an astute man, recognized that the Oslo Accords had changed the political landscape. In May of 1994, Jordan and Israel had reached agreement on a peace treaty and by June were holding meetings in London to refine its details. Rabin and King Hussein met in Washington, June 25, to sign a declaration ending twenty-five years of war.

The breakthrough had taken place in November of 1993 when Labor Party leader Shimon Peres had reached an agreement with the Jordanian king in secret talks in Jordan. In the aftermath however, Peres had been indiscreet, and when the news leaked, the outcries were vociferous, and in Israel it had taken a while for sanity, calm, and reason to be restored.

Key Clinton staff like Dennis Ross; Martin Indyk, the NSC Middle East expert; and Bob Pelletreau, the assistant secretary of state for the Near Eastern Affairs Bureau, were among many key players in what was to occur next. In July, Ross told an aide to King Hussein that President Clinton, who was anxious for the completion of a full-blown peace agreement, wanted from the king a specific list of his most important needs, relief from debt being one. Hussein's aide said he would send to the White House that evening a letter to Clinton outlining the king's most urgent needs.

Before the meeting in the Oval Office between King Hussein and Clinton, Indyk prepared a briefing for the president and attached to it King Hussein's letter and a long annex. When Hussein met with Clinton, his performance displayed his enormous talents of memory and eloquence at their best and most effective. As Ross noted later, "Clinton's style and command of detail typically had an effect on those with whom he was meeting. Nowhere was that more evident than at this meeting. He conducted the meeting without any notes. His ability to go over all the points in the King's letter and annex without any notes wowed the King and his key aides. Indeed, by going over some issue of assistance to Jordan and pointing out what we could do and what we could not do, he persuaded the King that he had personally delved deeply into Jordan's needs and was personally looking for ways to respond." Ross concluded, "The President's mastery of detail convinced the King that the President placed a high priority on Jordan and the King."[11] The treaty would be signed in Jordan in October, but few were aware that the growing menace of a belligerent Iraq wouldn't wait.

On October 17 of 1994, Saddam, as he often did, put his worst foot forward. On that date, the Iraqi dictator massed heavy forces within a few miles of the border of Kuwait. Clinton's reaction was stern. After a tense Principals meeting, the president deployed 36,000 troops to Kuwait, backed up by an aircraft carrier group armed with advanced Tomahawk cruise missiles. Clinton had his finger on the trigger, he wasn't about to blink, and Saddam reluctantly sucked back. Clinton was in a fury—now he had another score to settle with Saddam.

By mid-October, Israel and Jordan were ready to sign the agreement. On October 27, more than four thousand guests from Israel, Jordan, and neighboring countries met under the blazing desert sun at Arava. A huge black tent provided some shade, while out in the open, military officers from what had been hostile armies exchanged chatter and war stories. Rabin, a former tank commander, was wearing a heavy wool sweater in the sweltering heat. King Hussein had ridden his motorcycle the 170 miles from Amman. When the ceremony was finished, Clinton and Christopher joined the king on the royal yacht for a tour of the Gulf waters. Hussein was at the wheel and responded to the shouts and cheers with repeated blasts of the craft's whistle.

From Amman, Clinton flew to Israel; he then went to Kuwait to thank the emir there for his support, and to talk about Saddam. After that, he went on to Saudi Arabia. There on October 29, while visiting King Fahd at a northern air force base, the threat represented by the sinister figure of Saddam had assumed a definite, frightening shape, and Clinton informed the king that Saddam must be removed if there was to be peace in the Middle East. The president then signed a "Memorandum of Amplification" that replaced the earlier lethal finding of Bush, authorizing a program of covert action that, once fully developed, would be driven home with ruthless force.[12]

22

SHADOW WAR

"Migraine Hussein," former Secretary of State Madeleine Albright called him, and she would complain, "We would spend eight full years grappling with issues left unresolved at the end of the Persian Gulf War."[1]

One such issue had been the appearance after the war of dozens of Iraqi exile groups. They were another headache that President Bill Clinton had inherited.

"Be very cautious in dealing with exiles," said longtime former agency covert operator Jack Devine, a black-haired, quick-witted Irishman. "Exile groups are penetrated top to bottom."[2] Another former CIA official, Tyler Drumheller, said that the agency had "a real flaw" in letting itself be "duped and co-opted by such dubious groups which all have their own agenda."[3] After Saddam's 1991 defeat, Iraqi exile groups sprouted everywhere like poisonous toadstools, at least seventy, attempting to obtain United States backing, funds, and resources for getting rid of Saddam. Many were tiny in membership. All were self-exalting, cantankerous, and grasping, and all stubbornly refused to cede any authority to rivals. There were Arab dissident groups, there were groups that had ties to Iran like the Supreme Assembly for the Revolution in Iraq, and Shia organizations formed earlier continued to exist. There were two chief Kurdish groups, the Kurdistan Democratic Party (KDP), led by the Barzani family, and the Patriotic Union of Kurdistan (PUK), led by Jalal Talabani. All the leaders of the various groups proved to be men of ideals but no principles.

But they might be used. "The idea was to mount a general, broad-based

propaganda effort involving the CIA, DOD, and other agencies in the U.S.
government to support and finance keeping pressure on Saddam. There
had never been an umbrella opposition organization before," a former longtime CIA operative said. "The original impetus was not coup planning at
all. We wanted to bring in credible people to speak against the Saddam regime to dramatize and publicize its abuses."

The agency first contacted the wily, charming, brilliant Iraqi exile
Ahmed Chalabi on May 11, 1991, when Whitley Bruner left the U.S. embassy on Grosvenor Square in London and met the exile at his palatial flat.
Chalabi had headed the Petya Bank in Amman, Jordan's third largest, then
fled after the Jordanian authorities seized the bank because of "questionable
currency transactions." Chalabi had been convicted in absentia of having
embezzled $60 million, and according to former CENTCOM commander
Gen. Anthony Zinni, "There are warrants outstanding for Chalabi in Lebanon" for other dubious financial dealings.[4] Chalabi was also known to be an
Iranian agent. (His Jordanian bank had helped advance Iranian interests,
former CIA officials say.) When Frank Anderson, chief of the CIA's Near
East Division of the clandestine Directorate of Operations, was asked why
he tolerated Chalabi since the man was a proven crook, Anderson replied
that "he was an excellent day-to-day administrator."

By 1992, the agency had finally decided there were only about twenty-
five Iraqi groups of any useful significance. It was then that the CIA moved
in June to set up and pay for a conference for exiles held in Vienna, out of
which emerged an umbrella organization called the Iraqi National Congress, the INC.[5] In spite of later claims by Chalabi, the INC was a direct
creation of the CIA, according to Tom Twetten, the CIA's former deputy of
operations, a slight, dry-humored man who looks like TV's meek and mild
Mister Rogers but whose character contained a vein of pure iron. Twetten,
like Anderson, had been a big player in the vast covert operation that had
run the Soviets out of Afghanistan, and Twetten would later say that it was
a Washington-based public relations firm, the Rendon Group, employed by
the CIA that created the INC. He recently told a journalist, "The INC was
clueless. They needed a lot of help and didn't know where to start. That is
why Rendon was brought in."[6] Rendon was John Walter Rendon, Jr., the
head of the Rendon Group, a man who lives in a multimillion-dollar home
in the exclusive Kalorama area of Washington, close to the home of former
Secretary of Defense Donald Rumsfeld. The son of a stockbroker, he grew
up in New Jersey and worked on the presidential campaign of Senator
George McGovern before graduating from Northwestern University. He
began consulting in the 1980s after the election of Ronald Reagan. Within

a few years he had founded his own company with its headquarters at Du-
pont Circle and two other offices, one in Boston, the other in London. His
wife, Sandra Libby, the sister of "Scooter" Libby, the indicted former White
House vice presidential aide, handles the books and is a "senior communications strategist." In the late 1990s, after having fallen out with the CIA,
the Rendon Group maneuvered to become a favorite tool of the administration of George W. Bush, obtaining some thirty-five Pentagon contracts,
worth many millions of dollars, between 2000 and 2004.

According to former CIA official and Middle East expert Whitley Bruner,
Rendon's group got the INC job "because of what they had done in Panama,"
during the December 1989 invasion producing propaganda to help oust
Panamanian dictator Manuel Noriega, a former $700,000 per year CIA em-
ployee turned renegade and drug smuggler. When Rendon finally met Chalabi, both recognized in the other a slick, unprincipled hustler just like
himself. Rendon told a reporter, "From day one, Chalabi was very clear that
the basic interest was to rid Iraq of Saddam."[7] But Bruner, who dealt with
both Rendon and Chalabi in 1991, said that Chalabi's primary, secret focus
had always been "to drag us into war with Iraq." Ned Walker, former assistant secretary of state for the Near Eastern Affairs Bureau agreed: "There is
no doubt that Chalabi's chief aim was to involve us in some low-intensity
conflict with Iraq, and finally into all-out war."[8] This sinister design would
only become clear much later, when the ability to prevent it was impossible.

From the beginning, the CIA knew that Chalabi's INC had been penetrated by Iraqi double agents. "No one was concerned about Iraqi penetration," said another former CIA official with knowledge of the operation.
"We wanted Saddam to know that we were doing these things. It was basically a Rendon-type PR exercise—sort of a covert op done in public. Only
the amount being spent was secret. The point was to raise the profile of
exiles, not plan a coup. Chalabi was kept away from anything secret."

On October 27, 1992, 234 of the Iraqi opposition met on U.S.-controlled
Iraqi soil in Kurdistan in the city of Salahudin, and the basic structure of the
Iraqi National Congress was set up, its job to transmit "gray propaganda."
Black propaganda meant U.S.-crafted acts or statements carefully made to
look as if Saddam was their author in order to discredit him. Gray propaganda is similar to a commercial advertisement. "All of INC's stuff was basically gray," said a former operative in the program.

In Kurdistan, another of Chalabi's main tasks would be helping to keep
the Kurds, then engaged in a civil war, from tearing at each other's
throats. The INC forces would also feed and shelter and debrief defecting
Iraqi military, arriving in a constant trickle from the south, so many by

1994 that Saddam ordered that any who were captured were to have their ears cut off.

When it came to attempting a coup in Iraq, Washington had been consumed with apathy. Shortly after President Bush signed his finding to remove Saddam, a classified copy was forwarded to CIA headquarters at Langley, Virginia, where it reached the desk of the chief of the agency's Near East Division, Frank Anderson, who, after reading it, scrawled on the document, "I don't like this at all."[9]

Anderson was experienced enough to know when a plan wouldn't work. He saw in a glance that Bush's plot had no chance of success. Topple Saddam? How? With what? Anderson knew the CIA had no penetrations or reliable sources in Iraq. Neighboring countries like Jordan, Saudi Arabia, and Iran hated Saddam, and they had some intelligence resources, but the agency had none. Anderson saw that too much had been left undone. Iraq shared a border with enemies like Kuwait and Kurdistan, which helped—a border didn't simply separate two nations, it was also a point at which they came together. Of course, a covert operation was a way to keep the heat on an opponent and avoid a military collision; it was a means of limiting U.S. involvement abroad while making changes favorable to your interests. But you didn't run a covert action without congressional support or some prior debate. There needed to be a detailed covert plan and operational security, and agents had to take care only to deal with cutouts, not sources, to disguise the role of the agency. How could that be done in Iraq?

Anderson was a man who followed orders, he knew he had been told to try and get some sort of coup up and running, but from the moment he'd read the Bush plan he realized the hand he'd drawn was not a winning one. The CIA had no agents in Iraq, but Anderson knew Washington very well. Congress had given the agency $20 million to spend on preparing a coup, and in Washington, the rule for handling money was simple: "use it or lose it." So he began to disburse the funds to an agency front called the Rendon Group.

Since Iraq was not a priority, efforts made to implement the secret Clinton finding began in very low gear. Christopher wanted Clinton to steer clear of it, and Lake embodied misgivings, "Don't give us sweaty palms," over Iraq, he repeated again and again.[10] Out at the CIA, there was only Director James Woolsey—neutral, inflexible, out of step and out of style. For months, he had made intermittent efforts to increase the networks of paid agents inside foreign governments and foreign intelligence services, but the intelligence they offered was usually low-grade, mainly bits of biographical gossip. A handful of White House hawks were for it, including U.N. ambassador Madeleine Albright, Vice President Al Gore, his NSC advisor, Leon Fuerth, and his NSC deputy, Martin Indyk, but they were voices more at the periphery than the center. As a result, operations directed against Saddam were not only a sideshow, but they would be a sideshow of a sideshow. In the White House, the Arab-Israeli problem enjoyed precedence as *the* major issue in the Middle East.

Initial anti-Saddam explorations were limited at best. By October of 1994, the first of two CIA teams arrived in Kurdistan, their mission approved personally by Indyk. The first four-man team was headed by Warren Marik, a frank, outspoken Chicagoan with a big, thickset frame and ruddy face from the Iraq Operations Group. Marik's friendly manner belied his toughness and his relish for taking risks. He had been an intelligence specialist with the U.S. Army in Vietnam and then joined the CIA, serving in Afghanistan after the Soviet invasion. He later joined the CIA's Afghan Task Force, and following that, he had been an undeclared CIA case officer in Karachi, Pakistan, processing European and Asian adventurers who arrived to fight in the war. After that operation ended, Marik was assigned to Baghdad during the Iran-Iraq War.

Bob Baer, head of the CIA's secret Iraq Operations Group, would lead the other. Baer was a top field agent with a forceful independence of character and a will of single-minded tenacity. He had brought his own bright dream of glory to Kurdistan, harboring a hope of making a mark, for he detested mediocrity and loathed any performance lacking in vigorous energy and skill. He was impatient of restraint, had a sharp tongue, and didn't bother to control it when he spotted defects in a superior, a trait that often got him in trouble. Now, without realizing it, he was entering a situation that appeared full of promise of solid accomplishment, but which was, in fact, a tract of treacherous quicksand, abounding in invisible disasters.

Kurdistan remained very important to U.S. policy. The U.S.-protected area set up by President Bush in northern Iraq and protected by no-fly zones provided a secure base for organizing anti-Saddam elements. Secondly, the Kurds were the only groups on Iraqi soil with their own significant military forces. Also the involvement of the Kurds with the Iraqi exile groups, distracted the former from their obsession of establishing an independent state carved out of Turkish territory, an idea that Ankara had resisted for decades. Baer's and Marik's teams, which alternated, were assigned the job of baby-sitting Chalabi, to work with the Kurds and the INC, to assess the latter's capabilities. Unforeseen complications occurred in January 1995, when a former Iraqi director of military intelligence, Gen. Wafiq al-Samarrai, defected to Baer in Kurdistan. Samarrai was offering to use crack military units to help depose Saddam, and, as part of the plan, Chalabi would launch his INC militia to seize two Iraqi cities. This placed Baer in a painful dilemma. Baer and Marik were working to their utmost limits in Kurdistan, both men believing that any problem yielded to persistence, attention, and ability. But without realizing it, they stood within a very small, lighted circle of knowledge. Neither had the remotest idea that both their plans and the INC's activities were filling Langley with alarm.

As Baer pressed ahead with coup plans, discussing options and refining timing, he thought that he had the full picture, when, without knowing it, Baer was involved in an office dispute, and in an office dispute, no faith is kept, no decency is displayed, and no mercy is shown. Working from the shadows, Steve Richter, the new chief of the Near East Division, Directorate of Operations, having read Baer's cables on the Samarrai-Chalabi plan, put forth all his formidable powers of obstruction. The INC had a rival, the Iraqi National Accord, and when it came to Clinton's secret finding, Richter had bet all his chips using the INA to topple Saddam, not the INC. "The INA were the chosen ones to topple Saddam," said Marik. "They were the first team. They bragged about it openly." Meanwhile, to conceal its support for the INA, Richter and the White House were making misleading statements, telling INC officials it had no interest in "the dictator option"— in other words, toppling Saddam and putting in another Iraqi strongman. This was mere dust to blind Chalabi's eyes because Richter was in the stages of preliminary planning for just such a coup—one that, if approved, would have meant Iraqi INA-led rebels seizing control of the traditional centers of power in Iraq, including the armed forces, the police and security forces, and TV, radio, and other communications networks, plus key government ministries.

Richter was controversial. Opinions of him were to be found only in extremes. "He's an asshole, but by no means is he a dope," a former senior CIA official said. Richter had a lot of Middle East expertise. He spoke fluent Arabic, and he'd been in Pakistan, India, Egypt, Turkey, and Syria where he'd been chief of station. After Syria, he was promoted to chief of station in Jordan. A CIA operative who knew Richter when he was a clandestine operator working in Syria, described him as "looking just like Regis Philbin," the TV talk show personality. Richter, he said, had brownish gray hair, was moderately tall and very military in his bearing. Baer said that Richter liked "wearing gold jewelry and diaphanous shirts."

It was Richter's personality that proved prickly. "He was very dictatorial, self-assured to a fault," said Rick Francona, a former Defense Intelligence Agency officer who had worked with him. "He could be so very charming to your face and then stab in you in the back." Judith Yaphe, a former senior CIA Iraqi analyst, said, "Richter wanted people to admire his plans, obey his orders, and shut up. He weeded out everyone promising from the operation groups." However, Richter did have one defender who had worked with him in the European Division in Frankfurt. "Listen, Richter didn't hold people down. He appreciated talent."

Richter *had* been involved in one indisputable and unfortunate failure. In the late 1980s, when he was at the CIA's European Division, he ran an intelligence collection program that used Iranians who were spying for the agency at great personal risk. In the grip of ambition, he suddenly ordered that agents in Iran double the amount of their reporting, discounting the warnings of colleagues because Richter knew that success of a chief of station was measured by the volume of intelligence reports his unit could produce. Unfortunately, the letters from Frankfurt to Richter's Iranian agents, written in invisible ink, were addressed in the same hand and mailed in batches that included the return accommodation addresses, and Iranian counterintelligence "blew the network apart," costing the lives of more than thirty brave operatives, according to former sources.

Journalist Seymour Hersh in a *New Yorker* article blamed Richter for being impatient and overambitious and cited "a subsequent internal CIA counter-intelligence investigation" that claimed Richter was reckless.[11] There is still a debate about this. A number of former senior Directorate of Operations officials told me that the later investigation into the matter determined that the calamity was not Richter's fault, but that the error was made by personnel in the operation's technical unit—especially one individual whose "tradecraft got sloppy." In any case, the CIA internal investigation moved so slowly that it wasn't Richter but his successor, Jerry Bunton (now deceased), who "took the hit," said these sources. (Another former CIA official said a more inferior kind of invisible ink had been used.) Ken Pollack, a former CIA analyst on Iran, said that as a result of the failure, "Tehran had systematically rolled up American assets in Iran, and the Agency was left with effectively nothing in Iran that might have done anything if there were something for it to do."[12]

Now, ensconced at Langley headquarters, Richter's outlook was upbeat. He could see a magnificent triumph unfold in his mind, could picture the brutal and callous Saddam imprisoned, disgraced, shattered, and alone, out of power. Soon the possibility of success began hammering away at him. The first meetings to plan the coup had occurred on the Isle of Wight in 1994 and included members of the British elite MI-6. Another meeting was convened in the summer of 1994 at a resort in the Plains, Virginia, with CIA and MI-6 officials in attendance. Richter was at the center of everything, receiving, digesting, exchanging views, issuing assignments and requests for analyses. At agency headquarters, an office or "planning cell" was quickly established on the sixth floor. The group contained two officers from CEN-TCOM, the defense organization tasked with deploying U.S. forces in the Middle East. CENTCOM is divided into six directorates, known as "Js" for "joint." One CENTCOM official in the new program was an Army colonel from J3, Operations, and the second was an Air Force captain from J5, Plans and Programs. In addition to the CENTCOM officials, the cell contained eight to ten CIA analysts and field officers.

"CENTCOM was there because it had a definite part to play," said one former Directorate of Operations operative involved in the planning. In the case of a coup, CENTCOM would launch U.S. combat aircraft that would turn the skies over Iraq into a no-fly zone. "We had seen in 1991 how effective Saddam's helicopters could be in killing bushels of people. CENTCOM was going to clamp a real tight lid over the whole country," the former official said. "Nothing in the way of helicopters or gunships was going to get off the ground."[13]

From the beginning, Baer had seen Richter as a bully. No sooner had Frank Anderson retired than Richter, the new director of the Near East Division, held a meeting where he told Baer and others there would be no cables sent from the field to the NSC, a practice often done in the past. Richter made clear that if anyone were to send any cable to the White House, it would be Richter and Richter alone. Many stories were retailed of Richter on a secure phone, administering scathing tongue-lashings for violators, outbursts meant to put the erring employee in his place once and for all. In brief, Richter wasn't about to be defied with impunity by his employees.

"Richter made it clear he was boss in the kitchen, and if we didn't like the heat, we could get out," Baer said.

Convinced of the worth of his aim, Baer redoubled his effort. From January to the end of February, Baer, lonely, harassed, and increasingly desperate, sent eight cables to Richter outlining each development of the new coup plan as it emerged. His only reply was silence. Baer clearly believed in the coup, and with each hour the degree of Baer's nervous fury sharply increased. What Baer feared most was that the knees of Washington would go weak just when the Kurds and INC were finally manifesting some backbone about really going after Saddam. (Baer seemed unaware of the agency's low opinion of Chalabi and the strict limits of his mission there.)

On March 3, the fatal blow finally fell. When a Baer team member, "Tom," a former Special Forces operative, entered his room, Baer saw instantly from the man's face that he had bad news.

"They're pulling us out aren't they?" Baer asked in despair.

"You're not going to believe it," Tom said.

Baer's eyes fell on the cable in his hands and he stared. He had spent nineteen years in the CIA, and yet he had never seen anything like this. It wasn't from Richter. It was a cable directly from the White House. It said simply: "THE ACTION YOU HAVE PLANNED FOR THIS WEEKEND HAS BEEN TOTALLY COMPROMISED. WE BELIEVE THERE IS A HIGH RISK OF FAILURE. ANY DECISION TO PROCEED WILL BE ON YOUR OWN." It was from National Security Advisor Tony Lake.[14]

Richter had kept the NSC and the White House in the dark until the very last instant. The next paragraph of the cable instructed Baer to contact Washington immediately. The operative gazed at his watch. The coup was to begin in less than thirty-six hours. Washington had known about the coup since the end of January, and it was March. No argument of his had any effect. The plan collapsed.

23

A REAL STEP UP

Common sense required that you have the right people in place to handle the right problems, and in May of 1995, a ray of hope had dawned at last at the White House when it came to the CIA. James Woolsey was out, and, President Clinton, after numerous discussions with National Security Council deputy Sandy Berger and Secretary of Defense William Perry, had come up with the perfect replacement in John Deutch, a deputy secretary of defense under Perry. Deutch was a large, bearish man with a severe, earnest bespectacled face, topped by an almost forbiddingly high forehead with receding dark hair. He had a bright, quick analytical mind and like Perry was at home in the impersonal certainties of science and math. He was close to Perry, Berger, and Clinton's Russia hand, Strobe Talbott, whose children tenderly referred to Deutch as "big guy."[1]

Deutch had been Clinton's first choice, thanks to advice from Perry, but Deutch hadn't wanted the job, partly because as number two at the Pentagon he enjoyed enormous power. He endured a blizzard of imploring calls from Clinton, plus lobbying from Berger and Perry, and at last gave in. "I'm told the president really twisted his arm out of his socket," said a close friend of Deutch. Deutch's meeting at the White House with Clinton had gone well, the president showing him around, full to the brim with ideas and observations about U.S. history and former presidents. The two men got on well, and Deutch suddenly found himself the new CIA director. Publicly Clinton called Deutch "a dynamic, brilliant leader with all the necessary skills for this critical assignment," but more importantly, Deutch also found himself a member of the cabinet, a strict condition that he had imposed for accepting the job.[2] In addition, Deutch had also been granted a broad role in setting national security policy. This upgrading signaled a major organizational shift. Only William Casey, President Reagan's CIA director, had been accorded Cabinet rank, and that had led to the disasters of the Iran-contra scandal.

Unfortunately, Deutch was a vain and theatrical personality, bold and cocky. He was addicted to doing things his own way. He would startle agency colleagues by coming to work through the front door, while it had been the habit of most previous directors to take the private elevator from the garage up to their paneled office, and at lunch he would push his own tray through the cafeteria line. He arrived at the CIA at a time of disarray.

The Ames case had cast the agency under a terrible cloud. Aldrich Ames was a longtime career CIA agent, working in counterintelligence, who, on June 13, 1985, at Chadwick's restaurant in Georgetown, managed to give the Russians a complete list of CIA assets in the Soviet Union contained in a seven-pound bag. Ames was paid $2.7 million by a grateful KGB, and twenty-four agents lost their lives, most of them shot in the back of the head so that their faces would not be recognizable from the effects of the bullet. Deutch saw the agency as riddled with incompetence, timidity, sexism, corruption, and the lack of any fixity of purpose. The Directorate of Operations, he said, had forgotten the basics of espionage. They weren't living up to the old standards. They also weren't much good at what they did. They weren't good at recruitment or at intelligence collection.

In general, Deutch appeared to feel that human agents were a bit out-of-date. Deutch, a chemist, had once been provost of the Massachusetts Institute of Technology, and was a man infatuated with organizational innovation who believed the future of intelligence lay with technical means of collection. He described himself as "a technical guy, a satellite guy, a SIGINT guy," referring to electronic interceptions of sensitive data. During his confirmation hearing, Deutch had promised to reform the agency "all the way down to the bones."

As soon as he arrived, Deutch replaced top management in the Directorate of Operations. Stephen Kappes, the deputy director of operations, resigned before he could be fired. He also brought in the staff director of the Senate Intelligence Committee, a sharp Greek-American by the name of George Tenet whose father owned a diner in Queens. Deutch, taking his cue from the White House, put in place an arrangement where the new deputy director of operations would report to him through a woman, a former assistant secretary of the Navy, Nora Slatkin, and he made clear that racial and gender diversity were prime hiring goals. Since there were a great many white middle-aged males in the agency, this attitude was despised as mere posturing for political purposes. Deutch disliked human spies and felt the culture of the Directorate of Operations was too closed off, too inward, too self-feeding. A new culture was put in place: employees should feel free to criticize superiors, there would be focus groups, more discussion of the agency's purpose, more interaction with the media, all labeled "California hot tub stuff," by one veteran.[3]

Deutch streamlined twenty-eight competing intelligence programs, and he used his early budget requests to channel more money to the National Reconnaissance Office at the Pentagon and the NSA, CIA rivals. He disliked aimless briefings and pointless task forces, and he quickly began a housecleaning of the clandestine DO.[4]

The Directorate of Operations was at one of the lowest points in its history, a victim of endless budget cuts, one of DO's biggest coming in 1995 when a third of the clandestine budget was cut (hadn't we won the Cold War?). The DO was also woefully lacking in Arabic or Farsi (Persian) speakers, lacking experts in Iranian or Arab culture, and facing transnational threats of a new and sinister kind it hadn't fully analyzed yet. It was at this time that Deutch, allegedly ordered by Clinton, began a "scrub" of clandestine sources—to weed out agents that might embarrass the agency. A disqualifying act might be a foreign dictator on the payroll dumping toxic waste or an agent who indulged in domestic abuse. "If your asset [paid agent] has stepped on some poison ivy, he's out," said a former station chief. Clearly an asset who had infiltrated a terrorist group was hardly going to be someone you wanted your daughter to marry, but all that mattered was: was he the kind of person who got the job done? Lists of all its full- and part-time informers were gathered and culled, eliminating valuable sources of intelligence. Then Congressman Porter Goss told a reporter, "No smart career officer was going to send in a little cable to headquarters saying, 'I've got this really great guy; now, he's killed his wife and murdered his children but he knows what the [Reds] are doing.'"[5] What the agency's human spies felt for Deutch was disgruntled disdain, repulsion, and stored-up rage. They were weary of barely disguised impatience that implied his subordinates were a lower, more stupid form of life. They abominated his dominating, omniscient, presiding manner, his mindless arrogance that spat on them as something unclean and inferior; they were full of glum outrage at the dismissal of two top covert action experts for not informing headquarters about an agent's human rights violations in Guatemala. Some spies began wearing black armbands to show their solidarity with the fired men, and when Deutch entered the "Bubble," Langley's impenetrable and leakproof auditorium, the assembled group did not get to its feet, an unparalleled breach of protocol. When Deutch urged the agents to be more aggressive and "forward-looking," they broke out in derisive laughter.

Deutch soon began looking for other victims, scouring lists to identify those agents whose length of service made them eligible for early retirement. These men were encouraged to take the package, hardly a ringing endorsement of their value, and many did. The departures ate away at morale, poisoned loyalty, spread disquiet and vindictive suspicion. There were at the time only eight hundred spies worldwide, and the feeling in the agency was that it was being rolled by the FBI, NSA, and the Pentagon. Soon fires of fierce bitterness flared up. As one former agent said of Deutch: "We were waiting for him to be here long enough for him to fall hard on his ass. And we knew he would, and he did."

One of the agency's most seasoned and astute Soviet analysts, Fritz Earmarth, took the retirement package and, during his exit interview, he asked the Human Resources person the kind of question that was typical of him. "You process four to five hundred people in a year, right? What's your portrait of the place?" The abashed woman's eyes filled with tears. "I've never seen it so bad," she said. Earmarth wanted to know in what way. "Everybody says it's hard to put your finger on it," she replied, "but it's the growth in the importance of stuff that shouldn't matter relative to the stuff that should."

Deutch, clad in authority, was unfazed by the hostility. A man of enormous, supreme self-assurance, he seemed proud of his management. "I've never had any problem asserting control," he said pompously.[6]

As the defects of his personality began to emerge, they undercut his designs to revamp and reenergize the agency. Deutch had no equanimity of temperament. At the least error in a subordinate, he would erupt in a fit of furious, savage temper, plus he liked to carelessly toss off tactless remarks. Once he told a group of DO officials, "From what I hear, junior officers are waiting for some new direction. Now I may be unhappily surprised." In a casual conversation at an agency event, early after his appointment, Deutch snapped the breezy, careless comment that he thought Pentagon intelligence officers were brighter than his CIA colleagues. The attitudes of his listeners instantly hardened against him like bacon fat going cold on a plate.

Soon, the pace of the Saddam program began to pick up. Deutch declared the program had to have "milestones," rigidly scheduled markers of progress. The 1996 presidential elections were many months away, but President Clinton had wanted a foreign policy success by the spring of the election year. The relentless Richter was no easy taskmaster, and there was a perceptible tightening up, an increasing pressure to produce, and the operation's swelling staff now found they were working flat-out, to the full extent of their capacity and endurance.

The signs of future success were there. A National Intelligence Estimate, NIE, completed in 1992 said that, although Saddam Hussein was weaker, the "only real threat" to his remaining in power is from a sudden, violent effort to remove him by one or more people with access to him."[7] Economic sanctions alone would not be enough, as the Bush administration had hoped. Saddam had maintained power by providing "his core group" with goods and services not available to the masses. Another difficulty was that no leader had emerged inside Iraq to challenge him, since any sign of opposition was met by "arrest, execution, or confiscation of a family's property." But the estimate then goes on to say that its conclusion could be wrong if the NIE underestimated "the current degree of unhappiness in military circles and in the Sunni core" that were the base of Saddam's power.

The NIE ruled out a popular revolt, then ended by saying, "If important individuals in the inner circle or within the Republican Guard are ready to act against him, a coup by these groups with access to him is the most likely scenario."

In 1993, another NIE put forth the conclusion that if Saddam were to be toppled, the impetus would have to come from within his most sensitive military ruling circles. There the conclusion sat, like a freshly laid egg, until 1994 when the Iraqi military's dissatisfaction was transformed from a hypothetical speculation to a quickening fact. In June, there was an assassination attempt on Saddam that came very close to success, and it was an event that was to have a profound influence on the new Clinton administration's policy toward the Iraqi dictator. Suddenly U.S. interest in Saddam's demise became infused with fresh energy and new life. Numbered U.S. intelligence reports coming into the White House made clear that members of Saddam's elite Republican Guard tried to bushwhack his personal motorcade and had barely missed. Referring to U.S. intelligence assets, a former U.S. official said: "We almost had him."

What impressed U.S. analysts was how well organized the attempt was. The hit had been put together in Baghdad by officers of the Republican Guard. The design was for Saddam to be killed as he moved under protection from one secret haunt to another. The Iraqi leader was tipped off about the plot's existence with only twenty-four to thirty-six hours to go. Saddam deployed a dummy motorcade, and as it proceeded, he was jarred to see that the Iraqi president's car in which he was supposed to be riding was blown up and badly damaged. The would-be assassins had revealed themselves and were out in the open, and Saddam with tough impassivity oversaw their slaughter. Within the U.S. intelligence community interest was aflame because the core of the failed scheme centered on twenty to thirty senior Republican Guard officers, the elite of Saddam's armed forces. Clearly treason had gained a foothold among them and treason was infectious.

Deutch was more convinced than ever that Saddam could be had, and in reality, throughout the summer of 1995, Deutch and Richter were maturing a very sophisticated plan. It had three aspects. Called the Silver Bullet Coup, the silver bullet was literal. U.S. intelligence was looking for someone in Saddam's ruling circle who would poison or shoot him, according to Ned Walker. "The United States made a major effort to try and assassinate Saddam," he said. "It wasn't halfhearted, we wanted him killed." Unfortunately, "we couldn't find a way to get to him, we lacked the penetration, but we were really looking for a way to assassinate him—it would have been easier than a coup."

The second aspect of the plan was Richter's revival of a discarded idea of a popular insurrection to unseat Saddam. One of Chalabi's Washington backers, Laurie Mylroie, a former advisor on Iraq to the Clinton campaign, would from time to time spread the word that Chalabi had come up with some master military plan to liberate Iraq from Saddam. Unfortunately the White House viewed her with disdain and had no interest in Chalabi's grand designs. Said former CIA official Bob Baer of Chalabi, "He'd shop me military stuff from time to time, none of it much good."[8] But Mylroie, a neoconservative, openly mocked "the Arabists," as she termed them, who were "wedded to the notion of changing the Iraqi regime through a coup," she told *The Middle East Intelligence Bulletin*.[9] A coup would be impossible, she claimed, because Saddam's "multiple, competing and overlapping security services" made the regime "virtually coup proof." The only thing that would work would be a huge popular insurrection, she said. The CIA and other U.S. intelligence analysts disagreed. "If you had a popular uprising in Iraq, all that would happen would be that the people in the streets would be slaughtered like partridges," a former DIA official said. So the idea was quietly dropped.

Surprisingly, Richter and Deutch had rescued Mylroie's idea from the Dumpster. The key element, they thought, would be a revolt by Saddam's military and security officers combined with a popular rising. If the insurrection occurred first, it might act to mask a military uprising or if the military revolt occurred first, the insurrection might act to support it and divide and confuse, and possibly paralyze Saddam's forces. With no American embassy active in Iraq, it was decided that the four central sites for operational planning would be the CIA chiefs of station in Ankara, Amman, London, and Kuwait City. The Kuwait role would be chiefly to recruit. Ankara was to provide intelligence and counterintelligence on the Kurds helping the agency. The chief of station in Cairo would have a role of subsidiary support.

The agency chief of station (COS, pronounced "coss") is the personal representative of the director of Central Intelligence, and the COS was always tasked with the intended area of operations and was also responsible for all counterintelligence. The COS in London would also play a critical part since that was where the INA, the Iraqi National Accord, was based. London has always been a hub for the collection/reception of U.S. intelligence on the Middle East. In the old days of cables, London was always the first stop on the list. From there it went to specific country desks at the State Department and various government agencies. Tom Twetten, the Mister Rogers with the iron spine, had moved to become London COS, replacing longtime covert operative Jack Devine.

The operation was ready for battle.

24

CONTENDING WITH GHOSTS

The matter of a coup in Iraq hardly had the president's full attention. Consumed by his domestic agenda, President Clinton was told of details by CIA director John Deutch during cabinet meetings. Vice President Al Gore was explaining the mechanics of planning and new developments as well, and his National Security Council advisor, Leon Fuerth, had been put in charge of the "Iraqi Study Group." In the meantime, planning for the coup went ahead. "Any time we were going to move to a different stage of op it would have to be cleared through Lake's office," a former participant said of the national security advisor, Tony Lake. The group at Langley headquarters submitted written summaries every Friday. Done on computer, they were "pretty pro forma," he said. Lake, alas, had never manifested more than tepid interest in the scheme. He was far too preoccupied with Bosnia to take much interest. "Lake was basically an Africa man," said CIA case officer Warren Marik. "He had no deep interest in the Middle East."[1] But there were others who harbored a sincere fervor when it came to helping plot the downfall of Saddam: James Pavitt at the agency was a hawk as were Fuerth and Gore. On the NSC, the hawks were George Tenet and Martin Indyk. They read the plans, assessed the options, evaluated the tactics, discussed them, then sent drafts back. "The word from on high was 'Stay with it, improve it,'" State Department official David Mack said. "People did."[2]

Within a short time, plans for intelligence collection began to assume a definite shape. One of the CIA people searching for possible assets within the Iraqi military and security forces was a man in his forties by the name of Regis

Matlak. Matlak started as an analyst at the Directorate of Intelligence and had moved over to the Directorate of Operations. His current position had landed him in the agency's Bureau of Leadership Analysis. It was a targeting office and Matlak was very good at his job. In the 1980s, Libyan leader Muammar Qaddafi had been a major troublemaker, stepping up efforts to get a nuclear weapon, declaring Libyan sovereignty of the Gulf of Sidra, launching military adventures in Chad, and other disturbing actions. Matlak had focused his efforts to develop sources within Qaddafi's inner circle. Before long, the agency learned a lot about the Libyan leader—that he used female bodyguards, knowing an Arab assassin would have trouble killing a woman; that he was emotionally unstable, at times sending signals that he wanted to talk to the United States, at others sending out assassination squads to deal with dissidents. He was a man with "big, big dreams, but a leader without a base or a center, a man in search of a country," a DO officer had observed at the time.

Matlak had helped to procure the sources that could come up with this kind of detailed biographical information. A former longtime agency case officer described Matlak's methods: "Sometimes a minister in a senior position is merely a political hack who knows less about internal affairs than the office manager or office director. The second person is more important because he knows more, probably feels unappreciated, and is easier to get to. So you would target him. That's what Matlak did for DBAchilles—the code name for the operation, DB indicating Iraq. Matlak went down lists of senior Saddam people. He was really very good."

A critical requirement for the proposed coup was acquiring information on the middle levels of the Iraqi military, mainly colonels and brigadiers. "Anyone above that rank was considered to be a problem," said a former agency plotter. The intelligence gathered on Iraq's military was to center on Iraqi army brigades because they "were the only units capable of independent movement," a former DO operative said, meaning they could, for a brief while, escape Saddam's eye. The original intelligence collection teams in the field were to ignore data dealing with Iraq's order of battle—the massed formation of Iraqi military units—"We could get that by technical means," from satellite imagery and intercepts, said a former DO program participant. What *was* wanted, he said, was intelligence on the attitudes of the middle Iraqi military leadership toward a possible overthrow of Saddam. If a coup was fomented or an insurrection occurred, how would they respond? Would the generals and corps commanders join the coup and turn on Saddam, or would they fight to defend him? CIA teams, working with the Kurds, also tried to acquire this kind of data.

"We were starting to get a picture of which division would not fight or which would defend the capital. We began to gain an impression of the status of the Republican Guard versus the Special [Republican] Guard, that sort of thing. Some of it went all the way to highest levels of the military. We were also convinced that the right level to pitch wasn't the division, but the brigade," said a former CIA recruiter for the program.

The agency discovered that intelligence from the Iraqi tribes would be key. Iraq was a society of 150 tribes, from the Dulami, centered in Anbar province, to the Jabor, the Bani Lam and the Bani Malik tribes down by the southern city of Basra. From the time Saddam had taken power, he had re-cruited young tribes from his home of Tikrit and other nearby areas into his internal security forces and the military. The Kurds ran excellent networks made up of tribesmen inside Iraq who had relatives in Saddam's military. Some of the best intelligence came to the CIA from Talabani's Kurdish mi-litia group, the PUK. "I don't know why, but the stuff we got from them was always great," said one former spook, chiefly, he said, because the group's members lived in cities close to the Iraq border like Irbil and Sulaimaniya. More importantly, the PUK also had connections with Iran, said a program participant. Within Iraq, Tehran ran a lot of first-class agent networks who passed their information to the Kurds, who passed it on to the CIA.

Along with CIA case officers, tribesmen would be given the job of re-cruiting agents. Once a large enough number of tribesmen had joined the plot, the goal was to infiltrate them into Iraq from Kurdistan, with their orders being to recruit more counterparts willing to rise against Saddam once the signal was given. "We looked at the tribes very carefully. We got good analysis out of the agency DI. We would send in a certain member of a tribe, and once he'd got in he'd begin to recruit," said a former recruiter. Some of the agency's best recruits came from the Dulamis, said the former DO official. "You have to be really careful. Some were loyal and some weren't—you had to know which clans. The DI had a two-hundred-plus page document on clans and subclans, and we were using that."

Great shrewdness on the part of recruiters was a must. A tribesman or dissident who joined the fight because his whole soul was filled with loath-ing for Saddam and who idolized the United States was considered a dubi-ous quantity. His cover had to work, and his real feelings had to be absolutely undetectable by the people he was infiltrating. A violently anti-Saddam in-dividual would probably give his convictions away and would not prove able to successfully penetrate a pro-Saddam organization. And if he gave the most minuscule indication of any pro-U.S. feelings he would fail and be put to death. Manipulating a person's ideological convictions was a real headache, and the coup's planners rejected many hotheaded candidates.

The centerpiece of the Deutch plan was the exile outfit the INA. With the backing of British and Saudi intelligence, it was founded in the early 1990s by a reformed Baath Party member, Iyad Alawi, and Salih Omar Ali al-Tikriti or Salah Umar al-Ali as he was also called. Salih Omar, a Tikriti, had enjoyed a career with Saddam that ranged from arranging public hangings of Saddam's enemies to becoming Iraq's ambassador to the United Nations. He later was based in London as "a cat's paw" for Saddam according to a former senior CIA official. In their excellent book, *Saddam Hussein: An American Obsession*, Andrew and Patrick Cockburn write that both Ali and Alawi began as assets for Saudi intelligence. But former U.S. intelligence figures with close knowledge of events told me that Alawi "was never a Saudi asset." One of these sources added, "The Saudis used Alawi during that period, but he was never an asset of theirs." Saudi intelligence took an immediate interest in Salih Omar, not Alawi, because Salih Omar "was a strutting Sunni Tikriti who appealed to their primitive tribal ethos." According to a former agency station chief, "The Saudis didn't really buy Alawi; they bought Ali, whom they thought could lead a Sunni coup against Saddam, from the inside." This, however, was "poppycock," he said, especially since CIA counterintelligence people and liaison services of foreign governments believed Salih Omar to be a double agent.

He was. By 1990, Salih Omar occupied the highly paid post of the London office of the Iraqi Freight Service where he displayed a wall-sized poster of Saddam. At that time he was still an agent for Iraqi intelligence. Then, in 1992, thinking Saddam about to fall, knowing that sanctions would put his office out of business and seeing a wide-open opportunity for himself, he resigned, making his disloyalty public.

According to Whitley Bruner, a former head of the CIA Iraq Task Force, there was "no way Ali [Salih Omar] could be trusted, but he took a lot of people in, including the Saudis, the Brits, and Alawi." The Saudis were burned, and Alawi was burned, and because of this the Saudis distrusted Alawi, thinking him an accomplice, but the agency had not been fooled, Bruner said. With Alawi, the CIA quickly laid down a few inalterable rules. If Alawi wanted to deal with Langley, he had to dump Salih. It was that simple. He did, and by 1992 Alawi was working for the agency.

Alawi's past life is a dim silhouette lost in deep shadow—the bedrock facts are hard to come by.

Alawi claimed that he broke with Saddam in 1971 during a visit to Lebanon after a friend told him Saddam had threatened to kill him. This is not true. According to several former senior CIA sources, when he moved to

London from Lebanon, Alawi was still very much a member of Saddam's secret intelligence, working for what would, in 1973, become the Mukhabarat, his job to head the Iraqi Student Union in Europe, a key intelligence-related post that required him to cultivate the elite Arab students who were being schooled at the best universities in London. Operating out of the Iraqi embassy in London, and using his medical studies as a cover, Alawi tracked Iraqi dissidents and student dissenters throughout Europe and is alleged to have been an assassin of the rebellious among them. Alawi worked at this job until 1975.

"He was definitely a paid Mukhabarat agent," said former CIA counter-terrorism chief Vince Cannistraro, who also contends that Alawi worked as an assassin.[3] "I know he was a hit man for a time, so if you're asking me if Alawi has blood on his hands from his days in London, the answer is yes, he does."[4] Former Middle East Institute president Phil Stoddard told the author that Alawi had been a hit man and was "a basic thug." A former CIA official who asked not to be named also said the account was true. "Alawi definitely used to do wet work [killing]," he said. (Alawi's office has never made any response to this and did not respond to my request for comment.)

To this day the opinion is that no one knows the real cause of the Saddam-Alawi rupture. Marik, in any case, remains of divided mind about it. "In the [CIA] file on Alawi, which I read, it is never clear why the break between the two [Alawi and Saddam] occurred. It could have been that Alawi was doing assassinations—I don't discount it, but I'm saying I personally don't believe it."[5] Neither does David Manners, the former chief of station in Amman. "I don't think it happened," Manners said but did not elaborate.[6]

There *is* one discreditable episode that does not easily lend itself to a facile recasting of the facts. Former U.S. intelligence officials, who asked not to be named, said that from 1992 to 1995, Alawi's organization, the INA, smuggled car bombs and other devices in from northern Iraq to Baghdad where they exploded, including one that blew up in a movie theater. Former U.S. intelligence sources weren't sure of the dates, pointing out the lack of U.S. sources in the country.

Although Alawi never publicly addressed the matter, one INA member did. In 1996, Amneh al-Khadeami, who claimed he was chief bomb maker for the organization, talked of the bombings in a videotape in which he complained of having been shortchanged supplies and money. Former CIA Iran-Iraq analyst Kenneth Pollack, who recalled the bombing campaign, quipped, "Send a thief to catch a thief."[7] The consensus is that not many people were killed.

It is of substantial interest that the CIA's first contact with the Alawi

family occurred in the early 1990s when Gary Shroen, then a CIA operative and deputy chief of mission to Hugh Turner at the U.S. embassy in
Riyadh, met and befriended Alawi's brother, Sabah, a man who at that time
was working for the United Nations Development Programme. The UNDP
works through a network of 134 country offices, and "helps people in 174
countries to help themselves, focusing on poverty elimination, environmental regeneration, job creation and the advancement of women," according
to its Web site. But UNDP also has key offices in all the Middle East and
North African countries, ranging from Saudi Arabia, Jordan, Egypt, and
Iraq, to Algeria, Tunisia, Somalia, and many others. Throughout the 1980s,
Alawi, like his brother, also worked for the UNDP, a perfect cover for his
new real job as a spy, making visits to Colombia and other places in Latin
America but also to many parts of the Middle East, gathering information
for the British. The British are said to have set him up with oil deals in Ye-
men to enable him to make money.

According to former CIA agents who have read the agency's file on
Alawi, in 1978, he defected to the British Secret Intelligence Service (MI--
6), offering his services. Alawi had a talent for favorably impressing people,
especially intelligence officers, and the MI-6 soon had him in tow. But Alawi
was lazy and feckless of nature and "didn't do much," Marik said. However,
Alawi did convey to the British some information that stimulated their ap-
petite, and they liked him. Bruner said caustically, "It's amazing how romantic the British are about some people. They get seduced by guys like Alawi."
Said Marik, "They suffered from case officer's disease—falling in love with
their agents."

Once Bush Senior had signed his finding about getting rid of Saddam,
"the British brought Alawi in to us," said Bruner. "Of course, they played a lot
of games with us first," Marik said. "By then, they really didn't know what to
do with him. He wasn't exactly a go-getter."

25

THE GREAT GAME BEGINS

According to Miles Copeland, one of the CIA's experts on coups, as he had executed one singlehandedly in Syria in 1949, it is official U.S. policy not to interfere in "the internal affairs of a sovereign nation." When it needs to, however, the United States finds means *outside* the normal channels of government that are able to "define a problem, and release forces which, largely on their own power, can effect a solution," allowing the U.S. to "disclaim any responsibility."[1] The point of DBAchilles was not simply to put in power in Iraq someone who would be seen as a U.S. stooge, who was then likely to be assassinated or overthrown and replaced by someone worse. The saying in the agency was: "Better a wise enemy (by whatever standards) than a stupid friend."

The ultimate candidate for a coup would be a man "intelligent enough to know what they should do for the good of their countries with the guts enough to do it."[2] What was wanted in the case of Iraq was a leader who knew that the "commander's principal function is to maintain conditions in which subordinates have no alternative but to accept them."[3] In replacing Saddam, the United States was looking for a less reckless leader who would enjoy the backing of Iraq's ruling class. The new leader could not be an isolated individual. The United States did not want a man in power who represented no one but himself. He had to be inseparably bound to an elite that had roots in a subelite that, in turn, had roots in the populace. This clearly meant a candidate from the Iraqi army. The actual recruitment would be done by elders of his own country with whom America could come to some sort of arrangement. The elders, or the elite, as Copeland explained, "would hear U.S. suggestions, argue with us, drive some bargains, and finally succumb to our overall argument—sweetened as it would be by economic aid and promises that once a constructive minded oligarchy got into power we would be appreciative of what it had to do to stay in power and would stop short of actual pressure . . . about how the country should be run."[4] In the agency's mind, there was "no question of a 'democratic' or 'popular' revolution. We would want to gain the support of the politically conscious and active urban populace, and that the rest of the country could be won over thereafter." The problem was not about bringing about a change, "but making the change stick," said Copeland.[5]

"We were going over all those considerations," a chief planner of the Alawi operation said after hearing Copeland's list.

The Clinton administration would set up its own strongman in Iraq after arresting some leading members of Saddam's family and a few key Iraqi commanders. Who was Iraq's new strongman to be? At first several candidates were discussed, and a consensus was produced by the Principals that America would rely on a retired general from the Iraqi Special Helicopter Force, Mohammad Abdullah al-Shawani, a native of the northern city of Mosul. In 1994, the CIA first contacted Iyad Alawi in Kurdistan about Shawani. Shawani was living in Amman when Amman Chief of Station Steve Richter had first met him and it wasn't long before Shawani disclosed breathtaking plans to rid Iraq of Saddam. The retired Iraqi general proposed that Saddam be overthrown or killed by his military. Shawani's three sons, Anmar, Ayead, and Atheer, a major, captain, and lieutenant respectively, were still residing in Iraq and still active in Saddam's Republican Guard. They were tough, seasoned men who had key links to others inside Saddam's military and security forces who could prove effective in toppling Saddam. (Versions differ of this—some say Alawi was first given the details of the proposal, and he passed them to MI-6, which finally briefed the CIA. Others maintain Richter heard it first.)

Shawani has been described by former CIA program participants as a man of the highest character, honest, direct, with a frank, straightforward style, always held in high honor by the people of Jordan and his former military colleagues in Iraq. "He was the kind of guy you liked to be around," said a former agency operative. "Everything about him was genuine."

If there were anxieties about the possibility of a Shawani failure, there were also misgivings about his enjoying success. Participants in a discussion on a post-Saddam Iraq included National Security Advisor Tony Lake, Secretary of State Warren Christopher, NSC staffer Martin Indyk, the Pentagon's Middle East expert Bruce Reidel, George Tenet, deputy CIA director, and various Middle East experts. Meetings stretched out over weeks.

The Principals and Deputies committees knew that a covert action could work if the plan were in conformity with basic, publicly announced administration policy. That way if it leaked it would not come as any great surprise and criticism would be minimal. Former CIA director William Colby, as cool and courageous an operator as there ever was, had once observed that "there must be a natural political base of support in the country where the covert action is carried out—a true resistance or political opposition. The CIA cannot create one."

Saddam's base of power had been at its weakest at the end of the Gulf War, yet no one had acted. That posed a problem. Many senior people in the White House wondered what the opposition amounted to. They were only too aware of the squabbling exile groups. Iraq itself was a tribal society, over 150 of them. Did the United States know what that meant politically? By destroying a leader who was a center of power, would the United States release anarchic chaos? Any society was a mechanism, with interests competing with each other, with different centers of force, everything held in balance, incessantly interacting. As the historian Herbert Butterfield pointed out, to render a country leaderless meant not simply to remove an unjust force but also to take away inducements, restraints, and safeguards that heretofore had kept that society from sliding into anarchy. If such safeguards were removed, wouldn't people suddenly discover that it was possible to do horrible things with impunity? People would take to crime who had been previously kept on the rails by a certain balance existing in society. "A great and prolonged police-strike, the existence of a revolutionary situation in a capital city, the exhilaration of conquest in an enemy country are likely to show up a seamy side of human nature amongst people who, cushioned and guided by the influences of normal social life, have hitherto presented a respectable figure to the world," said Butterfield.[6]

If Saddam had produced order by means of fear, it had still been order. Pat Lang, the first U.S. military analyst to predict the invasion of Kuwait, sent an e-mail to DIA director Lt. Gen. Harry Soyster, on July 30, 1990, saying, "I do not think he is bluffing." Lang was invited to a meeting in the Oval Office on January 8, 1991, only days before the war. The gathering was attended by President Bush, Gen. Colin Powell, National Security Advisor Brent Scowcroft, Richard Haas, chief of the NSC's Middle Eastern division, and others.

When it came his turn, Lang said he assumed he'd been asked to the meeting because he'd predicted the invasion. Then he said that Americans had a "perennial inability to comprehend alien cultures, even marginally alien cultures." Lang, an expert on Iraq and a man whose scholarly demeanor disguised an instinct for the jugular, added: the United States usually made two mistaken assumptions, the first that Iraqis were cowards, the second, that because Saddam was a "criminal, brutal and inhumane," he was not a legitimate leader. This was not true, said Lang. Saddam had either the support of his people or such tight control over them that he was legitimate in their eyes. A war with this small country with its overdeveloped military and entrenched leadership would be long and difficult, he warned.[7]

When Bush replied that Israeli prime minister Yitzhak Shamir, Egypt's president, Hosni Mubarak, Syrian president Hafez al-Assad, and Saudi Ambassador Bandar were all telling him, "it will be a pushover," Lang replied, "Sir, if I may say, that sounds to me like a collection of the ill-informed and self-serving."[8]

April Glaspie, the U.S. ambassador to Iraq, also already told Bush that while in the West Saddam wasn't recognized as legitimate, a great many Iraqis supported him. "They may not like him, but they like his program," she said. "It's an illusion to think he's not supported."

That had been back in 1990. Since then, U.N. sanctions hadn't turned Iraqis against Saddam but rather against the West. The hidden U.S. hand in any coup that toppled Saddam would eventually be revealed. Would Shawani be compromised? Would he be seen as a foreign tool, a serious worry in a xenophobic country like Iraq? Saddam's removal would cut across class, tribal, religious, ethnic ties. Under his rule there had been a great sense of inequities and fear and hatred of tyranny, but would a coup result in an unfocused struggle for power among the factions finally freed of authority? Was there in Iraq a galvanizing force of moral responsibility for the public good that Saddam's removal would release? Would there be a desire to maintain order and administer justice? Or with the safeguards gone, the inducements missing, would it be every man for himself?

There were many other issues that might emerge if Saddam were gone. Unless killed, he could grow into a hero, and the tensions would intensify over issues that Saddam had exploited, the Palestinian question, deep suspicion about neocolonialism, the divisions between rich and poor Arabs.

No administration official knew the answer.

Now a new more focused, driven spirit began to emerge among the CIA planners, and as resources mounted and multiplied, they began to obtain a clearer idea of the terrain they were going to operate in. Soon, "We were starting to get a picture of which division would not fight or which would defend the capital," said a former senior program operative. "We began to get a feel for the political currents active within the top leadership of the regular army, the tensions between the Republican Guard versus the Special Guard, that sort of thing." It was not long before the agency was trying to recruit "at the division level," because a defection of a general of a division "would take off the board three Iraqi brigades," said a former Pentagon official.

The CIA analysts were also doing a precise, dispassionate study of Iraqi military units, especially the ones that could intervene at the time of the coup to thwart it. Some would ask for detailed knowledge of an Iraqi general's office: the personalities, the intrigues, the cliques. At other times, they would ask questions like: What is the list of dangerous units? Who were their leaders, what was the technical structure of the unit, and who were its key technicians?

A particular Iraqi unit, an armored brigade in the Medina Division of the Republican Guard near Basra, emerged as a possible candidate to play a decisive part. It would seize key symbolic locations like TV stations, power centers, military installations, the Presidential Palace, the airport, and important ministries. The plotters would also arrest leading regime figures. It would close roads to forces attempting to counterattack.

More information poured in and the momentum continued to build.

As early as January 1996, there was a meeting in Riyadh that included a clutch of high-level intelligence officials from MI-6, the CIA, and Kuwait. The gathering was hosted by Prince Turki, head of Saudi intelligence, and the Saudi intelligence desk officer for Iraq, Gen. Abu Abdul Mohssan. In an unusual spirit of resolve, enterprise, and unanimity, those present all pledged their support.

By the spring of 1996, Kurdish, Iraqi, and other dissidents, about three hundred of them, were brought back to secret CIA training camps in America for instruction in explosives, sabotage, special weapons, and the like. One such camp was Camp Hale in Colorado, there was another temporary camp set up in the Southwest, about six in all. At headquarters and CENTCOM between two hundred and three hundred people were working on DBAchilles at its height.

What was especially clear was that the capital of Jordan, Amman, was going to be at the center of the action.

For years after World War II, Amman had been a pleasant backwater in the Arab world, picturesque and languid, until the advent of Desert Storm forever altered the character of the place. Suddenly it became like Lisbon or Casablanca during World War II or Berlin and Vienna during the Cold War—Amman was transformed into a "sort of holy city" for spies, as one former agency official put it. Iranians, Palestinians, Iraqis, Egyptians, Hezbollah, Americans, were all stirring throughout the crowded, busy, noisy place. Following the Gulf War, Amman was bursting with modern hotels, restaurants, offices, mosques, and public parks. Hordes of Palestinians, expelled by the vindictive Kuwaitis after the Gulf War, used to sleep in the open, green parks, and a garish building boom was going on all over the city. Crowning the crest of the high, imposing hill above Abdoun sprawled the vast, newly constructed compound of the U.S. embassy, while below, on Jebel Amman, the chief thoroughfare that ran down the city's center, was the embassy of Iraq, Saddam's most important diplomatic outpost (with the exception of the mission to the United Nations in New York). There were plenty of CIA agents and their counterparts in the Mukhabarat, the latter's presence making the town an edgy place, for it was the Iraqis' main objective to murder Iraqi dissidents. In 1992, for example, the Iraqi nuclear physicist Muayad Hassan Naji had been killed in front of his wife and children while on his way to Libya. In 1996, Amman was a tense, unpredictable, dangerous place. Multitudes were trying to get out of Iraq, and long lines of them would collect and thicken at the U.S. embassy.

Most were frauds, claiming knowledge of WMD simply to gain a U.S. visa, according to former CIA operatives who dealt with them. Some informants provided valuable information, yet most were simply angling for a way out of Jordan, and in one case lazy skepticism bred tragedy. An earnest, agitated Iraqi said he was in danger and wanted desperately to get a visa, explaining to his American interviewer that he had real knowledge of Saddam's WMD programs and wanted to impart what he knew to the U.S. government. The American official had heard it all before, and said listlessly that he would check it out; the Iraqi was told to return the next day. Unfortunately, Saddam's spies had the U.S. embassy staked out the way the FBI did in the Cold War days when the Soviet embassy in Washington had been kept under incessant surveillance. In any case, the Iraqi, greeted with something far less than enthusiastic warmth, went away, nervous and disconsolate. When Jordanian agents found him later that night in a street, he was dead, his throat cut.[9]

A city seething with plots and counterplots, Amman was a battleground of that world of mirrors whose major scenes of warfare took place in dreary alleys or ordinary streets, whose clashes were part of a grim, remorseless fight to the finish. Now thanks to Steve Richter and David Manners, Amman's secret wars were soon to be thrust before the world in a blaze of unwanted publicity. King Hussein had once been on the CIA payroll, being paid $700,000 a year "for security," according to a former senior intelligence official, but in

1977, after *The Washington Post* made this public, President Jimmy Carter canceled the operation, believing it unsavory, and for a time it had been policy to keep heads of state off the agency payroll. Then, in the 1980s, under CIA director William Casey, a joint CIA-NSA program for collection and intelligence sharing had resumed in the region, even though the king had not been happy about it. (Memories are long in the Middle East.)

Repairs were made, however. In the fall of 1995, King Hussein visited President Clinton. Hussein had taken a very collaborationist line toward Iraq during Desert Storm, but since then Clinton had met and talked bluntly to the king, requesting his full support for the coup, making sure it was all right to have the key base of planning in Amman. Clinton's fluency of persuasion worked its magic. The wounded feelings of the 1970s, having healed, Hussein once more agreed and once more opened himself and his country to America in his pursuit of what he defined as his country's best interests.

In January of 1996, David Manners, the new chief of station for Jordan, was dispatched to Amman along with a special team, including a CENTCOM Air Force officer who never left his side. Manners knew he was bearing the brunt of a large load and that he was the central figure in a precarious situation. He was experienced and expert, said a former colleague. Manners had worked in the agency's European Division and been COS in Prague, and was described by a former colleague as "tall, thin, with large hands and short gray hair and very intense piercing eyes—a high-energy guy, very intelligent, who doesn't take prisoners." A former senior Directorate of Operations official called him "a very highly charged guy—very aggressively operationally. Very." Another man who knew Manners well said, "He had an inner steeliness behind the courtesy."

As COS he was the personal representative of the director of Central Intelligence and he was responsible for all civilian intelligence and counterintelligence in his area of operations. The only person senior to him would be the U.S. ambassador, who would rely heavily on Manners for his judgment concerning intelligence matters. Under Manners were the embassy case officers who had people spying for them, and these officers were responsible for their assets' security and production (assets being paid agents). The station in Amman was not established to support the planning for the coup. The CIA officers in Amman already had a full-time job going after their assigned intelligence targets, and Manners's assignment was in addition to what they were already doing.[10]

Manners had a great deal to do and not enough resources to do it with. Saddam's agents had the U.S. embassy under constant Iraqi surveillance, yet it was not Iraqis who posed the greatest trouble for Manners, it was his boss, Near East Division chief Steve Richter. They had been at odds since the first time they met. Richter was the previous Amman station chief, replacing Geoff O'Connell, who had done clandestine work in Syria before Amman. O'Connell was a man described by colleagues as a "by the book" guy who disliked the military and was "difficult to know," according to one. After Richter moved to Washington, David Manners was slated to take his place in Amman. It was an old quarrel. After Manners had been assigned to Langley, he headed the DO's Iran Operations Group where he first encountered the overbearing Richter. The situation was ripe with possibilities for misunderstanding, and from the first, they clashed like hostile species. Manners was a hard man with a hard head and he saw Richter drifting into a shadow land where hard facts had to be adjusted to vaporous doctrine, infected by wishful thinking that could picture sunny results. To Manners, the idea of a coup was dubious. Amman was a hopeless place, yet day-by-day pressure was piling on, and they were being forced into a tightening circle of events. Impossibilities were to be rendered possible.

From the outset, their methods differed as much as their characters. To Manners, time was of the essence. He had to recruit operatives, train them, and send them into Iraq, and this took time and Manners hadn't any to spare. CIA director John Deutch was getting more and more impatient as his access to Clinton grew. Both Richter and Deutch were giving weekly updates to the Principals, and what they wanted even more than success was to avoid some embarrassing public failure. The failure of a subordinate reflects badly upon his superior so there is a strong instinct on the part of both to cover it up; it is only when the knowledge of the failure is out in the open that the superior becomes responsible so there must be no failures. When it came to recruiting, Richter was painstaking and methodical, the niggling soul of methodical caution. The more aggressive Manners preferred the more risky method of "cold pitching" potential agents. Cold pitching meant any Iraqi serving at any Iraqi embassy or Iraqi trade mission in the world could provide a target. Manners or his agency recruiters would usually work through the U.S. military attaché at the U.S. embassy. The spymasters would wait for Armed Forces Day in Amman or some similar occasion, and then make sure the U.S. embassy got the targeted person on the guest list. Then the agency recruiter "always got dressed up in the proper uniform to win recognition with Iraqis that I met socially." The contact would seem accidental, and the recruiter would try to set up a meeting, a lunch, a walk, a visit to a museum, and, once at the site, he would then ask the Iraqi, "Will you work for us?" Most said no. Sometimes, the approach sparked panic. "I had one Iraqi guy scream at me, 'Get out of my face! You're going to get me killed!'" a former coup planner said.

But some would say yes.

By contrast, Richter wanted a slower, more cautious approach where the contact was less bald, the pitch less blatant, the meaning more ambiguous and oblique. Recruitment for Richter was a choice fruit that took time and patience to ripen. As a former recruiter for the op put it, Richter wanted to "Spot the guy, assess him, try and get paper on his background, then gradually develop contacts—indirect at first, and then gradually start tasking the subject, and only doing that after you really knew where his allegiances lay." It was a slow, painstaking process.

Richter was especially alert to targeting a potential asset who was likely to cooperate and not report the approach to his superiors. Any pitch was risky. Your contacting a prospect put him on the horns of a painful dilemma—he had to envisage greater benefits by supporting the coup than by reporting your approach to his superiors. The rewards of disloyalty had to be greater than remaining loyal. A shared political outlook was important, but so were ethnic links, which oftentimes in the Middle East outweighed political affiliations. It was safest if you stated the objective of the coup in terms of political outlook rather than disparaging ruling personalities or specific policies. A common and usually successful tactic was to tell the prospect that most of the members of his unit "were already with us," said one former CIA operative. The recruiter had to assure the prospect no harm will come to him. The prospect was to be given no information beyond the minimum required, and the pitch was always verbal, never written. A former recruiter noted, "We would say to a guy, when the overthrow comes, you want to be part of the winning side. You'd also appeal to their patriotism—you'd say, 'You're a real Iraqi—stand up for Iraq—fight for the real Iraq, not this guy Saddam.'"

The number of recruitments was kept small because of security. The fewer who knew of your plans, the more likely you were to succeed. So ran the rules.

Manners, however, was in charge and he would do as he saw fit. He was not a careless man, he knew the dangers, respected his enemy, and from the first took steps to establish and safeguard the security of his network. Inside Jordanian intelligence, there was a special unit whose job was to work with the Americans by facilitating secret meetings with dissident Iraqis, supplying transport, and providing interpreters and the like. The Jordanian in charge of this group, Samih Batikhi, the new director general of Jordanian intelligence, had been helped into his position by "American pressure," said a former White House official, but he was good at his job.

Special emphasis was also placed on security and spotting countersurveillance. Manners's own agents would abruptly reverse direction when walking down a street, pause constantly to use the reflections from shop windows to spot tails, enter a store, wait to see who entered, then abruptly leave to wait outside to see who came out or else try to gain vantage points (like standing on the center of a bridge) to better see foot traffic coming in all directions, and so on. According to one former U.S. operative, "The Jordanian intelligence agents were first-rate—the Jordanian service is fabulous." Even Alawi's people observed security procedures "very rigorously," he said. But the tension of the situation was extreme.

When Manners was told his people were the object of a five-man Iraqi counterintelligence group, he instantly found a way to neutralize them. The aggressive, high-energy Manners had developed a sensitive source inside the Iraqi embassy. At some point that source complained to Manners that he was being harassed and threatened by an Iraqi intelligence major who headed a counterintelligence unit that hunted for U.S. spies. The major was "your basic thug," said a participant. So Manners, his deputy, and another operative arranged for another CIA team member to meet with the major, talk him up, then hand him some money, the transaction being lovingly photographed. "In an instant, he had changed from killer to a cowering, whimpering little kid," a former agent said.[11] Manners and his team kept up the remorseless pressure; the source in the Iraqi embassy was left alone. Back at headquarters at Langley, they grew nervous. Richter or some other superior said to Manners that the tactics he'd employed on the Iraqi major were "too aggressive" and "were inviting retaliation." According to one source, Manners replied that he'd stop when he was ordered to stop. Langley replied he might be ordered to stop, but the orders never came.

26

OPERATION BACKFIRE

David Manners, the new CIA chief of station for Jordan, was hard at work building up a system of spies, contacts, and informants who kept Langley abreast of progress in Amman when a surprising incident opened everyone's eyes to the nature of the vastly careless, unstable, reckless character of Iyad Alawi and émigré groups in general. In February 1996, Alawi, a paid CIA agent and head of the INA, held a press conference to announce he was opening a headquarters in Amman. A complete stranger to modesty, Alawi announced that his arrival was "a historic moment . . . a beacon of light into Iraq, a light from which Saddam will find no hiding place." After hurling invective at one of Saddam's murderous sons, Alawi did concede that there were areas of the work of his organization that "must remain secret," if they were to succeed. This was bad enough but other announcements followed, including one about the upcoming launch of an INA radio station called al-Mustaqbal or The Future, that would broadcast from Amman. In a broadcast for CNN, a channel that was required watching in Baghdad, Alawi called Jordan "a door to Iraq."

Panic reigned in the Jordanian ministries. Alawi's announcement was a dangerously provocative indiscretion. Short of a formal declaration of war, allowing hostile, covert actions to be waged from its soil meant that Jordan had gone about as far as any country could, and Iraq was, after all, a neighbor. So the nervous Jordanian government issued immediate denials: "We will not be involved in any plans to overthrow the regime," and other dramatic protestations.

As sure as the coming of night and old age, Alawi opened his headquarters, the festivities marred only slightly by the appearance in the British newspaper *The Independent* disclosing the INA's bombing campaign inside Iraq.

A former U.S. program operative said of the whole episode, "It was eye-rolling, truly stunning in its crassness and stupidity."

Manners knew from the beginning that by operating from Amman his operation faced an especially daunting threat to its success: sheer distance. Six hundred miles away and out of sight lay the menaces of Baghdad. The courier-agents of Manners had a long way to travel to their safe houses across a hostile, closely scrutinized territory. There was no choice. Phone service was patchy. International calls were routed via telephone exchanges to Rasedia, north of Baghdad, instead of being dialed directly. Not only were all phone calls taped by Iraqi intelligence, they were later examined carefully by a special committee made up of the representatives of Saddam's numerous intelligence services. Manners had no choice—it was couriers or nothing.

So the agency experts devised an ingenious plan. The Iraq-Jordan border was alive and busy, sometimes clogged by long strings of oil truck convoys going in and out, many part of the huge smuggling operation whose spoils had put the Kurdish groups of Barzani and Talabani at odds, plus there were constant streams of people coming back and forth. Amman was the home of a lively, profitable black market in auto tires. Apparently because of some loophole in the U.N. sanctions, Iraq taxis were allowed to come across the border into Jordan where they could buy new tires and exchange their old ones, and often they put the old ones back on, and returned to Iraq to sell the new ones at extortionate prices. "We were taking advantage of every chink in the system," said a former program operative. The CIA couriers would become part of the oil smuggling and taxi traffic, using trucks or taxis for their transportation.

In May, the signal was finally given for the first infiltrations into Iraq from Kurdistan. The CIA was using "ratlines"—centuries old smuggling routes—to get in and out. "It was eye-watering to watch these guys work," a former U.S. source said of the tribesmen. "They were very gutsy guys." Secrecy, anonymity, discretion were the watchwords.

To foil Iraqi eyes and ears, the CIA provided its couriers with Inmarsat satellite phone systems. Inmarsat is the system used worldwide by the U.S. Merchant Marine. According to its Web site, an Inmarsat phone, or terminal, "contacts the [geosynchronous] satellite and communicates to a ground station through the satellite. It provides reliable communications services . . . in remote regions or where there is no reliable terrestrial network."

In fact, it does a lot more than that. It is a computer that can look like an ordinary briefcase, and it can transmit both streaming and digital data. It comes with a little dish that can be placed on the hood of a car and then transmit images in real time back to a receiving ground station. It can also transmit notes: the operator writes a scrawl, a scanner is used, and those can go back in real time to the CIA. For DBAchilles, the agency's phones for its network couriers were heavily encrypted and assets were provided with very precise schedules for burst transmissions. Case officer instructions included verbal ciphers, meaning certain code words or phrases that had to be used or their omission would mean the courier was under Iraqi control.

In addition, the couriers going back and forth from Iraq to Jordan and vice versa were not only instructed in the use of these instruments, they were given directions about how to safeguard their own and the operation's security. The Inmarsat communications gear was disguised to look like a regular notebook computer carried in a briefcase. "We would tell couriers that when you go across carrying a computer, don't be conspicuous in the way you dress, and above all, don't carry too much money or do anything else that will attract suspicion," said one former case officer. "Of course, it only takes one guy who doesn't get the message to ruin it all."

All through May the infiltrations continued and the White House was keeping close tabs. Deutch, powerful, experienced, and extremely self-confident, by now was all reckless, headlong drive. The uprising was scheduled for the third week of June, and the outcome of a whole chain of small crescendos was quickly gathering to a climax. What no one detected in all the bustling activity was the silent running out of time. Thinking they were on the brink of success, no one noticed that the current of circumstance was flowing now with irresistible strength toward a disastrous culmination. The agency believed it had cast a snare to trap Saddam when in fact it was walking into one.

There had already been warnings. In March, a source of Chalabi's INC in the Mukhabarat had alerted the exile that the planning for the coup had been compromised. The source claimed that in January, one of Manners's couriers, an Egyptian, had been captured, his Inmarsat equipment seized, and he had been closely interrogated. Many of the plotters' names were known to Iraqi spy hunters. In fact, the INC informant said that the Inmarsat phone had been installed in a Mukhabarat headquarters in Baghdad. Highly excited and full of urgent concern, Chalabi hastened to Washington where he was given a hearing by Deutch and Richter. Richter looked at Chalabi the way a family man might look at a leper on his doorstep. Chalabi was a swindler, a liar, and a scoundrel, why should he be believed? The exile was seen as cunningly revengeful, a man of atrocious spite, merely trying to wreck a rival. Besides, the agency had invested too much to stop now.

So they had listened but they had ignored him, and Chalabi made hot tracks to Capitol Hill to talk to his right-wing Republican backers, who had no love of Alawi or the agency. To old Iraq hands, it was on the Hill that the plot leaked. "Chalabi betrayed the plot by his warning," Whitley Bruner said.[1]

By June, the entire scheme had crumbled to powder. Alawi had given another infamous interview in which he bragged to *The Washington Post* that the uprising "should have at its very center the [Iraqi] armed forces," and the furor from that had hardly begun to die down when agency people realized the venture had gone horribly wrong. Acute anxiety spread as arrests began in what had been until then Sunni loyalist strongholds like Ramadi, Fallujah, Tikrit, and Mosul. "We knew instantly it was falling apart," said a former agency operative. According to a colleague of theirs, the Egyptian courier gave Saddam's agent five names. Saddam's police "arrested the five and got more names. Then they would look at new names and their circle of friends might be part of a plot and they began to track them. The Mukhabarat began profiling people on the assumption they might be part of this network."

Within three weeks to a month, Saddam had exposed much of the underground organization. Then the Inmarsat equipment carried by the Egyptian began to come alive with taunts. "They would call and say 'We just arrested so and so,' and we'd get another call and they said, 'We just arrested so and so.' They were really enjoying themselves."

The first 120 of the plotters captured were members of the extremely elite Special Republican Guard, the Republican Guard, the General Security Service, and the regular army. Saddam had a special communications intelligence unit called the B32, which was tasked with ensuring the security of the communications from the Presidential Palace with military units around the country. The commander of that unit, Brig. Gen. Ata Samawal, was arrested, tortured horribly, and executed for treason, and some of his fellow officers were arrested and packed off to prison. Even the senior levels of the Mukhabarat were not immune to penetration. Col. Omar al-Dhouri, a section director for Ahm al-Khass, the special security service, and Col. Riyadh al-Dourhi, both members of a tribe considered solidly loyal to Saddam, were seized. Muffawaq al-Nassiri, a Tikriti general, was arrested. The Dulamis, the tribe within which so much recruiting had been done, was a special target, and many members fled into neighboring countries. Saddam's own personal household staff had been penetrated. Boutrous Eliya and William Matti, two of Saddam's personal cooks from the Assyrian Christian community, confessed to being part of a scheme to poison Saddam. In short time, the number of arrested had swollen to eight hundred.

As news of the fiasco emerged, many in the Western press gloated, comparing DBAchilles to Kennedy's Bay of Pigs in the magnitude of its disaster. Yet the fact was President Clinton never gave the go-ahead for a coup. As a former major actor in the plot said, "We never attempted a coup. We never had the backing. We never had a go-ahead. All we had was a piece of paper from the president," meaning the lethal finding. Others remain bitter to this day. Said one organizer of the failed plot, "I have a lot of resentment. I don't think the Clinton administration ever really put their back into the effort. They went through the motions to satisfy their critics in Congress and their political opponents. The INA people were very brave and did their part. We never did ours."

Many believed that the major failure lay with Deutch. His was a blind urge to simply forge ahead. All he could see was an opening that offered a great prospect for advancement and could be readily exploited. He brushed aside serious considerations, and in general exhibited a little too much haste, and a little too much impatience, a little too much zeal, an incapacity to question his own methods, his ideas, his intensity of purpose. His ego was much too inseparable from his aims, former associates said.

Richter was a pain, said former U.S. diplomat David Mack, but the main push for a coup was coming from CIA director John Deutch. "In his eagerness to get something going, careful tradecraft was overruled," Mack said. "Clinton would ask 'How are we doing?' and Deutch bustled to comply and please. Things got sloppy."[2]

David Manners resigned from the CIA over the poor planning for the operation. "We entirely let them down," sources close to Manners said of the plotters. Because Manners is a man of high conscience with the un-spy-like ability to feel keenly another's suffering, he felt the agency had betrayed the Iraqis and he could not go to work anymore although he was only forty-three and had a wife and six children fourteen years and under. He told his wife that he would take early retirement if Langley gave him the opportunity. He then was told by DO sources that the agency was planning to offer early retirement to all eligible employees, and he resolved to leave the service. "He hated his job," a source close to Manners said.

When the new chief of the agency's Inspector General's Office sent Manners an eyes-only cable requesting his candid comments on the Iraq program, Manners, according to a colleague, responded with a devastating blast, "the cable equivalent of a flamethrower." Although Manners's critique was valid, it put harshly and bluntly what others might have said in smoother words. A source close to Manners criticized the response as being "unnecessarily personal in some parts" such was his rage at the headquarters types who "Manners felt had failed the officers in the field."

To everyone's amazement, Richter, Manners's *bête noire* at headquarters, never mentioned a word to him about the critical blast of which he'd been the chief target. Yet the damage was done. Cherished designs and careful plans lay in fragments on the floor like shattered china. The DDO politely asked Manners if he would like to make a lateral move to become the Moscow chief of station, but the offer was marred by a request by headquarters that Manners postpone taking the new post for a year, ostensibly for the agent to brush up on his Russian. Manners stunned the DDO when instead he took early retirement.

Before Manners left Amman, CIA deputy director George Tenet came to town as part of a Middle East swing. Amman was the last stop on his trip. Because Manners was poised for his final departure, and this roughly coincided with Tenet's schedule, the deputy director offered to fly Manners and his family back to the United States with him on his Air Force plane. It was a kind and gallant gesture, and it saved Manners the hassle of moving six young kids through a European transit. During the fourteen-hour trip to Andrews Air Force Base, Manners and Tenet talked a great deal about Manners's future plans. Tenet, describing Manners as a "leader," urged him to stay with the agency, saying that he would one day be a future director of the clandestine operations. Manners was touched, thanked Tenet for his support, but wasn't having any. His decision to move on had been made.[3]

Tenet then asked Manners to take some leave to decompress and then reconsider whether it was the right step. Manners did take three months of leave but "never looked back," according to a source close to him. Some CIA agents like Whitley Bruner blame Chalabi's warning to Deutch and then the Republican congressmen on the Hill. Said Bruner, "Remember the rivalry between the INA and INC. If Alawi [of the INA] had succeeded, it would have been end of the INC and Chalabi. As it was, the CIA cut him off, so he went to the Pentagon and the checks kept coming."[4]

"We had strong suspicion that INC betrayed it," a former senior agency official said. Others doubt it. According to David Mack, the code name for the program, DBAchilles, had never changed from 1994 through the spring of 1996. "That's way too long for a code name to remain secure," Mack said.[5]

But perhaps the most puzzling aspect of the Amman operation lies with the fact that the agency knew, in advance, that Alawi's organization, just like the INC, *had been penetrated* by Iraqi agents; however, they felt they had "rewired" the operation, compartmentalized it in such a way as to screen out the double agents. Manners knew of the penetration, according to a source formerly close to him. "Manners knew, we all knew. We tried to re-wire the INA so that only a very few knew what was going on."

Manners, Richter, and others were aware that the Egyptian courier was an Iraqi agent, but "the courier was Shawani's man, and Shawani felt he could control his man," said a former program official. Former Middle East Institute president Phil Stoddard summed up: "I had no idea of how the agency thought it could succeed with a penetrated group."

The conclusion of many is that the Egyptian intelligence service tipped off Saddam about the coup plan. "It was purely economics," said Ned Walker.[6] He explained that at the time Egypt was experiencing alarmingly high levels of unemployment. Senior Egyptian government officials feared social insta-bility or a spike in the activities of Islamic fundamentalists, so it was with relief that Saddam was willing to import huge numbers of Egyptians for work in Iraq. "Hundreds of thousands of Egyptian workers were working Iraq's arable land," said a former senior CIA official. "In the beginning, they were able to remit all of their earnings back to Egypt." If Saddam had been toppled, "the whole neat, prosperous bilateral arrangement would have gone down the tubes."[7]

27

STARS THAT SHINE AND NEVER WEEP

The disaster of the coup planning for Iraq was only one bitter setback for Clinton that spring and summer. He would suffer two more: failing to finesse the election of Shimon Peres as Israeli premier, and the bombing in Saudi Arabia of a U.S. barracks by Iranian-trained agents.

Israeli premier Yitzhak Rabin did not live to see his dream of peace. He was killed on November 4, 1995, by a young Israeli zealot. Just before he died, he had signed Oslo II in October 1995, which provided for the withdrawal of the Israeli army from nine of the most populous cities on the West Bank. Secretary of State Christopher had been alone with Clinton when the word came that Rabin had been killed. The news hit Clinton very hard. He had developed a profound affection for Rabin. Christopher said he had never seen news affect the president so profoundly. Clinton was silent for a long minute, rendered mute, and Christopher felt the president was pondering his own mortality. When he regained his poise, Clinton said quietly he wanted to go to Rabin's funeral.[1] At the service, Jordan's King Hussein was the main speaker, but Clinton spoke briefly, ending somberly with the Hebrew words, "Goodbye, friend."

Rabin's successor was Shimon Peres, his old rival, and Peres wanted to ensure that Rabin's legacy lived on, and that momentum and progress in the peace process were not sidetracked. Peres was seventy-eight years old, born in Poland, and had arrived in Palestine at the age of eleven, in 1934. Most Israelis at the time were Ashkenazis, from Eastern Europe, cultured and refined people who looked down their noses at the poorly bred Peres with his heavy accent. Where Peres yearned for equality of status, what he encountered was haughty superiority. Like Clinton, his sole obsession was politics, and he was sly, shrewdly insightful with a talent for intrigue.[2] He knew how to assume the character that best served the designs he harbored and the situation in which he found himself. Fame, self-interest, service to the state dominated his mind. Of his special role in Israel's history he had no doubt.

Most of the "New Hebrews," as they were called, thought themselves if not to be above politics, to be outside of it and held it in contempt. Not Peres. Like Clinton, he was the supreme political animal endowed with a sound, active mind. When he'd been twenty-nine, he was appointed minister of defense by Israeli president David Ben-Gurion, but he lacked military experience, and many of the military felt him an outsider, not up to the job.

Peres was a seasoned politician, and above all things, he wanted peace. It had been his Foreign Ministry that fashioned the Oslo breakthrough. In 1994 further progress had occurred: Palestinian self-rule was established over Jericho and the Gaza Strip following the withdrawal of the Israeli Defense Forces. Not that the reign of joy and harmony had arrived on earth because of the accords: since 1993, hundreds of innocent Israeli civilians had been killed and injured by terrorist attacks by Arab diehards, and there had been savage, punishing clashes between Israeli soldiers and Israeli settlers.

Where Rabin had been practical and taciturn, Peres was expansionist and visionary, but both manifested unbreakable stubbornness when it came to the issue of settlements. When Rabin had become Israeli premier, he acted quickly to freeze contracts to build seven thousand new settlements in the territories. He intended to cancel the contracts and remove the incentives and subsidies Yitzhak Shamir had used to get people to become settlers. The settler movement had flown into a fit of furious temper, but Rabin wasn't fazed and didn't deviate a hairbreadth from his resolve. Rabin's great achievement was to commit Israel to a different, tougher policy toward the settlements. The government of Israel would not create or sanction any new settlements and would even attempt to prevent settlements by private individuals. As Rabin had once said to Secretary of State James Baker, "For the sake of 3.9 million Jews and a million Israeli Arabs who should not have to mortgage their future because of 100,000 settlers in the territories, I intend to persevere."[3]

Peres was determined to take up where Rabin had left off. Throughout 1995 and 1996, the promotion of settlements and the manipulation of people's fears of terror and undermining public confidence in the Oslo Accords were the chief agenda items of Benjamin Netanyahu.[4] In 1997, in an act of defiant spite, Netanyahu approved the Har Homa project envisioning the construction of housing for 312,000 Jews on a disputed hillside known in Arabic as Jebel Abu-Ghneim south of Jerusalem.

Clinton, through position papers first put together in the State Department's Policy Planning Department and by means of U.S. intelligence estimates and field reports, summaries, and briefings given him by his excellent negotiator, Dennis Ross, had gained an absolute determination not to see Netanyahu sabotage the peace process for which Clinton's friend, Yitzhak Rabin, had paid the ultimate price. Beginning in December, and continuing on into the spring, Clinton put in motion a plan to help Peres obtain the premiership.

By the spring of 1996, Peres and Netanyahu were locked in a tight race. It was already clear that Netanyahu was not going to trade land for peace. He would also work to dash the Arab hopes that compliance with the Oslo conditions would eventually result in Palestinian statehood.

Peres, like Rabin, still steadfastly opposed the spread of Israeli settlements. One example makes clear the fixed and unmoving character of his outlook. As the price for renewing peace talks that had stalled after an Israeli settler, Baruch Goldstein, massacred thirty-one Palestinian worshipers inside the Cave of Patriarchs in February 1994, in Hebron, Arafat insisted on the removal of five hundred Jewish settlers from the heart of the city and demanded he be allowed to dispatch a Palestinian police detachment alongside an international contingent.

The idea raised strong objections among officers in the Israeli Defense Forces. When he heard the stubbornness, Peres blew up at one group in a surge of fury: "You want 150,000 Hebronites to remain under our control because of 400 Jews? There's a limit to arrogance and a limit to timidity.

"I'm telling you that we can break Arafat, if that's what you want. But then we'll be left with Hamas, an intifada, and terror. We've made the decision to strive for a political settlement. Today we must decide who's in charge in this country: the government or a handful of settlers. And to you generals, I say: you too must weigh this matter from the standpoint of security. Enough of this dread of how the settler will react."[5]

With so much at stake, Peres embarked on a series of blunders. U.S. Middle East negotiator Dennis Ross, a man with a superb, penetrating, and humane mind, was upset by what he saw as he observed Peres's campaign. Perhaps because Peres had lost so many elections in the past, he appeared to shy away from accentuating the stark differences of outlook and policy between himself and Netanyahu. The right wing Likud leader was crying that Peres was "soft" on Israeli security, the one campaign charge likely to stick with Israelis, and Peres could have countered it by using in the campaign his friend Ehud Barak, the ex-military chief of staff, yet Peres did not. Peres did not confront his weaknesses, but instead ran away from them, Ross said. It was clear that the Israeli public was ready to make compromises with the Palestinians for peace, and Netanyahu talked out of both sides of his mouth—no compromises with the Palestinians even as he continued to press for peace. Instead of pointing out these ludicrous contradictions, Peres ran as if he had already won. With a far shrewder mind, Netanyahu kept hammering at Israeli's need for a leader tough when it came to security. As the election proceeded it was clear that to Netanyahu and the Likud, the Palestinians were simply renegade and hostile, and the mere exchange of consideration, and any warmth of courtesy were hardly possible. As Ariel Sharon had often said, the best way to solve the problem of the Palestinians was to get rid of them. So whatever else the Likud stood for, Netanyahu had no use for the peace treaty or for the whole series of confidence-building measures put in place by the Oslo talks.

Rabin had always taken the stand that outbreaks of violence should be powerless to sidetrack peace talks, but Iran now moved to derail the peacemaking process. Any sort of peace with Israel was the last thing Tehran wanted, and in February of 1996, the Palestinian Islamic Jihad, clearly an instrument of Tehran, struck savagely at Israel—four suicide attacks in four days, killing fifty-nine. A month later Hezbollah accelerated its attacks on Israeli targets in southern Lebanon. There was a satanic insidiousness in the way the assaults were done—they were launched from civilian sites in Lebanon so that Israeli retaliation would kill Lebanese civilians and inflame the public mood.

With every terrorist attack, Peres lost popularity and in April, accused of being soft on Arabs and Hezbollah, and in an act of stark misjudgment, Peres launched Operation Grapes of Wrath, a sixteen-day assault against Hezbollah offices in Lebanon. In a strategically clumsy move to pressure the Lebanese to rein in and hobble the Iranian terrorist proxy and end the attacks on Tel Aviv, Israeli forces struck at Lebanese power plants, then attacked Lebanese villages after Hezbollah fired Katyusha rockets into northern Israel. Soon, 400,000 Lebanese had fled south, and the tempo of Hezbollah attacks stepped up. The Israeli assaults damaged Lebanese infrastructure and disrupted the country's efforts at economic reconstruction. Politically, Grapes of Wrath blew up in Peres's face. Over 150 Lebanese civilians were killed, a U.N. compound was shelled, and thanks to Israel's callousness in damaging Lebanon's buildings, roads, and water supplies, instead of Hezbollah being reined in, its popularity dramatically shot up.

Peres, now running neck and neck with his rival, looked on in dismay as his popularity plummeted.

Clinton was appalled by the Israeli attack and in private harshly condemned Peres's inability to control his forces, especially since it would make it harder for the U.S. administration to assist him in the election. The president toyed with the idea of extending a guarantee to Israel "if she took risks for peace"—in other words, the United States would take measures to protect the borders Israel left exposed in any agreements it made in exchange for peace. In the end, no formal agreement was reached, but Clinton publicly made the promise, which came as close to endorsing Peres as he felt he could.

Above all, the Clinton administration, fearful that Netanyahu's election would mean the end of the peace process, moved to active measures. Clinton now resorted to using covert means to ensure that Peres, not Netanyahu, won the election. Said former U.S. Assistant Secretary of State Ned Walker, "We tried to buy the election. Hell, we try to buy every election we can lay our hands on."[6]

The first sign of how serious Clinton was about a Peres win was his assigning Doug Schoen, a partner in the polling firm of Penn & Schoen, who had been hired by the White House at the urging of Clinton advisor Dick Morris. The job of Morris and Schoen was to devise questionnaires, get White House approval, then use the research as the basis for writing ads that were factual, emotional, and effective. Schoen was the consummate professional, but at the beginning of their acquaintance Clinton hadn't trusted him, and since Schoen had worked once for an opponent, the growth of confidence came slowly. During his first two years, Clinton had become paranoid about leaks, observing, "I have learned never to say anything—anything—in a meeting larger than three people." But Clinton hired Schoen on Morris's say-so, and the bond eventually became trusting and deep.[7]

Schoen had then been a personal pollster and advisor to Rabin, and with Rabin's death, Peres took on the American, not understanding the importance of Schoen's role. As the race unfolded, Schoen became a regular, informal channel to Clinton, and both Clinton and Peres thought it a good idea. Every night in Washington, after Clinton and Morris ended their meetings on the president's own reelection strategy, Clinton would talk to Schoen about the political situation in Israel, with an absorbing passion going over new developments in comprehensive detail.[8] (Schoen allegedly had knowledge of the origins of the secret U.S. support and how it was being channeled.) Through Schoen, Clinton followed with enthusiasm the

inside details of the Peres campaign. Schoen's polls showed Clinton to be
the most popular international figure, even more popular than other Israeli
candidates running for prime minister. With that kind of political cash in
the bank, Clinton's backing of Peres could be made to count.

Israel is a direct representative democracy in which virtually every
social group has its own political party, if not several. As a result, Israeli governments are unstable multiparty coalitions subject more to political whims
or agendas than the national welfare. U.S. covert monies were being funneled into minor partners of the Labor coalition, with some of the monies
being laundered through several front companies and accounts.

The Israeli campaign was like an American one, that is, a battle of false
simplicities, a duel to the death with pillows by Tweedle Dum and Tweedle
Dee. Suddenly the contest was between "Peace versus Security." As a columnist for *The Nation* said, "The Likud is running a scare campaign: two-
faced Arafat can't control the extremists, Peres relies on Arafat, and you're
afraid to ride on a bus and send your children to kindergarten. On top of
that, Peres will establish a Palestinian state, give back the Golan Heights
(the Syrian army will swim in the Sea of Galilee), and divide Jerusalem. But
don't worry—we, the Likud, will give you 'Peace with Security.'"[9]

At the end of April, Clinton was clearly piling in resources and support
for Peres. Washington had helped extract him from Operation Grapes of
Wrath, with Christopher playing a strenuous role in obtaining a cease-fire.
Secretary of Defense William Perry announced that the United States would
sell an improved early warning system for Israel to alert it to hostile missiles. The Pentagon would also spend $50 million in additional funds to de-
velop a laser able to shoot down the Hezbollah Katyusha rockets fired into
northern Israel from Lebanon. In addition, and despite cuts in the foreign
aid budget, Israel would still receive its annual $3 billion, Clinton pledged.

In a late April meeting with Arafat, Clinton praised the Palestinian's
boldness in removing a vow to destroy Israel from the Palestinian Liberation Organization charter. "He's proven a reliable partner in the peace process, and we want to do what we can for him," a White House official said.

Clinton promised to try and unblock $10 million currently being held
by the House International Relations Committee. The money represented
the U.S. contribution to operating expenses of the Palestinian Authority,
dating back to 1989.[10]

The ploys and covert funding may have worked if it hadn't been for a
loose-lipped American diplomat. According to Ned Walker, the covert operation to buy the election was blown when then U.S. ambassador to Israel

Martin Indyk, somewhat elevated by liquor, indiscreetly spoke of the plan at a Tel Aviv cocktail party.[11]

It was a closely run thing, but on May 29, Netanyahu won. In one of his first announcements as prime minister, he pledged to expand Israeli settlements on Palestinian land.

28

THE ALMOST WAR

On June 25, 1996, at a private FBI meeting at Quantico, Virginia, agents were sitting around eating hot dogs and hamburgers. After lunch, some had gone to play a round of golf when suddenly everyone's beeper went off.

The news wasn't good. America servicemen of the 444th Airlift Wing had been stationed in Saudi Arabia since the end of the Gulf War, tasked with enforcing the no-fly zones in Iraq. The men were housed in a barracks at Khobar Towers, a military complex in the eastern town of Dhahran when, without warning, a five-thousand-pound bomb carried in a tanker truck exploded, killing nineteen of the servicemen and wounding scores more. The blast was so powerful it tore off the front of the compound and was felt twenty miles away in Bahrain.

The next day a team of forty FBI agents and members of various police agencies were aboard a military transport plane for the seventeen-hour flight to Riyadh. The personnel included no less than Louis Freeh, the FBI director, and his top counterterrorist expert, John O'Neill. The two men could not have been more different. Where O'Neill was elegant, sophisticated, and worldly, Freeh liked suits off the rack and wore scuffed shoes. Slender and sober-faced, standing about five feet, eight inches tall, his hair in a crew cut, Freeh was a conventional man of orderly habits who left the office at six to be home with his wife and four children. He disliked and distrusted technology and getting rid of the computer on his office desk had been one of his first acts. The FBI in general disdained computers, and reporter Larry Wright noted some FBI models were so ancient that even church groups declined to accept them as gifts.

When the FBI team arrived at the attack site, what opened out before them was a vast crater, eighty-five feet wide and thirty-five feet deep. It was dark, yet the location was lit up bright as day by lights positioned on stanchions. The year before there had been another attack upon the Saudi National Guard Training Center, but this bomb had been far larger and far more viciously destructive. Lying inside circles of red paint were body parts of the victims. Investigators were reconstructing fragments of the truck that had been used to carry the bomb, the cluster of technicians sheltered under a tarp as they worked.[1]

Richard Clarke, Clinton's counterterrorism czar, quickly came to the conclusion that Iran was the likely culprit rather than Osama bin Laden. Clarke's specialists and NSC counterterrorism experts had examined two year's worth of NSA, CIA, Defense, and State Department reports on threats to America within the Saudi kingdom amounting to thousands of pages. A clear pattern had emerged. Iran's Al-Quds Force had set up cells of Hezbollah in Bahrain, Kuwait, and Saudi Arabia, and had trained terrorists in Iran and Beirut. The day after the attack, Clarke's counterterrorism group presented National Security Advisor Tony Lake with a report naming Iran's Revolutionary Guard Quds (Jerusalem) Force and its front group, the Saudi Hezbollah, as responsible for the attack. After reading it, Lake thought Clarke's conclusions were on the money.[2]

Clarke's response was swift and implacable. He urged Clinton to write to the Saudi king, asking full cooperation into the Khobar attack. He also urged Clinton to appoint four-star Gen. Wayne Downing to probe the military laxness that had made the facility vulnerable. Clinton signed off on both actions, but the matter had puzzling aspects. Was the Iranian government truly at the bottom of the plot? There was Iranian involvement, but the key question was: had Tehran *sanctioned* the attack? Lake believed the Clarke report to be accurate but there were skeptics. CIA director John Deutch dismissed Clarke's conclusion as only one of many theories. Clarke was undeterred. He was intent on amassing ironclad evidence that would stand up in court, and he knew the White House was far from having that kind of evidence.

At the time of the attack, the relations between the FBI and the White House had fallen near the freezing level. A corrosive mistrust had poisoned the relations between Clinton and his FBI director, Louis Freeh. As we've seen, skill and perceptiveness in making appointments was not a Clinton talent. Before Freeh, there had been CIA director James Woolsey, picked as a sop to the Reagan Republicans, and now there was Freeh, another Republican and a man who would prove an utter disaster as FBI director.

Freeh disliked politics as a species of worldly contamination, and he had cautioned his agents against White House officials, branding them "politicals," to his mind a word equivalent to something irrevocably tainted and soiled. Given his invulnerable sense of moral superiority, Freeh felt he could exercise the freedom to offend and had refused to attend weekend high-level meetings. Once, in a display of his indifference to the presence and benefits of power, Freeh had turned in his White House pass, saying that he preferred to go there only as a visitor. When it came to Clinton, Freeh manifested an incessant disposition to find fault. He was a sanctimonious man, given to public disagreements with his president. For example, the FBI director had fiercely pursued the appointment of an independent counsel to probe possible fund-raising abuses during the 1996 election, alleging that China had snuck in money for Clinton's reelection. If true, it would have had major implications for U.S.-China policy. Attorney General Janet Reno had refused to appoint a prosecutor, thinking the charge unwarranted, but Freeh doggedly continued to make it all the same. When he heard Freeh's remarks, Clinton's edgy temper exploded in black wrath, the president showering Freeh with epithets including "that little shit." To aggravate matters, Freeh conscientiously kept Republican senators and House members apprised of his misgivings, yet never seemed able to find the time to honor White House requests for a briefing of the evidence or even a summary of it. Clinton was angry and bitter: "That bastard is trying to sting us," Clinton snarled.

Freeh believed himself the most righteous man in government, an idea that only made him the most boring. He was also involved in another controversial case, pushing hard for the indictment of Wen Ho Lee, a Chinese nuclear scientist the FBI suspected of passing on secrets to Beijing. It was an investigation that a federal judge later said "embarrassed our entire nation." Lee was later proved innocent and entirely cleared.[3]

Freeh nonetheless still saw himself as a formidable figure. Speaking of the White House he once said to a friend, "They are terrified of me."[4] Now, however, the White House was paying Freeh a lot of attention, and he was delighted. Freeh tried to snub the White House whenever he could, but his counterterrorist specialists ignored Freeh's determination to feud. The FBI men were savvy and sophisticated and had been working closely with the White House on terrorism and counterterrorism for some time, and they simply continued with their meetings with Clarke or the NSC, not bothering to keep Freeh informed.

Unfortunately, while Freeh may have taken pride in his assignment, he was entirely out of his depth. His previous fields of expertise had been organized crime and narcotics, so when it came to the Middle East, his mind was basically shallow. Since he knew nothing of foreign affairs, Freeh was not aware that Middle Easterners rarely open their hearts to foreigners. Hospitality and courtesy of manners were important to people like the Saudis, and they could be flattering and agreeable to the point of sycophancy while telling you what you wanted to hear, all the while concealing what actually was happening. This they now did to Freeh. The Saudi ambassador to the United States, Prince Bandar, had invited Freeh to be his guest at his Virginia estate, and it had turned Freeh's head. What Freeh did not understand was that among people like the Saudis or Iranians the concept of "face"—of not allowing any compromise of one's public image that would damage one's prestige—was an obsession as essential to them as to the Japanese. The Khobar Towers attack had revealed Saudi internal weaknesses that were embarrassing to the Kingdom and no foreigner was to know about them. Because of this, the Saudi interior minister, Prince Nayef, who felt little warmth for Americans, resolved to deny Freeh and O'Neill access to any witnesses or evidence they'd collected. As far as the Saudis were concerned, the Americans were on their own.

Although Freeh's conversations with the Saudis were pleasant and breezy, no hard facts had emerged about responsibility for the plot. The Saudis promised to help, but didn't go into details. Freeh, a credulous, even gullible, man, said to O'Neill on the way home, "Wasn't that a great trip? I think they're really going to help us."

The abrasive O'Neill impaled him with a stare. "You've got to be kidding," he said. "They didn't give us anything. They were just shining sunshine up your ass."[5] Insulted, Freeh wouldn't speak to O'Neill for the rest of the flight. He did send O'Neill back to try and cobble together intelligence-sharing arrangements, but even O'Neill, famous for his wiles, agile strategies, and untiring, stubborn persistence, received no help from the Saudis.

The FBI did not understand that in Saudi Arabia, religious or Sharia law forbids the interrogation of natives by foreigners. Plus, since the judges are clerics, they have a tendency to suppress evidence they don't want to hear, especially if a foreign country is its source. They were full of questions that seemed to ask for America to drop its front of pugnacity and to retreat. One of the Saudi officials had questioned O'Neill about the possible U.S. reaction. What would America's response be if Iran's complicity was proved? "If it is a military response, what are you going to bomb? Are you going to nuke them? Flatten their military facilities? Destroy their oil refineries? And to achieve what? We are next door to them. You are 6,000 miles away."

In the meantime, the Saudis soon had the Americans chasing their tails. For Louis Freeh there was one story; for Sandy Berger, there was another. When the unremitting Berger pressed the Saudi ambassador, Prince Bandar, for some solid information, Bandar said he believed the Iranians were behind it, but the Kingdom could not allow access to the suspects apprehended by the Saudis or other assistance. To Freeh, Bandar said that there was no genuine interest on the part of the White House in pursuing the case, and, because of that, the Saudis were reluctant to share information. Bandar asserted that what Clinton wanted was to end his administration's deadlock with Iran. The president did not want war, and, because of that, any U.S. response would be tepid.

This was a very clever perversion of the facts, a Saudi version of the Elizabethan tactic of "turning the cat in the pan"—attributing to others what are really your own views. It was the Saudis who did not want nor could they afford a U.S.-Iran war. The Persian Gulf War had almost bankrupted the Kingdom; American forces on Saudi soil had augured the rise of bin Laden and spread internal destabilization. A war with Iran would be even more destabilizing because Americans would arrive en masse. So the Saudis, skilled at double-dealing, did what they did best. Crown Prince Abdullah had quietly entered into talks with Iran, and the two countries reached an agreement. Iran was not to launch any more terrorist attacks inside the Kingdom, and the Saudis would allow no military operations to be launched against Iran from its soil.

Freeh, however, was not about to drop the case. He and Berger talked every other week about the bombing, and to Berger's face Freeh was pleasant, but behind his back, Freeh considered the administration a weak sellout for not taking a tougher stand. In other words, Freeh swallowed the Saudi's lies about Clinton wholesale, yet the opposite was the case: Clinton was itching for a war with Iran. When the news of the bombing surfaced, the president made clear he wanted the offenders punished. He wrote to King Fahd, requesting cooperation, and flew to New York to meet with Prince Abdullah, the king's half-brother, personally requesting their cooperation. Personal appeals were also made to the Saudi royal family by U.N. ambassador Albright and the secretary of defense, former Republican Senator William Cohen.

Clinton's mood grew foul. In late June, the president was in the grip of the same combative truculence he had exhibited in the case of North Korea. The president called a meeting of "the Small Group," consisting of CIA director John Deutch, Defense Secretary William Perry, Secretary of State Warren Christopher, and NSC staffer Leon Fuerth to reexamine options for all-out war. "I don't want any pissant half-measures," Clinton said with some heat.[6]

Lake had sent his deputy, Sandy Berger, to talk with the head of the Joint Chiefs, John Shalikashvili, but Berger came away empty-handed. The Joint Chiefs were not in the habit of showing civilians their war plans, but the ingenious Clarke had somehow obtained the number of the plan. He asked Lake to call Shalikashvili and asked for a briefing on it, and by July of 1996, Shalikashvili was talking at a Pentagon meeting of starting a war to the finish with Iran. During the Eisenhower administration a plan had been drawn up for Iran's invasion by U.S. troops that required several divisions of Army and Marine forces to sweep over the country in the course of several months. This would take months and months to assemble, it would be difficult to supply, and would cost billions of dollars.

The ever-cautious Berger asked, What if the United States attempted something less?

Shalikashvili got out another map. "CENTCOM also has a plan to bomb their military facilities along the coast, navy ports, air force bases, missile installations." There were also plans to divert satellites to get better coverage of the country, and there were plans to take out two launch sites southeast of Tehran. After clearing the air corridor around the cities of Tehran and Qom, where Iranian missile command centers were located, B-1 and B-2 aircraft bombers from the island of Diego Garcia in the Indian Ocean and perhaps Turkey would drop bombs on these targets, while the Navy would hit targets near the Gulf ports of Bandar-e-Bushehr and Bandar Abbas.

Berger then asked, What would happen next?

The coast of Iran bristled with a huge array of fast patrol boats and Silkworm and other missiles. There were also Iranian forces throughout the Gulf islands of Abu Musa, Sirri, Queshem, Khark, Larak, and Hengam, and Iran would probably try to close the Strait of Hormuz, only twenty-nine miles wide and the conduit for the transport of most of the free world's oil. There would be a slew of attacks against Saudi oil installations, and Iranian assaults against Persian Gulf states like Dubai, the United Arab Emirates, and Abu Dhabi. Hezbollah attacks would occur all over the Middle East and perhaps even in America where the group was known to have sleeper cells.

Berger didn't like the sound of that at all. Clinton had already made clear to advisors like Clarke, Lake, and Berger that he didn't want to get into a series of gradually escalating mutual attacks. If America was going to go after Iran, Clinton said he wanted a massive attack that would "frighten Iran into inaction." Clarke had then proposed the old nuclear strategy of escalation dominance, where "you hit the guy the first time so hard, where he loses some of the things he really values, and then you tell him that if he responds, he will lose everything he values."

"We could do that," said Shalikashvili. "Let me talk to the boys in Tampa," meaning CENTCOM.[7]

The Small Group now began to examine other options as well. One involved a brigade-size force (1,200) that would invade Iran from Azerbaijan in the northwest while a heavy armored force would slide over the border from Iraq. Why Iraq, suffering under tough U.N. sanctions and at loggerheads with the United States, would allow this transit wasn't made clear. However, it was agreed that the United States lacked adequate intelligence on Iran's nuclear facilities making it hard to target them. If Washington knew what to hit, there could also be a huge air strike involving B-52s, F-117s, F-15s, and B-1 bombers that could damage Iran's nuclear development sites, destroy its air defense system, damage its air force and navy and its offensive missile forces. The strikes would also knock out Iran's key command and control centers.

There was also discussion of flattening terrorist training camps in Lebanon. Another was to send U.S. envoys to Europe and Japan to ask them to join in an economic boycott of the Persians.

Clinton, however, lost interest. "It was hard to keep the president's mind fastened to one spot for very long," said a former senior advisor. Aides said he was distracted, his mind on the Monica Lewinsky scandal, his attention ranging over a dozen subjects, bouncing ideas off aides, listening to objections, arguing viewpoints to which he was opposed, just to make certain he felt them wrong. Discussion of options dragged along among the Principals for some months. "The White House always began with this—who can we get for this? Who can we nail to the wall? But the anger was never fortified by any coherent depth of thought or planning. Every tactic brought up soon ran out of support or was forgotten. It was all momentary."[8]

In 1992, Hezbollah coordinating with the Iranian embassy detonated a bomb at the Israeli embassy in Buenos Aires killing twenty-nine. In 1994, working with neo-Nazis, Hezbollah exploded a bomb at a Jewish community center in Buenos Aires, killing eighty-five and wounding hundreds of others.

Iran had begun to target Saudi Arabia because the Kingdom had not thought Iran much of a threat after the Iran-Iraq War.

The Saudis continued to turn a pleasing face and be everything to everyone, but in fact they had proved quite proficient. Even before the Khobar

Towers attack, they had assembled a great deal of information on the terrorist network. It had all started at a customs post when a border guard noticed that a car arriving from Jordan was squatted on its springs, much too close to the ground and clearly heavily loaded. When the car was searched it was found to be bursting full of explosives. Under questioning, the driver admitted he was part of a loosely linked group of cluster cells. The Saudis scooped up the network one member at a time until twelve captives outlined a broad plan, headed by an officer in the Iranian Revolutionary Guards, to hit targets inside Saudi Arabia. In the aftermath of the Khobar blast, the Saudi questioner returned to collect more names and information from their prisoner. (The United States would only learn of this much later, and Clinton, Clarke, and Lake were infuriated by the holding back of information that might have prevented the attack.)

Iran was a hated and serious rival, and the Saudis had traced the Khobar attack to a Saudi operative known as "Mugassal" and the Iranian Quds Force. They had also scooped up evidence, witnesses, and even members of the cell. They had even discovered that the plotters had used a bomb expert from the Lebanese Hezbollah to fashion the explosive. Yet the royal family was badly divided, and debate dragged on for three years, one faction urging that America be given everything, expecting a full U.S. assault against Iran, the others refusing any disclosure, fearing that a U.S. strike would bring more U.S. forces into the Kingdom and such forces would only galvanize internal dissent. In addition, the Saudis were touchy about revealing to America that it was its own Shia population that provided the chief manpower for such plots.

So with the obdurate Berger, Prince Bandar promised that if the United States launched a massive strike against Iran, Saudi Arabia would open its files and give full access. Berger said the United States could hardly pledge a military action based on evidence it hadn't yet seen. Berger was only being lawyerlike and canny, but the Saudis doubted the steadiness of Washington's resolve. Frustrations grew so intense that during one bilateral meeting Vice President Gore gave full vent to his famous temper by pounding on a table and asking an appalled Saudi prince what sort of country hid the identity of people who had killed American military personnel stationed in that country defending it and the royal family.

America kept remorselessly tightening the vise of pressure, but the Saudis only worked through consensus and it couldn't reach one, and the matter floated dead in the water.

Then the whole political picture rook a sudden, drastic turn. In May 1997, Mohammad Khatami, a moderate, was elected president of Iran. Iran's fragmented political system, overrun with too many obscure and ineffective parties, was united by one passion—the need for drastic change. The majority of the Iranian people wanted everything its clerics were denying them, rock music, material goods, glamour, sensualism, movies from the West, more freedom of expression.

Two hundred thirty candidates had run for president and the Council of Guardians disqualified all but four. Supreme leader Ayatollah Khamenei had endorsed the Majles (parliament) speaker, Ali Akbar Nateq Nuri, and a CIA analysis had predicated Nuri's victory. The Council of Guardians thought Khatami a cipher and had ignored him. The authorities banned Khatami from TV, they shut down his campaign headquarters, but on May 23 Khatami won anyway.

Khatami knew his victory had left the hard-liners off balance, shocked at their own unpopularity, and he attempted to use that period of disorganized bewilderment to try and gain some control over the country's security institutions. He put liberals in his cabinet and ousted hard-liners including some virulent anti-American officials. The new president moved immediately against Iran's Ministry of Information and Intelligence, a stronghold of reactionaries, realizing the public projected onto him all their dissatisfaction with the hard-line clerics, all their pent-up frustrations with the status quo. Khatami talked of the rule of law, of curbing corruption, of ridding the government of "superstition and fanaticism." He sought to empower civilian society, which everyone knew meant weakening Tehran's religious dictatorship. Khatami also moved to liberalize the public, removing censorship, and not enforcing regulations on music, dress, and social affairs. Khatami swiftly signaled a desire for a rapprochement with the United States. When his foreign minister, Kamal Kharrazi, was asked about improving relations with America, he replied, "We are ready to work with all nations, provided they are ready to establish relations with us based on mutual respect." Khatami went further. While saying that the time was not ready for direct talks, he said he wanted exchanges of academics, authors, athletes, and artists. He even talked of a dialogue among civilizations. Throughout this time, Khatami displayed cunning, cleverness, and courage.

The flow of intelligence on the Khobar matter dried up instantly, which the CIA, Defense Intelligence Agency, State's Bureau of Intelligence and Research, and other U.S. intelligence agencies immediately noticed. Anything through the pipeline abruptly stopped. "We were getting updates all the time, and suddenly there was nothing—truly nothing," said former INR official Wayne White. Richard Clarke blew up, wondering what in the hell was going on, and the agency was in a rage, and it was discovered that

Clinton had given the order to Berger, "Don't let anything leak. Don't antagonize the Iranians," White said.[9]

According to several sources, Berger then sealed up in the NSC at least 150 documents that contained the words "Khobar Towers."

Clinton was suddenly saying conciliatory things such as, "I have never been pleased about the estrangement between the U.S. and the people of Iran," and a few days later added, "What we hope for is reconciliation with a country that does not believe that terrorism is a legitimate expansion of political policies."[10]

Then, in an interview with CNN, when Khatami attacked terrorism, Clinton did one of his remarkable backward somersaults on Iran: "I personally believe that only those who lack logic resort to violence. Terrorism should be condemned in all its forms and manifestations; assassins must be condemned." There was no unanimity among the Principals. Lake was a hawk and thought talk of reforming Iran a waste of time and words. Yet Albright, Gore, and others had always felt Iran was the real geopolitical prize in the region and knew that it presented a dilemma to America because it was an Islamic country where both democrats and totalitarians wielded leadership at the same time. What gave them pause was the pro-American sentiment so widespread among Iran's population. Albright had always entertained the possibility of appealing to the Iranian public over the anti-American heads of government, feeling that the chance of a genuine thaw in relations was a real one. She too was acutely aware that Iran was a divided government, on one side moderates seemingly eager to find common ground for reconciliation, the other the hard-line religious leaders like Khamenei who loathed the United States and all its ways.

Further startling changes took place. A Khatami official gave an interview to an Israeli journalist for the first time since the revolution. Informal Khatami intermediaries told Clinton officials that Iran's president was trying to shut down terrorism operations and gain control of the Ministry of Intelligence and Security. In the Persian Gulf, Iranian warships stopped harassing U.S. Navy vessels.

The administration replied by proposing sending Iran a message via the Swiss that would be delivered by high-ranking White House and State Department officials. There was no response from Iran. The Saudis, who had made their own separate peace with Iran, were jubilant over developments, offering to serve as a go-between the two countries. There was no response from Iran. The White House sent American wrestlers to Iran, and Clinton proposed more exchanges of American academics, religious figures, athletes, and the like with their Iranian counterparts. The White House put an anti-Iranian terrorist group, the MEK, operating from Iraqi soil, on the terrorist list. Iran barely stirred.

The FBI was skeptical of Khatami's authenticity. The FBI counterterrorism chief, Dale Watson, said that he believed Khatami would turn out to be Khamenei's puppet, a judgment grotesquely mistaken. In supreme leader Ayatollah Khamenei, Khatami had a sinister and unrelenting enemy. Khamenei was one of the people most responsible for the suppression in Iran of human rights, its pursuit of nuclear weapons, aiding the jihadis waging war against Israel, and the regime's murder of its dissidents. Khamenei loved to whip up crowds chanting "Death to America," and he controlled Iran's political, intelligence, and military institutions. He would soon have the intrepid Khatami fighting for his life.

However, as usual, the Clinton policy toward Iran tried to do two things at once. Watson also saw that Freeh's aim and White House policy about the matter faced collision, even though Berger later denied this. "We said this in no way means we're not going to go after Khobar. These two policies weren't in conflict."[11] As Clinton's overtures continued, Clinton and Berger were convinced that any military action to punish Iran for the Khobar Towers attack would cut the ground from under Khatami's feet, and so the bottom fell out of the American anti-Iranian effort.

What is perhaps most disturbing is Clinton's odd laxity toward the impertinence, the bald lies, the jeering slanders of his appointee Freeh. Clinton was not a corrupt public servant, yet he allowed Freeh to call him one without moving to destroy him root and branch. Clinton would be incensed and he would shout, yet he wouldn't take him out.

"It was all fear of Freeh's big-time Republican friends on Capitol Hill," said a former senior White House official.

Clarke said, "Clinton simply should have fired him and taken the shit."[12]

But whatever the reason, the insults remained unanswered.

SINISTER DESIGNS

President Bill Clinton had been sworn in for his second term on January 20, 1997, by Chief Justice William Rehnquist. Clinton reported later that Rehnquist had looked at him pityingly and said in a sarcastic tone, "Good luck."

The Whitewater probe was finally subsiding, and Special Counsel Robert Fiske, Jr., appointed to investigate White House aide Vince Foster's death, had ended his probe after four doctors ruled the death a suicide. Foster's death had been sharply painful for Clinton, but it was one hardship in a growing sea of them. Talking with Washington attorney Lloyd Cutler, Clinton had said, "Look, frankly I'm genuinely worried that Congress and the press and my enemies are going to make life miserable for me," and he spoke of the need to find a coherent defense to counter the various charges. If the shadow of Foster's death was gone, Clinton was still contending with the Paula Jones case and other allegations of womanizing when an event occurred that would have a profound effect on the rest of his presidency.

In August, as Fiske flew to Florida and was walking from the plane to his wife, his beeper went off. A three-judge court had just appointed someone named Ken Starr to replace Fiske as independent counsel. Starr, forty-eight, was the son of a Baptist minister from Texas, a pleasant man with a liking to talk in terms of moral abstractions. Starr had been a finalist for the position of attorney general, taken by Janet Reno. Hearing of the appointment, Clinton advisors were nervous. The lead judge was a conservative Republican, Judge David Sentelle. Starr was a Republican pawn, screamed Clinton's aides. In any case, Starr's first chore would be to reopen the Fiske probe on Foster's death, regarded by the panel as biased.

Clinton's first reaction to the news of the Starr appointment was to remark to an aide that he'd like to double up Starr with a punch to the stomach. The breadth and intensity of the scrutiny on the president's past, the multiplying areas of his activities thought suspicious or illegal by his enemies, was getting on Clinton's nerves. With his advisor Dick Morris, Clinton's rage would emerge in towering, self-pitying tantrums: "You can't tell me that the drip, drip, drip of this innuendo, of lies and defamation and slander and totally concocted, fictitious stories, one after the other after the other, that this isn't going to have an impact!" His face red and enraged, he would pound the arm of his chair, shrieking his frustrated dismay.[1]

Unknown to Clinton, in September, the Jones lawyers had received a tip from one Linda Tripp, forty-eight, a former White House assistant in the counsel's office now working as an $88,000 a year public affairs specialist at the Pentagon. They were told that she had tapes with a "female co-worker talking of having a sexual affair with the president." The Jones lawyers added the name given by Tripp to their witness list. She was witness number 80, someone named Monica Lewinsky.

When Iraq's Saddam Hussein began his duel with Clinton in the summer of 1997, he was brilliant in his timing. Whatever other talents he had, Saddam had always been able to subject his enemies to a pitiless analysis, gifted as he was with an incredible instinct to sense any weakness. If there were a soft spot in a U.S. policy that would collapse when touched, Saddam always seemed to know where to find it, and he had spied one in the summer of 1996 when he attacked Ahmed Chalabi's INC in Kurdistan, scattering the exiles to the winds, and prompting an awkward, ineffectual U.S. retaliation from an administration caught off balance.

During the summer of 1997, Clinton never saw the new crisis coming. By then, the president was exhibiting an eclipse of nerve, a profound and gloomy spiritual discouragement. Sunk in scandal, trapped in a sleet storm of petty malice and scathing, belittling allegations, the president had lost his ardor. Hostile Republicans had undervalued and misinterpreted his success in Bosnia, and, prey to a fresh storm of gross, callous partisan virulence, he was manifesting a wounded spirit. The president was still maintaining that the U.S. position vis-à-vis Iraq was a strong one, but it had steadily lost credibility, strength, and coherent support, especially when it came to sanctions.

President Clinton had used sanctions more than any other U.S. leader in history, and they were being viewed by more and more as failed and ineffective. The roots for sanctions date back to Woodrow Wilson, who in 1919 said that "a nation boycotted is a nation that is in sight of surrender." Clinton seems to have believed this, and he used sanctions so often that his critics called him "sanction-happy" and accused him of substituting them for genuine diplomacy. Slapped on Iraq in August of 1990, sanctions had remained the chief pillar of U.S. policy toward that country ever since.

Unfortunately, the allied coalition formed to wage the war of Desert Storm had pretty much frayed to ribbons. It was made up of countries with nothing in common. On the one hand, you had Saddam's Middle East neighbors: Saudi Arabia, Turkey, Egypt, Syria, plus the ministates of the Gulf. On the other hand, there were Britain, France, Germany, Japan, and a disintegrating Soviet Union, since becoming mainly Russia. All had different vital interests and national agendas, and all were pulling away from support of sanctions.

In terms of inflicting suffering on an innocent population, the chief villain was U.N. Resolution 687, passed in 1991, which related specifically to Iraq's weapons of mass destruction and which Madeleine Albright had described as an attempt to have a country disarm itself without a foreign power having to occupy it. What had resulted was not disarmament but a devastating humanitarian disaster inside Iraq. Iraq's electricity was intermittent, making it risky to store food in refrigerators; its water wasn't clean; its cars couldn't be repaired because of a lack of spare parts, compelling people to ride bicycles. Since the sanctions forbade business mail, doctors were not even allowed to receive medical journals.

By the mid-1990s, when at last Saddam agreed to comply with the United Nations, the daily Iraqi intake had fallen to one thousand calories, even though the sanctions had included provisions for providing humanitarian relief. Thanks to these sanctions there had been a spike in the malnutrition rate, child deaths numbered in the hundreds of thousands, and there had been a breakdown in health and other basic services, according to U.N. statistics. According to a UNICEF report, Iraq had the worst infant mortality rate of all 188 countries monitored by that agency.[2]

Strategically, U.N. sanctions severely limited Iraq's financial resources and raw materials, so that new equipment and expertise became increasingly scarce. As Charles Duelfer, the U.N. Special Commission official, noted, "The effects of the sanctions reverberated throughout the [Iraqi] scientific community and affected all aspects of industry within Iraq. Many scientists were underemployed or had access to neither research and production materials nor professional development."[3]

If Iraq's middle class were struggling with privation and hardship, the ruling class Baath Party members had access to whatever they desired. Controlling the black market, they were able to import all the medicines or luxury goods, cars, and appliances they wanted.

The hard-line Albright described the sanctions as a determination "to do the right thing in a tough way." The French ambassador to the United States, François Bujon de l'Estang, disagreed, likening the situation to "two doctors called to a sick bed who agree on the diagnosis but [were] prescribing different treatments." Where the U.S. stance was always relentless, implacably tough, designed to irk and frustrate Saddam, the French and Europeans wanted to provide incentives for obtaining Iraqi cooperation "by offering goodwill and a willingness to cooperate," in the words of a French official.[4]

Clearly to some, the United States was losing the battle for hearts and minds. "The idea that we are engaged in a constant battle for perceptions, and that the key perception is the welfare of the Iraqi people, seems to be absolutely beyond the comprehension of the State Department," said Middle East expert Tony Cordesman. "If you look back on [Secretary of State] Madeleine Albright's tenure, this will probably be recognized as one of the greatest single failures for which she has to be held responsible."

By the summer of 1997, Saddam had sensed the shift in sympathy toward him within the European community and the Arab world, and he issued a direct challenge to the United States. It was done silently at first. That summer, U.S. intelligence analysts were startled to discover Saddam's air defense systems had been deployed in new and ominous patterns, and they concluded that Saddam was preparing a plan to shoot down a U-2 surveillance aircraft, used to monitor and verify weapons inspections.

Clinton loathed Saddam Hussein as devious, unstable, brutal, corrupt, and wildly unpredictable, and one of the unspoken aims of U.S. policy had been to make the crafty, predatory Iraqi leader's conduct at least more restrained and calculable, if nothing else. CIA estimates concluded that Saddam was vulnerable and his regime confronted the "constant possibility of sudden and violent change." Yet Saddam's security services were as formidable as ever and the agency said that any successor regime might move to conciliate international opinion but would still maintain a strong military establishment.

Nothing seemed urgent or threatening, but then in September Saddam put several inspection sites off-limits to U.N. inspectors, announced that no Americans would be allowed on inspection teams, followed by the pronouncement that all American inspectors would have to leave Iraq forthwith, claiming that Iraq wanted "balance" on the inspection teams. Saddam also warned America not to use its U-2 aircraft.

In response, Clinton ordered Secretary of Defense William Cohen to deploy the USS *Nimitz* battle group to the Persian Gulf to deter any attack on the U-2s and be ready to counter any new menaces from Saddam. In reaction to Saddam's latest muscle flexing, the U.N. Security Council averted its face, warning only of "serious consequences" without hinting as to what those might be. The Clinton group was stunned by the indifference of the United Nations. Saddam wasted no time. Having met with a flaccid U.N. response, he was now prepared to up the stakes. On October 29, the Iraqi government announced the expulsion from Iraq of all American inspectors. Richard Butler, the Australian who had become the executive chairman of UNSCOM, said he would suspend all inspections until Americans were included.

Clearly, Iraq and the United States were squaring off, yet in a case where a resolute, imperturbable stance was required, the United Nations instead dispatched three mediators to Iraq, seeing a chance for diplomacy. When Clinton strongly argued that the United States needed no further authority for taking action against Iraq, the Russians strongly disagreed. Clinton could not afford an open clash with the Security Council and so sullenly acquiesced in the mediation. The mediation team came up empty, and the Security Council managed to retreat still further on its own. On November 12, it finally voted for travel restrictions for the Iraqi officials obstructing the inspections, named by the administration seven months earlier and who were already forbidden to travel by Saddam. The Security Council warned vaguely of "further measures," but a campaign by Albright and Berger to toughen up the terms went nowhere.

War clouds were piling up, and although Clinton had a profound interest in preventing a coalescing of the anti-American forces in the United Nations or among allies that could shackle him when it came to executing U.S. foreign policy, it was too late. The political landscape was in motion, currents were flowing in a different direction, and where there should have been focus in the White House there was only alarm. As a former advisor said, Clinton's aim should have been to impose his view and appraisal of the Middle East situation on his allies but they were imposing theirs on him. In America, he needed to channel public opinion into approval of a firm course of action, yet he had no plan.

The situation required leadership, both in concept and execution, and the president was fluctuating and unsteady. Clinton did not want a war. Any military action would be long and costly, its outcome uncertain, or worse, have unpleasant consequences. The president was soon spending hours on the phone with French president Jacques Chirac and Russian leader Boris Yeltsin, looking for a diplomatic exit from the confrontation. What Clinton heard he did not like. The position of France and Russia was that the rigidity of U.S. opposition, with its state of continual belligerency, offered Saddam no incentive for compromise and provoked him into defiance. Both Chirac and Yeltsin held the view that Iraq had to be offered an eventual solution that would end the sanctions—a light at the end of the tunnel, said Chirac. Clinton's reaction was a display of unvarnished anger: sanctions, he shouted, would be in place "till the end of time," but he quickly backed down, telling both men that the United States did not want sanctions to last forever.[5]

By now Clinton realized he faced a whole new spectrum of difficulties when it came to his Middle East policy. Besides sanctions fatigue, Arab support for the United States had waned because of the stalled peace talks. The new Israel prime minister, Benjamin Netanyahu, was busy undoing the Oslo Accords, making statements that the West Bank was "Israel proper," adding, this "is not alien land. This is the land of our forefathers." Unlike Rabin, Netanyahu wanted no sovereign Palestinian state, seeing it as a mortal threat to Israel. Instead he wanted "self-rule" for the Palestinians. Clinton, described as "impatient and frustrated," exhibited a personal loathing for Netanyahu, and Israel and America were at the brink of stark rupture, while the moderate Arab world was withdrawing support from Washington, seeing U.S. policy as more of an anti-Arab political agenda than a strategic necessity to ensure Persian Gulf security. In November, when the United States sponsored a regional Arab-Israeli economic conference in Doha, Qatar, many American Arab allies including Saudi Arabia, Morocco, and Egypt, boycotted it. An Egyptian newspaper, *Al-Ahram*, usually pro-American, declared: "The American position toward Iraq cannot be described as anything but coercive, aggressive and unwise and uncaring about the lives of Iraqis, who are unnecessarily subject to sanctions and humiliations." The paper specifically cited the Middle East peace talks, noting that America had a double standard, eager to pressure and force Arabs but unwilling to pressure Israel.[6]

On November 8, NSC deputy advisor Sandy Berger convened a meeting in the Situation Room with Clinton and a dozen or so of the Principals and their deputies. The advisors all agreed that sanctions had to be maintained and weapons inspections continued as the only way to curb Saddam and prevent his rearming. The choice was stark—unless firm action was taken, the current enforcement framework could collapse. Clinton, talking incessantly to his advisors, peppering them with questions, his reading glasses on his nose, listened intently to their opinions. Berger spoke up, telling Clinton, "You have to make the last decision first. Are you prepared to use military force? If you can stare that in the eye and say, yes, then we can commence a diplomatic campaign to make the need for it less likely."[7]

The new Chairman of the Joint Chiefs of Staff, Gen. Hugh Shelton, then briefed Clinton on a strike plan developed by the Defense Department. It relied largely on cruise missiles and was designed to inflict punishment. Strikes had been made against Iraq in 1995 and 1996, but this was a far larger, harsher attack. The previous strikes had not deterred Saddam and were now seen as being mere "pinpricks."

The meeting adjourned with no immediate response from Clinton, but two days later, in a private meeting with Berger, Clinton told him, "Let's go forward."

The question was, Would it work? Would Saddam be forced to slink snarling into the background by a convincing display of U.S. military strength? Clinton's advisors couldn't agree. Berger, Albright, and Undersecretary of State Thomas Pickering all said they believed that Saddam would back off and cave in. The military felt Saddam would stand fast and the Pentagon would be compelled to proceed with the strike. "You don't have a lot of aircraft around, if you're a great power, for show," said a Pentagon official at the time. "You have to have a decision."

One decision had been made: to use force, but what, when? What were the objectives of a strike to be? When angered, as in the case of North Korea and Somalia, or whenever U.S. lives had been lost to terrorism or combat, Clinton could mobilize a will of terrible force. However, that unabashed, driving, relentless desire to inflict punishment seemed to have deserted him. Clinton's rare capacity for rapid decision about what to do and his drive behind the command that forced the matter to success were nowhere to be seen.

He had plenty of company. The debate about goals dragged on. The options ranged from using military power to coerce Saddam to readmitting the inspectors, to bombing him to remove any capability for any production of weapons of mass destruction. These goals were considered too ambitious, and so the attack would be aimed at damaging Saddam's suspected WMD sites and mauling his conventional forces that might pose a threat to his neighbors.

All these plans were called the Pol-Mil Plan Iraq, a white binder with timelines for each stage of rhetorical escalation and deployment of military assets. The military developed three different plans over a period of three months, "down to the last drop of water," one DOD official said.

A new obsession was quick to develop over the fear of casualties. One former advisor said, "Clinton had a horror of seeing shots of wrecked houses and civilian bodies lying about," and the Pentagon officials took their cue from him. An aide to Shelton made clear that if hitting a target meant too many casualties, the target was removed from the lists in the binder.

On November 14, Secretary of Defense William Cohen ordered the USS *George Washington* battle group into the Gulf. Together with the *Nimitz*, the two battle forces had 288 cruise missiles, more than the total fired in the Gulf War. Clinton also sent an additional forty thousand military personnel to the region. He then wrote to Senator Trent Lott, the Republican majority leader, saying that the large military presence was "a demonstration of our resolve," but the military, like the president, was still basically "planless."

What were to be the strategic objectives of an attack? They still remained unformulated.

The military realized that if the goal was to get UNSCOM back into Iraq, it could not be done with a military objective "short of a full-scale Desert Storm that's followed through to completion," according to General Shelton. Slowly the senior civilian advisors abandoned the idea of their major goal to force the return of UNSCOM to Iraq. Many of these advisors now thought that the best course would be an escalating sequence of ultimatums and strikes until Saddam came to terms or was replaced by a leader more amenable to Washington's demands. The Pentagon officials thought this strategy naive, too reminiscent of Vietnam where America had bombed, then waited to see the impact and evidence on the part of Vietnam to change, an utterly unproductive strategy.

In the meantime, diplomatic efforts continued. Russian foreign minister Yevgeny Primakov called Albright back from a state visit to India, and met with her and other members of the Security Council at 2 A.M. in Geneva, November 20, 1997. Russia's motives were not disinterested. Moscow was owed billions of dollars by Saddam, and Primakov, who was close to the Iraqi leader, crafted a deal under which Saddam would let the weapons inspectors back in return for a vague promise to lift sanctions.

Clinton's reaction was dour. "We'll wait and see," he said.

As the costs and risks of a military strike were explained and expanded, Clinton's reluctance to act increased. His personal eclipse, his loss of prestige, had left him feeling battered, beaten, and betrayed. He had not reneged on his decision to bomb, but serious drawbacks might be suffered if an attack went ahead. The greatest fear rested on a further souring of U.S.-Arab relations, a backlash from the bombing that could result in undermining the Gulf kingdoms or allies like Saudi Arabia or Jordan denying the

United States basing rights for its planes on their soil. Any attack might also accelerate the decline in international support for sanctions, already seen by many as a thoughtless, crushing machinery.

An important aspect of the Clinton crisis would be to pick the strategy, the method, most likely to generate widespread public support. Fear mongering would be the tactic and a threat of horrible dimensions would be used and portrayed to the public. In a November 13 meeting of the Principals, Cohen made the argument that Iraq's weapons of mass destruction were a vital national interest.

Clinton pricked up instantly. He asked Cohen to "raise the profile" of the danger looming from WMD, and the next day, Cohen appeared on the Sunday TV program *This Week* with a five-pound bag of sugar and said the same amount of anthrax could kill half the population of Washington. The goal of the air strike then became the destruction or degrading of Saddam's WMD. Cohen's tactic was similar to that of President Harry Truman, who had sold the Marshall Plan to Congress, not by going into the complications of Europe's economy but by painting the continent as about to be overrun by the communist menace. It had the crudity of a cartoon, but it had worked.

Unfortunately, this tack transformed the whole conception of the operation, and threw the Defense Department planners for a loop. Speaking of neutralizing Iraq's WMD, General Shelton said, "You just can't do that," explaining that you could degrade the arsenal or take out plants, delivery systems, storage sites, and the like, but added with clear misgiving, "This is not something that a lot of people have a lot of experience with."[8]

Cohen was going to use Saddam's nonexistent WMD as the rationale for the U.S. military savaging of him. Cohen was not alone in portraying as evidence what was simply a guess. The truth was that the whole topic of Iraq's WMD was riddled with propaganda, poisoned by misinformation and unsubstantiated assertions, and it had spun entirely out of control.

30

UNDER WESTERN EYES

In May 1991, under the cover of Operation Provide Comfort, the U.S.-run military relief effort in Kurdistan, the CIA had begun an intensive program to debrief Iraqi defectors about Saddam's weapons of mass destruction, including their locations, quantities, and capabilities. The discovery after the Gulf War that Saddam had progressed much further in nuclear and other dangerous weapons of mass destruction came as a startling shock to U.S. intelligence organizations.

The U.N. cease-fire resolution passed in April 1991 said the ban on the sale of Iraqi oil would be lifted when Iraq had destroyed all its chemical and biological weapons, all missiles with a range of more than one hundred miles, and all material usable in a nuclear weapon. Two agencies tasked to carry out this mission were the U.N. Special Commission, UNSCOM, and the International Atomic Energy Agency.

For a year, Saddam evaded, dodged, feinted, sidestepped, but then in 1993 began to cooperate in inspections. As *The Economist* noted, the inspection system "was extraordinarily intrusive on many levels," involving "keeping an eye on the whole country, daily helicopter patrols, ground inspections, and tags and sensors attached to bits of sensitive equipment."[1]

Unfortunately, the weapons inspections by UNSCOM were to have been a multilateral effort, not an adjunct to Clinton's policy, yet from the first the operation had been penetrated by the CIA. As early as May of 1991, a senior Iraqi scientist defected to the United States, making his way through Kurdistan. He was called "Defector source DS-385."[2] The CIA debriefed him but would not share the information with UNSCOM chairman and former Swedish ambassador Rolf Ekéus, a career diplomat, who asked for a list of priority WMD sites inside Iraq. The CIA initially stonewalled Ekéus but, after prodding, the agency revealed the existence of the defector and the fact he'd brought documents pertaining to several "caultrons" or centrifuges used to enrich uranium that Saddam's engineers had developed.

Soon, at Clinton's orders, the CIA's extremely secret Operations Planning Cell was busily gathering intelligence to pass to UNSCOM, under the cell's leader, Doug Englund. The agency's connection to UNSCOM was kept secret, the CIA personnel being identified only as "State Department employees" seconded to UNSCOM. Inspections had to strike hard and hit fast, so the 1st Detachment of the Special Forces operational unit based at Fort Bragg, North Carolina, a Delta hostage rescue team, were used in the raids. Some were concerned that the involvement of U.S. intelligence would compromise the integrity of UNSCOM, but dissent was crushed, and the agency ties stayed in place. CIA teams would hold U.S.-only briefings for Americans working for UNSCOM staff, affronting non-Americans on the commission. After reconsideration, the CIA teams based in Bahrain invited the U.K., Canada, and Australia to send representatives to the meeting to "internationalize" the effort.[3]

With the tenure of CIA director John Deutch, covert efforts were stepped up in an attempt to better monitor Iraq's internal condition. By 1996, Near East Division chief Steve Richter was pushing hard to make sure UNSCOM's activities aided plans for a Baghdad coup. At his direction, the agency and close U.S. allies began using UNSCOM as a cover to isolate and intercept radio frequencies used by the Iraqi Special Security Operation. This was further evidence of a dramatic rethinking of America's Iraq policy inside the CIA. The Clinton administration had switched from attempting to contain Saddam to getting rid of him.

Richter soon had a team of five intercept operators using high-quality commercially available communications scanners and digital audiotape with the antennas mounted on the roof of the Baghdad Monitoring and Verification Center giving the analysts 360 degree coverage. Soon there was a system of five intercept stations, two manned by specialists in traffic analysis—all part of a covert communications intercept team operating inside Iraq reporting directly back to UNSCOM. There was also a National Security Agency team in Bahrain to review the work of the teams, called "B441," a special unit under NSA's "B" group responsible for the Middle East. Final Curtain was the name of the intercept program.

The intercepts were sent by satellite relay to Bahrain and forwarded to the NSA at Fort Meade, Maryland, where they were decoded and translated into English. Other targets of U.S. monitoring were the Iraqi special security apparatus, the National Monitoring Directorate, the Special Republican Guard, and the Office of Presidential Security. At one point, NSA black boxes that would automatically track targeted Iraqi frequencies were installed at sensitive locations.

The CIA techniques were extremely sophisticated. One Special Collection Element or SCE, a five-man team, was able to intercept not only the calls of senior Iraqi leadership but also their security detachments, enabling anyone listening in to determine the precise location and activity of those being listened to (a method very useful in tracking Milosevic in Serbia).[4] For example, in addition to being able to tap a phone call by Iraqi deputy prime minister Tariq Aziz and another official, the CIA was able to pinpoint their respective locations, which were then programmed into the guidance computers of the cruise missiles on station with U.S. ships in the Persian Gulf. British secret intelligence, MI-6, was also feeding the CIA team in Iraq information about the location of senior Iraq officials.

The surprise inspections of UNSCOM had proved invaluable. The UNSCOM teams destroyed so much WMD equipment that in July of 1994 UNSCOM head Ekéus gave an assessment to the Security Council in which he noted that with so much progress having been made, he would be embarrassed, "if the council does not at least show Iraq that there is light at the end of the tunnel," adding that Iraqi officials should be given some hope of sanctions being lifted.[5]

No one knew what the exact status of Saddam's WMD arsenal was. From the beginning, UNSCOM had been bedeviled by faulty information. There was one DIA analyst who was always peddling worst case scenarios, and his latest allegation was that Iraq had squirreled away a large batch of Scud missiles. The claim would prove false; however, many like it were made. There was a blizzard of supposition being paraded as fact and to obtain a clear, unobstructed view of Saddam's WMD was like being stranded in a furious gale trying to stare through gusts of sprays with rain driven into your face.

On August 8, 1995, the obscuring murk vanished when Saddam's son-in-law Gen. Hussein Kamel defected from Iraq, and the whole landscape was lit up bright as day as if by sheet lightning. Kamel's defection was kept quiet, even from the usual U.S. intelligence agencies, and his debriefing was done in deepest secrecy, on the royal grounds of King Hussein's palace in Amman. Kamel may have indulged expectations of a warm welcome but his reception was not friendly. Like most defectors, he had an "incredibly inflated sense of his own importance, almost delusional, a megalomaniac," according to a former senior U.S. intelligence official, but he had an incredible story to tell.

Kamel's position in Saddam's WMD program had afforded him a view unsurpassed in its access to the intricacy of its processes, its inventory, the performance of individual weapons, a depth of knowledge, not only about the weapons but where they were made, by whom, when, and where they had been deployed within Iraq. Kamel's major revelations were so unexpected, some fell on the inspectors like blows from an ax. In an August 22, 1995, interview with Rolf Ekéus, director of UNSCOM, who was accompanied by two technical experts, Kamel said that Iraq had *unilaterally* destroyed its WMD in the summer of 1991. The questioners were stunned. When asked again, Kamel nodded and said, "All weapons—biological, chemical, missile and nuclear were destroyed," adding, "You have an important role in Iraq with this. You should not underestimate yourself. You are very effective in Iraq."[6]

The story was this. After one aggressive IAEA inspection in June 1991, Saddam ordered a senior scientist, Dr. Mahmoud Faraj Bilal, former deputy of Baghdad's chemical weapons programs, to destroy all hidden biological and chemical weapons. This was promptly done, ridding Iraq of all precursors and hidden chemical weapons, according to official reports.

When Kamel was asked about VX chemical weapons bombs, he said that they had been built in the last days of the Iran-Iraq War. "During the Gulf War, there was no intention to use chemical weapons as the allied air force was overwhelming." There had been no VX production since the war, he said.

Not only did Kamel admit to having destroyed Iraq's WMD, he did something even more momentous. As Swedish ambassador and UNSCOM chairman Rolf Ekéus was about to depart from Baghdad, he received a phone call from an Iraqi official asking him to delay his departure for Jordan and the debriefing. The Iraqi had something to show the U.N. official, he said. Ekéus was annoyed but went along. When he got off the plane, he was taken to a chicken farm belonging to Kamel. As former UNSCOM inspector Scott Ritter said, "The farm was stuffed with crates and boxes containing hundreds of thousands of pages of documents on paper and stored as microfiche, dealing with Iraq's weapons of mass destruction programs." It was in fact, the legendary gold mine—the exclusive file of the Military Industrial Committee archive, which UNSCOM had heard about since 1992.[7]

Saddam's reaction was immediate. With Kamel's defection, Baghdad dropped its truculent chip-on-the-shoulder manner and adopted a new meekness. Within a very small group in the White House and CIA, there began a series of hasty meetings, discussions, questions, a rush to develop new avenues of inquiry and procedure and assemble more specialists.

Skepticism plagued many. How did you get a real accounting of what had been destroyed? What proof did you have? The most disconcerting feature was that Iraq had earlier tried to conceal the existence of their WMD. Before the Gulf War, U.S. analysts knew Iraq had WMD, but Iraq had lied. Would it now account for all its prewar stores? It was too hard for U.S. analysts to believe. As a Senate report said, "The Intelligence Community (IC) suffered from a collective presumption that Iraq had an active and growing . . . WMD program." This was clung to "in spite of evidence that Saddam had made the decision to declare virtually all hidden information they felt was significant on Iraq's programs, turning over WMD documentation including 21 trunks of documents," the Senate report said.[8] According to top U.N. weapons inspector Scott Ritter, when the Iraqi official directed Ekéus to the documents, Saddam was surrendering Iraq's final hope to go on with any WMD programs.

Albright's statements in her memoirs that Saddam's goal was "to foil inspectors by gaining relief from sanctions without giving up his remaining weapons" is wildly inaccurate, as is her belief in the recitals of "Iraqi defectors who detailed Saddam's manic pursuit of ever-more-lethal arms."[9] The information proved fabricated.

Not only did Saddam *not* have any WMD, his intelligence service, the Mukhabarat, wanted Baghdad to display complete openness to the United Nations on strategic grounds. To the Mukhabarat, the sanctions passed by the U.N. Security Council on August 6, 1990, which cut off all exports and imports between Iraq and the rest of the world, were the greatest security threat to the country, and after them came the presence of U.N. inspectors on Iraq soil. The Mukhabarat did not want Saddam to hide any WMD or remnants of WMD programs or in any way hamper or impair the work of inspectors. The Mukhabarat's only concern was to keep the weapons inspectors under the closest possible scrutiny and get them out of the country.

Other Iraqi security organizations disagreed. One, called the National Monitoring Directorate, was refusing to publicly acknowledge the range and depth of Iraq's WMD programs, feeling it would make it more difficult to get sanctions lifted if the existence of such programs were ever known to the West. Hussein Kamel, Saddam's son-in-law and director of Iraq's Military Industrialization Corporation, the home of most WMD projects, had argued that Iraq could not admit to having had a biological weapons program, even though Saddam had ordered it destroyed. "The world would not understand, and condemn us even though it has been destroyed," he said.[10]

As UNSCOM went about its work, its inspectors had no idea "that there were no weapons of mass destruction left in Iraq" or "that there were no dedicated programs related to the manufacture of weapons of mass destruction; these had been dismantled," according to the U.N.'s top weapons inspector, Scott Ritter. Further, there was another Iraqi security outfit that was stonewalling, the Special Security Organization, which felt that anything relating to Saddam's security could never be discussed with U.N. inspectors.[11]

Much of this resistance was simply Iraq's own pride in its being a sovereign country.

31

WMD MIRAGE

Did the Clinton administration know the contents of Kamel's debriefing? Acknowledging it did would weaken its argument for mounting strikes against Saddam, thus in in February of 1998, Clinton, when sending out his top foreign policy team to try and prepare the country for war, had discarded any appeals to reason in favor of marketing stark fear. The country wasn't buying. Facing a jeering crowd at Ohio State University chanting, "One, two, three, four, we don't want your racist war!" Defense Secretary William Cohen was asked about Saddam's WMD. In his reply, he said that before the Gulf War, Saddam had produced 2,100 gallons of anthrax and that "U.N. inspectors fear he may have produced 300 times that."[1]

The vague wording is everything.

Where many accounts portray Saddam's defiance of the international community as further evidence of his infinite capacity for perverse wickedness, there was quite another equation in play, one of national prestige. Saddam's son Qusay, who also said that the 1991 unilateral destruction of WMD should never be disclosed, partly on strategic grounds because Saddam would go to any lengths not to reveal any military or strategic weakness to Israel but especially because of Iran, with which Iraq had fought a terrible war of atrocity for eight long years. Like the rest of the world, Iran had to be deceived. National pride required it. On the other hand, Saddam was being weakened by sanctions and wanted them lifted. This then left Saddam with a strategy: stonewall and suffer sanctions or admit he didn't have WMD any longer, get the sanctions lifted, and secretly try to reconstitute the

program over time. Saddam feared the U.N. inspections would simply un-
veil to Iran his own vulnerability and leave him open to new forms of Iranian bullying. He used the analogy that the inspections were "like a savage
strike on the wrist of such force that it could immobilize the larger muscles
of the arm and shoulder."[2]

By December, the head of the Joint Chiefs, Gen. Hugh Shelton, brought to
Clinton a major revision of the military plan that included targets like dual
use sites and nonconventional weapons, especially places forbidden to U.N.
weapons inspectors. The military had begun to backtrack from the beginning. Clinton was extremely concerned about civilians, and that was reflected in the Pentagon. Shelton's group presented Clinton with lists of
possible civilian deaths if such and such a target were attacked. Shelton
said, "If the target was in such a place that it would result in the deaths of a
large number of civilians, then we did not recommend it."[3]

As weeks dragged by there were no clear-cut objectives to accomplish
by using force. The debate was windy and endless. An argument would be
offered, it would be debated, slashed to pieces, defended, defeated, and
then, in two weeks at another meeting, it would reappear like a corpse rising
from the grave. Slowly the purpose of using force changed from coercing
Saddam into some sort of un-aggressive behavior, to degrading or denying
his capacity to use WMD. At the time, there was no hard evidence that he
had any such weapons, but the reasoning was that the strikes would still
degrade Saddam's ability to ever get them.

Clinton was given no fewer than three separate Pentagon plans in a period of three months; however, no decision was in the offing. The white
loose-leaf binder with timelines for each stage of deployment and escalation
of forces grew thicker and thicker. Yet the U.S. position was eroding. The
more Clinton pondered the target lists and tried to calculate the results, the
less heart he had for proceeding, and the more misgivings he suffered about
the aftermath—from fearing a backlash in the Arab world that might deny
the U.S. basing rights in key countries, or further deterioration in U.S.-
Israeli relations, to perceived U.S. weakness causing a rise in terrorism in
the friendly Persian Gulf kingdoms.

Cohen, seized by a passion of impatience, wanted to strike before December 31, the beginning of the holy month of Ramadan. At a Principals
meeting, he told his colleagues that what was at stake was the credibility of
the U.S. threat. Albright and Berger thought there was not enough time to
prepare the public, and that the administration should raise the volume of
the threat to alter Baghdad's course.

Everyone breathed easier. Clinton had not reneged on his decision to bomb, but he wanted to try other measures when an act of Saddam's wrecked any calm. On January 12, the Iraqi ruler halted UNSCOM inspection team 227, which was investigating allegations that he had used human beings as experimental subjects. The deal with Russian foreign minister Primakov was in ugly pieces and the new UNSCOM head, Richard Butler, flew to Baghdad and announced a three-month freeze on inspections. When he returned he complained of the Iraq officials' "abuse and denunciation."

By then Shelton had completed the third and final plan to build momentum for a strike while trying to leave a door slightly ajar leading to a diplomatic solution. Clinton dispatched Albright to European and Arab capitals, her message to be "the diplomatic string is running out."

However, squabbling among the Clinton advisors continued. They could not agree on details of the plan and Shelton's top generals were suffering cowardly qualms. Finally, in a sudden stiffening of spine during a Principals meeting on February 6, they decided to shift from the threat of force to final preparations to launching the strike. The time for bluffing was finally over. On January 29, in Paris, Secretary of State Albright forged the pivotal diplomatic link when the French foreign minister, Hubert Vedrine, told reporters that "all options were open" if Saddam refused to cooperate with U.N. weapons inspectors. The message was ominously clear: in the Persian Gulf a gigantic thundercloud was stacked higher than anything so far in the U.S.-Iraq conflict, and whatever was coming was going to smash into Baghdad when it came.

To avert this, the French promoted a mission to Baghdad by new U.N. secretary-general Kofi Annan to fashion a compromise deal that would break down Saddam's reluctance to allow inspection of eight of his palaces. (Saddam was afraid intelligence obtained at those palaces was not intended for disarmament but for his assassination; and there were two lethal presidential findings that sought to overthrow him.) Clinton advisors were still divided on the value of sending Kofi Annan to Baghdad. U.S. ambassador to the United Nations Bill Richardson told Annan privately on February 11, "You can't go. . . . You can't box us in," but Albright and Berger favored it, and even Prime Minister Tony Blair was not at ease sending British aircraft to Baghdad without a final U.N. effort to bolster a deal.

Clinton too had felt the mission dubious, but he was going to leave little to chance. He had opposed the mission on February 11, but the next day had changed his mind. Clinton had earlier blocked an Annan mission out of fear Annan would negotiate a deal that would let Saddam off the hook (Annan said publicly there was no need to humiliate the man), but now Berger

Apolog

had a suggestion that Clinton approved. The United States would support the Annan mission if the U.N. official took with him a set of *written* instructions crafted by the Principals. When discussed at a meeting of the Security Council, the majority rejected it as high-handed: America was not going to use the United Nations to dictate its own conditions. So the plan for written instructions was discarded. Instead there would be "agreed advice."

What began now was a bit of skillful deceit, an act to fool the world. Prior to Annan's departure, a series of secret conference calls occurred between Richardson, Undersecretary of State Tom Pickering, and Albright, who, on February 15, secretly flew to New York and met with Annan at his Sutton Place townhouse to precisely draft "his compromise settlement." When Annan left for Iraq, he had gone from minister to messenger; he had with him an American-authorized mandate as to what he could or could not say to Saddam. Saddam could be low, gross, and sordid to a visitor, yet Annan returned with an agreement verbally endorsed by Saddam with the announcement to be made to the world on February 22. Immediately there rose the jubilation that comes with the end of excruciating tension.

The accord came just in time. The Arab anti-Saddam coalition, already fragile, received a new blow on February 20 when senior Saudi officials notified the White House that Americans could not fly bombers, only support aircraft, from Saudi air bases. In addition, the Clinton group had never managed to envisage what the aftermath of a strike might require in terms of policy. No matter. Relief swept over everyone at the news of the agreement. In Tampa, at CENTCOM headquarters, a crisis action team that had been on alert twenty-four hours a day waiting for the word to launch stood down. Clinton always led by only a step, and he had his eye on an uncertain, skeptical Congress, and a public hardly unanimous in its support for war.

Unfortunately, the duel wasn't over.

32

BRILLIANT VICTORY

The Annan accord was a symbol of past trouble and was to quickly be a cause for fresh trouble. No sooner was the Annan agreement made public than the U.N. Special Commission denounced it as a betrayal and a sham, and soon in the Congress, the tiny sparks of dislike, the little, licking flames of suspicion of Clinton, erupted in a sudden flare-up of savage denunciation. Politics had lost its flexibility, and the air was filled with so much distorting heat waves of malice and animosity that objects could no longer be clearly seen.

Republican Senate Majority Leader Trent Lott saw the accord as the U.N.'s "capitulation" to the Iraqi dictator. "It's always possible to get a deal if you give enough away," he said. "After years of denying that Saddam Hussein had any right to determine the scope of inspections or the make-up of inspection teams, this agreement codifies his ability to do both."[1]

Others accused Clinton of abandoning confrontation for appeasement, and there was anger at Clinton's having allowed Annan to dictate the pace and nature of U.S.-Iraq dealings and stern disapproval for the United States entrusting its foreign policy interests to the United Nations. None of which was true, but it didn't matter. The national temperature was boiling over. The din of gloating, belittling criticism knew no rest, and the administration team realized that the secrecy of Clinton's diplomacy had opened the door to a great tempest, and Clinton had been left standing in the wind's path.

His situation was made worse by the Monica Lewinsky scandal, made public on January 21, 1998, which provoked a perfect storm of nastiness. The assault on Clinton's character became enormous, bitter, and unending.

260 * CLINTON'S SECRET WARS

The sheer virulence of foul-mouthed abuse exhibited a great fallacy in pro-
portion on the part of his enemies, but no one cared. The tumult became
ear-splitting that summer when the prosecutor's 445-page report to Congress laid out allegations that included "abundant and calculating lies" under
oath, obstruction of justice, and other sins. In the provincial town of Washington, smug, insular, its people unshakable in their belief in their own
freedom from sin, Clinton found he had lost his standing, his credit, and his
prestige. The president was now suffering to the full the bitter misfortune,
misfortune beyond remedy, caused by his own fault. "There is a cloud over
this presidency," said Republican Senator John Ashcroft;[2] and Speaker of
the House Newt Gingrich had said to Clinton's face, "Mr. President, we're
going to run you out of town."

Yet if he were angry, faltering, and hurt when it came to the scandal, on
the subject of Iraq, Clinton was alert, tough, and pitiless. While the Republicans were busy accusing him of being weak, Clinton had moved quickly
and in secret to make revisions in Annan's "Memorandum of Understanding" relating to the inspection of Saddam's eight palaces. National Security
Council deputy advisor Sandy Berger and Secretary of State Madeleine
Albright subjected UNSCOM to remorseless pressure, obtaining terms that
said if Saddam tried to block another surprise UNSCOM inspection, the
automatic result would be a week of sustained bombing. In the meantime,
UNSCOM continued to collect intelligence on Saddam's security forces.

But WMD was no longer the real issue. According to a former senior
operative in the CIA's Directorate of Operations, "Iraq had no WMD. It
had produced none since Desert Storm. The inspectors knew that."

Unfortunately, the people with the best intelligence, the soundest knowledge, were being edged to the margins of the issue. To the great and lasting
discredit of the CIA, a rash and fractious manner began to prevail in the
agency. A new spirit of dogma had arrived. The idea that intentions are one
thing and capabilities another began to be lost. Ritter saw an emerging tendency on the part of analysts to assume that "an unaccounted-for VX nerve
agent program [had become] an active nerve agent program, and a potential
to manufacture powdered anthrax became a de facto capability."[3] At one
point, Ritter had written a paper theorizing that if the Iraqis *had* hidden
some WMD materials, what were the quantities likely to be? Ritter's document was a mass of supposition and hypotheticals, not facts. Yet no matter
how many verbal qualifiers Ritter used, like "suspected" or "possible" or "potential for," when the CIA returned his document to him, the agency had
rewritten it, and what Ritter had posed as questions had been changed to flat
statements of fact. The tension between inspectors like Ritter and bureau-

crats at the agency would signal the outbreak of an extraordinary intestinal war that would rage without intermission until the United States went to war with Iraq in 2003 and discovered no WMD.

"It was the WMD analysts at the CIA who got it completely wrong," said a former senior agency analyst. "There was a sort of momentum that built up." The lead agency analyst, a female, ferociously ignored "anything that challenged her pet assumptions or unwarranted conclusions. When new information came in, she acted like a college professor with a grad student who had had the nerve to question her doctoral thesis. You simply didn't get a hearing. The UNSCOM inspectors like Ritter were discredited by everybody, and yet they had the best intelligence."

The CIA had thus begun to assess WMD in terms of fixed and unchallengeable notions, ignoring and trying to destroy contradictory evidence or uncompliant facts. "It was all hot blood and muddled heads," said a former senior Directorate of Operations official.

One former DO agent who had access to defector Gen. Hussein Kamel's debriefing said, "Saddam had definitely destroyed them in 1991. For one thing, his economy was in bad shape, and one of the reasons he destroyed his stockpiles was to be spared the expense of having to maintain them and move them around."

Another former CIA agent said, "Saddam thought the United Nations would halt the program of inspections. He was warned the United States was crazy on this subject, but he didn't believe it."

Still another former senior administration official said, "When it came to WMD, the agency analysts began to embrace absolutes; no compromise was possible."

What continued to worry the CIA was the mechanism that Iraq had used to conceal the weapons prior to their destruction. What was it and how did it work? Was it dismantled or was it still in operation and what threat did it still pose? In addition, the agency analysts were worried over a Kamel statement (not revealed until this book), when he told the debriefers, "We tried to destroy them all, we tried and failed. We were stopped in 1995." What did that mean? What was still out there?

Kamel had told of how the Special Republican Guard had been used to hide WMD early in the decade, and UNSCOM wanted to clarify the Guard's role. A fresh round of inspections was mounted whose target was presidential palaces, offending the Iraqis, who had been far more cooperative after Kamel's defection. "Why does UNSCOM need to inspect these sites?" an Iraqi official asked inspector Ritter. "These are sensitive to the security of Iraq . . . this has nothing to do with weapons of mass destruction." He was right.[4]

According to several former intelligence sources, the chief but ignored fact in all this was that U.S. intelligence had *no solid evidence* of Iraqi WMD. UNSCOM was uncovering and destroying some, but it was clear that they had been produced before the Gulf War. They weren't new. According to the evidence, there was no current manufacture of WMD in Iraq.

A former senior CIA official said, "Saddam did have some VX shells and chemical weapons that he gave to Sunni tribal sheiks because he didn't trust his army. The sheiks buried them in the desert, and they had degraded and were unusable."

Bridling at incessant U.N. intrusions, the Iraqis hunkered down to protect the country's security, resisting UNSCOM's efforts to unravel the Iraqi concealment mechanism and the organizations it used.

All the while, in spite of the evidence, Saddam's WMD continued to be a growing, alarming menace to the agency. The path to error, folly, and war was paved by blindness fed by blatant disinformation.

Throughout the summer, Clinton went through his Lewinsky ordeal acting distressed at times, so much so that he seemed not to hear or see anything, and yet he never lost his pugnacity. He had once asked Gingrich, "Do you know who I am? I'm the big rubber clown doll you had as a kid, and every time you hit it, it bounces back. That's me—the harder you hit me, the faster I come back up."[5]

That summer the real work of the president was not only having to endure the ceaseless racket of deriding, holier-than-thou opposition, but the far more difficult task of rebuilding his emotional ties to his family. Hillary was a difficult woman. When it came to getting what she wanted, she was a person of unrest, hurry, and impatience, and now resentment had entered her innermost recesses. Knowing her husband had lied to her, she could barely stand to be in the same room with him. Clinton was simply shut down by this. His relation with his daughter, Chelsea, was not much better. As days went by, he floated isolated, like a spar on an empty sea.

He was getting good advice from aides. Aide Rahm Emanuel told Clinton bluntly: "People don't care about you or your problems, they only care about what you are doing for their problems."[6] The public wanted Clinton to get on with the ordinary business of being president. On August 17, Clinton celebrated his fifty-second birthday, and there was a poignant image of the wounded family, setting out for their vacation on Martha's Vineyard, Chelsea walking across the White House lawn between them, holding their hands. (It was at that time that he launched cruise missile strikes at Osama bin Laden in Khost, Afghanistan.)

When they returned to Washington, Hillary was still cold, hostile, and distant, and the staff could detect no deference or kindness in her dealings with her husband. Worse, Clinton's political fortunes continued to fall. By September, rumors flew that he was only a few days away from having a delegation of Democrats come down from Congress and demand his resignation. The question that reigned in people's minds was, Did Clinton regret his misdeeds or did he only resent having had them exposed? Advisors made clear to their chief that defiance, shrewd moves, or sly maneuvers were not required—simple, abject groveling was. Clinton gave a tearful apology to the White House staff, but one of his cabinet members, Secretary of Health and Human Services Donna Shalala, was not very forgiving or receptive. A former chancellor of the University of Wisconsin, she did not think tinkering sexually with a young, inexperienced woman a trivial matter. She listened coldly to Clinton's talk of struggling with personal demons and thought it self-justifying rubbish. To Shalala, Clinton was basically sending them a message that "he had no obligation to provide moral leadership." When she said this, the roomful of listeners froze at the tone, and he snapped, "By your standard, Richard Nixon would have beaten John Kennedy."

After the long meeting, Clinton hugged Shalala.

"You're always on my ass," he said, slightly bitter.

"Yes," she said, "and about the right things."[7]

The next morning, Clinton met with a group of ministers in the East Room for breakfast, and said humbly, "I don't think there's any fancy way to say 'I have sinned,'" adding that he knew "legal language must not obscure the fact that I have done wrong." But humility did not come easily to him.

Meanwhile, the kaleidoscope of fortune had been given a sharp turn. For one, Clinton enjoyed some budget triumphs in the Congress, and then he flew to the Wye River Plantation along the Chesapeake Bay to meet with Israeli Prime Minster Benjamin Netanyahu, PLO chairman Yasser Arafat, and King Hussein of Jordan, who was dying of cancer, to mount an effort to rescue the earlier Israeli-Palestinian peace agreements. Endurance, indifference to pain, emotional stamina, are all required of a president. A World War II British general who was an opponent of Rommel's in North Africa talked of the "robustness" required in a leader, noting that "delicate mechanism is of little use in war," adding that this applied "to the mind as well as the body." Military historian Ronald Lewin said that a leader had, "in his mental and emotional capacity, to accept very large responsibilities and, in consequence, to absorb very large shocks over very long periods of time."[8] In this crisis, Clinton was robust—he spent eighty-five hours over the next nine days cloistered head to head with the three Middle East leaders.

264 * CLINTON'S SECRET WARS

It was grueling. Often his helicopter would not land at the White House until many hours after midnight. The talks aimed at obtaining agreement to implement the Interim Agreement of September 28, 1995, brokered by the United States between Israel and the Palestinian Authority signed on October 23. The talks weren't going well; everyone was eager for concessions as long as they were made by the other side. The summit was about to collapse, but Clinton had always been able to imbue others with enthusiasm for his own purposes because of the effectiveness of his own personality, and he did so now.

Until the final evening, the talks had exuded a feeling of futility. The sides were far apart, rigid and fixed in their viewpoints, and the participants were about to admit to failture. On the last night of the collapsing talks, just as the sky was starting to redden in the east, lighting up the undersides of the cottony clouds, Clinton somehow managed to coax out an accord. Netanyahu, who was close to Gingrich and no admirer of Clinton, said later in admiration, "I mean he doesn't stop. He has this ability to maintain a tireless pace and to nudge and prod and suggest and use a nimble and flexible mind."[9] Jesse Jackson remarked, "This man's survival skills are of a different order."

The agreement was one piece of good news, and another was the midterm elections. Gingrich had expected large gains of up to forty seats in the House. He sat back with complacency to await the results. Clinton was in the White House eating pizza. Hillary had always believed that trading early returns was a jinx and left to watch the movie *Beloved*. Clinton wasn't a big fan of technology and had never learned how to operate a computer. That night, to his delight, his political director, Craig Smith, showed him how you could use the computer to go on the Web and track election results in real time, and the more Clinton watched, his pulse began to quicken. Gingrich, instead of gaining seats in the House actually lost five, barely hanging on to the majority. There was also good news in the Senate. One of Clinton's most dedicated tormentors, Republican Alfonse D'Amato, a very powerful man, lost his New York seat to Charles Schumer, a Democrat.

Not long after that Gingrich resigned as speaker of the house.

However things were going at home, when it came to foreign policy, Iraq was still the heart and center of trouble in the Middle East, and a showdown was in the works. For the last few months, there had been a whole series of unreasonable demands made on Iraq by the administration in the hope of provoking noncompliance by Saddam and providing a pretext for a military strike. UNSCOM chief Richard Butler, in close conjunction with Albright and Berger, had worked on engineering some sort of crisis. At one point, they had demanded that Saddam allow inspection of his Ministry of

Defense, certain Saddam would go to war. When Ritter went to Baghdad, Saddam gave in and war was averted, but the well was dry. The time for drift and indecision was over. A series of complicated crescendos was gathering to a climax.

The skills required of a congressman are different from those of a manager of one of the largest, most conservative, and contentious institutions, the Pentagon, yet William Cohen seemed to have made the switch with polish, ease, and skill. He was a moderate centrist Republican from Maine. He had caught the national eye when, as a freshman member of the House Judiciary Committee, he and a handful of other members had broken ranks to cast a key vote for Nixon's impeachment.

As the Reagan fundamentalists gained strength in the Republican Party, Cohen's distaste increased and he saw himself becoming inexorably boxed in and politically impotent. In 1996, he refused to run for a fourth term, having became a senator in 1979, disillusioned by the sordid methods of political fund-raising and bearing emotional scars from the Iran-contra scandal and the disgrace of his friend, Senator Gary Hart, being forced out of the Democratic primaries by an extramarital affair. President Clinton very much wanted to keep some Republicans in his second administration for coloring and balance, and he had called Cohen just as the former senator was packing up his office. Several conversations followed, and the two men came to like and respect each other. They talked of books. Cohen was a man of serious mind who had written sentimental poetry and spy novels. Cohen told Clinton that he would agree to become a member of the administration on two conditions—he would leave if he found himself undermined, or if he disagreed with the administration on a matter of principle. Clinton said fine.

At one point, the two had a remarkable conversation about scandals and the missteps Nixon and Reagan had made in handling theirs. Cohen thought Clinton should get Whitewater off his back, and advised that the most efficient, satisfactory way to do that would be to release everything to the public. "Nothing held back," he said. He believed that Clinton might have to give a national mea culpa speech, but at least the probes would be ended. Cohen believed it to be tragic if the country had to endure four more years of investigations. "No further surprises," he said.[10]

Clinton hadn't really replied, but several days later he offered Cohen the Pentagon job and he accepted. Cohen said, "I don't intend to be a Lone Ranger," and pledged that he had never accepted any Republican social agenda and would be a loyal member of the group.[11]

Cohen had shared the military's reluctance to be drawn into some bottomless morass in the Balkans. His caution urged him to steer clear, and he disliked the tough talk of some of the civilian hawks like Albright, because he felt it irresponsible. The stakes were too big. Cohen unfortunately had a magisterial manner, derived from his years in the Senate, and was in the habit of addressing the Principals as if he were still a member of Congress. He brought to the administration all the doubts of Congress, and referred to Congress as "us" and to the White House group as "you." Sandy Berger finally took him aside and said gently, "I will regard this administration as a success when you refer to the administration as *we* and not *you*."[12]

What concerned Cohen that morning of December 16 of 1998 was the state of Clinton's nerve. Since October the Iraqis had repeatedly denied access to weapons inspectors, and Saddam was due for a sound and sustained bombing. Clinton had approved a huge bombing raid in November, but when Saddam promised to comply, Clinton had stepped back. Surprisingly, General Shelton had agreed. Now Cohen wanted to go ahead. Wanting to avoid the highly public buildup of forces done in January, Shelton told Cohen that arrangements were being made to have the assault launched without any advance notice to Saddam that it was on the way. With the president's permission, Cohen gave the forces twenty-four hours' notice and scheduled the raid the day the full House was to begin impeachment proceedings.

Cohen figured that Saddam would perform a charade of appearing to cooperate the first two weeks of December, then renege as usual. It was silly in a way. Saddam was about to suffer hard punishment over half a dozen sites denied to the United Nations out of three hundred. By 7 A.M., Cohen was seated in the Situation Room with the Principals. They reviewed a U.N. report that said Saddam was not in compliance. President Clinton then joined the group. All the advisors present urged that the president launch the attack at 5 P.M. that day. Cohen said, "A failure to act now would undercut our credibility."

Clinton paused, then said, "I can't consider anything else. I have no choice."

When Clinton asked the members of the National Security Council if they would proceed with the attack if there were no impeachment hearings, all said they would.

Called Operation Desert Fox, it would involve 650 bomber or missile assaults against fewer than one hundred targets during a seventy-hour period. It would only constitute between 1 to 2 percent of the bombing of the Gulf War, but its effects would be devastating. Administration officials had been quietly lining up support for the air strikes with the Gulf states and working in the Security Council to harden the line on sanctions. The French and Russians were given last-minute notice of the strikes. Ironically, Clinton's success at Wye had convinced the Arab world that there was progress for an Arab-Israeli peace and their mood changed for the better.

When the time came, Clinton signed the order. Gen. Anthony Zinni, who had become CENTCOM commander in 1997, launched over two hundred cruise missiles from ships and subs in the Gulf along with B-52 heavy bombers. In all, one hundred cruise missiles were fired. When the bombing ended on the fourth night, a total of ninety-seven targets had been struck, the major ones being suspected sites for the production and storage of chemical weapons and the missiles that could deliver them.[13]

The effects were unexpected and momentous. The target list had been stunningly precise. One principal target had been Saddam Hussein's sleeping quarters on the outskirts of Baghdad, only one of the sites of CENTCOM's list. Bombs were dropped on separate buildings that housed secret units of the infamous Special Security Organization and the Special Republican Guard that included units like the 5th Battalion of the 1st Brigade, the 8th Battalion of the 2nd Brigade, the Armored Battalion of the 4th Brigade, all very bad actors.

Cohen had publicly given the rationale for the raid as designed to degrade Iraq's ability to produce WMD. The target list gave the lie to the supposed anxieties about WMD as the object of attack. Only thirteen targets hit were associated with Iraq's supposed production of WMD including biological, chemical, or ballistic missiles. By contrast, thirty-five targets were destroyed because they were part of Iraq's air defense system, always the first target in the event of war. Perhaps the most dramatic change was General Zinni's targeting of the pillars of the regime's power, the desire to inflict damage on Saddam's inner circle. Forty-nine of one hundred targets were six palace strongholds, including units of secret police, guard, and transport organizations. A site at Radwaniyah, a complex adjacent to the airport, had been designated "LO1" in Desert Storm, indicating a target in the senior leadership. Special barracks and units in and around Baghdad or outlying provinces were all hit.

The message was, "We have penetrated your security and are inside your head," as one official at the time put it. And it was all made possible by U.S. information on the regime gathered by the CIA under the cover of UNSCOM. The strike had its origins in the Principals' discussions of October of 1997 when people had come to believe that a military strike was not only unavoidable but might accomplish something. Shelton had his group map out seven general target categories including "WMD Industry and

Production" and "Command and Control." By striking at Saddam's pillars of power, the bombing was intended to shake the regime to its core, to destabilize it, if possible.

U.S. intelligence had discovered that Saddam was using short-range missile facilities, attacked in Desert Storm in 1991 but now being used as a cover to develop long-range missiles. The suspected facilities were at places like Kindi in Mosul, Shahiyat, Ibn al-Haythem, and others, all being monitored by UNSCOM. That agency had made lists of equipment that was irreplaceable and, if hit, would severely set back the new program. All were left wrecked. Non-WMD targets included the Biological Center at Baghdad University, suspected of producing chemicals that could be delivered by drones. Yet in the main, Zinni did not bomb suspected dual use facilities for commercial and military purposes because chemical agents in small amounts could be manufactured for terrorist use too easily. Instead, Zinni was going to attack the "visible symbols" of the regime: the Iraqi intelligence and Baath Party organizations, Saddam's entourage and advisors like Abed Hamid Mahmoud, the dictator's chief of staff; the Special Security Organization's computer center; as well as intelligence archives. Centers of control such as the two corps and four division headquarters of the regular Republican Guard, along with helicopter bases at Samarra East, K2 airfield near Baiji, Taji, and Kut were smashed to bits in revenge for the slaughters of the Kurds and Shia in 1991. The headquarters of the Special Republican Guard was left a ruin. The Mukhabarat headquarters was also hit. Other targets included telephone exchanges and TV transmitters in Abu Ghraib and Baghdad, which were destroyed along with intelligence stations and secret police archives in an effort to thwart Saddam's ability to track what was happening internally.[14]

To achieve surprise, the attacks were mounted at night and some targets like electrical power sites were deliberately avoided for fear of causing panic among civilians and producing bad publicity.

Another target specifically passed over was the Iraq army, considered the "soul of the country," according to former DIA analyst Pat Lang. "I did not drop a single bomb on the army," Zinni said.[15] The Iraqi war of 2003 lasted only from March 20 until April 9, and British military historian John Keegan described it as a "lightning campaign so complete in its results (as to be) almost unprecedented.[16]

Keegan also called the war "mysterious." He noted that although Iraq fielded an army of 400,000, it faded away from confronting an American force only half that size. The explanation lies with the failed Richter/Manners coup of 1996. Everyone extolled the brilliance of Tommy Franks's campaign, but it occurred to few that perhaps General Franks had enjoyed help from the Iraqi army, which had opened some sectors of the front and stood down to enable Franks to make progress. This occurred thanks to Iraqi military assets developed during the coup and because of agreements made between the United States and Iraqi army commanders. At least four former senior U.S. officials, including Zinni, told me that this was so. These sources said that the Iraqis were told that if they agreed not to fight, they would not suffer in the event of surrender. On the contrary, U.S. officials promised that they would retain their grades, their ranks, pay, and privileges in the event of American victory. These promises were not oral, but, according to Zinni, "were made in writing," and he claimed to have seen them.[17]

When the 2003 invasion occurred, the Iraqi assets recruited by Iyad Alawi remained in place. Said David Manners, Franks was aware of these arrangements, "which is why he took in the kind of light force that he did."[18]

The Iraqi army had 385,000 personnel, and was known as "the soul of the country," according to former DIA Col. Pat Lang. The army had great popular standing in the country, and was seen as one of the country's few unifying forces. Keeping the Iraqi army in being, even if America conquered the country, was central to CENTCOM's planning. Gen. Jay Garner had wanted to get the Iraqi army back on its feet as quickly as he could. And key U.S. commanders in Iraq had agreed. Even the Saudis had recommended that America find some way to keep Iraq's army intact, and Alawi saw in it a new power base.

Unfortunately, the neocons saw the Iraqi army as a hostile force because its members belonged the ruling political party in Iraq, the Baath, which was seen by the neocons as akin to the Nazi Party in Hitler's Germany. When the U.S. administrator, L. Paul Bremer, disbanded the army, "We went from liberators to occupiers in an instant," said former CIA official Vince Cannistraro. Bremer had been warned by a CIA chief, "Do it and by nightfall, you'll have driven 30,000 to 50,000 Baathists underground." Bremer disbanded not only the army but all the civilian ministries, casting into poverty about half a million Iraqis, and the insurrection began.

Although derided by most military experts at the time, the Desert Fox operation had had profound effects. Former CIA analyst Ken Pollack wrote, "Saddam became so concerned about a coup that he overreacted, ordering emergency security measures including the arrest and assassination of several important Shiite clerics, that set off an uprising among Iraq's Shi'a communities." His regime was destabilized for months afterward, Pollack said.

Zinni added, "We had these reports of Iraqi generals sitting on the curb holding their heads in their hands."[19]

In an interview, Zinni said he was surprised by the results. The Polish mission in Iraq was acting as the eyes and ears of the United States, and it informed Zinni of the unexpected impact the bombings had. "There were a lot of good reports coming out afterward on how Saddam changed his command and control very quickly. It was especially clear in areas involving internal control," Zinni said.

Asked about WMD, Zinni said, "If Saddam had any WMD, it was only tactical stuff, old Soviet artillery rounds, and those things tend to degrade quickly. There was no indication of his doing WMD. The targets we were hitting could support WMD, but the Iraqis weren't producing WMD or storing WMD. Saddam had no WMD."

His conclusion? "Containment was working effectively. Saddam was contained. His military over time had become a shell. There had been no modernization of weapons; there had been no modernization of structure."

The attack weakened Saddam so much that the fear was "not of explosion but implosion" of the Iraqi state, said Zinni. Neighboring countries were worried that if Saddam collapsed, there would be "a spillover of refugees. There was no problem with taking down the Republican Guard or even taking down the regime. We could have," he said. "But everyone said the problem was after the victory. Everyone said there would be a disaster. So we didn't. No one wanted to occupy Iraq."

33

GOOD AND EVIL IN HISTORY

By the close of the decade, Saddam Hussein was clearly a despised, derided, diminished figure, no longer a menace, merely a manageable nuisance pushed to the sidelines.

How that view of Saddam became obscured, how unstable assertions and the purveying of the wildest and most unsound assertions about Iraq led the United States into a disastrous war, was due chiefly to two parties—the neocons, the neoconservatives, along with Ahmed Chalabi, the man who was diabolically brilliant in using the neocons' own unexamined assumptions to mislead them.

Clinton's handling of Iraq and Saddam had been a constant target of Republican ridicule. The conservative Republicans never let Clinton forget Iraq. Their contemptuous disdain for the president's handling of Saddam was made clear in a slew of jeers, innuendos, and outright attacks. To the conservative Republicans, the Clinton group was impaired, coarsened, and degenerate, and it was from a sense of moral imperative, of acting from a desire to rid the world of wickedness, that the Republicans had sought Clinton's humiliation, his abasement, his banishment.

To conservative Republicans, America was enjoying an unprecedented time of supremacy, and Clinton's responses to challenges to that supremacy had been ambivalent, weak, and inadequate. The Clinton years, they felt, had been easy, soft, pleasure-loving, profit-taking years, years in which a priceless new world order could have been forged and a great deal could have been accomplished. Instead, the time had been squandered in distracting scandal and indecision. The Republican group about to assume political power embraced a policy of utopian optimism backed by unlimited force. They believed that America was the last, best hope for the world's regeneration, "mighty but good," and that creating a fresh, rich, and more promising future meant having to turn their backs on the past, the past meaning the Clinton years. ABC was the rule—Anything But Clinton. If Clinton had sailed hard in one direction, they would sail hard in exactly the opposite one.

The Republican predominance in Congress after 1994 had quickly brought the neocons, many based in far-right pro-Israel think tanks like the American Enterprise Institute or the Washington Center for Near East Policy, into prominence and they were exerting formidable influence on any debate on Middle East policy. These were organizations that tended to see American national interests as being identical with Israel's. One group made up of people with this mind-set in 1996 published a paper, *A Clean Break—a New Strategy for Securing the Realm*. It was written by Americans who were then in the employ of Israeli Prime Minister Benjamin Netanyahu. Heavily funded by right-wing benefactors, the power, visibility, and clout of the new group quickly drowned out the more liberal voices of discussion.

The chief neocon tenets for reform were straightforward: the Middle East could only progress if the old support for tyrannical regimes was repudiated; only if the Arabists in the State Department and CIA were ignored; and America had the guts to topple Saddam, create a democracy in Iraq, then, one by one, change regimes in Iran and Syria and other countries regarded as enemies of Israel. In the mid-1990s, Richard Perle introduced the exile Chalabi to Dick Cheney, to the views of the American Enterprise Institute, the Project for a New American Century, and the Gingrich Congress.

Perle was a classic insider, a man who, over the years, had collected a lot of keys to Washington's back doors, doors that would open quickly when he appeared at them, allowing him to glide into some central chamber of influence or intrigue. Chalabi saw that Perle and company had a shrewd grasp of the workings of Washington. The neocons liked to stay in obscurity, to remain in the shadows, out of sight of public scrutiny, working in secret the threads that set the governing machinery in motion. Besides Perle, the group included Paul Wolfowitz, fifty-eight, with long, thick, graying hair, and a mild, likable manner. He was a former senior DOD official and former U.S. ambassador to Indonesia where he had ruined the career of a star Foreign Service officer, Bob Gelbard. Gelbard had been a special presidential envoy to the Balkans and "a major player," according to

Peter Galbraith. Gelbard had been ambassador to Bolivia and assistant secretary of state for international law enforcement and narcotics. According to Richard Clarke, Gelbard "knew about armed helicopters and communications intercepts. He had fought drug lords and Serbian thugs." Indonesia was a breeding ground for al Qaeda, and Gelbard was concerned, far too concerned for Wolfowitz's taste.[1]

After Wolfowitz arrived, he heard from acquaintances that Gelbard was stirring things up, that he was making too much of a fuss over al Qaeda, and people were uncomfortable. Wolfowitz didn't know much about al Qaeda, and felt Gelbard was alarmist; he urged that Gelbard be removed. Soon after, Gelbard went home and retired from the Foreign Service. In October of 2002, al Qaeda struck Indonesia, attacking nightclubs in Bali and killing 202, most of them Australians. (Wolfowitz was sometimes in error but never in doubt.)

For years, Wolfowitz had been a virulent hawk on Iraq. To him, Saddam was pure evil and must be removed and a liberal, free market democracy must replace him in Iraq. Wolfowitz had been saying this since 1998. He disliked the Clinton policy of containment of Saddam. For one thing it was expensive, about $30 billion, and it had cost American lives, plus the U.N. sanctions had inflicted unnecessary suffering on the Iraqi people. Wolfowitz also believed that Saddam was attempting to build WMD, in spite of the fact that Saddam's son-in-law General Kamel, who ran those programs, said that they had been destroyed.

Besides Wolfowitz, there was Doug Feith, a former member of Reagan's National Security Council, once the subject of an FBI probe that alleged he had passed information to Israel, a charge never proved. Nonetheless, he had been discharged from the NSC according to two of his colleagues at the time, Michael Ledeen and Vince Cannistraro. Feith would soon occupy the number three spot in the Pentagon as undersecretary of defense for policy. Wolfowitz would land the number two spot, deputy secretary of defense. Before the election of George W. Bush, most had been roosting in various think tanks. With Bush's election, they came into their own.

The neocons like Perle and Wolfowitz displayed an odd mental weakness. When it came to Iraq, they suffered from a hankering for a political deliverer, a leader who could bring freedom to the country and raise his followers and backers to prosperity and power.

The neocons found their savior in Ahmed Chalabi. "Ahmed came, and all of a sudden, we had an angel!" gushed Mey Wurmser, an official at the conservative Hudson Institute which did papers on the Middle East, and wife of

David Wurmser, who was a friend of Wolfowitz and Perle, and a former naval intelligence analyst, who would become a Pentagon official involved in distorting U.S. intelligence to exaggerate the threat of Saddam.

Both Wurmsers believed in toppling Arab dictatorships and installing regimes friendlier to Israel. Mey Wurmser certainly was no friend of Arabs. Her expertise "is Palestinians," and she claimed a lot of experience. "I've met some of them and got to know some of them. Always the little genie comes out: they are anti-Semites or they want 'the right of return' and the destruction of Israel."[2]

With the coming of Chalabi, relief was at hand. Chalabi detested Arab nationalism. He validated her and her fellow neocons' dream of a democratic Iraq. "This intellectual idea that we were believing in, regardless of him, all of a sudden we are like, here is this Arab democrat. See, they exist. Not all Arabs have horns. You know God sent us this Arab democrat."[3]

Many con men are astute and cunning enough to manipulate people through their vanities. Chalabi's genius was to perceive that in the case of the neocons, their vanity had its root in the belief of their own rectitude, in the invulnerable nobility of their ideals, and Chalabi exploited them through those. Politics would be the means to register ideological judgments. Arthur Schlesinger had once observed that "Little has been more pernicious in international politics than excessive self-righteousness," but little thought was given to that. The neocons loved the good and were full of moral indignation at Arab wickedness, ignoring Herbert Butterfield's warning that "moral indignation corrupts the agent who possesses it and is not calculated to reform the man who is the object of it." What the neocons wanted was power, and as Butterfield said, the passing of a moral judgment was really a "demand for an illegitimate form of power," a weapon to rouse hatred against a rival or an enemy. In very little time, the neocon party of principle would have become a party of ambition and interest.

Chalabi had arrived in Washington in the early 1990s. Chalabi knew Americans brought to politics simple emotions and complicated ideas. Like the neocons, he chose to cloak his will to power in idealism. No one was more deft in staging history as a melodrama than Chalabi. He had noticed in his study of the South African struggle that the rebel African National Congress had portrayed apartheid in South Africa as tantamount to slavery. It wasn't at all accurate, but it had worked to poison and undermine the white regime's position in world opinion. From that topic, Chalabi had moved to the careful, tireless study of the way Jewish-American groups organized themselves to support Israel. In 1998, he began to tell pro-Israeli audiences what they had longed to hear: that Saddam should be toppled, and then the new government of a democratic Iraq would put back on line the oil pipelines that ran from Iraq's northern oilfields to Haifa in Israel, disrupted since the 1948 war.

He certainly sensed money to be made in promoting Saddam's downfall. He said to a friend that America had paid $500 million for an insurgency in Afghanistan, and that if Iraqi exiles could come up with a plan, they also might come up with the same kind of money. Former senior CIA Middle East analyst Judith Yaphe commented on Chalabi, "They are always in it for revenge or for Rolexes or for women or federal funding. They don't do it for love of country. Guys like Chalabi don't have a disinfested bone in their body."

Since the neocons regarded any differing opinion as a corrupt opinion, better ignored, they began to build a rosy scenario that had no basis in fact. No one seemed concerned if Chalabi had any popular base in Iraq. Nor had the neocons done a major assessment to determine which was the most important political group in Iraq. There was no need for it. By now it was clear to almost everyone that Ahmed Chalabi was going to head a free market Iraq that would become a liberal democracy in a region that, except for Israel and, in a limited way, Turkey, had none. Former Reagan Deputy Defense Secretary Richard Perle, chairman of a Pentagon advisory group called the Defense Policy Board, told European parliamentarian Daniel Cohn-Bendit before the invasion of Iraq of the U.S. confidence in the Iraqi exile. After which Cohn-Bendit remarked that it was only "the French themselves, not an American general [that] could remake France after the shame of the country's collaboration with the Nazis."

Perle had replied, "We have Ahmed Chalabi, chief of the opposition Iraqi National Congress, to enter Baghdad. Ending the current regime will liberate the Iraqis. . . . And I expect the Iraqis to be at least as thankful as French president Jacques Chirac was for France's liberation."[4]

His ascent had been smoothly engineered: thanks to a quiet conference here at a cocktail party, and with knots of influential people meeting at some event. Long before Clinton had left office, Chalabi was soon on a first-name basis with thirty key members of Congress including such Republican stars as Trent Lott, Jesse Helms, and Newt Gingrich, and he always had the right word or the right silence, and his influence spread rapidly.

PART THREE

A SPECIAL KIND OF EVIL:

AL QAEDA IN THE BALKANS

34

A CHANGING WORLD

It was a new posting for Daniel Coleman, an FBI agent experienced in handling foreign intelligence cases. It was St. Patrick's Day 1996, a day that usually holds hints of spring and heralds the finish of winter's bleak imprisonments, a day of fun if you are Irish and savor being able to drink to excess and do it with a sense of authorized mission.

So it was, for Coleman, a day of optimism and expectancy, especially if you are about to take up a new posting. But this St. Patrick's Day any signs of spring were lamentably late. The sun was anemic, and the sidewalks still lay littered with melting gray banks of spattered and soiled snow from a late blizzard a few weeks before—1996 was not a good year for mild weather. Coleman drove to Tysons Corner, Virginia, to a bland, undistinguished, almost East German–looking government tower called the Gloucester Building. He went inside, crossed the lobby, got on the elevator, and headed up to the fifth floor. The office there was formally known as the "Bin Laden Issue Station" code-named "Alec."

Located not far from the agency headquarters at Langley, on the agency organization chart it came under the heading of "Terrorist Financial Links." It was a subsection of the agency's Counterterrorism Center, and if its focus sounded vague and broad, the subsection was obsessed with a single mission—tracking an obscure Saudi by the name of Osama bin Laden whose obsession was destroying the United States of America and Israel, which he saw as being the two great sources of evil in the world and Islam's most deadly enemies.

It had been in 1993 when a foreign informant spoke about "a Saudi prince" who was supporting a cell of Islamic radicals or jihadis in a plot to blow up New York landmarks including the Holland and Lincoln tunnels, and Federal Plaza, when Coleman, then in the FBI's New York office, first heard the name bin Laden. Now, three years after the plot, the FBI had finally decided to send someone over to talk about this Saudi prince with the odd and unfamiliar name.

Alec Station was home to thirty-five volumes of transcripts of National Security Agency intercepts of conversations by bin Laden, who used a cell phone that employed "Pretty Good Privacy" technology, which lived up to its name: it fell far short of being excellent. There was a rich mine of information in the station waiting to be explored. Coleman was a scholarly and inquisitive man, suffering from asthma, but his mind was extraordinary. Once his interest was aroused, all his energies and stamina of attention came into play. He didn't skip over the surface of things—his mind could float on a vast ocean of particulars and then it would suddenly lower down into the depths here and there, a little bucket that brought up to the light some priceless specimen to be examined with meticulous curiosity. As it stood, knowledge of bin Laden remained vague; in one file Coleman had read, bin Laden was designated merely "as an Islamist financier." That was hardly adequate.[1]

The term "state-sponsored terrorism" was widely used but hardly ever understood. Iraq sponsored terrorism, but mainly against its own dissidents. Directed against foreigners it usually failed. Before the outbreak of Desert Storm, Iraq had sent forty-one hit teams across the world to assassinate U.S. diplomats. According to Stan Bedlington, a superb former CIA analyst who had worked with the British MI-5 and been active in Malaysia, the closest Saddam came to hitting a U.S. target was in Indonesia, where a team managed to penetrate the house and grounds of the U.S. ambassador, planted a bomb in the flower pot on his back porch, and left undetected. The ambassador liked every evening to go out on the porch in the mild twilight and drink a martini while he enjoyed his tropical garden. The plot would have worked perfectly, had it not been for an alert Indonesian gardener who found a bit of cut wire left lying out atop the garden wall. Forces were alerted, the bomb was discovered and detonated, and that was as close as Saddam's great state-sponsored terrorist team would ever come to harming an American diplomat.[2]

For Dan Coleman, his own view was that terrorism was more of a nuisance than a genuine, sleep-disturbing worry. His outlook would change when, in 1996, he flew to Stuttgart, Germany, with two U.S. attorneys, Kenneth Karas and Patrick Fitzgerald, to talk with a defector from some unfamiliar organization called al Qaeda. The informer was a nervous, jumpy Sudanese by the name of Jamal al-Fadl, who said he had worked with bin Laden in Khartoum, Sudan. Defectors are always of a certain type, casting themselves in heroic roles, making themselves the heroes of all their tales, and the Americans sat with patience as their man endlessly struck attitudes.

But then came a moment of stupendous importance. The man used a term his listeners had never heard before, "al Qaeda," or "the Base" in Arabic, and he began to describe sleeper cells and training camps. Coleman's curiosity was by now more than aroused. It was riveted. Fadl said that members of al Qaeda had been responsible for a 1992 bombing in Yemen aimed at Americans and it was also responsible for the two Black Hawk helicopters being shot down in Somalia, killing eighteen Americans. Al Qaeda, however, was no state. Fadl now began to outline a new, novel, and disquieting menace. He said that bin Laden was attempting to obtain nuclear weapons, and to the agents' astonishment, Fadl began to give names and draw organization charts. The impact on Coleman was formidable. For two weeks, six or seven hours a day, stunned investigators went over every aspect of Fadl's story, reinterviewing him again and again, yet the details he gave never changed.

During the next year and a half, using wiretaps of bin Laden businesses, Coleman was able to begin to chart the organization, to draw a map of its networks, horror growing over his mind as he saw how al Qaeda spread throughout the Middle East, Africa, Europe, and Central Asia. This was an amazingly far-flung organization obsessed with inflicting mass casualty murders on America, but when he tried to pass on his alarm and knowledge, no one paid attention. The thing that chilled the blood about al Qaeda lay with the fact that U.S. law enforcement and intelligence communities didn't take it seriously. They saw it as a quirk or a fluke. Here was a Saudi dedicated to destroying America yet Coleman could not get agents or officials to return his calls.

Given the nuclear might of the United States, its expertise in electronic warfare, its lethality in conventional weapons just displayed in Desert Storm, the threat of bin Laden seemed outlandish. The organization was like a man on a subway track giving the finger to an onrushing train. Yet Coleman could not rid his mind of a growing disquiet and unease. The picture of al Qaeda lay like a weight on him.

When the World Trade Center was bombed in February 1993, Serbia was one of the first suspects. White House official Richard Clarke picked up his phone to find National Security Advisor Tony Lake at the other end, asking frantically, "Did the Serbs do it? Did the Serbs bomb it? Was it a bomb?"

In 1993, President Clinton would have two clashes with al Qaeda and lose them both. There had been the attack on the World Trade Center, which was a relatively low-budget operation, so when the truck bomb went off in the massive parking garage, blowing through six stories of structural steel, only six people had been killed and 1,042 wounded. Then in October of 1993, al Qaeda operatives had worked with the followers of a warlord in Somalia, targeting U.S. helicopters, downing two and killing six U.S. soldiers.

Al Qaeda had attempted to attack U.S. targets as early as 1992, planning to blow up an American plane, and the following year had plotted to blow up a U.S. building in Karachi, Pakistan, the scheme collapsing when two of the plotters were arrested. There had been other projects in development: attacks on U.S. embassies in Tirania, Albania; Sarajevo; Kampala, Uganda; and Singapore.

If al Qaeda had America squarely in its sights in early 1993, no American had heard of it, and the perpetrators of the World Trade Center bombing enjoyed the vast advantage of anonymity. But U.S. education in al Qaeda would be swift, even if it came piecemeal. In the aftermath of the 1993 World Trade Center attack, the FBI had, with amazing skill, pulled from the wreckage of the garage remnants of a rented Ryder truck and determined that it had been the vehicle that transported the bomb. When an Arab returned to the Ryder agency in New Jersey to collect his deposit on the truck, he was arrested and the case broke wide open.

The FBI was soon untangling the threads of a Brooklyn, New York, terror cell made up of Egyptians, a Jordanian, an Iraqi, and a Pakistani. Its leader was a blind sheik from Egypt, Omar Abdel Rahman, who had been involved in the 1981 assassination of Egyptian leader Anwar Sadat. When White House official Richard Clarke called the FBI, he was told the feds had a bunch of overseas phone numbers, but they didn't match any known suspects from Hezbollah, Palestinian Islamic Jihad, or other ominous anti-American organizations. The probe kept on and within two weeks of the bombing, the FBI arrested four men, who would be convicted of the crime. Among them would be El Sayyid Nosair, the first al Qaeda operative to be arrested by America, a fanatic who had killed Rabbi Meir Kahane, head of the radical Jewish Defense League, famous for its extremism.

Oddly enough, as the FBI focused its forces to unravel the World Trade Center bombing, the name of Osama bin Laden was never mentioned.

It would only later be discovered that the blind Egyptian Rahman had spent time with bin Laden in Afghanistan, and that his organization, based in Brooklyn, was affiliated with the Afghan Services Bureau, run by bin Laden, and that bin Laden had paid Nosair's legal bills. FBI surveillance would uncover another Rahman plot to bomb the Lincoln and Holland commuter tunnels as well as the United Nations and other New York landmarks that finally sent him to prison.

Throughout this time, the mastermind Osama bin Laden remained a nobody to the U.S. law enforcement and intelligence communities. To old CIA operators of the Afghan program in Pakistan, men like Milt Bearden and Frank Anderson, the name bin Laden was familiar but hardly impressive. Born in 1957, Osama was the seventeenth son of Muhammed bin Laden's fifty-four children. In many ways, Osama was a typical young, rich Saudi prince whose family was a powerhouse in the Saudi construction industry. During the war with the Soviets in Afghanistan, Osama bin Laden had been known as a logistics man, a financier, who helped run funds and supplies to the anti-Soviet mujahedeen factions in the field. At a meeting in 1993, National Security Advisor Lake and CIA director Woolsey had discussed bin Laden's importance as an Islamic financier, but nothing came of the talk.

Then in April 1993, there had been a CIA paper that described bin Laden as "an independent actor" who sometimes tried to promote "militant Islam" using various governments or individuals, but that hardly made the hair stir on one's head. Almost everyone in the U.S. intelligence community was slow to see the tall, soft-spoken, bearded man emerging as a single-minded menace capable of inflicting great and merciless devastation on America. During most of Clinton's first term, the CIA, which was responsible for dealing with foreign threats, had been poorly managed, and experienced great difficulty in developing anything in the way of a detailed or comprehensive knowledge on any new threat that involved a new and sinister brand of radical Sunni Islam. The thinking of the intelligence community was still handcuffed to Cold War thought that depicted terrorism as state-sponsored in most cases.

Washington was beginning to use Saudi financial support to help arm the Bosnia Muslims, and the Clinton administration was settled comfortably into the preconception that the Saudis were valuable and irreplaceable regional allies when in fact most of the money going to the new Islamic terrorism was also flowing straight from Riyadh. Saudi Prince Turki al-Faisal remained the CIA's chief source of intelligence for the area on terrorism within the Kingdom. Clinton and Turki knew each other from Clinton's days at Georgetown University. Before he ran for the presidency, Clinton had looked up the names of old classmates and written them letters asking for their support. He had written to Turki, who had gotten Clinton's request in his office at the General Intelligence Department in Riyadh.

Turki recalled Clinton very clearly but had discounted his political prospects since Clinton came from such a poor, small, Southern state, and he didn't reply for some time. After Clinton was elected, things changed. Turki quickly opened a correspondence and, accompanied by the CIA's Near East Division director, Frank Anderson, and Prince Bandar, the Saudi ambassador to the United States, they went to the White House where they sat and talked with Clinton, who, in his usual loose way, nattered on about the benefits of globalization. When Clinton did take up the topics of Central Asia or the Middle East, he asked Turki what the Saudi thought his policies should be in those areas like Kazakhstan and Uzbekistan. Used to being told rather than consulted, Turki felt certain dismay. In fact, both men felt Clinton's ideas unfocused and came away shaking their heads, saying, He's asking us? The president was asking when he should have been telling.

Still, as a courtesy and gift of friendship, Turki and Bandar sent $20 million to a Middle East studies group at the University of Arkansas to help a program in which Clinton had once manifested interest.

The first alarm in the war on terror would ring in North Africa beginning in 1991, when a series of events exploded like a line of dishes falling off a shelf. Odd doings were observed in Algeria, Egypt, and Tunisia. Groups of Islamic radicals were organizing and gaining political power; however, no one really knew who they were. One of the first CIA analysts to try and decipher the meaning of the outbreaks was a quietly articulate former U.S. Army officer in Vietnam who had degrees from Dartmouth and Oxford, as well as a doctorate from Princeton named Paul Pillar. He was a writer of scholarly articles and books and within a few weeks of the World Trade Center attack, he was at the CIA Counterterrorism Center, studying North Africa.

Did connections exist between these new, very violent groups and did they pose any threat to either the United States or its allies? The North African countries were important, pro-Western, secular, buffer states, reasonably stable, especially Egypt with its vast resources and population. Soon intelligence began to pour in from Cairo, Tunis, Algiers, and Tel Aviv via liaisons with their intelligence services.

Even PLO leader Yasser Arafat was providing the United States with intelligence. Whatever else he was, Arafat was secular, and he saw in the Islamic militants an up-and-coming rival out to challenge his supremacy and leadership. Arafat was especially disconcerted by Hamas, an organization that Israeli prime minister Ariel Sharon described in 2002 as "the deadliest terrorist group that we have to face."[3] Active in Gaza and the West Bank, Hamas strove to liberate all of Palestine and establish a radical Islamic state in the place of Israel. It had gained notoriety for its car bombs, assassinations, and other acts of terrorism. If Hamas and Israel were locked in deadly combat, it was a little known fact that Tel Aviv had given both direct and indirect financial aid to Hamas over a period of years.

Tel Aviv "aided Hamas directly—the Israelis wanted to use it as a counterbalance to the secular Palestine Liberation Organization," said Tony Cordesman, Middle East analyst for the Washington-based Center for Strategic and International Studies. A former CIA official said Israel's support for Hamas "was a direct attempt to dilute support for a strong, secular PLO by using a religious alternative."

According to Israeli intelligence documents, Hamas had evolved from cells of the Muslim Brotherhood, founded in 1928.[4] According to Israeli documents Hamas was legally registered in Israel in 1978 by Ahmed Yassin, the movement's fiery spiritual leader, as an Islamic association named the Al-Mujamma al-Islami, which widened its base of supporters and sympathizers by means of its religious propaganda and social work.

Funds for the movement came from the oil-producing states and directly and indirectly from Israel. The PLO was left, secular, and promoted nationalism. Hamas wanted to set up a transnational state under the rule of Islam, much like Khomeini's Iran, and, indeed, Israeli leaders expressed their surprise at the revitalized Islamic movements after the success of the Iranian Revolution when armed resistance to Israel sprang up in southern Lebanon vis-à-vis Hezbollah, an Iranian proxy, to Israel a disconcerting development.

A further element in the growth of Hamas was the fact the PLO moved its base of operations to Beirut in the 1980s, leaving the Islamic organization to grow unimpeded within the Occupied Territories as a "court of last resort," a former CIA official said. Israel was certainly funding Hamas at the time, said U.S. officials. By then Israel was not only using Hamas as a counterweight to the PLO, it saw in it a way to channel toward Israeli agents Hamas members who were dangerous terrorists.

In addition, by infiltrating Hamas, Israeli informers could listen to Hamas members debating policy and identify the dangerous hard-liners who could be targeted for assassination. Hamas, however, was aware of the Israeli presence. It set up a comprehensive counterintelligence system, and many Israeli collaborators were weeded out and killed. After that, savage acts of terror against Israel became a central tenet of the organization. Even then, some Israelis saw benefits in trying to continue Israel's support for Hamas. "The thinking was on the part of some right-wing Israelis in the establishment that Hamas, even if it gained control, would not have any part of the peace process and would torpedo any agreements already in place," another former CIA official said. "That way Israel would still be the only democracy in the region for the United States to support."

All of which disgusts U.S. intelligence officials.

Former head of CIA counterterrorism Vince Cannistraro said, "The thing wrong with so many Israeli intelligence operations is that they tend to be too clever." Larry Johnson, former State Department counterterrorist official, agreed: "The Israelis are like a guy who sets fire to his hair then tries to put it out by hitting it with a hammer. Such operations do more to incite terrorism than curb it."

Cordesman added that a similar attempt by the government of Egypt to fund Egyptian fundamentalists had also come to grief because "officials misread the situation."[5]

Only slowly was an antiterrorism ferment to be seen at work in the federal bureaucracy. As the great historian Bruce Catton observed, people "rarely notice the onset of fog. It comes on gradually, the sum total of many small uncertainties that hardly seemed worth a second thought . . . then suddenly, the horizon has vanished altogether, there is fog everywhere, and the noises that come from the invisible landscape are unidentifiable, confusing and full of menace."[6] That fog was the new jihadi terror.

One person who had a sense that a new and ominous future was taking shape was State Department director of policy planning James Steinberg, whose job included planning for national nightmares. After the collapse of the Soviet Union, he commissioned a series of cables tasked with defining what new threats the United States might face. The results were disquieting: crime, drugs, terrorism, weapons proliferation were all there, staring out from the pages. "The dark side of globalization," Steinberg said. What was ominous was America's lack of concrete knowledge.

The White House needed to move fast and move boldly, but move where? For the moment, there was no foresight, no activity, no energy, no sense of urgency.

35

HEAVY HOUR

America was abruptly shaken out of its complacency on April 19, 1995, at 10:02 A.M. when Clinton was on the phone talking to Turkish prime minister Tansu Ciller, and was handed a note. It read: "Half of the federal building in Oklahoma City blown up. Expect heavy casualties." It was from Attorney General Janet Reno. Clinton's first act was to chair Richard Clarke's Counterterrorism Security Group, CSG, since Clarke was out of town. When Clarke asked a staffer who was chairing the meeting in Clarke's absence, the staffer said wryly, "Oh, it's in good hands. Bill Clinton's chairing the CSG."[1]

Shortly after the bombing, President Clinton signed Presidential Decision Directive 35, the document that declared the administration's intelligence priorities. Occupying top place was support for ongoing military operations and analysis of potential enemies such as China, Russia, Iraq, and Iran. Fundamentalist Islam was missing.[2]

Clinton had displayed poise, compassion, and calm in the aftermath of the Oklahoma blast. As horror and dismay spread across the nation, Clinton's reaction was instant, tough, and visceral. It is in hours of crisis that character comes to the fore, and Clinton's actions over the next few days showed that he had evolved from an unsteady, callow, uncertain newcomer to a leader of tested, expert powers. When he addressed the country, he was not only resolute but determined to steady the country. He said, "The bombing in Oklahoma City was an attack on innocent children and defenseless citizens." He went on to say, "I will not allow the people in the country to be intimidated by evil cowards."[3]

Later on that day, after describing the measures being taken—the teams of investigators being sent in and the like—he said justice would be "swift, certain and severe. These people are killers and they must be treated like killers." Then Clinton used his eloquence not simply to unite the country but to calm it and restore its heart. He added, "Let me say that I ask all Americans tonight to pray—to pray for the people who have lost their lives, pray for their families and the friends of the dead and the wounded, to pray for the people of Oklahoma City. May God's grace be with them. And meanwhile, we will be about our work."[4]

It was his finest hour, the one he had been born for. He proved able not only to dominate the occasion, but steady and strengthen the spirits around him.

Unfortunately, there were other dark shapes rising in the distance. Oklahoma City was horrible, but America was looking in the wrong direction, and few knew that America's most deadly modern enemy, far more destructive than any American terrorist, was already far in the lead.

Still, Clinton acted. Only two months later, on June 22, 1995, he signed PDD 39, titled "U.S. Policy on Counterterrorism." It ordered the attorney general, the director of the FBI, the director of Central Intelligence, and the secretaries of state, defense, transportation, and the treasury to enact measures to reduce U.S. vulnerabilities to terrorism. The Government Accounting Office and General Services Administration were to erect or create structures that would aid in this as well. While the traditional focus would be to bring terrorist suspects to the United States for trial, the PDD put in place the mechanism for sending a suspected terrorist to a third country known as "rendition."

"When terrorists wanted for violation of U.S. law are at large overseas, their return for prosecution shall be a matter of the highest priority and shall be a continuing central issue in bilateral relations with any state that harbors or assists them," it said.

Yet a majority in the White House was dismissive of the tall, bearded Saudi who they depicted as a flake and negligible eccentric, while, by contrast, Richard Clarke and Tony Lake thought it worth their time to drive out to the CIA in 1995 for a briefing. They were not comforted by what they heard. Throughout the early 1990s, it was clear to Clarke and Lake, there was some coordination between radical Islamists in North Africa, and the rise of radical Islam. To Clarke and Lake, bin Laden was an extremely dangerous man, and if he were funding projects, those undertakings needed to be laid bare, derailed, and the participants scattered or killed. To do that meant the White House and CIA needed to know who was funding bin Laden and who or what bin Laden was funding, and the agency had to know what bin Laden's ties to various terror groups were. It was largely as a result of Clarke's and Lake's untiring efforts that the agency put together its bin Laden station that the FBI's Dan Coleman would finally join.

One thing was clear. Whoever Hezbollah and groups of that ilk were, they played for keeps. As early as 1993, Hezbollah had set afoot a plot to assassinate Tony Lake, using the resources of Sudanese intelligence, dispatching a hit team, and setting Washington on edge. Lake had been put under protection and he stayed in a series of safe houses until the threat had passed. Unfortunately, there were a lot of failed countries out there, Somalia and Sudan with its radical leadership proving to be a notorious pest hole, infested with all sorts of shady, renegade, and dangerous characters that would come to include bin Laden.

Al Qaeda may even have been plotting to kill Bill Clinton. In 2002, in the Shomali compound near Kabul, Afghanistan, documents and videos were discovered that included notes on "presidential protective details and what vulnerabilities to look for," according to J. Keith Idema, an American civilian advisor to the Afghan United Front. There were also sketches of other Secret Service procedures, and the documents disclosed which streets or open areas were the best locations to stage a presidential assassination.[5]

The handwritten notes also revealed that al Qaeda members had been given specialized training in assassination and hostage taking. These same documents showed the attack would have been launched at a high-level conference or international summit. Sequences of presidential motorcades had been analyzed, noting which vehicles were heavily armed reaction teams that followed the presidential limousine. The weapons would have been rocket launchers and machine guns.

In one captured al Qaeda video, a mock assault on a golf tournament is shown, with terrorists jumping down from carts to pull weapons out of golf bags to shoot at players. Clinton was well known for his love of golf. What was also disturbing was that the Shomali compound used mock-ups of city streets and golf courses. Most of the sources interviewed said they believed the attempt on Clinton was to have been made when he was still in office although there is no evidence of the date of any attempt.

By 1996, an enduring anxiety about terrorism had sunk deep roots in the U.S. intelligence establishment and the White House. Some, like Clarke, saw with disturbing lucidity the inevitable development of events and began to amass resources and inaugurate programs to stop the new terrorist movement in its tracks. People spend their money where their fears are most intense, and at the beginning of that year the Office of Management and

Budget wasn't even sure of what was being spent on antiterrorism efforts. An accounting was done, and it was found that a total of $5.7 billion was being allocated, that figure destined to shoot up like a rocket. By the end of Clinton's second term, the figure had almost doubled to $11.3 billion.

Accompanying the increase of funds, the level of activity to prevent terror attacks went up as well. "Terrorism is a rough game, a very rough game, and sometimes to win it, you have to use very tough tactics. These are not nice people, these are not the citizens of anyone's country, they live in a gray area," said Graham Fuller, a former CIA official.

The FBI and the CIA both use the practice of rendition: of kidnapping terror suspects and spiriting them out of their sanctuaries, either for trial in America or in their countries of origin. To do this, the CIA owns a fleet of Gulfstream V jets, registered to a series of dummy corporations, one being Bayard Foreign Marketing of Portland, Oregon. All have clearance to land on U.S. military bases. But the usual destination for such trips is overseas, in places like Jordan, Syria, Morocco, or Egypt, all of which have legal systems that employ torture as a matter of course.

The agency program for renditions was in place by the mid-1990s, set up by CIA officials including Mike Scheuer, who was at that time head of the agency's Islamic Militant Unit. Its job was "to detect, disrupt and dismantle," terrorist operations. Before 1993 and Clinton, there had only been three renditions to the United States, but suddenly renditions became a growth industry, a total of forty taking place within a short space of time. Perhaps the most satisfying was the 1995 FBI capture of World Trade Center bomber Ramzi Yousef in Pakistan and his transport to the United States.

Clinton first briefed the congressional oversight committees on the fugitive transfers in 1995, after he had signed a secret bilateral agreement between Washington and Cairo under whose terms the United States offered intelligence assistance, advanced communications, and other technology to Egypt, and in return, America would deploy a small fleet of aircraft to track down suspects and return them to Cairo. The program began when then ambassador to Egypt, and later assistant secretary of state for the Near Eastern affairs bureau, Ned Walker, walked into the "secure" area of the U.S. embassy to meet with the CIA chief of station.

Walker was extremely knowledgeable about the Middle East. He had been in Egypt a year and watched with dismay the growth of new terror threats: in 1990, an Islamic group, Gama'a al-Islamiya, had attacked and killed eleven Israeli tourists and wounded nineteen more. A total of forty-two more terror attacks, mainly on tourists, had followed. Walker had Washington's support to assist the Egyptians in any way possible, and Walker and the agency matured a clever plan. Without their knowing it, a great many of the senior leadership of al Qaeda were Egyptian. That the United States would actively locate and render Egypt's most wanted terror suspects would prove to bear fruit beyond anyone's expectations.[6]

"We developed this question of rendition with the Egyptians, where we would bring people who were suspects for further interrogation in Egypt and we did so," Walker said. Each operation was approved by a large team of lawyers at the CIA or the Department of Justice. The national security advisor also had his own legal team that scrutinized each proposed operation. In the case of Egypt, each operation was carefully arranged to ensure the target was already wanted in Egypt on a criminal charge. Mike Scheuer, then head of the agency's al Qaeda desk, said later that never had he seen "a set of operations that was more closely scrutinized by the direction of central intelligence, the National Security Council and the Congressional intelligence committees" or "that was more blessed (plagued) by the expert guidance of lawyers."[7]

Clinton's interest in the program was intense, and he was strongly supported by Clarke, Feurth, Gore, Albright, and CIA director Deutch. In 1993,when Clarke had first proposed a rendition or "snatch," White House Counsel Lloyd Cutler felt such transfers violated international law and hustled in flabbergasted to demand a meeting with Clinton. Clinton listened to Cutler and seemed to agree with him when Gore arrived late at the meeting, and Clinton recapped the arguments of Cutler and Clarke. "That's a no-brainer," said Gore. "Of course it's a violation of international law, that's why it's a covert action. The guy was a terrorist. Go grab his ass." (The White House tried and failed.)[8]

One of the first renditions was to take place on September 13, 1995. Ned Walker handled the negotiations through the CIA chief of station, who then dealt with Omar Suleiman, chief of Egyptian General Intelligence Service. Suleiman would be the one who arranged meetings between Walker and the Egyptian Interior Ministry officials, including Hassan El-Alfi, the minister, or even at times with Egyptian president Hosni Mubarak. The agency at Langley had carefully gathered, assessed, and assembled the targeting data on Talaat Fouad Qassem, one of Egypt's most wanted terrorists, who had been found guilty of involvement in the 1981 murder of Egyptian president Anwar Sadat and sentenced to death in absentia. The CIA specialists who were to snatch Qassem came from the agency's Special Operations Group–Special Activities Division, and were basically well-trained paramilitaries. It was a mixture of people, both men and women, skilled in the use of explosives, all kinds of pistols, rifles, knives, and expert

in hand-to-hand combat. They had their own special equipment and avia-
tion assets, and could deploy promptly to any place in the world. On the
appointed date, Qassem was seized in Croatia, flown to the USS *Adriatic*, a
Navy warship, interrogated, then flown to Egypt for execution.

The planes used came from a CIA front company, Aero Contractors,
located in Johnston County, Arkansas, near Pope Air Force Base. This was
handy because, in addition to the CIA direct action people, Pope was near
Fort Bragg where special Delta or SEAL Team Six operatives could be assigned as well. The military bases also helped to act as cover for the agency
activity. The pace of renditions quickly picked up.

Eager to move in other areas, Clinton, who at this period was increasingly concerned about American vulnerability to biological terror, told
Clarke to hold meetings, the results of which moved the Department of
Health and Human Services into the antiterrorism world, funded by an
emergency budget supplemental approved by Congress.

Tightening the focus to bring out the role of the Saudis was still off in
the future. The chief strategy of Clinton when it came to the Middle East
was to contain Iran and frustrate Iraq. Clinton signed Executive Order
12947 on January 23, 1995, naming twelve groups of Islamics as the target
of sanctions for impeding the Middle East peace process. Bin Laden's name
was absent from the list. The National Intelligence Estimate late that year
didn't mention him either.

Up until 1996, the federal mainspring worked only spasmodically when it
came to terrorism. The Clinton administration's antiterrorism policy remained
vague, diffuse, vacillating. Much of this was due to Clinton's style of management. What was needed was leadership and instead Clinton drifted, seeming
to thrive on disarray. But soon the power of a directing mind began to make
itself felt. It belonged to the utterly unbridled character of Richard Clarke.

As deputy chief of Intelligence and Research (INR) at the State Department, Clarke's head buzzed with wild and crazy schemes. He wanted to
unnerve hostile and arrogant Libyan leader Muammar Qaddafi by having
low-flying U.S. planes detonate sonic booms over Tripoli, or wash ashore a
horde of rubber life rafts, spreading alarmist stories of coming strikes by
U.S. commandos. Such schemes thankfully went nowhere. Clarke later was
embroiled in a bitter scandal in which his critics alleged that he had turned
a blind eye to Israel's selling NATO-capable equipment to China. The inspector general's report at State alleged that Clarke had usurped his superiors' authority and had run his own foreign policy with China, going over
their heads to make decisions he wasn't qualified to make. In response, Sec-

retary of State James Baker fired him. Clarke battled back and was rescued by Brent Scowcroft on the NSC, who gave Clarke a home on his staff, coordinating military and political affairs connected with Haiti.

Clarke irked superiors by refusing to attend the twice weekly staff meetings. Instead, he sent e-mail messages in bold red "that ranged from the snide to the insulting."[9]

Opinionated and cantankerous, he was not one to humor bureaucracy and established chains of command. Instead Clarke worked out of channels with the commanders in chief at the Central Southern or Special Forces Command when he wanted something done. "Dick drove the [Joint] Chiefs batshit," said a former assistant secretary of defense. People were always urging that Clarke be fired. Serving under Clinton, a colleague said that one of the few sentences uttered with appalling regularity was "This time Dick has gone too far." He was abusive, impatient, tyrannical with his staff.[10]

But Clarke was also a man of relentless, tireless drive who knew how the system worked "from the particular images a specific satellite could prove, to what hardware could be transferred to a friendly country without congressional approval, to the mechanics of imposing economic sanctions."[11] When it came to the murk of intelligence, Clarke was excellent at being the first to hear the melody through the haze of background noise, the first to devise a set of policy options, and he was always for prompt, direct, decisive action.

"Dick was a pile driver," said National Security Advisor Sandy Berger. "He got things done." When Clarke took the job at the NSC at the White House, he also played a major role in the U.S. withdrawal from Somalia, the campaign to remove Boutros Boutros-Ghali as U.N. secretary-general, the refugee crisis in Rwanda, and issues that required careful coordination with vast, divided government departments.

As writer Steve Coll said, Clarke "understood in a precise disciplined way how to use his seat at the White House to manipulate money in the federal budget to reinforce policy priorities that he personally championed."[12] Clarke also was a master of the interagency process—getting key groups together for discussions on issues, keeping careful minutes while he worked the issues via back channels with key operators and managers. When caught out, he would go into an expert "aw shucks" routine, implying that he was simply trying to get good people together.

Clarke had a major talent: a great ability to sense when a topic was about to be transformed into a major issue. In 1997 he was already deep into counterterrorism just when it was becoming a growth industry. Using his position at the NSC, at a time of budget cuts in a penny-pinching Congress, a

dozen federal departments were voted huge new appropriations for antiterrorism. He was urgent and anxious. Clarke said the United States was woefully unprepared for a new era of terrorist threats, and he proposed a group
with real clout, the Counterterrorism Security Group to be chaired by an
NSC official—and with a straight face he said he was looking for the person best qualified and to his surprise that turned out to be himself.

The new group he would chair would include the counterterrorism departments of the CIA, FBI, Joint Chiefs of Staff, and departments of Justice,
Defense, and State. Critics said this was a blatant attempt at self-aggrandizement,
that he would end up being another Oliver North (a Reagan NSC staffer
involved in the Iran-Contra affair), and the NSC, and instead of being an
advisory group, would "go operational." Clarke declared his critics paranoid
and said he was trying to simplify decision making. When he set up the
CSG, Clinton was forced to insert language that Clarke had "no operational power," and Presidential Decision Directive 62 was signed May 22,
1998, appointing Clarke as the White House's new counterterrorism em-
peror with unprecedented authority. He became a Principal—a cabinet
member equal in authority to the secretary of state or defense whenever
the topic was terror. No other NSC staffer had flown so high and had his
star fixed in the dazzling firmament.

At the White House, fuzziness still reigned when it came to bin Laden, and
in 1995, the Saudi slipped away from his residence in Khartoum into Afghanistan and disappeared into the "reformist" movement called the Taliban.
It was a serious mistake in U.S. strategy. By pressuring Sudan to rid itself of
bin Laden, the Saudi terrorist left an insecure place where he was vulnerable
and exposed for a safe haven from which to operate with relative invulnerability. Although Iran still remained the top worry when it came to attacks
against the United States, bin Laden was gaining notice.

By Christmas of 1997, Clinton and members of the Small Group decided that definite, clear effective measures to counter bin Laden had to be
made, yet no one had defined a strategy, plus, except for one incident, there
was no solid evidence of bin Laden's involvement in any terror plots directed against the United States.

Though that one incident was bloodcurdling enough. U.S. oil companies were active in Afghanistan, and the U.S. embassy in Islamabad, Pakistan, received an alert that at a meeting in Afghanistan, bin Laden had ordered
the assassination of a U.S. senator, Hank Brown. By early 1998, the intelligence on bin Laden was at flood tide, with reports of all kinds pouring in. It
was at this time that Clinton approved a plan to use tribal proxies to capture

bin Laden. Bin Laden traveled with bodyguards and stayed at a compound called Tarnak Farm with one of his wives. Thanks to Indian intelligence, the CIA was given the number to bin Laden's satellite phone, which the NSA, the agency tasked with intercepting foreign communications, began to tap. The strategy to capture him required the proxies to storm the house and yank bin Laden from his bed. Preparations dragged on until June of 1998. Tensions erupted between the CIA and Clarke. There were arguments made that civilians could be killed during the raid. Some critics called the plan "reckless," and others doubted if the tribesmen could deliver. The plan eventually fell apart like wet blotting paper.

That the CIA was not the only one ratcheting up its efforts was made clear in February of 1998, when bin Laden published his fatwah, "Jihad Against Jews and Crusaders," a militant Islamic document that basically declared war on America. The CIA analysts saw this was a clear escalation and issued a memo of alert. Oddly enough, the fatwah quickened no pulses at State, which was concerned with poverty in Bangladesh, corruption in Pakistan, and the nuclear competition between Pakistan and India. Nothing, it seems, could break the immobility of State's hard, narrow horizon.

A major turning point in the U.S. confrontation with bin Laden was reached on August 7, 1998. On Friday, at about 10:30 A.M., two teams of bin Laden operatives arrived in Nairobi, Kenya, and Dar es Salaam in Tanzania. In Nairobi, a brown, wobbly Toyota truck laden with two thousand pounds of TNT drove to the rear of the U.S. embassy. One of the attackers got out, flung a stun grenade at a guard and fled. In a blinding flash, a huge explosion sheared off the entire rear of the embassy building leaving dead people still sitting at their desks. In the street, people died in their tracks from the force of the blast, while inside, pieces of furniture, shards of glass, chunks of concrete beheaded, killed, or mangled score upon score of employees. A total of 213 people would die, twelve of them Americans, and four thousand would be wounded. Luck lightened the toll at Dar es Salaam. When the truck bombers brought in their vehicles, a water truck was parked between the embassy building and the bomb. When the explosion took place, the water truck was blown three stories into the air, deflecting the main force of the blast.

Bin Laden's henchman and major strategist, Dr. Ayman Mohammad Zawahiri, an Egyptian, had bestowed his own special and gruesome touch on the Kenya atrocity. He had ordered the assailant to throw the stun grenade because he knew the noise would bring the curious to the windows where they would be vulnerable when the big bomb went off. They were: many were decapitated by flying glass. It was a lesson he had learned from an earlier bombing in Egypt.[13]

In the White House, at a Principals meeting, senior officials became aware of the attack when their beepers all went off at once. Immediately, the Situation Room staff, consisting of people from the military and intelligence communities, whose job was to route cables, diplomatic phone calls, and intelligence reports to the White House, wasted no time in alerting the Transnational Threat Directorate. Gathered in a conference room in a West Wing basement, they went into a permanent session that dealt with countermeasures, rescue coordination, and an intelligence review. The CIA had seized faxes and satellite phone calls between East Africa and Afghanistan, and its specialists, mainly women, were busy assessing the evidence. It took only a week for the new CIA director, George Tenet, to personally deliver to Clinton the verdict: bin Laden was responsible.

The meaning of bin Laden's attack was chilling and unmistakable. As Steve Simon, one of Clarke's staff, later said, "No previous terrorist operations had shown the kind of skill that was evident in the destruction, within 10 minutes, of two embassy buildings separated by hundreds of miles."[14]

Investigating the East Africa attacks, the FBI investigators felt a momentous new phase was opening up in their war on terror. Within eight hours of the blasts, FBI investigators arrived in country. Acting on a tip, the agents went to a hotel where they encountered a slender Arab whose pants were spotless but whose forehead was leaking blood from jagged cuts. He said his name was Saleem bin Rasheed from Yemen. The only thing in his pocket was a packet of eight new $100 bills.

One of the FBI agents, Stephen Gaudin, talked briefly to the Arab, then had a restless night turning over details in his mind, and renewed the questioning the next day. What bothered Gaudin had been the Arab's inexplicable neatness. Gaudin had been flying for hours and was rumpled and coated in dust, yet the Arab hardly manifested a wrinkle. Gaudin, who had gone through counterinterrogation training at Fort Bragg knew that a basic tenet of lying coherently was to make sure there were no illogicalities. In talking to Rasheed, he had spotted one, and told the Arab that he had.

"What was illogical?" the man challenged.

Gaudin pointed at the man's shoes, scuffed and soiled. He pointed to the cuts on the man's hands. Then he pointed to the Arab's pants. There was not a spot of blood on them. They were perfectly clean.

"Arab men are cleaner than American men," the Arab sneered.

I'll give you that," said Gaudin, but what puzzled him was this: "Maybe you've got a magic soap that gets the blood out of your clothes."

The Arab was unfazed, but so was Gaudin. The FBI agent stood up and put his hand on his belt, which was old and worn. There were two things a person didn't wash, Gaudin said, your shoes and your belt. "Look at yours. It's pristine! Stand up and take it off!" he ordered.

The Arab did.

Another FBI agent, John Anticev, came in. A member of the I-49 squad, he said quietly, "There is another person we haven't talked about. Osama bin Laden."

Rasheed stopped talking, his eyes narrowing. Anticev suddenly thrust a pen under Rasheed's nose. "Write down the first telephone number you called after the bombing."

Amazingly enough, Rasheed did. It was a number in Yemen, and as Lawrence Wright says in his book *The Looming Tower,* "The Yemeni telephone number would prove to be one of the most important pieces of information the FBI would ever discover." The number belonged to a large villa from which a call had been placed a half hour before the bombing. When the forensic experts arrived, explosive residue lit up their swabs. The villa was where the bomb had been made.

Rasheed then lost his poise. He began screaming that he was not Rasheed but Mohammed al-Owhali and he was a Saudi. If he had any regret it was that the attack had not taken place within the United States. "The big attack is coming," he warned them. "There's nothing you can do to stop it."[15]

GLORIOUS DEATH

Clearly this was a new kind of terrorism. In the past, killing was used to advance a political aim by capitalizing on publicity. This new terrorism was a mass casualty and catastrophic terrorism meant to punish, not convince. It was based on a perverse interpretation of Islam that basically established a cult of death, a sinister glorification of suicide, of martyrdom, promising the terrorist a glorious death for the Islamic faith and certain entrance to Paradise.

After the East Africa embassy attacks, every hesitation was swept away, and Clinton began to direct a campaign of increasing scope and deadliness against bin Laden that would last until the end of his presidency. Under the provisions of the 1974 Hughes-Ryan Act, Clinton authorized the intelligence agencies to fund covert operations against bin Laden. In addition, he signed three highly classified Memoranda of Notification, classified as sensitive compartmented intelligence, Top Secret/Codeword.

The first MON authorized bin Laden's arrest, capture, and rendition for trial, using whatever force was required. The first finding had begun with a statement, called "laying the predicate," which retailed how bin Laden and his henchmen had attacked the United States. It also detailed possible repercussions of the proposed covert action. The MON made clear that the president was aware of all the deficits of taking such action, operations could go sour, there could be diplomatic consequences if they succeeded or if they failed. There could be civilian casualties, although "every effort must be taken" by the agency to avoid such casualties. The MON then authorized bin Laden's capture for trial.

The second MON authorized not just capturing the Saudi but killing him within a very narrow set of hypothetical conditions, without countermanding the first MON. The second MON also added as targets fewer than ten of bin Laden's lieutenants who could be captured in the absence of bin Laden. These included Ayman Zawahiri, for whom Clinton had a strong personal aversion. The henchmen were to be captured for trial, but without excluding the use of lethal force.

The last MON authorized the shooting down of any private civilian aircraft on which bin Laden was a passenger. Bin Laden was known to move around Afghanistan in helicopters and planes that were part of the Taliban's small air force. The aircraft were now targets. Each MON was a document about six to seven pages in length, and as their terms grew tougher, so did the risks increase since the operation probably violated international law and innocent civilians might die.

A key participant in the formulation of the different memoranda was Jamie Baker, the legal counsel to the national security advisor, a position established after Iran-contra, who had an office on the third floor of the Executive Office Building, next to the chief White House advisor on intelligence policy. Under Jamie Baker's hand, highly secret interagency meetings were held relating to covert actions or findings. Baker's office had certainly helped put together the October 1994 finding that authorized the ousting of Saddam Hussein. Just as the CIA had required of the finding authorizing the Milosevic ouster, it wanted the White House to be very clear in what it wanted to be done. Further, the agency wanted each step to be approved by the president and wanted his signature on a document verifying that fact. For example, deadly force might have to be employed, and the Memorandum of Notification made clear that the president approved this as long as force was employed in self-defense in the course of attempting a legitimate arrest.

The MON was not an unrestricted license to kill. Department of Justice lawyers had already said they would oppose the MON if it contained such language. On the topic of force, the lawyers at times resorted to hedging—"to apprehend with legal force as authorized" is an example.[1]

According to Clarke, the White House "preferred the arrest" of bin Laden but "we recognized that probably wasn't going to be possible." There was some leeway here: Clinton's Justice Department had ruled that Executive Order 12333, which banned assassinations, did not apply to legitimate military targets, which bin Laden had become. Nor did rule 12333 apply where the United States had solid intelligence of an imminent threat of attack on itself.

Although the ostensible goal of any covert operation was bin Laden's capture, the legal authority was there for him to be killed in the course of attempting his arrest.

For the Clinton administration, the attacks on the African embassies had crossed a line, and, unlike Clinton's failure to hit Iran after the Khobar Towers attack, the president had an overmastering resolution to kill bin Laden at one of his Afghan training camps. The CIA's covert satellite mapping system had produced a whole new set of targets in Afghanistan. One of these was Tarnak Farm, the desolate place of mud-brick shacks and a few rope sleeping cots where bin Laden went with one of his wives. After the Principals Committee reviewed the list of military targets in Afghanistan, Clinton reviewed the list as well and gave his personal approval. They included six bin Laden terrorist training camps and a tannery in Sudan, thought to be making chemical weapons.

Clinton's conduct at this time was tough and unswerving. The Lewinsky scandal was at high tide, he was sinking deeper and deeper into it, and he was aware that critics would cry that he'd launched the strike to divert attention from his disgrace. Nonetheless, aides described him as "stalwart and focused." In a Principals meeting on August 19, he asked, "Do you all recommend that we strike on the 20? Do not give me political advice or personal advice about the timing. That's my problem. Let me worry about that."[2]

Unfortunately, bureaucratic infighting marred the success of the planned attack. America's chief means for keeping track of bin Laden's movements was by National Security Agency taps on the cell phones of bin Laden's leadership, and the NSA had kept busy. Information in Washington is power and to everyone's surprise, the NSA refused to share its monitoring of al Qaeda phones with the FBI, the CIA, or Clarke's group in the White House. When a nettled CIA learned that bin Laden's calls were being taped, it demanded complete transcripts. The NSA refused, merely handing over summaries of calls that were often days old and useless. The science and technology office of the agency was brought in to cobble together its own monitoring system, and although it could only obtain one side of the conversation, the agency was able to conclude that bin Laden was going to be at a camp near Khost in Afghanistan. The intelligence was good, completed only the night before.

Because the Saudis refused the use of their airfields, thanks to Khobar, the attack would come from ships launching Tomahawk cruise missiles in what was called Operation Infinite Reach. As it turned out, no less than Zawahiri was talking on bin Laden's phone to a reporter at a Pakistani paper, the *News*, when sixty-six Tomahawks, each costing $750,000, hurtled toward Khost. Bin Laden had just reached a crossroad pointing to Khost or Kabul. When he asked his bodyguard which city to go to, he replied "Kabul," where they had friends. The group headed toward Kabul, thus saving bin Laden's life. If he had not heeded his bodyguard, he would have been at Khost in a meeting with his top leadership, the consultative council.

In the aftermath of the attack, everyone blamed everyone else. U.S. intelligence officials told the author that the Pakistan government, whose intelligence service had direct links to bin Laden, had warned him off of Khost after U.S. Gen. Joe Ralston alerted Pakistan that it would be overflown by U.S. missiles. So half a billion dollars' worth of U.S. missiles exploded in the desert, killing six jihadis, and transforming bin Laden into a heroic figure in the Arab world. "By the grace of God, I am alive!" he said in a radio transmission after the attack.

The failure of the strike displeased the president. "Nervous irritability doesn't begin to describe his behavior," said a former aide. "I mean he was *pissed*."

Afterward, Clinton said publicly that bin Laden had launched "a terrorist war" on the United States and Clinton made the decision to strike back.

When the strike was seen by his critics as the greatest foreign policy blunder of the Clinton presidency, key Clinton advisors on terrorism like NSC staffers Daniel Benjamin and Steve Simon "were extremely distressed." But some in the administration and agencies felt the failure impugned the credibility of U.S. intelligence and counterterrorism forces. Clinton would never launch a second such attack although on three occasions he geared up for one.[3]

Bin Laden promptly relocated the training camps. Clearly part of Clinton's problem lay with defective intelligence. To land munitions on a target in Afghanistan, the U.S. military needed at least thirty-six hours of advance notice, and the missiles would be in the air for six hours. Because of Arab aversion to the United States, attacks could only be launched from U.S. air bases in the Persian Gulf or by flights of B-2 bombers based in the United States. Clinton used what means he had, ordering two Los Angeles–class ballistic missile submarines put on station in the Persian Gulf and northern Indian Ocean. Still, the targeting data proved elusive.

Clinton kept discussing other options. He rejected a proposed Pentagon operation as being too big and too costly, and the Pentagon rejected a Clinton plan to drop a small group of Special Forces into a bin Laden camp and capture him. The Pentagon thought this idea naive and "going Hollywood," as one official said.

In the weeks that followed, Clinton's attention was like a great sea bird, a storm petrel, swooping low over the waves alert for any prey. The President's Daily Brief would come back to Transnational Threats with Clinton's unmistakable question marks, jottings, or comments in the margin. Soon the NSC was holding thrice weekly "threats" meetings, where the dispatch of security teams to embassies, the closure of embassies, and other measures were discussed. The United States also pushed ahead with programs that would disrupt bin Laden's financial networks. The day of the cruise missile attacks, Clinton announced an executive order freezing the assets of bin Laden and al Qaeda.

37

HIGH-STAKES GAME

President Clinton had ordered action taken against terrorist financing the day of his 1995 U.N. speech but for months nothing was done. Rivers of money were flowing out of the Gulf states into regional banking centers, especially Dubai, and wire-transferred or carried by hand to Pakistan and Afghanistan. Islamic charities and NGOs were being used as conduits. The U.S. effort was headed by the Treasury Department's Office of Foreign Assets Control and directed by a canny, resourceful, strategically talented man by the name of Rick Newcomb. When Secretary of the Treasury Robert Rubin heard of the plan he bridled.

The United States was known around the world as the guarantor of the international finance system. If the knowledge surfaced that America was conducting covert operations against banks, there would be an unprecedented international crisis of confidence, perhaps a flight of capital from the United States or even legal challenges. Treasury, under Rubin, also opposed monitoring terrorist money transfers outside the formal banking system such as the hawala (Hindu for trust) network used by bin Laden. The department also opposed funding for a White House–sponsored National Terrorist Asset Center.

The FBI also balked because it had a bad case of political correctness, concerned that Arab-American groups would think themselves victims of racism. After a series of stormy sessions, the Treasury plan died out but was replaced by another more insidious and diabolical.

By 1999, Richard Clarke, aided by Will Wechsler, the NSC director who handled money laundering and international crime, decided that the best course would be to approach individual governments with incriminating knowledge about target institutions and individuals. The work would be done by Treasury's Financial Crimes Enforcement Center. FinCen, as it was called, had a large database and a formidable analytical and technical capability.

For example, the United States was able to manufacture "all the indices of authentication" required to make a validated withdrawal from a terrorist account, and, if needed, had the electronic means to paralyze whole financial networks. That would be one weapon—looting an account by hacking. Disruption tactics were employed—jamming cell or satellite phones in parts of Afghanistan, illicitly entering accounts to shift or delete funds.

In addition, governments confronted with solid evidence would be shamed into taking action. For months, the Newcomb team planned approaches to governments, selected financial targets, and built a solid body of incriminating information. This approach would later be used against Serb dictator, Slobodan Milosevic, but in the case of bin Laden, it went nowhere.

The Clinton White House did get one break when an extremely valuable informant appeared by the name of Sayed Tayib al-Madani. Madani had been bin Laden's chief financial aide and he either defected or was planted into bin Laden's retinue from the very first. (Sources have their preferred versions.) Thanks to information provided by Madani, the FBI seized accounts and assets stashed in banks located in Detroit, Jersey City, Brooklyn, and the Caribbean.

In addition, by 1999, American agents located three bin Laden holding companies in Luxembourg and Amsterdam. They also found a major Saudi money man, allegedly a top figure in the Kingdom's auto industry, and he was shut down. The State Department's Office of Counterterrorism was also able to identify members of the royal family who were anti-American and secretly funding bin Laden, according to Dick Gannon, former deputy director of operations for that office.

To everyone's surprise, the Pentagon backed a vigorous program to undermine financial networks used by terrorists, pushing it through representatives like Defense Secretary Cohen and Gen. Hugh Shelton, chairman of the Joint Chiefs. In spite of this, Treasury dawdled and delayed as much as it could. Secretary Rubin was opposed to these new measures as well, arguing that cyber-attacks could be seen as acts of war.

But the financial reserves of the jihadis are formidable, as much as $16 billion spread through banks in the Persian Gulf states, the Benelux states, the

Middle East, Algeria and North Africa, Pakistan, and Switzerland. Bin Laden is also known to launder money through the Chechen and Russian Mafias.

As the CIA's Directorate of Operations began to develop new sources, Clinton met more frequently with Small Group experts consisting of the top officials of State, DOD, the CIA, and NSC, the meetings chaired in his absence by Deputy National Security Advisor Sandy Berger. Liaison between the NSC counterterrorism officials and their agency counterparts increased in volume so that they were in contact many times a day. When a new threat emerged, either meetings were held in the Situation Room or White House officials drove out to Langley. Clinton made it clear that in the tracking of bin Laden, thwarting and derailing his plans, capturing his operatives, the CIA was to have the lead.

But diversity of opinion and differences of emphasis began to emerge. By the spring of 1998, the United States still had not put in place a solid covert plan to capture bin Laden nor did it have ready any legal indictment of his activities.

The CIA's Paul Pillar saw terrorism as a kind of low-grade infection of the body politic—something that could be retarded or weakened or held at bay but never eliminated entirely. Pillar's plan of attack was to get rid of terrorism by a steady, ominous buildup of resources that allowed you to destroy it cell by cell, relying on the resources of foreign intelligence services. Yet he doubted the effectiveness of his own strategy. He said bluntly, fighting terror "is a war that cannot be won." Clinton said basically the same thing: it would take a long time to defeat terror.[1]

The State Department's counterterrorism expert, Mike Sheehan, arrived in his job not long after the East Africa embassy bombings. He was a hard man, a West Point graduate, a counterinsurgency advisor in El Salvador in the 1980s, a leader of U.S. Special Forces in Panama. His strategy was well thought out. To take a law enforcement approach to terror was to ensure your own defeat, he felt. To try and destroy a decentralized network of terrorists cell by cell was like swatting at individual mosquitoes. What had to be done was drain the swamp where they lived and bred.

Bin Laden was using Afghanistan as a safe haven, and Afghanistan was being aided and bolstered by Pakistan's intelligence service, who saw the country as a buffer against India. The Saudis also aided terrorists by providing free trips to Afghanistan, not really caring about much except the fact the terrorist killers were no longer inside the Kingdom.

What the administration was doing was using its ties and liaison with

foreign intelligence services to disrupt networks and capture terrorist operatives, successes that remained anonymous and unsung because of the high
level of anti-American feeling among the publics of the assisting countries.

Clinton was obsessed with bin Laden obtaining weapons of mass destruction, but to Pillar, the president's concern was almost hysterical. Pillar
told associates that he believed that the determination to capture bin Laden
had narrowed to obsession after the East Africa bombings. In the White
House, Clinton performed in his usual manner. One minute, he was full of
aggressive energy, all fire and dash, talking about fighting bin Laden effectively and with the greatest speed and savagery, and in the next expressing
misgiving over possible political damage if an operation against bin Laden
misfired. CIA director George Tenet was more in step with the White
House. He wanted, he said, to devote every resource to destroying bin
Laden, and yet what financial resources he could command were meager at
best. The only thing Tenet could control was the very modest CIA budget.
Among the rest of the huge, fragmented agglomeration of American bureaucracies, bin Laden was a mere blip. The Pentagon and the NSA had
their eyes on a huge spectrum of threats to U.S. security: rogue states like
North Korea, Iran, Iraq, and Libya, and issues like drugs, nuclear proliferation, and organized crime, the internal weaknesses of Russia and China—
not simply the demise of one renegade Saudi prince.

In November of 1998, the CIA had one or possibly two agents inside al
Qaeda, and, thanks to their information, American agents arrested twenty
bin Laden associates in twenty-eight countries and subjected them to intense questioning. Not long after, Saudi Prince Salman bin Abdul-Azziz, the
governor of Riyadh province, recruited an assassin called Sadiq Ahmed to
poison bin Laden. Ahmed received technical and other assistance from U.S.
intelligence agencies. By using a middle man, the agencies avoided prohibi-
tions on assassinations. Ahmed's poison collapsed bin Laden's kidneys and
videos after the attempt showed a frail bin Laden leaning on a stick.

Surrogate forces in Pakistan, Uzbekistan, and Afghanistan were recruited,
paid, equipped, and trained by the CIA, their assignment to kill or capture bin
Laden. Although these forces fought small skirmishes with bin Laden's forces,
they produced no significant results. The CIA's paramilitary group, the Special Activities Division, made a foray into Afghanistan in 1999 and built an
airfield for use in evacuating proxy allies, while the Special Collection Service
of the NSA slipped in to set up listening posts near bin Laden's forces.

The odd fact is that for all his efforts—Clinton was the first president to
develop a systematic counterterrorism program, doubling counterterrorism
spending across forty agencies and departments—he never attempted to

bring military pressure against Afghanistan, never threatened the Taliban, and was not particularly forceful in dealing with Pakistan.

Yet the CIA never gave up plans to kidnap bin Laden.

By 1999, the White House had a clear picture of exactly what al Qaeda was and how it saw its political and historical mission, thanks to the FBI's Dan Coleman and John O'Neill. What the world faced in al Qaeda was a global Salafi jihad whose goal consists of "reestablishing past Muslim glory and predominance in a great Islamic state stretching from Morocco to the Philippines, eliminating present national boundaries," in the words of former CIA official Marc Sageman.[2]

Clarke, the FBI, and the CIA were carefully piecing together what the al Qaeda leadership consisted of. Soon they found that it was a loose coalition with its own command and control structures. There were four in all. A pyramidal structure stood at the top, its purpose to give strategic and tactical direction. The second was the global network, the third was a force inside Afghanistan, the fourth was a coalition of international terrorist groups.

Within the pyramid, the top position is that of emir-general or bin Laden. Just below that is the consultative council including bin Laden and his right-hand commander, Dr. Ayman Zawahiri, whose Egyptian Islamic Jihad or al-Jihad group formally merged with al Qaeda. As a result, almost two thirds of the consultative council (sometimes called the Central Staff) comes from Egypt. Most of these were involved with the Soviet-Afghan war, according to Vince Cannistraro, former CIA counterterrorism chief, along with Sageman, Steve Simon, and others.

After the Egyptians, the second largest Salafi group of terrorists is a large cluster that comes from the core Arab states including Saudi Arabia, Egypt, Yemen, and Kuwait, he says. The third largest comes from North Africa, from Morocco, Algeria, and Tunisia, known as the Magreb Arabs, according to Sageman. The fourth cluster is Southeast Asian and consists of members of the Jemaah Islamiyah centered in Malaysia and Indonesia.

President Clinton was briefed on this information by Berger, Tenet, and Clarke. Updates were included in the ten–twelve-page President's Daily Brief, sources said.

To return to the pyramid, after the consultative council come the financial, military, and business committees. Each committee is compartmentalized into working groups that are assigned special missions. It is the military committee that appoints handlers of agents or management of cells outside Afghanistan. The cell system is based on the cluster model, and members in many cells don't know each other and they never meet in one place.

Al Qaeda also relies on a group of subagents whose task is to infiltrate emigrant communities in the United States and Europe, and recruit new agents for strikes against sensitive targets. New recruits are provided safe houses, secure communications, and transportation.

But there are other small, lethal Salafi cells that spring up on their own, such as the one headed by Ahmed Ressam, an Algerian who formed an organization that was to have carried out the Millennium bombing of Los Angeles International Airport, and the Hamburg cell, which was key to the September 11 attacks, and which evolved from a group of nine young men who were members of an upper-middle-class expatriate student community. This group originally planned to go to Chechnya to fight the Russians when a lieutenant of bin Laden urged that they go to Afghanistan for training.

CIA officials make the point that small networks pose a real problem and display amazing resilience because they exhibit such "dense interconnectivity." If the small network has a weakness, one said, it lies with its hub, which he defines as "a collection of nodes connected through links." All the major groups of Magreb and core Arabs, the central staff, and the Salafis of Southeast Asia are clusters built around hubs.

After 1996, the consultative committee or central staff was no longer directly involved in international terror operations, but the other three large clusters remained connected to the central staff or consultative council by their senior commanders and operatives in the field. Some of these were in Bosnia.

An outstanding individual of a small network can become a hub. The hub then becomes the point of attack on a small network because most of its communications take place through the hub. An elimination of a hub breaks the network down into "isolated, noncommunicating islands of nodes," says Sageman. That appears to him to be the best way of countering networks. The jihad "is resilient to random arrests of its members but fragile in terms of targeted attacks on its hubs," according to Sageman and others.

Because a network is always growing, always self-organizing, attacks against large hubs must be undertaken simultaneously. Given that many hubs are linked to each other, the degradation of the network into ineffectual islands of small, unconnected nodes requires that between 5 and 15 percent of hubs be taken down at one time. Otherwise, "new hubs will take the place of the eliminated ones and restore the network's ability to function."[3]

For the remainder of his presidency Clinton wanted sudden, bold, forward, determined war against al Qaeda.[4] His advisors were fertile in schemes, but some of the fire slowly went out of the program. The military grew tired of having the two ballistic missile submarines patrol off Pakistan's coast; these surrogate forces produced no results and while, at the last, direct threats were made to Taliban leaders for shielding bin Laden, they were empty ones. There was no public support for a military assault at home, plus it would cause a huge backlash in the Arab world, and would costs billions of dollars and demand too many resources.

Bin Laden never left Clinton's mind, right up to the end of his presidency. In Clinton's last year, the Small Group put together a summary of government-wide efforts to kill or capture bin Laden. The document came back with Clinton's handwritten reply, "Not enough. Unsatisfactory."[5]

Although Clinton had not made terror the number one U.S. security threat, he had a number of victories to his credit. Working through allied intelligence services and acting on U.S. intelligence, a number of senior al Qaeda members had been captured and sent to other countries for execution. Cells were detected and neutralized in Italy, Germany, Britain, Canada, and the United States as well as South Africa, Tanzania, Kenya, Yemen, and Albania. Still, al Qaeda was active in sixty-seven countries, taking its time brewing plots against America and the West.

However, there was one area where bin Laden had mounted an ambitious program of penetration, and where, at the hands of Bill Clinton, he suffered his greatest defeat. That area was Bosnia.

38

CALIPHATE

When Osama bin Laden gazed out upon the world, he saw Bosnia as a perfect place to allow new Islamic terrorist groups from many countries to come to the aid of religious brethren in Western Europe as part of the establishment of a new Muslim empire. When presidential advisor Richard Clarke looked, he saw that Bosnia, long discriminated against by Christians, was now being brutalized by Serbs. Clarke also noted the region's importance, "Bosnia was the center of attention during its struggle with Serbia. It was also a center of scrutiny by Western European and American intelligence." What America saw unfold there, he said, was "a guidebook to the bin Laden network."[1]

Bin Laden had set up a large, horizontal organization of cells using regional nodes. One such node was in Bosnia, another in Albania, and another in Turkey, the three handling not only coordinated operations in Bosnia, but also in the Caucasus. Bin Laden was expert at having his operatives penetrate U.S.-based Islamic nongovernmental organizations. Two of these were the global Benevolence International Foundation and the Global Relief Foundation, which was founded in 1992 by terrorist Enaam Arnaout, alias Abu Mahmud, a U.S. citizen born in Syria. Both organizations were based in Chicago but had offices all over the globe including Saudi Arabia, Pakistan, Chechnya, the Sudan, Bosnia, and in the Croatian cities of Zagreb and Zenica. A Benevolence International employee from Croatia was arrested in Kashmir in July of 1995, following an operation in which six people were abducted and murdered. In October 1995, another Benevolence

International employee left Pakistan, traveled to the United States, then left for Bosnia, having worked for bin Laden's Afghan Service Bureau. As part of his duties, he visited the conflict zones in Bosnia until Benevolence International was shut down by the U.S. government in December 2001.

Another organization that provided cover for bin Laden agents, the International Islamic Relief Organization, attracted CIA attention, and soon the Croatian security service placed it under surveillance. The foundation had connections to a bin Laden affiliate, Al-Gama'a at al-Islamiyya, and also funded and supported the mujahedeen battalions in Zenica. In an attempt to clamp down on the charity, the Croatian security forces raided its Zagreb office, after the CIA claimed the organization was raising funds through smuggling, prostitution, and narcotics trafficking.

Another dubious group was the Third World Relief Agency, headquartered in the Sudan with offices in Sarajevo and Split in the Balkans. The CIA claimed the agency raised millions of dollars for foreign fighters in Bosnia and Croatia. When the Croatians arrested one of its employees, who was also a member of the Egyptian Islamic Jihad, which had carried out a suicide bombing of a Croatian police station at Rijeka in mid-October 1995, Croatian security killed the leader of the plot, Anwar Sheban, a former mujahedeen leader in December. His death interrupted a plot to bomb NATO forces that were about to be deployed to Bosnia as part of the Dayton Accords. When the agency's weapons smuggling operations in Zagreb were exposed, they hastily relocated.

It is worthy of note that some of the first jihadis bound for Bosnia were trained in America. During the 1995 trial of plotters conspiring to blow up New York landmarks, Rodney Hampton-el, who had trained in Afghanistan, confirmed that he had set up a terrorist camp in New Bloomfield, Pennsylvania. Hampton-el had been smuggling monies from the Third World Relief Agency into the United States to pay for the training of the mujahedeen destined for Bosnia. The men were mainly Egyptian or Sudanese, and some of the graduates of New Bloomfield went to train Arab and Bosnian fighters near the town of Tuzla, the team led by Abu Abdullah, purportedly a former colonel in the U.S. Army. Camps in New York and Connecticut also sent Arab-Afghan mujahedeen to Bosnia. Several graduates of these makeshift camps had helped organize and carry out the 1993 bombing of the World Trade Center in New York.

The infiltrations continued. Soon a jihadi team turned up near Tuzla, led by foreign mercenary Abu Adullah. The team was there to train fighters, most of whom were Sudanese. They perceived their initial mission to be the rescue of the oppressed Bosnian Muslim population, but that idea was quickly dropped, replaced by the idea of using Bosnia as a springboard for attacks in Western Europe. A jihadi fund-raiser, Shaykh Abu Abdel Aziz Barbaros, who led a fund-raising tour across the Middle East, proclaimed Bosnia "a great opportunity now to make Islam enter Europe via Jihad."[2] A new chain of Kuwaiti charities began to send financial support to the area.

Jihadi activity began to increase, attracting the attention of Bosnia's neighbors both near and far. States bordering Bosnia, which were mainly Christian, grew uneasy with the increasing influx of the foreign fighters, who they felt were violent and disorderly. They began to make sure that routes through their countries were not being used by these foreigners. With Bosnia landlocked, the most efficient way to get to the central area of the country was through neighboring Croatia. Frictions soon grew raw. Bin Laden complained that the Croats "won't allow the mujahedeen in through Croatia as the Pakistanis did with Afghanistan."

In September 1992, the Croats struck out harshly at the arms traffic traversing its territory. The Third World Relief Agency's weapons pipeline being run from the Croatian ports was attacked and crushed. The Croats then began to make clear that their visitors weren't welcome. In one operation in 1993, the Croats stood aside as the Serbs took the town of Jajce, a major Muslim outpost. Croat forces also began to steal weapons and money at gunpoint from the mujahedeen traveling through their territory. The Croats also tried to arrest and jail the foreign fighters' leadership, obtaining covert advice and assistance from the CIA. In Srebnic, near Travnik, a pitched battle ensued when the Croats attempted an arrest. When a group of mujahedeen, refugees from Afghanistan, were killed, the surviving jihadis flared into a grim and murderous rage. Soon they had kidnapped four suspected Croatian intelligence officers in Travnik; they then abducted the vice commander of Croat military forces in Bosnia along with six recruits. A war broke out, sending twenty thousand refugees fleeing headlong. A truce between the jihadis and Croats was declared on May 17, 1993, but the fact was that the religious zeal of the mujahedeen was estranging the inhabitants.

The Croat-Muslim war then broke out in April 1993, sending the region into uproar until the Washington Agreement of 1994 was signed. Shortly after Peter Galbraith became ambassador to Croatia, the foreign fighters began to have difficulties there. Some senior officials, not realizing they were up against al Qaeda, knew only that the foreign fighters were torturing and mutilating Serb prisoners. In the case of some Serb prisoners, they were given knives and made to fight to the death. Other prisoners were held like animals for days, slowly starving to death or killed by torture. The jihadis used cleavers and chain saws to decapitate prisoners, the remaining captives then forced to kiss the dead lips of the corpses. Other prisoners were hung upside down by ropes, had weights attached to their testicles, and were then lowered into barrels where they slowly drowned.[3] The U.S. government and Croatia made secret covenants that the Croats were allowed to disrupt or arrest or kill mujahedeen operatives as part of assisting U.S. counterterrorist policy.

With U.S. assistance and thanks to a strong CIA station in Zagreb, the Croatians also tried to cripple the mujahedeen movement by destroying and arresting its senior leadership.

In the early 1990s, the CIA discovered that there was a very troubling organization in Bosnia called Al-Jihad—not yet part of al Qaeda but very much in tune with it, set up by Mahmoud Zawahiri, the brother of bin Laden's main strategist, Ayman Zawahiri. Over the years, the CIA had been keeping track of Ayman's close associates. When the agents felt the time was right, they trailed one and in July 1998 kidnapped Ahmed Salama Mabruk and other members of a jihad cell outside a restaurant in the oil city of Baku in Azerbaijan.[4] Mabruk was a prize catch. He had been Zawahiri's closest political confidant for some time, and as the agents cloned his laptop computer, there opened before their astonished eyes an organizational chart and a roster of Al-Jihad members in Europe. It was "the Rosetta Stone of al Qaeda" as FBI agent Dan Coleman said. But for months, the CIA wouldn't turn the information over to the FBI. In intelligence as in politics, the interplay, the attractions and aversions of personalities are everything, and the chief CIA official, Mike Scheuer, hated the aggressive, flamboyant John O'Neill, the top FBI bin Laden expert. As a result, neither would help the other. Finally, after a careful series of delicate maneuvers, the FBI got the computer, but the feelings that remained were very raw.

The FBI, however, was not guiltless when it came to selfish hoarding of information. Institutionally, the fifty-six FBI offices talked only to U.S. attorneys around the country, and there was also some communication between field and FBI headquarters, but less between FBI headquarters and the Justice Department. As Clarke observed, "It is easier to waste time on bureaucratic reorganization (turf battles) than it is to accomplish something concrete." When Clarke and the National Security Council asked the FBI for some information about a case, the FBI officials explained that information developed in criminal investigations could not be shared with "civilians."[5]

In the meantime, back in Albania, the CIA began to map out "the chains of contacts" for Zawahiri in that country. The jihadi ring there had involved the usual phony charities that didn't provide humanitarian aid as much as they tried to recruit. The ring used threats and intimidation, and was involved in grisly bombings. Surveillance was begun. To strike at Zawahiri's circle was to strike at him, so the agency had supplied eavesdropping equipment to the Albanian police, but it is believed that National Security Agency intercepts also played a part. As tapes of militants piled up, the agency suddenly realized a group from Al-Jihad was planning to blow up the U.S. embassy there. The terrorist ring in Tirana was led by another friend of Zawahiri named Abu Hajer aka Mamoud Salim, a swarthy, sinister-looking man with dark, fiercely arched eyebrows and a hulking, unsmiling face. Hajer, who had urged that unbelievers be killed, however innocent, reasoned that if a Muslim was killed in a bombing, if he were a good Muslim, he would go to Paradise. If a bad one, to Hell. "Thus the dead tourist and the hotel worker would find their reward," said a reporter.

Abu Hajer had issued two fatwahs, the first approving attacks on American troops, the second, the murder of innocents. The U.S. agents asked for assistance, and Egypt issued a warrant for his arrest. The Americans tightened security but then closed the embassy. Thanks to CIA assistance and technical support, agents of the Albanian intelligence agency ShIK (pronounced Shish) tapped the phones of the terrorists in Tirana while search teams began a grid search. Scrutiny of the tapes revealed lengthy conversations between Tirana and Zawahiri. The United States then put pressure on Egypt, which responded with an arrest warrant for Shawki Salama Attiya, an important militant of the cell. U.S. covert operatives began to work the search for the jihadis in Tirana, their efforts finally taking them to the city's outskirts—a place of unpaved streets with potholes the size of small ponds, shabby and run-down houses, and frequent power outages.

The Albanian agents arrived at a darkened house, and, then, after preparations, the assault team burst in. They could hear someone moving in the dark, and went from room to room, guns at the ready. One agent eyed an old washing machine, went over to it and flipped up the lid. Shots flashed from inside the machine, wounding the officer, before the suspect died in a hail of bullets. The search continued over the next few months until ShIK had in custody five Egyptians, whom they turned over to the Americans, who blindfolded, bound, and took them to an abandoned air base where they were interrogated by CIA agents. From there they were flown to Cairo. U.S. intelligence had given the Albanians the information about the jihadis' whereabouts. The four suffered terrible fates, hung from the ceiling and given shocks, another kept in a room for thirty-five days in water up to his knees and tortured with electric shocks. Two were hanged. Purportedly, they produced twenty thousand pages of invaluable confessions. Both

Zawahiri brothers were condemned to death in absentia. The leader, Zawahiri's friend, Hajer aka Abu Hazir aka Mamoud Salim, disappeared.[6]

On August 6, in an access of hideous rage, Zawahiri replied to the kidnappings: "We are interested in briefly telling the Americans that their message has been received and that the response, which we hope they will read carefully, which is being prepared, because, with God's help, we will write it in a language they understand."

A day later, truck bombs were on their way to the U.S. embassies in Kenya and Tanzania. The man who built the bombs was an Egyptian called only "Saleh." He was an excellent bomb maker, probably trained to make shaped charges by Iranian experts, according to U.S. intelligence officials. Saleh had added oxygen tanks or gas canisters to induce big secondary explosions. He escaped and was never found.

Yet the damage to Zawahiri and al Qaeda was considerable. By 1999, both of Zawahiri's brothers were captured, and both of them rendered for interrogation in Egypt. Then, in the spring, Mohamed al-Zawahiri, a military commander in the Islamic Jihad, was captured in the United Arab Emirates, and disappeared into Egyptian prisons where he was interrogated. He later surfaced in Al Torah prison. Husyn al-Zawahiri was captured in Malaysia in November or December 1999. He was released in 2000, after six months of Egyptian interrogation. Years later he remained under house arrest and forbidden contact with his immediate family, and he had defected from al Qaeda.

In the end, the jihadis' efforts in the Balkans petered out. Another major jihadi gang was exposed in 1998, and by 2001, when another plot was broken up, the mood of the foreign fighters was weary and oppressed. As Sabri Ibrahim al'Attar, a member of the Egyptian Al-Gamat al-Islamiyya, said, "After the signing of the Dayton peace agreement, we the Arabs felt that our stay in Bosnia was not desirable any more. . . . We were compelled to flee to Kosovo. On the way there, I was arrested by the Serb intelligence services and I believe CIA agents. . . . I was handed over with the others to Egyptian authorities."[7]

Although the Dayton Accords had compelled Bosnian president Alija Izetbegovic to expel his foreign fighters by 1996, in 1998 the French forces raided one of the remaining jihadi outfits still operating in Bosnia in violation of the accords. They arrested eleven: nine mujahedeen and two Iranians. Clinton was forced to threaten Izetbegovic with cutting off military aid and added that if the Bosnian did not act, Clinton would stop American assistance. In spite of the pressure, Izetbegovic did not evict the last major jihadis until 2000, the last week of Clinton's office. It was the mujahedeen leader Abu al-Maali, once described by U.S. officials as "a junior Osama bin Laden." He was an Algerian famous for his personal fearlessness, called "a lion in fighting." He was welcomed in the Netherlands.

As Clarke says, "Despite Izetbegovic's lapses, Bosnia was largely a failure for al Qaeda. They invested men and money, but they were unable to establish a major, permanent base nor were they able to turn another country into part of the Caliphate. The local populace spurned them. The jihadis did, however, gain further experience and burrow deeper into Western Europe. Yet for the United States, Bosnia was largely a success. Although late to address the issue, the U.S. was the main reason that the Islamic government in Bosnia survived. Moreover, the CIA was able to cripple parts of the al Qaeda network and uncover others."[8]

Al Qaeda was merely one element working among many Islamic organizations involved in Bosnia, including charities with official backing from more moderate sections of Islamic and Middle East opinion, and it is unclear whether there was any very precise boundary between who was linked to al Qaeda and who was not. It should be made clear that bin Laden had no direct involvement in the mujahedeen operations in Bosnia, although he had visited the Balkans. However, his close associates like Zawahiri were directly involved. This was a case of a minority of extremists attempting to latch on to a much larger Islamic movement of support for the Bosnian Muslims—one that united different shades of liberal, conservative, and radical Islamic opinion—to manipulate it for their own ends. Most mujahedeen in Bosnia had no such complicated long-term ambitions, but were merely concerned with the immediate struggle to defend Muslims in Bosnia.

Ironically, although Clinton was the first president to overcome the overpowering fear of Iran that characterized so much of previous U.S. policy, by supporting the Bosnian Muslims and the Kosovars, in much of the Muslim world America was perceived as acting as a proxy for the Serbs. Although not widely known, Tel Aviv took Serbia's side in the war, and up until the end, in 1999, Israel was selling arms to Belgrade. In the Muslim world, the myth prevailed that Israel did nothing without U.S. approval and there was a wide perception among Islamic radicals at this time that the United States was supporting the Serbs to exterminate the Muslims. In the words of one such radical at the time, "Who is the one who is fighting the Muslims? And, who is the one who wants to destroy them? There are two main enemies. The enemy who is at the foremost of the work against Islam are America and the Allies. Who is assisting the Serbs? And who is providing them with weapons and food? Europe, and behind it is America."[9] The United States, for its part, played no role in arming or organizing the mujahedeen in Bosnia, and indeed looked with suspicion upon their presence there. This presence would not be tolerated once the United States was in a position to end it.

39

ETERNAL ALIENS

Kosovo, a province about the size of the state of Connecticut, was a predominantly Muslim country occupied by the Serbs, part of the rump Yugoslavia called the Federal Republic of Yugoslavia consisting of Serbia, Montenegro, and Kosovo. The Serbian police ran the province with great brutality. There was never any attempt by the Serbs to win Muslim hearts and minds. To Serbs, Muslims were subhuman, dirty, some form of vermin; a biological mistake.

Since 1990, the Kosovars had lived as an underclass when, thanks to Milosevic, they had been ousted from public jobs. Their university had become a Serbian one, courses on Muslim culture were no longer taught, and their great library with its priceless artifacts and treasures had been burned. Those who had remained employed were compelled to sign loyalty oaths.

As a result of their dispossession, Kosovo's Muslims lived in constant expectation of insult, injury, and mistreatment, their lives ones of incessant surveillance, interrogation, arrests, beatings—an endless succession of ordinary people brought into police stations to have confessions extorted from them by means of torture. Serb police would surround whole villages and subject them to unrestrained, brutal searches for weapons. One Muslim man testified that eight police entered his house where they kicked him until he fell down. As they beat him, they kept asking him, "Where are your bunkers . . . your hiding places for weapons?" As he lay helpless on the ground, they kicked him in the mouth and left ear. He later lost most of his hearing in that ear, but the worst thing for the man was that he was brutalized in front of his wife and children.[1]

However, there are always a small number of men who find their supreme expression in resistance, men who have deep within them an indestructible, almost mineral streak of rebellious defiance, who cannot bend the knee, who would rather die than submit to subjugation. Such a one was a young Kosovar by the name of Hashim Thaci. In his late thirties, he dreamed of the deliverance of his people from oppression.

Until Thaci, anti-Serb opposition among the Muslims had been laughable: defacing government buildings, overturning gravestones, disfiguring heroic monuments—acts rarely accompanied by terror. Thaci was going to change all that. He was going to found the Kosovo Liberation Army, the KLA. The group began with fewer than fifty members. The Dayton Accords had forced them into a mood of desperation because at Dayton their fate had been overlooked. "We all felt a deep sense of betrayal," said one KLA leader. "We mounted a peaceful, civilized protest to fight the totalitarian role of Milosevic [and] the result is that we were ignored."[2]

"After Dayton, the mood in Washington was, we just wanted the Balkans to go away," said a former senior administration official.

To Thaci, this was unendurable. In the fall of 1996, the group finally decided that using terrorism would prove the only effective way to attract the world's attention and sympathy, and one night they launched simultaneous grenade attacks against Serb cafés and restaurants in six Kosovo cities.

At first the KLA focused solely on assaulting Serb police or military personnel, but as their attacks grew in number, the Serb paramilitary police hit back. On February 26, 1998, the bodies of twenty villagers from Drenica were found with bullet wounds. One was a twenty-seven-year-old pregnant woman.

Then an event would shake to its foundations the rickety order in Kosovo.

Adem Jashari was rumored to be the commander in chief of the KLA. He was a strong, impressive-looking man, with a full, bushy beard, a wild, thick-flourishing head of curly graying hair, and a hearty, winning personality. He felt delight in his family, pride in his people, and he dreamed of the freedom of his country. Jashari and his family lived in a hollow at Prekaz, in a compact, snug cluster of farm buildings that sat amid spindly trees. There were dirt roads sloping down to the main house and its adjoining buildings spread in wings to both sides. In the distance the dun-colored mass and power of the mountains were rising in uneven profiles at the edge of the plain.

It was March 5, 1998, when the Serbs struck. For hours on end they poured a murderous fire into the place, reducing it to a smoking shambles. At last the scene finally fell completely still. The Jashari house was roofless, white smoke rising straight up in a thin, broad curtain into the bleak, gray sky. Soon, the bulky, squat Serb tanks advanced close to the house, their engines groaning and whining, sending up huge clouds of white smoke in the cold, dry air.

Everyone in the house was dead. Jashari would be found with his green clear eyes open, his throat bloody. During the battle a handful of women and children had taken shelter in a cellar. A Serb paramilitary opened the door, stood aside, tossed in a grenade, and ran. In the cellar, Beserta Jashari, a lovely eight-year-old girl with dark hair and great, touching, black eyes, the only one to survive, would later talk in a low, composed voice of seeing "my granny being blown into the next room." Her sister had called for water before she died, crying, "Mama! Mama!" but her mother was already dead. In the end, the Serbs had killed forty-five members of the Jashari clan, including Jashari, all the males, twelve females, and eleven young children.

Within days, six of NATO's foreign ministers met in London. They wasted no time in fruitless bickering. They decided that full U.N. sanctions had again to be imposed in Serbia. Milosevic was to begin talks with the KLA about autonomy, and the most effective way for Europe and America to make their disapproval felt would be to reimpose a full range of economic sanctions.

That at least was clear, but who were the KLA? U.S. intelligence didn't know anything about them, what they stood for, how they were financed, what their goals were. "We had no phone numbers for these guys," said U.S. ambassador to Macedonia Chris Hill. Albright quickly sent Richard Holbrooke as her envoy to ferret out about the guerrillas. Soon, Holbrooke was on his way to the border village of Junik. When he reached the village elder's house he went upstairs to talk, and was seated talking when a poker-faced man entered and wedged himself in next to Holbrooke. This was Lum Haxhiu, a KLA leader, unsmiling, bespectacled, with a healthy brown beard, wearing a beret with a badge, clad in a green uniform, with an AK--47 between his knees. Holbrooke thought him "dashing" although he had no idea who he was. Chris Hill later said the man "practically sat on Holbrooke's lap as if he were Santa Claus."

Someone had taken a photo, and it flashed instantaneously around the world, becoming, as Holbrooke said, "a part of the Kosovo legend." When an aide had shown it to Jacques Chirac, the French president was exceedingly displeased. From his early days of daring in his presidency when he had impetuously wanted to drop French paratroopers on Srebrenica to retake the town, Chirac had lost his fire. The calculations, compromises, accommodations, and adjustments required by his job had changed him from "the bulldozer" into a creature cautious, judicious, and legalistic. He was now the one to get worried, the one to want to adapt, to adjust, to modify, to propitiate, to keep his head down in a fit of temper. Chirac called Clinton, expressing his dismay at discovering a U.S. envoy sitting next to a "terrorist." It was not "a wise initiative," Chirac scolded.

Clinton listened, but Chirac's annoyance had no effect. Clinton's advisors as well as the Europeans knew the Kosovars were being vilified, swindled, imprisoned, murdered, robbed, harassed, and their abuse had to be stopped. The State Department never branded the KLA as a terrorist organization, and Ambassador William Walker, the top U.S. official in Kosovo and a longtime CIA operative, said when asked his impression of the KLA: "I had been told that a lot of KLA leaders were former bandits or warlords, or engaged in contraband over the frontiers, but those weren't the guys I saw. The guys I dealt with were military commanders. . . . What they wanted was independence."

As far as Clinton was concerned, America was going to move hard and move fast on Kosovo. It was not going to spend months "nibbling around the edges doing nothing," as he told now National Security Advisor Sandy Berger. Yet Clinton's position was not strong. He had just been impeached, there was little public interest in Kosovo, and he still had plenty of enemies in Congress just waiting for him to make a mistake.

In the meantime, Holbrooke announced he was going to Switzerland to attend a conference. This was merely a device to disguise his secret meeting with a young, clean-shaven, dark-haired KLA man named Bardhyl Mahmuti, a plump and personable man in his early forties, married with two children and living on Social Security. The men sat down at the hotel table and Mahmuti told Holbrooke that the KLA "sought a democratic Kosovo." Whether it was right-wing or left-wing didn't matter, he said. What the KLA wanted was independence for their country whose villages were currently "being bombed and shelled" by the Serbs. Holbrooke said that independence just might happen if the KLA exercised some restraint in their attacks on the Serb police, inwardly thinking it unfair to ask people to moderate their attacks "when they are already fighting for their lives." Then he added grandiosely that America "will force constitutional changes on Milosevic" that would result in Kosovo obtaining independence "in three to five years." It would hardly prove that easy.

By the summer of 1998, the KLA had killed about eighty Serb police and taken two towns. Unfortunately, the KLA still had no army and the Serbs did. The Serb paramilitary police began to target whole towns, surrounding them with artillery and tanks, shelling them, capturing the people, taking the men and boys away from the women, then executing the men and burning the houses to the ground.

The West was becoming convinced it had to take action, the question was how? Chirac wanted the U.N. Security Council to pass a resolution approving the use of force. Hearing this, Clinton, who was becoming more aggressive in mood, flared out in brisk impatience. America had to move in a hurry, he said. Going to the United Nations for approval would mean "we'd still be sitting there," since Russia would veto any such resolution. The United States was not going to wait while the United Nations and especially NATO "nibbled around the edges for two and a half years," as it had done in Bosnia, he repeated.

As usual, the United Nations was stricken by its inveterate reluctance to act. It passed a U.N. resolution that stated a list of demands Milosevic had to meet and then adjourned for the summer. Back in Belgrade, Milosevic started huge sweep operations against an array of Kosovo towns, and by September over 100,000 Kosovars had been driven out of their homes and were hiding in the woods. Reports of massacres proliferated.

Then a door of opportunity unexpectedly opened. On September 23, the Russians backed a proposal for a cease-fire in Kosovo, including the right of return for refugees. The very next day the NATO defense ministers met in Portugal. The NATO secretary general, Javier Solana, wanted a clear signal sent to Milosevic. If nothing was done, Milosevic would keep destroying villages, killing people and driving them off their land.

The question was, What legal basis would NATO have to issue a warning and threat of force? Suddenly a light switched on in the brain of the British defense minister, George Davidson. The U.N. resolution had said Milosevic had to withdraw troops, stop attacks, and let refugees return— why shouldn't these be the basis of an ultimatum? If the conditions of the resolution weren't met, then NATO would bomb.

All nineteen of the NATO foreign ministers agreed.

Back in Belgrade, Milosevic met with his Supreme Defense Council, who were in an ugly, mutinous mood. To many senior Serb generals the choice was simple—they must do what NATO demanded. NATO meant business. Milosevic scoffed: NATO was a joke, a paper tiger. It would bomb for two days and peace would come.

When these remarks were reported to Holbrooke, he hardened to stone. The American asked for an immediate activation order—this was the next-to-last step before war and the first in NATO's history. It meant NATO member states would turn over all their planes and other equipment to the NATO supreme commander. Milosevic had ninety-six hours to comply with the U.N. demands or face a rain of destruction. "We were through bluffing," Holbrooke said.

B-52s were flown in from the United States to fields in Italy. Ships moved into the Adriatic. The world held its breath.

Milosevic caved in.

But even as he agreed to withdraw his forces and allow international monitors to be deployed, Milosevic tightened his repression at home, banning the broadcasting of Serbian language broadcasts from Radio Free Europe, the BBC, and the Voice of America.

In Washington, a mood of edgy gloom deepened. There was a sense of something sinister building up.

40

MADAM SECRETARY

Madeleine Albright was asleep in the dim gloom of a Saturday morning when her clock radio clicked on at 4:30 announcing the WTOP news headlines, and she groggily heard a voice reporting about an atrocity five thousand miles away. It was January 16, 1999.

For months Milosevic's forces had displayed ceaseless, ominous activity. Throughout the previous summer villages and towns in Kosovo had been burned and crops destroyed. Kosovar Muslims had been rounded up and remained unaccounted for while Serbian troops were machine-gunning cattle, and a vast horde of Muslims had fled to hills or deep woods to save their lives. People down in the towns could hear the reverberating thud of artillery fire up in the mountains.

After the fall cease-fire, like a rising flood, the Serbs began to seep back into Kosovo, towns and landmarks disappearing into chaos as they came. The slaughters and displacements began anew. The latest Balkan horrors would come to a climax in Racak, a picturesque, compact town with brown-roofed, white-faced houses and a minaret slim as a needle rising from the center of the huddled buildings, all set amidst a pleasant rolling country of low hills.

The Serb Special Police under the command of the mild, charming, graying, Maj. Radosavljevic, had approached the place at night. The nervous and on-edge Radosavljevic had suffered a night of agonized suspense, feeling that the barking of a single dog could betray his operation, but there were no barking dogs that night. In the morning, the undetected police moved in with slaughter on their minds, going from house to house, shooting people.[1]

Albright didn't like leaving anything to chance, and she had infiltrated CIA agents into Kosovo observers, many of them members of the Organization for Security and Co-operation in Europe (OSCE), to keep tabs on what was happening and to gather accurate information. Albright had specifically chosen William Walker as the American Ambassador to the OSCE mission for this purpose. A longtime CIA operative, Walker had a thin, alert intelligent face with a light brown beard.[2] He wore wire-rimmed spectacles, which made him look mild and bookish. Walker's British deputy had called the afternoon before to say he'd heard that a KLA-Serb police clash had occurred in a village called Racak. Walker had never heard of it.

The next morning, Walker asked his deputy for the latest news, and the deputy said, "I'm telling you, Mr. Ambassador, there's something fishy here. Something doesn't smell right." He suggested Walker go see for himself. Accompanied by his deputy and his protective detail, the Polish Delta unit called GROM, Walker, with journalists in tow, walked to the village. He was clad in a padded blue ski coat against the cold. It was bleak winter, all "snow, ice, cold, and frost," he said later.[3]

As he was walking up a ravine, a sort of empty riverbed full of rocks and stony debris, Walker came upon the first body. It was a man dressed in the dull, ordinary clothes people wear in winter except it lay on its back with a small blanket covering its head. Walker removed the blanket, starting as he saw it had no head. As Walker continued to stride up the sloping grade, he found one body after another, little unmoving, dull bundles lying here and there.

Walker stalked on, passing ten more bodies. Finally, he came upon a pile of nineteen bullet-riddled corpses scattered helter-skelter in the gully. All wore civilian clothes and had been shot at point-blank range, usually in the head. They wore no uniforms and had no weapons. They were peasants, obviously. What sickened Walker was the brutality of it. "An awful lot of shots were to the top of the head or the eyes blown out. It was absolutely horrible. It was very, very hard to take."[4]

The total number of dead was forty-five, including a twelve-year-old boy and two women.

Walker, in a fine fury, sat down at a typewriter and labeled what he had seen a "massacre" and a "crime against humanity" and angrily blamed the Serbs. When he called Gen. Wesley Clark later that day he told Clark he'd seen massacres before and this was one. "These aren't fighters, they're farmers," said Walker heatedly. Clark believed him. He had worked with Walker in Latin America. "The man was experienced; he didn't exaggerate."[5]

Walker's chief of staff, U.S. Army Lt. Col. Michael Philips, had dialed the State Department's Operations Center from the scene and began to dictate a graphic report, which moved to the White House Situation Room, which forwarded it to National Security Advisor Berger. James Steinberg, Berger's youthful, hard-driving young deputy, took a call direct from Racak at 6 A.M. It was Walker, giving him the gruesome and distressing report, sparing nothing. When Albright learned of the details, she called Berger, saying dryly, "Spring has come early to Kosovo."

Clinton had the news by morning.

The U.N. Security Council, pushed by the United States on March 31, passed Resolution 1160, which laid economic sanctions on Belgrade, and Clinton froze Yugoslavian assets in the United States. None of this had much of a restraining effect. At a June NATO meeting, Secretary of Defense Cohen had urged that NATO begin to authorize the military committee to put together preliminary plans for a military intervention.

Drowned in rage, Walker took a step of a very incriminating kind. He denounced the killings as a massacre and loudly blamed the Serbs, and his statements so incensed Milosevic that the Serb, in a fit of atrocious fury, ordered the American out of Kosovo. Walker was persona non grata. This raised hackles. General Clark wanted the decision reversed immediately, and in addition he wanted Milosevic to permit investigation of the massacre, and for the Serb to comply with promises he'd made as conditions of the October 1998 cease-fire. He soon met with the Serb leader.

Milosevic was in a foul mood, nasty and brazenly insolent. When Clark asked him if the chief prosecutor for the International Criminal Tribunal, Louise Arbour, could come to investigate Racak, Milosevic resumed his pigeon-strutting manner: "Well, General Clark, as you know, we do not recognize the jurisdiction of the tribunal here."

Clark listened to more affronting gibberish, then he said evenly, "Please understand, Mr. President, that if I carry your answers back to NATO, they are going to start moving aircraft. They are going to ask, who is this man who is destroying his own country, who has crushed democracy, taken a vibrant economy and wrecked it, forced [Muslim] university professors to sign loyalty oaths." Clark continued until Milosevic, red-faced, burst out savagely, spitting out his words. "Who are you to accuse us? Those are lies—Serbia is a democracy—there are no loyalty oaths. You are threatening—you are a war criminal." As Clark departed, Milosevic appeared drained and indifferent.[6]

The day before the Racak massacre, on Saturday afternoon, January 15, Washington had been locked fast in an ice storm as the Principals Committee straggled wearily into the Situation Room. The subject was Kosovo.

Every day there was some new bit of disturbing intelligence in the President's Daily Brief about Kosovo. Albright said that the Serb leader was "shredding" all the 1998 promises of restraint against his seccessionist Muslims, muddling through wasn't working, and to get a comprehensive settlement between Serbia and Kosovo they needed to use the threat of force.

She drew skeptical silence for her pains. They were willing, however, to approve a thirteen-page classified "Kosovo Strategy" that was referred to informally as "Status Quo Plus." The lack of action put Albright in a foul, irascible mood. "We're just gerbils on a wheel," she said outside the meeting. Now the news of the massacre gave a fresh twist to the kaleidoscope and nothing would ever look the same again. Everyone knew that any effort to contain the conflict in Kosovo was futile. The only way to end Serb aggression would be to thrash Milosevic in war.

When the Principals met again on the 19th, the mood was fixed and unyielding. It was time to discuss an ultimatum with the allies, said Albright. It was also time to stop straddling the fence on whether the United States would participate in a ground force if peace in Kosovo were agreed on. Cohen immediately objected that any talk of ground forces was premature. Plans took shape. America and its allies would make a credible threat of the use of force. Principal demands on Milosevic would be agreed on in advance of a meeting of the Contact Group, including Russia. The demands were nonnegotiable, including deployment of a NATO force. Berger presented Clinton with the new plan and on January 21, the president outlined it for British prime minister Tony Blair. "If we do military action without a political plan, we'll have a problem," Clinton said.[7] Clinton knew that the KLA was viewed as unsavory by most of the European allies. "One thing to do is to go to [the KLA] and say, 'Look, if you want us to do any more, you have to help too.'"

On January 30, NATO approved its second activation order, and on February 1, Clinton, in a meeting with his foreign policy staff, approved.

Albright was in her element. She was sixty-two year-old, the first woman to become secretary of state.

Her appointment was groundbreaking and greeted with friendly, welcoming acclaim. She was also the first secretary of state to have an e-mail address. She received two hundred messages a day at that site and her popularity was soaring. She threw out the first ball at an Orioles game in Baltimore, and took calls on *Larry King Live*, presiding over an electronic town meeting. While Warren Christopher would speak at one graduation ceremony every year, she received dozens of invitations the spring of 1997 and accepted four.[8]

Popularity, however, is not equivalent to effectiveness, and her tenure as secretary did not begin well. As usual, the president had dithered over his choice for someone to replace Christopher. Clinton put off his selection until December 7, when he called outgoing White House chief of staff Leon Panetta and said, "I think I've come to a conclusion here." She slipped in by a hair. Vice President Al Gore had quietly pushed Richard Holbrooke for the job, although he liked Albright as well. Both Albright and Holbrooke told the president that if one of them didn't get the job, the other should have it. Hillary Clinton, a Wellesley alumna like Albright, had pushed for a female in the job, and the decision was made.

However, many of her colleagues considered her repetitious and weak as a secretary, lacking a grand strategic long-term vision of U.S. policy. "Madame Half-Bright," said her enemies at the United Nations. She had an obsessive love of the spotlight and never met a camera she didn't like. When colleagues like U.S. ambassador to the United Nations Bill Richardson or Richard Holbrooke began appearing in the press, Albright would be screaming inside. Clinton had said that he preferred a "team" approach when it came to his cabinet, but every team had to have a captain, and there was no doubt in Albright's mind who that captain was to be.

When it came to Bosnia, she had been one of the earlier hawks, writing a 1993 memo urging action, "Why America Should Lead."[9] As the U.S. ambassador to the U.N., she advocated the view that the crisis in Bosnia was coming to overshadow everything the administration was attempting to do and that force was the only language the Bosnian Serbs understood. She saw clearly in the case of Bosnia that America had a moral victory at stake that it could not afford to lose. Few others saw it. Defense Secretary Aspin was wishy-washy; Warren Christopher was the embodiment of the horror of risk. Her constant agitations began to bore National Security Advisor Tony Lake, who could be seen drumming his fingers on the desktop as she talked. Whatever the case, she was having little influence on the Bosnian debate. Even though her views came to be seen as farsighted, her influence at the time was peripheral. The decisions on Bosnia were going to be made by Lake, Berger, Gore, and Clinton. They listened to her "interventions" with increasing politeness and deepening indifference. To them, Albright was a phonograph needle stuck in one groove.

She began to hit her stride in early 1997, even though she still bored people. She soon clashed with William Cohen over Bosnia—Albright wanted to keep U.S. peacekeeping troops there, and Cohen wanted them out by June of 1998. Cohen had told Clinton, "I voted against your Bosnia policy," and Clinton now returned the gesture. Ignoring Cohen, pledging the administration would "work like crazy" to implement the Dayton Accords, Clinton added, "I want [to] stop talking about what date we're leaving on, and talk about what we're going to do on the only date that matters, which is tomorrow." Albright commented, "I've never been Madame Nice Guy on Bosnia."[10]

With the news of the Racak massacre, it was perhaps Albright who felt the most let down. For almost a year she had tried "to lead by rhetoric," as she put it. If Milosevic continued to maul, savage, despoil the people of Kosovo, hounding them to the last ditch, it wasn't going to pass unnoticed. What was going to matter, she felt, was the resolve, the clarity of allied policy, and the direct force and efficiency of its execution. On every foreign trip, Albright tried to impress on people that she meant business. On a visit to Rome in March of 1998, alongside an uncomfortable Italian prime minister Lamberto Dini, Albright had said, "We are not going to stand by and watch the Serbian authorities do in Kosovo what they can no longer get away with doing in Bosnia."[11] This far exceeded what her peers felt about the violence spreading through the Muslim province. For one thing, the Kosovo Liberation Army was not a peaceful, sleepy unarmed populace. They were killing Serbs, Serbs in cafés, killing mail carriers, but Albright's purpose had been to discomfit the Europeans, to try and prod them from their inert halfhearted attitude into some stiffening of the spine. In a meeting in London at Lancaster House, she had said, "History is watching us, and we have the chance to make up for the mistakes we made four or five years ago."

Albright's colleagues like Secretary Cohen and General Shelton had thought this colorful but intemperate and irresponsible. Another of her colleagues, Sandy Berger, had acted to rein her in. Clinton, in selecting advisors, always sought balance, putting an impetuous, hard-driving Albright in as secretary of state but installing as her counterpart, Berger, a lawyer, an alarmist alert to the nature of unintended consequences and burdened by the knowledge that even when policy looked simple and clear-cut, implementing the simplest facet of it had always proved to be far more difficult to carry out than it seemed. Berger, endowed with a soul that by instinct faced a crisis in low gear, had cautioned, "Let's not get too far ahead of ourselves in terms of making threats."[12] His line was that promising more than Clinton could deliver would only act to damage "our credibility" with Europe. What we said we had to mean and act on.

Yet Albright was nothing if not persistent. Throughout the previous year, in spite of the worsening savagery in Kosovo, and in spite of Albright's efforts, there had been no administration enthusiasm for threatening the use of force. In May of 1998, Albright and Ambassador Bob Gelbard had gone into the office of the national security advisor, Sandy Berger, urging the use of air strikes to pressure Milosevic. They were backed by Wesley Clark, who was then NATO's Supreme Allied Commander Europe (SACEUR), who had drawn up a list of targets. Gelbard, a principal actor in the CIA–State Department plot to topple Milosevic and a man who had the outspokenness of a bluff integrity, did the talking. Berger's reaction was swift and ferocious. He retorted, What would America do if the air strikes did not have the intended effect?

Berger's outburst had the desired refrigerating effect. However, a hardy few persisted, and one was Albright. The administration's caution angered and exasperated her, but not enough to have any effect on her level of effort. For eighteen months she tried with furious single-mindedness to get her way, not by using a bludgeon but by subtly building consensus. She would work and persist, persist until success came. In August of 1998, ambassador to NATO Sandy Vershbow sent a "no distribution" (NODIS) cable to the NSC, arguing that in Bosnia, the Clinton administration had staked all its chips on a single throw, and the gamble had worked—by using surrogates on the battlefield, America had helped to end the war. To Vershbow the stakes were the same in this instance. The situation required that clear, ruthless, energetic, intelligent steps be taken.

Berger bitterly disagreed. NATO allies already had troops in Bosnia implementing the Dayton Accords, and the idea of threatening force when NATO troops on the ground were vulnerable to retaliation was a nonstarter to him. Only Albright was unfazed. She would do anything in pursuit of a goal except stop short of achieving it. Throughout the rest of 1998, Albright, undeterred, hunkered down and began to build a consensus for using force on Milosevic. "The victories of diplomacy," said Lord Palmerston, were won "by a series of microscopic advantages; a judicious suggestion here, an inopportune civility there, a wise concession at one moment and far-sighted persistence at another; of sleepless tact, immoveable calmness and patience that no folly, no provocation, no blunder, can shake."[13]

These tactics became Albright's and by January 1999, Albright, Vershbow, and Berger finally had been able to arrive somehow at a consensus, and suddenly Albright had everyone's ear. To her, diplomacy was not a separate ream of puffed-up and grandiose abstractions. Once when asked about Kosovo, she said that what had brought America there was "the greatness of the crime." In the end, to Albright words like "state" or "nation" or "public welfare" really stood for so many people. To Albright the glory of people lay with the fact they were so highly differentiated. There wasn't a single "real" but a "plurality of reals." "We need to be true to our principles in describing how we believe various societies should operate for the benefit of their people," she said. "I believe the best role for the United States is as a partner and as somebody who respects the operating procedures of various countries."

41

BUCKEYES AND RAZORBACKS

Hardened by suspicion and dislike, the Clinton administration, operating with the greatest secrecy, once again showed that it could drive for a goal with uncommon ruthlessness. If Dayton had brought the Bosnian war to an end, there still was unfinished business to do with the indicted Serb war criminals. Richard Holbrooke had brought up the question of war criminals when meeting with Milosevic in September 1995, during Operation Storm. "Mr. President," he said, "there is one matter I must raise with you now, so that there is no misunderstanding later. That is the question of the International War Crimes Tribunal." Ratko Mladic and Radovan Karadzic had been indicted as war criminals because of the massacre at Srebrenica, the first instance of genocide since World War II.

However, as Holbrooke and Milosevic talked, the Serb blithely denied any involvement in or knowledge of the massacre, and Holbrooke, his temper rising, stuck implacably to his point: "I want to be sure . . . that you understand that we will not, and cannot, compromise on the question of the war crimes tribunal."[1]

John Shattuck, the assistant secretary of state for democracy, human rights and labor, had flown to Tuzla to begin the investigations into Srebrenica. He was, said Holbrooke, a man who "masked grim determination with a dispassionate manner.[2] Shattuck had taught at Harvard Law School and served on the board of Amnesty International. He endured a squabble with the European Bureau in the Department of State, which said that human rights questions should be handled by embassies in the regions. This left Shattuck entirely cold. Shattuck was a man of high morals, and he wanted to make sure that if we sought peace in Bosnia, we were also seeking justice as well.

It finally fell to Shattuck to visit the site of war crimes sites and towns, and once again, the bulk of the leadership at State had resisted this at first.[3] The Human Rights Bureau had a long history of ruffling feathers and stirring things up, and few were surprised when senior State Department officials demanded that Shattuck to stay clear of involvement in Bosnia. Holbrooke strongly disagreed. Shattuck's trips could focus attention on ethnic cleansing and other war crimes, and most important of all, his efforts would be highly publicized. They were needed. Period.

The *only* potent mechanism for dealing with war criminals was the International Criminal Tribunal located at The Hague. It had been established by the United Nations Security Council in 1993, and it originally was viewed as little more than a public relations device. In fact, one former senior U.S. advisor told me the tribunal had been set up chiefly to act as a "bargaining chip"—to be given away as part of an offer of amnesty to the Bosnian Serbs in return for them entering serious peace talks. Its existence was initially "symbolic," he said.[4]

Nothing could have vexed Albright more. She was resolved that the body have an effective and genuine function. These criminals were not going to do such monstrous wrongs and escape suffering the consequences. The tribunal wasn't to be a decoration or an enticing bit of bait to be traded away, it was to be real. So she and Holbrooke and Shattuck began to fight a hard, wearying struggle to increase its funding. Other countries, especially the Germans and Dutch, gave it substantial support from the outset, but no one yet knew how it was to function. There was no established mechanism to effect the arrest of indicted criminals. It was a symptom of the tribunal's growing stature that its chief prosecutor, Richard Goldstone, a forceful fiery South African jurist, had the whole weight of initiative and responsibility on him. Soon he had installed in The Hague a secure phone connecting him directly with the NSC's Tony Lake, CIA director John Deutch, and Secretary of State Warren Christopher. Goldstone was going to singlehandedly change the direction of the court.

By October of 1995, the tribunal had handed down over fifty indictments, including those for Mladic, Karadzic, and the terrorist Arkan, yet the court had stalled like a freight car on a siding. Goldstone began to heatedly complain about international peacekeeping forces who were not making the faintest exertion to try and arrest major war criminals. His anger sparked nothing and moved no one. The problem was senior officials at the Pentagon had been strongly opposed to NATO troops being used to hunt down war criminals. It was mere "police work" and not fitting for troops to do, they said. Christopher and Holbrooke, knowing that Congress was opposed to involvement of any U.S. troops in such an operation, felt they lacked the clout to counter the Pentagon's position and congressional position.

This period of inaction would end sudden appallingness, thanks to the advent of Wesley Clark. In 1997, Clark became Supreme Allied Commander, Europe. After Dayton, Albright and Shattuck had talked, and she had underscored the fact that since the United States had brought key pressure to found the tribunal, it was not to be sidelined. The administration had to exert all its effort to strengthen it, Albright said, and an Albright advisor, Jim O'Brien, a lawyer and an exceptionally brilliant man, had drafted language into the accord that "all competent authorities in Bosnia and Herzegovina cooperate with and provide unrestricted access to . . . the International War Crimes Tribunal."[5]

As part of the Dayton Accords, Milosevic had signed a military annex. Although it was silent on whether the new International Force could arrest indicted war criminals in Bosnia, there was plenty of ambiguous language to support an enterprising commander who chose to interpret it as a mandate. IFOR's first commander, Admiral Leighton "Snuffy" Smith, had made clear he had no plans to act on the matter at all: "I have no authority to arrest anyone," he said.[6]

In fact, he viewed such arrests as threats to his mission. His cautious approach to his mandate merely reflected the earlier and habitual Pentagon reluctance to risk casualties in Bosnia. Even in Bosnia, U.S. commanders were taking pains to keep their troops from even coming into contact with war criminals or appearing to assist the tribunal in its work. For almost a year after Dayton, they were able to block any significant or effective action.

It was then that the frustrated Shattuck enjoyed a piece of good luck. In January of 1996, he went to Bosnia with Holbrooke and General Clark, and Shattuck and Clark became allies. Clark was a maverick, a striver after results, who always preferred his own views to his superior's, and he wanted the war criminals caught. The intensity of Clark's determination swept everyone headlong. While Pentagon leaders continued to insist that tracking down war criminals was not a part of their charter of authority, Clark sided with Shattuck in saying such views acted to undermine the Dayton peace process. To Clark, "The failure of the Pentagon, the White House, the Congress and the governments of the other IFOR contributors sent a dangerous signal [to the war criminals] that they and their political patrons were safe in Bosnia and beyond the reach of IFOR."[7]

By the summer of 1997, the first raid on Serb criminals struck like a bolt of lightning. In a venture called Operation Tango, in June of 1997, a group from SEAL Team Six were brought into the Croatia airport of Tuzla aboard a C-17 transport. As the plane landed, all the SEALs were inside containers that were used as Trojan horses. The containers were unloaded, invisible to the surveillance from Serbian spies near the airport, and once taken inside a hangar, the SEALs climbed out. After organizing their equipment, they were then taken in vehicles to a nearby safe house. The target was Simo Drljaca, a former police chief of the Bosnian Serb town of Prijedor. Drljaca was being probed by The Hague for having taken part in ethnic cleansing operations against Muslims and Croats in 1992. While a police chief, Drljaca had unbridled power, forcing prisoners to perform sexual acts on each other before killing them, for example. Drljaca also enjoyed torturing his captives, inserting clubs into their anuses or forcing them to sit naked on broken bottles. As police chief, he had run Prijedor with rigid brutality, demanding kickbacks and police protection for Serb businesses and skimming Red Cross funds. After killing Croats and Muslims and evicting them from their homes, Drljaca had sold the stolen properties and pocketed the proceeds to swell his personal fortune. In March of 1997, he had finally been indicted.[8]

Throughout the time before the raid, Drljaca had treated NATO forces with contempt. In the fall of 1996, he had quarreled with Czech peacekeepers, threatening them at gunpoint. He was forced to resign as police chief as a result, yet still kept his office and secretary even though he had been reassigned.

The first task of the SEALs was to perform surveillance on the war criminal. The surveillance was conducted from the safe house using miniature unmanned aerial vehicles that looked like model airplanes called the RQ-11A and the RQ-11B Raven. They were so tiny they could be hand-launched and they came equipped with state-of-the-art video cameras and were controlled by two special advanced technology laptops. Thanks to a satellite link, the tiny aircraft could relay data in real time, not only directly to U.S. installations in Croatia, but in Germany and the White House Situation Room. A mobile guard unit also performed surveillance of the Serb by the roadside.

What the flights disclosed was dismaying. Drljaca was always accompanied by two to four armed guards. Capturing him could prove to be a bloody business. The question was, "Where would he be most vulnerable to capture?" a former SEAL team member said. As surveillance continued, ths SEALs discovered that Drljaca lived near Omarsk, near Prijedor, and he liked to fish on a lake near Pale, which could only be reached by a single back road. On these trips Drljaca always went alone or with his son and brother-in-law, leaving behind his usual contingent of armed guards. Finally, after studying maps and plotting routes, a mixed team of SEALs and British Special Air Service (SAS) forces readied themselves to take him down. They had surveillance on Drljaca and a truck convoy traveling down the back roads brought them to Drljaca's favorite fishing place. The Serb's indictment from The Hague was sealed, but Drljaca had been cocky and defiant. In an interview in 1996 with *The Boston Globe*, he had crowed, "At any time of the day or night I am ready to resist."

The SEAL and SAS team deployed accordingly. "We were more than happy to kill him," said a former Special Forces operator.[9] When the SEALs and SAS piled out of their vehicles, weapons at the ready, Drljaca, accompanied by his relatives, pulled a pistol and began firing, standing on the dock. He wounded one SAS trooper slightly in the leg, but was shot to rags by an incredible volume of return fire, "dead before he hit the dock," according to one former SEAL participant. U.S. newspapers said that the SAS had staged the assault and that America provided only transportation and logical support. No U.S. troops were involved, U.S. officials said.

The next target for The Hague was Milan Kovacevic, a leading political boss in Prijedor, who headed a hospital clinic a hundred miles from where the assault on Drljaca was taking place. Kovacevic had been involved in the Srbrenica massacre. The convoy included a van for prisoners and a chase car of heavily armed men. The SEALs carried forged papers that identified them as members of a local medical organization The SEAL A Squad, a team of eight to nine men, were to act as backup. At 9:20 A.M, SEAL Team Six Squad B arrived at the hospital. They posed as medical suppliers and were under orders not to engage local forces. The receptionist said, "No admittance," but the men insisted they had to deliver the supplies as ordered and that all they needed was a signature from the doctor on the receipt. Once they entered the doctor's office, one SEAL shut the door while another clamped a cloth full of chloroform over the doctor's face. Once rendered unconscious, the doctor was put in a wheelchair, his head wrapped in a towel, and taken to a loading dock at the rear of the hospital. He was bundled into a truck and raced down one of the dozen escape routes the operation had mapped out. He finally arrived at a landing zone and was put on a helicopter and flown to Tuzla. From there he was put aboard an aircraft and flown to The Hague. In another case, the SEAL-SAS team captured a Serb war criminal, dumped him unconscious in a rubber boat, floated it down the Drina River, and later got the man to The Hague as well.[10]

Bosnian Serb radio had referred to the killing of Drljaca as "a brutal murder," but Clinton, who was visiting Warsaw, said the arrests and raids "were the appropriate thing to do." Clark, who was in Germany at the time, read the newspaper accounts and noted that the European reaction was approving. The public tide had turned. The Serbs replied with ugly, harrowing intimidation. Small bombs were exploded at various locations, unarmed members of the international community received death threats, an unoccupied car belonging to the U.N. was burned. In Clark's words, 'It was a sustained campaign, by various warnings and threats. It had to be answered."

By then Richard Goldstone had left. His successor, Canadian judge Louise Arbour, found Clark felt no compunction about going after the Serbs. In a meeting with Bosnian Serb leaders, Clark declared NATO would not be intimidated. Clark then flew on to Belgrade to meet with Milosevic. Serb hard-liners in positions of power were hindering the implementation of the Dayton Accords, Clark said. Milosevic was stung. "General Clark," he said, "it would not be good if more actions were taken against Serbs. Trying to seize these 'war criminals' is like holding a lighted match over bucket of gasoline."

Clark reminded the Serb that he had agreed to cooperate with the International Criminal Tribunal. Milosevic, with his usual talent for putting his foot in his mouth, said, "General Clark, please believe me. You must not continue actions like this or the Serb people will view you as an army of occupation. And occupying armies have not done well historically" in Serbia.[11]

It was a threat. Clark bridled and issued a sharp, harsh warning of his own, and the two left it at that. But afterward, angered, Clark was boiling with plans. The Bosnian Serb hard-liners were the staunchest opponents of the Dayton Accords. Clark was going to take away their instruments of power, make fools of them in front of their own people, and the best way to do this was to shut down the Serb special police. When the special police in Banja Luka made threats, Gen. Eric Shinseki ordered the station surrounded, the guns of the U.S. tanks pointed at the building while its inhabitants came streaming out barefoot and in pajamas. In another case, a takeover failed, and U.S. troops replied with tear gas, destroying a radio tower that was inciting people to violence. But the rioting of the Serbs had made the Americans look ill-prepared, foolish, and weak. Then Clark got unexpected support. Secretary of Defense Bill Cohen called the general to tell him not to let U.S. troops "be forced off the field of battle."

Tensions between Clark and Milosevic reached a new level when, in a September meeting in Belgrade, Milosevic scolded Clark about "trying to split the Serbs." Clark said he had no recollection of any discussion like that with Milosevic. Milosevic went on blandly: "Yes, and I warned you last time not to go after Serb 'war criminals.' Yet you still talk about this. It is dangerous."[12]

Clark was deeply perplexed and puzzled. He hadn't discussed these things, and he asked for Milosevic's source of information. "Your letter," said Milosevic, showing Clark a letter Clark had given to General Shinseki at his office in Sarajevo only a few weeks earlier. It was a confidential document.

"How did you get it?" asked Clark.

Milosovic was smug. "Let us say that we have many friends, General Clark."

To Clark, that was it. From then on, he was going with his throttle wide open. The war criminals were going down. The general was all focused, tireless, energetic activity. Said a former member of a U.S. Special Ops team, "Clark wanted these guys in hand by Christmas of 1997—there was a lot of pressure to get something done." So under Clark's direct supervision, U.S. Special Forces began a campaign to kidnap Serbian war criminals on their own soil and send them to The Hague. The man Clark put in operational control of the plan was Brig. Gen. William "Jerry" Boykin. (Boykin has since become three-star general.) Boykin had come from the CIA where he had been an associate director for military support. After moving to Clark's command, Boykin was soon on his way to Europe. He reported directly to Clark outside of regular NATO channels.

Tracking down fugitive Serb targets was a secret cooperative effort between the United States, France, Britain, Germany, and the Netherlands. As Shattuck pointed out, logistically the greatest challenge in tracking down war criminals is having the precise intelligence. Operationally, their arrest requires a combination of careful planning, surprise, targeted use of force more suited to police work than peacekeeping. There was also the possibility of casualties, and you had to keep an eye peeled for the effect an arrest could have on the peace process.

But Boykin was good at his job. By September of 1997, over one hundred people met at Fort Bragg, North Carolina, to draw up plans for seizing Mladic, Karadzic, and a dozen others. Boykin also began to assemble Special Ops snatch teams who would kidnap war criminals right off the streets of their towns. They were made up of DELTA Forces. The two key groups of these commandos were called the "Buckeyes" and the "Razorbacks," named after American college football teams. The code name for the operation was Amber Star, according to two different participants.[13]

They would be flown into Sarajevo on C-17s, going into a hangar at the far end of the field. Then they would move out of the hangars into nearby

CIA safe houses. The special teams also got additional support from a highly secret unit called "Torn Victor," from the Pentagon's Intelligence Support Activity or ISA, known basically as "The Unit," sources involved said.

One participant noted, "There were two female soldiers [in torn Victor], and they were truly scary, really bloodthirsty. They made the rest of us nervous."

As to their targets, "We knew exactly where they were supposed to be, who they were, and we eventually got all of them."

Another former operative said, "We had to do all the old detective work, looking up old addresses, working through circles of old associates to extract information, tracking paper trails, the works."

On this one mission, the French were briefed about the operation, but they were not part of it. The U.S. Special Ops teams were moving in the French sector to make their arrests, and so Boykin had to tell them. The Dutch, British, and Americans all had their own operations afoot to take down war criminals. Each team had been assigned five to seven targets, and by December of 1997, both teams had identified all their targets and were doing "good surveillance on them," a participant said. The teams not only had access to a wide range of communications intercepts, they also had helicopter support, and the long-range surveillance of the Centra Spike system, which had been used in Somalia to track strongman Mohammad Aideed and in Colombia to track the drug czar Pablo Escobar.

Finding people who didn't want to be found was the specialty of Centra Spike. Using sophisticated listening equipment, it could pinpoint radio telephone conversations from the air to an amazing degree of accuracy. The technology was an outgrowth of the German radio direction finding of World War II where the Germans tracked resistance fighters by setting up three radio receivers in a triangle, and then, from each point, the detectors, moving in trucks, would project lines to where the signal was strongest. The place where the three lines intersected on a grid was the place where the radio would be found. The Germans then sent in trucks of troops to make the arrest. With Centra Spike, operators could trace the origins of a call to within a few hundred meters. Instead of having to triangulate using three receivers on the ground, the search was done from a light plane, a Beechcraft, flying high overhead. The three separate ground locations were provided by the computers aboard the plane. As the plane loitered, the computers would plot three points along its flight path.

As soon as a signal was received, the pilot began flying around it in an arc, and, using the precise calculations from its computers, it was able to detect the key point in its arc within seconds. If the aircraft completed a half circle around the site of the strongest signal, the location of origin would be known to within two hundred meters. Coded calls could not foil the system. A coded message still had a location revealing the origin of its transmission. In addition to its Beechcraft flights, Centra Spike had a ground-based listening post in the Tuzla suburbs to supplement its flights, and the teams had ground-penetrating radar and hidden cameras. The key to the success of the Centra Spike flights was their not being noticed; they blended in, staying up at thirty thousand feet where they were not seen. The crews of the planes worked from the embassy or from safe houses they changed with great frequency.

They also used top secret high-tech equipment, portable GPS satellite positioning devices, microwave imagery platforms, and video cameras with powerful lenses for remote ground surveillance to pinpoint origins of calls.

In addition to Centra Spike, NSA had assigned dedicated units consisting of a team with a "CIA guy in charge, with a DOD second in command, plus a SEAL Team Six group including three intelligence guys plus two operators." In addition, there were SEAL Team Six intelligence analysts who would do an analysis of the intelligence collected. But the mix could vary. On the Razorback team were six SEAL Team Six operatives plus two intelligence guys, a former member said.

The intelligence was extremely precise. In one case, a team kept track of a suspect for days, and noticed that every Sunday morning he went to a specific café for coffee. The actual surveillance of him was done by the CIA or DIA. He was sighted one Sunday and the team went and took him down.

Take-downs were painstakingly rehearsed. In one case, one indicted war criminal went around town in a garish yellow late model Mercedes. Special Ops went and bought one in Stuttgart, Germany, at the Army's EURCOM headquarters. There team members gave it to members of Delta Force, who ended up building a model of the roadway in Bosnia where they rehearsed how to crowd the car in, block its escape, and run it into the curb. When the time came, the snatch team pinned the indicted suspect's vehicles on both sides, crowded him to a stop, and "dragged him out the window on the driver's side and sent him to The Hague," according to a participant.

"We wanted him alive. In one operation, the British got sloppy and killed their target. We wanted to avoid that," he said.

The Buckeye's first capture was of Goran Jelesic, a Bosnian Serb who liked to call himself "the Serbian Adolf." He was taken down on January 22, 1998. Jelisic pled guilty to thirty-one of the thirty-two charges against him, which covered twelve murders, four beatings, and the plunder of private property, all of which took place in May 1992 at the Luka concentration camp. Jelisic pled not guilty to the final charge against him of genocide. In October 1998, however, Jelisic said he had voluntarily pled guilty to the twelve charges of murder to "cleanse [his] soul."

Another Buckeye's target was Blagoje Simic, commander of a Serb police squad that had murdered one man and tortured and beaten and abused several others in 1992. The Buckeyes had tried for Simic the previous December. They had flown into Tuzla and begun setting up when Clark held a videoconference with Gen. Eric Shinseki, the commander of all peacekeeping troops in Bosnia. Shinseki listened and then declared he didn't think there was enough "actionable" intelligence for the raid. He began to pepper Clark with questions: Did Serb police live in Simic's building? How many? What were their arms and weapons? How many stories did the building have? Were his bodyguards likely to fight? What were the staircases made of? Were there dogs that lived in the building?

Shinskei gave Clark and his team three days to supplement their intelligence or cancel. Then a Bosnian Serb told a soldier that they knew that a Special Ops raid was in the works and Shinseki looked sick to his stomach and called it off. The team flew home. The source of the leak was never determined. But the team returned within a couple of months and captured Simic.

In another case that same month, the Buckeyes had three targets in their sights. Said a former member of the team, "We had been working with the CIA chief of station and had good intelligence. We wanted to take them all at once. If you just take one of these guys, the rest run for cover. They get people on the phone and warn them and they go to ground. We wanted to bag them all in one shot." The team leader and his men were asked to brief Shinseki and his J-2 or intelligence group. Members of the Torn Victor unit attended as well. One of the Buckeyes observed that one of the PICWICs was "dead meat." The Special Ops soldier had been resourceful and recruited an informant in the suspect's house. The informant had even provided the team with house plans. The team leader wanted to take the indicted war criminal at night.

Shinseki interrupted: "We are not going to take him or anyone else at four in the morning, and we are not going to take him in front of his family. Take him on the street." The team leader protested that taking him in the street was "five times as dangerous." But Shinseki was stubborn. "Go back and come up with a better plan," he said. But the team leader persisted. Could they at least show the surveillance film they had? So they showed the film that had collected on the subjects. When they finished, Shinseki was shaking his head. "I don't see what's behind you," he said.

The team leader had no idea what he meant.

Shinseki said, "I don't see what's behind you." Baffled, the team leader asked what the general meant. Shinseki said, "I want to see 360 degrees, I don't see 360 degrees." He turned to the members of the Torn Victor unit. He asked them what was going to happen if they saw a cop. "If a cop comes up when you're doing this, are you going to kill the cop?" he asked. Without hesitation, the Torn Victor people said, "Yes. If the cops raise their weapons, we'll fire."

Shinseki threw a fit. He dismissed them all. "Go back to the drawing board!" he shouted.

In another op, C-17 cargo planes were flown into Tuzla in Croatia, and before the plane was unloaded, members of SEAL Team 6 climbed into eight-foot-high metal containers, taken to a nearby hangar, and there climbed out, beyond the sight of French, Serb, or other allied spies. They were joined by others who drove in from Germany, all of them heading to nearby CIA-run safe houses. This was part of an operation named Green Light whose sole focus was the capture of Karadzic, the former Krajina Republic president. Its intelligence component was called "Buckeye" and involved personnel from the NSA, the State Department, and a Germany-based secret unit called "Torn Victor," intelligence collectors. NSA was monitoring Karadzic's cell and mobile phones and many technical means were employed with no result.

According to several sources, the French were believed to be leaking information to Karadzic and a female French officer was discovered having unauthorized contacts with Bosnian Serbs. Her phone was tapped and a tracking beacon was put on her car, and she was heard arranging a meeting with Karadzic associates. But at the last minute, she switched her car, abandoning the one with the bug, and she lost her surveillance. In a public statement, the Clinton administration had already accused a French army major of exposing pending raids to Karadzic in a series of secret meetings. The French apologized, claiming the major was a rogue, and his actions had not involved French government approval.

But for this book, two U.S. officials said they believe both Mladic and Karadzic are at large because they are being protected by the French and "living in the French zone."

In the end both teams got their targets. The Buckeyes arrested Simic, Simo, Zaric, Miroslav Tadic, Stevan Todorovic, and other indicted war criminals.

In the papers, the kidnappings were attributed to "Bosnian mercenaries."

Supposedly Todorovic was seized after he had driven into Serbia, and he tried to argue that his seizure was illegal before pleading guilty.

Most got sentences of forty years or more. Todorovic later committed suicide. All were charged with crimes against humanity, violation of the rules of war, unlawful detention and confinement of people, murder, beatings and tortures, and other "inhumane acts" done to non-Serbs.

Karadzic was finally captured in 2008. Mladic is still at large.

42

KILL, CONFISCATE, DESTROY

Clinton's initial performance in the confrontation with Milosevic over Kosovo appeared to be that of a man not quite able to measure up. Having been impeached, the president had tumbled from a height he would never regain. He had lost much of his standing, his credit, his prestige. The blight of futility seemed to lie on any attempt to rescue his good name and reputation.

In brief, throughout the summer and fall of 1998, Clinton hardly embodied dash, energy, or enthusiasm. In fact, his spirits were desperately flat. As the Serb onslaughts on the Kosovars spread greedily like fire in grass, Clinton was kept busy preparing his case to counter accusations in the House and Senate about his misconduct. The whole load of the scandal had been placed on him, and its demands drained him of energy and focus. He would not be acquitted by the Senate until February and much of the time he was in an agony of apprehension as he waited for the verdict.

Incessant, venomous carping came from the Congress. In October of 1998 the Senate majority leader, Republican Trent Lott, after an administration briefing, wanted to know how Clinton was going to pay for military action in Kosovo, alleging that Clinton had already hurt U.S. military preparedness by involvement in Bosnia. Further, he said, Clinton "had no plan" for Kosovo, and if Clinton did act it would be a ploy to manipulate the polls. So Lott would seem to be opposed to action and capped his case by saying, "We have huffed and puffed [his characterization of diplomacy] and done nothing," adding that the "Serbians have done what they wanted and now they're pulling back." Lott added that there was no point in bombing "some Serb artillery" inside Kosovo "when 90 percent of the population is Albanian."[1]

This is all puzzling. So was Clinton wrong in *not* acting on Kosovo if he already knew he couldn't pay for a military intervention? Or was Clinton aware he had already drawn down and damaged U.S. military readiness by putting forces in Bosnia? Was Clinton now belatedly trying to act responsibly in the matter of U.S. military readiness? But if Lott was opposed to action how could he at the same time be critical of inaction? Why allege that any Clinton attempts to act would further injure U.S. military security and that any plan of Clinton's would be promoted by only the most base and self-seeking political motives, and would be of no benefit to Serb victims? Lott condemned Clinton for having "no real plan of action" on Kosovo, yet Lott had confidently asserted the Serbs had already won. The garbled stupidity of these remarks, the false inferences, the phony alarms, the colliding assumptions, the fatuous conclusions, and suggested contradictory courses of action made the Republican comments a sure recipe to induce paralysis and they did.

Sometime later, a more sensible and compassionate Senator Bob Dole would say the Lewinsky matter was "all consuming" and that Kosovo may have been one of the casualties, but it wasn't quite that simple. Clinton was already overwhelmed. He was coping with Russia's economic collapse, Russian leader Yeltsin's pending impeachment, a confrontation with China over a case of alleged espionage, a crisis in Africa, plus the midterm elections were coming up, and his aides feared that, as Lott had said, any attempt to urge the use of force against Milosevic would smack of a blatant manipulation to boost his popularity.

The massacre at Racak was clearly a call for a sharp, pulverizing blow, yet at the White House there was no system of coherent concepts in place to deal with the growing crisis. Everything seemed impulsive, intermittent, and ad hoc. On January 19, when Clinton's top aides met in the Situation Room to discuss Racak, Clinton was absent, busy preparing to deliver that night's State of the Union address and also staying in constant touch with his attorneys regarding their arguments to be presented on the Senate floor. Clinton's national security team knew the deceitful brutality of Milosevic, and they were aware that the October 1998 agreement had been habitually ignored by the Serb leader.

At the time of the crisis, Sandy Berger was a fifty-three-year-old Washington trade lawyer who had been an advisor to Clinton since the 1980s but his influence over the president was at its highest peak. His work ethic was legendary. In Washington, a town where a twelve-hour workday is the norm, Berger would work three hours longer. White House aides giving friends tours over three-day weekends would be startled to find Berger in his office, head bent, forehead furrowed, gaze contracted, face severe, poring over notes, memos, and speeches, making exhaustive notes and editing changes in his notoriously legible handwriting.

Berger grasped issues quickly thanks to his outstanding ability to penetrate to the heart of a complex problem in a second or two. He had a pigeonhole mind and could carry a vast amount of information. Often he could leap from fact to fact in an instant, relating the most unlikely pieces of information to one another, allowing him to quickly reach the exact crux of an issue.[2]

Unfortunately, Berger at times could be commanding, cocky, and bossy. Gen. Anthony Zinni had gone to the Hill to scorn the Republican plan expressing the belief that a small band of Iraqi exiles, headed by Chalabi, could bring down Saddam Hussein, saying that the end result would be "a Bay of Goats, most likely." On hearing this, Berger wanted Zinni fired and sent Gen. Hugh Shelton to convey the advisor's displeasure. "What gives you the right to say that?" Shelton asked Zinni, scandalized.

The unfazed Zinni simply chuckled. "Well, for starters, the First Amendment," he said.[3]

One fact, however, was indisputable. Of all Clinton's advisors, the personalities of Clinton and Berger fitted together as neatly and closely as two flagstones. Berger had an uncanny ability to read his boss's moods, desires, and likely approach to a problem. Like his boss, Berger was slow in forming his plans because, like his boss, Berger shrank from irrevocable steps. Like his boss, Berger wanted as many options open before him as possible and wanted them open for as long as possible. Like his boss, Berger was a singular mixture of tenacity and hesitation, of daring and timidity. Scorched by the Vietnam War and Somalia, Berger was strongly opposed to any military intervention in Kosovo, and Clinton had placed unusual and exceptional powers in the hands of Berger and his young deputy James Steinberg. Unlike Clinton's first term where the State Department had been predominant, it was now the NSC that was making policy. From their West Wing offices, Berger and Steinberg had been hammering away at subjects as diverse as State Department briefings to overseeing the Pentagon's planning for a possible Kosovo peacekeeping force. What aides from both State and the NSC admired was Berger's ability to gently remove the fangs of prerogative and professional envy and contests for precedence from the process.

In any case, at the January 19 meeting, Berger and Clinton's other chief aides ruled out any unilateral air strikes, deciding that any action would be done in concert with the NATO allies, who, like America, had troops on the ground in Bosnia. U.S. bombing would endanger friendly troops on the ground, they said. In fact, Berger was against making any threat to use force at all. He wanted to put pressure on Milosevic to comply with the October agreement of the year before including some protection for allied monitors on the ground. Beyond that he refused to go. Certainly in the Congress there was little support for clear, decisive energetic steps. Republican leaders were opposed and Senate Democrats were coming up to Senator Joe Biden saying, "Don't include me in . . . Don't include me in."

By January 21, Clinton was on the phone with Tony Blair, and aides saw that his energy and focus had returned. There were no good options but two of the least bad were either to launch an immediate bombing raid in reprisal for Racak or to get Milosevic to agree to admit a force of NATO peacekeepers to the province. Blair stipulated that ground troops would only be used as part of a political strategy, not as combat troops, and Clinton concurred. "I completely agree with you on that. If we send a ground force without some sort of an agreement beforehand, sooner or later they're sitting ducks for either side who is willing to provoke something."[4]

Yet never, perhaps, had there been such a total misreading of such an explosive strategic situation, both in NATO and the White House. In Milosevic, there was to be found no more astute, pitiless, and calculating observer of the Western alliance. No weakness in the Western array ever escaped his hard, glossy spider's eye, and each defect he saw was subject to a most searching and painstaking analysis. Even at the time of Racak, Belgrade was facing the threat of air strikes, but Milosevic paraded genuine indifference. With calm, malign lucidity, he saw that his criminality in Racak had sparked in the West no desire to dominate, overthrow, or even to punish him. The Serb saw that the widespread public reaction of the West to the massacre had been lacking in the genuine energy of hatred, replaced instead by an urge to accommodate and smooth things over.

The West's flame of resolution had almost gone out.

On February 6, the six key countries of the Contact Group agreed that Racak had been a massacre and that those responsible had to be brought to justice. The NATO-Serb talks that would result in NATO's first war in its history were held at Rambouillet, a château thirty miles southwest of Paris. The talks were a snare set for Milosevic. What NATO demanded was that the Serbs allow a foreign military presence on their soil in Kosovo—NATO vehicles, troops, forces—which Milosevic promptly rejected as an unacceptable diktat. The Serb leader had stayed home, only sending low-level personnel, who spent most of their time at the conference drinking and singing nationalist songs. But gaining the Serb leader's agreement wasn't the true object of the talks. As a close aide to Albright said, the talks "were to get the war started with the Europeans locked in."[5]

Yet if there was to be war, an additional moral and unselfish underpinning was needed. The allies needed the endorsement of the underdogs in the conflict, the KLA, which was seeking independence. Helping the KLA lent the war a certain nobility, a humanitarian pretext, but Albright proved maddeningly dense when it came to truly understanding the KLA's real agenda. Official U.S. policy only wanted Kosovo to remain a self-governing part of Serbia. It was not to be independent. Unfortunately, Rambouillet meant do-or-die for the KLA delegation. Headed by the boyish-looking twenty-nine-year-old Hashim Thaci, the dark-haired KLA leader was in fact negotiating with a loaded gun to his head. Without Albright knowing it, Thaci was daily being told by old radicals back home like KLA leader Adem Demaci that there must be included in any Rambouillet agreement signed by the KLA a clause that said within three years the fate of Kosovo would be determined by a referendum that "expressed the will of its people." Albright was unaware of this nor could she know that Thaci was being threatened with death on a daily basis. He had been told that if he failed to meet Demaci's conditions or if he accepted anything short of a guarantee of a referendum on independence, Thaci's plane would be shot down by a shoulder-fired missile as it returned home, as KLA leaders would acknowledge later on. (Thaci became so unnerved by the threats that when offered a glass of wine, he refused, afraid it might be poisoned.)[6]

As the KLA displayed inexplicable inflexibility, all forward movement stalled in the talks, time was running out, and Albright began to feel the first stirrings of panic. Thaci wouldn't budge, and pleas by Albright to "show some realism" fell short of any effect. Exasperated impatience quickly rose on the American side. As a former U.S. official said, "Here we had the secretary of state being stiffed by someone who no one has ever heard of." Only thanks to some very nimble last-minute footwork by Albright staffer Jim O'Brien and a crafty Kosovar delegate did Albright finally agree that a referendum on Kosovo's final status would be held within three years *only* if the Kosovars signed on at Rambouillet. On March 18, they finally signed.

Yet even after the early February talks at Rambouillet had locked the Europeans into war, the positions of the chief Clinton actors were marked by uncertainty and ambivalence. If stopping Milosevic from committing atrocities in Kosovo was a common aim, no one seemed able to agree on any of the several roads that proposed to lead to it. Albright, Gore, and other senior state advisors wanted to launch cruise missile attacks, but Clinton and his other advisors were still reluctant to employ force, even if limited to air strikes. Clinton had been acquitted by the Senate on February 12, and still believed that war could be avoided. He *would* resort to a short burst of bombing, but only if absolutely necessary. When Clinton and Berger met with the new Italian prime minister, Massimo D'Alema, in the Oval Office, the president was upbeat. Milosevic had "accepted almost everything" the allies were demanding, he said.

D'Alema was dubious. What if there was no deal? What if air strikes failed to halt the Serb leader? Milosevic's attacks would send a vast tsunami of refugees, as many as 400,000, boiling into Albania, then across the Adriatic and into Italy. What then?

Clinton looked over to Berger, who was in the room, to make a reply.

Berger said simply that NATO would continue bombing.[7]

As Milosevic kept building up his forces in Kosovo, unanswered questions continued to abound. What was the actual strategic goal of the war? Would air strikes force Milosevic to a political settlement? (Many hoped for that.) But if air attacks didn't work, then what? If the United States threatened Belgrade directly, wouldn't the Albanian guerrillas, the KLA, gain morale and take advantage and step up their attacks on Serbs? Wouldn't the war simply widen? Was Kosovo worth the life of a single American soldier? There was little American sympathy for Kosovo. It didn't register on any U.S. opinion poll, and even though America had committed troops totaling only 15 percent to the Bosnia peacekeeping force, Clinton had been engulfed by a stiff, bitter storm of sneering criticism for making the move. On Kosovo, as much as 70 percent of the U.S. public was against involvement.[8]

In any case, for Clinton, NATO unity was, at the moment, the primary aim, along with avoiding further clashes with the Congress and evading any additional damage to his presidential career.

Unfortunately, many Clinton advisors foresaw only a short war. Lying behind that conclusion lay a sheaf of flawed premises. Albright, as did many, harbored the shallow reading of Milosevic's character that saw him as a species of schoolyard bully, who, if hit by a solid blow, would cave in, cringe, and conform. Albright had announced publicly that she thought air attacks would force Milosevic to surrender "in a relatively short period of time," probably within two to three weeks. She did not see that Milosevic's hold on his political power in Belgrade was at stake, and that if he failed in Kosovo, his dream of a Greater Serbia would be like a wave down the slope of failure, and his political career would be finished.

The West had decided that the great, overarching goal of this war must be to protect the lives of the Kosovars, but beyond that vague and noble profession there was endless division, fragmentation, second-guessing, and confusion. As precious time ticked away, the White House advisors, like the members of NATO, muddled on, without coherent vigor or focus, conviction or adequate resolve.

43

THE STAKES AT CHESS

NATO would stumble into war with no plan B.

"We called this one absolutely wrong," said Adm. James Ellis, the officer directly below Supreme Allied Commander Gen. Wesley Clark.

As the allies bickered, squabbled, and fumed, on March 20, Milosevic struck at Kosovo with all he had, remorselessly piling his forces in a huge, slaughterous sweep through villages that suffered mass rape, pillage and murder, mutilations, throat cuttings, the burning of crops and villages— assaults that would cause 800,000 Kosovars to flee in terror into Albania or Macedonia.

The Belgrade offensive, called Operation Horseshoe, had been carefully designed over a period of months by Milosevic and his senior officials in what a NATO official called "a pre-planned, premeditated and meticulously executed military campaign."[1] The Serb idea was to seize control of all main roads in central Kosovo, and then, using three hundred tanks, 1,500 artillery pieces, and more than forty thousand army or paramilitary groups, race across the Muslim provinces to destroy seven major KLA strongholds, damage or destroy over 250 villages, and ended by forcing 800,000 Kosovars into permanent, rootless exile. With satanic insidiousness, the Serbs took care to destroy any claim to the right of return by meticulously confiscating birth certificates, property deeds and titles, and even identity cards to sever any connection between the refugees and their homeland. Once again families were herded into the street, realizing they were seeing each other for the last time. There were hugs, handshakes, kisses into which people put all their love, their appreciation, their despair, their fear, their pain. Men were shot where they stood, women were raped; one had her breast cut off. Then amid shouted orders, the transport of the Muslims began.

Horrified, Western analysts watched as Serb army and paramilitary units attacked from the west and south, to create an avenue for refugees, and suddenly the intelligence agents understood the meaning of the secret operations used earlier that winter by the Serbs to stash fuel in various depots. Clearly, such huge migrations of refugees threatened to destabilize the whole region, and Kosovo could be sucked into this terrible, enveloping storm, a maelstrom likely to pull Greece, Turkey, and Bulgaria loose from their moorings into a general war. Viewing the savagery of the attack, senior Washington officials were like a duck struck on the head, "stunned at the ferocity" of Milosevic's rampage, according to a former senior advisor.

Yet Milosevic had made no secret of his design. What Milosevic had planned was genocide, a huge, well-conceived military plan, mind-boggling in its scale, to despoil and expel the Kosovars en masse. In a conversation with German NATO Gen. Klaus Naumann, Milosevic had said that the higher birth rate of the Muslims of Kosovo had made the Serbs there a minority and all-out action had to be taken so Serbs would never again find themselves outnumbered. The Serb leader's utter indifference to the value of human life gave him another card to play. The Serb leader had told German foreign minister Joschka Fischer in March, "I can stand death—lots of it—but you can't."[2] As Clark's top U.S. Air Force commander, Gen. Mike Short said, "Body bags coming home from Kosovo didn't bother [Milosevic], and it didn't bother the [Serb] leadership elite." In other words, Milosevic would send his military forces to their doom as indifferently as a butcher pushing raw material into a mincing machine—even slaughter of his own meant nothing to him. But he knew that the West was horrified by the possibility of casualties, and if war came, NATO would splinter and give up.

In fact, the NATO allies including the United States knew of Milosevic's Horseshoe plan, but they had mislaid the fact they knew. The government of Austria spends 90 percent of its intelligence budget on operations to spy on parts of the former Austro-Hungarian Empire, and ties between Vienna's military intelligence and the CIA were extremely close, with agency officials allowed to attend Austrian intelligence briefings. In the fall of 1998, the Austrian military intelligence gave the CIA chief of station in Vienna the complete Horseshoe plan, which laid out a day-by-day account of the proposed movements of various Serb military and paramilitary units into

Kosovo. It also provided a list of Muslim towns that were to be attacked and the times of the attacks and their point of origin.

The COS had immediately alerted Washington, but skeptical officials, minds benumbed by stale preconceptions, thought the find too good to be true, and both NATO and U.S. analysts, lapsing into habit, thought that as Milosevic had done, so he would do. They expected that the Serb leader would launch only another broad attack on the KLA strong points and towns as he had the previous summer. U.S. leaders could not conceive of the operation as a plan to deport most of Kosovo's population. Those who feared the worst got no hearing. As late as February, when CIA director George Tenet in congressional testimony had warned of large-scale attacks on the Muslims of Kosovo, the alert had simply not penetrated the thickened hides of the intelligence committees.

The truth was that Berger, Clinton, and Albright had all misread Milosevic's designs. The most drastic misreadings of the administration lay in seeing Kosovo as basically a repeat of Bosnia, when it fact the situations were entirely incompatible. Bosnia was an independent republic, recognized by the United States in April 1992, but Kosovo in 1999 was still an integral part of Yugoslavia, recognized as such by the international community. The majority of Serbs were implacably opposed to granting independence to the Muslim province. For Milosevic and most Serbs, Kosovo was seen as the vital heart of Serbia, the cradle of Serb nationalism, and therefore a territory not to be surrendered whatever the cost in blood. The last U.S. ambassador, Warren Zimmermann, had said that Kosovo was "to the Serbs what Jerusalem and the West Bank are to Israelis—a sacred ancestral homeland now largely inhabited by Muslims."[3] Kosovo was home to the patriarchate of the Serb Orthodox Church and contained hundreds of important monasteries. U.S. officials did not understand the depth of patriotic emotion the Serbs brought to the province or their fanatical determination to rid it of Muslims.

The faculty of being able to discern the probabilities is a key skill for the working statesman, and Albright lacked it. As hard as she worked, as earnest and implacable as she was, she was victim of a disabling misconception due to her reasoning from a false historical analogy. Albright believed that it was the 1995 NATO bombing of the Serbs that brought Milosevic to the Dayton talks, when it had been thanks to the U.S.-manipulated and assisted Croat *ground* offensive against the Bosnian Serbs that had made Milosevic eager for a diplomatic solution. The NATO bombing that followed gave an additional push. The crisis the White House faced now was totally different in kind. In the case of Kosovo, Clinton administration advisors were banking on a plan to use a credible threat of force to bring Milosevic to the conference table, extract critical concessions, install a cease-fire, and then get the KLA to rein in their attacks, after which the dark clouds would clear and all would be well.

This ignored the fact that Clinton's advisors were now dealing with a different man in Milosevic. Whereas in 1995 Milosevic had been eager to be seen as a world-class diplomat, his regime had since begun "to turn inward," in the words of Jim O'Brien, a former Albright advisor. By early 1999, Milosevic now had surrounded himself almost exclusively with hard-line, anti-Western advisors, including his sinister wife, Mira Markovic. He no longer had or would tolerate candid, disinterested advice. What didn't conform to what he wanted to hear was viewed as hostile and subversive. Officers within his army and security forces that were opposed to his harsh persecution of Kosovo's Muslims were fired. Throughout late 1998, Milosevic's army and police forces had launched wide-scale and devastating attacks on Kosovar villages and towns, forcing hundreds of thousands to flee for their lives, but it never occurred to the Europeans or the White House that Milosevic would resort to his usual brutal frightfulness to evict the majority of the population of Kosovo from its home.

For NATO and the United States, this was a time to move fast and hit hard, yet in the West, spirits were flat. In the whole alliance, there was no one in charge of policy, no single controller of focus, function, and resistance, no concerted effectiveness that derives from grim, calculated unanimity. Instead, confused political weakness reigned in every quarter, and nowhere more so than in the White House. NATO not only had lacked any coherent campaign plan and target but also lacked the staff necessary to generate a detailed plan if one was needed.

NATO struck at Serbia on March 24, and never was a war so ineptly begun. NATO and the United States were like a cat that wanted to fish without wetting its paws. American leadership was going to be key to any success, but what that leadership required most of all was what historian Bruce Catton called "the hard, flaming spirit of war—the urge to get on with it at any cost and drive on through to victory."[4] Yet not only was there no blind urge to fight on the part of Clinton or Berger, by contrast, the reactions of both appeared flighty, disjointed, and ineffective. Adm. James Ellis, the officer directly below Supreme Allied Commander Gen. Wesley Clark, explained that NATO not only had lacked any coherent campaign plan and target but also lacked the staff necessary to generate a detailed plan if one was needed. NATO Gen. Klaus Naumann was equally critical, alleging that the alliance had accepted a war plan developed in the fall of 1998 meant to coerce Milosevic into negotiations. When Milosevic accepted war, it caught everyone off balance.

For over a year, a U.S. air assault plan had been on paper, revised a total of forty-one times. Its intent was to land a blow of such sharp, punishing impact that it would cause Milosevic to halt his massacres of his Muslims. NATO's initial attack was to neutralize Serbian air defenses, and then attack Serbian ground forces mauling the Kosovars. Unfortunately, in the end, it was all just so many words.

When the bombing began there were only 350 NATO planes within Serbia's range, and they missed scoring a knock-down, much less a knock-out blow. Since Washington assumed the war would be short, it had compiled only three days' worth of targets, and only forty were hit the first night. As Holbrooke said later the target list was so "disgracefully weak" it would have been better not to have bombed at all. Perhaps because a French officer had betrayed the initial bombing plans to the Serbs, the air defense radars weren't turned on, and they escaped bombardment. NATO did shoot down three Serb MiG fighters on the first day, but on the second day, Belgrade once again did not activate its air defense systems. On the third day the weather was poor and made bombing impossible. Since NATO had run out of targets, it went back and rebombed the initial set, "turning rocks into littler rocks," in the words of one U.S. pilot.

Thus, the world's most powerful alliance with four million active duty miliary personnel and a combined annual defense spending of $450 billion had accomplished little against a small, poor country with a defense budget of $2.5 billion and a total of active duty personnel of 110,000 not including thousands of heavily armed internal police.

There were other blunders.

The night of NATO's initial bombing, Madeleine Albright had invited an admiral and three generals to a private dinner at the State Department's elegant seventh floor dining room. Albright's guests, including former CEN-TCOM commander Gen. Anthony Zinni, retired Army Gen. George Joulwan, the previous SACEUR, and Adm T. J. Lopez, former commander of U.S. naval forces in Europe. The three all stepped deftly off the elevator into the James Monroe Reception Room. The military men were glum. The commanders still harbored grave doubts about the Kosovo operation. A war of small steps, driven mainly by politics, was not to their taste.

After dinner a few guests lingered as Clinton appeared on television, speaking to the nation from the Oval Office. "I do not intend to put our troops in Kosovo to fight a war." At this a great groan went up.[5] One of the critical elements of war was surprise. If you did not intend to use a weapon in your arsenal, you did not publicly tell your enemy about your decision. As a commander and strategist, your job was to scatter your enemy's focus, not simplify it, to distract his attention, not concentrate it, to provoke in him frantic efforts on behalf of threats that did not exist, to multiply his confusions and concerns, not annul or clarify them.

To many historians, it was *the* major military blunder of the Clinton administration. In other accounts, it was also a political necessity, given the hostility of the Pentagon and Congress and the indifference of the public. Clearly, the "no troops announcement" was the price of keeping the frail allied consensus from disintegrating. The "no troops" statement had originated from a former NSC staffer, Ivo Daalder, a resident scholar at the Brookings Institution.[6] Before Clinton was to give his speech on Kosovo, NSC staffer Miriam Sapiro called Daalder to outline what Clinton was going to say about the crisis, and Daalder asked about the use of ground troops. Sapiro answered that Clinton was going to announce "there were no plans" to use U.S. ground troops. Daalder warned that for the president to say he had no plans was in essence to announce that planners were incompetent and should be fired. Daalder suggested that what Clinton had best say that America had no *intention* of using ground troops, Sapiro took this down and Daalder's addition was inserted by National Security Advisor Sandy Berger at the last minute and without any approval from Albright.

In fairness, Clinton and Berger had acted under the despotism of necessity. The Berger statement was simply giving voice to the prevailing reluctance of America's NATO allies and only outlined what was politically workable. The alliance was all gingerly caution, going to war like a barefoot man trying to cross over a floor littered with broken glass. There was nothing *approaching* any allied consensus, nor would there would be until weeks had passed. The air effort was ineffectual, the target list was pathetic, and the mass of procedures prevented any effective application of airpower. The truth was that *no* European support for using ground troops existed and there was no determination to do more than a limited air operation meant to inflict "a taste of bombing" on Milosevic to get him to sign an agreement. Within NATO and the Clinton group a powerful undertow existed for NATO to wage the shortest war possible. Indeed, the word "war" was studiously avoided by both NATO and the Clinton group. What air strikes were designed to do was "Demonstrate, deter, damage, degrade" Milosevic's murdering forces in Kosovo. In fact, the bombing was powerless to do any of these.

As NATO wobbled off to a weak start, a major strategic overhaul was clearly needed for Operation Allied Force, and the spotlight now fell squarely on the gifted talents of Gen. Wesley Clark. He had spent a year lobbying allies to get approval of a meager list of targets for what was called Phase 1 of the campaign. Holbrooke had called the target list "disgracefully weak," and no one knew that better than Clark. Clark knew that NATO was an obstructive monster, a nest of bonds and fetters, and that trying to get its nineteen members to act in unison was like attempting to carry a tray of marbles across a sheet of ice. Clinton and Clark were not close, but through their own contacts and intermediaries had established excellent terms of understanding each other. Clinton and the White House now tactfully stood clear as their general went into action.

Clark had dealt with Milosevic for five years and saw him as the predatory monster of selfishness that he was. Like Gore, Leon Feurth, Albright, and Holbrooke did, Clark saw that the Serb "moved always where opposition was weak. He stops where opposition is strong. He puts out pseudopodia like an amoeba. . . . If the pseudopodia meet no obstacle, [he] flows on."[7] To Clark, NATO's war was a response to aggression. His temperament had a bias for action, and he had been waiting for Milosevic to overreach himself. When he heard of the killings at Racak, he had said through clenched teeth, "I have them [the Serbs] where I want them now." The massacre, he saw, had weakened the position of the doves.

From boyhood, Clark had been a volcano of restless, vital energy that incessantly sought outlets in worthwhile accomplishment. His whole career exhibited a voracious hunger for prestige. He loved power, he loved admiration, and he loved grandeur. He graduated first in his class at West Point in 1966, and was known then as a coming star. He was forty-three when he got his first star, and at forty-six commanded the 1st Cavalry Division. Whether it was swimming, tennis, or academics, everything for Clark was a contest, a trial, with his talent, his grit, his fixity of intent, pitted against everyone else's, with triumph the only acceptable outcome. He believed that crisis afforded the supreme and authentic reevaluation of what one was worth.

Wherever he was, his drive made things happen. After the war in Bosnia, during a visit to Banja Luka, Clark had met with his subordinate commanders on how to handle peacekeeping matters there. "Use your martial law like authority," he said to them, adding, "You can impose any law." He instructed them to detain Serb nationalist hard-liners. He said not to fear disorder or attacks against NATO troops, plus they were to funnel funds to projects of the moderate opposition, create pretexts to disrupt Mafia-like criminal networks and jail suspected ringleaders for seventy-two hours, the limit allowed by law.[8] Nor were they to wait and ask Washington, Berlin, Rome, or Ottawa for leadership or direction and they weren't to wait until they got it. "What you have to do is try to see the larger problem and see where you can modify your instructions from civilians back home. You have to push the envelope. If you put this strategy down [on paper] it's dead," he cautioned.[9]

As SACEUR, Clark reported directly to Secretary of Defense William Cohen, who approached having to act decisively with the utmost reluctance—and who soon found that Clark's overpowering efficiency set his teeth on edge. Before becoming SACEUR in 1997, Clark had played a key role in defining the military duties required by the Dayton Accords, but much of what he did was off the books—not illegal but not done right out in the open either. Clark wanted to close the offices of the MUP, the special police, who harassed political moderates. He wanted the U.S. troops to support the president of Republika Srpska Beiljana Plavsic, a highly controversial figure. He requested that the police station in Banja Luka be closed by British troops. His bias for vigorous action was always in play.

Javier Solana, the NATO secretary general, was delighted by this endless, audacious energy, the spirit of attack, but all Cohen could see in Clark's actions were further headaches. Cohen lacked Clark's energy of life, and he knew he lacked it, and the two men began to distrust each other. "Sir, I am within your intent, aren't I," Clark anxiously asked Cohen at a meeting about his activities in Bosnia. "Just barely," Cohen said.[10]

As the opening days of the war exhibited drift, deadlock, defeatism, NATO's efforts at times seemed to dwindle to utter slackness. The Pentagon disliked the way the war was run, in the White House no one seemed to have a clear direction to offer or measures to take, the flood of refugees had caught everyone flatfooted, and there was a feeling that the State Department had blown it. "I'm getting killed in those meetings," Albright complained.

As the early confused days drifted by, the rifts, antagonisms, hostilities, and bitter differences between the Americans and Europeans erupted with fresh intensity. The French wanted no bombings of northern Serbia, where they had interests, the U.S. military and Congress and others worried over collateral damage in Kosovo, and the Germans especially wanted no bombing of Serbian cities. The pro-Serb Greeks opposed the bombing entirely. Clinton's fear of killing civilians verged on the phobic.

Clark realized that while he would agree to the original paltry effort at bombing, it had to be discarded for something more sustained, severe, and robust. Fierce, purposeful, and relentless, he began to work to get this done. Unfortunately, NATO's chain of command was a monstrosity of bonds and fetters so complex that Clark could hit no targets without first consulting Clinton, the British, the French, and NATO secretary general Javier Solana. British prime minister Tony Blair retained the right to veto targets to be hit by American B-52s flying from British bases. Chirac reserved the right to review targets in Montenegro, Serbia's partner, which was pro-West. Together with President Clinton, they reserved the right to veto targets that would affect or kill large numbers of civilians. This left off the target list key command and control nodes and telephone exchanges. At times, the approval for targets of air strikes came down to President Clinton, Gen. Hugh Shelton, and Solana, who were compelled to okay targets already reviewed by a vast host of NATO and American lawyers. Clark was working amid a command system that exhibited the most blatant civilian meddling in warfare since Lyndon Johnson and Vietnam, an ominous echo of the American civilian leadership and its disastrous meddling in that war.

One failure bred another. Unable to destroy Serb air defenses in Phase 1, General Short ordered his pilots to avoid losses by flying at fifteen thousand feet where they had no way of targeting Serb police or special forces committing atrocities. As the ineffectual bombing continued, Milosevic escalated his attacks on the Kosovars while Clark frenziedly sought approval from all nineteen NATO members to enlarge the targeting list. On the ground, the slaughter of innocents mounted, and U.S. officials said that the Muslim monthly death rate soared like a high fever, up twenty-fold, over the previous fifteen months. The disheartening truth was that the weak bombing only emboldened the Serbs.

Clearly, the NATO war plan had run aground. Hitting Belgrade's infrastructure sounded tough and two-fisted enough, but almost all the Europeans were opposed to such a step, fearing a threat to their governments if the attacks were undertaken. In the meantime, General Clark was screaming inside. Furious and quick-tempered, Clark was frantically trying to expand targets, driving his staff without regard for human frailty. Since the beginning of April, he had argued for hitting bridges, petroleum facilities, oil refining plants. He wanted to bomb Serbia's highway network, its railway network, its tunnels and bridges across the Danube. When French president Chirac heard of the plan to attack bridges, he was extremely upset. The flamboyant, audacious Frenchman had lost some of his fire and nerve since he'd become president. The office had tamed him, drained him of some of his previous singularity of intent and strength of resolution, replacing those things with caution, prudence, the necessity to try and think of all objections and risks before embarking on action.

Clinton had seen Chirac's lack of pugnacity during the Bosnian conflict. One morning before the Dayton talks, consultant Dick Morris encountered a pale, mortally tired Clinton. "I was up all night talking to Chirac. . . . It's getting there. . . . I'm bringing him around to the idea of massive air power."[11] He knew that with Kosovo he would be faced with allies like Chirac who would flutter like shaken leaves in a storm wind, and that it would take all of his talented skills to manage and master so many opposing constituencies and bickering factions.

Now, made nervous by Clark's intention to hit the bridges, Chirac anxiously protested to Clinton in a phone call, saying: "This is absurd and unnecessary given our mission." They talked some more, came to no agreement, and then Chirac left for his Easter break at a chalet up on the French Riviera where a calm, unswerving Clinton tracked him down. Two U.S. Army technicians flew in from Germany to establish a secure "Stu 3" line, but the attempt failed, and the two leaders ended up talking in the clear. Chirac again argued that if NATO bombed Serb infrastructure it would simply make the Serbs "more angry."

Clinton disagreed. He told Chirac: "I think this bombing can work, but we have to have enough muscle to have impact."

Chirac then made a slip. As he again urged moderation, the French leader reminded Clinton that NATO did not want to "wage a traditional war," but added that it was of course acceptable to "neutralize" Milosevic's military command and control capability. Clinton instantly saw a door ajar, and he hastened through it. He had Berger call Defense Secretary Cohen, who called Clark. The general, furiously dissatisfied, was looking to hit targets that were symbolic and directly connected with the heart of Milosevic's oppressive rule. In downtown Belgrade stood the headquarters of the Serbian Ministerial Special Police and the Yugoslavian Ministerial Special Police, both implicated in atrocities and ethnic cleansing in Kosovo. Clinton alerted Chirac of the attack, and Chirac gave his okay.[12]

In the middle of a weekend night, on the eleventh day of the war, April 3, both targets blew up, huge fires flaring up from what was left of the ruined building frames, chunks of stone rubble heavily dotting the street. They were no civilian casualties. With Chirac on vacation, Clark, like a mischievous but dangerous schoolboy, seized the chance to also bomb two bridges over the Danube south of Belgrade. Milosevic began to position civilians on bridges wearing bull's-eyes.[13]

Nonetheless, Clark was pleased. "The strikes were effective and precise," and they "sent a signal of NATO's resolve," he said later.

The driving combativeness of Clark would more and more come to play a key part. If any man had the killer instinct it was Clark. When the wife of NATO Gen. Klaus Naumann had raged at her husband, wondering why NATO could not get rid of "this center of evil" named Milosevic by using some James Bond assassination plot, Naumann dutifully explained to her that a head of state was *not* a proper military target. But when intense, remorseless Clark heard the story, he had an idea. Milosevic was living in enormous, luxurious rooms of the old Tito villa at Dobanovci, and NATO intelligence showed clearly that Milosevic had had a command and control bunker built under his new residence. Milosevic, as head of state, wasn't a proper target, but in Clark's eyes, that compound made it a military facility and since Clark had approval to neutralize Serbia's command and control, he was resolved to bomb Milosevic's mansion, yet getting agreement took a month to conclude. The chief source of opposition was the Dutch government, which protested that the Serb presidential palace contained a painting by Rembrandt. General Naumann retorted acidly that it wasn't a very good Rembrandt, and the Dutch finally gave way. Early in the morning of May 1, he gave the order: a Tomahawk cruise missile slammed into the house, destroying an entire wall of the elegant residence and scattering huge chunks of concrete, shards of glass, and tree limbs over the surrounding garden. Since Milosevic and Mira slept in a different bunker every night they escaped but she complained, "Our curtains were up in the tree tops. They destroyed all our belongings except our grandson's cot."[14]

THE RUTHLESS TRUTH OF WAR

As the war wore on, Clinton was no longer the earlier president, tentative and unsure. As his biographer John Harris said, the earlier Clinton "would stammer and second-guess his own judgment," preferring to listen to others. Those days were gone for good. Adversity had hardened him, and he had gained a new, masterly sureness. He had "developed his own instincts about the world and the confidence to trust them."[1] When his advisors fell into despair over the poor start of the war, it was Clinton who put heart into them, telling them "to take a breath, and that everything would work out in the end. There was no point in having high poll numbers if you were not prepared to spend capital on something like this," he said.[2] Clinton no longer had illusions—he knew he would be faced with allies that would balk or hang back, or when difficulties emerged would think the task hopeless and make only a halfhearted attempt to do it before declaring that it couldn't be done. Now, facing the worst political crisis of his career, Clinton was sustained by a faith, an inner certainty that the allies would win the war, which gave him resolve and direction. The president would prove to be the origin of a persistent effort to bring about a victorious result. One of the U.S. war aims was to continue to work closely with Russia, and Clinton's new inner poise was on display in his handling of the unstable and explosive Russian leader, Boris Yeltsin.

On March 24, as the first attack planes lifted off the base in Aviano, Italy, early in the afternoon Washington time, Clinton had called Yeltsin two hours before the event to alert him. Clinton told the Russian leader that NATO was acting unilaterally against the Serb forces committing atrocities in Kosovo, and Yeltsin's reception displayed the ugliest kind of wrath. Clinton had worked with extraordinary care to build a friendship with Russia and had even used a covert operation to ensure Yeltsin's election in 1996.[3] Unfortunately, by 1999, Yeltsin's domestic situation had soured. He was being impeached, he had a very pro-Serb public who would use his stand on NATO to further undermine him, and even though he and Clinton still retained a genuine feeling for each other, the Russian had been roused by irritation to a blind fury. Yeltsin tensely denounced the NATO action, then shouted at Clinton that all the good that he and Clinton had tried to do together, all their joint ventures and mutual exertions in foreign policy, "had gone down the drain."

Clinton stood his ground. He told Yeltsin that he believed that NATO's actions had taken and would take "a lot of heat" off Russia, and listed all the opportunities for good that Milosevic had wasted that could have avoided war. Yeltsin rudely cut the call short, and then phoned French president Chirac. According to Chirac aid Jean-David Levitte, Yeltsin shouted at Chirac "in a voice of thunder" that the NATO bombing was "a gross blunder of American diplomacy and Clinton. . . . A gross blunder!" Levitte said that Yeltsin was shouting so loud that Chirac had been forced to hold the phone away from his ear.[4]

Still Clinton didn't yield, even though keeping Russia on board had been a chief U.S. policy aim, and Yeltsin in a fit of atrocious spite canceled all Russian cooperation with NATO. Yeltsin put a Russian division on alert and sent spy ships into the area.

Clinton remained unmoved. As he would later say of the bombing, "I felt very strongly that we had to move quickly." Clinton refused to suffer a repeat of the Bosnian war where for two years "NATO had nibbled around the edges."

Milosevic had been as utterly muddled as to NATO's true intentions as America and NATO had been to his. According to a former senior Clinton advisor, Milosevic felt that America and NATO would drop a few bombs, grow red-faced and winded, succumb to fear of casualties, and abruptly end its war. He did not believe the unity of the NATO alliance would long survive any enticements, and so all he had to do was hold out. Milosevic told associates that he expected the bombing to be "polite," and his wife, Mira, told intimates she expected the bombing to "last little more than a day or so." Milosevic had watched with keen interest General Zinni's Operation Desert Fox, the earlier U.S. attack on Iraq, and the Serb leader had even met with Iraqi military and intelligence officials to talk about the operation's phases, targeting, and tactical methods. The Serb leader believed that any NATO assault would only seek to "degrade" his military, not smash it, and he began to move aircraft from their bases, dispersing tanks and helicopters from their bases and hiding them under trees or in tunnels and putting in their place an elaborate system of cheap decoys.

The lack of any NATO ability to ruthlessly drive home its attacks simply encouraged further massacres of the Kosovars and defiance on the part of Serb citizens. Belgrade was certainly paying no price for anything. There were hardly any casualties. People packed cafés and restaurants, shops were open, buses ran. Daily life was not at risk, plus with his control of state media, Milosevic was far ahead in the "information war," issuing a surging flood of false reports about civilian deaths and damage, many cleverly aimed at sowing dissension within the alliance. Milosevic's propaganda was so deftly composed and aimed that it put the alliance on the defensive from the first and it remained there.

Early in the year, Clinton had ordered the CIA to produce a psychological profile of the Serb, and after poring over videotapes, transcripts of his media interviews, photographs, and surveillance tapes, it was clear Milosevic would not prove easy to corner, short of a coup or a major upheaval inside Serbia. Milosevic was subject to wild mood swings stemming from back problems and adult onset diabetes. He grew stubborn when contested and gained weight when under stress, said the report. His smoking and drinking tended to increase at such times as well. He became most blindly stubborn when he felt bullied, the report said.[5]

He would be difficult to locate since he could move constantly between a series of command and control centers or presidential palaces, bunkers and residences, and government buildings. He had his personal physician near him at all times, the report said.

Although he could be charming and affable, his personality was frighteningly cold. There was very little human about the Serb leader, so he remained in Belgrade at the former Tito mansion, which Mira had renamed Uzicka. Far away from his posh suburb were the shabby shantytowns where the Serb refugees from Bosnia and Croatia, the flotsam of his wars, huddled together in ramshackle squalor. Even though his own forces were fighting hard for him, he never visited any of the wounded, never went to any areas damaged by the bombs, and manifested an obliviousness and total hardheartedness. All of his public appearances were staged, and he gave only two TV interviews in the course of the war.

Milosevic was waging his war impaired by two fatal delusions. The first was that Russia would come to his aid, giving him intelligence and perhaps even providing him with advanced surface-to-air missiles to counter NATO airpower. Certainly, the anti-Yeltsin hard-liners in the Russian military sided with him. In fact, after the bombing started, Moscow sent an intelligence ship into the area to spy on NATO, and an army division was put on alert. The other delusion involved his perception of NATO, whose rifts and divisions he felt confident to exploit. The Serb felt time was on his side. "What Milosevic was counting on was splitting the alliance." Rich Serbs affiliated with the Republican Party were "giving Milosevic bad advice," telling him that if he could outlast Clinton, Milosevic would find a Republican administration "much easer to deal with," according to a former senior Clinton advisor.[6] Milosevic would bide his time and count on the steady withering away of NATO's strength.

Meanwhile, the war was widening. Clark urgently wanted to take out Serb installations in Montenegro, the junior partner of the FRY, Federal Republic of Yugoslavia (the rump of Yugoslavia that consisted of Serbia and its junior partner, Montenegro), because they based Belgrade air defense networks, but Chirac objected. Clinton, full of fight, replied that if NATO had "a high level of certainty that we were not going to kill civilians but [the bombing] goes to the heart of what they are doing, we should not rule targets off the list."[7] Clinton approved the raid, defying Chirac. It was typical of his temper throughout the war.

Clinton liked to speak of the "consensus" within NATO while in fact nothing of the sort existed. Clinton knew from the first that if NATO's weapons were ready, its will was not. Yet what Clinton consistently retained was a full awareness of the complexity and range of his responsibilities as commander in chief. He knew the White House was the center of history and that presidential power depends as much on the appearance of effective power as on direct control of the mechanisms of power. Clinton knew that NATO was an alliance weighted in favor of America, that American generals would lead it, and that advanced weapons such as the B-2 bomber, a technological miracle not under NATO's jurisdiction, would eventually win the war, and that, given American predominance, he would slowly gain a grasp over the levers that made the power of the alliance work effectively. He would guide NATO the way a mahout guides an elephant, with a delicate but wise and discerning touch; he would use every artifice to galvanize the sluggish monstrosity into some form of effective life.

Yet the effectiveness of NATO was not Clinton's only problem. As the NATO summit approached in late April, the atmosphere within the White

House and the alliance was ridden with troubled suspense and uncertainty. Critical decisions had to be made and made quickly, and the reflexes of NATO had not been trained for speed. In Belgrade, the people had united behind Milosevic, as Chirac had warned. Thanks to well-orchestrated demonstrations, they could be seen in the streets burning dollar bills and American flags. NATO had enjoyed not victory but simply a few minor successes. It needed victory. In addition, it had made gruesome, calamitous errors. On April 14, NATO was bombing from fifteen thousand feet and, mistaking a Kosovar refugee column for a Serb military formation, struck it, killing seventy-three people and leaving the roadside strewn with ghastly bundles lying in the grotesque indignities of violent death.

After the bombing of the refugee column, protests began to spread across Europe like an ugly rash. The German coalition government wobbled on the brink of collapse; the publics of Greece and Italy were infuriated. "Throughout Europe, there was a real fear of what I would call 'the return of the right wing,'" said a former senior CIA official. "Europe had had enough tensions during the Reagan years, and there was real fear that Europe was being dragged into a war because of American moralism." Clinton's own moral strength was being tested as never before.

The date of the summit was set for Washington on April 28, and as Washington's five-star hotels began to fill up, and as growing hostility to the bombing spread across Europe, on April 22, British prime minister Tony Blair, who had a superb sense of public relations, phoned Clinton as he did almost every day, declaring: "We are losing the propaganda war big time," he told Clinton.[8] Throughout the war, Milosevic manifested a total absence of interest when it came to his people, yet his shrewdness as a liar never left him. When a reporter spoke to Milosevic about Kosovar refugees, the Serb blamed the homeless refugees, not on his slaughters, but on NATO's bombing: "The people are running, dogs are running, animals are running, birds are running," he said.[9]

Blair knew this wound had to be stanched. He told Clinton: "You have to set an agenda, correct lies of opponents, run this as though it were an election campaign." With Clinton's approval, NATO secretary general Solana had already advised General Clark to explore ground troops options, and over the phone, Blair urged Clinton to propose a U.S.-U.K. plan for ground troops to the rest of the allies.[10] Clinton found Blair too impatient and lacking in shrewdness. No topic in NATO was more touchy and liable to splinter the alliance than such an act. It was all right for Blair to talk tough—the British were providing only 4 percent of the NATO airpower for the campaign,[11] but the idea was extremely dangerous to preserving alliance unity and the only way for Milosevic to win was to disrupt that unity. While Blair liked action and quick decision and felt that Clinton was weak and equivocating, Clinton hung tough and while not addressing the issue of troops, his message was blunt: "Let's be clear," he told Blair. "We're not going to lose."[12] He also requested Blair tone down his rhetoric about the use of ground troops.

To Blair, Clinton may have seemed to be given to delay, but behind the scenes, both Clinton and Berger had sharply revised U.S. policy. He and Clinton had established the means of an excellent mutual understanding and no advisor had a more uncanny grasp of his boss's desires. Berger suggested that what Clinton had to tell the NATO group was that the administration was prepared to use all necessary means to prevail in Kosovo, including ground troops. Clinton agreed. Berger then took a tough line—victory would be secured "in or outside of NATO."[13] He also wanted to make clear that America would go it alone if it had to. As he said, "A consensus within NATO is valuable. But it is not a sine qua non. We want to move with NATO, but it can't prevent us from moving."[14]

Reluctance to these ideas came from the usual quarter. Secretary of Defense Bill Cohen as a former Republican senator from Maine, articulate and amiable, but narrow and territorial, said he didn't like having U.S. troops on the ground in Bosnia, and he liked this idea even less.

But for Clinton the war had to end. In addition, there had not been a groundswell of support in America for the war, for one thing, and for another, Milosevic was launching peace offensives, and the alliance was increasingly faltering and infirm. (Clinton's nightmare was that a dovish country like Germany might make a separate peace with Milosevic.) More importantly, the costs of an extended war in terms of refugee suffering, allied unity, and domestic politics were proving very high. Clinton was politically losing ground as polls showed the public losing confidence in the way he was handling the war: the majority wanted an immediate negotiated settlement, not escalation. However, Clinton knew the war couldn't be *settled*, it had to be *won*. He was also receiving many credible intelligence reports about how the Yugoslav people had soured on Milosevic. The allied bombing would soon move to bridges, power plants, TV stations, oil refineries, command and control centers, and it would continue without letup until Belgrade was badly damaged and Serbia's economy in ruins. In addition, all of Serbia's neighbors were fierce hawks supporting the war.

A worried Blair then flew to Belgium to talk to General Clark in a four-eyed meeting. Blair looked at him: "Are we going to win this thing?" he asked, startling Clark, who confessed that no one had ever asked him that question. Then, eyes flashing, Clark snapped, "Mr. Prime Minister, I've never lost anything of significance in my life. I'm not going to lose this one."

"Are we going to need ground troops?" Blair asked.

"Maybe," said Clark.

"Then we need to prepare."

"That would be your job, Mr. Prime Minister," Clark said.[15]

Clinton knew any proposal to use ground troops would fracture the alliance, and it would redouble his domestic difficulties. Clinton's first concern was to put heart into NATO's will to win. That done, he might propose the use of troops, although he feared, he said, that the Congress, mainly Republicans or his enemies, would pass a resolution forbidding the use of troops and trying to curtail his support. Clinton said that if Congress tried to hamper him, he would battle back, but he said he believed that ground troops weren't needed. He believed in the ultimate success of the air war.

Perhaps Clinton's war leadership reached its peak at the NATO summit. "The partnership in NATO in the Yugoslav crisis is simply weak, masking greater differences between the United States and its Europan allies," said a former high-ranking aide to U.N. secretary-general Kofi Annan, and he was right. Clinton was facing a war by coalition. The United States in Desert Storm had waged a war by coalition, but since its establishment in 1949, NATO had never fought a war. Yet Clinton knew NATO was indispensable. He also knew that the NATO system of command must be perfected, the targeting improved, more planes massed for strikes, and the pillars of Milosevic's power must be assaulted and weakened.

Clinton by now had taken the Serb leader's true measure. Clinton also saw that Milosevic and his circle were men of a type used to casually inflicting the worst kind of punishment, but he suspected they would not prove as good in enduring it. Clinton well knew that war was often a question of which party could hold out the longest. If Serbia was a puny opponent and Clinton knew that NATO and American airpower would win the war, the only way for Milosevic to win would be for him to exploit and manipulate the rifts and captious rivalries among the allies. To prevent this he applied all the energy of his character and his acute and restless mind. Clinton understood that his first job was to win the confidence and respect of the allied leaders he worked with, and this he did.

Whoever he dealt with, the leaders of Italy, Germany, Greece, Clinton exerted to the full his great powers of personality and expression. It was his capacity to persuade, to always be clear and distinct, to have a singular command of the most telling details of an issue, that enabled him to lead. He saw that if there was in NATO no identity of aims, there was an identity of outlook to which he could appeal. He also had the ability to frame consecutive questions that lured an opponent into agreement, and he used this deftly, former aides said. Since the crisis began Clinton made almost daily calls to Blair, Chirac, German chancellor Gerhard Schroeder, and Italian prime minister Massimo D'Alema. The high-level calls were critical to decision making regarding strikes on central Belgrade, the veto of a proposed Easter bombing pause, and the rejection of an early April cease-fire by Milosevic.

Most of the allied leaders were young and, like Clinton, had formerly been antiwar. The phone calls were used to steady each other's nerves. If the leaders made a tough decision, the phones began to ring as they checked to make sure everyone was still on board. They would nervously ask for a meeting of NATO ambassadors to discover if everyone was still hanging tough, calmed when they found they were, and vowed to hang on.

There were "a lot of reality checks going on," said a former diplomat.[16] France, Britain, and Washington were able to make the key contacts at the highest level and then work in unison to sell them to the alliance as a whole.

As critics jeered that allied unity had become "an end in itself," Clinton knew that maintaining NATO's unity was the absolute and essential key to military success. The air war had to be launched from twenty-two air bases in seven NATO countries. When it came to the issue of troops, the objective of his policy was to win the war, but to win meant preserving the alliance. According to a former senior advisor, the president was, in private, certain that NATO would prevail. Clinton believed that NATO would win because of "its unfaltering will, its endurance and tenacity, and because of its absolute refusal to lose."

When Clinton and Blair next had discussions in Washington on the eve of the NATO meeting, Berger spoke directly to Blair, in Clinton's presence, so there would be no record of Clinton and Blair having disagreed. Berger knew that European governments could fall over the issue of ground troops. "We were getting pretty shaky reads" regarding the stability of the alliance, he said later, and were being asked that the United States not raise the issue of ground troops. "The only way we can win is to back the unity of the alliance," said Berger, who felt it was simply a matter of time before the air war, if it were fierce, unrelenting, and terrible, would wear down Milosevic.

Clinton at this time exhibited his inner flintiness, his deep springs of mental courage. He told Blair that using ground troops would divide the United States and cause fresh outcry, but that he was willing "to absorb it" if he had to. He still maintained he didn't think NATO would need ground troops to win the war.

Blair replied that perhaps they didn't need to use ground troops, but NATO shouldn't hesitate to threaten their use.

Berger was exceptionally nervous. The national security advisor coun-
seled Blair and Clinton not to raise the troop issue at the NATO meeting—
tensions were already white hot. A NATO summit was not a place to show
the group's unity fraying to ribbons, but Blair insisted that NATO had to
manifest *something* that showed "our total will to win." Cooperation, he insisted, was not an end in itself but an avenue for action. Berger remained
conscious of the risks, but Blair said the idea of troops must remain visible
in the background as a credible threat. There was some bickering, but what
seized these men was the common conviction that if they didn't put their
backs into winning, they were going to lose the war. Finally Berger, Clinton, and Blair came up with a formula: without mentioning troops on the
ground, the allies would pledge to do "whatever it takes to win," Clinton said
later. According to a former senior advisor, the president was, in private,
"determined to win." Clinton believed that NATO would win because of its
unfaltering will, its endurance and tenacity, and because of its absolute refusal to lose, he said.

The very next day, with Washington packed with diplomats, Clinton
presented the nineteen NATO ministers with the proposal that NATO declare its unalterable resolution to prevail in the conflict. After this was proposal was made, a great calm descended, quieting all the feverish bickering
and speculation among the ministers. Uncertainty and doubt were gone.
The many had fused into one. As Berger said later, "looking each other
straight in the eye," all nineteen leaders made a personal commitment that
NATO would not lose. NATO was now in the war with both feet.

Soon, air operations became round-the-clock attacks, direct and savage.
As NATO's assaults gained in force, intensity, concentration, Milosevic began to lose his military infrastructure, the ability to sustain his forces, his
air defense system, and a loss of morale could be detected in Belgrade's
forces. There were command and control problems, leadership gaps, increasing desertions. Up until that time, the rate of assault had allowed "periods when everyone [in Belgrade] can come out of their shelter and take a
breath," an official said. "When you get to the point where you can't come
out," luck had changed in your favor. "Right now, every time you give them
a breather, life flows back in" the Serbian ground forces.[17]

It was the next day that Berger's deputy, James Steinberg, entered the
huge room where the summit was under way, Clinton seated at a U-shaped
table, to tell the president that Yeltsin was on the phone. In a seventy-five-
minute conversation, the Russian leader was alarmed at the increasing destruction of Belgrade's infrastructure and also worried that Moscow's
influence was being pushed to the margins. Yetlsin was requesting a bomb-

ing pause to show that the Russia still wielded some influence. Clinton would have none of it. "I knew [Yeltsin] was mad at Milosevic too," Clinton said later. Clinton told Yeltsin there would be no bombing pause until Milosevic "cried uncle first," adding, "There has to be a clear unambiguous defeat [of the Serbs] in Kosovo" before Clinton would agree to any bombing pause.[18]

It was at that point Yeltsin came up with his diplomatic master stroke: he would send his special envoy, Viktor Chernomyrdin, to begin to hammer out a diplomatic solution that would result in Milosevic's surrender.

45

BREADTH OF DESTRUCTION

One cannot grasp the complexities of the NATO-Serb war without keeping in the back of one's mind the August 1995 finding Clinton had signed pledging to use any and all means short of assassination to remove Milosevic from power. According to a former senior Clinton advisor, the ouster of the Serb leader had never been a NATO war aim "because we knew the allies would never agree." Yet getting rid of Milosevic had been publicly talked of by a few American officials, and the idea was always there. In 1998 congressional testimony, U.S. envoy to the Balkans Robert Gelbard, a key player in waging the wartime covert operation, said: "A truly lasting solution to the problems of Kosovo will require the development of strong democratic institions in Serbia and the FRY [Federal Republic of Yugoslavia]. A new generation of political leaders."[1] Albright had also said publicly that removing Milosevic would end Serbian aggression and result in the democratization of Yugoslavia, but it was dismissed by most as mere rhetoric. It wasn't.

As the alliance pressed the air war with mounting intensity, one of Milosevic's chief liabilities had become the enormous increase of U.S and allied intelligence assets pouring into Albania and Kosovo from Bosnia.[2] By early 1996, in order to implement the Dayton Accords, U.S. military commanders in Bosnia deployed advanced spy planes, sensitive RC-135 "Rivet Joint" flights able to monitor highly protected and classified communications between Bosnia and Belgrade. CIA and Defense Department human intelligence programs were run from a single office, the heart of these operations a brigade-sized unit from the U.S. Army's V Corps consisting of over one thousand intelligence officers, signals analysts, and counterintelligence officers. Small teams composed of NSA, CIA, and Defense Intelligence Agency officials supplemented the larger group. At the start of the war with Belgrade, the bulk of this group transferred to Albania with some elements entering Kosovo.

Of increasing importance was the Special Collection Service, the five-man CIA/NSA signals intelligence teams, formed in the 1970s, that worked out of U.S. embassies and fused the talents of human spies and ultra-high-tech eavesdroppers whose job was to get close to very difficult and inaccessible targets. NSA analysts now began to study Serbia to try and understand how its communication systems worked, what its Internet addresses were, and how its traffic was routed, not only domestically, but around the world. Sophisticated NSA Internet surveillance techniques made it possible to acquire data "in motion" across the world or at rest in databases. "Volume, velocity and variety are key," said one NSA official.[3]

During the Cold War, the prime targets of such operations were usually sensitively placed code clerks, but by the time of the NATO-Serb war, the espionage bull's-eye had come to focus on systems administrators who could plant trapdoors in computer systems enabling U.S. spooks to have access to the system from the other side of the world. Such technical experts were also able to provide encryption keys to NSA operatives, and some of these Serb intelligence assets were bought outright. "You want the technicians of your enemy's system working for you as defectors in place," said a former NSA official.

NSA computer hackers played a critical role in the military side of Operation Allied Force, producing "a success so astounding, so monumental that even the most optimistic of us have been stunned," said information warfare expert Frederic H. Levien.[4] By planting viruses inside Serb air defense computers, or by insertion of deceptive communications into the microwave net, the Serbs couldn't log in and they could not fire missiles reliably. "If you break the missile lock every few seconds, they can't function," said Levien.[5]

In addition, the KLA was working closely with the CIA, whose key wartime location was in Kukes, Albania, in an effort to plot and target the disposition of Serb forces in Kosovo. This was an effort that, at best, produced only limited success, yet because Milosevic's view was ruinously distorted, the program had beneficial effects. The Serb leader now saw U.S. forces building up in Macedonia and knew that a flight of twenty-four Apache attack helicopters was on the ground in Albania that could be used to savage his own troops in the field. Additional U.S. forces were pouring into Albania, their main duty actually to repair the main road from Tirana to Kukes, but Milosevic feared the effort was connected to invasion preparations. As *Washington Post* reporter Dana Priest put it, "The ground planning was one key thread . . . as it unfolded inside the headquarters and secure communications bunkers of NATO's high command."[6]

In spite of Clinton's wariness over the use of ground troops (he felt it might stir up pressure by Congress to use the War Powers Act), before the NATO summit, Clinton had given a quiet okay to NATO secretary general Javier Solana and General Clark to upgrade secret NATO ground options, and Clark had wasted no time. Berger would later say that Clark was very clever in putting pieces on the board for a possible invasion, launched not from Hungary, but from Albania and Macedonia, which would avoid having to occupy of all of Serbia.

As usual, Secretary of Defense Cohen and most of the Joint Chiefs of Staff strongly opposed any talk of ground troops, taking away the very element of psychological uncertainty for which they had excoriated Clinton when the president made his "no troops" speech in March. The Pentagon had tried to keep Clark from attending the NATO summit in an effort to isolate him and his promotion of an invasion, but the effort failed. As a result, Clinton, not trusting his military, refused to consult with the Joint Chiefs of Staff except for the chairman, Gen. Hugh Shelton, who went to the White House every day with huge lists of new targets to be approved. (The approval of fresh targets remained excruciatingly slow throughout the war.)

The Pentagon, which had opposed the air war, now abruptly shifted ground and declared that the air war would work. In the meantime, the edgy, unremitting Clark, with White House approval, outwitted any allied hesitation relating to targets by excluding NATO from such missions, instead using American planes not assigned to the alliance. Congress began to bridle. As U.S. efforts intensified, Representative Ron Paul and a bipartisan team of seventeen members sued Clinton over Kosovo, alleging he had violated the law, was putting American lives at risk, and, as a result, denied any support for the air campaign.[7] Congress kept complaining it could not understand what U.S. interests were in the struggle. "We should not even be in the Balkans," said Representative Floyd Spence.[8] On May 3, the Senate killed a resolution authorizing Clinton to use all means necessary to win the war.

In the days since the covert finding was signed in 1995, secret measures and fresh channels to infiltrate the regime had been developed, completed and put in place to advance its implementation. "Milosevic was an expert at divide and rule, so we were going to wage war to undermine his power, isolate him from his backers, split his cabal of cronies from a solid block of supporters into doubters looking out for themselves, uncertain about Milosevic's long-term survival," a former senior Clinton advisor said.

The covert segment was kept out of the sight and hearing of Clark and the U.S. military. On the covert side, the chief targets were not the military, but the Serb ruling elite, especially the cronies of Milosevic. According to David Leavy, spokesman for the NSC, early in the war, Clinton determined on broadening the Belgrade target list "to include the things Milosevic values most."[9]. Milosevic's ruling circle was made up of the most idle, vicious, and degenerate parts of society, used to pampering themselves with weekend jaunts to Paris or Budapest or the Greek islands. The Serb leader had no friends, only accomplices, and for his elite, privileges and rank were awarded based on their robotic, mindless loyalty and practical usefulness to Milosevic and his family. If you were trusted, you prospered, and had access to the choice apartment houses, country dachas, foreign cars, the best neighborhoods, special rest homes, fleets of expensive cars, squads of security guards. In brief, the political-criminal elite of Serbia lived a life of obscene ostentatious luxury in contrast to the Serb public. That was about to change.

Pressure on Belgrade inexorably tightened all that May, especially after the European Union banned 305 key Serbs from traveling to or doing business with Europe, beginning with Milosevic and including Nikola Sainovic, Serbian president Milan Milutinovic, Milosevic's wife, Mira, his daughter Marija and others. America quickly did the same. The EU plan was called the Black List, according to one former senior U.S. official.

"I want to see the rapid economic death of Serbia," Deputy National Security Advisor James Steinberg had told reporters.

To produce this result, an initial Clinton proposal planned to target the finances of Milosevic's close associates using U.S. computer experts to hack into the various offshore bank accounts of his chief henchmen, employing an elaborate plan of information warfare. Clinton had used such hacker programs before, having personally approved the penetration of Haitian government computer networks during the 1994 Haiti crisis, although those operations were done mainly to collect intelligence. Unfortunately, this first hacker plan was knocked to pieces by horrified Defense Department lawyers who produced a fifty-page internal "Assessment of International Legal Issues in Information Operations," which concluded such hacking would be absolutely illegal. The United States had the capability, but there had been a lack of operational vision and strategy in the framing of the operation.[10]

Now another plan emerged that would use NATO bombing to target the economic holdings of key Milosevic backers, to make the members of his power elite reevaluate their loyalty. One part of the program was called Elephant Blanket, named because its elements were laid out in diagrams on a five-foot-square piece of paper, the details meticulously printed in six-point type. It had been drawn up and developed by the Special Technical Operations (STO) cell at the U.S. European Command headquarters at Stuttgart. The operation used a combination of hijacking, espionage, special weapons, and psychological operations to gain its effect. (Each major combat command now has an STO cell, coordinated by a high-level panel on the Joint Chiefs of Staff.)

At a top secret facility near Washington, a diagrammatic model of Milosevic's inner circle was completed with painstaking care, using the inputs from dozens of intelligence and aid agencies, much in the way the Iraqi leadership had been targeted by the CIA listening units within UNSCOM. The information it presented would prove crucial in weakening the Serb leader. It showed in detail who within Milosevic's ruling circle managed what, who owned what, who had hidden holdings and where those were. It also listed the front companies that were being used to move and launder money in violation of allied sanctions. In this way, U.S. intelligence provided an intricate diagram of the Serbian leadership organization that would later prove the basis for enacting its downfall in 2000.

When Elephant Blanket was being prepared, security swiftly emerged as a major problem. Elephant Blanket was a "Special Access" program, meaning that it was so highly restricted only a minuscule number of people were allowed to see it, and, strangely enough, not a single European officer, excepting a few British, had the required number of clearances. The plan was then revised by a number of secret U.S. and British agencies, and what emerged was called, the Day 54 Plan.[11] Yet it would be easier said than done because Yugoslav telephone networks and cell phone operations could not be bombed because Italian and Greek NATO allies held financial stakes in them. (In fact, the Serb telephone network was actually left functional because the NSA was monitoring conversations of the top Serb political leaders and military commanders.)

In any case, the approach was changed yet again. In something called Operation Matrix, managed by Robert Gelbard, Serb owners of plants or other economic facilities would be given advance warning via e-mail, fax, or cell phone that their cherished facility and source of vast personal profit was about to disappear from the face of the earth. According to someone with knowledge of the operation, the response of Serb business owners to having been contacted was often panicky and unnerved, some asking, "How was I tracked down? How did you find me?"[12]

Two such attacks, on Bor and Smederevo, provide examples of the effectiveness of the U.S.-British campaign. The NATO bull's-eye at Bor in Serbia was a copper smelter; at Smederevo, the steel plant was the key target. Former deputy prime minister Nikola Sainovic, the manager of Bor, was using his position to operate an elaborate kickback scheme to drain off gold from the plant, then smuggle it to offshore sanctuaries. At Smederevo, an ex-deputy of Milosevic's Socialist Party had a similar operation going full blast.

The U.S. announcements to the Milosevic cronies sent shudders down their backs. NSA, CIA, and DIA computer intelligence operators would hack into Serb communications and computer networks to insert NATO surrender terms and other unsettling messages, then NATO planes would promptly appear over the facilities and reduce them to smoking piles of rubble.

As an official involved in the operations said, "It is a tool of extreme intimidation to tell a factory owner when his factory will disappear and tell him in time for him to be able to do nothing except watch it happen."

There was another U.S., Clinton-approved measure that had almost the same devastating effect, called the White List, never made public, which specifically targeted the finances of the top ruling circles in Serbia. "Replacing the Black List with the White List was an important and critical step," said a former senior administration official. The White List meant that any Serbian business on it was forbidden to do business with the EU or America unless it proved it had *no* connections to the Serb government and was doing *no* business with it. This meant that the CIA and Department of the Treasury, along with the financial agencies of the European Union, would begin pressuring neighboring states to freeze their Serb accounts and deny transit of funds.

In addition, the Department of the Treasury's Office of Foreign Assets Control suddenly appeared in Cyprus, the major Serb money laundering center where 7,500 Serb companies had their offshore accounts. As part of the new offensive, America acted to keep oil from going to Serbia, kept any cash out of the food aid program, and kept donations away from the Yugoslavia Red Cross because monies were always diverted to the Milosevic family. In another step, America had Carla Del Ponte, a forensic accountant for the International Criminal Tribunal, begin to unearth the disguised Serb assets hidden away in Cyprus, China, Russia, and other locations. As the monies began to be tracked, it caused a panic in Belgrade, said a former very senior U.S. official. Serbia had banks and trading companies in Russia that suddenly found their assets frozen. Credit being extended to Serbia by Moscow was abruptly cut off.

One of the first Milosevic henchmen to feel the humiliation of impotence was Bogoljub Karic. On May 21, he tried to go to Cyprus where he owned a bank, headed several companies, and was chief of a branch of the Karic Foundation. At the airport, he was refused entry and forced to return to Serbia.

Another bonanza for Washington was the indictment of Milosevic as a war criminal by The Hague on May 27, 1999.[13] Arrest warrants were issued for the Serb leader and his top four aides. Milosevic was no longer a "reputable" head of state, but a pariah, shunned, belittled, and despised. The indictment resulted in intelligence bonanzas as rich Serb criminals, thugs, former generals, paramilitary leaders, and the like began to use cutouts to establish back channels to the West, trying to have their former standing restored and their names removed from the hated White List.

As Milosevic's political base shrank to a smaller and smaller circumference, his cronies seeing their names on the EU list did much to drain any remaining fervor and dedication from their support. The elite close to Milosevic began to grow restive. At the beginning of the war, their posh cars could be seen cruising the streets and life went on as usual, but by mid-May, many family members of the political elite had left. NATO dropped fifty-five Serb bridges, ending the smuggling on which the proceeds of Milosevic's cronies depended for their wealth, and their families began to emigrate. The inner circle wanted an end to the war.

Meanwhile, the destruction was only becoming more widespread. By May 1, NATO was flying 150 sorties per day. By the end of the month, this had risen to more than 250, and the number of aircraft involved had climbed to 535 from 350. In addition, NATO had acquired new bases in Hungary and Turkey, which enabled the allies to bomb twenty-four hours a day. Both allied and U.S. officials made clear that NATO would inflict more and more pain on the Serb nation until it reversed course in Kosovo.

Some of the threats made the hair stand on one's head. German Gen. Klaus Naumann observed that Milosevic was daring the risk that "his entire country would be bombed into rubble.[14] Many in the Serb leadership recalled the warning given by Air Force Gen. Michael Short in October of 1998 when he told Milosevic, "The speed and violence of and the destruction that is going to occur is beyond anything you can imagine. If indeed, you're not going to accept my terms, I suggest you go outside, get in your car and drive around the city of Belgrade. Remember the way it is today. . . . Belgrade will never look that way again—never in your lifetime."[15]

NATO considered dual use facilities, including bridges, steam plants, electric power facilities, highways, as legitimate military targets, and one by one such facilities were systematically destroyed. Oil refineries, petrol depots, road and rail bridges, military communications sites, and factories that produced weapons were also smashed. On May 17, NATO attacks temporarily knocked out electrical power grids leaving 70 percent of the country in darkness with no water, and more assets of the elite were left in ruins. Worse, probes by allied agencies into the Serb elite's shady financial activities were being stepped up, fresh sanctions were in place, and by the second week of May, more pro-war and antiwar camps had appeared inside the ruling circle.

In the meantime, Clinton was meeting daily with Cohen, Gen. Hugh Shelton, CIA director George Tenet, and Berger to view damage from the previous night's attacks. While trying anxiously to avoid civilian deaths, Clinton still aimed to inflict a certain amount of pain on the Serb people. It was clear from a host of U.S. intelligence reports that the public mood in Serbia had soured. By the third week of the war, the cold, steady rain of disillusion and weariness fell in the Serbian soul. The focus of about 70 percent of the people was on their own hardships and chances of survival. Signs of despair were everywhere. The crowds at the open-air rock concerts had dwindled from 100,000 to a few dozen. Since many bombings occurred at night, the Serbs were getting no rest, plus they were afraid for the welfare of themselves and their families, they were suffering physical hardship, and they were exhausted and demoralized, knowing NATO was not going to let up until it prevailed. As the bombing intensified and spread, their mood grew more disheartened and spiritually discouraged. The hardships were real—some 42 percent of people had been forced to leave their homes and seek safety, and 71 percent suffered privations from shortages of oil, sugar, soap, and diapers. A total of 86 percent reported psychological problems within families. Mass anxiety for the future rose like water in a glass. There was only one question: how long was it all going to go on this way?

For Milosevic, it was becoming more and more clear that nothing and no one in Belgrade was safe. By May, the accumulating attacks on Interior Ministry buildings, command and control bunkers, MUP police, and military headquarters around the country were weakening and degrading Belgrade's political control. The cruise missile strikes that took out Milosevic's Socialist Party headquarters and the JUL party of his wife, were all devastating to the morale of the elite, who realized the bombing would continue until their holdings were destroyed and the economy was a wreck. Perhaps the most decisive strike of the war occurred May 24, when bombs took down Serbia's power grid for good. Disabled were the computers that ran the country's banks to command and control and air defense installations to the pumps that ran the country's water systems. NATO had destroyed Serbia's central nervous system.

Soon profound disaffection began to spread within the Serb armed forces as the families of senior Serb army or VJ officials began to emigrate. There was concern among top commanders that the war would prove to be a loser. Some VJ officers openly rebelled and bluntly told Milosevic to take NATO's terms. The relations between Serbia's military and the Milosevic circle had never been easy, and the bombing was expanding its damage dramatically. NATO blew up oil refineries, it destroyed fourteen dual use factories owned by close associates, nine major electric generating plants. Businesses closed. As many as 100,000 Serbs were out of work and Serbia was losing so much infrastructure, it was turning into a failed state.

NATO inadvertently added to Serb public pressure to end to war. On May 7, NATO mistakenly bombed a Serb passenger train, and as the target list kept expanding, a U.S. missile hit the Chinese embassy, killing three employees. Since Milosevic's wife, Mira, supported the Chinese as a counterweight to U.S. might, many in the Serb leadership thought the strike to have been deliberate. (U.S. intelligence confirmed a Chinese INTEL unit had been operating from the building.) But the strike had been a mistake, due to an out-of-date map, and CIA employees were fired over the matter.

Yet the Serbs thought U.S. technology so advanced, they were fixedly convinced that it could not make mistakes, and the Serb leaders began to fear that every city in Serbia would be razed and that NATO, displaying vindictive ferocity, was preparing to demolish the country's entire infrastructure and destroy its economy. This wasn't true, but the United States launched psychological operations using leaflets and broadcasts that blamed Milosevic for the continuing destruction. "How long will you suffer for Milosevic. . . . Don't let Milosevic hold you hostage to his atrocities."[16]

NATO would fight a wearing, dogged war, yet more and more its strength appeared swift, certain, irresistible to the Serbs; NATO was gaining ground, and its forces were inflicting a fearful mauling on Belgrade as they came.

The end for Milosevic was not long in coming. In secret, the United States, Russia, and Finland put together an ultimatum. Working from a draft put together by State Department official James Dobbins, one inexorable U.S. demand was the withdrawal of "all" Serb forces from Kosovo, meaning all Serb regular forces, all Serb special police, all Serb paramilitary units. Viktor Chernomyrdin, Yeltsin's special envoy,[17] having to contend with the mulish stubbornness of the accompanying Russian military, resisted the word "all," for several days. Then, without warning, as a fatigued and frustrated American diplomat, Strobe Talbott, Clinton's top Russia hand, was about to explode in exasperated wrath, Chernomyrdin gave in and agreed. Shortly thereafter, the Russian and the president of Finland, Martti Ahtisaari, a former senior official of the United Nations, left for Belgrade to meet with Milosevic.

Presented with the ultimatum, a cocky, smug, imperious Milosevic tried to dodge and duck. "May I make an amendment?" the Serb asked at one point. "Unfortunately, not," said Ahtisaari. When the Serb again hesitated over a point, a boiling, furious Chernomyrdin suddenly swept the conference table clear of its documents, water glasses, and pads, saying intensely, "Reject these terms, and Serbia will look like this table."[18]

That was it. Clinton was hard at work on the ground option, and the U.S. attitude had hardened. On June 2, in a senior policy meeting, Berger made four points. The first was: "We're going to win," and the fourth was: "All options are on the table." When asked if Clinton would support ground troops, Berger said, "Go back to point one." He spent the night of June 3 working on a yellow legal pad on a "go/no-go" memo that was officially formatted and sent over to the president for approval.

Clearly, the doors had closed on Milosevic. His country in turmoil, his popularity plummeting, deserted by the Russians, Milosevic knew the only way for him to hang on to any vestige of his power was to surrender. He did so on June 3.

46

SOWING THE WIND

After his defeat in war, Milosevic's position was awkward, and yet oddly unassailable. After his indictment as a war criminal, Milosevic's American and European enemies hungrily prowled around him like cats beneath a bird cage, but the Serbian president in fact could not be touched. In spite of his indictment, Milosevic remained a sovereign head of state, and even though an arrest warrant for him and four chief aides had been authorized by The Hague, those warrants could not be served until Milosevic left office when his term as Serb president expired in 2001. Until then, his position made him immune.

In any case, Serbia's international status and reputation meant little to Milosevic, who, during his whole adult life, had cared about only power, not status. In Serbia, he still ruled supreme, and he had not the slightest intention of allowing that supremacy to be diminished one iota. What usurped top priority now was Milosevic's own political survival. His intention to prolong his political longevity was an agenda that dominated and absorbed all others, and the Serb began to embark on a wide spectrum of sweeping administrative changes that, if carried through, would give him a hold over Serbia as hard to break as the grip from a pair of pliers. Milosevic had a shrewd knowledge of the state's administrative machinery, and he used it now with an adroit and destructive effectiveness. His focus fell first on Serbia's judiciary, and here he was pitiless. Suddenly, all the constitutional, supreme, and district courts in the country became his targets. As early as 1997, Milosevic began a major purge of his judges, and by the time it ended three years later, a total of nine hundred judges out of two thousand had been replaced. It appears that judges were to resemble his cronies; they were to be dogs all nicely on a leash. If a judge disapproved of a Milosevic decision and said so publicly, he or she was promptly out of a job. No means of redress existed. As Serbian justice minister Dragoliub Jankovic once blandly remarked, "The state pays the judges; they cannot work against the state."[1] So much for the rule of law.

Unfortunately, the result of Milosevic's reshuffling of judges and other measures was that it made him more difficult to remove from power than ever. Under the new system, Milosevic could only be removed from office if the Constitutional Court ruled that he had violated the constitution. Two thirds of both houses of the legislature then had to vote to remove him, and since both courts and legislature were entirely subject to Milosevic's personal control including their systems of coercion and intimidation, any chances of his removal verged on the far-fetched.

Milosevic now turned his attention to muzzling his critics. Until Kosovo, Milosevic had kept up the pretense of tolerating a tiny amount of internal opposition, but that veil was cast aside and what was now clearly revealed was a regime that was basically criminal and determined to have compliant servility at all costs. As a political colleague said, after Kosovo, Milosevic's system changed from one based on "the power of authority" to one of employing "the authority of power."[2] Another colleague would say, "Milosevic has no ideology, and his only goal is to rule unchecked for as long as possible."[3]

For most of Milosevic's career, there had been little coherent opposition to his rule, and it had consisted chiefly of a mix of unpaid soldiers, political insiders whose careers Milosevic had ruined, generals he'd milked dry, shelved, and discarded, along with a scattering of domestic political parties, all of which were divided, ineptly led, and at odds over everything. Milosevic displayed expert skill in keeping them divided and at each other's throats.

Yet after Kosovo, Milosevic had seen the storm coming, the sinister cloud bank building ahead, almost like a solid obstacle, the brief, bright flutters of lightning, the feeble daylight failing, the ship of state beginning to pitch and lurch in increasingly rough seas. During the war, Sandy Berger had observed to a State Department official that the Serb leader "was feeling the heat from the military campaign: we are seeing in the intelligence increasingly as we got into May, the noose tightening around Milosevic. There was a shift in the public mood in Serbia that happened about the time the lights went out. People realized this wasn't a grand cause; it was simply causing them suffering."[4]

Milosevic saw this shift in the public mood and realized disaffection with his rule was spreading, hostile forces were building up, his own prestige was dwindling, and he was determined not to be caught unprepared. According to biographer Leonard Cohen, his new target was Serbia's independent media, which had three times the number of listeners than the state-controlled radio and TV stations. Until then, Milosevic had tolerated their operation as a sort of safety valve so when critics called him a dictator, he could always point to the private media as proof of his broad fairness. Now he suddenly viewed them as subversive filth whose existence threatened Serbia's very survival, and his methods of attack included "fines, closures, and personal threats." The reporters and owners were staggered by extortionate fines and labeled "terrorists"; they saw their fees raised and were deprived of supplies and newsprint; and they were even denied the right to attend parliamentary sessions. Over 250 unlicensed stations were shut down, and one of the most influential and popular, B-92, was run off the air, continuing to broadcast thanks only to satellites and the Internet. Clearly, Milosevic's dictatorship had coarsened from soft to one that was hard, merciless, and all-pervasive. And Milosevic was not simply silencing his opponents, he was also assassinating them: "People were being hunted down like rats," said former mayor of Belgrade Zoran Djindjic.[5]

For Albright, the Serb leader was insufferable and disgusting. The repulsive obnoxiousness of Milosevic, his brutality and corruption, haunted her like a nightmare. In a meeting she told her young and devoted advisor, James Rubin, that getting rid of Milosevic "is my top personal priority. I want him gone before I'm gone." Elsewhere she had said, "Milosevic *is* the problem," adding, "There will be peace in Kosovo when there is democracy in Belgrade."[6]

President Clinton's mood certainly exhibited a new unshakable fixity of intent. The president was far from being through with Milosevic. "The Serb people are going to have to get out of denial," he said. "They are going to have to come to grips with what Milosevic ordered in Kosovo."[7]

By then he had taken Milosevic's true measure—a man who would rather rule "over rubble" than not rule at all, he said.

Milosevic was clearly a marked man, but the CIA plan to take him down had run into unforeseen complications. The Clinton covert operation for Milosevic's overthrow was derived from the model put in place by CIA director Bill Casey when he and President Reagan had supported Solidarity, the free Polish union, in 1980. Covert CIA support had proved essential in preventing Soviet counterintelligence from destroying or decapitating the union. Since Serbia, like Russia, was in the hands of a centralized authoritarian, the CIA knew that in Serbia, the opposition was going to have to concentrate on creating a structure that would be invulnerable to Milosevic's counterspy organizations. Opposition members had to have mobility and fast, secure communications among their units in different cities and provinces. Anti-Serb groups including unions, Serbs from overseas, and civic organizations were already sending funds to the regime's opponents, but one of the actors of surpassing importance would be nongovernmental organizations or NGOs.

The National Endowment for Democracy, set up by President Reagan in the 1980s, had employed an assortment of organizations across the political spectrum, including the AFL-CIO and U.S. Chamber of Commerce, to help funnel U.S. tax dollars to overseas organizations working to develop democracies in their respective countries. In the 1980s, especially in Poland, the NED had proved an effective tool in loosening and weakening Soviet power by supporting dissidents. Where Poland had been the focus of its effort, its new target would be Serbia.

The plan briefed to Clinton by CIA director George Tenet, National Security Advisor Sandy Berger, and others was intricate and comprehensive. Basically, it would work through the NED's two subordinate wings, the International Republican Institute (IRI) and the National Democratic Institute (NDI), as well as the Center for International Private Enterprise, an offshoot of the U.S. Chamber of Commerce. The IRI would focus on dissident students, while the NDI would work closely with the different opposition parties. The State Department and U.S. Agency for International Development would play lead roles in channeling funds through commercial contracts and nonprofit groups. Under the authority of AID, other money would be funneled to opposition groups and the mayors of opposition cities.

Because of their freedom to travel and move in closed areas, the CIA recruited the staff of other NGOs, mainly relief agencies and human rights groups, which produced a great deal of useful intelligence. According to former CIA officials such recruitment was done very selectively. "We didn't want organizations discredited or people killed, nor could they afford to be seen as foreign vassals," said one former Directorate of Operations official. Another said of the NGO recruitment, "There was a lot of reluctance in this area."

This former operative emphasized that the coup operation "had to be very tightly controlled from beginning, middle, and end. You had to support one group against another; you helped the people who were going to help you."

So the Clinton plan was to use covert/overt, insider/outsider elements simultaneously, which meant employing NGOs in coordination with sophisticated espionage. Said one former senior agency official who was closely involved: "We planned to do to Milosevic what he'd done to us. We went in to create trouble spots, support dissidents, circulate subversive literature, beam in anti-Milosevic broadcasts, recruit and neutralize his army and security forces, especially the police and security forces. Solidarity was the model."

The agency plan had several general goals: first, the program should be a region-wide effort, making use of a Central European network of banks, corporations, political, and social organizations to fund coup assets plus use the intelligence services of countries like Austria, Germany, Albania, and Italy, and even Greece, for recruitment and penetration. All these nations had their own excellent intelligence collection networks inside Serbia. Forward planning was going to be done in places like Pristina, Kosovo; Vienna; and Stuttgart. At one point when opposition leaders were squabbling, they were flown on U.S. aircraft to Berlin or Stuttgart and Ulm in Germany for a sit-down and sober scolding by the Americans. Another source of key intelligence came from the former Kosovo president, Ibrahim Rugova, a mild man and a poet, a man who collected rocks and who always wore his trademark scarf. After he had lost power and been supplanted by the Kosovo Liberation Army (KLA), Rugova had set up an exile government in Ulm that provided invaluable intelligence, and the CIA kept in close contact with it. The agency also had a network in Kosovo involving a broad range of sources and contacts. "Our intelligence collection there was excellent," a former senior CIA official said.[8]

There was another crucial element. Following the war, U.S. recruitment of Serb army officers, political leaders, labor leaders, police, and security officials soared. A prize catch had been Gen. Momcilo Perisic, former chief of staff of the Yugoslav army or VJ. In the spring of 1997, Perisic suggested in a clear jibe at Milosevic that "less than one percent of the people who head institutions" were really working for the public good. Perisic had deeply opposed intervention in Kosovo, wanted to keep the army out of politics, and asserted that Milosevic's agreement with Holbrooke in October 1998 that averted war was a product of Belgrade's military weakness, not diplomatic cunning. Intensely disliked by Milosevic's wife, Mira Markovic, Perisic was fired in 1999, remarking, "This establishment does not like officials with high personal integrity who use their own heads."[9] He would play a key role in keeping the army on the sidelines during the October revolt.

More importantly, Perisic and other key senior Milosevic officials were the results of an accelerated program of recruitment intensified after the Kosovo defeat when State Department officials, CIA officials, and others had with cunning and tireless energy developed contacts inside Milosevic's ruling circle, security forces, and his army. "We were talking to everyone we could lay our hands on," said a former senior State Department official. Exortion was a common undercurrent. The indictment of Milosevic had unnerved many of the Serb's cronies, and U.S. recruiters were saying to them, "The war crimes indictment list will be extended to 600 names, so you betray the big boss when I tell you, or you'll go to The Hague."[10] The increase in those willing to cooperate "was truly startling," said one former operative.

If neutralizing Serbia's security services was one goal of the coup, another was the creation of shock troops for the street. Even before the Millennium, as the agency had hammered out more details of its strategy, planners knew that the coup would rely for its success on the creation of a massive nonviolent resistance movement, just as Reagan had done in Poland with Solidarity. The CIA had found these in a Serb student organization called Otpor, Milosevic's newest enemy.

Beginning in the spring of 1998, Milosevic, in a fury of energy, had tried to smother any circulation of free opinion by brutally intimidating or expelling university professors and students as well as by continuing to harass and persecute independent newspapers and radio stations. Unfortunately, he inadvertently provoked a small group of students to act. No innocent person unjustly insulted ever forgets his grievance, and in October of 1998, at Belgrade University, a half dozen disgruntled students came together to form a coherent anti-Milosevic organization that would not be simply a gesture to annoy Milosevic but pose a genuine threat to his continued existence. This small group decided to fight the Serb dictator by raising a storm of fury, revenge, and hostile strength against him. The question was, how to go about it? Until that point, Serb student dissidents had proved utterly ineffective as a political force, but that night six students sat together drinking and talking together until one of them, tousled, dark-haired Srbja Popovic, came up with a brilliant idea. Symbols were important, he said. They bypassed thought, but they had to capture the attention—they had to stir and arouse emotions but they also had to have a name or use a symbol that would hold people's attention and resound afterward in their minds. Popovic suggested that their symbol be that of a clenched fist—the classic symbol of Communist worker's resistance. After vigorous discussion, the group decided it would call itself "Otpor" or "Resistance." Its slogan would be: *"Gotov je!"* or—"He's finished!"[11]

It wasn't long before Otpor displayed its own unique flair for making an impact.

One night, to celebrate the Millennium, the group, declared illegal by

Milosevic, scheduled a rock concert in central Belgrade. As a preliminary act, there was a band on stage with an energetic, talented drummer given to dramatic flourishes, and he played until midnight to keep the crowd amused. About 25,000 had turned up to listen, and when the music stopped, everyone was eager for the concert to begin. The lights were turned down. Then on a giant TV screen behind the stage, images of faces appeared, and a somber male voice began to read a list of names. Confusion first overcame the crowd, but as the baritone voice went on evenly and emphatically reading the list of names, degree by degree, the audience realized what was happening. The names were ones they recognized. They were the faces and names of those who had died in Kosovo, Bosnia, Croatia in Milosevic's futile wars. They were, said the voice, the names and faces of the "beaten, the betrayed, the dead."[12]

When the reading ended, there was no rock concert. "Go home," said the deep, spectral voice. "There is nothing to celebrate." The crowd quietly dispersed. But at last the students had found their grimly resolved and inalterable purpose—they were going to conquer the peace.

Very quietly the group began to receive money. Of the almost $3 million spent by the National Endowment of Democracy in September of 1998, Otpor was "certainly the largest recipient," said Paul McCarthy, an official of the Washington-based group. From August 1999 on, the amount of funding continued to rise. The money was transferred to accounts in countries outside Serbia, mainly in Hungary and Austria. Since Milosevic had nationalized the Serb banks, a lot of it came over the Serb border in suitcases from Hungary. The NED would not know how the money was going, and would receive a receipt signed by a dissident as to how the funds were used. For example, money going to underground publications would be acknowledged by a secret code printed on one of the pages.

Clearly, a new, unifying force was coming into its own.

The only thing missing now was an organized Serb opposition. If there were to be a coup, there had to be a concerted, focused, coordinated campaign to remove Milosevic and the core of that campaign had to be a genuine Serb leader who embodied Serbia's real aspirations and aims and who would not be viewed as an American or European tool. At the moment, that leadership did not exist.

At the end of the war, two opposition leaders had emerged, yet they were divided, ineptly led, and given to venomous squabbling. One of these leaders was Zoran Djindjic, a brilliant, West-leaning intellectual who wished Serbia to join a liberal, pro-democratic Europe. His opponent was bearded

Vuk Draskovic, a corrupt ultra-Serb nationalist, tainted by government service under Milosevic, who was set on becoming president of Serbia. Djindjic, who called for Milosevic's overthrow by means of "peaceful change," felt that the spectrum of opposition should expand to include students, activists, businessmen and professionals, and others from the private sectors of Serbian society. Unfortunately, this program drew scanty crowds, and Djindjic's efforts were constantly undermined by Draskovic, who Washington saw as greedy, authoritarian, anti-Western, and consumed by a gross craving for power.

The feud of these men drove Albright to extremes of exasperation. All America wanted was something "to happen in Serbia that we can support," she said. To overthrow Milosevic required a disciplined, focused, well-organized group of Serb dissidents, and although Albright had made untiring efforts to create a "unified, stable" opposition, she had failed. As she said of the two bitter Serb rivals, "They couldn't figure who would sit at the table, who would stand behind, who would talk."[13]

Albright decided to send State Department official John Shattuck to the Czech Republic for a meeting in August of 1999 to try and talk Draskovic into improving relations with his rival. The pressure put on Draskovic "was enormous," said a former U.S. official, and Draskovic agreed to cooperate more with Djindjic. It was no sooner said than it was forgotten. Draskovic was a "Serbia first" man, Serbia meaning himself in power. He continued to upstage his rival and energetically build his own following, unaware that as far as Washington was concerned, he had no future.

"We did not want Draskovic in there, or any other Serb ultranationalist. He was a nonstarter," said a former CIA covert operative.

Said another former agency operative, "We were going to avoid ultranationalists at all costs."

Who did that leave?

It was hard to tell. By the fall of 1999, the spectrum of Serb opposition was still faltering, timorous, hesitant, unable to commit to a course of action. For Djindjic, the prospects of success seemed to have dwindled to the vanishing point. The wind was blowing lustily at Draskovic's back, and after obtaining Clinton's and Albright's approval, Deborah Alexander, an official for the National Democratic Institute for International Affairs, a nongovernmental organization, quickly ordered a Clinton political operative, Doug Schoen, to the scene. Schoen, a Harvard professor, was a pollster who had worked for Clinton in Israel and had experience dealing with a variety of foreign political leaders. Having spent several years polling the Serbian electorate, Schoen arrived at the Marriott in Budapest and in a softly lit conference room, before an audience of twenty key opposition leaders, he flashed a PowerPoint presentation of an in-depth opinion poll of 840 Serbian voters onto a huge projection screen. It outlined a strategy for toppling Europe's last remaining communist-era ruler.

Wearing a jacket and open collar, Schoen announced his findings: "Based on reliable survey data," he declared that the anti-Milosevic opposition "could win a solid majority" without Draskovic. That was the good news. The bad news was that America's favorite candidate, Djindjic, had very high negative ratings. Milosevic had always ruled by diktat, through fraud, coercion, and bribery, and had used the war as an occasion to kill his enemies. Not long after the bombing began, Djindjic and an independent journalist, Slavka Curuvija, a bearded, thoughtful, bespectacled man in his early forties who published *The Telegraph*, wrote an article criticizing the regime. The paper was closed, and its offices emptied of desks and equipment. Soon after that, Djindjic and Curuvija found they were at the top of a state assassination list.

Djindjic and Curuvija and their wives met in an abandoned restaurant to discuss what to do. Both men decided to stay, but Curuvija, coming home with his wife after a beautiful Easter Sunday out in the city of Belgrade, was killed in the hallway of his apartment, shot in the head in front of his horrified wife. Djindjic attended the funeral but then fled to Montenegro. The Milosevic-controlled press had a field day. A man supposed to be a Serb patriot had fled his country in its hour of need. Djindjic was a tool of the Americans, a foreign lackey, and Milosevic's state media had alleged that Djindjic had even requested that NATO do "three weeks more bombing," an infamous but discrediting lie.[14]

The White House understood that for the covert operation against Milosevic to succeed, it needed to coalesce around someone not linked to Milosevic, someone who was not a Milosevic target, but someone that the majority of the Serbs could trust and respect. In brief, the opposition needed a front man, and one wasn't hard to find. American analysts soon settled on Vojislav Kostunica, a forty-six-year-old lawyer who headed the Van Party, so small people said that all its members could fit into a single van. Kostunica, a sober Serb lawyer, was perceived by the public as middle-of-the-road, a democratic nationalist, with personal integrity, who had never met or negotiated with Milosevic, and who was also free of foreign ties. He had his own decided views. Kostunica had wanted Belgrade to take a tough line on the KLA in Kosovo, maintaining that Kosovo was an integral part of Serbia. When NATO bombed his country, Kostunica never forgot or forgave, declaring, "In my soul the attacks will always remain an open wound." He loathed the establishment of the international protectorate in Kosovo, and the tone of his remarks was often anti-American. To CIA planners, however, his remarks and stance would add to his credibility and make it more difficult for Milosevic to brand him an American sycophant advancing American colonial interests in his country.

When he was offered the candidacy, Kostunica was completely stunned, and he asked for time to think it over. Saddened and oppressed by the thought of the responsibility, he left for a small summer home he had fifty miles from Belgrade. Kostunica had lived in Belgrade too long not to know what lay in store for him. On October 3, Milosevic's special police had crashed a sand-filled truck into Draskovic's car, killing three of his staff. The shaken Draskovic escaped to Montenegro. So Kostunica knew just how dangerous the stakes were, and for days he brooded in uncertainty and anxious gloom. In fact, it would take him five days to reach a decision and he would later frankly say, "I agonized over it."[15]

But he accepted.

Kostunica would be the candidate, but he would be guided and backed by a small, potent group of former Milosevic insiders, led by Djindjic, the king maker in the shadows, who would pull all the levers, activate the U.S.-recruited networks and sleeper cells, keep tracks of assets. Djindjic was key to U.S. plans to not only topple Milosevic, but at some point have him captured and taken to The Hague. Outwardly, then, Kostunica would still appear the chief actor and powerhouse, but through Djindjic, he enjoyed formidable U.S. auspices.

CRISIS OF FATE

By the spring of 2000, President Clinton for weeks had received a steady stream of intelligence reports, which he read sitting in the Oval Office or in the residence. They indicated that Milosevic was proving less and less able to satisfy the legitimate aspirations of his people. Serb society was collapsing. A sinister gangster class had appeared and was increasing in number. The public was sinking into fatal apathy, fascinated by astrology and the occult. For Milosevic's enemies, the growing despair held the promise of change. For years the Serbs had appeared to manifest a single personality, seeing, feeling, and willing in common. They had appeared to ignore the low, gross, brutal nature of the Milosevic regime for so long they had become like people who are so used to living next to a cataract, they cease to hear its noise. Now that was rapidly changing. It was typical of Milosevic that he had portrayed his military defeat at the hands of NATO as a victory, labeling his forces "invincible." That insulting lie was succeeded by another, almost as impudently audacious, in which he asserted that he hadn't lost Kosovo to NATO, and he soon began with some energy to paint "little Serbia" as the noble underdog "David," heroically leading the resistance to the power-mad "Goliath" of a suffocating, strait-jacketed, America-dominated new world order. "The West wants to conquer the whole world," he told his country.[1] Ignoring the fact that world opinion saw Serbia as one of the last, festering abscesses of the communist world system, Milosevic boasted that his country was not isolated but had flourishing relations with regimes such as Cuba, Libya, Iraq, Ukraine, and Vietnam. Milosevic once confided that China was perhaps the country closest to Serbia.

Unfortunately, no matter how grandiose his professions, Milosevic's credibility was ebbing away. Among the bulk of the people there was manifest a sluggishness, a lack of the energy of life. Most were bleak and inert. Every war Milosevic had started had begun badly and ended in catastrophe. The destruction in Belgrade and other Serb cities had been terrible— fifty-five Serb bridges lay ruined, backs broken, dumped in the Danube. Public buildings in downtown Belgrade and Serbia's economic infrastructure had been savaged to the tune of $4 billion, its military was in ruins, and here was Milosevic declaring Serbia "victorious." People knew better. Under Milosevic's leadership, Serbia had gone from almost a First World country to a failed Third World one. Half the population lived at the survival level. Serbia's Gross Domestic Product had fallen to about $1,400 per person a year and unemployment was up by 50 percent. People in the street were wearing shoes that were ten years old. When it came to Kosovo, some of his citizens defied the lie about victory. At a football match that hosted a crowd of sixty thousand, onlookers shouted, and they would chant, "You lost Kosovo, Slobo!" or onlookers chanted, "Slobo, you sold out Kosovo!" or "Slobo, leave!"[2] Milosevic tried to posit Serbian "reconstruction" as the shining, glorious motive for future accomplishment, and briefly, this flame tossed brightly to and fro, but fed by no real fire, it quickly went out. There began to dawn the feeling among the public that Slobo was not invincible, a sense that if you pierced the shell of menacing boastfulness, you would find hollowness within. Nothing alters the soul of a people like the the discovery of ineptness and fallibility in its leaders and the public's own gullibility in having admired them.

In the meantime, the final pieces of the CIA/State Department plan were being put in place. Before the operation began, the CIA completed classified studies of domestic unrest in Serbia, and the plan was to make the Serb public aware of internal dissatisfaction and thereby create more of it. This could be done by promoting "disaffection between people and rulers, underscoring the lies and denials of rights; inefficient management of the economy, corruption, indifference to the real wants and needs of the people, suppression of cultural diversity. . . . We should seek to drive wedges of resentment and suspicion . . . we should extol the merits of our system."[3]

Clinton not only read the CIA studies, he discussed their contents with advisors like Berger and Albright and CIA director Tenet. "The agency wanted really clear-cut goals. They asked a lot of questions, very detailed questions," a senior participant in those meetings said.[4]

According to former agency officials, Clinton, eager to push forward, wanted America to send its message straight to the people of Serbia whom he saw as an irreplaceable ally. They had to win their own freedom; the United States couldn't win it for them, he said, but we could aid them in their struggle to be free. Clinton wanted to forge a direct bond with the Serbian public by speaking past the Milosevic government, encouraging the masses to have confidence that defeating Milosevic was truly possible and their backing of the dictator was not in their best interest. Since Milosevic controlled the media, the United States would counter with radio broadcasts emphasizing Milosevic's decay. In addition to manipulating Serb opinion, such broadcasts could also send coded messages to agents by playing a song or using certain words. The NGOs would smuggle in tons of printed materials, and organize a get-out-the-vote campaign.

What was clear was that the operation "had to be very tightly controlled from beginning, middle and end. You had to support one group against another; you helped the people who were going to help you," said a former program operative.

Another former participant said, "You had to be very careful, you had to look at every aspect, every facet. Mike Sulik was key."

Mike Sulik, former chief of station in Warsaw and Moscow, was to head the team working with Doug Smith, COS in Bosnia, Bill Murray, former COS in Athens and then Bosnia, and COS Tyler Drumheller in Vienna, all old pros. Where the old Casey plan for Poland had been run out of the CIA's European Division in Frankfurt, Germany, this would be run out of the Budapest embassy in close cooperation with what former CIA agent Bob Baer calls "the CIA's Central Eurasian Division" at Langley, which deals with Eastern Europe and the former Soviet Union (also called the Central European Division, or CE Division). The division was headed by John Bender. Key support points would be U.S. embassies or facilities in Austria, Hungary, Kosovo, Croatia, Germany, the Czech Republic, Bulgaria, and Romania. Support would also come from the major German political parties, all of which had action arms that would contribute resources to the effort. Vienna would be the major focus of intelligence collection for the operation. According to former CIA sources, thanks to U.S. "liaison partners," intelligence poured into Vienna like a torrent through an open sluice. Austrian military intelligence had given America the Operation Horseshoe, and it had the countries of Central and Eastern Europe wired, sources said. "Vienna's information was amazing. So was Germany's," said one former participant.[5]

In addition to those resources, there were between 300,000 to 400,000 Serbs then living in Austria. When war with NATO was declared, Milosevic had called all males of military age to return to Serbia and join the Serb armed forces. Many had, but both during and after the war, many were agency walk-ins that provided the agency with extremely detailed assessments of troops, lists of security and police officials, deployments of special units or security police, and other valuable information. Many were willing to return to Kosovo and continue to report, according to one former CIA official. Throughout the war, other Serb deserters went by refugee channels or ratlines to Germany, and ended up being debriefed at Westport a former center east of Munich, once an actual military base but now a series of safe houses.[6]

The diktat of ambition is that it must expand, says Pascal. Ignoring the rising aura of decay and increasing public distrust, on July 27, Milosevic called for elections for the Yugoslav parliament, the federal presidency, and the local governments. All through the spring, the Serb had been bolstering his power as president by passing rigid and oppressive new laws, especially draconian antiterrorism legislation aimed at Otpor and the private media. By March of 2000, fifty of the students had been beaten and 190 had been detained for handing out posters drawing anti-regime graffiti or simply for wearing Otpor T-shirts.The police had files on 630 of them.

Having learned from the attempts by the Soviets to decapitate the Polish union's leadership back in the 1980s by mass arrests, Otpor set up a brilliant horizontal structure, exactly the opposite of Milosevic's centralized hierarchy of authority. Instead, Otpor was made up of small cells, and to escape capture, the cell members shifted constantly to a sophisticated network of safe houses. Operations were launched from these. A safe house used signals such as a raised blind or a closed window or a raised flag on a mailbox to indicate that all was well. If such a detail were missing, it meant the house was no longer safe.

In the meantime, the U.S.-funded NGOs bought thousands of cell phones, radio transmitters, and fax machines for the students. Calls and e-mails went through servers outside Serbia to escape Belgrade intelligence interception. Otpor was also supplied with printing equipment and supplies, and the publications and leaflets soon had an impact. The students would end by printing over sixty tons of material.

Establishing a money conduit to fund Otpor and other Serbian defectors in place had been the most urgent priority. Much of it was cash gathered in Hungary and smuggled in suitcases over the border into Serbia, preferably U.S. dollars or deutsche marks, which were widely used in Yugoslavia and had far more value than the worthless dinar. In addition, a complex web of international financial institutions was employed. To avoid detection, the money trail moved constantly. Several American and European companies unwittingly had funds transferred into Hungary through accounts already established for legitimate purposes, mainly using electronic transfers because the money could be converted more easily. By the end of the operation, even Serb businesses were active in funding dissidents, as had U.S. corporations in Hungary and neighboring countries.

Regarding the funding of certain persons and groups, the agency took pains to act through intermediaries or make recruitments while pretending that U.S. agents belonged to another country since Clinton and Albright did not want Serbians to be exposed as American lackeys and be discredited with the Serb public. Said a former operation participant, "I don't think a lot of our assets had a sense of working for the United States. It's a very gray area letting them know where their resources are coming from." Eventually $70 million was paid to the opposition, a lot of it coming over the border from Hungary.

Communications gear came next. The dissidents had to be supplied with advanced CIA communications equipment such as Inmarsat scrambler phones to organize a command, control, and intelligence (C3I) network so they could stay underground yet keep in touch and stay a step ahead of capture. Training for a few specific opposition leaders and key individuals was provided. U.S. assets within Serbia would serve as the eyes and ears for key dissidents as well as provide security and funds.

By now Otpor had developed a crisis committee to coordinate resistance activities that enabled networks from different regions to keep in close touch. U.S. intelligence was going to serve as an early warning system for the students: the NSA and CIA Special Collection Elements in neighboring countries had hacked into Milosevic's key security bureaucracies and were reading Ministry of Internal Affairs orders for police raids against the demonstrators. This intelligence was passed to dissidents, who gave advance alerts to Otpor cells, which allowed them to disperse and avoid arrest. By now, the student group even had a committee to deal with administrative tasks such as lining up safe houses, cars, and fake IDs. As the election campaign went on, money kept pouring in to Otpor, $30 million from the United States alone. An election-monitoring force of twenty thousand was trained with three people assigned to each polling place, and the huge get-out-the-vote campaign began.

"It was the humor and fearlessness of the students that really made this work," a former senior Albright advisor said.

Feeling his grip slipping, Milosevic was not going to leave any card unplayed. By July, through intricate maneuvering, Milosevic managed to set up arrangements that withered into inanition the powers of Serbia's FRY partner, Montenegro, in order to curtail any aid that pro-West republic might tender toward Otpor. Still obsessed by his political longevity, Milosevic then forced the passage of new constitutional provisions that allowed him to run for two more presidential terms, not one as established previously, which meant that if he won both, he would be in office until 2009. This move at this time was puzzling because Milosevic's current term didn't end until 2001. Yet, thanks to the new law, from now on, the Serb president would be elected by direct vote, not by majorities in the assembly, at a stroke changing the government from a parliamentary to a presidential system and enabling Milosevic to avoid dependence on any party affiliations.

Distorting the constitution in his favor did not mean Milosevic was going to leave behind any loose ends. He was going to deal with danger from whatever quarter it came, and in June, Draskovic, who lived in Budka, Montenegro, was wounded in an attempted assassination.

Throughout this spring and early summer, Milosevic had displayed the cold, scheming egotism, the invulnerable conceit, of a great and dominating will. From having been periodically the victim of the doubts of alienated solitude, Milosevic now felt triumphant and impervious—able finally to make his value felt, and it was, at this moment, quite inexplicably, that he would take a step that would inflict on himself a setback of mammoth dimensions—his bid for the presidency via direct elections. Unfortunately, Milosevic had completely misjudged the time like a man who stays on a train as it goes past his stop. Just how far opposition infiltration of Milosevic's security forces, special police, and other pillars of his regime had already progressed became clear when secret e-mails from dissenters within the regime alerted Otpor of this news twelve days before Milosevic made it public.

Since he was certain of victory, the Serb leader's campaign began lamely, restricted to platitudinous speeches during perfunctory visits at friendly factories that hardly stirred the pulse. "The West wants to rule the world," he said, and that remained his basic theme.

He told the crowds that the West was trying to conquer everything and that his opposition was subversive and working for NATO and that a victory for the "NATO mercenaries" would mean poverty and chaos. His wife also made many speeches, talking to large crowds "like a schoolmarm," as she said later. She tried to attract the youth vote by running funky rock and roll commercials featuring sexy, bare-bellied young women.

Unfortunately, the tide of circumstance was flowing in irresistible strength toward a different consummation. In August of 2000, right under Milosevic's nose, U.S. diplomat William Montgomery opened the Office of Yugoslav Affairs, a five-person satellite office of the U.S. embassy in Budapest. The OYA had been a personal and pressing priority for Albright. There were now seventy thousand Otpor students in 130 groups with twelve regional offices, and Otpor leaders were schooled in nonviolent techniques designed to undermine authority by a retired U.S. Army colonel, Robert Helvey. Helvey taught the principles of Gene Sharp's book *From Dictatorship to Democracy: A Conceptual Framework for Liberation*. Translated chapters were handed from cell to cell throughout the country. Seminars for activists were held in the sumptuous Budapest Hilton. The courses for the students began in August, lasted ten days, and dealt with general strikes, fraternization, the principles of asymmetric warfare. As Sharp said in an interview, his nonviolent method "is not ethical. It has nothing to do with pacifism. It is based on an analysis of power in a dictatorship and how to break it by withdrawing the obedience of its citizens and the key institutions of society."[7]

To Sharp, the first step in undermining a brutal regime was to stop being afraid of it. Seeing their own brutalization as a means of creating sympathetic support and exposing the regime's weakness, Otpor members began to provoke police and were sometimes kicked or beaten by booted, flak-vested, helmeted police armed with truncheons. A milestone occurred in a small town in southeastern Serbia, Vladicin Han. On September 8, 2000, under cover of darkness, four Otpor activists were out spray-painting clenched fists or *"Gotov je"* or *"Vreme je"* ("It's Time"), when they were caught by police and briefly detained, then allowed to go home. When they returned the next day to be photographed and fingerprinted, they were confronted by three drunken policemen. The violence was triggered by a T-shirt worn by a twenty-two-year-old that had printed on it *"Promene,"* "Changes." His shirt was ripped off, and he was shoved into an office and beaten to the brink of unconsciousness. His twenty-year-old friend was sporting an earring. The liquor-ridden police chief shouted at the young man that he was "a decadent Muslim and hater of Serbs" as he was assaulted. Another young man the same age was half-strangled by the police chief. A twenty-three-year old was also almost strangled. All were threatened with "liquidation" at the Kosovo border.[8]

The news of the beatings was like an electric spark spreading through the town. By late evening, three hundred infuriated adults had gathered outside the police station, demanding answers, but the three young men had already been released to a local health clinic. The rage didn't abate—what had surfaced among the parents was a cauldron of unsatisfied hatred. "These were not slum kids," said a former senior Clinton advisor. "They were solid middle-class kids, and when they showed up at home dripping blood, or with a hen's egg on their forehead from a club, it radicalized their parents."

"Every student beaten up meant 1,000 new votes for Otpor," said a former administration official.

The beatings accomplished something more important than crystallizing the opposition's outrage: they dissolved the animosities among the adult opposition leaders that had left them rudderless and divided for so long. The young had shamed them. The students had taken the lead in defying with intrepidity and fearlessness all the corrupt brutality of a vicious leader. Without the student group, the Milosevic opposition had been a gray ember red at the center. The ember now began to brighten.

Using its covert monies, the student group began to buy T-shirts, stickers, leaflets that bore its dramatic emblem. Soon the clenched fist of Otpor appeared on the walls, postal boxes, cars, the sides of trucks, statues, all over the cities of Yugoslavia. The group had an imaginative, boldly innovative streak. They painted red footsteps on the ground to symbolize Milosevic's bloody departure from parliament; passersby in the street found thrust into their hands cardboard telescopes that described a falling star called "Slobo-tea." They also used a wide range of public relations techniques including polling, leafleting, and paid advertising. "The poll results were very important," said Ivo Andric, then a marketing student at Belgrade University. "At every moment, we knew what to say to the people."[9]

As the days went on, recruitment was expanded, new assets were acquired, and in cities such as Banja Luka in northern Bosnia, in Pristina in Kosovo, in the provincial cities of Serbia, activity was mounting to a climax. All the beatings of crowds, the fixing of the 1997 elections, the suppression of newspapers, the disbanding of parties, the dismissal of officials, the snubs, the humiliating defeats, the arrogant indifference of Milosevic had been piling up, generating a pent-up violence that was going to be discharged in one shattering explosion of revolt.

In the meantime, the United States, Britain, and others were seeing to it that Serbia felt encircled. Covert operations continued and gained momentum as meetings to ensure support were held in Szeged, in Hungary, in Croatia, in Ulm, Germany, and in Montenegro. In addition to Hungary, the U.S. embassies in Bulgaria and Romania were involved. The United States and others now got busy attempting to create a new post-Milosevic elite. Suddenly the Western-financed Political Academy for Central and Southeastern Europe established a program for training the opposition. The academy had ties to Vojislav Kostunica's Van Party. Another Western-financed organization was the Balkan Academy of Leading Reporters, which gave financial and expert assistance to opposition media prior to the election. There was another such program run by the British Foreign Office.

When Milosevic grew ugly and threatened to destabilize Montenegro, Wesley Clark put elements of U.S. forces in the republic, with a contingency option to launch a military assault to rescue Montenegro's pro-Western president if Milosevic were reckless enough to invade. To make the threat real, the NATO allies were in movement all over the map. In Italy, the allied leaders signed a lead contract to begin training exercises in October at the Koren training ground near Kosovo in southeast Bulgaria. The French signed a similar agreement that would use French forces including tanks to train in central Bulgaria at Novo Selo. Plans were afoot for U.S. forces to lead the Shabal training grounds in northeastern Bulgaria as well, while near Split in Croatia, there were joint exercises between U.S. and Croat forces. Very quietly British warships were sent to the region.

Everywhere the Serb ruling circle looked, it saw only a deepening darkness.

48

THE GAIN THAT DARKENS

One of the most remarkable of Milosevic's innate characteristics was his belief, mistaken or not, in his own supreme ability not only to survive but to prevail. As the elections approached, he'd lost none of his predatory ruthlessness and worked to mobilize every corrupt government mechanism to ensure his victory. Every senior official in his government was dependent on him for his or her job. Replace him, and Milosevic's close associates knew that their house, their life, their advantages, their position, would be destroyed and cast away, and since many were people of selfish and reckless enjoyment, Milosevic had no worries about being obeyed. The Serb had also carefully pruned and weeded the army of dissidents and skeptics, and he felt he had little fear from his military since they would be reluctant to bite the hand that fed it so well.

Milosevic was also complacent because the suspense of the outcome had been removed. In running, his weapons would be dissimulation, deception, and outright fraud. Elections to Milosevic had always been a fundamental form of buying, selling, and exchange. His major concern now was to ensure his fraud would not be detected and so he barred international electoral observers from Serbia. Only those from countries friendly to his regime were to have access. In addition, Montenegro, Serbia's junior partner, was so wounded by being stripped of its status, it was boycotting the elections entirely, removing another obstacle. Spying, deception, corruption, entrapment had always produced for him in the past, and Milosevic had every reason to believe that there would be no defense against the avalanche of theft he was about to unleash.

Yet he was making a drastic miscalculation. He saw himself as a glorious leader, but the obligatory reverence Milosevic usually received from his military had vanished. It no longer esteemed him as a great Serb patriot. In addition, Serbia was a small country where everyone in the upper ranks knew everyone else, and recruitment of assets by the United States had reached very deep. U.S. and other intelligence agents had discovered a cache of forged ballots that Milosevic planned to use to win the elections for the municipalities, provinces, and presidency. The insidious scheme involved a horde of "fabricated votes from Kosovo," a former senior U.S. intelligence official said. "There was always a big stash of phony votes there."

Clinton was told by CIA director George Tenet that Milosevic's plan was to move the bogus votes out of Kosovo municipalities and into the Serbian presidential election at the last minute. Milosevic would then "gerrymander the opposition areas with the fake votes and ensure that the opposition lost," according to a former senior U.S. advisor. U.S. special envoy to the Balkans Jim O'Brien put it this way: "He has redrawn electoral districts so that cities and towns with opposition support will elect fewer members in the federal parliament than will those where pro-Milosevic forces predominate." In addition to seizing materials, and intimidating media outlets or beating students, O'Brien said that Milosevic was telling government workers they might not receive pensions if they did not produce evidence that they voted for Milosevic or his party.[1]

As the days blurred by, Albright and Berger, Gore, and the whole U.S. covert operation went on high alert. Extreme care had been taken to create a system to monitor the elections to guard against just such blatant rigging. Operating under the authority of Djindjic's Democratic Opposition of Serbia (DOS), three U.S. or National Endowment of Democracy–trained monitors would be provided for every polling place, a total of twenty thousand across Serbia. They kept in touch via cell phones that again used servers outside the state to prevent tampering by Serbian counterintelligence, using U.S. technological assistance. The creation of a parallel vote count "was one of the most outstanding achievements" of the U.S. dethronement plan, said a former senior official who was one of its architects.

On September 24, the turnout for the election was large, not good news for Milosevic. His plan to fix the election had abruptly collapsed, when, at the last minute, he discovered that because of an error of procedure he could not shift the bogus Kosovo ballots from the municipal to the presidential election. At 2 A.M. the next day, the DOS independent voting results were announced but in a way designed to entice Milosevic into taking an incriminating step. When the DOS gave the results, they deliberately exaggerated them, declaring that Kostunica had won 52 percent of the vote, with Milosevic coming in second with only 33 percent. When Kostunica heard the results, he said, "Dawn is coming to Serbia."[2]

An infuriated Milosevic then grabbed fellow war criminal Nikola Sainovic, ordering him to fix the results. Milosevic supporters claimed that Slobodan, not Kostunica, had won. Raucous squabbling arose, and the matter was referred to the Federal Election Commission, which was under Milosevic's domination. Yet the edginess of the public mood disconcerted that body. Kostunica was immensely popular with a multitude of extremely discontented minds, and rather than immediately obeying Milosevic, the commission unexpectedly hung fire. The tension of the situation was extreme. The whole country was riveted in pin-drop suspense As pressure mounted, the commission was finally coerced into a compromise. It lamely announced that Kostunica had won only 49 percent of the total, just under the 50 percent required by the constitution. Milosevic had won 39 percent, it said. This meant that a second round of voting would be required.

The Djindjic group dreaded this the way a dog dreads fire. The opposition was certain to lose in a second round. Only Milosevic, with his cold, conniving egotism, would delight in the prospect of a second round, convinced he could secure it employing the same unsavory means that he'd used in the first. Or, as some feared, he would claim foreign interference, and cancel another round altogether and move to an all-out dictatorship. As the country awaited Kostunica's reply, the restive people of the country passed through every possible stage of anxiety, hope, distress, and fear of consequences. Events were clearly hurtling toward a crossroads.

Matters were still up in the air, when on September 26, seven opposition leaders, including Djindjic and Nebojsa Covic, the former mayor of Belgrade, met at a sports club in Belgrade after having had the place swept to ensure there were no bugs. All were members of the DOS opposition, and before the election had met to produce a strategy that would provoke a revolution. Covic was a pleasant-faced, appealing, dark-haired man, a Serb patriot, a person of decent uprightness, possessed of a formidable force of will. He was also an extremely able organizer who was part of a ring of dissatisfied well-connected men, all outcasts from the government like himself, but who, like him, retained sources in key government positions, able to induce paralysis in the machinery if and when the right moment came.

The discussions exhibited a grim singleness of purpose. All the plotters knew that Milosevic would not leave office voluntarily, but, if pushed, would callously put Serbia and its people through the most horrific pitch of harsh intensity in order to come out on top. Even if Kostunica participated in a second round, it would be so completely rigged, he would be sure to be defeated. Already U.S. intelligence knew that in the city of Nis one of the election commissioners had recorded votes from penal and correctional institutions, and that the security guards were not allowing the commissioners to view the full results of the ballot papers, claiming they were acting on the orders of commission headquarters. Milosevic's vote totals from Kosovo showed 145,000 votes cast for him even though members of his regime had said publicly there were only 45,000 votes in the entire province. The plotters knew they had to shun any second round. Instead, there had to be a revolution.

A revolution was possible. The plotters knew that although Milosevic could be counted on to rig the vote in Belgrade, in cities like Novi Sad, Cacak, and Nis, he had no following. The opposition would win the elections in these places, hold them, and barricade themselves in the cities. They would then organize mass demonstrations, throw up roadblocks around Belgrade, and finally push a mass march on the capital. Covic, for one, said he believed such a march would be necessary. As he later said of Milosevic, "I knew the man. I knew he would never concede."[3]

Violence was a common Milosevic tool, and the Djindjic plotters decided that if assaulted by Milosevic goons, they would respond with the same level of force. If it meant clubs and bats, then it would be clubs and bats. If they were shot at, they would shoot back and shoot to kill. The decision was made with everyone aware of the possible consequences. Covic knew the country was awash with guns. He already had a party that was well armed. So then and there the plotters decided it was all or nothing. If Milosevic attacked, they would attack in return, energetically and determinedly, relentlessly. Djindjic felt the same about what was coming—it was make or break. "The winner will stay, the loser will be finished, both physically and as a party," he said.[4]

The group took care not to invite Kostunica to either meeting.

Although Kostunica himself was being subsidized by the United States, he used the aid unhappily and disapproved of the covert U.S. support. He disliked Otpor because he believed its funding was dubious. When Ambassador Montgomery had opened the satellite embassy in Budapest to assist in the covert plan, Kostunica had condemned the move as blatant interference in Serbia's internal affairs. He wasn't wrong. Indeed, so much money was pouring in from Hungary that a British diplomat said at the time Milosevic would have been within his rights canceling the second round on the grounds of foreign interference. But Kostunica knew that Milosevic had lost the consent of the governed and that he had won it fairly. At the news of his win, protests were rising in the international community with leaders calling for Milosevic to resign. "You lost. Go," Britain's Tony Blair told him. Clinton contacted Milosevic and asked him to leave, promising to lift the economic sanctions when he did. The Serbian Orthodox Church weighed in, calling for a peaceful transfer of power and announcing Kostunica as Serbia's new ruler. When the election commission called for a second round of voting October 8, Kostunica made up his mind. He would be willing to have a fair recount, but to consent to a second round would be to betray the people who had voted for him.

Convinced that he had a clear field, Milosevic was preparing for a new campaign, as usual hiding his true designs behind the camouflage of phony legal procedures. As Belgrade analyst Bratislav Grubacic has remarked, Milosevic "was more of a 'semi-dictator' always trying to have some legal basis for what he did."[5] Meanwhile, disquieting reports spread rapidly— that Milosevic's family had fled to Moscow, that his daughter had suffered a nervous collapse. More and more the Milosevic government was seen as a mass of slops and pestilence, a swamp of impenetrable vines and twisted creepers infested by poisonous spiders and snakes, emitting the vile stench of rotting growth. The peak of the crisis came when, on October 4, the commission announced that it had annulled the September 24 election results, sweeping away any pretense of government legality. At last the diverse hatreds had coalesced into a formidable mass. Djindjic and the DOS leadership knew that to succeed it had to declare a general strike, and once the strike had succeeded, they had to seize key symbolic government buildings to make clear Milosevic's loss of power. As the men bent over to study maps, they made their decision: they would seize two essential symbols of Milosevic's rule, the Federal Parliament Building and the hated state-run TV station Radio Television Serbia.

For Milosevic, a menace more frightening to his power than ever before was on the march.

49

GOTOV JE!

Gustave Le Bon once observed that, "It has been very justly said that governments are not overthrown, but that they commit suicide," and Milosevic's rule would do just that.

Serbia began to slide into rebellion on Friday, September 29. Otpor had announced a general strike, and traveling like a vast wave across the country businesses shut down, primary and secondary schools closed their doors, cinemas were dark, roads were blocked. The country's western border was closed. The Kolubara mine forty miles southwest of Belgrade was on strike, halting coal deliveries for the country's thermonuclear power stations. Milosevic felt it coming and warned: "I consider it my duty to warn of the consequences of the activities supported and financed by the NATO governments. It should be evident to all that they are not attacking Serbia to get at Milosevic, but attacking Milosevic to get at Serbia." Belgrade had ignored the strike announcement.[1] The capital was a busy, energetic hive of activity. Big, hulking city buses, packed with people, were breezing by, the major roadways were choked with trucks and cars, the street vendors had begun to open their stalls, and shops were open, while on the walks droves of trooping people headed to work. The blockades that had brought the rest of the country to a standstill were clearly having no effect here.

Plans were in place nonetheless, the actors tensed in readiness, and on Thursday, October 5, it happened. By 7 A.M. Belgrade time, five convoys were on the road, headed for Belgrade, all coming in from cities in the provinces. Two thousand people from Uzice riding twenty-four buses and 135 cars; fifteen minutes later, 230 trucks and fifty-two buses and hundreds of cars leave Cacak, a total of ten thousand people in the fourteen-mile-long convoy; then another convoy with 230 cars, a thousand more people; then another convoy with 230 cars with at least a thousand people; and another moving in twenty-five buses and about 250 cars.

U.S. intelligence operatives or assets among the dissidents alerted the CIA chief of station, who called the watch officer at the agency on a secure phone. It was 1 A.M. in Washington. The watch officer called the duty officer, who called James Pavitt, deputy director of operations, who then called National Security Advisor Sandy Berger. At the State Department, William Montgomery, the U.S. ambassador, called the State Operations Center, which alerted Albright. Someone called Al Gore, and one by one the Principals were alerted, and finally, President Clinton. Some of the data and pictures of the scene were being sent in real time via satellite relay and the images appeared on the screen in the Situation Room. There were hastily called personal conferences, reports from U.S. embassies, summaries from various U.S. intelligence agencies, e-mails flying back and forth, Clinton always in close consultation with Berger and Tenet.

Then came a key intercept that sent a stab of anxious pain in the stomach. Milosevic had issued orders: "At any price stop the demonstrators." In Serbia, the opposition knew of this because Djindjic's party was reading all orders issued to police by the Ministry of Internal Affairs, thanks to U.S. Special Collection Elements and NSA taps. Covic and Djindjic kept in constant touch by CIA-supplied secure scrambler phones. Covic had been busy. The night before he and the other opposition leaders had held meetings with Serb police to obtain assurances that they would not fire. In one last-minute unnerving encounter, Djindjic was summoned to a meeting with one of Milosevic's most brutal operators, a young, handsome, but sinister colonel of Serbia's Special Operations Unit named Milorad "Legija" Ulemek. When Djindjic met Legija secretly in a side street and asked the colonel where he stood, the unemotional solider said simply that the demonstrators were not to fire at the police, adding, "I'm not going to shoot people for the man who stole the elections."[2]

For the city of Belgrade, October 5 began as just another day. Strikes in the provinces had paralyzed the cities, yet beneath the surface, something unusual was developing. Certain inexplicable events had begun to occur within the Milosevic power structure. For example, many Serb police had not shown up for work that day, and even with swirling rumors that a large number of menacing convoys of protesters were on the way, the Belgrade police were ordered to arm themselves only with batons and tear gas, not rifles. In addition, the police were told not to operate in massed formations but to break up into widely dispersed small units—an entirely puzzling way to proceed.

Jarring deviations of procedure were not limited to the police. The Army chief of staff and the head of Serbia's armed forces, Gen. Nebojsa Pavkovic, would wake up on the day of the revolution to discover that there were few soldiers in Belgrade because, unknown to him, major units of the army had been transferred to other barracks days earlier. Even at the Ministry of Internal Affairs there had been a sudden, unexplained break in the chain of command. Gen. Vlastimir Djordjevic, who wielded the major authority over the Belgrade police, had casually said of Milosevic, "He's lost the elections and should step down." When the remark reached Milosevic's ears, Djordjevic was abruptly removed. His replacement was Gen. Radovan Stojilkovic, who was talking to police units and issuing orders that morning, but who unfortunately had no police authority. Confusion reigned. Other anomalies began to crop up. The careful recruitment of defectors within Milosevic's security forces by Djindjic, Covic and other activists and intelligence agents was starting to take effect.

Said a former senior CIA agent closely involved with the event, "That's the whole idea of a blocking mechanism—that when the target pushes the panic button for help, none ever comes."

Details began to appear on the screens in the Situation Room as the digitalized images arrived. In Belgrade on the police screens, the first gathering of citizens occurred at 8 A.M. near the Belgrade railway station near Belgrade University. By now blockades had sprung up all over the city, blocking all routes that could be used by military or police reinforcements. Garbage containers, the City Transport Company's buses and trams, water tankers for the city's parks, machinery from the road workers division, protesters had seized them all.

By 9 A.M., news came that the demonstrators were using roadside garbage containers to block streets in a Belgrade suburb. All of this was relayed in real time to the White House.

According to a U.S. intercept, Gen. Nebojsa Pavkovic, the chief of staff of the Yugoslav army, was listening to news on the police bands when he received a police call asking for assistance and claiming people had been killed at the state-owned television station, RTS. Pavkovic heard the report and retorted with calm disdain, "No one is dead." The army was going to stand aside.

Milosevic as yet had no clue that his most valuable pillars of support were no longer in place.

Hordes of excited people were pouring into Belgrade, converging on it from all sides. Otpor was waiting. Each person knew what his particular task force should be doing, where the group should be positioned, and what the rest, armed with stones, arms, or antitank weapons, should do if attacked by police. Trained by their U.S. intelligence handlers, they were drilled in how to use the equipment and had mastered their communications network, a new energy flowing through the groups.

At noon a crowd of three thousand began to drift in an uneven mass from the main railway station to the Federal Parliament Building, a bulky, imposing structure that covered an entire city block. It was a bright, fine, clear day, and the Parliament looked like an American state capitol, with graceful faded green domes and thick yellow walls. It was surrounded by long islands of green hedges, and in front were long bulky concrete planters full of colorful, blossoming flowers. Bright sunlight lay on the whole scene, lighting up an impressive sculpture, *Black Horses at Play*. The Parliament was an important target, "the symbol of might, the power that has dictated our lives for fifty years," as a Serb observer called it.

Soon thousands of angry people swarmed in to form a solid mass in front of the Parliament Building, sending up an ear-splitting din. Confronting them was a force of menacing, stern-faced police clad in flak jackets and equipped with riot shields. Smoke already hung in a choking haze over the city from burning trash containers. The animated, agitated crowd was constantly growing in numbers.

In the White House, Clinton stayed in close touch with events, once again voicing his concern to Berger over possible civilian casualties. The president displayed a high level of mental energy, and constantly asked questions of advisors, several about the whereabouts of Milosevic and what the latest intercepts were.

Back in Belgrade, a sea of screaming people choked the street. Soon, the broad thoroughfare in front of the Parliament was jammed full by an enormous mass of incensed and agitated people. One of the men in the front rank of the demonstrators was a U.S. agent of influence and top Djindjic deputy, Ceda Jovanovic.[3] The twenty-nine-year-old was dressed in his battle gear, wide black trousers with big pockets on the sides, a flak jacket, a sweater, a thick rustling jacket, and Nike sneakers. His outfit had been a trademark since the 1996 demonstrations over the stolen elections. Jovanovic had nothing to lose. Milosevic had put an assassination team on him; and there were nine charges against him for "undermining the state," and he faced a five-month sentence on the same charge. Jovanovic had organized the strike at Kolubara, removing and destroying key equipment to render the mine inoperable, just in case Milosevic planned to use troops or strike-breakers to get it up and running.

The crowd's din was unendurable. It grew and grew until there were 500,000 intent, furious demonstrators, held back by four thousand nervous police. The tension tightened a notch, then clicked up another. Time seemed to hang fire, then an opposition member brought a bottle down on a policeman's head, and there was a sudden rush and commotion, the police charging, veering here and there, hitting and chopping, as people fled wildly, ducking, stumbling over one another. The police ceased. The two groups drew apart. An empty space of only a few yards separated them, like a line that separates two hostile armies.

The police with their tight faces stared in hatred at the mob.

The police attack was greeted with rabid fury. There was a lull, then the police fired tear gas. In a rippling movement of unreasoning panic, people fled. More gas was fired until a white, milky, poisonous fog covered much of the scene. People held handkerchiefs or clothes to try and cover their lower faces, some on their hands and knees, dazed, long strings of phlegm dangling from their noses. When the gas would clear, and the thick, billowing fog would lift and thin a bit, the forward ranks of protesters again suddenly surged forward, people crushing one another, shouting and squeezing desperately, in an attempt to reach the front doors. The tall, massive front doors remained tightly locked. After a flailing rampage of police fury, the demonstrators were driven back.

Meanwhile, out in the streets, protesters were turning over cars and setting them afire, and suddenly the crowd again hurled itself forward in another sharp rush, pushing and panting. The screaming mob, its members trampling one another, were all tightly packed together in front of the locked Parliament doors, trying to force their way in. The doors stayed locked. The wild, ear-splitting uproar reached a new height; the people were not to be stopped. Within them lurked the determination that could mount one final, supreme effort. One of the Otpor leaders said later their mood was one of unadulterated rage, and he was ready to be killed, but he was determined to win if he lived.

The police, making short dashes, clubbing and pummeling, once again drove the crowd back, and it halted for a moment, stricken with indecision, when suddenly the clogged, howling masses drew apart, and a bulldozer appeared. With a large hump in his back from a spine broken in childhood, wearing an Otpor T-shirt, the operator, Ljubisav "Joe" Djokic (or Dujukic), from Cacak, had joined the convoy because he felt that it had been Milosevic's corruption that had caused the collapse of his cement and sanding business.

Now he was out to even the score. He owned a bright yellow bulldozer, an American-made 538, a front-loading, earthmoving machine. He had joined the Cacak convoy accompanied by a seventy-two-year-old pugnacious baker named Milan. Djokic had led the charge up one of the major Belgrade thoroughfares and reached the Parliament only to find the ground floor windows heavily barred, the doors locked, and the way blocked by the bulky cement planters out front.

Djokic eyed the obstacles, his temper rising. "Fuck it," he said. He gunned the engine of his machine and drove straight in. He smashed into the planters, then lowered the bulldozer's blade to allow the young protesters to swarm aboard the scoop. He steered the machine in as close as he could to the building, then raised the blade just above the heads of police, allowing the Otpor people and protesters to scramble over the second floor balcony railings and vanish inside the building.

Soon, the front doors were unlocked, and the wildly excited mass began to funnel through the opening like water pouring through a lock. As the protesters entered the building, there opened before them the large, orange, high-ceiling halls, richly carpeted, the walls lined by graceful statues on pedestals. The crowd consisted of men, women, and kids of all ages and sizes from all walks, states, and conditions of life, clad in sport coats, in T-shirts, in colorful ski jackets and sweaters. When they burst inside, the people had expected a formidable, bristling phalanx of police but initially found only a meager fifty of them, some frightened and crying. In droves, the students ran in joyous triumph through the building, taking TV sets, office chairs, computers, phones, a palm tree.

Milosevic had lost none of his taste for slaughter. He now ordered his favorite butcher, Maj. Goran Radosavljevic, the killer of Adem Jashari and the author of Racak, to drop tear gas canisters from helicopters on the shouting, screaming sea of humanity outside. The major knew that a gas canister weighed at least twenty-five pounds, and that dropped from a hundred feet, would kill anyone instantly. Radosavljevic, who was hovering in the air over the vast mob, made a decision. As a frantic Milosevic kept shouting at him to drop the canisters, Radosavljevic replied, "There is too much smoke to be able to see." Milosevic insisted. "There is too much smoke to be able to see," he lied again. Radosavljevic kept repeating his lie until, on his order, the mission was aborted. The butcher of Racak had had enough of killing.

Inside the Parliament Building, a few terrified police began to retreat, firing rubber bullets or tear gas. The sound was like the pop of bursting bottles. Gas canisters landed hissing on the carpeted floors, and the poisonous milky layers began rising again, the view was obscured, and people were soon coughing, choking, and vomiting, blinded. A few fled in confusion back outside, but most of the clogged sea of people stayed and re-formed, still in the grip of unappeasable rage. More doors suddenly swung open, and people rushed in, swarming over the floor like ants. The police broke and ran for their lives.

The Parliament was soon ablaze. A dense bank of smoke billowed from it and rose as a huge dark smudge into the blue sky. The protesters would be seen withdrawing after the battle, dragging off cooking oil, bottles of mineral water, chairs, racks, paintings, furniture, liberated police helmets sitting at a jaunty angle on their heads, but some of the opposition still had work left to do. The most determined like Jovanovic gained the top floor, discovering the hundreds of boxes of forged ballots that Milosevic had intended to use in the second round. They grabbed these and tipped them over the balconies. The phony ballots fluttered and twinkled down through the air as lightly as fish scales. The Parliament Building had fallen in thirty-seven minutes.

It was late in the afternoon as the other government strongholds toppled one after another. The crowd first burned the offices of Mira Markovic's Yugoslav Left party, leaving its walls a blazing mass of flames. A huge pall of soiled smoke hung over the street in front of the building. Milosevic was up in his white, fortified compound of a house, which sat high on the side of a heavily wooded hill. His situation was growing worse with each hour. With frantic urgency, he called General Pavkovic—Milosevic wanted to call out the army. Pavkovic said calmly that the army was not trained for street warfare. That was a matter for the police. Milosevic said to him, "You are refusing to obey my orders," but Pavkovic repeated what he had said. In a furious temper, Milosevic hung up on him.

Radio Television Serbia was an especially hated target. Called "The Bastille" by the public, it stood on No. 10 Takoska Street, and for years it had been a key tool in Milosevic's seduction of his populace. RTS for years had "reinvented reality, falsified it, glamorized it, faked it, varnished and re-painted it," a Serb journalist said. The first assault began at 4:35 in the afternoon, but the place was swarming with blue-uniformed police. Two cordons of police were working their way along the street, firing tear gas in all directions, but they were a disorganized rabble, and the crowd realized the police were trying to retreat. Two police buses followed slowly along, and the cops bent, dodged, ducked, cast wild looks about while from behind buses, cars, garbage containers came a heavy rain of missiles: bricks, stones, bottles, even pieces of wood torn from the benches that lined the walks of the park. Everywhere the police were surrounded by shouting faces full of atrocious rage. They began firing. Rubber bullets flew thick and fast.

People scattered and dashed for cover. Part of the TV station was already on fire, the burning curtains flapping through the jaggedly shattered windows.

The idea of getting inside had gripped the people with desperate urgency, stirring the crowd to fresh effort. Some police were trying to get out of the place, but a roaring, impassable mass of shouting humanity barred the way. And suddenly a yellow bulldozer appeared, rumbling at full speed up the street. Police inside the building fired at it, but it came on and crashed into the building at full speed, reversed and crashed again, smashing at it a total of four times. When the police fired bullets or tear gas, the canisters and shells bounced harmlessly off the scoop and the driver's cab. The fury of battle on him, Joe Djokic yelled, "Let them fire everything they've got. Fuck them!"[4]

The building was on fire, and thousands of people moved in a sluggish flood toward it. Finally, after he reversed his bulldozer a final time, Joe's machine crashed inside. The protesters poured in, grim-faced, carrying clubs, stones, or sticks, hunting for police tormentors. Unlike the police at the Parliament who hadn't fired, Joe would find eighty police bullet holes in his cab. (It is remarkable that only five people were wounded in the melee.)

People were milling about when suddenly horror spread through the crowd and everyone froze. Heads pivoted as if on sticks. At 5:35 P.M., Col. Legija Ulemek's dreaded legion, the Red Berets, the Special Operations Unit, popularly called "The Boys from Brazil," appeared. Legija was in the lead vehicle. One person yelled, "We're finished, they'll shoot us all like rabbits!" Panic swept through the people. A large rock had almost shattered the windshield of Legija's vehicle, which came on and finally jerked to a stop. Legija stepped out of his vehicle, and removed his gas mask, the people starting to call out his name. He replied, "What's this all about, brothers? Why don't you stop shooting?" Then he gave the crowd the Serbian three-fingered salute and got back in his car. The armored column pulled back and disappeared.[5]

It was over. The RTS building was left a burning wreck as were Milosevic's Socialist Party headquarters. It wasn't all noble or pretty. Hatred is the dominant force of a mob. Staffers at the TV station had been punched and brutalized. In a fit of vindictive malice, the crowd had particularly enjoyed trashing the perfume store of Milosevic's son, Marko, located on a posh downtown street.

But by 6 P.M., the government of Yugoslavia had changed hands. The RTS building was burning from the top down, its steel and timber structure sagging to collapse. Howling in happiness, a wild, delirious mass of humanity poured into the streets, a flood tide converging from every streetcorner. The streets were choked solid by joyous, exalted celebrating people, their eyes and faces radiant with happiness. Some were ecstatic, hugging, crying, holding their arms over their heads, jubilant and triumphant. They danced, drank, kissed, cried, savoring to the full the unexpected freeing of their spirit. *"Gotov je!"* they shouted. "He's finished!"

50

TO CURE AN EVIL

Milosevic returned to his fortified house, living with his family in the old Tito residence at 13 Uzicka for which he paid no bills or charges, using state monies to fund a private army of heavily armed bodyguards. His son, Marko, had fled to Russia to escape criminal probes, and the ousted Serb leader was adrift in a strange, self-isolated, disordered existence. In the parliamentary elections that fall, his socialists garnered 13 percent of the vote, making them the largest opposition group in the new Kostunica government. Now and then Milosevic would make the odd speech damning NATO or vilifying his enemies, but they were of little effect, like casting a stone into a marsh. Sealed up in himself, Milosevic seemed a failed and futile figure.

Throughout his tenure, Milosevic had been immune from the actions of courts of law and other forms of interference, but he was no longer part of a system driven by the compulsions of power. Since his indictment by The Hague in May of 1999, he was a wanted man and alleged war criminal, yet he did not seem to grasp his dawning predicament. "Our circumstances may change, but our ideas of ourselves do only slowly," said the English essayist William Hazlitt. Failure in a leader makes his subject people question his viability, and as Le Bon said, "The moment prestige is questioned, it is no longer prestige."

Rivalries quickly emerged within the new government. Who was going to dominate the stage and direct the action? Once the threat that had created unanimity of purpose had evaporated, the victors had split into hostile camps and greedy, self-seeking factions, and there was a lot of hauling and pulling in different directions. One group, made up of conservative Serbian nationalists like Kostunica, wanted Serbia to find its own path in its own way and in its own time. Pitted against this were energetic pro-Western reformers like Prime Minister Djindjic, who wanted Serbia to hurry and end its isolation and join the West.

Kostunica was ambivalent about the West when he wasn't hostile to it. One irreconcilable issue between the president and prime minister lay with The Hague, war crimes, and what was to be done with Milosevic. The stiff, humorless Kostunica had wanted Milosevic left alone. Kostunica disliked NATO, had opposed the bombing, and thought The Hague an anti-Serbian institution "selective in its justice." Kostunica had vehemently disapproved of the CIA covert operation that had been run from the satellite U.S. embassy office in Budapest. He thought it imperialist, he thought it meddling, he thought it "egotistical" and inappropriate, although when U.S. intelligence had actively aided his presidency before and after the election, he hadn't complained, former U.S. officials said.

Djindjic was of a different mind. Both Kostunica and Djindjic saw the preservation and aggrandizement of their own positions as their chief mission, but Djindjic's position was ambiguous. He had come to office thanks to covert American backing in the hope that he would prove key to creating a new, more liberal political order based on democracy and free markets; but he was operating at least in part under American auspices, and the Americans wanted Milosevic in The Hague.

Upon Kostunica's victory, President Clinton had called to express the usual pro forma congratulations. Washington, it appeared, was pleased, but in politics appearances are everything. Behind the scenes, Kostunica was to receive a much sterner American message. Secretary of State Madeleine Albright sent to Belgrade her special envoy to the Balkans, one of her best advisors, Jim O'Brien, who had played a key part in setting up the overthrow of Milosevic. When he met with Kostunica, the American had been exceptionally blunt. The extradition of Milosevic "is a clear marker of your acceptance of the rule of law," he told the new president. O'Brien added, "This is not a subject about which you have much of a choice."[1]

In Clinton's view, the huge debts of blood Milosevic had run up during his campaigns of aggressive war, massacre, rape, and plunder had to be paid in full. In the closing days of the Clinton administration, a series of meetings began with the new Bush group, especially between Albright and the new secretary of state, Colin Powell, to ensure the covert seizure of Milosevic, including his capture and transport to The Hague, would go ahead as planned.

Berger was involved, Gelbard, and representatives from the CIA, the Army, and Special Forces. The logistics of the plan were discussed, the assets weighed, routes argued about, strategies debated. Milosevic was to face trial in The Hague for genocide and other war crimes. There was no compromise to be had, no accommodations to be made, no bargaining to be done. The new Serbian government was coerced into compliance. At stake was $100 million in congressional funding for Serbia's reconstruction. In addition, the United States would vote against Serbia at donor meetings in Europe promising aid packages and block Belgrade's attempts to get loans from the World Bank or International Monetary Fund or any other international financial institution able to help Serbia restructure its debt or obtain low interest loans. The deadline for action was March 31.

In January, Kostunica met with Milosevic, indicted in 1999 for the mistreatment of Albanians in Kosovo. During the meeting, the ousted leader sought assurances that he, Milosevic, would not be extradited. Although Kostunica had set aside time to talk to Milosevic, he couldn't spare any time that same day to talk to Carla Del Ponte, The Hague's International Criminal Tribunal's chief prosecutor.

This angered Washington. The Congress had already said Belgrade must take concrete steps in cooperating with the court, citing U.S. laws that required the Belgrade government to "surrender and transfer" war crimes indictees or offer "assistance in their apprehension."

However, Kostunica had no intention of moving on Milosevic. Earlier that year when he'd been asked what he was doing about arresting Bosnian Serb war criminals like Radovan Karadzic and Ratko Mladic, the new president replied coldly that he had other priorities. In a sense, this *was* true: he had to establish the country's stability, deal with unrest in Albania and possible succession by Montenegro. Then there were old Milosevic supporters determined to hang on at all costs. So if he was not America's enemy, Kostunica was hardly its friend. He disliked America's pressure, and he had his own streak of obstinate resolve. He saw Djindjic as a spear carrier for the Americans and wanted Serbia to stay clear of any association with a foreign power. For all of his moral courage and intelligence, Kostunica seemed amazingly unaware of the larger strategy at work, and with his unfortunate need to be right at all times, he dug in his heels. Paralyzed bickering produced embittered bafflement which produced dead stalemate.

Weeks drifted past like clouds, while, far off in Washington, Albright and the new Bush group fretted and fumed with frustration. Unfortunately for Milosevic, disapproval of him had intensified within his own country and around the world. The proceedings at The Hague were gathering in earnestness and resolute decision. Milosevic hardly realized it, but the shadow of his captivity was creeping ever closer.

It did not take long for the depth of the official rot in Milosevic's inner circle to emerge. The Milosevic regime had been a "criminal enterprise," an unabashed, totally heartless pursuit of personal enrichment and power that had ignored legal or moral restraints of any kind. As probes began, horrific discoveries were made centering on Milosevic's control of the key Serbian bureaucracies—the national bank, Belgrade city hall, the customs bureau, a few state-owned enterprises. What became clear were the outlines of the protracted crime spree that had been the Serb leader's reign. The degree of wanton plunder and pillage that had taken place against the Serb people under his rule had reached a new level of callous venality. The average monthly salary had fallen to $35 from $75, and all the while the elite had been living a lavish and illicit life based on gifts to itself of billions of dollars in stolen state assets.

In one case, 750 apartments that belonged to Belgrade were given to relatives and friends with no payment having been required. In another, an office building, valued at $1 million, was given to Milosevic's Socialist Party by the city of Belgrade, which demanded no payment. Investigators said they believed billions and billions worth of state-owned property had simply been seized by Milosevic cronies out to enrich themselves. As the ousted Serb leader was increasingly connected with money laundering, pyramid schemes, murders, more and more Serbs began to call for his arrest.

In Washington, Albright and Clinton were gone, but in January, the new U.S. ambassador in Belgrade, William Montgomery, had delivered to Kostunica a demand for Milosevic's arrest, including recommendations that his government share documents with the International Criminal Tribunal and no longer provide safe harbor for Serbs wanted for war crimes, two steps the new president had hesitated taking.

Kostunica's reluctance would matter very little. The administration of George W. Bush was pursuing the same policy as the Clinton administration with undeviating intentness. In January, the joint Clinton-Bush discussions had agreed Milosevic might be tried in Yugoslavia first, but there needed to be "international justice as well," according to O'Brien. On February 3, Djindjic, along with a handful of Balkan leaders, visited Washington for a meeting with Secretary of State Colin Powell. Powell brutally snubbed Montenegro's president, Milo Djiakanovic, a clear manifestation of Washington's disapproval of any scheme of succession.

When Djindjic met with Powell and Deputy National Security Advisor Stephen Hadley, Djindjic said he wanted a trial for Milosevic to take place in the Yugoslav courts before his extradition to The Hague. Kostunica was saying in Belgrade that Milosevic's extradition "would destabilize Serbia," and Djindjic had asked Powell, "We can send Milosevic to The Hague, but what about the consequences?"

According to former CIA official Larry Johnson, to the new Bush White House, Milosevic "was still a high priority target," and the March 31 deadline for extradition still stood. Powell told Djindjic that on June 29 there would be a meeting of international aid donors and the United States would vote to approve that aid if Djindjic would promise Powell that Milosevic would be in The Hague by then. Djindjic promised; he did not inform Kostunica of his pledge.

Under the Yugoslav constitution, there were clear channels of authority. The Serb president commanded the national army, and the prime minster controlled the police and special forces under the authority of the Ministry of the Interior. Under Milosevic, the police and security forces had been built up as his personal instruments, and Milosevic neglected his army. When he turned to them to rescue him on October 5, they had simply turned their backs. As we have seen, Gen. Nebojsa Pavkovic, the army chief of staff, had acted to keep the army from intervening in the October 5 rebellion, telling Milosevic that his forces were not trained to confront people in the streets, the police were.

The rift between the army and the office of the president had healed since the election of Kostunica. The new president had developed his own ties with Pavkovic, partly as a counterbalance to Djindjic and the police, and the general had assigned an army detail to protect the palatial Milosevic compound on grounds it was an "official" residence. It was also guarded by a contingent of police, and, in addition, Milosevic had his own private bodyguards headed by paramilitary leader Sinisa Vucinic, who commanded the Falcons, a group responsible for vicious ethnic cleansing in Bosnia. Vucinic had turned the residence into a fortress. The compound had reinforced walls, thick bulletproof glass, underground passages. Everywhere were weapons: two machine guns, a rocket grenade launcher, cases of ammo, a sniper rifle, thirty assault rifles, pistols, two cases of hand grenades.

As the March 31 deadline on U.S. aid approached, Kostunica was in Geneva attending a conference. The drama in Belgrade had begun on March 30 when Interior Ministry officials ordered Milosevic's police to leave the residence. An anxious Milosevic had offered quadruple pay if they stayed, but only one did. That evening, a rumor had spread like a wind over darkening water that Milosevic was going to be arrested. Soon a noisy, lively crowd of his supporters, mainly pensioners, had appeared at the tall, broad, high white house, and Milosevic had come out and mingled with them. Whatever fuse had been lit had sputtered out.

However, Djindjic not only controlled the police but the Special Operations Unit commanded by the ruthless young colonel, Legija, once described by Djindjic as "the iron fist" of the old regime. Djindjic had taken pains to have Ministry of the Interior officials negotiate an agreement with the army generals to hand over the keys to the presidential villa and allow Milosevic's arrest to take place. Instead, the generals gave the keys to Vucinic and blocked the doors to the residence. Surprised, the police didn't know what to do and began to pull back to the cheers of Milosevic supporters in the streets. A frantic Djindjic sent negotiators, and finally wrangled an agreement by which the federal soldiers would stand aside at 1:20 A.M. According to reliable accounts, Kostunica had ordered the army to block the way.

On March 31, 150 police in full riot gear appeared to block the entrances, control the crowd, and clear a path. Some fire was exchanged and two policemen were wounded. The attack stalled. Then at 2:40 A.M., a train of six black jeeps and one white van arrived at the back of the house, and the passengers sat inside without moving. A police prison van and two ambulances were parked far down the street. Several hundred Milosevic supporters then arrived, mostly elderly, clapping and calling "Slobo, Slobo."

Suddenly, men in blue jeans and bulletproof vests wearing black masks piled out of the vehicles. They were met with a sleeting of bullets from Milosevic's bodyguards, but some of the vehicles crashed through the gatehouse. They were on the grounds to stay, but by 4 A.M., no one had gotten inside.

There was an edgy, nerve-testing lull, and negotiators presented Milosevic with an arrest warrant. Inside the house, he had already brandished a cocked pistol and counted twenty-five bullets, twenty for his enemies and the rest for himself and his family. He was clearly disturbed. Refusing to accept the warrant, Milosevic said he didn't "recognize the police or these authorities," since they were all "NATO servants."

Shortly after daylight, the police pushed all bystanders, press, and Milosevic's supporters about a half mile down the street; the Special Forces poised for a major assault. Officially, the raiding party was composed of the

Red Berets led by Colonel Legija along with some Serb police, but not all were Red Berets. Some were also members of a highly classified U.S. Navy hostage rescue team SEAL Team Six, based at Dam Lock, Virginia, near Norfolk. The group knew its business. SEAL Team Six had been sent to Grenada during the 1983 U.S. invasion and was dispatched to the Middle East during the 1985 hijacking of the *Achille Lauro* cruise ship. They were also in Beirut during the same period helping in the search for kidnapped CIA station chief William Buckley. SEAL Team Six gets its orders from the Joint Special Operations Command at Fort Bragg, North Carolina, the home of its U.S. Army counterpart, the Delta Force.

They were expert killers of men. They worked in squads of eight or nine or platoons of sixteen to eighteen. Their plan was simple: "Our doctrine is to kill everybody within sight or hearing," in the words of one. Another said: "We hit hard, overwhelm everything with annihilating fire, and get out quick! That's the way we stay alive."

The strike plan was developed in Germany, at the headquarters of EuroCom, the U.S. Army, in Stuttgart. The SEALs reported to a chain of authority that began with the Joint Special Operations Command to U.S. Special Operations Command at MacDill Air Force Base near Tampa, Florida. They always worked closely with the regional or war-fighting commanders in chief of the U.S. European Command, SOUTHCOM, and CENTCOM and other major commands.

SEAL Team Six was supported by a special tactics team of Team Six operators. For this mission they had rehearsed incessantly. Informants had been developed inside the Milosevic hillside house sheltered behind its high metal fences. The SEALs had built for practice a model of the interior of the compound as well as a model of the grounds. Soon the SEALs were familiar with the layout of the place—the secret tunnels, the weapons caches. Milosevic was to be taken alive, if possible, but he was increasingly surrounded by heavily armed and unstable people.

What followed was a thirty-three-hour siege. The Special Forces first tried to storm the residence, hitting hard, smashing in the windows as Milosevic bodyguards opened a fearsome fire. The commandos were driven back, but finally the SEALs had gained the back garden and were readying an all-out assault. They were in a finish fight. "There were people there who simply wanted to kill the bastard," a former U.S. participant said. They came very close to doing just that. Under authorization from Djindjic, the mixed team of SEALs and Serb Special Forces were to use "whatever force necessary" to storm the house. The order was issued after the first Serb

SWAT team had been fired on. Djindjic said later he was prepared to level the fortified villa and kill Milosevic to end the standoff. "We were not going to mess around," said a former SEAL operative.

Colonel Legija met with Milosevic and told him to give up or he would be taken by force. Milosevic said he would die first.

A strange lull descended. From time to time, one of Milosevic's bodyguards would let loose a shot and set off a storm of returning volleys, then everything would fall still. "They were trying to get Milosevic out of there alive," said former CIA official Larry Johnson.

Suddenly a new actor of importance appeared. Cedomir "Ceda" Jovanovic, the former Otpor leader, and a U.S. asset, wearing a sweater and a thin, rustling jacket, asked to go in and try to talk Milosevic into surrendering. When he entered the house, Jovanovic, now a key Djindjic deputy, saw instantly the place "was an armed fortress." The room was filled with as many as fifty people, numerous friends of the Milosevic family. All had been drinking heavily and taking drugs. Milosevic's daughter, Marija, having drunk most of a bottle of brandy and who was euphoric from taking many sleeping pills, was brandishing three pistols, a derringer, a Beretta, and a Walther. Vucinic, head of security and a friend of Mira, was manning a machine gun.

Jovanovic said later that everyone in the room "had lost touch with reality."[2]

Milosevic, quite soused, with a cocked pistol in his hand, said to Jovanovic. "They won't take me alive." Jovanovic peered anxiously around. With the imprisoned followers becoming frantic, a general frenzy was increasing.

Jovanovic saw instantly that Milosevic was suicidal and unbalanced. The full fury of the storm was about to fall on him, and yet he seemed to have no real grasp of events. The SEALs had that irresistible, furious energy that feels equal to surmounting any obstacle, to brushing aside any hindrance, yet Milosevic appeared to some to be sealed inside a queer, trancelike state, where the real and unreal danced in and out of his understanding.

Jovanovic patiently began negotiations. He knew the house had no water, no electricity, and its phone lines had been cut. SEALs were now in the backyard. It was only a question of time.

One of the first things Jovanovic said to Milosevic was, "Don't shoot at the police."

Milosevic again retorted, "I won't be taken alive," and he made more threats to kill himself and his family. Since both his parents had killed themselves, this was sobering. Outside, there were psychologists on the scene, and Jovanovic went and talked with them. They asked if Milosevic was saying things like "when I'm no longer around," and Jovanovic said he was. The psychiatrist concluded that Milosevic's ramblings were suicidal.

Jovanovic then returned, trying to calm Milosevic, while inside the house, chaos had become complete. Mass desperation was rising higher every minute. After lengthy discussions, Jovanovic told the former leader that to millions of Serbs he was still a role model.

This image of himself seemed to calm Milosevic.

For hours the discussions continued, Jovanovic going out to consult with experts and military leaders, trying to find a way to hit the right note. Finally, after talking with the police and SEALs, Jovanovic once more returned to the house to try and help Milosevic see what his true situation was. The Otpor leader explained that if the commando team attacked, the former Serb leader's fifteen bodyguards would be killed instantly, perhaps two of the attackers would die, but certainly all of Milosevic's family and the Serb himself would be killed. Jovanovic went and stood before Mira, Milosevic's wife, with her small eyes, fat, white, doughy face and black bangs, and told her the same thing. As she would later relate, "This messenger of the people said that if we did not surrender, everyone in the house would be killed, so [Milosevic] surrendered."[3]

Just before Milosevic surrendered, an investigating judge entered the house and read the charges. Milosevic and his family were then guaranteed safety, and two key annexes said that Milosevic "will not be handed over to any judicial or other institutions outside the country."[4] Milosevic went over every line with his lawyer, Mira frequently objecting. The annexes were signed by Serbian prime minister President Djindjic and DOS official Jovanovic. The problem for Milosevic was that the guarantees of no extradition were valid only for that date.[5]

Milosevic had been had. As he sped away in his Audi, to be lodged in the central prison in Belgrade, inmate 101980, his daughter, still drunk and irrational, took a shot at Jovanovic, which missed, then fired five shots at the departing convoy, "Why didn't you kill yourself and us as we agreed?" she screamed.[6]

Kostunica had not known of the raid. He had been in Geneva on business. When he got back, he was tight-lipped and furious. He made a public statement saying the raid "put the law at risk," and that it amounted "to a coup d'état." Djindjic, Covic, and the others had "broken the law in numerous respects,"[7]

Several days passed. Finally Kostunica reappeared, worn and glum. "No man," he said wearily, "not even Slobodan Milosevic, is worth a civil war.

We will not allow the safety of one individual to endanger the security of the state."[8]

Milosevic had lost his last defender.

The Serb dictator was now ensconced in a comfortable wing of the Belgrade central prison, making fruit tea, smoking cigarettes, getting visits from his wife.

However, in the early summer of 2001, there was a gruesome discovery of a series of mass graves of Kosovo Albanians. When this news spread, it sealed Milosevic's fate and turned the public tide against him. On March 26, 2000, Serbs had surrounded the village of the Berisha family, ordered the people out, separated the men from the women and children and shot six on the spot. The rest were then herded into a coffee shop. Once inside, the Serb troops fired steadily, indiscriminately killing forty family members. Serb officials had warned Milosevic that the bodies would be discovered, and so the corpses had been exhumed and then moved secretly into sites at several Serbian locations including one at Batajinca military base just outside Belgrade. In the case of the Berisha family, the work of Serb officials had been lazy and inept. Sanitary workers were awakened in the middle of the night and driven to a rifle range in the town of Prizren and, as officers looked on, loaded the dead bodies into a white refrigerator truck. In April of 2000, a fisherman saw the truck floating in the Danube. When local police opened the door, a human leg fell out. Inside were eighty bodies, which were then taken to the Batajinca air base. Many belonged to the Berisha family and even more bodies were in the mass grave found at the air base. Serbs who had participated in the ghastly operation confessed, and it created a devastating shock in the minds of many Serbs, who had, until then, believed in Milosevic's protestations of innocence.[9]

It would be discovered in April of 2003 that he had murdered his former mentor and choice friend of his heart in his early career, Ivan Stambolic. Stambolic had been living in Montenegro, and in 2000 had planned to re-enter politics and run against Milosevic for the presidency. One day he had been out for a jog and stopped to rest on a bench when a van appeared and men in black bundled him inside. His remains were found south of Belgrade, shot twice in the head.

When investigators attempted to question Mira, she fled to Moscow where she remains.

A process had begun that could not be stopped. On June 28, 2001, without the presence of Kostunica, Djindjic chaired a meeting of the Serbian government and by a vote of 14–1, the group authorized Milosevic's extradition to The Hague. The document was signed by Djindjic, who argued that a provision to the 1990 constitution "empowered the Serbian government to overrule Yugoslav law if it was in the best interest of Serbia." Called Article 135, it was penned in Milosevic's own hand, and it cleared the way for his extradition. (Kostunica had secretly agreed to the deal once Djindjic had threatened to resign.)

When the public prosecutor entered Milosevic's cell in Belgrade and for twenty-five minutes related the charges against him, Milosevic just sat on his bed in unbelieving silence. An hour later Legija's Special Operations unit arrived. "Prepare to leave," the police ordered. Stunned, Milosevic asked, "Where I am supposed to be going?" "The Hague," said a voice. Then, "Start packing."[10]

Milosevic retrieved a black leather bag from under his cot and put in it two books on Serb history and an Orthodox Bible. Djindjic had arranged a special aircraft as a decoy, to draw out any proposed intervention that might try and rescue Milosevic. Instead, the former Serb leader was taken by motorcade to a police base where a helicopter was waiting. The police read Milosevic his rights and the tribunal's indictment. Asked if he had anything to say, Milosevic said The Hague was "a political circus" whose aim was to endanger the Serbian people "until it destroyed them completely." He described his arrest as a kidnapping. He was flown to the U.S. air base in Tuzla, in Bosnia, where not too many years before the anguished victims from Srebrenica had gathered. He was put on an RAF twin-engine jet and flown to Eindhoven, a Dutch military base, and put on a police helicopter.[11]

Kostunica claimed that he had not been consulted and publicly attacked Djindjic, saying that Milosevic's transfer was not "legal or constitutional" and that it "seriously jeopardized" the constitutional order of the country, but it was all hollow posturing.

At 11 P.M., Milosevic passed through the gate of a U.N. detention center. He would die in prison in March of 2006 before his trial was complete. Former President Clinton was disappointed that Milosevic's death occurred before a verdict had been reached. Nevertheless, Clinton said, "His capture and trial will serve as a reminder that egregious crimes against humanity will not be tolerated."

It was an operation well coordinated by Washington, London, and Belgrade. Milosevic was the first head of state to be charged with genocide relating to Croatia, Bosnia, and Kosovo. From its beginning as a bargaining chip to get the Bosnian Serbs to peace talks, the U.N.'s International Criminal Tribunal on the former Yugoslavia was now a major international organization with an annual budget of $90 million employing 1,188 staff members.

Today there are over one hundred accused war criminals detained there.

EPILOGUE

Clearly in the beginning of his presidency, Clinton's knowledge of foreign affairs was not sufficient for competence. Yet it is fair to say his earlier failures were a defect of inadequate past interest, not a lack of present capacity. The initial and major Clinton foreign policy failure of his first term was allowing it to be sidelined to advance his domestic agendas. In the service of these, Clinton's abilities were at their peak. According to his advisor David Gergen, Clinton had the firmest, most subtle grasp of public policy of any president he had known, and he had served as an advisor to both Nixon and Reagan. Usually politicians know the *politics* of an issue but not the issue itself. This was not true of Clinton, Gergen said. Various city or state officials were astonished to find that Clinton was often more well versed in their subjects than they were, whether it was education, health care, or urban affairs. On the subject of economics, for example, Clinton listened to his experts but was never satisfied until he had mastered the intricacies of their thought and understood the smallest facets of the issue. He did not take the word of experts, but came to his conclusions, for better or worse, by an authentic process of thinking things out.

Throughout Clinton's first term, his foreign policy was never able to capture and invigorate the president's interest the way domestic issues did. Many of his advisors noted with alarm that geostrategic and national security concerns in Clinton's mind had been replaced by concerns for advancing trade schemes, by his fascination with globalization, or by his early obsession with cutting the deficit, which was a major accomplishment but which came at a high cost.

A national leader ignores foreign policy at his or her peril. As a Clinton aide said "You don't do foreign policy, foreign policy does you." In foreign policy, to ignore difficulties and challenges is to be left at their mercy, as Clinton's difficulties with Milosevic proved.

A more disturbing trait was Clinton's tendency to select figures of mediocrity to handle his foreign policy because Clinton shrank from having any competing influence or rival strength to contend with. Observing his foreign policy team, Clinton once said that there "wasn't a winner among them." Yet one of the critical gifts of leadership is to recognize where you're weak or your abilities fall short. His first secretary of state, Warren Christopher, was a person of mediocre vision who secretly harbored a self-seeking ambition, and an ambitious mediocrity is a very dangerous mediocrity. Once Clinton gained in self-confidence and felt increasingly secure in his instincts, he began to dominate even exceptionally strong and self-willed personalities. As the tragedy of the Balkans unfolded, it is interesting to note how Clinton moved from the un-aggressive, timid, and fatally cautious in his cabinet to relying on those who had the killer instinct and who demanded diplomacy backed by force, switching from the Lakes and Christophers to the Galbraiths, the Holbrookes, the Clarks and the Albrights. By 1995, he acted with great hardihood of resolution on Bosnia, and would be a more dominating figure during the Kosovo war. Unfortunately, hundreds of thousands of Bosnian Muslims had died, thanks to his slowness in asserting command.

However, by the end of Clinton's first term, he had learned to impose his own personality on the crises, stamping his own imprint on them, and not only author his own major decisions but make them stick. He learned to do what a president is supposed to do: he declared a direction in policy, and was able to explain to his public why it would benefit the people and make more secure American national interests, and he was persuasive in gaining at least temporary support among a mainly indifferent public.

The attention span of the American public in the mid-1990s does not reflect much credit on itself. After Clinton had lost eighteen soldiers in Somalia, and even as the horrible genocide in Rwanda was unfolding, Democratic Representative David Obey described the American masses. "The American people's hope," he said, was for "zero degree of involvement and zero degree of risk and zero degree of risk and self-sacrifice."[1]

This mood had not changed much seven years later at the time of the Kosovo clash. Yet in making war on Milosevic over Kosovo, Clinton had made a cannily accurate judgment of the culture and political temperament of his time. "Better than any other player on the national political stage, he understood what Americans want, how much they will pay, how much they will put up with," according to Andrew Bacevich, a retired Army colonel and professor of international relations at Boston University.[2]

Clinton saw clearly that the culture of the 1960s had reemerged in the 1990s. The right might rule finance, but the left ruled culture. Most Americans were addicted to the idea of personal, not national, development, and they wished to serve their own, not another's, purposes. These cultural attitudes had facets that were less than savory—a belief in the primacy of self-gratification, of giving obedience not to principle but to personal caprice, the vulgar worship of financial success. Americans no longer viewed wars as heroic enterprises, as mighty ennobling crusades to right a wrong. The military virtues of self-sacrifice, manliness, hardihood, endurance of discomfort, stoicism in hardship were no longer held in much esteem, even after Desert Storm.

Clinton then decided to avoid criticism of his plans for Kosovo by keeping them secret. Among all the presidents, Clinton most resembles FDR in his love of artifice, of the devious, the hidden. Clinton resolved to wage war without paying much attention to the public's aims and wishes. "Decoupling the people from military affairs" was Clinton's primary purpose, said Bacevich. As president, Clinton would wage war in a way that would do the least political damage while achieving the maximum effect. Clinton pretty much ignored the Congress, refusing to consult it because most of its members were ignorant of or indifferent to military affairs. (Republican leader Trent Lott was urging Clinton to "give peace a chance.") Nor did Clinton bother even to consult the Joint Chiefs of Staff as FDR had, dealing mainly with its chairman, Gen. Hugh Shelton, a mild, torpid, rather colorless man who was not likely to make waves or say no.

THE TEST OF COMMAND

Command is the test of the commander, as the saying goes, and as a commander in chief, Clinton has been vastly underestimated. When it came to Kosovo, many argued that the Clinton administration had no coherent war plan, that Clinton was strategically confused, and that, given his antiwar background, he was squeamish about using force. Perhaps at the beginning of his presidency, Clinton had misgivings about presidential power because it was connected with force, yet the fact is that Bill Clinton was not in the least dainty about using force. He used force in Haiti, and he had used force in Bosnia, first through Croatian proxies, and then by means of NATO bombing raids. Clinton at one point had also wanted a full-scale war with Iran over the bombing of the Khobar Towers in Saudi Arabia in which Iran was involved, and in 1994 had to be talked out of bombing North Korea.

In addition, for a year after Operation Desert Fox, the 1998 bombing of Baghdad, almost unnoticed by the public, Clinton had conducted a savage and incessant air war against Iraq, dropping two thousand bombs that reduced to a miserable shambles Saddam Hussein's entire air defense network. It also does well to remember that in 1994, Clinton signed a finding to remove or kill Saddam Hussein, and he signed a finding to remove Milosevic from power and either kill him or deliver him as a war criminal to The Hague. Clinton had also tried to kill Saudi terrorist Osama bin Laden. His decisions to center U.S. efforts in Bosnia and Croatia, to use Croatian proxies, to back and arm the Bosnia Muslims, were courageous and cunning. These are not the actions of a man averse to force or who suffers faint putters of the heart when faced with a lion in the path.

Clinton made war to inflict punishment on Milosevic to the degree that it would force the Serb to end his slaughterous persecution of Kosovars. As military historian Eliot Cohen noted, Clinton was going to use force as a way to shape the international environment, to inflict enough pain to coerce his enemy to adopt a new line of conduct. This was a new way of making war and a new way of applying force because you aimed to attain a diplomatic, not a military, objective. But the American public was fickle and distracted and unable to distinguish between war and mere force. In the first place, there had never been a popular groundswell of support in America for the war, and by May 18, with the war less than a month old, Clinton's poll numbers had begun to slip—incredibly, the public had already grown weary of it, and most were urging an immediate negotiated settlement. Fifty-six percent opposed sending any ground troops. By then the Serbs had taken 250 Kosovar towns and burned fifty of them to the ground. When the war ended in victory, Clinton's poll numbers actually dipped instead of rising.

Yet what Clinton had done was amazing. He had been gutsy enough to dump the Powell Doctrine and the Weinberger Doctrine and, using airpower alone, had instead embraced the tactic of gradual escalation, thought to have been discredited once and for all after President Johnson's failure in Vietnam. In spite of the ineptitude of Clinton and NATO that characterized the beginning of the Kosovo war, especially the failure to halt the Serb eviction of the Kosovars, NATO kept tightening the pressure, using attacks on Milosevic and his key political supporters, the Yugoslav army, and the country's infrastructure, until the growing despair and hardships of the

Serb people provided the decisive pressure that made the stubborn Serb submit.

Throughout the conflict, Clinton ensured that America was by far the major player in the NATO alliance, and he kept the coalition from paralyzing allied target selection by using American planes not subject to NATO's jurisdiction. For example, at the Vicenza air base in Italy there was an area for American assets and a second for NATO war planes. The two did not mix. In addition, the United States did not share much intelligence with its allies, and it sheltered its new technological wonder, the B-2 bomber, from prying European eyes by basing it at Whiteman Air Force Base in Missouri from which it flew to Serbia to bomb and then flew home again, a trip of twenty-eight hours.

The message was there for all to read. Under Clinton there would be no long, wearing campaigns, but instead, in the words of Andrew Bacevich, "brief, measured ripostes . . . calibrated, judicious, precise." As Bacevich goes on to say, force was used "not to achieve decision, but to signal, warn, contain, punish or at least to avoid the appearance of weakness and inaction."[3]

The use of airpower also means you can deliver direct and savage punishment almost with impunity, important in a culture where avoiding casualties is the ultimate measure of success. There would be no more Mogadishus on Clinton's watch.

Because of the deft skill with which Clinton "recast America's strategic purposes," and because of his new way of war, Bacevich asserts that Clinton's ability to fashion a "new post-liberal civil-military relationship," Clinton "deserves to be ranked along with FDR and Reagan as one of the most influential commander in chiefs in modern American history," a honor he has been unfairly denied.[4]

A WORLDVIEW?

Clinton was never thought to have any sweeping global strategy. As a leader he seemed to stumble from one place and then on to another, like a man in the street at night who has had too much to drink. This is misleading.

To begin with, Clinton from the first resisted any American retreat into isolationism after the end of the Cold War. With the fall of the Soviet Union and the information revolution, the way had opened wide for globalism—the abolition of borders, barriers, and boundaries that had acted to hamper free trade. It also presented the Clinton administration with the chance to promote personal freedom and the general human welfare in the newly born democracies of Eastern Europe.

As Charles de Gaulle observed of FDR: "He cloaks his will to power in idealism." Clinton's chief strategic aim was to expand America's world role, and the collapse of the Soviet Union afforded Clinton an opportunity to indirectly assert American predominance over a far wider area. His policy was far-seeing and intelligent. As Bacevich told the author, "Clinton had a very definite idea of what America's role in the world was to be and how he was to obtain it."

Like Franklin Roosevelt, Clinton saw the increase of economic freedom in the world as the surest solution to avoiding war, so free trade was replaced by promoting "globalism," a more sophisticated form of economic networking and exchange. Some of Clinton's vision included Jeffersonian nonsense that claimed prospering democracies were less likely to fight and that world peace was more likely to prevail, but Clinton was, at heart, very much a realist. The key to American security was a stable and secure Europe led by America. On October 27, 1999, at a luncheon for the American Society of American Newspaper Editors, Clinton said, "I have tried to lead America into a new century and into a whole new era in the way we live and work and relate to each other, and the rest of the world. And I have tried to build a world that was more peaceful, prosperous and more secure." He added, he wanted to build a Europe that was "united, democratic and at peace."

This lofty idealism disguised Clinton's strategic aims, which were increasing American influence and gaining new markets. "Growth at home, means growth abroad," he said.[5] But while building such a Europe meant avoiding war, it did not mean disavowing the use of force. Clinton saw all war as disruptive, but he saw military force as an instrument that could be used carefully, cautiously, moderately as a tool of statecraft, a way of shaping a more favorable global economic environment, an instrument for coercing outlaws like Milosevic into compliance with America's view of the necessity for the rule of law.

Certainly Clinton recognized NATO and continued relations with Russia as the central instruments in expanding American influence in Europe, for he knew that any rupture in U.S.-Russian relations would have adverse effects way beyond the Balkans. To keep Boris Yeltsin on board and in power, Clinton promoted him as a democrat when in fact Yeltsin governed by extremely authoritarian means. As I have mentioned earlier, the Clinton administration, by covert means, ensured Yeltsin's election of 1996. However purists may complain that such an act was unsavory, the bond that Clinton built to Yeltsin proved to be of surpassing importance when the clash in Kosovo came. Even though Yeltsin stormed and ranted, the Russians in fact did not arm the Serbs nor did they report NATO troop movements to the Serbs.

From the earliest days of his presidency Clinton had seen in NATO a way to reorient the European chessboard. He transformed NATO from a 1949 defensive alliance against a conventional Russian military onslaught against the West to an offensive organization able to enforce peace and put down disorders not only in Europe but in Central Asia and the Middle East, areas vital to U.S. interests. The fact that NATO is today operating in Afghanistan is due to the vision of Bill Clinton.

WHAT MANNER OF MAN

Clinton had so many sides to him, so many facets to his personality, that to many it rendered him almost incomprehensible. To many he was a divided man whose head battled with his heart, his instincts with his reason, his appetites with his conscience. How does one convey that complexity with a few broad strokes in a simplified outline?

First and perhaps most important, Bill Clinton was possessed of an extraordinarily winning personalty. He was an attractive, warmhearted man with a vastly responsive intelligence. People kindled in him fires of real affection and liking. The force and vigor of his personality were extraordinary, his personality a genuine power, "a primal force," one former aide said. When Clinton locked on a fresh subject with full concentration, he could produce the effect that FDR's speechwriter Samuel Rosenberg wrote of Roosevelt, "He could make a casual visitor believe that he had been waiting all day for this hour to arrive. Only a person who really loved human beings could give that impression."[6]

Like FDR, Clinton knew by instinct that what the people required in a politician was a down-to-earth leader who could touch their hearts, and his sense of hitting the right note was uncanny for its emotional rightness and perceptive sincerity. This requires the ability to make subtle, accurate reads of receptivities of the moment, and to possess a valid insight into his hearers' set of mind that allows the leader like himself to fashion the appropriate reply that will please, using all his political skills to stay in step with an audience and not get out in front of it. This means knowing what matters to people most. That ability to discern the mental and emotional make up of the hearer is key to any president's ability to persuade, hardly a trifling power.

Since a democratic leader can only lead by consent there can be no leadership without skill with words. However, there is a traditional American suspicion of the person who speaks well that goes along with the suspicion of anything seen as fancy, new and unfamiliar. Only recently President Barack Obama was derided for his skill with words. This is understandable because when we attempt to express ourselves on a topic, we usually rely on the words that lie nearest to hand, which are usually words others are already using continually, dull, hackneyed words like "at the end of the day," or "moving forward" or "closure," which immediately put any listeners to sleep.

But Clinton's power over words was enormous, not seen since the days of Reagan or John Kennedy. Secretary of Labor Robert Reich said of Clinton, "The president has an extraordinary capacity to empathize and also to preach. I don't mean in terms of telling people what to do, or in a self-righteous way. I mean in terms of making people aware that the cosmos works in strange ways. . . . he is extraordinarily able to feel the emotions in a situation and to express those emotions in a very articulate way." (Hamilton, *Bill Clinton, Mastering the Presidency*, pp. 448–9.) We have not had many recent presidents with the skill to quicken the pulse of the American people, to fill it with fresh, aspiring energy.

Clinton also had great powers of exposition, tremendous gifts of fluency, including ingenuity of illustration combined with solid knowledge. He seemed to have a way of putting things that was vivid, clear, shrewd, and unexpected. They were words not just made up for the public occasion, but words that expressed emotions that he carried in his heart. Clinton was an earnest man of deep feeling, agree with him or not. To move the coarser nature, you need the finer one, and Clinton could light up the imagination and move the inner soul as he did at Oklahoma after the terrible bombing.

Nor was it simply what Clinton *said*, but what he *believed* that gave him such power over so many people. What Roosevelt, Kennedy, and Reagan had was a real faith in the higher parts of human nature, and each believed with all his heart and soul and strength that there is such a thing as the truth. When any of these men spoke, it didn't matter that we heard things we did not agree with, it was thrilling simply to hear such things so well said. But these abilities of persuasion enabled Clinton to gain a direct control over the masses of people, and by his words and deeds, hold their attention and interest, in spite of the clamor of critics, and to arouse their energies to focused activity and support. He could guide them gently the way a mahout guides an elephant, and his direct command over many Americans was immense.

Someone once noted that "administration is the foundation of strategy." If they were referring to Clinton as a manager, there is no doubt that he had an extremely undisciplined and disorganized style of leadership. He did not like to impose decisions by means of authority, but preferred to forge a consensus. He had an accommodating, conciliatory streak to his temperament. His nature shrank with dread from wounding the feelings of others, except when he was annoyed or suffering a reverse, when he lost control of his temper, often blaming others for his own mistakes. Yet his basic instinct was to build consensus.

His mental gifts were prodigious. Clinton was interested in everything, a genuine polymath. Yet to know so much all at once can breed murk and confusion as well as enlightenment. Dick Morris described Clinton as having a tendency toward "intellectual clutter—he was so quick to absorb so much information that he lost track of his purpose and was seduced by the last person he talked to." Morris said Clinton lacked the ability to distinguish the important from the subordinate, and his mind could not easily form a hierarchy of values among what he was being told. Morris credits himself and Hillary with helping Clinton sort and impose a conceptual framework on his facts. Yet even Morris concedes that once Clinton made a decision, he was "devastatingly effective." Clinton seems hardly alone among presidents in having this difficulty. John Kennedy was known to be a conciliator, coming to decisions with caution, and Roosevelt, when the crisis arose over Lend-Lease, for example, "seemed unable or unwilling to concentrate" his thoughts on a matter crucial to his presidency.[7]

George Stephanopoulos notes that Clinton used study to avoid having to make decisions. As for framing his own policies or deciding on what course of action to take, Clinton would call many people at all hours of the day and night and would pass on some of their thoughts while concealing their origin—"a kind of blind market testing," Stephanopoulos said. Clinton, he says, possessed a formidable force of will when it came to keeping his independence of mind so that no single advisor could ever fully own him, that Clinton was "too smart and too stubborn for that." For instance, in trying to deal with affirmative action, Clinton devoured with his usual voracity position papers, monographs, and opinion pieces, and made pithy observations about them. But he was indecisive, because he had to think multidimensionally, to grasp the effect any action of his would have on two dozen parties, on making enemies of people he might need for future approvals for eighteen different topics. The Victorian novelist George Meredith said, "It's a terrific decree in life that one must act who would prevail," and no one knew that better than Clinton. But the action had to be right, it had to bolster his prestige and increase his power and the mainstays of his support, not estrange them. A president must adapt much of what he does to the "tendencies of the hour," as a great commentator said. And so in the face of difficult decisions, Clinton balked and prevaricated and waited for his moment, knowing always that people or associates only follow a leader who produces results.

THE LEADERSHIP MIND

Clinton had many roles, party leader, commander in chief, the chief of the people of the United States. He was never a man of fixed methods or inflexible principles or frozen procedures, but did he have within him what many said he lacked, that "compass of certainty and rightness"?

To me it's clear that he did. I have not covered the domestic side of his presidency, but it seems clear that Clinton had a genuine idealism when it came to common people. He felt as their president, not only responsible *to* them, but responsible *for* them. His shiftiness, his manipulations, his compromises and pieces of expediency do nothing to dim that claim. Clinton cared very much for the ordinary human life and sought to better it, gladden it, relieve it of its burdens and broaden and enrich its prospects. He believed in the basic goodness of people and felt that the obligation of government was to do for them what they could not do for themselves. To him the government was not the Wizard of Oz. It was not a miracle worker. But if the government wasn't everything, it could be *a* thing of decisive importance to ordinary people in the race of life.

Clinton never went at anything in a straight line, but was always ready to hear options, always appearing to be open for a trade, a compromise, a delay. Yet it is in the hours of crisis that character comes to the fore, and it is much to Clinton's credit that in any great crisis, woolliness of thought or indecision of purpose fell away, and the president seemed to rise to his full height and, by means of moral force and a remarkable strength of will, proved able not only to dominate the occasion, but steady and strengthen the spirts around him. Robert Reich said he was awed by the president's "instinctive leadership"[8] at the time of the Oklahoma City bombing, where his spirit rose to its full height, calming, comforting, healing. But his leadership strengths are displayed at many critical points. Clinton was not a man whose decisions were direct, simple, and to the point, yet Clinton for all his retreats and irresolute hesitations was a man who was at his finest in emergencies, a master of predicaments. He liked to pit his will against impossibilities, and adversities such as the Mexican currency crisis or Kosovo seemed to rouse him to shed his vanity or timidity and at such times he lost any doubt he may have had of his abilities.

Although it took him what seemed an eternity to decide America's course on Bosnia, Clinton used to ruefully point out that it had taken Truman, for all his greatness, two years to come up with the Truman Doctrine of offering aid to all countries threatened by communism. Yet Clinton learned from his mistakes. By the time of Kosovo, Clinton had passed from a callow, insecure novice to a leader of expert and tested powers. His leadership during the Kosovo war would prove bold, steady, and fearless. The problem is that his contemporaries, his peers, couldn't see him clearly because unconscious biases and partisan aversions distorted their view.

I am not a Democrat and I harbor a great suspicion of politics. Alexis de Tocqueville said that people in America can't converse but discuss instead. I am suspicious of opinions, even my own, since mine have changed so often from being wrong to hopefully being less wrong. I have done this book because I feel Bill Clinton had admirable qualities, and that the petty malice of partisanship and quarrels over power acted to obscure them. It seemed an act of fairness to try and present them clearly.

NOTES

1: THE DILEMMAS OF LEADERSHIP

Interviews with principals.

1. George Stephanopoulos, *All Too Human*, New York: Little, Brown, 1999, p. 156.
2. Richard Clarke, *Against All Enemies*, New York: Free Press, 2004, p. 80.
3. Ibid.
4. Warren Christopher, *Chances of a Lifetime*, New York: Scribner, 2001, p. 336.
5. Colin Powell, *My American Journey*, New York: Random House, 1994, p. 423.
6. Ibid, p. 569.
7. Clarke, *Against All Enemies*, p. 83.
8. Powell, *My American Journey*, p. 570.

2: PRESIDENT OF ALL THE PEOPLE

Interviews with principals.

1. Nigel Hamilton, *Bill Clinton, Mastering the Presidency*, New York: Public Affairs, 2007, p. 97.
2. Joe Klein, *The Natural: The Misunderstood Presidency of Bill Clinton*, New York: Broadway Books, 2002, p. 39.
3. Ibid.

3: THE SPREADING OF DARKNESS

1. Tony Judt, *Postwar*, New York: Penguin, 2005, p. 716.
2. Warren Zimmermann, *Origins of a Catastrophe: Yugoslavia and Its Destroyers*, New York: Times Books, 1996, p. 5.
3. Ibid, p. 4.
4. Former administration official.
5. Richard Hofstadter, *The American Political Tradition: and the Men Who Made It*, New

York: Vintage Books, 1947, p. 33. See also, Arthur M. Schlesinger, Jr., *Cycles of American History*, Boston: Houghton Mifflin Company, 1986, p. 52, p. 55, p. 70, p. 89.

6. William G. Hyland, *Clinton's World: Remaking America's Foreign Policy*, New York: Praeger, 1999. p. 33.

7. Dick Morris, *Behind the Oval Office: Getting Reelected Against All Odds*, Los Angeles: Renaissance Books, 1999, p. 246.

8. John Harris, *The Survivor: Bill Clinton in the White House*, New York: Random House, 2005, p. 43.

9. Ibid.

4: A STARLESS DARK

Interviews with principals.

1. Mary Curtius, "Ex-State Dept. Official Widens Attack on U.S. Foreign Policy," *Boston Globe*, Sept. 4, 1992, p. 1.

2. *The Guardian*, Sept. 7, 1992.

3. Zimmermann, *Origins of a Catastrophe*, p. 234.

4. William Perry, Secretary of Defense, "Remarks Prepared for William Perry," www .defenselink.mil., Dec. 15, 1995. See also James Baker, *The Politics of Diplomacy*, New York, G. P. Putnam's Sons, 1995, p. 634–637.

5. Zimmerman, *Origins of a Catastrophe*, p. 234.

5: THE PRESENT STATE OF EVIL IN THE WORLD

Interviews with principals.
Material on Richard Holbrooke's trips to Bosnia from e-mails with author. See also, Richard Holbrooke, *To End a War*, New York: Modern Library, 1999.

1. Elizabeth Drew, *On the Edge: The Clinton Presidency*, New York: Simon & Schuster, Modern Library, 1994, p. 147.

2. Rieff quoted in Mark Danner, "Clinton, the U.N., and the Bosnian Disaster," *New York Review of Books*, Dec. 18, 1997, p. 13. See also, David Rieff, *Slaughterhouse: Bosnia and the Failure of the West*, New York: Touchstone, 1996, p. 174–175.

3. Henry Kissinger, *Diplomacy*, New York: Simon & Schuster, 1994, p. 638.

4. Laura Silber and Alan Little, *Yugoslavia: Death of a Nation*, London: Penguin, 1996, p. 270.

5. David Halberstam, *War in a Time of Peace*, New York: Simon & Schuster, 2001, p. 21.

6. James Woolsey, interviews and e-mail exchanges with author.

7. Richard Holbrooke, *To End a War*, New York: Random House, p. 31.

6: AN ECHOING CAVE OF WINDS

Interviews with principals.

1. Zimmermann, *Origins of a Catastrophe*, p. 215.

2. Powell, *My American Journey*, p. 578.

7: DANSE MACABRE

1. Drew, *On the Edge*, p. 149.

2. Silber and Little, *Yugoslavia: Death of a Nation*, p. 270.

3. Drew, *On the Edge*, p. 67.

4. Edward Vulliamy, *Seasons in Hell*, New York: St. Martin's, 1994, p. 281.

5. Ibid, p. 282.
6. Judt, *Postwar*, p. 284.
7. Drew, *On the Edge*, p. 157.
8. As an example of British pressure on the Bosnian Muslims to capitulate to Serb demands, Lord Peter Carrington, chairman of the European Community's open peace conference, at a meeting in April 1992, as 286,000 Bosnian refugees fled a Serb onslaught, Carrington urged Izetbegovic not to resist Serb pressure. As the Bosnian recalled, "Carrington advised me to negotiate to find the solution while their forces were attacking us. I told him that was impossible. (The Serb) demand, their objective was to destroy us as a country. He asked me, 'What will you do?' I told him we would fight back. Carrington paused. He looked me in the eye and said, 'What makes you think you can fight back? Do you know what you are talking about, Mr. Izetbegovic? Do you know what you are fighting against? Do you know what weaponry they have?' I told him we had no other choice but to fight back or to capitulate. If we capitulate, we will either be captured or killed. We have no choice, no alternative. He told me 'You, Mr. Izetbegovic, are not aware who you are dealing with.'" (See, Laura Silber and Alan Little, *Yugoslavia: Death of a Nation*, p. 253.)

8: THE PRINCE OF TENNESSEE
Interviews with principals.
1. David Maraniss and Ellen Nakashima, *The Prince of Tennessee*, New York: Simon & Schuster, 2000, p. 267.
2. Jacob Heilbrunn, President Gore's Foreign Policy (Vice-President Gore), *World Policy Journal*, June 22, 2000.
3. Thomas Lippman, "An Obscure Force in National Security Edges into the Limelight," *Washington Post*, June 16, 1998.
4. Maraniss, *The Prince of Tennessee*, p. 270.
5. Arthur Kengor, "The Foreign Policy Role of Vice President Al Gore," *Presidential Studies Quarterly*, Jan. 1, 1997.
(See also, Alexandra Starr, "The Stiff Man Has a Spine," *Washington Monthly*, Sept. 1, 1999. Elaine Sciolino, and Todd S. Purdum, "Al Gore One Vice President Who Is Eluding the Shadows," *New York Times*, Feb. 19, 1995. Bill Torque, *Inventing Al Gore*, Boston: Houghton Mifflin, 2000, pp. 265–281.

9: THE COURTIER
Interviews with principals.
1. Drew, *On the Edge*, p. 217.
2. Confidential interview.
3. James MacGregor Burns, *Roosevelt: The Lion and the Fox*, New York: Harcourt, 1956, p. 259.

10: SHAPING A SECRET STRATEGY
Interviews with principals.
1. The Deputies Committee was a group of emerging importance made up of senior officials of the National Security Council, State Department, Defense Department and other deputies of the principals. It was run by Sandy Berger and met in the White House Situation Room for two and three hour sessions in which options were discussed, analyzed, and hammered out. It was a Clinton innovation.

2. Andrew Cockburn and Patrick Cockburn, *Saddam Hussein: An American Obsession*, London: Verso, 2000, p. 41–42.

11: MARK OF DESOLATION

Interviews with principals, with special thanks to General Joe Hoar, General Anthony Zinni, and former CIA operatives including Ernest Shanklin.

1. Clarke, *Against All Enemies*, p. 85.
2. Interview with Marine Gen. Joseph Hoar, ret.
3. Ibid.
4. Interview with former CENTCOM commander, Gen. Anthony Zinni.
5. Ibid.
6. Former White House official.
7. Interviews with former Ambassador Robert Oakley.
8. Interviews with Gen. Hoar.
9. Interviews with former CIA operative Ernie Shanklin.
10. Confidential interview.
11. Zinni interview.
12. Former White House official.
13. Former White House official.

12: THE WANT OF SUCCESS

Interviews with principals.

13: HAMMER ON THE ANVIL

Interviews with principals.

1. Peter Galbraith interviews.
2. Louis Sell interview.

14: FACING ADVERSITY

Interviews with principals.

1. Former administration official.
2. Arthur M. Schlesinger, Jr., *Cycles of American History*, p. 175.
3. Strobe Talbott, *The Russia Hand: A Memoir of Presidential Diplomacy*, New York: Random House, 2003, p. 175.
4. Silber and Little, *Yugoslavia: Death of a Nation*, p. 309
5. Roger Cohen, *Hearts Grown Brutal: Sagas of Sarajevo*, New York: Random House, 1998, p. 247.
6. Ibid, p. 258.
7. Former administration official.
8. Former U.S. intelligence officials. See also, Cees Wiebes, *Intelligence and the War in Bosnia*, Berlin: Lit Verlag, 2006, p. 211.

15: TO BE USED AND PUSHED ASIDE

Interviews with principals, including interviews and e-mails with former CIA director James Woolsey.

1. Former administration official.

2. Steve Coll, *Ghost Wars*, New York: Penguin, 2004, p. 244.

3. Former NSA officials.

4. Multiple interviews with former senior DIA official, Col. Pat Lang, ret.

16: THE RETURN OF HELL

Interviews with principals, including Peter Galbraith and his wife, Tune Bringa, who was kind enough to read the relevant copy.

1. John Harris, *The Survivor*, p. 149.

2. Bob Woodward, *The Choice*, New York, Simon & Schuster, New York, 1996, p. 235.

3. *Srebrenica: A 'Safe' Area*, a 3,000-page report by the Netherlands Institute on War Documentation, 2005. See Part 3, Chapter 1, Section 4; Part 3, Chapter 2, Section 2. See also, *Report of the Secretary-General Pursuant to General Assembly Resolution 53/55*, Srebrenica Report, p. 190.

4. Madeleine Albright, *Madam Secretary*, New York: Hyperion, 2003, pp. 182–83. See also, Michael Dobbs, *Madeleine Albright: a Twentieth Century Odyssey*, New York: Henry Holt, 1999, p. 362 and pp. 186–188.

5. Interviews. See also, *Srebrenica: Safe Area*, Appendix 6, Chapter 7, Section 2. This appendix deals with imagery intelligence. See also Appendix 2, Chapter 5, on the "Signals Intelligence War." The odd fact is that because of poor weather there was imagery intelligence of the area before and after the executions, but *no picture was found of the killings themselves*. See also, Appendix 6, Chapter 7, Section 6, and Appendix 6, Chapter 8, Section 7, of the report. See also Part 3, Chapter 6, Section 10. In all cases I was able to verify assertions in the report by my own reporting.

6. See above.

7. Former administration official.

8. Interviews. Also see, Appendix 2, Chapter 7 of Netherlands report on how Albright's satellite photos were discovered, verified by former U.S. intelligence officials.

17: THE RIVALS

Interview with principals, Ivo Daalder, *Getting to Dayton: The Making of Bosnia Policy*, Washington, D.C.: Brookings Institution Press, 2000, p. 88.

1. Former administration officials.

2. Ibid.

3. Ibid.

4. Milos Stankovic, *Trusted Mole*, London: HarperCollins, 2000, pp. 250–251, and former U.S. officials.

5. Stankovic, ibid.

6. Halberstam, *War in a Time of Peace*, p. 304.

18: "COVENANTS WITHOUT SWORDS BE BUT WORDS"

Interviews with principals.

1. Material on London from Daalder, *Getting to Dayton*, pp. 72–79. See also Carla Ann Robins, Thomas E. Ricks, and Mark M. Nelson, "U.S. Seeks Bosnian Airstrikes," *Wall Street Journal*, July 19, 1995, and Ann Devoy and Michael Dobbs, "U.S. Unity Must Proceed Balkan Action," *Washington Post*, July 18, 1995.

2. Former senior U.S. officials.

3. Daalder, *Getting to Dayton*, p. 120.
4. Former administration officials.
5. Former U.S. intelligence officials.
6. Interview with Galbraith.
7. Former U.S. intelligence officials.
8. For details on "Operation Storm," see Daalder, *Getting to Dayton*, pp. 22–24, also Adam LeBor, *Milosevic*, New Haven: Yale University Press, 2005, pp. 228–330; Mark Danner, "Operation Storm," *New York Review of Books*, Oct. 22, 1998, and Steve Engleberg, "U.S. Took Calculated Risk in Not Curbing Croat Attack," *New York Times*, Aug. 13, 1995, p. 11.
9. LeBor, *Milosevic*, p. 239.
10. Holbrooke, *To End a War*, p. 73.
11. Lake said to Holbrooke, "This is the kind of thing we dreamed of doing together thirty years ago in Vietnam. I'm going to be with you all the way. And if this thing fails, it's my ass more than yours." (Holbrooke, *To End a War*, p. 74.)
12. Holbrooke, *To End A War*, p. 73.

19: "THE STRIFE OF WILLS, THE WARS OF PRECEDENCE"
Interviews with principals including U.S. diplomat Louis Sell.
1. Louis Sell, *Slobodan Milosevic and the Destruction of Yugoslavia*, Durham, NC: Duke University Press, 2002, p. 230.
2. Holbrooke, *To End a War*, p. 234.
3. Ibid, p. 207.
4. Interview with Larry Johnson.
5. LeBor, *Milosevic*, p. 244.
6. Participants and Halberstam, *War in a Time of Peace*, p. 255.
7. LeBor, *Milosevic*, p. 240.
8. Sell, *Slobodan Milosevic and the Destruction of Yugoslavia*, p. 211.
9. Ibid.
10. Holbrooke, *To End a War*, p. 290. Also, Sell, *Slobodan Milosevic and the Destruction of Yugoslavia*, p. 253. See also, LeBor, *Milosevic*, p. 251.
11. Ibid, *To End a War*, p. 291.
12. Ibid, p. 295.
13. It should be noted that the CIA had every room at the Dayton Talks thoroughly bugged. The agency at the time located a Milosevic advisor who suggested that a coup against the Serb might be possible. The CIA sent an agent to Belgrade who met with a high-ranking potential defector who was then flown to agency headquarters at Langley. The man had numerous connections to Milosevic's inner circle, but the plan was thought premature.

20: "HUMAN ALL TOO HUMAN"
Interviews with principals.
1. Lt. Gen. Bernard Trainor, ret., e-mail, March 5, 2007.
2. Former senior CIA official.
3. United Nations Web site, April 8, 1991. See also, Nancy Soderberg, *The Superpower Myth: the Use and Misuse of American Might*, New Jersey: John Wiley & Sons, 2005, p. 204.
4. Barry Lando, *Web of Deceit*, New York: Other Press, 2005, p. 196.

21: DUAL CONTAINMENT

1. Douglas Jehl, "Clinton bluntly warns Iraq to yield to arms inspectors," *New York Times,* June 28, 1993.
2. Sharon Waxman, "France Criticizes Attack on Iraq: Paris Contends U.S. Strike Went Beyond U.N. Resolutions, *Washington Post,* Jan. 21, 1993.
3. William Safire, "Essay: Memories of Yitzhak Rabin," *New York Times,* Nov. 6, 1995.
4. Zbigniew Brzezinski, *Power and Principle,* pp. 90–91.
5. Dennis Ross, *The Missing Peace: The Inside Story of the Fight for Middle East Peace,* New York: Farrar, Strauss & Giroux, 2004, p. 90.
6. The Palestine Liberation Organization was the political and paramilitary organization regarded by the Arab League since October 1974 as the sole legitimate representative of the Palestinian people. Founded in 1964 in Jerusalem and led by PLO chairman Yasser Arafat, its goal was the liberation of Palestine through armed struggle. It had used terror tactics to attack Israel from bases in Jordan, Syria and Lebanon as well as the Gaza Strip and West Bank. Israel and the PLO had been the deadliest of enemies until August 1993 when a new era of Israeli-Arab relations began. Without notifying the United States, the two enemies signed a peace agreement in Oslo, Norway. This was the same PLO that previous Israel prime ministers had refused to see as equals and rejected any dealings with them. Never before had the Israelis sat down for talks with the PLO, but under Rabin's leadership they had.
7. Bill Clinton, *My Life,* New York: Alfred A. Knopf, 2004, p. 541.
8. Ibid.
9. Christopher, *Chances of a Lifetime,* p. 293.
10. Ibid.
11. Ross, *The Missing Peace,* p. 173–176.
12. Former CIA official.

22: SHADOW WAR

Interviews with principals including former CIA official Whitley Bruner, Warren Marik, and Bob Baer from November to April 2007 as well as program participants.

1. Albright, *Madam Secretary,* p. 272.
2. Interview, former CIA official, Jack Devine.
3. Interviews with Tyler Drumheller.
4. Interview with General Anthony Zinni.
5. Former CIA official.
6. James Bamford, "The Man Who Sold the War," *Rolling Stone,* Nov. 17, 2005, p. 8.
7. Bamford, ibid.
8. Interview with former State Department official Ned Walker.
9. Cockburn and Cockburn, *Saddam Hussein,* p. 31.
10. Former administration official.
11. Seymour Hersh, "Saddam's Best Friend," *The New Yorker,* April 5, 1999.
12. Kenneth Pollack, *The Persian Puzzle: The Conflict Between Iran and America,* New York: Random House, 2004, p. 74, and interviews.
13. Former DIA official.
14. Robert Baer, *See No Evil: the True Story of a Ground Soldier in the CIA's War on Terror,* New York: Crown, 2002, p. 173–175.

23: A REAL STEP UP

Multiple interviews with former senior officials.

1. Evan Thomas and Victoria Gregory, "Spooking the Director," *Newsweek*, Nov. 6, 1995.
2. Former White House official. See also, "A Profile of CIA Director John Deutch," *NPR Weekend Edition*, May 19, 1996.
3. Former CIA official.
4. Evan Thomas, "Cleaning up the Company," *Newsweek*, June 12, 1995.
5. Ibid.
6. Former CIA official.
7. Former CIA officials.
8. Interview with Baer.
9. Interview with prominent neoconservative Laurie Mylroie.

24: CONTENDING WITH GHOSTS

Interviews with principals.

1. Interview with former CIA operative Warren Marik.
2. Interview with former U.S. diplomat David Mack.
3. Interview with Vince Cannistraro.
4. Interview with Middle East specialist Phil Stoddard.
5. Marik interview.
6. Interview with former CIA Jordan chief of station David Manners.
7. Pollack interview.

25: THE GREAT GAME BEGINS

Interviews with principals.

1. Miles Copeland, *The Game of Nations*, New York: Simon & Schuster, 1969, p. 12.
2. Ibid, p. 42
3. Ibid, p. 53.
4. Ibid, p. 60.
5. Ibid, p. 66.
6. Herbert Butterfield, *Christianity and History*, New York: Scribner, 1948, p. 30.
7. Interview with Lang. See also, Bob Woodward, *The Commanders*, New York: Simon & Schuster, 1991, pp. 360–361.
8. Woodward, ibid.
9. Former CIA operative.
10. Interviews with CIA officials.
11. Member of CIA action team.

26: OPERATION BACKFIRE

Interviews with principals.

1. Multiple interviews with former CIA official Whitley Bruner.
2. Manners interview.
3. Manners interview.
4. Bruner interview.
5. Mack interview.
6. Walker interview.

7. It is important to note that the Iraqi and tribal assets of the failed coup were to play an important part in the 2003 war with Iraq. The CIA continued to use General Shawani and his tribal associates in concert with leader of the American forces, General Tommy Franks to protect supply routes and keep Saddam's men from torching the southern oil fields. In fact, the CIA incessantly predicted mass capitulations of the Iraqi army which unfortunately did not occur. But the expectation of such surrenders determined the small size of Franks's forces, which turned out to be inadequate. See, George Tenet, *At the Center of the Storm: My Years at the CIA*, New York: HarperCollins, p. 388–389.

27: STARS THAT SHINE AND NEVER WEEP

Interviews with principals.

1. Christopher, *Chances of a Lifetime*, p. 299.
2. Thomas Segev, *1967: Israel: The War, and the Year That Transformed the Middle East*, New York: Metropolitan Books Henry Holt, 2005, p. 299. See also, Ross, *The Missing Peace*, pp. 235–236.
3. Baker, *The Politics of Diplomacy*, p. 121.
4. Benjamin Netanyahu, of the far right-wing Likud Party, was, along with former Israeli Prime Minister Ariel Sharon, the most important figure of Israel's far-right wing. The U.S. diplomatic and intelligence community had had little to do with Sharon ever since he had been identified as one of the recruiters in 1981 of U.S. Navy field intelligence analyst Jonathan Pollard by the Israeli Ministry of Defense when Sharon was defense minister. With Sharon's knowledge, Israel began to trade U.S. intelligence data with the Soviets whose penetration of Israel's intelligence establishment occurred in the early 1980s and involved "right-wing defense officials close to Ariel Sharon," in the words of senior FBI counterintelligence officials and corroborated to me by former Secretary of Defense Caspar Weinberger. U.S. intelligence officials said they were aware of reports of meetings between Israeli and Soviet officials in Cyprus, a well-known Soviet base for espionage operations against Israel. The stolen Pollard information was traded to the Soviets in return for promises of increased emigration of Soviet Jews to Israel. "It began as a straight data-for-people deal," said a former State Department official, but the result was that "the Soviets penetrated the Israeli defense establishment at the highest level," the State Department official said.
5. Michael Rubner, "Making Peace with the PLO: The Rabin Government's Road to the Oslo Accord," *Middle East Policy*, Oct. 1, 1998.
6. Interviews with Ned Walker.
7. Morris, *Behind the Oval Office*, p. 24.
8. Ibid, p. 256.
9. Hillel Schkener, "A house divided: Israel Votes (1996 elections)," *The Nation*, June, 10, 1996.
10. Clinton advisors were recommending that to sweeten the pot for Peres, the White House and Peres would pressure the chairman of the House International Relations Committee, Rep. Benjamin Gilman, R-N.Y., to unblock $10 million for the Palestinian Authority, being blocked by the Republican majority. The money represents the U.S. contribution in 1995 to the operating expenses of the authority. Gilman ignored Clinton's pleas.
11. Interview with Walker.

28: THE ALMOST WAR

Interviews with principals.

1. Larry Wright, *The Looming Tower: Al-Qaeda and the Road to 9/11*, New York: Alfred A. Knopf, 2006, p. 238.
2. Clarke, *Against All Enemies*, p. 113.
3. Elsah Walsh, "Louis Freeh's Last Case," *The New Yorker*, May 14, 2001, p. 30.
4. Ibid.
5. Wright, *The Looming Tower*, p. 238.
6. Clarke, *Against All Enemies*, p. 118.
7. Ibid, p. 120.
8. Former White House official.
9. Interview with former Intelligence and Research official Wayne White.
10. Walsh, ibid. See also, Pollack, *The Persian Puzzle*, p. 323.
11. Walsh, ibid.
12. Former White House official.

(See also, Bradley Graham, Dana Priest, and Barton Gellman, "Diplomacy and Doubts on the Road to War: US Prepared to Bomb Iraq While Wondering if the Aftermath Would Be Worth It," *Washington Post*, March 1, 1998.)

29: SINISTER DESIGNS

Interviews with principals.

1. Morris, *Behind the Oval Office*, p. 287. See also, Bob Woodward, *Shadow*, New York: Simon & Schuster, 1999, pp. 240–243.
2. There were blizzards of figures. According to Clinton aide Nancy Soderberg, a UNICEF report estimated that five hundred thousand children had died, of which 100,000 to 227,000 were children under the age of five. Another study by the Red Crescent Society of Iraq estimated that food shortages had already caused 3,000 infant deaths. An October 1991 study by a Harvard University team estimated that a million children were starving to death. By March 1996, a World Health Organization study said that infant mortality had increased by 600 percent. Barry Lando, *Web of Deceit*, p. 305, quotes authorities that children were dying at a rate of 4,500 per month. A later 1996 UNICEF study said that Iraq had the worst infant mortality rate of 188 countries monitored by that agency.
3. Lando, *Web of Deceit*, p. 213.
4. Soderberg, *The Superpower Myth*, p. 206.
5. Hyland, *Clinton's World*, p. 178.
6. Robert O. Freedman, "U.S. Policy Towards the Middle East in Clinton's Second Term," *Middle East Review*, November, 1997.
7. Graham, Priest, Gellman, "Diplomacy and Doubts on the Road to War: US Prepared to Bomb Iraq While Wondering if the Aftermath Would Be Worth It," *Washington Post*, March 1, 1998.
8. Ibid.

30: UNDER WESTERN EYES

Interviews with principals.

1. "Saddam Bows, Clinton Doesn't," *The Economist*, June 18, 1994.

2. See Scott Ritter, *Iraq Confidential: The Untold Story of the Intelligence Conspiracy to Undermine the UN and the Overthrow of Saddam Hussein*, New York: Nation Books, 2005, p.11.

3. Ibid, p.16.

4. Former CIA officials.

5. Ritter, *Iraq Confidential*, p. 42.

6. Former CIA officials. Also Ritter, *Iraq Confidential*, p. 116.

7. Craig Whitney, *WMD Mirage*, New York: Public Affairs, 2005, p. 251. Economic sanctions were starting to pinch Milosevic severely by then.

8. Ibid, p. 110.

9. Albright, *Madam Secretary*, p. 274, pp. 276–277, plus former U.S. intelligence officials.

10. Former CIA officials.

11. Ritter interview.

<h3 style="text-align:center">31: WMD MIRAGE</h3>

Interviews with principals.

1. The town hall meeting took place at the University of Ohio, Feb 18, 1998. See Barry Schweid, "Albright, defense team seek to sway U.S. opinion," *Chicago Sun-Times*, Feb. 18, 1998, and Thomas Oliphant, "The Real Story on the Albright Show in Ohio," *Boston Globe*, Feb. 23, 1998.

2. Whitney, *WMD Mirage*, p. 251.

3. Former administration official. See also, "Intelligence on Iraq's WMD Faulty," *China Daily*, March 29, 2004; Paul Kerr, "Duelfer Disproves U.S. WMD Claims," *Arms Control Today*, Nov. 1, 2004; Peter Pringle, "A Deadly Cloud of Paranoia Drifts Across the U.S., Mr. Clinton has cleverly conflated domestic panic over terrorism with an exaggerated report of Saddam's arsenal; THE THREAT," The *Independent*, Dec 20, 1998; Al Venter, "Iraq's 'Nearly' Bomb," *The Middle East*, April 1, 1998. See especially, "The Clinton Administration's Public Case Against Saddam Hussein," *Project for the New American Century*, 2004. This is full of statements providing alleged details of Iraq's WMD capabilities, all of which were wildly wrong. These claims included accusations that Saddam had "twenty-five biological warheads for missiles and one-hundred fifty-seven aerial bombs," and talked of tons of chemical and biological agents. Yet on Dec. 16, 1998, as Clinton launched Operation Desert Fox, he said: "Our mission is clear: to degrade Saddam's capacity to develop and deliver weapons of mass destruction." The phrase "to degrade Saddam's capacity to deliver" is weakening and puzzling to Clinton's meaning. Either Saddam Hussein *had* the arsenal Clinton and his chief advisors said he had or he didn't.

<h3 style="text-align:center">32: BRILLIANT VICTORY</h3>

Interviews with principals.

1. Helen Dewar and John M. Gosko, "Lott Criticizes Iraq Deal as 'Appeasement,'" *Washington Post*, Feb. 26, 1998.

2. Harris, *The Survivor*, p. 345, and meeting participant.

3. Ritter, *Iraq Confidential*, p. 215.

4. Ritter interview.

5. Meeting participant.

6. Harris, *The Survivor*, p. 343.

7. Meeting participant.

8. Ronald Lewin, *Rommel as Military Commander*, New York: Ballantine, 1968, p. 206.

9. Harris, *The Survivor*, p. 353.

10. Woodward, *Shadow*, p. 490.

11. Ibid, pp. 490–495.

12. Halberstam, *War in a Time of Peace*, p. 440.

13. Interview with General Zinni. See also William Arkin, "The Difference Was in the Details," *Washington Post*, Jan. 17, 1999.

14. Ibid.

15. Ibid.

16. John Keegan, *The Iraq War*, New York: Vintage, 2005, pp. 1–5.

17. General Zinni interview.

18. Manners interview.

19. Kenneth Pollack, "Next Stop Baghdad?" *Foreign Affairs*, March/April, 2000.

33: GOOD AND EVIL IN HISTORY

Interviews with principals. I also drew on valuable data from Jane Mayer's, "The Manipulator," The New Yorker, June 7, 2004.

1. Clarke, *Against All Enemies*, p. 233.

2. Aram Roston, *The Man Who Pushed America to War*, New York: Nation Books, p. 135.

3. Ibid, p. 137.

4. One wonders what Richard Perle was thinking. Jacques Chirac was born in 1932, and so was only twelve years old at the time of France's 1944 liberation. Perle appears to confuse Charles de Gaulle with Chirac, which is not reassuring.

34: A CHANGING WORLD

Interviews with principals.

1. Wright, *The Looming Tower*, pp. 2–8.

2. Interview with former CIA operative Stan Bedlington.

3. Former U.S. intelligence officials.

4. Hamas evolved from the cells of the Muslim Brotherhood, the oldest and largest Sunni Arab political movement whose goal was to turn Egypt into a Muslim State. It was founded in 1928 and has branches in Syria, Jordan, and many Arab states. Originally nonviolent, it turned to terrorism after the Egyptian government obstructed attempts by the Brotherhood to field candidates for elections.

5. Richard Sale, "Hamas History Tied to Israel, *United Press International*, June 18, 2002.

6. Bruce Catton, *The Coming Fury*, New York: Doubleday, 1961, p. 404.

35: HEAVY HOUR

Interviews with principals.

1. Harris, *The Survivor*, p. 179.

2. Former administration officials.

3. See also, Hamilton, *Bill Clinton: Mastering the Presidency*, p. 439.

4. Ibid.

5. "Al Qaeda May Have Tried to Kill Clinton," *United Press International*, Feb. 6, 2002.

6. Walker interview.

7. Stephen Grey, *Ghost Plane: The True Story of a CIA Torture Program*, New York: St. Martin's Press, 2006, p. 126.

8. Clarke, *Against All Enemies*, p. 144.

9. Daniel Benjamin and Steve Simon, *The Age of Sacred Terror*, New York: Random House, 2002, p. 232.

10. Ibid.

11. Ibid.

12. Stephen Coll, *Ghost Wars: the Secret History of the CIA, Afghanistan, and bin Laden from the Soviet Invasion to Sept. 10, 2001*, New York: Penguin, 2004, p. 387–389.

13. Former administration officials.

14. Benjamin and Simon, *The Age of Sacred Terror*, p. 257.

15. Wright, *The Looming Tower*, p. 279.

36: GLORIOUS DEATH

Interviews with principals including terrorist expert, Rohan Gunaratna, *Inside Al Qaeda: Global Network of Terror*, New York: Columbia University Press, p. 85.

1. Coll, *Ghost Wars*, pp. 423–427.

2. Ibid, p. 409.

3. Former administration official.

37: HIGH-STAKES GAME

Interviews with principals including former CIA officials Larry Johnson, Milt Bearden, Vince Cannistraro, Marc Sageman; David Long, former chief of State Department Counterterrorism; former DIA Middle East expert, Pat Lang; Judith Yaphe, e-mail exchanges with former senior India intelligence official B. Raman, Rohan Gunaratna, and others who declined to be named.

1. Former administration officials.

2. Sageman interview.

3. Ibid.

4. For those who insist on claiming that Bill Clinton was weak in confronting bin Laden, it is interesting to consult the 9/11 Report that concluded: "Policymakers in the Clinton administration, including his national security advisor, told us that the President's intent regarding covert action against bin Laden was clear: He wanted him dead." See Thomas K. Kean, Chair and Lee Hamilton, Vice Chair, *The 9/11 Report: The National Commission on Terrorist Attacks Upon the United States*, New York, St. Martins, 2004, pp. 194–195. Whether this was communicated to the CIA remains a matter of controversy.

5. Former administration official.

38: CALIPHATE

Interviews with principals.

1. Clarke, *Against All Enemies*, p. 137.

2. Evan F. Kohlmann, *Al-Qaida's Jihad in Europe*, Oxford, U.K.: Berg, 2004, p. 75.

3. Kohlmann, *Al-Qaida's Jihad in Europe*, p. 130.

4. Wright, *The Looming Tower*, p. 268.

5. Clarke, *Against All Enemies*, p. 91.

6. Jane Mayer, "Outsourcing Terror," *The New Yorker*, Feb. 14, 2003, p. 4. Also Wright, *The Looming Tower*, p. 268.

7. Kohlmann, *Al-Qaida's Jihad in Europe*, p. 20.

8. Clarke, *Against All Enemies*, p. 140.

9. Kohlmann, *Al-Qaida's Jihad in Europe*, p. 172.

39: ETERNAL ALIENS

Interviews with principals.

1. Tim Judah, *Kosovo: War and Revenge*, New Haven: Yale University Press, 2002, p. 84.

2. Sell, *Slobodan Milosevic and the Destruction of Yugoslavia*, p. 278.

40: MADAM SECRETARY

Interviews with principals.

1. Norma Percy, Angus Macqueen, and Paul Mitchell, producers, *The Fall of Milosevic*, Brook Lapping Associates for BBC, London, 2001. Three episodes: *Defiance, War, Finished.*

2. Former CIA officials.

3. Percy et al., *The Fall of Milosevic: War.*

4. Frontline, *War in Europe*, Oct. 27, 1999.

5. Wesley Clark, *Waging Modern War*, New York: Public Affairs, 2001, p. 160.

6. Ibid, p. 161.

7. Barton Gellman, "The Path to Crisis: How the United States and Its Allies Went to War," *Washington Post*, April 18, 1999.

8. Former administration officials. See, Thomas W. Lippman, *Madeleine Albright and the New American Diplomacy*, Boulder: Westview Press, pp. 27–28.

9. Albright, *Madam Secretary*, pp. 178–182.

10. Former administration officials.

11. Gellman, "The Path to Crisis."

12. Ibid, p. 6.

13. Barbara W. Tuchman, *The Proud Tower: A Portrait of the World Before the War, 1890–1914*, New York: Scribner, 1966, p. 35.

41: BUCKEYES AND RAZORBACKS

Interviews with principals.

1. Holbrooke, *To End a War*, p.107.

2. Ibid, 189.

3. Former administration officials.

4. Former senior administration officials.

5. Former administration officials.

6. Holbrooke, *To End a War*, p. 118. Smith also told Holbrooke, "I have no dog in this fight," ibid. Other quotes from principals. There was at the time no method of arresting Serb war criminals.

7. John Shattuck, *Freedom on Fire: Human Rights & America's Response*, Cambridge: Harvard University Press, 2005, p. 215.

8. Program operative, Special Forces. See also Elizabeth Neuffer, "NATO Seeks Suspects in Bosnia Raids: Alleged Serb War Criminal Killed; Second Arrested, British Soldier Hurt," *Boston Globe*, July 11, 1997.

9. Program operative.
10. Former White House official.
11. Clark, *Waging Modern War*, p. 92. Notes from meeting by participants.
12. Ibid, pp. 92–93, and participants.
13. Rest of material to end of chapter from interviews with program operatives.

42: KILL, CONFISCATE, DESTROY
Interviews with principals.
1. Dana Priest, "Lott Questions Timing on Kosovo: Administration Has 'No Real Plan' of Action, GOD Leader Says," *Washington Post*, Oct. 5, 1999.
2. Interviews with former officials. It was Berger who in the mid-1990s was acutely aware of the threat posed by bin Laden when few in the White House were. It was thanks to Berger that the CIA prepared a daily report on bin Laden that included the latest overnight intelligence on the Saudi terrorist. Berger was as obsessed as Richard Clarke was, Clarke being known derisively as the "Chicken Little" of the Islamic terrorist question. Once speaking of Clinton's virulent hatred of bin Laden, Berger said to George Tenet that "Clinton wanted him dead." This startled Tenet who replied that the agency hadn't been authorized to kill bin Laden, only to capture him. But Berger informed Tenet of the Memorandum of Notification that approved the Saudi's assassination.

When Clinton ordered the bombing of the bin Laden camp in Afghanistan, Berger warned it would prompt an outburst of cynical sneering since the Lewinsky scandal was white-hot at the time, but Clinton said, "We're going to get crap either way, so you do the right thing." (From interviews)

Clark and the Counterterrorism Security Group reported directly to Berger's Small Group made up of Cohen, Albright, Attorney General Janet Reno, and a tiny number of other officials. Berger's predominance had come at Clarke's expense, and Berger and others tried to soothe the ruffled feathers of the fiery Clarke.
3. Dana Priest, *The Mission: Waging War and Keeping the Peace*, New York: W.W. Norton, 2004, pp. 97–98.
4. Elaine Sciolino and Ethan Bronner, "Crisis in the Balkans: How a President, Distracted by Scandal, Entered a Balkan War," *New York Times*, April 18, 1999; Gellman *The Path to Crisis.*
5. Ivo Daalder and Mike O'Hanlon, *Winning Ugly: NATO's War to Save Kosovo*, Washington, D.C.: Brookings Institution Press, 2000, p. 89.
6. Judah, *Kosovo*, p. 214.
7. Sciolino and Bronner, "Crisis in the Balkans," p. 13.
8. Hyland, *Clinton's World*, p. 33.

43: THE STAKES AT CHESS
Interviews with principals.
1. R. Jeffrey Smith and William Drozdiak, "The Anatomy of a Purge," *Washington Post*, April 11, 1999.
2. Daalder and O'Hanlon, *Winning Ugly*, p. 94.
3. Zimmermann, *Origins of a Catastrophe*, p. 4.
4. Catton, *This Hallowed Ground*, p. 152.

5. Priest, *The Mission*, p. 53.

6. Halberstam, *War in a Time of Peace*, p. 423.

7. Memo of William C. Bullitt, President Franklin Roosevelt's first Ambassador to the Soviet Union.

8. Priest, *The Mission*, p. 260.

9. Ibid., p. 260.

10. Ibid., p. 258.

11. Morris, *Behind the Oval Office*, p. 255.

12. Percy et al., *The Fall of Milosevic: War.*

13. Ibid.

14. Ibid.

44: THE RUTHLESS TRUTH OF WAR

Interviews with principals.

1. Stephen Mufson and John F. Harris, "Novice Became Confident Diplomat on World Stage," *Washington Post*, Jan. 15, 2001.

2. Harris, *The Survivor*, p. 368.

3. Interview with Dimitri Simes, Russian expert, Nixon Foundation; and interviews with former CIA officials.

4. Percy et al., *The Fall of Milosevic: War.*

5. Former CIA officials. See also, Robert Windrem, "Kosovo: CIA: Milosevic Difficult to Track," *NBC News*, June 26, 1999.

6. Former senior Clinton advisor.

7. Percy et al., *The Fall of Milosevic: War.*

8. Former administration official.

9. Percy et al., *The Fall of Milosevic: War.*

10. Former White House officials. See also, Harris, *The Survivor*, p. 373.

11. Daalder and O'Hanlon, *Winning Ugly*, p. 164.

12. Former White House officials. General Clark, e-mail.

13. John Norris, *Collision Course: NATO, Russia and Kosovo*, New York: Praeger, 2005, p. 180.

14. Ibid, p. 189.

15. E-mail from General Clark, and Percy et al., *The Fall of Milosevic: War.*

16. Former meeting participant.

17. Former Air Force official.

18. Percy et al., *The Fall of Milosevic: War.*

For additional data on air war see also, David Fromkin, *Kosovo Crossing: American Ideals Meet Reality on the Balkan Battlefields*, New York: Free Press, 1999; Andrew J. Bacevich and Eliot A. Cohen, editors, *War Over Kosovo*, New York: Colombia University Press, 2001; Earl M. Tilford Jr., "Operation Allied Force and the Role of Air Power," Parameters, Winter, 1999–2000; Benjamin W. Lamgeth, *NATO's Air War for Kosovo: A Strategic and Operational* Assessment, Santa Monica: Rand, 2002. Also the excellent James Kurth, Andrew Bacevich and Eliot A. Cohen.

45: BREADTH OF DESTRUCTION

Interviews with principals.

1. Ambassador Robert S. Gelbard, Kosovo, Testimony before the House International Relations Committee, July 23, 1998, p. 9.
2. R. Jeffrey Smith, "High-Tech Cooperation in Bosnia," *Washington Post*, Jan. 19, 1996, p. 1.
3. Vernon Loeb, "Test of Strength," *Washington Post*, July 29, 2001.
4. Frederic Levien, "Kosovo: an IW Report Card," *Journal of Electronic Defense*, Aug. 1, 1999.
5. Ibid.
6. Dana Priest, "Kosovo Land Threat May Have Won War," *Washington Post*, Sept. 19, 1999.
7. Ron Paul, office press release, April 20, 1999.
8. Representative Floyd Spence, CNN, April 28, 1999.
9. William Arkin, "Ask Not for Whom the Phone Rings," *Washington Post*, Oct. 11, 1999.
10. Ibid.
11. Former U.S. official.
12. Michael Hirsh, "NATO's Game of Chicken," *Newsweek*, July 26, 1999. U.S. intelligence played an outstanding part in the whole operation. In less than two weeks after Racak, U.S. intelligence included listening posts in Croatia in Tuzla and Brac Island along with sites in Albania; and dozens of U.S. signals intelligence satellites such as the Vortex, Magnum, Jumpseat and Trumpet had intercepted calls that showed the massacre there had been orchestrated by senior officials in Belgrade and the Serb military leadership in Kosovo. When three Serb soldiers were killed by the KLA on Jan. 8, officials in Belgrade ordered troops to "go in heavy," according to former U.S. officials who named Serb deputy prime minister Nikola Sainovic and senior Serb interior minister Gen. Sreten Lukic who kept in touch with Belgrade as the massacre was taking place, relating the number of executions. At one point Sainovic called Lukic from Belgrade asking how many Racak villagers had been killed. Lukic replied the total was twenty-two.

   When the massacre was over and forty-five villagers had been executed, Sainovic, who reported to Milosevic, tried to put a cover-up in place to defuse world outrage by portraying the killings as the result of KLA rebels attempting to engage Serb troops. When U.N. war crimes investigator Louise Arbrour was turned back from investigating the execution site, U.S. and other officials finally pressured Serbia to admit a team of Finish forensic pathologists to do autopsies on the dead. See R. Jeffrey Smith, "Serbs Tried to Cover Up Massacre: Kosovo Reprisal Plot Bared by Phone Taps," *Washington Post*, Jan. 29, 1999, "Serb Talk of Killing Was Intercepted, U.S. Says" *New York Times*, Jan. 29, 1999, all confirmed by former U.S. officials.
13. www.un.org.icty, May 27, 1999.
14. Stephen T. Hosmer, "*Why Milosevic Decided to Settle When He Did*," Santa Monica: Rand, 2001, p.100.
15. Ibid.
16. Ibid., p. 72.
17. Talbott, *The Russia Hand*, p. 309, p. 318.
18. Percy et al., *The Fall of Milosevic: War*.

46: SOWING THE WIND

Interviews with principals.

1. Leonard J. Cohen, *Serpent in the Bosom: the Rise and Fall of Slobodan Milosevic*, Boulder: Westview, 2002, p. 404.
2. Ibid., p. 393.
3. Ibid., p. 303.
4. Former administration official.
5. Percy et al., *The Fall of Milosevic: War.*
6. Albright, *Madam Secretary*, p. 500. Quoted by former aide.
7. Former administration official.
8. John Donnelly, "U.S. Spies Are Busy Recruiting Serbs to Overthrow Milosevic, but Lack of Viable Successor and Yugoslav's Leader's Strengths Complicate Efforts," *Milwaukee Journal Sentinel*, Aug. 31, 1999.
9. Cohen, *Serpent in the Bosom*, pp. 303–304.
10. Percy et al., *The Fall of Milosevic: Finished.*
11. Ibid.
12. Ibid.
13. Ibid.
14. Former administration official.
15. Percy et al., *The Fall of Milosevic: Finished.*

47: CRISIS OF FATE

Interviews with principals including Louis Sell.

1. Sell interview. See also, Cohen, *Serpent in the Bosom*, p. 394.
2. Sell, *"Slobodan Milosevic and the Destruction of Yugoslavia,"* p. 329.
3. See, CIA document quoted by Joseph E. Smith, *Portrait of a Cold Warrior*, New York: Ballantine, 1976, p. 229.
4. Former CIA officials.
5. Ibid.
6. Ibid.
7. During the Cold War, Israel's intelligence service, the Mossad, had developed an extensive network in Central Europe. Using Polish émigrés and sources in Poland, the Soviet Union, and Hungary, it ran a ratline, or escape route, from Albania to Poland and east into the heart of the Soviet Union. It helped Jews escape and while it did not produce valuable intelligence in the beginning, it was the ratline that smuggled out of Russia Nikita Khrushchev's historic speech debunking Stalin before the 20th Communist Party Congress. Throughout the anti-Milosevic operation, the United States and its allies ran agents into Serbia over similar ratlines, which I have been asked not to name.
8. For material on Sharp, see Pal Amitabh, Sharp interview, *The Progressive*, March 1, 2007; Laura Secord, "War by Other Means," *Boston Globe*, May 28, 2005; Tisa M. Anders, *International Journal of World Peace*, March 1, 2007.
9. Former U.S. intelligence sources.

48: THE GAIN THAT DARKENS

Interviews with principals.

1. "U.S. Confident of Yugoslav Opposition's Electoral Chances," *United Press International*, Sept. 20, 2000.
2. LeBor, *Milosevic*, p. 207.
3. Percy et al., *The Fall of Milosevic: Finished*.
4. Ibid.
5. Cohen, *Serpent in the Bosom*, p. 443.

49: *GOTOV JE!*

Interviews with principals.

1. Percy et al., *The Fall of Milosevic: Finished*.
2. Dragan Bujosevic and Ivan Radovanic, *The Fall of Milosevic: The October 5 Revolution*, London: Palgrave Macmillan, 2003, p. 28.
3. Identified by former CIA officials.
4. Bujosevic and Radovanic, p. 118.
5. Bujosevic and Radovanic, p. 128. Note on the salute from an eyewitness.

50: TO CURE AN EVIL

Interviews with principals including former CIA official Larry Johnson.

1. Percy et al., *The Fall of Milosevic: Finished*. Plus O'Brien interview.
2. Ibid.
3. Ibid.
4. LeBor, *Milosevic*, p. 313.
5. Former U.S. official. Also LeBor, *Milosevic*, p. 316.
6. Former U.S. intelligence officials.
7. Percy et al., *The Fall of Milosevic: Finished*.
8. Ibid.
9. LeBor, *Milosevic*, pp. 316–319.
10. See also, Cohen, *Serpent in the Bosom*, p. 9. Also Sell, *Slobodan Milosevic and The Destruction of Yugoslavia*, p. 356–357. Sell interviews.
11. LeBor, *Milosevic*, p. 318. See also Cohen, *Serpent in the Bosom*, p. 9–12.

EPILOGUE

1. *Reuters* "Clinton Moves to Limit U.S. Peacekeeping Plan," May 11, 1994.
2. Bacevich and Cohen, *War over Kosovo*, p. 171.
3. Ibid., p. 178.
4. Ibid., p. 172. Many military critics deplore the Clinton Doctrine, especially its emphasis on avoiding casualties. Earl M. Tilford Jr. notes that an air power only doctrine can be defeated by the enemy achieving its objectives before air power can be brought to bear. Tilford also says: "If avoiding casualties is the keystone to the strategic arch, that arch will crumble because war without casualties is an oxymoron." Also, he says, no credible foreign policy can be used to "build a lasting international security system as long as the United States seeks to impose its own will on other nations but is unwilling to shed the blood of its own people." Earl M. Tilford Jr., "Operation Allies Force and the Role of Air Power," Parameters, Winter 1999–2000, pp. 24–28.

Yet defenders of the doctrine include Gen. John Jumper, a senior Air Force advisor to Gen. Wesley Clark, and Gen. Joe Ralston, who succeeded Clark as Supreme Allied Commander Europe (SACEUR). Said Jumper, "From the air campaign planning point of view, it is always the neatest and tidiest when you can get a political consensus of the objective at a certain phase, and then go about achieving that objective with the freedom to act as you see militarily best. But that is not the situation we find ourselves in. We can rail against that, but it does no good. It is the politics of the moment that is going to dictate what we are able to do . . . If the limit of the consensus means gradualism, then we are going to have to find a way to deal with a phase air campaign with gradual escalation." He said it was "the probable reality for future conflicts." Quoted in Lt. Col. Paul Strickland, USAF, "USAF Aerospace-Power Doctrine, Decisive or Coercive?" in *Aerospace Power Journal*, Fall 2000.

Gen. Joe Ralston said: ". . . the U.S. Air Force no doubt will continue to maintain the massive application of air power that will be more efficient and effective than gradual escalation. Yet when the political and tactical contraints imposed on air use are extensive and pervasive—and that trend seems more likely than less likely—then gradualism may be perceived as the only option." (Ibid.)

The Clinton way of making war had its imitators. As a prime example, President George W. Bush adopted it when waging war against Al-Qaeda in Afghanistan in 2001, using a minimum of ground spotters to escalate attacks on jihadis and the Taliban till they collapsed. Air power, until the 2003 Iraq invasion, was the chief tool of conflict.

5. American Society of Newspaper Editors, October 27, 1999.
6. Goodwin, *No Ordinary Time*, p. 78.
7. Hamilton, *Bill Clinton: Mastering the Presidency*, pp. 448–9
8. Ibid.

BIBLIOGRAPHY

Albright, Madeleine. *Madam Secretary*. New York: Miramax, 2003.

Anonymous. *Imperial Hubris: Why the West Is Losing the War on Terror*. Washington, D.C.: Brassey's, 2004.

Bacevich, Andrew J., and Eliot A. Cohen, editors. *War over Kosovo: Policy and Strategy in a Global Age*. New York: Columbia University Press, 2001.

Baer, Robert. *See No Evil: The True Story of a Ground Soldier in the CIA's War on Terror*. New York: Crown, 2002.

Baker, James A. III, with Thomas M. DeFrank. *The Politics of Diplomacy: Revolution, War and Peace*. New York: Putnam, 1995.

Benjamin, Daniel, and Steve Simon. *The Age of Sacred Terror*. New York: Random House, 2002.

Bennett, Christopher. *Yugoslavia's Bloody Collapse: Causes, Course and Consequences*. London: C. Hurst, 1995.

Beschloss, Michael. *Presidential Courage: Brave Leaders and How They Changed America, 1789–1989*. New York: Simon & Schuster, 2007.

Black, Conrad. *Roosevelt: Champion of Freedom*. New York: PublicAffairs, 2003.

Brzezinski, Zbigniew. *Power and Principle*. New York: Farrar, Straus & Giroux, 1983.

Bujosevic, Dragan, and Ivan Radovanovic. *The Fall of Milosevic: The October 5 Revolution*. London: Palgrave Macmillan, 2003.

Burns, James MacGregor. *Roosevelt: The Lion and the Fox*. New York: Harcourt, 1956.

———. *Roosevelt: The Soldier of Freedom*. New York: Harvest, 1970.

Butterfield, Herbert. *Christianity and History*. New York: Scribner, 1948.

Canetti, Elias. *Crowds and Power*. London: Phoenix, 2000.

Carney Jr., Col. John, and Benjamin F. Schemmer. *No Room for Error: the Covert Operations of America's Special Tactics Units from Iran to Afghanistan*, New York: Ballantine, 2002.

Catton, Bruce. *This Hallowed Ground*. Edison, NJ: Castle Books, 2002.

Christopher, Warren. *Chances of a Lifetime*. New York: Scribner, 2001.

Clark, Wesley. *Waging Modern War*. New York: Public Affairs, 2001.

Clarke, Richard. *Against All Enemies*. New York: Free Press, 1994.

Cockburn, Andrew, and Patrick Cockburn. *Saddam Hussein: An American Obsession*. Verso, 2000.

Clinton, Bill. *My Life*. New York: Alfred A. Knopf, 2004.

Cohen, Leonard J. *Serpent in the Bosom: The Rise and Fall of Slobodan Milosevic*. Boulder: Westview, 2002.

Cohen, Philip J. *Serbia's Secret War: Propaganda and the Deceit of History*. College Station: Texas A&M University Press, 1996.

Cohen, Roger. *Hearts Grown Brutal: Sagas of Sarajevo*. New York: Random House, 1998.

Coll, Stephen. *Ghost Wars: The Secret History of the CIA, Afghanistan and bin Laden from the Soviet Invasion to September 10, 2001*. New York: Penguin, 2004.

Cook, Blanche Wiesen. *The Declassified Eisenhower: A Divided Legacy of Peace and Political Warfare*. New York: Doubleday, 1982.

Copeland, Miles. *The Game of Nations*. New York: Simon & Schuster, 1969.

Daalder, Ivo H. *Getting to Dayton: The Making of America's Bosnia Policy*. Washington, D.C.: Brookings Institution Press, 2000.

Daalder, Ivo H., and Michael O'Hanlon. *Winning Ugly: NATO's War to Save Kosovo*. Washington, D.C.: Brookings Institution Press, 2000.

Dobbs, Michael. *Madeleine Albright: A Twentieth Century Odyssey*. New York: Henry Holt, 1999.

Doder, Dusko, and Louise Bramson. *Milosevic: Portrait of a Tyrant*. New York: Free Press, 1999.

Drew, Elizabeth. *On the Edge: The Clinton Presidency*. New York: Simon & Schuster, 1994.

———. *Showdown*. New York: Simon & Schuster, 1995.

Donald, David Herbert. *Lincoln*. New York: Simon & Schuster, 2005.

DeLong, Lt. Gen. Michael, with Noah Lukeman. *Inside CentCom: the Unvarnished Truth about the Wars in Afghanistan and Iraq*. Washington, D.C.: Regnery, 2004.

Drumheller, Tyler. *On the Brink: An Insider's Account of How the White House Compromised American Intelligence*. New York: Carroll & Graf, 2006.

Fleming, Thomas. *The New Dealers' War: FDR and the War Within World War II*. New York: Basic Books, 2001.

Freidel, Frank. *Franklin D. Roosevelt: A Rendezvous with Destiny*. Boston: Back Bay/Little, Brown, 1990.

Francona, Ric. *Ally to Adversary: An Eyewitness Account of Iraq's Fall from Grace*. Annapolis: Naval Institute Press, 1999.

Fromkin, David. *Kosovo Crossing: American Ideals Meet Reality in the Balkan Battlefields*. New York: Free Press, 1999.

Gergen, David. *Eyewitness to Power*. New York: Simon & Schuster, 2000.

Glenny, Misha. *The Balkans: Nationalism, War and the Great Powers, 1804–1990*. New York: Penguin, 2000.

———. *The Fall of Yugoslavia: The Third Balkan War*. New York: Columbia University Press, 1996.

Goodwin, Doris Kearns. *No Ordinary Time*. New York: Simon & Schuster, 2004.

———. *Team of Rivals*. New York: Simon & Schuster, 2005.

Goodwin, Jason. *Lords of the Horizons: A History of the Ottoman Empire*. New York: Vintage, 1990.

Gordon, Michael R., and Gen. Bernard E. Trainor. *Cobra II*. New York: Vintage, 2007.

Gourevitch, Philip. *We Wish to Inform You That Tomorrow We Will Be Killed with Our Families*. New York: Farrar, Straus & Giroux, 1998.

Grant, Rebecca. *The B2 Goes to War*. New York: Iris, 2001.

———. *The Kosovo Campaign: Aerospace Power Made It Work*. Air Force Association, 1999.

Grey, Stephen. *Ghost Plane: The True Story of a CIA Torture Program*. New York: St. Martin's, 2006.

Rohan, Gunaratna. *Inside Al Qaeda: Global Network of Terror*. New York: Columbia University Press, 2002.

Gutman, Roy. *Witness to Genocide*. New York: Macmillan, 1993.

Haas, Richard. *Intervention: The Use of American Military Force in the Post-War World*. Washington, D.C.: Brookings Institution Press, 1999.

———. *The Reluctant Sheriff: The United States After the Cold War*. New York: Council on Foreign Relations Press, 1992.

Halberstam, David. *The Best and the Brightest*. New York: Ballantine, 1992.

———. *War in a Time of Peace*. New York: Simon & Schuster, 2001.

Hamilton, Nigel. *Bill Clinton: Mastering the Presidency*. (New York: PublicAffairs, 2007).

Harris, John F. *The Survivor: Bill Clinton in the White House*. New York: Random House, 2005.

Hofstadter, Richard. *The American Political Tradition and the Men Who Made It*. New York: Vintage, 1974.

Holbrooke, Richard. *To End a War*. New York: Modern Library, 1999.

Honig, Jan Willem, and Norbert Roth. *Srebrenica: Record of a War Crime*. New York: Penguin, 1996.

Hosmer, Stephen T. *Why Milosevic Decided to Settle When He Did*. Washington, DC: RAND, 2001.

Hyland, William G. *Clinton's World: Remaking American Foreign Policy*. New York: Praeger, 1999.

Ignatieff, Michael. *Virtual War*. Picador USA, 2000.

———. *The Warrior's Honor: Ethnic War and the Modern Conscience*. New York: Metropolitan Books, 1997.

Ridley, Jaspar. *Tito: A Biography*. London: Constable, 1994.

Johnson, Haynes. *The Best of Times*. New York: Harcourt, 2001.

Judah, Tim. *Kosovo: War and Revenge*. New Haven: Yale University Press, 2002.

———. *The Serbs*. New Haven: Yale University Press, 2000.

Judt, Tony. *Postwar*. New York: Penguin, 2005.

Kaplan, Robert. *Balkan Ghosts: A Journey Through History*. New York: Vintage, 1994.

Keegan, John. *The Iraq War*. New York: Vintage, 2005.

Kissinger, Henry A. *Diplomacy*. New York: Simon & Schuster, 1994.

———. *White House Years*. Boston: Little, Brown, 1979.

Kean, Thomas H., Chair, and Lee Hamilton, Vice Chair. *The Complete Investigation of the 9/11 Report: The National Commission on Terrorist Attacks upon the United States*. New York: St. Martin's, 2004.

Klein, Joe. *The Natural: The Misunderstood Presidency of Bill Clinton*. New York: Broadway, 2002.

Kohlmann, Evan F. *Al-Qaida's Jihad in Europe*. Oxford, U.K.: Berg, 2004.

Krepinevich, Andrew. *The Army and Vietnam*. Baltimore: Johns Hopkins University Press, 1986.

La Bruyere, Jean de. *Les Caractères*. New York: Penguin, 1970.

Lake, Anthony. *Six Nightmares: Real Threats in a Dangerous World and How America Can Meet Them*. Boston: Little, Brown, 2000.

Lambeth, Benjamin S. *NATO's Air War for Kosovo*. Santa Monica, CA: RAND, 2001.

Lando, Barry M. *Web of Deceit*. New York: Other Press, 2007.

Larrabee, Eric. *Commander in Chief: Franklin Delano Roosevelt, His Lieutenants, and Their War*. Annapolis: Naval Institute Press, 1987.

Le Bon, Gustave. *The French Revolution and the Psychology of Revolution*. New York: Transaction Books, 1980.

———. *The Crowd*. New York: Vintage Books, 1964.

LeBor, Adam. *Milosevic*. New Haven: Yale University Press, 2005.

Lewin. Ronald. *Rommel as Military Commander*. New York: Ballantine, 1968.

Lewis, Bernard. *Islam and the West*. New York: Oxford University Press, 1991.

Lippman, Thomas. *Madeleine Albright and the New American Diplomacy*. Boulder: Westview, 2000.

Lukacs, John. *The Passing of the Modern Age*. New York: Harper Torchbook, 1970.

MacMillan, Margaret. *Paris 1919: Six Months That Changed the World*. New York: Random House, 2001.

Malcolm, Noel. *Bosnia: A Short History*. New York: New York University Press, 1994.

———. *Kosovo: A Short History*. New York: New York University Press, 1998.

Maraniss, David. *First in His Class: The Biography of Bill Clinton*. New York: Touchstone, 1996.

Maraniss, David, and Ellen Nakashima. *The Prince of Tennessee: The Rise of Al Gore*. New York: Simon & Schuster, 2000.

Mattingly, Garrett. *Renaissance Diplomacy*. New York: Dover, 1988.

Morris, Dick. *Behind the Oval Office*. Los Angeles: Renaissance, 1999.

Morris, Dick, with Eileen McGann. *Because He Could*. New York: Regan Books, 2004.

Mazower, Mark. *The Balkans: A Short History*. New York: Modern Library, 2000.

Neustadt, Richard E., and Ernest R. May. *Thinking in Time: The Uses of History for Decision-Makers*. New York: Free Press, 1986.

Norris, John. *Collision Course: NATO, Russia and Kosovo*. New York: Praeger, 2005.

Owen, David. *Balkan Odyssey*. New York: Harcourt Brace, 1996.

Perry, William, and Ashton Carter. *Preventive Offense: A New Strategy for America*, Washington, D.C.: Brookings Institution Press, 1999.

Pollack, Kenneth. *The Persian Puzzle: The Conflict Between Iran and America*. New York: Random House, 2004.

Powell, Colin. *My American Journey*. New York: Random House, 1994.

Priest, Dana. *The Mission: Waging War and Keeping the Peace*. New York: W. W. Norton, 2004.

Reeve, Simon. *The New Jackals: Ramzi Yousef, Osama bin Laden and the Future of Terrorism*. Boston: Northeastern University Press, 1999.

Rieff, David. *Slaughterhouse: Bosnia and the Failure of the West*. Touchstone, New York: 1996.

Ritter, Scott. *Iraq Confidential: The Untold Story of the Intelligence Conspiracy to Undermine the UN and Overthrow Saddam Hussein*. New York: Nation Books, 2005.

Rohde, David. *Endgame: The Betrayal and Fall of Srebrenica: Europe's Worst Massacre Since World War II*. Boulder: Westview, 1997.

Ross, Dennis. *The Missing Peace: The Inside Story of the Fight for Middle East Peace*. New York: Farrar, Straus & Giroux, 2004.

Roston Aram. *The Man Who Pushed America to War*. New York: Nation Books, 2008.

Sageman, Marc. *Understanding Terror Networks*. Philadelphia: University of Pennsylvania Press, 2004.

Schlesinger Jr., Arthur M. *Cycles of American History*. Boston: Houghton Mifflin, 1986.

———. *Roosevelt Trilogy: Crisis of the Old Order: The Age of Roosevelt, 1919–1933*. Boston: Houghton Mifflin, 1957.

The Coming of the New Deal, 1933–1935. Boston: Houghton Mifflin, 1958;

Politics of Upheaval. Boston: Houghton Mifflin, 2003.

A Thousand Days. Boston: Houghton Mifflin, 1965.

———. *The Vital Center*. Boston: Houghton Mifflin, 1997.

———. *War and the American Presidency*. New York: W. W. Norton, 2005.

Segev, Thomas. *1967: Israel: The War, and the Year That Transformed the Middle East*. New York: Metropolitan Books/Henry Holt, 2005.

Sell, Louis. *Slobodan Milosevic and the Destruction of Yugoslavia*. Durham, N.C.: Duke University Press, 2002.

Shattuck, John. *Freedom on Fire: Human Rights Wars and America's Response*. Cambridge: Harvard University Press, 2005.

Shawcross, William. *Deliver Us from Evil Warlords and Peacekeepers in an Endless World of Conflict*. London: Bloomsbury, 2000.

Silber, Laura, and Alan Little. *Yugoslavia: Death of a Nation*. London: Penguin, 1996.

Simms, Brendon. *Unfinest Hour: Britain and the Destruction of Bosnia*. London: Allan Lane, 2001.

Smith, Joseph Burkholder. *Portrait of a Cold Warrior*. New York: Ballantine, 1976.

Smith, Sally Bedell. *For Love of Politics*. New York: Random House, 2007.

Soderberg, Nancy. *The Superpower Myth: The Use and Misuse of American Might*. Hoboken, N.J.: John Wiley, 2005.

Stankovic, Milos. *Trusted Mole*. New York: HarperCollins, 2001.

Stephanopoulos, George. *All Too Human*. New York: Little, Brown, 2000.

Sudetic, Chuck. *Blood and Vengeance*. New York: W. W. Norton, 1996.

Talbott, Strobe. *The Russia Hand: A Memoir of Presidential Diplomacy*. New York: Random House, 2003.

Tanner, Marcus. *Croatia: A Nation Forged in War*. New Haven: Yale University Press, 1997.

Tenet, George. *At the Center of the Storm: My Years at the CIA*. New York: HarperCollins, 2007.

Tenet, George, and Bill Barlow. *At the Center of the Storm: My Years at the CIA*. New York: HarperCollins, 2007.

Trinquier, Roger. *Modern Warfare: A French View of Counterinsurgency*. New York: Praeger, 1964.

Tuchman, Barbara W. *The Proud Tower: A Portrait of the World Before the War, 1890–1914*. New York: Scribner, 1966.

Turque, Bill. *Inventing Al Gore*. Boston: Houghton Mifflin, 2000.

Udowicki, Jasmina. and James Ridgway. *Burn This House: The Making and Unmaking of Yugoslavia*. Durham, N.C.: Duke University Press, 1997.

Vulliamy, Ed. *Seasons in Hell*. New York: St. Martins, 1994.

Whitney, Craig. *WMD Mirage: Iraq's Decade of Deception and America's False Premise for War*. New York: PublicAffairs, 2005.

Wiebes, Cees. *Intelligence and the War in Bosnia, 1992–1995*. Lit Verlag, 2003.

Woodward, Bob. *The Agenda: Inside the Clinton White House*. New York: Simon & Schuster, 1994.

———. *The Choice*. New York: Simon & Schuster, 1996.

————. *The Commanders*. New York: Simon & Schuster, 1991.

————. *Shadow: Five Presidents and the Legacy of Watergate*. New York: Simon & Schuster, 1999.

————. *State of Denial*. New York: Simon & Schuster, 2006.

Wright, Lawrence. *The Looming Tower: Al-Qaeda and the Road to 9/11*. New York: Alfred A. Knopf, 2006.

Zimmermann, Warren. *Origins of a Catastrophe: Yugoslavia and Its Destroyers*. New York: Times Books, 1996.

INDEX

Aero Contractors and, 292

Afghanistan and, 184

Alawi, I., and, 206, 214–16, 269

Albania and, 313–14, 373

Albright and, 135–36

analysis by, 65, 134–35

Baghdad Monitoring and Verification
 Center, 250

Bayard Foreign Marketing and, 290

bin Laden, O. and, 279–83, 288–89,
 295, 307

Bin Laden Issue Station of, 279

Black Hawk Down incident and, xiv–xv,
 84–86

Bosnia and, 146, 148

Bush, George H. W., and, 4–6, 121

Carter, J., and, 123

CENTCOM and, 190

Chalabi and, 184–85

Clinton, B., and, 116–25, 175

Counterterrorism Center of, 279, 284

covert actions and, 194, 291

Croatia and, 312

Dayton Accords and, 444

Deutch and, 192–97

Directorate of Operations, 194–95, 212,
 219, 260, 385

FBI and, 123, 313

Hamas and, 285–86

Hussein, S., and, 195–96, 205–14, 243

Hussein (king) and, 210

Iran and, 189

Iraq and, 183–91, 199–204, 211–21,
 250–54

Iraq Operations Group of, 187

Islamic Militant Unit of, 290

Jordan and, 211–17

Kosovo and, 340–41, 353, 386

in Kurdistan, 187–88, 200–201, 206,
 216, 249–52

Kurds, in Iraq, and, 200

Kuwait and, 198

Milosevic and, 393–96

Mukhabarat and, 210

NSA and, 340, 373

NSC and, 190–91

al-Qaeda and, 306–8, 313, 316

Reagan and, 121

recruiting for, 212–13

Richter and, 188–91, 250

Sarajevo and, 67–68

Serbia and, 376–77, 384–85, 407

sexism in, 193–94

Somalia and, 80

State Department and, 250, 330, 393

Syria and, 205

Tenet and, 193, 207, 220

UN and, 249–52

UNSCOM and, 249–52

USSR and, 193

WMDs and, 261

Woolsey and, 21, 33, 186, 231

Cervenko, Varimar, 147

Chalabi, Ahmed

 Alawi, I., and, 218, 220

 Cheney and, 272

 CIA and, 184–85

 Deutch and, 220

 Hussein, S., and, 197

 INC and, 217–18, 241

 Iran and, 184

 Lebanon and, 184

 Mukhabarat and, 217–18

 neoconservatives and, 271, 273–75

 Richter and, 217

 Zinni and, 184, 346

Cheney, Dick, 7, 13, 272

Chernomyrdin, Viktor, 174, 371, 380–81

China, and Serbia, 377, 380, 392

Chinese embassy bombing, in Serbia, 380

Chirac, Jacques

 Bosnia and, 144, 320, 360

 Clinton, B., and, 90, 137, 140–42, 245

 Montenegro and, 359

 Perle and, 275, 450

 Yeltsin and, 363

Chrétien, Jean, 114

Christopher, Warren

 Albright and, 327

 Aspin and, 50, 63

 Bosnia and, 27, 31, 38–39, 49–50, 73–74,
  132–33, 139